THE ATLANTIC REGION TO CONFEDERATION:
A HISTORY

The Atlantic Region to Confederation: A History

EDITED BY
PHILLIP A. BUCKNER AND JOHN G. REID

ERIC LEINBERGER, Cartographer
GRAEME WYNN, Cartographic Editor
MITCHELL A. McNUTT, Picture Editor

UNIVERSITY OF TORONTO PRESS
Toronto Buffalo London
and
ACADIENSIS PRESS
Fredericton

ISBN 0-8020-0553-5 (cloth)
ISBN 0-8020-6977-0 (paper)

Printed on acid-free paper

Canadian Cataloguing in Publication Data

Main entry under title:

The Atlantic region to Confederation : a history

Includes index.
ISBN 0-8020-0553-5 (bound). – ISBN 0-8020-6977-0 (pbk.)

1. Maritime Provinces – History – To 1867.*
2. Newfoundland – History. I. Buckner, Phillip A.
(Phillip Alfred), 1942–   . II. Reid, John G.
(John Graham), 1948–   .

FC2011.A75 1994   971.5′02   C93-095136-0
F1035.8.A75 1994

This book was published with the aid of grants from the Council of Maritime
Premiers and from the publications program of the Social Science Federation of
Canada, using funds provided by the Social Sciences and Humanities Research
Council of Canada.

Contents

Maps

Preface

PHILLIP A. BUCKNER AND JOHN G. REID

Some twenty-seven years have passed since the publication of the first and, until now, the only general history of the Atlantic region prior to Confederation. W.S. MacNutt's *The Atlantic Provinces: The Emergence of Colonial Society, 1712–1857* represented in its day an outstanding scholarly achievement, all the greater for being accomplished in an era when the secondary literature was sparse and primary sources frequently had to be unearthed from unorganized bodies of provincial records. Not for today's scholars the long, hot summer days that MacNutt spent in the dusty attic of the Legislative Building in Fredericton. Nor, or at least not so often, the stress and the exhilaration of venturing judgments on questions previously uninterpreted by historians. MacNutt's work was one of the inspirations for an upsurge of research and writing in Atlantic regional history that produced the journal *Acadiensis*, launched in 1971, and an impressive series of other articles and books. Years later, as a result, a new effort at synthesis is required to convey the state of our knowledge in the 1990s. Many of the themes that are important to today's historians have been fully developed only since the early 1970s. Also stemming from debates of the past twenty or so years have been important advances in our understanding of regional economic developments and their implications for social, cultural, and political life.

This book is intended to fulfil the need for a new synthesis. The decision to structure it as a team-written study also implies a hope that it will go even farther. All the authors have carried out substantial original research in their assigned areas, and all have been encouraged to regard their chapters as innovative essays in which the results of new work will be interwoven with syntheses of existing knowledge. The chapters are based on chronological periods, the time spans becoming shorter in the later chapters to reflect growing populations and larger bodies of surviving evidence. In all chapters, the authors have been asked to provide integrated treatments of the territories that ultimately became known as Newfoundland and the Maritime provinces. Within that general framework, the authors were allowed considerable freedom in deciding on the themes they wished to develop. Following the first drafts, and in the wake of an intensive, two-day workshop session, arrangements were made for adjustments that would add thematic unity to the book. In particular, some authors were requested to incorporate retrospective analyses of certain matters, such as immigrations that spanned lengthy periods of time, that would be more effectively dealt with in one place rather than spread out among successive chapters. As far as possible, in addition to making the normal editorial demands for clarity, precision, and as much conciseness as the complexities of the subject matter would allow, the editors sought to bring about consistency by reconciling interpretive differences between chapters. Intellectual honesty, of course, had to take first priority, and so some diversities of viewpoint persist. Nevertheless, taken as a whole, the book offers a new interpretive treatment that can be defined in both chronological and thematic terms.

The book is organized according to three overall time periods, the first of which encompasses the themes of 'cultures and coexistence' up until 1720. By that time, human habitation of the Atlantic region had been continuous for some 11,000 years. Cultures had gone through a series of evolutions, partly responding to profound environmental changes and partly reflecting new immigrations. Limitations in the evidence relating to the remote past prevent any confident assessment of the extent to which these changes may have involved conflict between newcomers and older inhabitants, but the general reality that emerges from archaeological study is twofold: that cultural change was an ongoing process for many thousands of years before any European set foot in the region, and that the coexistence of different cultural groups in different subregions was the norm. By the time that recurrent European contact began, around the year 1500, a complex pattern of Native cultures had emerged. The European presence brought, at first, very limited alteration to the prevailing evolutionary processes. For a hundred years, contact implied European resource exploitation – fisheries, whaling, and the first stirrings of the fur trade – rather than colonization. Even when colonization began in earnest, after 1600, the numbers were small. In Newfoundland, the entire notion of English resident communities remained controversial, and the French settlements in the vicinity of Placentia enjoyed little practical support from France, even though they were integrated into the civil structures of the French Empire in North America. French interest in the mainland colony of Acadia was also intermittent, and although the Acadian population reached some 1,500 by the year 1700, distributed for the most part in three well-founded clusters of settlement, Acadians were still far outnumbered by Native inhabitants.

Up to and even beyond the turn of the eighteenth century, the truth was that the European presence supplemented the existing Native order rather than displacing it. To be sure, such a sweeping statement needs some qualifiers. European disease brought epidemics that were unlike anything experienced in aboriginal times, though they were insufficient to break the cultural resilience of Native peoples. European trade, even though trade in itself was nothing new to the indigenous populations, did inaugurate new linkages to the merchant capitalist economy of western Europe. Over time, these connections would have profound environmental results, implying as they did the commercial exploitation of natural resources, and would prompt cultural changes among Native populations for whom the beaver hunt now assumed unprecedented importance. In Newfoundland, the Beothuk strategy of avoiding direct contact with either seasonal or resident English fishing populations began the process by which access to coastal resources was lost to the Native inhabitants, with ultimately fatal results. Yet European influence, destructive as it was in some respects, did not imply European control – either of Native populations or of the small but well-established non-Native settlements. Even so, the French and English – British, from 1707 – imperial authorities were rapidly attaching greater strategic significance to this part of North America, and the wars that led to the conquest of Acadia in 1710 both illustrated and contributed to this process. The aftermath included the Treaty of Utrecht, the departure of the French from Newfoundland, conflicting French and British pressures on the Acadians, and the start of construction of Fortress Louisbourg. The imperial presence, no matter how weak it might superficially appear in Newfoundland and for the time being in Nova Scotia, was more direct and intrusive than ever before. The autonomy of existing populations, and especially that of Native inhabitants, was not lost, but it was already more tightly circumscribed. These were the new realities that emerged from the turbulent events surrounding the turn of the century and that became clear by 1720.

Thus, the second major time division of this study comprises a century of 'the encounter with imperial militarism,' 1720–1820. Within that period, Britain fought four times with France, with the American revolutionaries, and then with the United States in the War of 1812. There were some stretches – the 1720s and 1730s, and briefer periods later on – when no major war was in progress, but none that was unaffected by the threat of war or its aftermath. Some of the consequences were directly military. British forces twice seized Louisbourg, and the French briefly held St John's. The British storming of Fort Beauséjour, on the Isthmus of Chignecto, was the prelude to the violent dispersion of the Acadian population. There were also lesser, though still bloody, affrays. The French defeat of a New England detachment at Grand Pré was one that gained especial notoriety in Anglo-American minds, as did the intermittent hostilities that arose from Micmac efforts to resist British encroachments. All these episodes belonged to the period before 1763, but violent conflict did not then cease to intrude on the populations of the region. Revolutionaries attempted unsuccessfully in 1776 to seize Fort Cumberland, the old Fort Beauséjour, and many colonists from Nova Scotia and the Island of St John (Prince Edward Island) served in Loyalist regiments; but the most direct impact on civilians, in this war and the next, arose from the activities of privateers. Warfare also had serious implications for the most basic configuration of settlement. Displacement of Acadian and Native populations was one obvious product. Wars and the terms of their settlement also profoundly affected immigration patterns. Not that all immigration of the period can be accounted for in this way. Irish and Scottish immigrations assumed crucial importance, beginning with the influx of Irish to Newfoundland and continuing with Scottish and Irish movements to the other provinces, and the origins lay primarily in economic circumstances prevailing in the British Isles. The arrival of the New England Planters in Nova Scotia during the 1760s, however, was prompted in large measure by the defeat of France and the availability of newly vacated Acadian lands. The Loyalist influx twenty years later was even more directly the result of war – the civil war within the Thirteen Colonies in which the Loyalists were the losers.

Such immigrations obviously had economic as well as societal implications, and war also unleashed powerful economic forces in other ways. Some of the effects were stimulating. Military spending was conspicuous in the major ports, while in Newfoundland the disruptions of war favoured the resident over the migratory fishery, and in New Brunswick the Napoleonic ascendancy in Europe brought a dramatic rise in timber exports. War-related prosperity was always treacherous, because each war eventually came to an end. The economic difficulties that followed the restoration of peace in 1815 testified to this simple truth. Even so, the population of the region had grown by 1820 to exceed 200,000, whereas a century before it had been less than a twentieth of that number. Within the population as it now existed were many complex divisions related to ethnicity, language, religion, and social class. Native and Acadian minorities coexisted with, among others, Celts, Germans, and – for want of a better term to describe the Planter and Loyalist immigrants

– Anglo-Americans. Languages varied accordingly, and so did religious affiliations. While the categories of Catholic and Protestant have some general validity, and already by 1820 had provided the stimulus to violent quarrels within the region, an Anglican attending King's College, Windsor, might well have as little in common – theologically or otherwise – with a Baptist from the St John Valley as did an Irish Catholic from St John's with a Micmac worshipper at Chapel Island on Cape Breton. Among the few general characteristics of a still-fragmented population was its largely non-English character. While there were, of course, significant groups who could trace their ancestry to English immigrants into the region – West Country settlers in Newfoundland, or Yorkshire settlers on the Isthmus of Chignecto – the large immigrations of the eighteenth and early nineteenth centuries had been Celtic or Anglo-American. Another characteristic lay in the inability of the population in general to attempt to shape a collective future with any assurance of stability when the exigencies of imperial wars were continually intruding. With peace restored in 1815, and the immediate post-war economic disruptions weathered by 1820, there was a possibility that this might change.

After 1820, despite occasional friction along the American border, the next half-century was a period of uninterrupted peace and general, if erratic, growth. The central theme of these decades is 'the consolidation of colonial society.' The population soared from 200,000 in 1820, the majority of whom had been born outside the region, to around 900,000, the majority of them native-born, in 1870. Immigration was particularly heavy from the 1830s to the 1850s, although to some extent offset by substantial outmigration in the 1840s, and by 1870 a sizeable proportion of the region's population consisted of immigrants from the British Isles or their immediate descendants. Few communities were untouched by the arrival of immigrants, and by the 1860s virtually every hectare of land that could support sustainable agriculture (and some that could not) was occupied. The sheer scale of immigration created enormous problems of social integration, and these were compounded by the ethnic and religious rivalries that the immigrants carried as part of their cultural baggage. Although chain migration reinforced earlier settlement patterns, increasing levels of intermarriage, the growth of urban centres, and the continual movement of people in response to changing economic conditions also ensured a substantial intermingling of different ethnic and religious groups. The persistence of ethno-religious tensions, particularly between evangelical Protestants and Irish Catholics, often led to friction and even violence in the aftermath of the exceptionally heavy immigration from Ireland in the 1840s. Nonetheless, despite continuing debate over such issues as the nature of the educational structures that should be given state support, slowly but steadily a sense of provincial identity began to take root among the majority of the British population in each of the four Atlantic colonies, and violence gave way to institutionalized political conflict.

Those most threatened by the rapid spread of population and least integrated into the emerging provincial cultures were the non-British minorities. The Acadian minority in the Maritime colonies was growing steadily larger through high rates of natural increase and was sufficiently residentially segregated in areas of comparatively limited interest to immigrants to be able to create its own institutional structures and begin to play a part in provincial politics. But the Native peoples of the region continued to be increasingly outnumbered in the face of the spread of European settlement. Only in the case of the Beothuk did population decline result in extinction, but everywhere the Native peoples found their movements and their access to resources increasingly circumscribed. That the Micmac and the Maliseet survived and preserved considerable cultural autonomy owed less to the concern of sympathetic Europeans than to these peoples' own resilience and determination. Although slavery had never taken firm root in the region and had largely disappeared long before its formal abolition by the British Parliament in 1833, Blacks in the region were also forced to fall back on their own resources and religious institutions in the face of the pervasive racism that permeated White society.

The rapid demographic growth of the four Atlantic colonies is sufficient in itself to explain the increasing discontent with a system of colonial government that left executive power in the hands of the governors and the small and unrepresentative provincial councils. All four colonies proceeded at a different pace, but one by one they struggled for and eventually received the introduction of a system of responsible government that brought the executive under the control of the elected assemblies. Confusion remained, as in the United Province of Canada, over how far colonial self-government would extend, over the role of the governor, and over the precise nature of the relationship between the executive and the Assembly. In the Atlantic colonies, this confusion was compounded by the fragility of the loosely knit party systems that emerged in the 1840s. By the 1860s, however, all four colonies had evolved party systems that operated at the provincial level, though they would be shattered by the issue of Confederation. The pressure for political reform of the old colonial system came largely from the colonies, but it was given greater momentum by the British decision to move to free trade, thus putting an end to the imperial tariff preferences on colonial products. The three Maritime colonies were particularly affected by this decision, since they had developed highly specialized economies that depended on access to the British market. The prolonged depression of the 1840s forced them to make a painful adjustment, by introducing technological innovations into the forest industries, by expanding interregional trade and their participation in the international shipping trades, by seeking markets in the United States, and ultimately by evolving new development strategies that included the building of railways and the promotion of domestic manufacturing.

Too much emphasis has in the past been laid upon the conservatism of the region, for both the entrepreneurial élites and the governments of the Maritime colonies showed considerable resilience in responding to the challenge of the 1840s. Undeniably, the benefits of growth and prosperity were unevenly distributed and class divisions became more pronounced. Whether this period should be seen as a 'golden age' rather depends upon whom one is talking about, and yet this was a period of sustained and substantial growth that lasted into the 1860s. For all that, the economic development of the region remained precariously dependent upon access to external markets and upon the ability of the colonial governments to find the necessary capital to finance further growth. The belief that union with Canada would provide a necessary element of stability, open new markets, and encourage investment in the region, as well as the fear of the consequences of the victory of the North in the American Civil War, together explain the initial enthusiasm, particularly among the Maritime élites, for Confederation with Canada. Newfoundland, from the beginning, was less convinced of the merits of union. Its economy was still tied to the Atlantic fisheries, and its politicians and people did not see themselves as having a continental destiny. Many Maritimers shared this feeling, and many more were concerned with the terms of union adopted at Quebec; but the three Maritime colonies decided that there was a more secure future within Confederation than outside it. With varying degrees of enthusiasm, they surrendered their status as self-governing colonies.

There was an irony in the transition. A recurrent theme in the history of Atlantic Canada, from the beginning of the colonial era until the early nineteenth century, was the effort of the resident populations – aboriginal, Acadian, Anglo- and Afro-American, and British- or European-born – to preserve the socio-economic integrity of their communities and to retain a degree of autonomy in the face of external threats exerted by conflicting efforts at colonization, rival imperial designs and assertions, and the demands and results of imperial wars. With varying degrees of success, the inhabitants of the region had succeeded in meeting these challenges. The emergence of British imperial pre-eminence after 1783 and the influx of unprecedented numbers of immigrants from the British Isles after 1815, however, irrevocably altered the balance of power within the region and ensured the predominance of the British element in the population. The tide of immigration declined after 1850, the proportion of native-born swelled dramatically, and the new settlers and their offspring joined with the descendants of the earlier settlers to seek a degree of autonomy for their colonies but within the larger framework of the second British Empire. Yet the provincial societies thus created could not escape the external pressures emanating from changing imperial policies and the emergence of the United States as the dominant force on the North American continent. Confederation appeared to many Maritimers as the only rational response to these pressures and held out the additional prospect of economic diversification and growth. Three of the Atlantic provinces therefore opted for union with the United Province of Canada. That union created powerful forces for integration that would lead inevitably to new threats to their autonomy and to the viability of their socio-economic structures. Once again the populations of the region responded to this challenge with varying degrees of success. But that theme lies beyond the time-frame of this book.

Acknowledgments

No book as long and complex as this one could be created without the help and collaboration of many people. As editors, we owe a great deal to the cooperation of the fourteen other contributors. Through successive phases of writing and revision, and despite our sometimes conflicting demands for extended coverage of the issues along with reductions in length, the chapters kept appearing with due regularity. The revision process was greatly assisted by intensive workshop sessions held in Fredericton in November 1990, in which, again, the authors of the chapters played a major role. So did a number of other participants who offered valuable comments. They included David Bell, Gail Campbell, Margaret Conrad, Gwen Davies, Ernie Forbes, David Frank, Colin Howell, Barry Moody, Del Muise, Brook Taylor, and Murray Young.

As the manuscript took shape, the organizational and secretarial skills of Beckey Daniel, Ruth Vallillee, and Marjorie Warren were essential. Crucial to the transformation from manuscript to book was the strong commitment of the publishers. On the part of the University of Toronto Press, Gerry Hallowell was a constant support; also fulfilling important roles were Agnes Ambrus, Theresa Griffin, and – reducing an unruly manuscript to order – Margaret Allen as copy-editor. David Frank, on behalf of Acadiensis Press, facilitated the manuscript's progress in many important ways, while Ernie Forbes and Del Muise were generous in sharing their experience gained as editors of the 1993 University of Toronto Press–Acadiensis Press co-publication, *The Atlantic Provinces in Confederation*. Also essential contributors of time and expertise were cartographic editor Graeme Wynn, cartographer Eric Leinberger, and picture editor Mitch McNutt. Financial support was provided at various stages by the University of New Brunswick and by the Senate Research Committee of Saint Mary's University, while publication was assisted by grants from the Social Sciences and Humanities Research Council of Canada – which also supported the Fredericton workshop – and from the Council of Maritime Premiers.

To all, we offer our sincere thanks.

PHILLIP A. BUCKNER
JOHN G. REID

Palaeo-Indian and Pre-ceramic artifacts. Bottom row (left to right), Palaeo-Indian artifacts: side-scraper, biface knife, fluted point, drill, end-scraper. Middle row (left to right), Late Pre-ceramic artifacts: ground stone axe, ground slate point, three projectile points. Top row, Late Pre-ceramic projectile points

Ceramic Period artifacts. Bottom row (left to right), three projectile points, ground stone axe. Second row (left to right), biface knife, two projectile points. Third row (left to right), biface knife, six small end-scrapers, large end-scraper. Top row, three rim sherds

Woodcut of Inuit woman and child, first published in Augsburg, 1567

A Norman vessel practising the green fishery. From Duhamel Du Monceau, *Traité général des pesches et histoire des poissons ...*

The dry fishery: splitting and salting. From Duhamel Du Monceau, *Traité général des pesches et histoire des poissons ...*

Acadians repairing a dyke, *c.* 1720. Re-creation by Azor Vienneau

View from a warship. Re-creation of Louisbourg by Lewis Parker

New England forces landing at Louisbourg, 1745. Print published in 1747

View of Halifax from Dartmouth, 1759. Print first published in 1764, from a drawing by R. Short

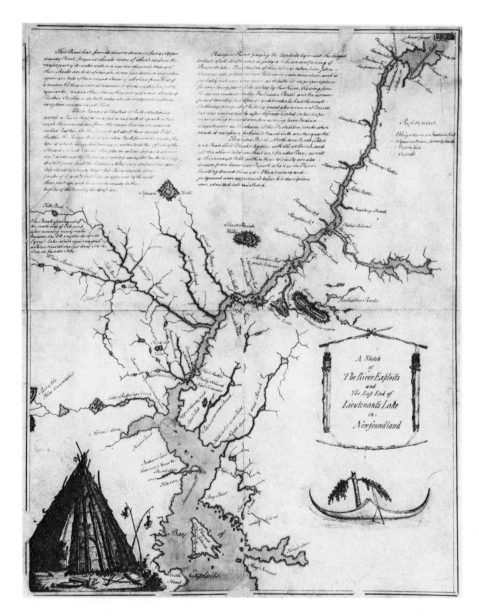

Map of the Exploits River, Newfoundland, by John Cartwright, 1773, with depictions of Beothuk material culture

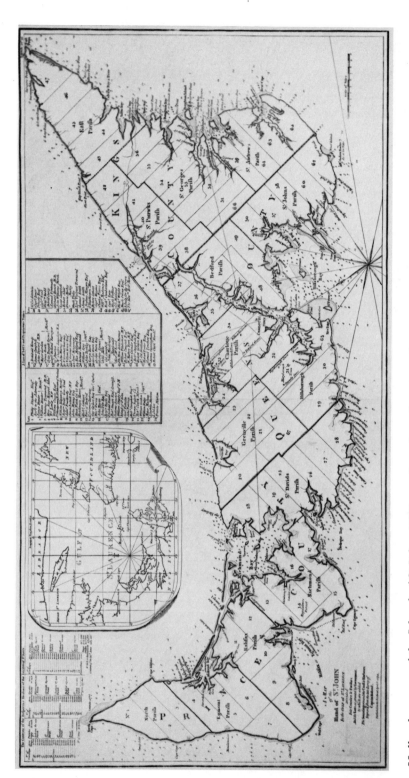

Holland survey of the Island of St John. 1775 map based on the original survey of 1765

Standard of the King's American Dragoons, a Loyalist American regiment

A Black woodcutter. Watercolour by William Booth, Shelburne, 1788

A Micmac encampment. Watercolour by Hibbert Newton Binney, *c.* 1790

Interior of a Micmac dwelling. 1837 lithograph, from a drawing by Robert Petley

View of St John's, late eighteenth century. Watercolour by an unknown artist

The *Shannon* leading the *Chesapeake* into Halifax Harbour, 1813. Print by
J.C. Schetky, from a design by R.H. King

Government House, Halifax, from the southwest. Etching by John Elliot
Woolford, published 1819

View of Saint John. Etching and aquatint by Ralph Stennett, 1815

Partridge Island, Saint John Harbour. Site of a quarantine station for immigrants. Sketch by A.J. Hill, published in *Canadian Illustrated News*, 28 January 1871

View on the Road from Windsor to Horton by Avon Bridge at Gaspereaux River.
Watercolour by John Elliot Woolford, 1817

View of the Cobaquid Mountains. Lithograph by Robert Petley, 1837

Lumberers on the Miramichi River, New Brunswick. Watercolour by J.F. Bland

View of Summerside. Watercolour by Robert Harris, *c.* 1866

Colonial Building, Charlottetown, *c.* 1860. Photographer unknown

Commemorative arch on Spring Garden Road, Halifax, 1860, built in honour of the visit of the Prince of Wales. Photograph by Wellington Chase

PART ONE
CULTURES AND COEXISTENCE, TO 1720

Early Societies
Sequences of Change

STEPHEN A. DAVIS

To analyse the development of the earliest human societies in the area now known as Atlantic Canada is a difficult task, partly because modern political boundaries bear little relationship to the realities of the remote past. The study of the past 11,000 years of human habitation of today's Maritime provinces is based on findings at a series of particular sites that represent events at a given time and place. Although these can be discussed in chronological order, the Maritimes have not produced, to date, any deeply stratified sites – that is, sites where remains from different periods are found layered one below the other – or areas that contain archaeological materials covering the entire length of human occupation. Newfoundland and Labrador, by contrast, have been studied in a more concentrated way, and southern Labrador is the only area within the whole Atlantic-Canadian region in which archaeological evidence approaches a complete representation of the sequence of culture change. Natural processes account for these differences. During the last phase of ice coverage in the Atlantic region, the land was depressed by the weight of the glaciers. As the ice melted and the weight was lifted, the land began to rebound. At the same time, the vast amount of water that had made up the glaciers began to flow into the Atlantic Ocean. Thus, land and sea were both rising. However, everywhere except in southern Labrador, the sea levels were rising faster. As a result, most of the coastal areas of human habitation began to disappear. This phenomenon was especially marked during the period from 7,000 to 4,000 years ago and, although not as rapidly, has continued to the present day.[1] Furthermore, except where unusual conditions have provided for neutralization, the acidic soils of Atlantic Canada are not kind to archaeologists. They quickly destroy organic material. Thus, although the prehistory of the region goes back for at least eleven millennia, the

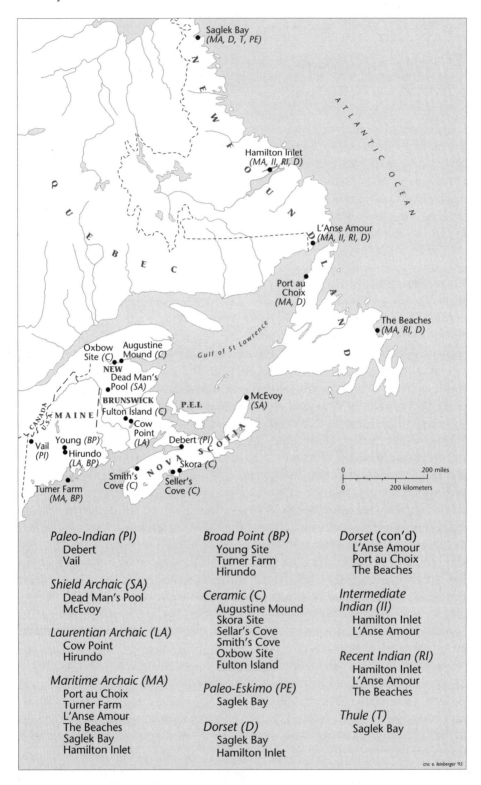

Archaeological sites in Atlantic Canada

evidence that would allow even the chronology of that long period to be accurately reconstructed is far from complete.

The earliest evidence of the human presence in North America has been found in Alaska and the Yukon Territory, supporting the argument that the first inhabitants migrated from Asia by crossing a land bridge between Siberia and Alaska during the last major glaciation. When the ice melted, sea levels rose, the land bridge was covered by the waters of the Bering Strait, and the inhabitants were isolated in North America. But access to the rest of the Americas was opened up by the retreat of the glaciers, and a slow southerly migration began. In general, the early human societies subsisted on big-game hunting. This phase, defined by archaeologists as that of the Palaeo-Indians, may have extended from 15,000 to 6,000 years ago. A more cautious estimate would be from 12,500 to 7,000 years ago. The period began with the hunting of such species as mammoths, mastodons, and long-horned bison; it persisted through and beyond their extinction, with later sites yielding evidence of the capture of modern species.[2] There were successive cultural adaptations. The earliest Palaeo-Indian cultural patterns were those included by archaeologists in the Clovis group, characterized by a distinctive type of chipped-stone spearhead known as a fluted (grooved) point. It was followed by the Folsom group, a pattern of Palaeo-Indian culture unique to western North America that also produced fluted spear points. The final culture of the period is known as the Plano, defined by a series of unfluted points. As the glaciers continued to retreat northward and ecological zones changed accordingly, the animals hunted by the Palaeo-Indians also moved. Human migration resulted, and as people spread in all directions across North America, the first small groups of hunters found their way into what is now eastern Canada.

The oldest generally recognized and accepted location of human cultural development within today's Maritime provinces is in the vicinity of Debert, Nova Scotia.[3] The first site excavated was close to the Debert airfield, and more recent discoveries at nearby Belmont have led to the use of the term Debert/Belmont Palaeo-Indian complex. The crucial artifactual discoveries were chipped-stone tools, most notably, fluted points belonging to the Clovis tradition. The Debert location, excavated during the 1960s, is one of the most important Clovis sites in North America, and radio-carbon dating of charcoal samples from the hearth areas indicated that the site had been occupied some 10,600 years ago. The wide range of Palaeo-Indian tools found there included fluted points, awls, spokeshaves, hammerstones, anvils, and abraders. No animal remains were excavated, but reconstruction of the palaeo-environment, the site location, and the hunting strategy known elsewhere suggests that Debert was occupied by caribou hunters and that the site was probably situated near a calving ground or along a caribou migration route.[4]

During the twenty-five years following the excavations at Debert, Clovis-type fluted points were found in eight locations distributed throughout the three Maritime provinces. These were isolated finds, but in the late fall of 1989 two sites were discovered at Belmont. Preliminary study during the summer of 1990 has revealed four more sites in this vicinity. Although none of the Belmont sites has been thoroughly excavated, limited testing and the first findings of artifactual materials confirm that they duplicate Debert in the material culture they reveal. Another noteworthy Palaeo-Indian location, the Vail site, has recently been discovered in one of the most mountainous regions of southwestern Maine. An early paper by Harold W. Borns had hypothesized that there were two possible routes by which human migrants may have entered what is today the Maritime region of Canada.[5] One was along the coastal plain, which has been drowned by the rise of the Bay of Fundy following the end of glaciation. The other was over the high country of the interior. The second possibility was long considered unlikely because of the presence of alpine ice caps and water drainage from them. But the Vail site gives new credibility to the seemingly unlikely route. The location has been radio-carbon dated to approximately 11,120 years ago, when southwestern Maine would have supported coniferous forests at low altitudes and a tundra-like landscape at higher elevations. Given these forms of vegetation and the terrain of the site itself, it is probably that caribou were hunted there. As at Debert, no faunal remains were found, but a concentration of fluted points 250 metres from the main living areas has been interpreted as indicating a kill site.[6]

As in the rest of North America, the Palaeo-Indians of the northeast were big-game hunters. Caribou was the most common quarry, although mammoth and mastodon teeth have also been recovered from the continental shelf.[7] These animals were probably contemporaneous with the Palaeo-Indians and were no doubt hunted for food when opportunity arose. It is also reasonable to believe that the rich coastal resources would not have been overlooked. Several authors have suggested, for example, that the large wintering herds of harp seals would have been hunted.[8] Archaeological evidence of Palaeo-Indian exploitation of marine resources along the coasts of southern Labrador has led James Tuck and Robert McGhee to conclude that a well-defined seasonal round of subsistence activities began in this period and continued through to the era of European contact.[9] Because of shoreline submergence, it is difficult to find equivalent evidence of the activities of people after the time of Debert in what are now the Maritime provinces, but the most convincing hypothesis is that human subsistence activities tended to be confined to marine resources, as the glaciers retreated and the landward environment changed radically from tundra to dense boreal forests that could not support large terrestrial mammals. The alternative hypothesis – that the area was simply abandoned for more favourable environments to the north and south – seems unlikely in the context of growing evidence of a transitional, or late, Palaeo-Indian cultural presence. Plano-type projectile points exist in private collections in New Brunswick and southern Nova Scotia. Although these artifacts cannot now be identified in the context of their original location, similar unfluted spear points have been found at sites on the Gaspé Peninsula and in Maine, where they have been attributed to the period from about 10,000 to 8,000 years ago.[10]

There is also a second form of possible late Palaeo-Indian occupation that has been defined by David Keenlyside for the southern part of the Gulf of St Lawrence. The key trait in this case is a distinctively triangular projectile point, of which Keenlyside has recorded twenty-two examples from Prince Edward Island and the north shore of New Brunswick. These specimens also cannot be placed in their exact location because all are either surface finds or are in private collections, but their assignment to a late Palaeo-Indian context can be made on the basis of their close similarity to points identified by Tuck and McGhee along the southern coast of Labrador and dated to a range between 9,000 and 8,000 years ago. Keenlyside suggests that the triangular-point form evolved from the classic northeast Palaeo-Indian fluted-point tradition, and that the distribution of the triangular-point types along coastal areas is an indication of a shift in resource utilization: whereas the occupants of Debert relied on large land animals, the makers of the triangular points depended more upon marine and estuary resources.[11] This intriguing hypothesis remains to be tested through the excavation of the points in a datable context.

The truth is that the archaeological evidence reveals the existence of people in Atlantic Canada during the Palaeo-Indian era but tells us very little about them. Even less is known about the period from 8,000 to 5,000 years ago, despite the discovery of some tantalizing clues. At least three times in Maritime waters, fishing vessels have recovered stone artifacts that may date back some 6,500 years. Scallop draggers working off Digby Neck brought up implements from a depth of some thirty fathoms, and similar vessels did so at comparable depths off the Bliss Islands, on the New Brunswick side of the Bay of Fundy, and on the northeast side of Prince Edward Island. In each instance, the artifacts were ground-stone ulus – tools used in the butchering of soft-tissue species such as fish and sea mammals – and their recovery in these disparate locations may well indicate that much of the evidence for human habitation in this period lies submerged. Not for nothing has the entire era from Debert to approximately 5,000 years ago been described by one researcher as the 'Great Hiatus.'[12]

The middle period of the development of human societies in what is now Atlantic Canada begins 5,000 years ago and is known to archaeologists as the Late Pre-ceramic. It corresponds in time to what is known elsewhere as the Late Archaic period. The concept of 'Archaic' is used to distinguish groups of hunters and gatherers in many parts of North America from later 'Woodland Period' horticulturalists, although this particular transition did not take place in the Atlantic region, where agriculture was not practised in the era prior to European contact. In this region, the most significant cultural change included the appearance of ceramic vessels. The evidence of human societies in the middle period is abundant, but it is also complex. No fewer than four broad cultural traditions have been identified, each of which could be further divided chronologically. Nevertheless, there are similarities that make the traditions comparable. One important common trait was the development of a new technology – the production of stone tools by grinding and polishing. Prominent among the implements produced by this method, which was developed in response to the changing environment that was now dominated by forestation, were woodworking tools such as axes, adzes, and gouges. Also important were ulus, bannerstones – flat, ground, and polished implements of which the function is unknown – and plummets, which resemble a modern-day carpenter's plumb bob. No one explanation of the plummet's function has gained full acceptance, although the most plausible suggestion is that it may have been used in fishing activities as a weight on a net or fishing line, since many Pre-ceramic sites are found at locations that were good fishing spots.

The four traditions that emerged during the middle period – which is considered to have continued until about 2,500 years ago – are known to scholars as the Laurentian tradition, the Maritime Archaic, the Shield Archaic, and the Broad Point tradition.[13] The Laurentian tradition was first defined from sites located in upstate New York, Vermont, and portions of western Quebec and southern Ontario. As well as sharing in the common prevalence of ground-stone tools, Laurentian sites are distinctive in their lack of pottery and in the frequent appearance of 'bayonets' made of ground slate. Laurentian research elsewhere has led to the conclusion that the tradition was adapted to deciduous or mixed-forest environments. Subsistence was based on species such as deer and moose, with smaller game also being hunted. Lake and river fishing was important, with anadromous species – those, such as salmon, that ascend rivers to spawn – predominating in the people's diet during migration runs. In all probability, vegetable foods, roots, and berries were collected at certain seasons of the year. Whether Laurentian inhabitants also exploited marine resources has been a controversial issue among scholars. A number of authors believe that the term 'Laurentian' should be reserved for interior populations, and that analogous cultures on the coast should be considered separately as the 'Maritime Archaic' tradition. The counter-hypothesis is that 'Laurentian' should be understood to include those whose seasonal harvests included specific marine resources.[14]

One major problem in assessing the evolution of the Laurentian tradition in Atlantic Canada is that few habitation sites have been excavated. More common have been burial sites, such as the important excavation conducted in 1971 by the Archaeological Survey of Canada at Cow Point, near Grand Lake in central New Brunswick. In all, sixty graves and 400 artifacts were found.[15] The graves and their contents were covered with red ochre and appeared to have represented two periods of burial activities. The radio-carbon dates on the last burials averaged about 3,800 years ago, with no dates available for the earlier ones. The common traits of these burials – which closely resemble those found in the state of Maine and known there as the 'Moorehead burial tradition' – include primary burial in an extended or flexed position, and secondary burial of disarticulated bones contained in a bundle. The primary burials represent people who died close to the cemetery in a season when their graves could easily be dug. The secondary burials, conversely, were of those who died far from the cemetery or when the ground was frozen and whose remains would later be gathered for interment. In either case, the inclusion of red ochre and grave goods consisting largely of ground-stone items suggests a high degree of ceremonialism. In the rare instances where bones have been recovered and analysed as to the age and sex of the individual, there has been no separation of different types of grave goods. Probably, therefore, the goods were deposited by members of the community rather than being possessions of the deceased. Most of the objects appear to be non-utilitarian or ceremonial in nature, rather than tools meant for use in another life. Most intriguing are the slate 'bayonets,' which in many cases are decorated with incised geometric lines on one or both faces and seem much too fragile to have served any utilitarian purpose. Some thicker bayonets made of slate and bone, however, may have served as the tips of spears and lances, and a distinctive type found in collections in southeastern Nova Scotia has a groove to enable the point to be secured to a haft. The prominence of red ochre has led to the coining of the term 'Red Paint People,' based on items from cemeteries in Maine and at Cow

Point. No cemeteries have been excavated in Nova Scotia, but many private collections contain examples of the distinctive grave goods, frequently still carrying the stains of red ochre and reported by the collectors to have been found among patches of red-stained soil.

The discovery in 1967 of an important site at Port au Choix, Newfoundland, led the Memorial University archaeologist James Tuck to propose the existence of a second major Pre-ceramic tradition in the region – the Maritime Archaic, so named because of the importance of marine resources. The site contained well-preserved skeletal remains of more than 100 individuals, of both sexes and a variety of ages. Because of the choice of the ancient raised beach as a burial site, there was a high degree of organic preservation, and the shells of molluscs provided calcium that leached through the gravels to neutralize the soil in an otherwise acidic environment. These conditions preserved not only the human remains but also hundreds of artifacts made of bone. It is this evidence of bone artifacts – harpoons, foreshafts, and lance points, all thought to have been used to capture marine resources – that defines the distinct character of the Maritime Archaic tradition. Various species were used in the making of these tools, including both sea mammals and land animals such as caribou, beaver, and bear. Fishing implements were found, perhaps used in taking the plentiful Atlantic salmon, and the remains of birds were also recovered, although it is not clear whether all of them were used for food. The clustering of the remains of a bird species in some graves suggests the existence of a special relationship between certain families and individual species of birds.[16]

With the recognition of the Maritime Archaic tradition, a complete cultural sequence has been defined for southern Labrador. Tuck sees the beginning of the Maritime Archaic adaptation to marine resources as developing out of the late Palaeo-Indian tradition. The evolution began some 7,500 years ago and continued until the entry of the later Dorset culture into Labrador and Newfoundland.[17] A key discovery in the elaboration of this argument came in 1974 at the village of L'Anse-Amour in southern Labrador. A burial site consisting of a low stone mound covering a stone cyst was found to contain the skeleton of a young adolescent, lying face down and apparently having been wrapped in an organic material such as bark or animal hide. Two hearths at the same level as the skeleton provided sufficient charcoal for radio-carbon dating to approximately 7,530 years ago. The grave goods included stone projectile points and knives, as well as three hollow-based bone points.[18] The most surprising items were an antler toggling harpoon and a hand-held toggle. These are the earliest discoveries yet found in North America of such a sophisticated seal-hunting technology. Beyond L'Anse-Amour, the Maritime Archaic sequence continues with a major northward expansion of the tradition. Investigations by the Smithsonian Institution, under the direction of William Fitzhugh, have revealed extensive Maritime Archaic occupations as far north as Hamilton Inlet approximately 6,000 years ago, and a thousand years later the expansion had reached the Saglek Bay area of northern Labrador.[19] One result was the discovery by Maritime Archaics of a unique, translucent grey silicate, known either as 'Ramah chert' or 'Ramah chalcedony.' Found only between Ramah Bay and Saglek Bay, its finely grained texture makes it an ideal raw material for lithic technologies, and it soon began to be traded throughout the Atlantic region.

Closely related sites have also been identified along the coast of Maine, most notably at the Turner Farm site. As at Port au Choix, bone preservation at this stratified site – which reveals a number of distinct occupations – is excellent. The economy was again varied, with faunal remains that included such land mammals as deer, moose, bear, and beaver, along with swordfish, grey and harbour seals, walrus, codfish, sturgeon, sea mink, and various sea birds. From this evidence, it appears that the Maritime Archaic peoples spent most of the year at or near the coast, with brief winter journeys inland to hunt deer, moose, or caribou. In southwesterly areas, perhaps in the vicinity of the present Maine–New Hampshire border, they may well have come in contact with Laurentian people, although further exploration of this interaction is hindered by the obliteration of many likely Maritime Archaic sites by the rise in sea levels.[20]

The third tradition that can be found within the middle period is one for which less satisfying evidence is available – the Shield Archaic. Named after the region where it was first defined, the boreal forest of the Canadian Shield, this tradition can be distinguished from the others by the presence of chipped-stone implements – projectile points, knives, and scrapers – that were relatively crudely made. Typically, they were produced from massive silicious deposits such as quartzite and rhyolite. Unfortunately, only one habitation site has been excavated, at Dead Man's Pool, in the north-central highland area of New Brunswick. David Sanger has concluded that enough traits existed at this location to distinguish it from the Laurentian tradition and that the subsistence pattern was largely oriented towards hunting the woodland caribou and taking the spawning Atlantic salmon, pursuits analogous to those found among Shield populations in the boreal forests. A small collection of Shield artifacts was also recovered from a ploughed field in the Cape Breton highlands, where the environmental setting is very similar to that of highland New Brunswick. This McEvoy site material fits well with other Shield Archaic assemblages in both the frequencies of the artifact classes and the specific attributes of the artifacts.[21]

Finally, another late Pre-ceramic tradition, the Broad Point tradition, has begun recently to attract attention within the region. The parent tradition was first defined in the middle Atlantic States, especially where the Susquehanna River flows through Pennsylvania, and the distinctive trait is a projectile point described as 'half as broad as long, or less';[22] hence the general designation 'Broad Point.' There are strong representations of the Broad Point tradition at sites in Maine, notably the Turner Farm site, the Hirundo site, and the Young site. North of this area, sites with the distinctive traits decline in numbers. The tradition derived from the southern and middle Atlantic areas of what is now the United States and spread northward in response to climate change.[23] Judging from the apparent displacement of earlier Laurentian/Maritime Archaic cultural characteristics at the Turner Farm site, the mechanism of the spread of the Broad Point tradition was actual movement of peoples.[24] The subsistence activities of the Broad Point people involved a mixed hunting-fishing-gathering economy. Because the culture encompassed both interior and coastal sites and used a varied technology, it apparently had neither the specialized marine orientation of the Maritime Archaic nor the complete interior adaptation of the Laurentian tradition. How far north the migration extended is uncertain, since distinctive artifacts are found only in the southwestern area of the Maritimes, notably in private collections in the Yarmouth-Tusket area, but it is at least suggestive that it occurred at the same time as the 'Red Paint' cemeteries stopped being used.

The middle-period traditions can all be considered as variants of mobile hunter-gatherer societies. Their social organization was at the band level, with communities numbering fewer than fifty people. The lack of archaeological evidence for substantive house features suggests that they did not stay at one location for very long. An intimate knowledge of the available resources within their territories led to a well-defined seasonal round of subsistence activities. This exploitation pattern continued into the early part of the next period. A number of technological changes occurred, however, including the disappearance of certain tool types – slate bayonets, gouges, ulus, and plummets – and, most importantly, the addition of a new technology centred on the production of ceramic vessels. The transitional process between the end of the middle period and the beginning of the late period in the Atlantic region remains an enigma for archaeologists. The principal change involved was the ending of the Pre-ceramic period through the introduction of pottery. To date, no evidence exists in the archaeological record of the Maritimes of an experimental stage in ceramic technology. The earliest vessels found reflect an intimate knowledge of pottery-manufacturing techniques, suggesting that the process was introduced by immigrants to the area or through close contact with peoples possessing the technology. The increased use of clay vessels through time is also an indicator of a change in lifestyle. Ceramic vessels are cumbersome and fragile and not easily transported, and thus peoples using such vessels would have had a more sedentary settlement pattern. Newfoundland and Labrador, however, never experienced the introduction of a ceramic technology. Whereas the peoples of the Maritimes were experiencing cultural contacts with groups to the west and south, those in Newfoundland and Labrador were coming under the influence of northern cultures.

The culture history of northern Labrador includes the earliest Inuit peoples, designated by archaeologists as Palaeo-Eskimos. Culturally and genetically distinct from North American Indians, these people were distributed from Alaska eastward as far as Greenland. Typical early Palaeo-Eskimo artifacts included small, triangular 'end-blades,' which formed a composite tool when fitted in the end of a barbed-bone or antler harpoon head, as well as lances tipped with contracting-stemmed projectile points, end-scrapers, and sharp tools known as 'burins' that were used in making a variety of bone, antler, and wood implements. Although the traces of these people in northern Labrador are scanty, it is assumed that their numbers were not large and that they were highly nomadic. Sites containing their characteristically small artifacts are known from Saglek Bay, and a few indications can be found as far south as Hamilton Inlet. The Arctic Small Tool tradition, although dated somewhat earlier for the Canadian High Arctic and for Greenland, can be placed in Labrador less than 4,000 years ago.[25]

Throughout the Arctic, changes took place over time as Palaeo-Eskimo cultures adapted to local resources. One local adaptation that had profoundly important results was the development of the late Palaeo-Eskimo culture known as the Dorset in the vicinity of Northern Hudson Bay, Hudson Strait, and Foxe Basin. From this core area, Dorset people migrated to northern Labrador and continued southward until they occupied the entire Newfoundland coast. The presence of this culture in Labrador can be dated from approximately 2,700 years ago, and it lasted for about 1,500 years. The decline began earlier in Labrador than in Newfoundland – northern sites are rare after 1,800 years ago, but there was a period of growth in Newfoundland between 2,000 and 1,500 years ago, with extinction occurring prior to A.D. 1000. Dorset sites have yielded a wealth of organic remains. In some respects, there is continuity from the earlier complexes, as in the miniaturization of tools and the use of two or more raw materials to create composite implements. A prime example of a composite weapon is the toggling harpoon, made of bone, antler, or ivory, and fitted with a stone end-blade. Occasionally a stone side-blade was slotted into the edge of the harpoon head, to increase its efficiency, while some harpoons were ground to a point and did not require an end-blade. The technology of grinding and polishing is evident in Dorset burins, and the Dorset also produced small, prismatic 'microblades' from chert and quartz crystals. New categories of artifacts now emerged. Whalebone sled shoes, for example, were likely fitted to the bottom of wooden sled runners to protect them from being damaged when pulled over ice. The absence of evidence of domesticated dogs leads to the further conclusion that the sleds were pulled by the Dorset people themselves. Other elements of the Dorset culture included soapstone bowls and lamps, both being typically flat-bottomed with angular corners and outsloping sides. The bowls were used for cooking, while the lamps provided light and heat. Evidence for the burial patterns of the Dorset can be found at sites on the island of Newfoundland, where several skeletons have been found in small caves and crevices in limestone cliffs. Study of these remains indicates an affinity with the Arctic Mongoloid physical type.[26]

At some time between A.D. 500 and A.D. 1000, Dorset people ceased to occupy Newfoundland and were replaced by Indian culture. The two groups must have been aware of each other's existence, and although the nature of any contact is unknown, it is not impossible that warfare hastened the end of the Dorset era. The end of this period also saw the brief intervention in Newfoundland of another culture – the Norse. Seven years of excavation by Anne Stine Ingstad and Helge Ingstad at the northern tip of Newfoundland demonstrated that L'Anse aux Meadows was a Norse site, and the finding was confirmed by a four-year re-examination by Birgitta Wallace of the Canadian Parks Service. The site consists of three dwelling complexes by the side of a small brook, with a smithy and associated kiln on the opposite side. All the dwellings were occupied at the same time, approximately A.D. 1000, and Wallace has interpreted the site as a centre for boat repair and thus as a staging point for exploration into the Gulf of St Lawrence. This brief occupation by the Norse represents the earliest evidence for European incursion into North America.[27] In addition to this single settlement site, a number of scattered Norse artifacts have been recovered during archaeological excavations. The Goddard site in Maine produced a Norse coin but no other Norse artifacts. The team investigating the site concluded that the coin was the product of a long coastal exchange network and not a reflection of direct contact between the Norse and the Native peoples of Maine. Other items of Norse material culture have been found in Inuit sites in the eastern Arctic. Robert McGhee has concluded that these have resulted from limited trading and possible mutual raiding between the Norse and Inuit. The search for the Norse settlements of

Vinland, so prominent in the sagas, has generated a large volume of literature. With few exceptions the evidence presented is highly speculative or based upon shoddy fakes. It seems reasonable to suggest that Vinland may have been somewhere in eastern Canada, but until substantial physical evidence is discovered, its location will remain uncertain.[28]

The direct ancestors of modern Labrador Inuit were the Thule people. Representing the last major migration of peoples from the western Arctic to the east, they moved rapidly and successfully on the basis of a whale-hunting technology that was especially effective in the context of a warming trend about A.D. 1000 and the consequent reduction of sea ice. This climatic phenomenon probably also facilitated the Norse voyages. The Eskimo peoples of north Alaska had developed by this time a technology for hunting the western Arctic bowhead whale through the use of large toggling harpoons fitted with lines attached to inflated sealskin floats. The whalers were able to pursue their quarry from kayaks and from large, open sealskin boats.[29] With the warming trend, the bowhead moved eastward into the High Arctic and overlapped with the range of the Greenland right whale. With a continuous spread of whale species, the whale hunters could apply their western technologies all across the High Arctic, and they arrived in Labrador about A.D. 1500.

On the basis of excavations near Saglek, Peter Schledermann has recognized distinct phases in the development of the Thule and the subsequent Labrador Inuit cultures. The earliest phase, dated from A.D. 1400 to A.D. 1700, can be represented by a typical Thule house. An oval-shaped, semi-subterranean structure with three levels, the house was entered by way of a tunnel leading to a slightly elevated flagstone floor. A raised sleeping platform was located at the rear, opposite the entrance. A low earthen exterior wall supported a whalebone interior frame, which was covered with baleen and sods to produce a domed roof. For archaeological purposes the houses have acted as deep freezes, providing excellent preservation of organic remains that reveal the material culture of the Thule to be similar to that of the Palaeo-Eskimo in types, but different in form. Objects have been recovered that were made from bone, antler, ivory, wood, baleen, and even the remnants of animal hides and bird feathers. The presence of whalebone snow knives is evidence that the Thule in Labrador built igloos. Other implements included the toggling harpoon with ground-slate end-blades. Ulus were also made from ground stone, while soapstone continued to be used in making lamps and pots. Towards the end of the early Thule phase, some European goods also appeared in the sites.[30]

While the rapid migration of the Thule is attributable to a warming trend, the dispersion and the subsequent definition of modern Inuit peoples resulted from the opposite climatic phenomenon. Between A.D. 1600 and A.D. 1850, the Arctic experienced its 'Little Ice Age,' and a series of local cultures developed that were adapted to the resources of specific areas. Conspicuous in Labrador was the disappearance of semi-subterranean houses and their replacement by rectangular, multifamily structures. Whaling and its by-products became less important, while seal hunting increased. European goods became increasingly influential in material culture and began to move towards predominance in the late eighteenth century, when Moravian missions were established along the Labrador coast. The last period in the history of Native American peoples prior to European contact is more obscure for Newfoundland and Labrador than for the Maritimes. Although at one time archaeologists suspected that the reasons had to do with the replacement of Indian by Inuit cultures, recent work has established that Indian cultures were not replaced but continued in Newfoundland and Labrador through to the era of European settlement. Accordingly, the occupation following the Maritime Archaic can be divided into two periods – the Intermediate Indian, from 3,500 to 2,000 years ago; and the Recent Indian, beginning some 2,000 years ago and continuing into the historic period. The Intermediate period is known only from sites excavated along the coasts of central and southern Labrador, and its material culture is represented in the archaeological record only by stone tools. Unfortunately, no bone, antler, or ivory items have survived, and thus it is difficult to reconstruct subsistence pursuits. The meagre record has led James Tuck to conclude that 'the Intermediate Indians represent a group of people, dispersed in small bands along the coast of central and southern Labrador, who represent a tenuous connection between earlier Archaic Indians and people who lived less than 2,000 years ago.'[31]

For the Recent Indian period in Newfoundland and Labrador, the archaeological record is more abundant and more complicated. Three cultural patterns have been defined. One of these, known as the Point Revenge complex, is found along the central and southern coasts of Labrador. The settlement pattern of these sites is similar to those of the Intermediate Indian period, and the stone tools have also been found to be similar, with the major exception that they are made from Ramah chalcedony. The sites are well south of the Ramah quarries in northern Labrador, and the almost exclusive use of this material may indicate either some form of trade with the Dorset Eskimos or annual northward excursions by the Point Revenge people. The excavation of a collapsed structure at the Big Island I site on Hamilton Inlet in central Labrador may link the Point Revenge people with the modern Montagnais-Naskapi. An alternative hypothesis, however, would see them as descendants of the Intermediate Indians who became extinct shortly after European contact. The two other Recent Indian cultures have been defined on the island of Newfoundland. The Beaches complex has many similarities to the Point Revenge pattern, except that here the stone tools were manufactured from local materials rather than Ramah chalcedony. The Little Passage complex, which may have grown out of the Beaches, is represented in coastal locations on both the north and south coasts of Newfoundland. The material culture, not unlike that found in Beaches sites, is characterized by small notched and stemmed projectile points, knives, and scrapers. Adaptive strategies included use of both marine and inland resources. There is a distinct possibility of a link between the Little Passage people and the historically known Beothuk, although very scant evidence of this connection has been found.

In the Maritimes, the late period of development prior to European contact began some 2,500 years ago and was characterized by the introduction of ceramic technology. Research to date has not provided a detailed sequence of changing styles within this technology, but the period is conventionally divided into three phases – Early, Middle, and Late Ceramic. It is generally recognized that the Early Ceramic period was characterized by clay vessels with cord impressions on the interior and exterior, known as Vinette pottery. Two fragments of Vinette ceramics have come to light in a collection gathered in the Gaspereau Valley in Nova Scotia, and others have been identified at Rafter Lake. Given the evidence from Maine, it is likely that ceramic technology began in Nova Scotia about 2,500 years ago. At the time that ceramic technology was being introduced into the Maritime region, a complex burial ceremonialism was reaching full development in the Ohio Valley. It is defined in the archaeological literature by the building of large earth mounds to cover ceremonial burial sites. Despite isolated finds of suggestive artifacts, this phenomenon was unknown in Atlantic Canada until 1972, when four skeletons and their associated grave goods, including more than 1,000 copper beads, were found at the Augustine site on the Southwest Miramichi River. Excavations revealed a human-made burial mound, and sufficient charcoal was recovered to produce radio-carbon dates ranging from 2,900 to 2,330 years ago.[32] These dates place the Augustine site as contemporary with the Adena mounds of the Ohio Valley. How did this kind of site come to be located in New Brunswick? Was it a case purely of cultural diffusion, or was there actual migration of people from farther west? These are difficult questions, and as yet the evidence permits no reliable answers. Nevertheless, a further discovery in 1986, at the Skora site near Halifax, showed that the Augustine site was no isolated phenomenon. An oval-shaped burial pit containing charcoal, cremated human remains, and artifacts was dated from 2,440 to 2,260 years ago. These dates, along with the artifacts and the mode of burial, show that the Skora and Augustine sites belong to the same ceremonial tradition.[33]

The archaeological record for the Middle and Late Ceramic phases has been defined primarily from shell midden sites found along the coasts of the Maritimes. Shell middens are accumulations of discarded shells of molluscs – clams, quahogs, mussels, and occasionally scallops and oysters. Beginning about 2,000 years ago, the aboriginal inhabitants began to exploit these resources of the intertidal zone. It may be that the practice was introduced by immigrants into the area, or that existing populations simply discovered the resource. The remains at a small site at Smith's Cove, in Digby County, Nova Scotia, primarily composed of thin paste made from shells of the common blue mussel, suggests that shellfish exploitation began when people were drawn to the most visible and readily available species. The blue mussel, attached in clusters to the rocks and outcrops of the intertidal zones, is easy to collect – by comparison, say, with digging for clams – but quickly becomes depleted. One can speculate, therefore, that harvesting began with simple discovery and that deletion of mussel stocks was followed by collection of other species.

Many shell middens have been excavated in the Maritime provinces. One that spans almost the entire Ceramic period – only the era of early Vinette pottery is unrepresented – is located at Sellar's Cove on the northeast side of Nova Scotia's St Margarets Bay. The first occupants of the site produced thin-walled, grit-tempered clay vessels, which were decorated by using a fine-toothed stamping technique. A number of the bone stamping tools were recovered from the lower levels of the midden. These inhabitants also produced the chipped-stone projectile points, with a contracting stem as a hafting device, that combine with bone and antler fishing implements to represent the essential tool-kit of the Middle Ceramic phase. The upper levels of the Sellar's Cove midden represent the Late Ceramic Phase. In general, clay pots in these levels show a decline in quality from their earlier counterparts. They are thicker, with a coarser-grained temper and less attention paid to firing techniques. Decoration reverts to the use of a cord-wrapped stick and is found only on the exterior of the vessels. The decline in vessel quality is considered an indication that people were becoming more mobile. These ceramics are associated with small, chipped-stone projectile points, notched to form an expanded stem for hafting. The small size of the points suggests that they were arrowheads, and thus that the bow and arrow had now been introduced. Also represented in the upper levels of the midden were fishing tools and an unusual section of a necklace made from rolled copper beads. In time, this and other Late

Ceramic sites persisted up until a few centuries prior to European contact, but no exact terminal date can be given. It is assumed that earthenware vessels disappeared from the cultural inventory of the aboriginal inhabitants before contact, as no mention of them is found in the ethnohistoric record.

This leads in turn to the problem of linking the pre-contact archaeological record with our knowledge of the post-contact era. Bernard Hoffman in the 1950s, later supported by David Christianson, suggested that the Micmac of the early contact period derived approximately 90 per cent of subsistence from marine resources, supplemented by marginal inland hunting during a short time in the winter months. Hoffman and Christianson relied extensively on the accounts of early European travellers – notably Pierre Biard's 1616 description of the annual Micmac subsistence cycle, but also the writings of Chrestien Le Clercq, Marc Lescarbot, Nicolas Denys, and the sieur de Dièreville.[34] Some recent analyses, however, have argued that archaeological evidence casts doubt on the validity of the written descriptions. The studies of Bruce Bourque, David Sanger, and Stephen Davis in northern Maine and southeastern New Brunswick indicate an opposite pattern. Faunal remains recovered from late-period shell middens strongly suggest a semi-sedentary form of settlement, with primary occupation of the coast lasting all year except for limited periods in the interior during the summer.[35] On the other hand, research conducted by Ronald J. Nash and Virginia P. Miller in northeastern Nova Scotia and by David Burley in northeastern New Brunswick has found 'a generalized Woodland economy more closely resembling that known from the fur trade period in which land mammals are an important part of the economy.'[36] Although the debate continues, it is likely that these divergences reflect, as Frances Stewart argues, 'different strategies adopted by the ancestral Maliseet-Passamaquoddies and Micmacs. Ancestral Micmacs may have exploited coastal resources most in the summer, whereas the prehistoric Maliseet-Passamaquoddies may have used the coast primarily in winter.'[37]

Although local groups adjusted to local conditions, there were broad similarities in the lives led by the late prehistoric peoples of the Maritimes. The ratio of marine to terrestrial species may have varied throughout the region, but the ancestors of the Micmac and the Maliseet were pre-eminently hunters and fishers. New Brunswick and Nova Scotia were at the northern limits of indigenous horticulture, and while it is possible that there may have been some experiments in growing one or more of the 'three sisters' – corn, beans, and squash – that formed the mainstay of the diet of peoples farther south, evidence for the spread of horticultural to the Maritimes is tentative at best. Similarly, there is little evidence that wild plants constituted a significant part of Native diets in the Maritimes – although this conclusion may be the result of inadequate archaeological data. The archaeological evidence for the late prehistoric period does reveal a widespread dependence on seals, small whales, cod, herring, salmon, smelt, gaspereau, eels, and shellfish. The land furnished beaver, caribou, and, especially, moose. On a seasonal basis there were ducks, geese, and a variety of sea birds. Small game such as hares and porcupines supplemented a diet rich in protein. The resources of the region also furnished most of the tools needed to catch and kill animals and to turn them into food, clothing, and shelter. Lances, arrows, and harpoons were tipped with stone; stone tools were also used to skin and butcher animals and to cut wood and peel bark. Animals themselves provided the means by which they could be converted to human use. Bones, antlers, and teeth were used as harpoons, projectile points, knives, needles, fish spears, hooks, and gorges, while skins and sinew were turned into clothing and containers. Although pottery had been made in the prehistoric period, by the time of European contact it had largely been replaced by bark and leather vessels. Maritime Natives also employed birch-bark to make light and strong canoes, seagoing versions of which were capable of making the hazardous voyage from the Nova Scotia mainland to the Magdalen Islands and across the Cabot Strait to Newfoundland. In winter, travel was by wooden toboggan and snowshoes made of wood and rawhide. The shapes, sizes, and coverings of houses in the Maritimes varied, but, winter and summer, the preferred dwelling throughout the region was a conical wigwam made by covering a framework of light poles with sheets of birch-bark. Although varying quantities of exotic stone from as far away as northern Labrador occasionally reached the Maritimes, the picture that has emerged from the admittedly incomplete archaeological record is of peoples relying on an intimate knowledge of their local environments for the bulk of their material needs.

The eleven millennia of human history in the Atlantic region prior to European contact produced richly diverse cultural experiences. Dramatic environmental changes took place, beginning with the unstable periglacial environment during the occupation of the Debert/Belmont Palaeo-Indian sites. These conditions limited occupation to the more favourable areas, but with their end people covered the region. The complexity of the Pre-ceramic period is related to the diverse economic pursuits of the inhabitants of this time. Their success in adaptation is reflected in their treatment of the dead. Sites like Cow Point and Port au Choix show a level of cultural complexity well beyond a mere hand-to-mouth existence. The movement of peoples, technologies, and cultural subsystems is clear from the archaeological record. Technologies were traded throughout the region along with certain raw materials. Especially remarkable was the introduction of an entire cultural subsystem derived from the very heartland of the continent. The burial mounds at Red Bank and White's Lake, with their exotic lithics and foreign treatment of the dead, emphasize that the Atlantic region was in contact with events elsewhere. The notion of isolation is further diminished when the origins of ceramic technologies are traced to New England. Overall, these events illustrate a sequence of profound changes through time. They serve to invalidate the foolish but still widely held illusion that Native cultures were timeless and unchanging.

CHAPTER TWO

The Sixteenth Century
Aboriginal Peoples and European Contact

RALPH PASTORE

Although it is possible that men from Bristol knew about the wealth of fish off Newfoundland even before Columbus' first voyage, John Cabot's discovery of those fish in 1497 probably began the early prosecution of the fisheries by English vessels. Four years later, Gaspar Corte Real reached Newfoundland and Labrador, and by 1506 the Portuguese had established a fishery in Terra Nova – which in the sixteenth century could be anywhere from the Strait of Belle Isle to New England. The French began fishing in the region by at least 1504, and Basques from both France and Spain had begun to arrive by about 1512. By 1524–5, when the explorers Giovanni da Verrazzano of France and Estevão Gomes of Spain had come as far north as Cape Breton, they regarded their mission of exploring the coastline of North America as complete – clear evidence of the geographical knowledge of the area surrounding Newfoundland that Europeans had gained from the fishery. European familiarity with the peoples and lands of the Atlantic region grew during the sixteenth century with the advent of a large-scale Basque whaling effort in the 1540s and an increased fur trade after 1580. By the late 1570s, the English merchant Anthony Parkhurst estimated that England, France, Spain, and Portugal together sent some 400 vessels and 12,000 men a year to the whale and cod fisheries.[1] Until more research is done in European archives, this can be only a crude estimate, but it gives some idea of the magnitude of the European presence in the Atlantic region. That presence would have a dramatic effect on the region's Native peoples.

When Europeans arrived off the shores of the lands from the Strait of Belle Isle to Passamaquoddy Bay, they began a process that would irrevocably change Native cultural development. Until recently, scholars have tended to emphasize what seemed to be the timeless nature of the coastal cultures prior to European contact. In reality, during the centuries that preceded the coming of the Europeans there were periods of significant cultural change, resulting both from radical environmental shifts and from the arrival of new ideas, and even new peoples, from outside the Atlantic realm. None of the changes, however, were as momentous as those that resulted from the arrival of the strangers from across the sea. To understand the magnitude of these transformations, it is necessary to understand the nature of the Native societies of what would become the Atlantic provinces. Unfortunately, the archaeological data needed to answer some of the most basic questions about the region's indigenous peoples are lacking and, because of rising sea levels in many areas of the Maritimes, may never be collected.

Fortunately, there is a growing amount of archaeological information about the Labrador Inuit, who periodically travelled from northern Labrador to the Strait of Belle Isle and may have encountered Europeans as early as 1500 or 1501.[2] Thereafter, there may have been occasional encounters between European fishermen and Labrador Inuit. Certainly, the woodcut of a woman and child captured by French fishermen in 1566 and displayed in Augsburg is that of two Inuit people, and it is likely that they were taken from Labrador. The fact that the fishermen killed the husband before taking the mother and daughter captive gives us a single, if suggestive, clue about the nature of Inuit-French relations of the period.[3] We have little more information about the nature of Inuit contact, if any, with the Basque whalers who came to the Strait of Belle Isle in the 1530s and remained on a seasonal basis until the beginning of the seventeenth century. Their vessels, up to twenty in number, left Spain for the strait as early as late April and stayed on some occasions until December. Once in the strait, the men erected or repaired structures on shore where the whales were processed.[4] Whaling carried out from shore stations required a great deal of metal – harpoons, flensing knives, copper cauldrons, and thousands of nails. Throughout North America, metal, especially iron, was eagerly sought after by Native populations to replace cutting and piercing tools made of stone and bone. The iron-rich whaling sites of the Strait of Belle Isle would have acted as a magnet attracting Native groups from a wide area, and there is no doubt that some adventurous Inuit acquired European goods from Basque whaling sites.[5] Writing in 1625, the Basque historian Lope de Isasti stated that there had been conflicts between the 'esquimaos' and the Basques, but it should be noted that the term 'esquimao' and its variants have been used to refer to a number of Native peoples, including Micmacs and Montagnais as well as Inuit.[6] Evidence of violence between the Inuit and the Basques in the sixteenth century is scanty and ambiguous, and the fact that European whalers were numerous and well-armed argues that the Inuit would have been foolhardy to attack them.[7] By the 1620s, however, relations between the Inuit and European fishermen – as opposed to whalers – were increasingly hostile. In Champlain's words, 'The savages of the north coast [of the Strait of Belle Isle] are very malicious, and attack the fishermen, who in self-defence arm small vessels to protect the boats which put to sea to fish for cod.'[8]

The Strait of Belle Isle about which Champlain was writing has been referred to as a 'resource funnel' for a variety of whales, seals, and sea birds.[9] Those creatures of the sea and air, in numbers that we can hardly imagine today, drew the hunters of the adjoining coasts to the strait every year. Some of the hunting groups belonged to what Europeans would later call the Montagnais.[10] The pre-contact ancestors of the modern Montagnais-Naskapi (Innu) were likely the people who left stone tools that archaeologists have assigned to the Point Revenge complex of Quebec-Labrador. These Point Revenge people probably repaired to the interior in the winter, perhaps to live in relatively more substantial, partially earth-covered, lodges and to hunt caribou and other inland game. When the ice broke up, the people may have gone down river and erected temporary wigwams in small settlements near river mouths and in the inner portions of bays. From these camps they would have hunted migratory sea birds, ringed seals, and harbour seals and fished for char and salmon. In July and August, they would have moved out to the outer islands where they might have lived in somewhat larger communities, occupying these camps for short periods of time while they exploited a variety of coastal resources. This might also have been the time when Point Revenge peoples traded for goods such as the highly desired Ramah chert, a stone found only in the Ramah Bay region of northern Labrador. As autumn arrived, it is probable that they left their outer-island camps for the inner reaches and a fall caribou hunt. In November, harp seals would have migrated southward, and it is unlikely that the Point Revenge hunters would have neglected such an abundant supply of food. Although this pattern of inner and outer coastal occupation and resource use is quite plausible, it was not characteristic of the Montagnais-Naskapi in the historic period. The reason for this discrepancy may lie in the spread down the Labrador coast of the Inuit in the fifteenth and sixteenth centuries, a movement that may have discouraged prehistoric Montagnais-Naskapi use of that coast. It is also possible that the Point Revenge people, although they may have been closely related to the historic Montagnais-Naskapi, simply became extinct.[11]

While the surviving archaeological evidence of prehistoric inhabitants of the Strait of Belle Isle and the lower north shore of Quebec is consistent with that of band society, to date archaeology has provided little detail about that society. By contrast, the historical record, most particularly the *Jesuit Relations*, contains sufficient information to allow researchers to construct at least the broad outlines of Montagnais society – keeping in mind that it was seventeenth- not sixteenth-century society that was described, and that the descriptions come to us filtered through the minds of seventeenth-century European clerics. The relevant documents depict a society functioning at four levels. The first was the fundamental social and economic unit, the multifamily lodge group, numbering from 10 to 20 people, who lived in a single structure. Several of these lodge groups (a total of 35 to 75 people) made up the winter aggregate, which might fracture into smaller groups, all of which tried to keep in touch so that the results of a good hunt could be shared. A number of these aggregates made up what has been called the 'named group,' often referred to as the 'band' – people whom Europeans called the Attikameks, the Papinachois, the Mistassini, and so forth. Such groups numbered anywhere from 150 to 300 people and thought of themselves as belonging to a defined entity. At least in the seventeenth century, several bands totalling up to 1,500 individuals clustered temporarily at trading posts, but it is not clear if groups of this size could have come together in the prehistoric period, when it would have been very difficult for such large groups to find sufficient food. Somewhat smaller aggregations, however, could have gathered at salmon or whitefish runs.

Seventeenth-century accounts make it clear that individuals and families moved easily between lodge groups, winter bands, and named groups. Marriage patterns are less easy to discern, but there is some evidence for matrilocality and a tendency to marry cross-cousins from outside the band.[12] These practices would have had the effect of strengthening ties among groups and would also have facilitated what appear to be two of the most significant values characteristic of Montagnais society – individual autonomy, and the sharing of goods, especially food. The result was a culture well adapted to a subarctic environment. When a local shortage of game necessitated moving, relatives could often be found in more productive areas, and the principle that food should be shared ensured that the risk of starvation would be spread as widely as possible. These values were held by an egalitarian society where obedience was owed not to an individual but to group norms – many of which, like the requirement that food be shared, functioned in a practical way to ensure survival. Such norms were enforced by pervasive joking and teasing. Band members were particularly concerned about open displays of anger, which could tear apart a group. In such a society, decisions were arrived at only after discussion and the achievement of consensus. While the Jesuits and others occasionally referred to individuals they termed 'captains' or 'chiefs,' these were actually people who simply spoke for the group. Leaders, in fact, appear to have functioned as such only in specific situations: one especially skilled hunter might lead a caribou hunt, another might act as an intermediary during the course of a commercial transaction, and a shaman would carry out a curing ritual or attempt to find distant game.[13]

While the political organization of a Montagnais band seems relatively apparent, the nature of relationships between men and women is less clear.[14] Montagnais women enjoyed a greater degree of independence than did European women,[15] but gender roles were clearly defined, and when men performed what was considered women's work, they were teased mercilessly. One of the central concerns of Montagnais life was food and its division. Wives appear to have had the freedom to apportion and give away food as they pleased, but they were not invited to major feasts and were not given the 'good pieces' of meat. On the other hand, the men who attended such a feast were expected to bring meat back, and on one occasion, failure to do so prompted the women of a band to criticize the offender harshly.[16] Another indication of the relative status of women is the fact that women who were dissatisfied with this sort of conduct on the part of their husbands could divorce them easily. Men could take more than one wife, however, a social practice that suggests an unequal relationship between the sexes. Even so, the degree of independence possessed by Montagnais women was disturbing to European observers. Equally upsetting were Native attitudes towards child rearing.[17] Accustomed to the rough discipline of early-modern France, the Jesuits were surprised that children were never struck or severely chastised. In fact, children absorbed group values and ideals primarily through teasing and by example. Most importantly, from an early age children learned that it was necessary to share, to suppress anger, and to exhibit patience and good humour.

It would be wise not to exaggerate the ostensibly idyllic aspects of Montagnais society. The virtues that the Montagnais displayed towards each other were not extended to their enemies. The anger that individuals suppressed within the group may have erupted, for example, in the torture of Iroquois captives. Not only enemies but non-Montagnais strangers as well were apparently excluded from the benefits enjoyed by members of Montagnais society. Although truthfulness was expected among the Montagnais, there was no compunction about lying to strangers. Nor was there any requirement that food be shared with outsiders. According to one knowledgeable observer, 'they are as ungrateful as possible toward strangers.'[18] Once again, however, it should be stressed that these descriptions of Montagnais society apply to a people already affected by more than 100 years of European contact, and at present it is simply not possible to determine the extent to which they applied to the pre-contact Montagnais.

In fact, we are not even sure when the process of European influence on the Montagnais began. One of the earliest European references to the Montagnais may be a French account of 1529, which noted that 'the inhabitants live in small huts and houses covered with tree bark, which they build to live in during the fishing season, which begins in the spring and lasts all summer. They hunt seals, porpoises, and certain sea birds called gannets [*margaux*] which they take on the islands ... When the fishing season ends with the approach of winter they return with their catch in boats made of the bark of certain trees called birch [*buil*], and go to warmer countries but we know not where.'[19] Some five years later, Jacques Cartier, the St Malo explorer who obtained royal support to search for a passage to Asia, left another description of a Native group on the north coast of the Strait of Belle Isle. In his words:

> There are people on this coast whose bodies are fairly well formed but they are wild and savage folk. They wear their hair tied up on the top of their heads like a handful of twisted hay, with a nail or something of the sort passed throught the middle, and into it they weave a few bird's feathers. They clothe themselves with the furs of animals, both men as well as women; but the women are wrapped up more closely and snuggly in their furs; and have a belt about their waists. They [all] paint themselves with certain tan colours. They have canoes made of birchbark in which they go about, and from which they catch many seals. Since seeing them [the Natives], I have been informed that their home is not at this place but that they come from warmer countries to catch these seals and to get other food for their sustenance.[20]

These people may have been Montagnais, or they may have been Beothuks – a distinction that may have had less meaning in the sixteenth century than it would at a later date.[21] While anchored off Natashquan point, on the Quebec lower north shore opposite the eastern end of Anticosti Island, Cartier encountered another group of some twelve Indians who 'came as freely on board our vessels as if they had been Frenchmen. They gave us to understand that they had come from the Grand bay [the western end of the Strait of Belle Isle].'[22] While it is obvious from the behaviour of these Natives that they were accustomed to trading with Europeans, their ethnic identity is less clear. They may have been Montagnais, or they may have been St Lawrence Iroquoians.[23]

The appearance of St Lawrence Iroquoians in the Strait of Belle Isle is confirmed by a report by Spanish officials, who, worried about French incursions in North America, conducted an investigation in 1542 that involved the interrogation of a number of Basque sailors. One of the latter said 'that many Indians came to his ship in Grand Bay, and they ate and drank together, and were very friendly, and the Indians gave them deer and wolf skins in exchange for axes and knives and other trifles ... they gave them to understand that one of their number was Chief in Canada. And that they killed more than thirty-five of Jacques' men ... '[24] The reference to the altercation between these Indians and Cartier's men is strong evidence that these were St Lawrence Iroquoians or, more precisely, Stadaconans, from the area of what is now Quebec City, who had turned against Cartier, probably because of his abusive treatment of them.[25] The testimony is also an indication of the amount of cultural change that had occurred in the Strait of Belle Isle within the lifetime of a person who had been alive when Columbus had begun the catastrophic process of bringing one-half of the planet to the attention of the other half.

By the 1540s, as the previous account indicates, there was already a trade in skins for axes, knives, and 'other trifles,' and eventually throughout North America it would be the lure of these edged iron tools that drew Native peoples to offer furs for them. Iron tools replaced stone, bone, and antler and significantly changed Native lives. Axes not only greatly reduced the time it took to cut down trees to make lodges; they could also be used to chop into frozen beaver houses in winter. Iron knives, while initially not as sharp as stone flakes, were superior because stone was brittle, quickly became dull, and was more difficult to sharpen. Nails and pieces of discarded iron and brass were also made into arrow, lance, and harpoon points that had similar advantages over stone weapons. These improvements must have increased the success rate of hunters and consequently made their lives that much easier. The participation in a European trade would also have meant that the need to travel to quarries to obtain raw materials would have been reduced or eliminated. This may or may not have resulted in a net saving of time for Native traders, who would also now have to spend time waiting for European vessels on the coast. In some cases, engaging in a fur trade would also have necessitated a change in seasonal movements.

An alteration in seasonal movements may not have been the only change to which Montagnais bands would have had to adjust. The presence of St Lawrence Iroquoian groups in the Strait of Belle Isle makes one wonder what sort of relations existed between these Iroquoians from farther west and the Algonkian-speakers in southern Quebec-Labrador. In any case, the St Lawrence Iroquoians were not a permanent fixture in the region. By the time Champlain described the St Lawrence Valley in 1603, the St Lawrence Iroquoians were gone and the region was a battleground between Montagnais and Algonkins on the one hand and Iroquois, mostly Mohawks, on the other. The evidence, both historical and archaeological, indicates that the last of the St Lawrence Iroquoians were destroyed by Five Nations Iroquois raiders bent on obtaining European goods either by pillage or by gaining access to European traders.[26] This pattern of intertribal warfare resulting from the arrival of trade goods may have begun in the Gulf, but eventually it would spread across the continent. Ultimately, the copper kettles and iron axes would cost a great deal more than beaver and otter skins.

In the sixteenth century, European goods were often supplied by the Basques, who appear to have built up a special relationship with the Montagnais of the Strait of Belle Isle, the other Algonkian peoples of the Gulf, and the St Lawrence Iroquoians. In the earlier part of the century, the fur trade carried on by Basque codfishers seems to have been a relatively minor sideline to the fishery itself, but by the last quarter of the sixteenth century the fur trade, while still less important than the fishery, had assumed much more significance.[27] The contacts between the Basques and the people of the Gulf had resulted in the growth of a *lingua franca* that was, in the words of Marc Lescarbot, the early-seventeenth-century chronicler of New France, 'half Basque.'[28] Basque fishermen-fur traders may even have made a practice of leaving young men with Native groups over the winter to learn the language and become interpreters.[29] Whalers as well as codfishers may have had equally close contacts with the Montagnais. Writing about events in the last decades of the sixteenth century, the West Country sea captain Richard Whitbourne stated, in reference to the 'naturall Inhabitants of the Countrey,' that 'the *French* and *Biscaines* (who resort thither [the Strait of Belle Isle] yeerely for the Whale-fishing, and also for the Cod-fish) report them to be an ingenious and tractable people (being well vsed:) they are ready to assist them with great labour and patience, in the killing, cutting, and boyling of Whales; and making the Traineoyle, without expectation of other reward, then a little bread, or some such small hire.'[30]

After 1580, with the demand by European hat manufacturers for felt made of beaver fur, the trade in the Gulf burgeoned, and Tadoussac, at the mouth of the Saguenay, replaced the Strait of Belle Isle as the most important rendezvous for the fur trade. From Tadoussac, a network of waterways served as highways for Native traders bringing down the furs of the interior to waiting European vessels.[31] But the increased dependency on the fur trade could bring about real hardship. In 1611, when Champlain arrived at Tadoussac in the middle of May, he encoun-

tered a group of Natives, presumably Montagnais, who had been waiting there to trade. Champlain described them as 'in a rather miserable
condition ... [with] only a few articles which they wished to barter
merely in order to get food. Furthermore, they wanted to wait until several ships had arrived in order to get our wares more cheaply.'[32] It is not
clear if this practice of waiting until enough vessels had arrived to make
the trade more competitive was common during the sixteenth century;
if it was, however, it suggests that Native hunting bands were having to
make significant changes to their seasonal rounds. A large concentration of people living for an extended period at a place such as Tadoussac
would have depleted the local food resources and forced the Native
people to rely on European foods to supplement their diet. The flour,
salt meat, and dried peas that were the staples of mariners' diets were
nutritionally inferior to indigenous food and may have contributed to a
decline in health.

On the other side of the Strait of Belle Isle, on the island of Newfoundland, contact with Europeans brought about different, if no less drastic,
changes to the lives of the island's people. The story of the Beothuk
begins with their ancestors, the possessors of the Little Passage complex. Unfortunately, there is relatively little archaeological evidence per-
taining to the Little Passage people, particularly those from the late
prehistoric period, but data from excavated Little Passage sites are consistent with the archaeological remains of a sparse, widely scattered
hunting people who lived in small bands and were heavily dependent
upon both caribou and marine resources.[33] There is a similar problem in
the historic period, where there is a parallel scarcity of information in
the documentary record. In that case it was because no European ever
`lived with a Beothuk group, and except for a few captured individuals,
contacts between the two peoples were fleeting. As a result, our understanding of Beothuk culture is more limited than that of other Native
peoples of the Atlantic region.

Although it is an archaeological convention that the term 'Beothuk'
can be substituted for the term 'Little Passage people' once the indigenous inhabitants of Newfoundland began to acquire European goods, it
is difficult to determine when this began. The group of Native people
kidnapped and taken to Rouen in 1509 are sometimes claimed to have
been Beothuks, but they could have been taken from almost anywhere
between the Strait of Belle Isle and New England.[34] The mysterious
author of the 'Discorso D'vn Gran Capitano di mare Franceseo del luoco
di Dieppa' described the people who lived on the west coast of Newfoundland in 1529 as 'more humane, and friendlier' than the Natives of
Newfoundland's south coast and Cape Breton,[35] suggesting, perhaps,
the former's greater willingness to trade with Europeans. It is signifi-

cant that when Cartier described the large flightless great auks, he referred to them as 'Apponatz,' a term recently recognized as a Beothuk word.[36] Cartier's use of a Beothuk word implies a friendly contact that had occurred before 1534, and perhaps a trading relationship between French fishermen and the Beothuk. There may have been a similar relationship between the Beothuk and the Basques, as evidenced by a Beothuk burial excavated near Comfort Cove, Notre Dame Bay, in 1974, that contained what appears to be a Basque whaling lance.

There is additional circumstantial evidence for the presence of a fur trade in the 1612 account of the English would-be colonizer John Guy, who met a group of Beothuks at the bottom of Trinity Bay, Newfoundland. After a friendly encounter, marked on the Natives'part by 'signes of ioy, & gladnes,' Guy's people found that the Beothuks had set up a small hut surrounded by poles upon which were fastened a variety of skins. Guy's men were not equipped to trade, but they left a few trinkets behind as a gesture of goodwill. In other deserted Beothuk houses, the colonists found a copper kettle and the dried inguinal sac of a beaver – a trade item from which *castoreum* was derived, a substance used by Europeans as a base for medicine and perfume.[37] Clearly, the Beothuks had previously carried on a trade, but it may have been in the form of 'silent barter' – an exchange of goods effected by one party that left goods at a predetermined place to be picked up by the other party at a later time. In fact, giving testimony before a parliamentary committee in 1793, the English explorer and entrepreneur George Cartwright testified that 'formerly a very beneficial barter was carried on between our people and the Indians ... by our people leaving goods at a certain place, and the Indians taking what they wanted and leaving furs in return.'[38]

These references hint at an unusual relationship with Europeans. Unlike the other Native peoples of the Atlantic provinces, the Beothuk did not go from a casual, opportunistic fur trade in the sixteenth century to a fully developed one in the next century. Instead, they withdrew from contact with Europeans in the seventeenth century, and after that, if they carried on any sort of trade, it was a very minor one – most likely with the Montagnais from southern Quebec-Labrador. The reasons for this unusual development appear to lie in the nature of the Newfoundland economy. Until the beginning of the nineteenth century, migratory fishermen from England's West Country and from France came to the island in the spring and built flakes, wharves, and stages. When they returned to Europe in the fall, they left behind nails, lost fish-hooks, and other debris. There are seventeenth- and eighteenth-century references to Beothuks' picking up those goods, and archaeological work at a number of sites reveals a pattern of Beothuks' working of nails and other European iron objects into projectile points, awls, and other tools. The long-standing presence of a migratory fishery allowed Beothuks to acquire these highly desirable European metal goods without trading for them. Scavenging metal was obviously less effort than spending time trapping fur-bearing animals, many of which would not normally be eaten. Once begun, this trend was strengthened by the emergence of European fur trappers (called 'furriers' in Newfoundland) who appeared as early as the early seventeenth century – a phenomenon not found elsewhere in North America until much later. By the latter half of the seventeenth century, migratory European fishermen in Newfoundland seldom saw Beothuks, and the few resident European settlers on the island had learned the skills of trapping and saw no need to seek out Beothuks with whom to trade. Because the last known Beothuk died in 1829, the popular – and scholarly – perception of the Beothuk is that of a doomed people, but this view is an anachronism. The laughing Beothuks whom Guy had met in 1612 did not know that their descendants were destined for extinction two hundred years later. In fact, one can argue that by choosing a strategy of obtaining European goods by scavenging, the Beothuks avoided the disease, alcoholism, violence, and cultural loss associated with prolonged contact with European fur traders, missionaries, soldiers, and officials.[39]

By contrast, all these things happened to the peoples who would be known as the Micmac and the Maliseet. In the early sixteenth century, the Micmac habitat appears to have included Cape Breton Island, Nova Scotia, Prince Edward Island, northeastern New Brunswick, and part of the Gaspé Peninsula. The Maliseet and the Passamaquoddy, two other Eastern Algonkian-speaking groups, are usually described as very similar peoples. In the eighteenth century, the Maliseet inhabited the St John River drainage in Maine and New Brunswick, while the Passamaquoddy lived along the coasts of northeastern Maine and southwestern New Brunswick.[40] Both groups are often thought to have been the direct descendants of the people whom the French called the Etchemin, but recent re-evaluation of the early-seventeenth-century French sources suggests that the Etchemin lived from the St John to the Kennebec River, and that, in fact, instead of being the direct descendants of the Etchemin, as has often been alleged, the modern 'Passamaquoddy and Maliseet tribes are better understood as products of ethnic realignments, shifts in residence, territorial loss, and the Indian policies of New England and New France.'[41] There is a better case for equating the modern-day Micmac with the Souriquois, the earliest seventeenth-century French term for the Native peoples east of the St John River. Partly because rising sea levels and coastal erosion have destroyed many coastal sites in New Brunswick and Nova Scotia, archaeological evidence for the origins of both the Souriquois and the Etchemin is not entirely clear. Both groups are probably the descendants of hunter-gath-erers who lived during the Late Ceramic period. By the time of Euro-pean contact, ceramics had largely been replaced by bark and leather vessels. Hunting-gathering remained – with fishing – the main subsis-tence pursuits, though with many local variations according to the availability of resources. Travel technologies were also based on local materials – such as birch-bark for canoes that could voyage as far from the mainland as the Magdalen Islands or Newfoundland, or wood for toboggans – as were the wigwams made of poles and birch-bark that were the preferred form of dwelling.[42]

Very early after the first European visits to North America, Native peo-ple began to acquire exotic goods from across the Atlantic. The Natives encountered by the Portuguese explorer Gaspar Corte Real in the course of his 1501 voyage, for example, were reported to have been in posses-sion of a broken sword and silver rings.[43] Although the identity of these Natives is not entirely clear, this information – if correct – indicates a very early, and possibly amicable, contact between Europeans and Natives of the northeast. When the King of France sent Jacques Cartier to find a passage to Asia in 1534, he met Micmacs in the Bay of Chaleur who held up furs on sticks in an effort to get his vessel to stop and trade – a clear indication that they were no strangers to a fur trade.[44] As the fishery and its attendant fur trade increased,[45] however, Micmac-Euro-pean relations took on a familiarity that ranged from easy friendliness to outright hostility – the latter probably occasioned by European arro-gance and failure to understand Native culture. A major source of fric-tion must have been the European explorers' habit of kidnapping the Natives they met. Corte Real had kidnapped a number of Natives, as had Gomes, Cartier, and others. The practice may have been responsible for the reception accorded Giovanni da Verrazzano, the Italian mariner in the service of the French king, when he encountered Natives, appar-ently on the coast of Maine, in 1524. While Natives to the south had been quite friendly, these people were very suspicious. They would not allow a small boat to land, and would only permit goods to pass along a rope to shore. Significantly, they were not interested in the bells, mir-rors, and trinkets that had enchanted Native groups to the south; these northern Natives wanted only knives, hooks, and edged iron tools. They made rude gestures toward Verrazzano's vessel, and when he sent a landing party ashore they shot arrows at it.[46] Although it is unlikely that these people were Micmacs, they were living not far from Micmac territory and had obviously experienced some prior unpleasantness in dealing with Europeans.

In this regard, the report of the 'great French sea captain from Dieppe' noted that 'Between Capo di Ras [Cape Race, Newfoundland] and Capo de Brettoni live a cruel and austere people, with whom it is impossible to deal or to converse.'[47] That description, possibly of the Micmac, was echoed later by the Rouen merchant Etienne Bellenger, whose trading and exploring expedition to the Maritimes in 1583 was marred by a clash with Micmacs on Nova Scotia's southern coast. The chronicler of that voyage noted that 'in divers places they [the Natives] are gentle and tractable. But those about Cape Briton and threescore or fowerscore leagues Westward are more cruell and subtill of norture [sic] then the rest.'[48] Similarly, when Marc Lescarbot talked to an old Basque fishing captain named Savalet near Canso in 1607, the captain described some of the difficulties associated with trading furs with Natives while carrying on a fishery. He had been coming to the region since 1565 and reported that 'he was at times troubled by the savages encamped there, who too boldly and impudently went on board his ship, and carried off what they listed.' They had desisted only when Savalet threatened to 'put them, one and all, to the sword.' He also complained that, when the fishermen were at anchor, Natives came on board and simply helped themselves to the fish they wanted. [49]

Some Micmacs may have been driven to expropriate fish in this manner because of changes to their seasonal round. For certain groups, the decision to spend more time in the interior securing fur-bearers than their prehistoric ancestors had may have resulted in periodic food shortages. The effect of European contact upon Micmac population levels is another significant question that cannot yet be answered with precision. It is certain that the Micmac lost much of their population to European disease; what is in doubt is the timing and the extent of the loss. Because New World and Old World populations had grown largely in isolation from each other, New World peoples had not developed the degree of resistance to many diseases that European peoples had. The result was that by the middle of the seventeenth century, Native populations in the northeast had experienced mortality rates ranging from 55 per cent to 98 per cent.[50] We do not know if such major epidemics began in the sixteenth century, but there is a strong argument that they did not strike the northeast until 1616 – although there may have been local outbreaks of disease in the region before then.[51]

Indeed, there is little convincing evidence for major epidemics anywhere in the northeast in the sixteenth century. Although European diseases had scythed through sixteenth-century Mexican populations, there were buffer zones of low population in North America beyond which such diseases probably would not have spread north to the Micmac. It is also unlikely that a virus such as smallpox, the deadliest seventeenth-century killer, would have survived in a small crew over the course of a typically long sixteenth-century voyage. In fact, since smallpox was such a common European childhood disease, it is probable that most adult fishermen would have contracted the disease as children and would not be a danger to New World peoples. This would change in the seventeenth century, with faster sailing times and the presence of colonists with children.[52] The size of the Micmac population in the early seventeenth century is a matter of considerable debate. In Biard's *Relation* of 1616, he estimated total Micmac numbers at about 3,000 to 3,500, but it is certain that this estimate reflects a people already affected by European disease. Biard himself noted that the Micmacs claimed that 'since the French mingle with and carry on trade with them, they are dying fast, and the population is thinning out.'[53] Recent estimates of pre-epidemic Micmac population have ranged from 4,500 to 50,000, but a figure of about 12,000 is more in keeping with conventional assumptions about the carrying capacity of their territory.[54]

Since population size is one of the factors that shape sociopolitical organization, it is not surprising that there is also a debate about the nature of Micmac society and government. Most hunter-gatherers have been members of band-level societies like that of the Inuit, Montagnais, and Beothuk. Many North American horticultural peoples, like the Iroquois and Huron, lived in tribal societies that consisted of larger units than bands – the Iroquois, for example, lived in villages of up to 1,000 or more people. Tribal peoples in North America usually practised horticulture and thus tended to be more sedentary than bands. They were also typically characterized by the presence of clans and various kinds of societies that linked communities of the same tribe together. Like bands, tribes were egalitarian and lacked full-time occupational specialists. Band leadership was typically temporary and specific to definite tasks, but in the case of tribes, within a community there occasionally were 'big men' or petty chieftains, who, because of their personal characteristics, exercised a considerable degree of leadership. In contrast to band or tribal societies, chiefdoms, such as those once found on the Pacific northwest coast, were characterized by social ranks – including that of the position of a chief who inherited his office – occupational specialization, the production of a surplus of food and other goods, the redistribution of those commodities by the chief, and the control of satellite communities from the chief's community.

Reality, of course, seldom corresponds completely with abstract models, and the descriptions of Micmac polity left to us by early-seventeenth-century observers do not fit neatly into any of the three forms of organization described above. The basic sociopolitical unit of the Micmac in the sixteenth century seems to have been the 'bilocal extended family,' consisting of a leader, some of his married sons and daughters and their families, other relatives on the side of both the chief and his wife, and some unrelated individuals.[55] This unit formed the summer village, and its population has been estimated at from 30 to 200 people.[56] The fullest description of such a village and its chief or sagamore, comes from Biard who stated that:

> There is the Sagamore, who is the eldest son of some powerful family, and consequently also its chief and leader. All the young people of the family are at his table and in his retinue; it is also his duty to provide dogs for the chase, canoes for transportation, provisions and reserves for bad weather and expeditions. The young people flatter him, hunt, and serve their apprenticeship under him, not being allowed to have anything before they are married ... Nevertheless they continue to live under the authority of the Sagamore, and very often in his company; as also do several others who have no relations, or those who of their own free will place themselves under his protection and guidance, being themselves weak and without a following.[57]

This account has been used to support the contention that Micmac society fell somewhere between that of a tribe and a chiefdom,[58] but the argument is not very convincing. Biard was not an ethnographer but a seventeenth-century European from a very hierarchical society. The references to the young people of a sagamore sitting at his table and serving their apprenticeship under him indicate that Biard was attempting to understand what he saw by placing it in a familiar framework. Biard also makes it clear that the sagamore did not enjoy the sort of authority exercised by the head of a chiefdom.[59] In addition, early-seventeenth-century accounts do not indicate that any leaders exercised authority over communities other than their own, or that the Micmac had occupational specialists.[60] It has been claimed that Micmac society was stratified into the ranks of chiefs, shamans, commoners, and slaves,[61] but these categories do not seem to have had the rigidity that would be the case in a true chiefdom.

Nor do the Micmac appear to have been organized along tribal lines. They lacked the clans, age-grade societies, moieties, and the like that served to knit separate communities of the same people together and to regulate their social life. On the other hand, Micmac society cannot be fitted precisely into the band model. Village chiefs seem to have possessed more prestige and authority – even if this was primarily in respect to their own family – than was the case with a band-level society. Micmac political structure was also more complex than one would expect for an aggregation of bands. According to Biard, in summer a number of sagamores gathered to 'consult among themselves about peace and war, treaties of friendship and treaties for the common good.'[62] Reports from the eighteenth century and later described the Micmac people as being divided into seven districts, each governed by a district chief who presided over a council of chiefs from the district's communities. The district chiefs in turn met in a grand council headed by a grand chief.[63] It is not at all clear if this formal division of Micmac territory into seven districts and its corresponding political structure was characteristic of the sixteenth century. In the latter part of the seventeenth century, a person who may have been the district chief was responsible for the allocation of hunting territories to individual hunters,[64] but both the existence of family hunting territories and the power of a chief to apportion them are unlikely to have been of indigenous origin. Throughout the northeast, European contact resulted in an increase in the power of those individuals who had special relationships with the newcomers, and the existence of family hunting territories, in the case of the Montagnais, for example, was a post-contact result of the fur trade.[65]

Given the lack of agriculture and the lack of a dependable, superabundant resource such as the Pacific salmon, it is unlikely that the Maritimes would have possessed the environmental requirements for the emergence of an indigenous chiefdom.[66] The descriptions of Micmac government by Biard, Lescarbot, Denys, and Le Clercq all suggest that more than 100 years of European contact had begun to transform a band-level society into one where certain individuals, because of their relationship to Europeans or their differential acquisition of European goods, had come to have a degree of prestige and authority greater than they would have in pre-contact bands of hunter-gatherers. This change in political organization was, of course, only one of a number of alterations in Micmac culture that had begun soon after the first European vessel had arrived off their coasts.

It should be stressed that much of indigenous Micmac material culture did not change throughout the sixteenth century. The superbly crafted bark canoes, the snowshoes, tobaggans, and bark-covered wigwams, for example, were retained because they were better fitted to local conditions than any conceivable European substitutions. Where European goods were perceived as superior, however, they displaced traditional articles. During the course of the sixteenth century, the Micmac replaced their stone and bone projectile points with iron, substituted iron axes for those made of stone, acquired European cloth garments, and replaced cooking containers of bark, wood, and skin with copper kettles. These substitutions changed everyday life significantly. Woollen clothes, unlike those made from skin, remained warm even when wet and dried out much faster. Copper kettles may have been even more important. Prior to their acquisition, Micmac women boiled water by heating stones in a fire and transferring them to a skin, bark, or wood container. Not surprisingly, the seventeenth-century Acadian entrepreneur Nicolas Denys concluded that 'above everything the kettle has always seemed to them, and seems still, the most valuable article they can obtain from us.' [67]

By the end of the sixteenth century, the food itself that went into those kettles was increasingly exotic. Now the Micmac also consumed flour, bread, peas, beans, prunes, and alcohol.[68] Exactly when the Micmac were introduced to alcohol is not known, but by the early seventeenth century they were reported as consuming it in excess, and later in the century, Denys recorded a horrifying description of the abuse of alcohol and its attendant violence and destruction to familial relations.[69] It is not surprising that the Micmac and other Native peoples of the northeast had difficulty coping with alcohol. Europeans had had centuries to develop cultural mechanisms to control the worst aspects of alcohol, and few would contend that those controls have ever been satisfactory. A parallel situation can be seen in European use of tobacco: when Europeans acquired it from the New World, it lost the ceremonial character that it had had among Native Americans and became a highly addictive, dangerous drug. Indeed, we need look no farther than the unsuccessful attempt by the western world to cope with a variety of mind-altering substances to realize the perils of incorporating new intoxicants into a culture.

Participation by the Micmac in a fur trade may have had other deleterious effects on social relations. Biard, for example, remarked both on the polygyny practised by the Micmac as well as the unenviable life led by women. In his words:

> These poor creatures endure all the misfortunes and hardships of life; they prepare and erect the houses or cabins, furnishing them with fire, wood, and water; prepare the food, preserve the meat and other provisions, that is, dry them in the smoke to preserve them; go to bring the game from the place where it has been killed; sew and repair the canoes, mend and stretch the skins, curry them, and make clothes and shoes of them for the whole family; they go fishing and do the rowing; in short, undertake all the work except that alone of the grand chase, besides having the care and so weakening nourishment of their children ... Now these women, although they have so much trouble ... are not cherished any more for it. The husbands beat them unmercifully, and often for a very slight cause.[70]

Even allowing for the seventeenth-century European observer's inability to understand the role played by women in a hunting and gathering economy, the description of wife-beating is unequivocal. Denys linked the abuse of women to drunkenness,[71] and it is possible that the place of women in Micmac society had changed as a result of the disruption of traditional Micmac society in the course of the sixteenth century.

The Micmac, of course, were not simply the passive recipients of cultural change. The fur trade also meant new opportunites for Native entrepreneurs. By the end of the sixteenth century, the Micmac had learned how to sail and were taking European-made shallops over impressive distances. There is good evidence that by the beginning of the seventeenth century, and probably earlier, the Micmac and the Etchemin had become middlemen who traded European goods for furs over an area that extended from Massachusetts Bay to the Quebec north shore. Judging by the archaeological evidence of Nova Scotia lithic material at prehistoric Maine sites, this post-contact trade may, in fact, have been an intensification of indigenous exchange networks.[72] As was so often the case in North America, traditional enmities, as well as traditional trade, may have been intensified by European contact. It is possible, for instance, that armed with iron-tipped weapons, the Micmac were able to expand westward and exclude the St Lawrence Iroquoians from the Gaspé Peninsula.

The coming of Europeans to the Atlantic region brought both good and evil to its first peoples. There was increased trade as well as increased warfare. A more efficient technology was now available, but so was alcohol. It cannot be stressed too highly, however, that neither Indians nor Inuit were the helpless victims of a superior civilization. In the sixteenth century, the trade partnerships between Native people and Europeans were not grossly imbalanced; indeed, it was clear that Europeans were not capable of living on their own on North American soil. This was a time when Europeans conducted their onshore activities at the sufferance of the region's indigenous inhabitants. During this period, as well, Natives picked and chose among the available elements of European culture, rejecting as much as or more than they accepted. The image of the Native peoples as broken, corrupted, and defeated societies – itself a distortion – began in the seventeenth century with the advent of European settlement, European disease, increased conflict, and population loss. For the sixteenth-century Beothuk, Micmac, and Montagnais, however, all that lay in the future.

CHAPTER THREE

1600–1650
Fish, Fur, and Folk

N.E.S. GRIFFITHS

European settlement in Acadia and Newfoundland during the first half of the seventeenth century followed at least three generations of transatlantic activity by explorers, traders, and, above all, fishermen. The ocean had not yet become a safe highway between continents in 1600, but even by that date 'the Atlantic realm of what is now Canada [had been] incorporated into the European economy as fishermen from many European ports came to catch and process cod.'[1] The migration of people and the founding of communities of Europeans in both Newfoundland and Acadia took place in a continuum of increased and increasing communication between western Europe and the rest of the world. The story of the European exploration of the world's oceans during the sixteenth century and the way in which the Europeans moved out across the world, is the background to the migrations that led to the founding of the tiny European settlements established on the northwestern shores of the Atlantic during the first half of the seventeenth century.

While there are significant differences in the ways in which English and French enterprises in these lands were envisaged and carried out, the results were almost identical. By 1650 the French and English settlements in Acadia and Newfoundland were still frail establishments. Whether one considers the Avalon Peninsula or the shores of the Bay of Fundy, the history is the same; grand schemes brought to nought as entrepreneurs battled not only ignorance of new lands and the realities of life in a different climate but also the jealousies at the courts of their respective monarchs. Those who sought to plant a settlement had both to raise the money for the enterprise and also to fight established merchants, whether in Bristol or in Rouen, who saw no new profit for them in such undertakings but rather a loss of monopoly and control.[2] Whether fish or fur was the product, those who were already involved

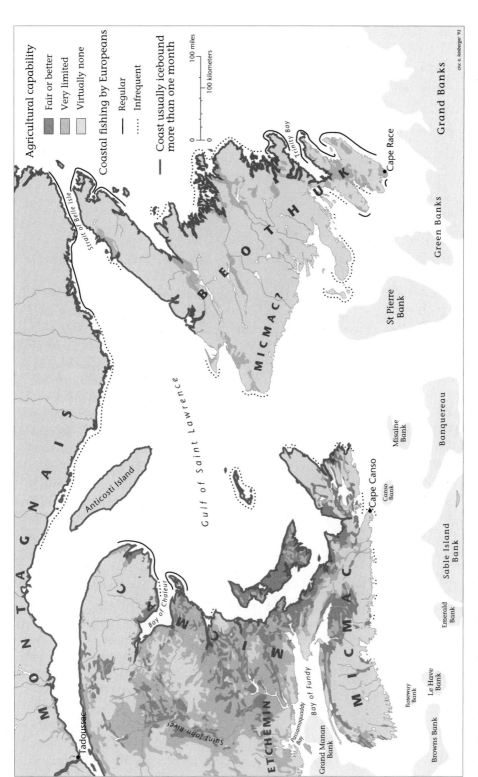

Agricultural capability

- Fair or better
- Very limited
- Virtually none

Coastal fishing by Europeans

—— Regular

······ Infrequent

—— Coast usually icebound more than one month

100 miles

100 kilometers

cvc e. lenberger '93

The Atlantic region in the sixteenth century

Labels on map:

MONTAGNAIS

Tadoussac

Strait of Belle Isle

BEOTHUK

MICMAC?

Trinity Bay

Cape Race

Green Banks

St Pierre Bank

Grand Banks

Gulf of Saint Lawrence

Anticosti Island

Banquereau

Misaine Bank

Cape Canso

Canso Bank

Sable Island Bank

Emerald Bank

Le Have Bank

Roseway Bank

Bay of Chaleur

ETCHEMIN

Saint John River

Bay of Fundy

Passamaquoddy Bay

Grand Manan Bank

Browns Bank

MALISEET

MICMAC

in transatlantic enterprise did not welcome the organization of year-round communities of Europeans in the new lands. Thus, those who gathered together people and supplies for the settlement expeditions had to struggle to obtain monopolies and patents from their respective monarchs in order to confront vested interests with legal authority. It is a moot point whether the adversities to be found in the new lands were more threatening to prospective settlers than the hostilities that proceeded from their original lands. The political systems of both France and England hampered rather than aided settlement ventures, while administrative ineptitude and bitter economic rivalries in a general economic climate of great instability impeded progress. In spite of all these obstacles, however, by 1650 European settlements had taken precarious root in both Newfoundland and Acadia and the communities established already contained most of the characteristics that would mark their future development.

These settlements were profoundly affected by the nature of the societies the newcomers had left. The overarching unity of European cultures and the strong contrast between the habits and customs of Amerindians and Europeans at the opening of the seventeenth century have tended to obscure the very significant differences between the polities of France and England at that time. It is true that the technological level of the two countries was much the same; that both countries were literate societies with largely illiterate populations; and that both were rural societies with agriculture the base of their economic life albeit in a context of major commercial and urban development. It is also true that both countries considered interpretations of Christianity to be the major factor of religious life, and that both countries considered religious belief a matter of crucial political and social importance. Further, both countries founded the organization of their political life upon acceptance of a final authority stemming from monarchical government and based upon a complex interpretation of property rights, both individual and collective, dependent upon a legal system given authority by the Crown.

Their particular interpretations of this general context of European civilization, however, made England and France very different cultures and the development of their overseas ventures reflected these divergences. Perhaps the most fundamental of them was in the realm of politics, and stemmed as much from the geographical and demographic differences of the countries as from different political ideologies. France was then, as it is now, an immensely varied country. The united kingdoms of England and Wales represented, then as now, a comparatively small and – though not uniform – relatively centralized collection of societies. In the seventeenth century, the geographical disparity of

England and France was matched by a very great demographic contrast: the population of France was close to 18 million in 1600, while that of England and Wales was no more than 3.5 million. The structure of government reflected these differences. The accession of Henri IV to the throne of France in 1589 brought to a close nearly four decades of civil war. Throughout the sixteenth century the Tudors had no serious challengers to their claim to the throne of England and Wales. The constitutional argument of seventeenth-century England would be about the limits of power and not about whether the core of legal authority rested with the Crown. There was no real argument about whether the Stuart monarchs were rightfully kings throughout their realms; the debate was whether kingship was limited in operation by the need to consult Parliament. Throughout the seventeenth century in France, however, the Bourbon monarchy was engaged in a struggle to have the Crown recognized as the source of law throughout France, to 'reduce' the authority of the greater nobles and to make the power of the Crown uniform throughout the state. The government of France at this time was not a powerful and rigid 'absolute' monarchy but a monarchy engaged in a constant struggle between its ambitious centralizing designs and intense local patriotism.[3]

The pattern for the development of the organization of colonial activity by the French Crown has to be understood against this background: a monarchy whose edicts and pronouncements were constantly challenged by the more distant parts of the realm. And so much of France was distant from Paris and the northern provinces. Local language, local customs, local rights, the organization of very strong local institutions of government differed so greatly from one another that Braudel considers it 'a commonplace to say that France is diverse to the point of absurdity.'[4] This diversity had two important results for French exploration overseas. First, offices that were developed to bring provinces into proper subservience to the monarch would be used, sooner or later, for the French communities established overseas. The outstanding example of this is the position of intendant. Second, the monarchy of France, anxious to bolster by every means at hand a position of primacy, sought to control colonial expansion to a very much greater degree than the English monarchs. By the opening of the seventeenth century there was already a strong French tradition of state intervention in colonial matters. 'Under Henri IV, under Louis XIII and Richelieu and under Louis XIV and Colbert,' E.L.J. Coornaert has pointed out, 'it was customary for the government not only to take its part in the foundation of companies, even to take the initiative, but for the government to recruit members, to name directors, to amass the capital needed, or at least to procure a large part of it.' It was the common practice 'for the French government to provide shipping and, as happened almost everywhere, to help by exemption from customs and other privileges.'[5]

In England, by contrast, the Tudor dynasty had established the power of the monarchy as the central and unquestioned authority for the government of England and Wales. In the seventeenth century, the debate between the Stuart kings and their realms was only very occasionally about whether any part of the kingdoms owed allegiance to the Crown. The constitutional issue of civil war was, above all, the issue of the extent to which the Crown must submit to the advice of Parliament. The very composition of the House of Commons, a body that in 1603 had 462 members, gave to England and Wales a link between the localities and the central government that had no parallel in France. The English monarchs might have to argue the extent to which their authority was unalloyed, but in the main they had no need to argue where their writ ran. Only in Ireland was there a fundamental challenge to the English Crown. Colonization for the English monarchs was primarily the expansion of kingdoms whose sense of being part of a single state was considerable. Colonization for the French monarchs was the expansion overseas of provincial enterprises whose commitment to the identity of France might very well be unenthusiastic to the point of anarchy. While there was a comparable granting of patents and other legal documents by both French and English sovereigns for overseas exploration, trade, and settlement, the English system was much more flexible than that of France.

The differences in constitutional structures and political traditions were paralleled by differences in the ways in which overseas ventures organized capital. The less-rigid structure of the English polity affected not only the way in which English ventures were financed but also, inevitably, the way in which such ventures were carried out. While England was not yet 'the leader of European commercial, industrial and overseas expansion' at the opening of the seventeenth century, 'all the foundations for that position had been laid.'[6] Above all, in England the joint-stock company, a type of enterprise almost unknown in France, was a common method of raising money, spreading the risk of investment, and providing the means to underwrite the costs of overseas ventures. This innovation had been developed in a society that had a much greater degree of social mobility than existed in France. While much recent research has considerably modified the previously held picture of France as a society that was close to a caste structure before 1789, it remains true that in western Europe generally, and in France in particular, the early seventeenth century was a time when the landed gentry considered commerce beneath its dignity.[7] In France, although the nobility were undoubtedly involved in the projects of trade and colonization, such entrepreneurial activity was the occupation of an exceptional few. Members of the Third Estate who gained their fortune from trade sooner or later established their families within the ranks of the nobility, but the path to translating wealth into social status took more time and was more tortuous in France than it was in England. It was an exceptional member of the French nobility who openly sought and made a fortune in trade and commerce during the first half of the seventeenth century.

By contrast, partly because the strong hold of primogeniture considerably restricted the formation of an exclusive nobility, the English gentry involved themselves thoroughly in trade. They controlled companies, worked with those who had no aristocratic family connections, and became familiar with the most minute details of trade and colonization practices. As a group 'they remained unique in this respect for centuries.'[8] In terms of overseas settlement, these political and social differences favoured the development of the individual entrepreneur in England; when and if successful, such a person would find a welcome among the élite of the country far more easily than in France. Colonial affairs in England had a considerably greater importance in the minds of the politically influential than was the case in France. This priority was both a stimulus for the interest of the gentry and one of its results.

England and France also had very different religious organizations. Both countries were, of course, nominally Christian, and both were convinced that 'non-Christians had no rights in the soil.'[9] Whether from devout belief or from more self-serving motivations, Europeans acted with the conviction that Christian Europe had legal rights to exploit and govern the New World.[10] Christianity and civilization, for most seventeenth-century Europeans, were inseparably linked. Whether Protestant or Catholic, the newcomers had no doubt that they had a moral duty to spread the Gospel, to trade, to settle and claim land in the New World, and to counter protest and hostility with military action. In many nineteenth-and early-twentieth-century writings about European exploitation of the New World, a strong contrast was drawn between 'Protestant acquisitiveness and Roman Catholic altruism.'[11] Recent scholarship has shown this division to be untenable and has demonstrated the common traits of the two interpretations of Christianity. But there are measurable differences in the colonial policies of France and England that came from the ways in which these countries accommodated varying Catholic and Protestant interpretations of Christianity in their political and social institutions. The differing ways in which the two countries tolerated variation in belief meant considerable differences in the nature of their settlements in North America, both in the daily lives of the

Euroamericans and in the relationship between Euroamerican and Amerindian.

In the matter of religion as in political institutions and social customs, England and France were polities of similar character but of differing pattern. In examining the colonial activities of the two countries there is as great a need to avoid explaining events by invoking supposedly national characteristics as there is a need to clarify those processes that do stem from the particular local traditions and customs of a given region. European colonization of what is today Atlantic Canada was both the expansion of a complex society and the action of many differing groups of individuals. As is the case for the history of Amerindians, a balance has to be kept between acknowledging common characteristics of European peoples as a whole and highlighting the distinctiveness of particular communities. Cornish and Breton are as alike, and as different, as Micmac and Beothuk.

One of the strongest of the common interests that drew English and French to present-day Atlantic Canada was fish. Whatever else enticed Europeans across the North Atlantic in the sixteenth century – the lure of the unknown to explore, the possibility of wealth from the fur trade, the quest to establish a new life in a new world – the pull of the abundant fishing resources was at the heart of the matter. The voyages of John Cabot, particularly the expedition of 1497, had opened the way for the exploitation of the fisheries from present-day Cape Cod to Labrador and Newfoundland. In a Europe where religious practices, as well as actual scarcity of meat, placed a premium on fish as an important protein, fish catches meant a vital hedge against starvation.[12] It was abundantly clear from the outset that the new fishing grounds would support a profitable enterprise most of the time for most of those engaged in it.[13] Over the next century, most of the communities of the European Atlantic seaboard sent fishing fleets to these new seas. Portuguese, French, and English fishermen set forth, as well as Spanish and Dutch. The records that remain of this period are by no means complete but are sufficient to provide an indication of what was happening. Harold Innis asserted that 'in 1577 the profits from the Newfoundland fishery as conducted from St. Jean de Luz, Zibura, Azcavin and Urnia were estimated at 60,000 ducats.' The French ports were fully as busy, and there are 100 recorded sailings to the Banks from Honfleur alone for the years from 1574 to 1583.[14] H.P. Biggar estimated that by 1603 the French had more than 300 ships in the waters around Newfoundland.[15] As for English participation, by 1580 '50 or 60 ships were said to visit the island annually,' and conservative estimates have the English-Newfoundland fleet at some 150 vessels in 1600.[16] By that date, English and French fishing fleets had become the particular rivals for the catches taken between Cape Cod and Labrador, although the interest of other nations would continue through the centuries.

Such was, and continues to be today – albeit in a changed climate of declining stocks – the importance of the North Atlantic fisheries that studies concerning their development seem, on occasion, to be as numerous as the fish that used to be caught. What is crucial for present purposes is a clear understanding of three major facets of the enterprise. First, the growth of the industry altered the place of the European fishing ports in the context of their hinterlands. The way in which the fisheries were conducted not only connected the Atlantic coast of Europe with that of North America but also wove a broad net of communications among differing European ports and in turn among the ports and their hinterlands. Second, the rapidly expanding economic importance of the fisheries very quickly made fish and all related matters an issue of European politics and diplomacy. Third, the technology of the fisheries needs to be grasped; the fishing methods themselves, quite apart from the ever-growing importance of the industry to the European homelands, greatly affected the development of settlement in Newfoundland and Acadia.

Most studies of the fisheries begin, sensibly enough, with the technical demands of the occupation and, in particular, with an analysis of the major ways in which the catch was obtained. Fish were caught either inshore or offshore, that is to say either very close to land or on the Banks, those relatively shallow waters that lie off the coasts from Maine to Labrador. Throughout the period under consideration, there were two main ways of bringing the fish back to home port in an edible state: as 'wet,' also known as 'green' or salted, cod and as dry, which was precisely what its name suggests. Dry cod also demanded salt for its processing, but by no means the quantity that 'green' cod demanded. In the 'wet' or 'green' fishery, lines were cast over the side of the ship and the fish so caught were taken to narrow tables on the deck to be cleaned and filleted. The salter would then layer them in the hold, head to tail and eachlayer well salted. In the late sixteenth century, ships sent out from France for this activity were, according to Harold Innis, on average around 100 tons and carried a crew of some fifteen to eighteen men. The ships would be out of home port from late January or early February until the end of May or the beginning of June, depending on weather and the state of fishing that year. Loaded with salt on the outward voyage, they returned with holds filled with fish. A vessel of some 100 to 150 tons could bring back some 20,000 to 25,000 fish.[17]

The dry fishery required more equipment, more labour, and larger ships.[18] The product was worth more than that of the 'wet' or 'green' fishery because the dried fish offered better food value and sold at better prices in the market. The dry fishery necessitated the use of the shore and thus occasioned temporary settlements, the seasonal establishment of communities of European men on what, for them, was the coast of a new world. While those engaged in the 'wet' or 'green' fishery might repair to land for wood and water, those who worked the dry fishery required good beaches, big enough to allow the fish to be processed and the men engaged in the work to be housed for the season. Ships for the dry fishery would seldom leave their home port before February and would often not return until the late summer. The technique was to catch fish close to the shore from shallops with three-man crews. Thus, small craft had to be brought out from Europe. Once the fish were brought to shore, they were cleaned and split before being lightly salted. After a few days, the fish were washed, drained, and then spread out on flakes to dry for some ten days, depending on weather conditions. This process was labour-intensive, and men and boys were brought out from the home ports for 'rigid specialized work in what were virtually unmechanized seasonal factories.'[19] While small ships did engage in dry fishing, the average vessel engaged in this type of fishery was at least 100 tons and could bring back to Europe as much as 200,000 cod a season.[20] The financial rewards for such a venture would bring a fair profit not only to the owners but also to those who provisioned the ship and to the fishermen themselves.

Neither method of fishing or preserving the catch was exclusive to one country. During the sixteenth century, however, offshore and 'green' or 'wet' fisheries were more popular with the French, while inshore and 'dry' fisheries were pursued more assiduously by the English. It is crucial not to make this division anything more than an approximate summary of sixteenth-century activity, an overall tendency rather than a hard and fast rule. Many boats would be outfitted and provisioned exclusively for either dry or wet stock, but many a ship provisioned and outfitted for one form of the industry returned to port with a cargo composed of both sorts of fish. For example, Charles de La Morandière has noted that in 1591 two English ships were captured and brought into St Malo: the *Croissant* with 32,000 dry fish and 19,000 'wet' fish on board, and the *Bonne Aventure* with 8,000 dry cod and 5,000 wet as her cargo.[21]

Whatever the type of voyage undertaken, the North Atlantic fishery was a dangerous, if potentially highly profitable, enterprise. It required risk capital. The hazards of the ocean itself presented challenge enough for even the larger sailing ships of the time, and the transatlantic voyage was dangerous indeed for the smaller boats that formed a significant part of the fleets. To the perils of the seas was added the threat of men. Piracy abounded, and the fishermen of all nations pillaged one another without scruple and with very little regard even for common origin, let alone for the international agreements signed and sealed in the capital cities of their world.

All vessels, regardless of size or fishing goal, had major areas of interest in common: the financing of their expedition, the provisioning and manning of the ship, and the marketing of the catch. The size of the ship was obviously a factor in the amount of investment demanded. Raising the money brought into the industry many a person who never set foot on board ship and, in fact, who might not have any great experience of life in a port. In the main, however, the expansion of the European fishing industry across the Atlantic was 'the extension of a well-established industry and the application of familiar techniques.'[22] At the same time, the increase in the quantity of capital investment demanded by the fisheries in the sixteenth and seventeenth centuries meant the organization of investment on a scale previously unknown. Harold Innis has described in detail how financiers in Rouen lent money to fishermen in Honfleur and Le Havre. Gillian Cell has examined in detail how London and Bristol supported the West Country fishermen in their trade.[23] The development of the transatlantic fisheries meant a broadening of interest and opportunity for the developing urban merchant class.

If the financing of these enterprises linked port with hinterland, the marketing of the catch connected countries. The fish caught and processed by West Country fishermen, financed by merchants in Bristol and London, 'could be sold in Marseilles, Spain, Portugal, the Biscay ports, in Nance [Nantes], Bordeaux, Rochelle, Bayonne, Rouen or in the British Isles.' Fishing vessels setting out from the French channel ports would most often destine their catch for Paris markets, but they would also find markets in Spain and Portugal. By the beginning of the seventeenth century, there existed two interconnected financial structures dependent on fishing activities. The first was a web of financial investment binding the ships not only to their ports for supplies and labour but also to inland cities and towns for the capital to mount the ventures. The second web was a marketing network that was international in nature and subject to very complex laws of supply and demand. The result of both these factors meant a very broad involvement in transatlantic activity by the emerging merchant classes in France and England.

In sum, at the opening of the sixteenth century, fishermen on the European Atlantic coast were engaged in a trade that was primarily locally financed and operated. At the opening of the seventeenth century, the trade had expanded to such an extent that its financing had repercussions in towns far removed from the home ports of the ships, and a considerable portion of the catch was destined for export. But while the hallmark of the sixteenth-century fishing industry was growth, the reality for the fisherman between 1560 and 1600 was still pre-eminently an enterprise demanding individual skills. Although the economics of the trade demanded complex agreements before the ship left port as well as on its return, during the voyage itself the captain had great latitude. If he was also part or full owner of the vessel, his freedom of action, provided he returned with some saleable cargo, was immense. It was in such freedom that the trade with the Amerindian for furs had its roots.[24]

There is still debate over when the first North American furs reached Europe, but by the 1580s many of those engaged in the dry fishery on the shores of the Bay of Fundy and at Canso had developed an interest in the fur trade as a profitable sideline.[25] Furs gathered by fishing ships sold in Paris in 1583 for more than 20,000 crowns.[26] Trying to estimate what such a sum represents leads rapidly into thickets of confusion, this being an English estimate of a French transaction but it is an amount that was sufficient to entice investment and by 1584 the merchants of St Malo, Rouen, and Dieppe were financing some expeditions dedicated exclusively to the fur trade. Until well past 1600, however, fur was more a matter of windfall profits than a product of systematic exploitation. The more common voyages until the end of the sixteenth century continued to be those whose first objective was fish and for whom fur was a secondary matter, even though as a commodity it was gaining all the time in value and importance.

By 1600, neither the fisheries nor the fur trade had led to the permanent settlement of Europeans in Acadia and Newfoundland. From the point of view of the financial and political élites of England and France in that year, Acadia and Newfoundland held their place in enterprise and policy because of the immediate and undisputed value of the fish caught. The fur trade was in its infancy, and the possibilities of settlement were barely under investigation. The catastrophic attempts by the French on Sable Island and in the Gulf of St Lawrence between 1577 and 1603 were indeed the fruitless initiatives that Marcel Trudel has named them.[27] For those already engaged in the fisheries and the fur trade, there might seem no good reason to alter the pattern of action established and much to say against change. Both these activities could be effectively exploited by seasonal expeditions. But the Anglo-French reach across the North Atlantic was not an isolated phenomenon. It was part of a massive European migration, a complex pattern of peoples and institutions on the move. The political rivalries and clashing economic dreams of the competing European states, their cultural antagonisms, and their ideological feuds led inevitably to the attempt at permanent settlement of Europeans in Acadia and Newfoundland. At its simplest, if the Spanish and Portuguese could grasp fortune and dominion across the southern Atlantic seas, the French and English would aspire to be no less successful across the northern oceans.

Amerindian views of these colonial attempts were greatly influenced by earlier phases of European contact. By 1600, the newcomers were no longer unfamiliar, even if they were still strangers. The immediate dangers involved in contact, as well as the present benefits to be obtained, were recognizable by the aboriginal peoples of the region. Episodic violence, the kidnapping of women and children, and the goods Europeans offered for trade were part of the known – if not everyday – experiences of the coastal peoples of Atlantic North America. The impact of the iron and copper goods that were acquired before 1600 certainly changed part of the material culture of the Amerindians, but did so without a fundamental disruption of the patterns of their lives. The quantity of new goods was, at this period, insufficient to make the production of the old unnecessary. At that time, even the greater efficiency of the new tools was not something that would cause, of itself, a major strain on the traditional fabric of Amerindian society. As James Axtell has written, 'adaptation [of artifacts] is less often a sign of capitulation than of capitalization.'[28] For the Micmac and the Maliseet, the sixteenth century was a time of controlled technological change, a time when the Europeans were the source of much that was new but not yet, apparently, the source of any overwhelming challenge to Amerindian powers.

What did pose a new and desperate challenge to the Amerindians were the diseases that arrived along with the newcomers. The impact of epidemic death-dealing illness on the functioning of societies demands major cultural efforts by the people who suffer. The consequences of epidemics are to be found not just in the immediate death toll but in the efforts that are required by the stricken communities to accommodate and interpret the aftermath.[29] The extent of the ravages of smallpox and influenza as major killers for the Micmac is a matter of ongoing debate, but there is no doubt that the Micmac themselves were aware of a recent decline in their population and so informed the Jesuits who were among them at the opening of the seventeenth century.[30] Few would disagree with Axtell's point that the impact of a smallpox scourge on Amerindian populations could be devastating. On the one hand, there would be the individual's 'psychological despair at having to watch family and friends cut down.' At the same time, such suffering would be community wide, and the social context of the individual would itself be one of trauma. The loss of family members greatly weakened the extensive web of clans and kinship that shaped individual identity quite as much as language and residence. Quite apart from the emotional shock, the death of elders presented a blow to the communities. The importance in oral cultures of the knowledge of the older adults, knowledge of technological skills and of political traditions, meant that their deaths could mean loss of particular skills for the community as a whole. The old and the young were often the most highly susceptible to the new diseases. Axtell has stressed the point that 'the natives' religious beliefs, cosmological assumptions and social morale were battered by the inexplicable fate that had befallen them, predisposing them to seek the material and spiritual help of the newcomers.'[31] While one might argue the extent to which the Micmac suffered such a cataclysmic fate within the time-span of three generations, there is no doubt that major depopulation was a Micmac experience during the contact, and especially during the early colonial eras. The Maliseet-Passamaquoddy also knew the onslaught of the new epidemics, though present estimation of the ravages these peoples suffered is less clear. Whatever the precise number of dead may have been, it is obvious that the early European settlers in Acadia and Newfoundland did not meet indigenous people at the height of their strength.

The European colonial attempts, while they need to be considered as part of the expansion of a complex and structured civilization, depended upon the actions of very specific groups of people. Individuals took initiatives, organized the ventures, sought government support, and in all essentials spearheaded the expansion of Europe.[32] Even in France, it was private individuals, not the state, who first established the contacts with what would be Acadia. The charter issued by Henry IV for the establishment of Acadia remarks in the preamble that one of the purposes of the action was to regulate the long-standing activity of fishermen in the new lands.[33] Institutions and regulations, theories of state rights, and organizations of political control followed after individual enterprise. In the beginnings of both Acadia and Newfoundland, their settlement was the business of private enterprise, organized and financed through the establishment of private companies. Government involvement of both France and England was more or less restricted between 1600 and 1650 to the granting of commissions and patents. It did not include the provision of money, goods, or salaried officials. The evolution of settlement was conditioned as much by individual ideology and ambition as by government design and policy, as much by the local ecology as by the settlers' previous experience and technology, and as much by the reality of Amerindian life at the time as by European dreams of future dominion. Considering the domestic history of France and England during these years – a civil war in one country and almost continual civil strife in the other – the official priorities of the Bourbons and Stuarts were understandably otherwise engaged.

Those who were members of the early expeditions to Acadia from France were, almost inevitably, veterans of the civil wars that had ravaged that country for close to forty years. Most of them had good service records. Pierre Du Gua de Monts was appointed in 1603 as Henri IV's viceroy and captain general on sea and land, in the countries of 'la Cadie, du Canada et autres terres de la Nouvelle France au 40° au 46°.' He was a Calvinist who had fought with gallantry for Henri IV.[34] His friend, Jean de Biencourt de Poutrincourt et de Saint-Just, who was to become the lieutenant-governor of Acadia in 1606, was a Catholic who had fought on the opposite side before joining Henri IV's cause in 1593. Champlain, also a member of the first expedition to Acadia, was yet another experienced soldier. Although there were exceptions, such as the lawyer and writer Marc Lescarbot, most of the leaders of the early French attempts at settlement had a military or naval background. Claude de La Tour, who played a major role in Acadia after 1610 (as did his son Charles), was a ship's captain in the religious wars.[35]

In Newfoundland, the typical background for the English élite was commercial. The leader of the first English settlement expeditions was an experienced merchant. John Guy, appointed as the first governor of that colony in 1610, was a member of the Bristol Society of Merchant Venturers.[36] The other leaders of the colony were either men of like background, such as Guy's two brothers, whom he appointed as his deputies when he returned to England, or those who can most easily be classified as gentry.[37] Both Newfoundland and Acadia had noble proprietors as the directors of early European settlement, but this was a similarity much more apparent than real. The authority conferred on the Newfoundland Company, which was set up as a joint-stock company, allowed for a simple enough succession of leadership among those men willing to invest money and energy in such an enterprise. There was a fairly rapid change of control during the first decades of English settlement in Newfoundland but the changes did not require those involved to face continual problems with court politics as well as commercial rivalry. Men like Sir William Vaughan, who purchased land from the Newfoundland Company in 1616, Richard Whitbourne, who went to Newfoundland as the governor for the Vaughan enterprise in 1618, and George Calvert, Lord Baltimore, who acquired rights to the development of the colony in 1621, certainly had to cope with competitors and adversaries in Bristol and London.[38] Their difficulties, however, were nothing compared to the troubles that soon bedevilled the Acadian expeditions. De Monts's royal patents and trade monopoly fell victim to the caprices of royal favour in 1607, and from that point on, many of those who had suffered the first winter, 1604–5, on St Croix Island in Passamaquoddy Bay turned their time and attention to the valley of the St Lawrence. As a result, the French settlement enterprise in Acadia was brought to a halt until 1610.

If the organization of European settlement in Newfoundland and Acadia was significantly affected by the different structures of the

French and English companies engaged in such enterprises, other differences of equal importance came from the nature of the lands settled. The geography of the two areas was sufficiently distinct to have a great impact on the ways of life of their inhabitants. For Newfoundland, nature's endowment had been of grandeur rather than of lavish and fertile lands. The cliffs and the low hills of the Avalon Peninsula made agriculture a wearisome business, the more so because the growing season was unpredictable and short. Nowhere was farming more than a matter of domestic supply. In contrast, the lands on the south of the Bay of Fundy, where the core of Acadian settlement would be built, were fertile river valleys among low, forested hills and with a lengthy and reliable growing season. Here, once established, farming would become a reliable source not only of domestic provisions but also of exports.

The effects of different topographies and climates were intensified by the way in which the fisheries were exploited. Newfoundland was, above all, a terminus for European fishing fleets, and the settlements of both English and French were interwoven into the prosecution of this activity. Settlement of what soon came to be known in international treaties as 'Acadia or Nova Scotia' was independent of the important fishing station at Canso, that beautiful place of sheltered bays and islands on Nova Scotia's Atlantic coast. Further, their respective positions led to very different geopolitical roles for the two colonies. As the dual name suggests, the actual lands that were claimed as Acadia by the French in 1604 were an object of Anglo-Scottish interest. By 1632, the territory so claimed, stretching from present-day northeastern Maine to the Bay of Chaleur and including the Gaspé, all of New Brunswick, and Nova Scotia, was well on its way to being a disputed borderland between New France and New England.[39] At least during the seventeenth century, French and English claims on Newfoundland were primarily claims to separate parts of the great island. Although inevitably there were skirmishes for dominance, at least in the beginning the competing interests in Newfoundland were a matter less of border warfare between settled communities than of intermittent hostilities between conflicting outposts of empire. A further profound difference between the colonies resulted from the relationship between settler and indigenous inhabitant. In Newfoundland, the Beothuk were, to all intents and purposes, an unimportant cipher for the newcomers. In 'Acadia or Nova Scotia,' the fact that the Micmac 'chose to offer toleration and support ... was essential to the persistence of French colonization.'[40] As the decades passed, the adherence of the Maliseet-Passamaquoddy to the French would also be of great importance in the border warfare waged between New France and New England.

Finally, the overwhelming difference between the two colonies was the way which their ties with Europe were sustained. In Newfoundland, the English efforts met with successive failures of the proprietors, and a painfully gradual establishment of communities.[41] The enduring myth that Newfoundland was not settled by the English in the seventeenth century conveys the reality of how slow and bitter the process actually was. The death toll from scurvy never reached the level that it had during the first winter spent by the French in Acadia, when thirty-five out of seventy-nine men died.[42] Nevertheless, it was present, debilitating, and often enough the cause of death. In the third winter of the colony at Cupids Cove, twenty-two of the population of sixty-two suffered the illness, and eight of those died.[43] In the same way as the raid of Samuel Argall hindered French efforts when he burnt the settlement at Port Royal in 1613, the raids of Peter Easton, while aimed more at the fishermen than the settlers, crippled the Newfoundland enterprise at much the same period.[44]

Permanent European settlement, as opposed to the exploitation of a resource, implied the presence of women. In Newfoundland, although women in the early years of colonization represented a tiny minority of a tiny population, their settlement had profound implications. The very existence of the Newfoundland Company had been resisted by merchants engaged in the fisheries, who were convinced that year-round settlers would interfere with their profits. While wintering over by small groups of men might provide them some small advantage 'because they shall be sure to be first here every yeare to take what stage they shall have need of for there own use,'[45] the settlement of families would mean that an unrestricted fishery must end. Settlement would bring institutions and regulation, and in all probability taxes as well. For at least two generations, the colony was overwhelmingly male, predominantly a seasonal labour force of people who could and would move easily if circumstances proved too hard. Yet, at the same time, almost from the outset some men brought their wives; census data from the 1670s suggest that some families therein recorded were descendants of the earliest expeditions. For example, it seems probable that the Cupids Cove colony, begun in 1610, and the settlement of Conception Bay during the 1670s are linked through the namesake of the first governor, John Guy. The genealogy has been traced by Gordon Handcock, who writes that Guy's 'brother Philip and kinsman Nicholas accompanied him to Newfoundland from Bristol, in 1610–1612. While John and Philip returned to Bristol, Nicholas, whose wife gave birth on March 27, 1613, to the first English child born in Newfoundland apparently stayed on but had moved to Carbonear by 1631, where he was reported to be farming and fishing with some success.'[46] On the other hand, the settlement of Ferryland – on the Avalon Peninsula south of St John's – in 1621

by Sir George Calvert, first Baron Baltimore, seemed to endure into later
years through successive arrivals of colonists rather than through the
children of the earliest settlers. It was only with Sir David Kirke's period
of activity, which began in 1637 and ended in 1653, that the beginning of
enduring family settlement in this locality can be discovered. Kirke was
as much a soldier of fortune as a colonizer and had been the leader of an
expedition that had temporarily captured Quebec in 1629. On November 1637, he was made a co-proprietor of Newfoundland, and in 1639 he
arrived there with some 100 colonists, most of whom he established at
Ferryland. Handcock has established that 'four of the eleven planters
recorded in Ferryland in 1675 and four of the eight in 1677 stemmed
from Sir David Kirke's period ... they included Kirke's widow and four
sons.'[47]

Throughout the early years, however, as Handcock has noted, 'the
volume of migration to the early colonies was small and confined to
four or five harbours as against the thirty to forty harbours and coves
visited by the contemporary seasonal men.' In the words of D.W.
Meinig, 'Newfoundland's population was [established as] ... an accumulation rather than an implantation. It began as a kind of flotsam
washed up on the beaches from the intensive seasonal harvest of the sea
and only gradually took on greater substance and a vaguely visible
shape as a settlement region. This was a strand culture, facing the sea,
each tiny village a jumble of simple houses and garden patches among
the rocks at the head of an anchorage along the eastern shores of the
Avalon Peninsular.'[48] Not until after 1650 was European settlement
more firmly established in Newfoundland.

The French in Acadia had produced by then a much more self-sufficient colony.[49] Its early years had been almost equally beset with problems. Its first proprietor, Pierre Du Gua de Monts, had been granted in
1603 a monopoly of the fur trade. Following the unsuccessful effort to
settle on St Croix Island in 1604, Port Royal was established in the following year. For the next twenty-seven years, the colony barely survived. French domestic rivalries saw the cancellation of de Monts's
monopoly in 1607, and the would-be settlers returned to France. Jean de
Biencourt de Poutrincourt led a second expedition to Port Royal in 1610,
but for two years religious antagonism was to prove a major handicap
for the settlement. Protestant merchants in La Rochelle were reluctant to
extend credit to Poutrincourt, a Catholic.[50] All these difficulties, however, paled in comparison with those of the year 1613, when Samuel
Argall, variously described as a Virginian pirate or 'the leader of the
first English expedition to contest French settlement in Acadia,' burned
Port Royal.[51]

After this action, Acadia as a European settlement almost completely vanished until the 1630s. A Jesuit mission was intermittently maintained at the mouth of the St John River, a desultory fur trade was pursued, and fishing boats appeared off the coast; but as an object of major French colonial effort the colony was neglected. Partly because of this, the area attracted Scottish interests. In 1621, James I of England (James VI of Scotland) granted to Sir William Alexander colonization rights over the area, now designated New Scotland or – in the Latin text of the charter – Nova Scotia.[52] No effective venture was made by Alexander to develop the colony until 1629, and his short-lived settlement at Port Royal was brought to an end by the provisions of the Treaty of St Germain-en-Laye, 1632, which restored the colony to France. With the international status of 'Acadia or Nova Scotia' settled for the time being, the French now made an effort to develop it. Over the next twenty years, Acadia developed from a territory claimed by France to a community that would remain French even when ruled from Boston during the years 1654–70.

The pattern of French migration to Acadia was, in some respects, similar to that of English migration to Newfoundland; a mixture of organized expeditions for settlement and individual enterprise. A major colonizing effort was mounted in 1632 by Isaac de Razilly, appointed governor of the colony that year by the French Crown. Razilly is though to have brought nearly 300 settlers, but there is little concrete information about who they were or from what part of France they originated. Geneviève Massignon, whose main interest was whether present-day Acadian speech is a dialect produced by particular genealogical descent from specific regions of France or the result of Acadian history in North America, demonstrated that the Acadian community was built by people from a number of different areas of France.[53] While many immigrants to Acadia, in common with immigrants to Quebec, came from areas that were integrated into France's participation in Atlantic fishing and trading, there were also families whose ancestors lived in the central and eastern districts of France.[54] The Loudunais region of France (the southern Loire Valley) provided many migrants, and by 1700, 46.7 per cent of names on the census returns of the colony can be linked to that region. Of the rest, 8 per cent can be traced to Aunis, 4.1 per cent to Anjou, 8.9 per cent to Brie, 25.6 per cent to unknown French origins, and 4.3 per cent to English or Scottish roots.[55] Those who came to Newfoundland during these years were overwhelmingly from the west of England, in many cases particular coves being the preserve of people from specific villages and making kith-and-kin chains that would stand the test of time. Migration to Acadia drew more broadly from across the whole of France.

The majority of those who came to Acadia had no pre-existing ties among themselves. They were part and parcel of the general movement of European peoples in the seventeenth century, of the complex population movements that saw, among other results, Scottish settlement of northern Ireland and emigration of French families to Spain. On the whole, those who moved were more often young single adults than families, and more often men than women. Nevertheless, families did migrate and so did single women. A number of those who came to Acadia from the Loudunais area were linked by family ties to one another before they emigrated, either by blood or marriage. Massignon reported at least eight families that were related by marriage prior to their departure for Acadia.[56] It is clear, too, that Jeanne Motin, whose first husband was Charles de Menou d'Aulnay and whose second was Charles de Saint-Etienne de La Tour – both early Acadian governors – made her way to the colony as a single woman in search of a better life than she could have lived in France.[57]

Evidence concerning the lives of women in early Acadian history is slim. Both Charles de La Tour's second wife, and his third wife, Jeanne Motin, played a considerable role in Acadian political life. Françoise Jacquelin was an effective diplomat for Acadian needs in Boston, and Jeanne Motin a good negotiator with creditors and their lawyers on behalf of her children. But the day-to-day occupations of the average Acadian pioneer women are recorded only as part of the general life of the community. Their essential role for the development of the colony, that of wife and mother, has been remembered mostly through the dry statistics of demographic growth, the establishment of families where infant mortality was astonishingly low. Yet, quite apart from the indispensable function of biological mate, it was the women who were mainly responsible for the comforts of living, the elements that helped the Acadian settlements become a developing colony rather than mere way-stations of migrants. It was above all the women who undertook the gardening, cooking, and preserving of food that resulted in meals that refreshed the spirit as well as the body, the making and mending of clothes, the organization of bed-coverings, – whether of fur pelts or of cloth – in sum, the work that made homes of shelters. By 1650, the settlers in Acadia, men and women, had built a community with a number of characteristics that would endure. While not yet demographically self-perpetuating, they formed a population of Europeans whose descendants would still be living within the bounds of Acadia 300 years later.

The community also had excellent relations with the Micmac. Not only was there no continuous warfare between Native and non-Native, but there was intermarriage, according to the rites of the newcomers, between the two peoples. As early as 1611, the Jesuits were commenting that men sent out to establish a colony of France had sought a different life among the Micmac: 'la plupart se marient a des sauvagesses et passerent le reste de leurs jours avec les sauvages adoptant leur manière de vie.'[58] The first marriage of Charles de La Tour, one of the most important men in early Acadian history, was with a Micmac.[59] Charles came to Acadia in 1610, at approximately age fourteen, with his father, Claude de La Tour. In 1626 he married a Micmac woman, with whom he had three daughters. The direct evidence for this relationship is contained in the declarations of one of his daughters, who married a Basque fur trader, Martin d'Arpentigny, seigneur de Martignon, who later owned land at the mouth of the St John River.[60] The indirect evidence that it was a marriage and not just a private liaison comes from the careers of the other two daughters. Both entered convents in France, a step for which legitimate birth was a necessity. This marriage was important beyond the lives of the individuals concerned. It attested publicly to a belief in the social acceptability of such a relationship. The very eminence of Charles de La Tour would serve as an argument in favour of the practice, and his example was to be followed during the 1630s and 1640s by members of the Lejeune, Thibodeau, and Martin families.[61]

If the importance to Acadians of their relationship with aboriginal people had quickly become clear, so too had the importance of their relationship with New England. After 1636 there was an intense rivalry between the two leading men of the colony, Charles de Saint-Etienne de La Tour and Charles de Menou d'Aulnay. D'Aulnay came to the colony in 1632 when he was twenty-eight, as an old friend and enthusiastic supporter of the new governor, de Razilly.[62] In 1636, on the death of de Razilly, d'Aulnay and La Tour both claimed that they held exclusive rights granted to them by the French Crown to govern and develop the colony. This feud did not end until the death of d'Aulnay by drowning near Port Royal in 1650 and the marriage of his rival to d'Aulnay's widow in 1653. During the years of dispute, both sides made appeals for aid to Boston. The New Englanders resolved the matter by allowing both to purchase what they deemed necessary.[63] By the end of the century, the interaction between Port Royal and Boston would be of considerable importance to those settled in Acadia.

Perhaps the most significant characteristics for the future to be found in Acadia in 1650 relate to the mixed economy being developed by the settlers.[64] The fur trade was important, especially in the coastal settlements of La Hève, Cape Sable, the mouth of the St John River, and Pentagoet. The fishery had limited importance for the colony, but the success of agriculture around Port Royal was crucial. It was based on dyking the land. 'There are numbers of meadows on both shores,' wrote

Nicolas Denys in 1653, 'and two islands which possess meadows ... There is a great extent of meadows which the sea used to cover and which the Sieur d'Aulnay had drained. It bears fine and food wheat ... below and above this great meadow ... they have again drained other lands which bear wheat in much greater abundance than those which they cultivated round the fort.'[65] This practice, which demanded not only particular skills but also considerable community activity, would allow the settlers to generate agricultural surpluses within two generations. It is tempting to continue to outline what can be seen in embryo in the colony in 1650: politics that were not a matter of feudal practices, religious beliefs that did not become fanatical, the absorption of English migrants into the community so that it became functionally bilingual.[66] The most important point is that Acadia by 1650 was a French colony of some 400 or 500 people. While by no means comparable in numbers to the settlements of Europeans in either New England or New France, it was a colony with its own distinctive patterns of social cohesion.

Gordon Handcock opened his work on Newfoundland by remarking that 'the peopling of any new world region from overseas is usually regarded as one of the most important cultural events in the human history of that region.' 'It establishes,' he continued, 'the character and norms on which the region develops.'[67] His vision of the new lands themselves, as a major factor in the history built by the Europeans who came to them, is enlightening. It is a needed context corrective: it is fatally easy to be caught up with the newcomers and give too little attention to those who were already present in the environment and whose characteristics would shape the future of the immigrants quite as much as the ideas imported by the latter. In the final analysis, the particular societies that emerged in Acadia, Nova Scotia, and Newfoundland were shaped as much by what was already present as by what the newcomers brought with them.

CHAPTER FOUR

1650–1686

'Un pays qui n'est pas fait'

JEAN DAIGLE

In 1688, a year after his arrival as governor of Acadia, Louis-Alexandre Des Friches de Meneval declared that the 'pays n'est pas fait': it was a country not yet formed.[1] This comment, which could equally well have been applied to Newfoundland, indicates the lack of sustained interest shown by France and England in the area comprising Acadia and Newfoundland. Between 1650 and 1686, that region experienced an ambivalent policy on the part of the two European powers. Lengthy periods of indifference alternated with sporadic bursts of interest, and the results were not favourable for the colonial development of the region. Among the settlers, the result of the marginalization of the Acadian colony and the settlements in Newfoundland, and of commercial and military policies that took no account of the settlers' interests, was to encourage the development of a sceptical attitude towards the colonial authorities. Settlers treated lightly the orders of administrators who were powerless to guarantee the security or the prosperity of the population. The motto of the ancestors of Jean-Vincent d'Abbadie de Saint-Castin, 'ni trop près, ni trop loin'[2] – neither too near nor too far – illustrates the thinking of colonists who, while still identifying themselves with the metropolis, mistrusted its demands. Their situation was comparable to that of the populations of the Basque country or Alsace, pulled in different directions by rival powers.[3]

The social and economic character of Newfoundland prompted vigorous internal debates in England and France. Some merchants opposed settlement on the ground that it was damaging to their interests and to the fishery as a whole. Other merchants joined with colonial promoters and certain state officials in regarding colonization as a promising route towards economic development, given the mercantilist economic theories of the era. They could not accept a policy of non-intervention in colonial matters. Acadia, however, with its few natural resources, was not attractive to any large number of colonists. Two main economic patterns developed in the colony, and neither one necessitated a strong influx of colonists. On the one hand, the development of a sedentary economy, centred on agriculture, evolved from the first settlement of Port Royal to the creation of a number of scattered farming establishments around the 'baie Française,' or Bay of Fundy. The first influx of settlers was followed by a trickle of new colonists in later years. The agricultural economy was still oriented primarily towards local consumption, although a small amount of agricultural produce was exchanged with commercial adventurers connected with the fishery and the fur trade. These commercial operations formed the second economic pattern: centred in outlying areas far removed from the agricultural settlements, they served as vital links for the sedentary population and brought manufactured European goods in exchange for agricultural produce. The French companies set up to exploit the fur and fish resources were unable to develop fully, as a result of military and economic pressures from the English interests in the region. Yet the two economies did develop simultaneously and meet at Port Royal, where Acadian demographic development would stem largely from the natural increase of the existing population.[4] The location of the colony, between the St Lawrence Valley and the Anglo-American colonies farther south, would arouse at times the strategic interest of France and England. Yet, in general, the residential colonies of Newfoundland and Acadia would develop without significant support from their respective governments. As early as 1650 they contained the seeds of their later evolution.

Several groups of fishers focused their interest on the rich fishing grounds of Newfoundland and effectively divided the island into spheres of influence. The southeast coast, from Cape Race to Cape Bonavista, was exploited by English migrant fishers. The banks of the northeast coast – the 'Petit nord' – were fished by French vessels from St Malo. French Basques could be found in the southwest, with Plaisance as their home port, while fishers from Normandy and Sables d'Olonne were active on the Grand Banks. According to a tradition that had evolved over the years, a rudimentary form of administration emerged during each fishing season. The first ship's captain to arrive in a harbour was recognized as 'admiral,' with powers to establish an order of precedence among later arrivals and to arbitrate disputes.[5] Both Versailles and Whitehall heard conflicting views on these arrangements. Many fishing merchants from the west of England – the 'Western Adventurers' of Somerset, Devon, and Cornwall – favoured free access to the coast of Newfoundland and the continuation of local administrative control through the system of admirals. So did their French counterparts from St Malo. According to this view, the presence of colonists was a menace to the traditional fish-drying operations on shore and a source of competition for the migratory fishers. Very different were the perceptions of London and Bristol merchants who were promoting the settlement of resident fishers. In spite of repeated setbacks, a number of these merchants succeeded in placing establishments in fishing harbours, and for their own security the colonists were in favour of the introduction of civil government.

In England, the Interregnum of the 1650s – following the overthrow of King Charles I by Parliament – saw the political balance tip in favour of the West Country merchants who opposed Newfoundland colonization. The island's cold and humid climate and its rocky subsoil, they argued, were insuperable obstacles to the settlement of any significant number of colonists. If a colonial population did manage to become self-sufficient, this would reduce the volume of West Country exports to North America. A policy that favoured colonization would not only be expensive for the state but would also weaken its naval power by inhibiting the ability of the migratory fishery to serve as a nursery for seamen. The London merchants who favoured colonization responded with arguments of their own. Resident fishing bases could be operated more efficiently than purely seasonal operations. The interests of those who had invested time and money in colonial schemes had to be respected. And Newfoundland colonies would represent the best means of containing French expansionism on the island.[6] Parliament, however, accepted the arguments of those who opposed colonization and believed with them that the cod fishery should remain under metropolitan control.[7] This policy was manifested during the 1650s in the establishment of a convoy system to protect the fishing fleet from possible attacks and in the naming of a 'commodore' as chief commander for the fishing season. Nevertheless, despite the absence of civil government, a number of colonists still persisted, with the support of the London merchants and notwithstanding the hostility of the migrant fishers, in establishing themselves on the coasts of the island. The principal site of fishing operations continued to be St John's, which offered security to the fishing fleet in its harbour as well as ready access to the fishing grounds.[8]

There was also debate in France between the advocates of a *laissez-faire* approach to the fishery and those who favoured greater government involvement in North American affairs. Only in the 1650s, with the inauguration of the partnership of King Louis XIV and his minister Jean-Baptiste Colbert – imbued with mercantilist ideas – did a systematic view of Newfoundland emerge. France, unlike England, opted for the establishment of a colony in Newfoundland, complete with civil government and a fortified port at Plaisance. This decision aroused complaints from shipowners in St Malo, who objected to a policy of settlement, but it reflected a wider French approach to colonization. French colonial policy aimed at the creation of a French society in North America, modelled on the provinces of France itself and supported by the family, religious institutions, and the granting of land.[9] As administrative structures evolved, the St Lawrence Valley became the cornerstone of French North America. Acadia and Newfoundland were subordinate territories, subject – at least in theory – to the authority of the governor in Quebec.[10] As for Plaisance, its selection as the administrative centre of French Newfoundland fulfilled a number of purposes. Its harbour and temperate climate offered protection to the fishing fleet, while its beaches were suitable for drying fish. Strategically, it was close to the English centre of St John's and could play a role in the military protection of French interests in the St Lawrence Valley and the Gulf. In other respects, however, Plaisance offered little to residents. The rocky soil gave no encouragement to agriculture and thus forced the population to depend on costly imported food supplies. This in turn worked against the establishment of industries other than the fishery.[11]

In 1662, Thalour Du Perron – a young and inexperienced civilian – arrived at Plaisance as governor, with a military force of seventy-five men. Early in the following year, he was killed by mutineers. Command was then taken over by military officers, culminating with the appointment of the naval lieutenant La Poippe as governor in 1670. An annual subsidy of 10,000 livres was set aside for the provisioning and military support of the colony, but this was not enough to extend to the costs of government.[12] The governor, inadequately paid, turned to trading in fish. The soldiers did not even have a barracks, and lodged in settler households. The fisheries of Plaisance, St Mary's Bay, and St Pierre, did well. Central administrative control ensured a rigorous check on the quality of the fish sent to France and to export markets. Although population growth was held back by competition between resident and migrant fishers, and by the monopolization of the beaches at Plaisance by administrative and military officers, the French resident fishers were shielded in the early 1670s from the effects of the Anglo-Dutch war, which resulted in harassment of the English fishery on the east coast. The alliance between Louis XIV and the restored Stuart monarchy in England ensured continued peace at Plaisance.

The English colonists in Newfoundland, meanwhile, were encountering frustrations that stemmed from the hostility of the migrant fishers and from the metropolitan ascendancy of anticolonial interests. In 1660, the English Parliament, with the goal of regulating trade contacts among English settlements in North America, reinforced the Navigation Act of 1651. The act had forbidden trade with foreigners and had included a list of products that could be traded only with England itself. Even new legislation in 1663, however, seemed to do little to curb illegal trade between the English and the French in Newfoundland. Much more limited were Native-European exchanges. Little is known of the Beothuk in this period. Avoiding contacts with non-Natives, they received no missionaries, and their language remained unknown to the colonizers. With limited access to fur-bearing animals, the Beothuk did not develop trade relationships with the Europeans. They continued to obtain metal goods – such as nails and fish-hooks – from seasonally deserted fishing installations, a practice that in turn aroused the hostility of European fishers, who took aggressive measures to safeguard their property. The existence of a Native fur trade on St Mary's Bay by 1662 raises the likelihood that Micmacs from Acadia had crossed the Gulf in order to extend the trading relationship they had already formed with the French, as well as to add to their hunting territories.[13]

The peaceful coexistence of the Natives with the French of Acadia can be explained by the type of establishments and the relationship between the two groups. The small French presence did not exert demographic pressure in the region. For example, the Pentagoet trading post, far removed from the Acadian settlements of the 'baie Française,' contained thirty-two Etchemin wigwams alongside two European buildings. The same can be said of the eastern seaboard of New Brunswick. The travels of the Recollet Chrestien Le Clercq in the 1670s illustrate the weakness of the European presence in the region: fortified trading posts, manned by about fifteen Frenchmen, at Bathurst and on the riverbank of the Miramichi, ensured the gathering of fur pelts.[14] Between Natives and French there were many forms of contact. Intermarriage can be exemplified by the cases of Charles de Saint-Etienne de La Tour at Cape Sable, Jean-Vincent d'Abbadie de Saint-Castin at Pentagoet, and Richard Denys de Fronsac at Jemseg. Borrowings between one culture and another included technological exchanges and the adoption by non-Natives of place names (such as Cobeguit or Pigiguit) that indicated the continuing presence of the first nations, while the use of French religious words like 'angeri' for angel and 'hostisin' for wafer were incorporated in the Abenaki language.[15]

The colony of Acadia had fallen into a state of anarchy during the 1650s. The accidental drowning of Charles de Menou d'Aulnay, in 1650, set three individuals in opposition to each other, all of whom had a strong interest in the matter of who would take over the debt-laden governor's control of the colony. Emmanuel Le Borgne was the chief creditor of the d'Aulnay family, but was unable to reach agreement with them. As a result, in 1652 he seized Port Royal and went on to attack the establishments of d'Aulnay's rivals, notably at La Hève, Pentagoet, and St Peter's in Cape Breton.[16] Charles de Saint-Etienne de La Tour, d'Aulnay's main enemy, was also active in attempts to consolidate his position and to recover the earlier loss of his posts at Cape Sable and at the mouth of the St John River. In 1653, La Tour married d'Aulnay's widow in order to assure, according to the marriage contract, 'the peace and tranquility of the country, and union and harmony between the two families.'[17] Nicolas Denys, the third of the contenders, moved to protect his investments in the fishery and the fur trade by obtaining, on 30 January 1654, a large grant of territory that took in all of the Gulf coast from Canso to the Gaspé.[18]

Armed conflict soon began between Le Borgne on the one hand, and Denys and the now-united La Tour–d'Aulnay interests on the other. But worse was to come. Robert Sedgwick, an English naval captain, pillaged most of the colony's settlements between July and September 1654.[19] This conquest of sorts, though its legal and diplomatic status was doubtful, led to many years of uncertainty, during which the Acadians maintained closer links with the English than with the French. An important element of their life in America was forged in that period; they learned to accommodate with their English neighbours. Receiving little help from either France or England, the Acadians had to rely on their own resources. That explains their independent attitude, perceived by European visitors and administrators. From 1654 to 1670, both France and England claimed – though barely exercised – jurisdiction over the region. Versailles continued to make land grants and issue permission for trapping and fishing,[20] while England renamed the conquered territory 'Nova Scotia' – the name deriving from the earlier efforts of Sir William Alexander – and conceded it to a partnership composed of three individuals, Thomas Temple, William Crowne, and Charles de Saint-Etienne de La Tour. La Tour gained few benefits from his participation in this venture. Even Temple, who was later named governor of Nova Scotia, made little progress in developing the colony. Soon legally embroiled with Crowne over the terms of their financial interests, he also faced a dangerous military rival in Emmanuel Le Borgne.[21] Inevitably, all of this was damaging for the colony. Immigration ceased. The girls' school operated by Mme de Brice was closed, and the Capuchins left their mission at Port Royal, to be replaced by Franciscans in 1664.[22] At the time of d'Aulnay's death, some forty or fifty families constituted 'the founders of the Acadian people,' as, 'with a few possible exceptions, no more French families came to boost the country's settlement.'[23] Most subsequent settlers were either soldiers or indentured labourers who chose to establish themselves permanently in the colony.

The strife over Acadia/Nova Scotia continued until 1670. The military and legal actions of Le Borgne, directed not only against Temple but also against Acadian colonists and entrepreneurs, provided revealing evidence of the role that had been played by La Rochelle merchants – of whom Le Borgne was one – in the development of Acadia. Merchants of this port town had advanced the funds for necessary supplies for the colony, on the understanding that they would be reimbursed from the profits of the fisheries and the fur trade. The colony had been run constantly on credit, and recurring deficits had led to the chronic debts of d'Aulnay, Denys, and the La Tours: debts that were owed largely to La Rochelle merchants.[24] The later lack of interest in Acadia on the part of the merchant class, and the resulting need for state support of the colony, can be attributed to the difficulties experienced in recovering investments from a colony that had a small population and offered relatively little access to easily exploitable natural resources.

For the Acadian settlers, the Sedgwick conquest opened the way for the strengthening of the economic influence of Massachusetts. New England merchants and fishing vessels brought provisions to the Acadians, who suffered no serious deprivations during this period.[25] For fifteen years, they saw little sign of the authorities of either France or England, although what links they had were more with the English than the French. A generation grew up to consider the necessity for reaching accommodations with their English neighbours, and with the representatives of whatever regime prevailed, as the key to their survival in North America. This pragmatic attitude, often perceived as dangerously independent by European visitors and administrators, was a product of the realization that the European powers attached little importance to the particular interests of the Acadians. It was also this attitude that strengthened the Acadians to continue their way of life on the Fundy marshes.[26] Dièreville, a later French visitor, marvelled at their ingenuity and commented that 'it is not easy to change the course of the sea, but the Acadians do so by strong dykes.'[27] The first efforts to dyke alluvial Fundy lands belonged to the years between 1640 and 1645, when families from Poitou settled in the area of Port Royal. The census of 1671 revealed that the colonists – of whom several were of Poitevin origin and had arrived with a familiarity with the cultivation of marshes and the techniques of producing sea salt – had already proceeded to drain the marshes of this vicinity. The construction of dykes, and the development of the necessary technology, made the Acadians 'cultivators of water.' Made of clods of earth, the dykes were built to different heights and widths depending on their placement along the water's edge. Wooden canals, known as *aboiteaux*, were installed at regular intervals along the base of the dyke, so as to allow water to run off from the fields into the sea. This marshland cultivation represented an experience unique in North America at the time.[28]

French administrators and outsiders frequently interpreted the Acadians' methods of land use as indicating a lack of ambition, since there was no evidence of any interest in clearing uplands.[29] The dykelands, as well as having their technological implications, also influenced Acadian social relations. The search for and cultivation of alluvial lands induced Acadians to favour a scattered pattern of settlement, within which groups of individuals – already familiarized with communal labour by living under French feudalism – would gather together in extended family units bound both by blood ties and by the bonds of affection.[30] The families that were established during d'Aulnay's regime came for the most part from Poitou and Loudun. This immigration produced an initial cultural homogeneity that facilitated the assimilation of later immigrants from elsewhere. An essentially agricultural people, some 350 of the 500 persons enumerated by Governor Hector d'Andigné de Grandfontaine in 1671 lived in the area of Port Royal and formed seventy family units. Others, mainly those involved in the fisheries and the fur trade, lived at Pentagoet, on the St John River, or at Cape Sable. Even though the French government had made land grants elsewhere, the remoteness of their locations and the preoccupation of the grantees with profit combined to discourage settlement. Even the practice of granting the same land to several individuals could by no means ensure its development.[31]

Acadia was finally restored to France under the terms of the 1667 Treaty of Breda, although it took another three years before a direct order from the English Crown forced Thomas Temple to turn over the various settlements to the new French governor, Grandfontaine.[32] The new governor brought settlers with him from Rochefort in 1671, and they were soon incorporated into the existing population. After that time, the flow of immigrants lessened. After 1671, only sixty-one men and five women, coming from Anjou and the Beauce, from Normandy and Brittany, and from other French provinces, were quickly integrated into the community. Some were brought from Canada by Governor Michel Le Neuf de La Vallière. Yet others were Huguenots who arrived by way of England, or, like the Caisseys, were of English origin.[33] Up until the conquest of 1710, new arrivals tended no longer to be families but single men.[34]

Yet the image of Acadia as the home of a peasant population that had withdrawn into itself is false. The Acadian experience was diverse, and Acadians encountered influences that combined to forge their particular identity. They had a continuing relationship with Native people, and were subject to the economic influence of Massachusetts. French authority over Acadia coexisted with the presence of New England merchants, even though French colonial policy dictated that the merchants of Boston and the fishers of Salem should be replaced with counterparts from France. The problem was all the more acute because New England interests regarded the Bay of Fundy as a 'Mare Nostrum,' and French business interests did not extend in the region. The slender resources that Grandfontaine and his successor, Chambly (1673–8), had at their disposal made it impossible for them to restore French authority with any real firmness. They had no naval protection for the coast, and an inadequate garrison. Indeed, in 1674, a small Dutch force under Jurriaen Aernoutsz was able temporarily to seize control of Acadia. Massachusetts, meanwhile, continued to supply essential goods and services. Grandfontaine bought supplies there in 1670, and brought a carpenter from Boston to build a boat. Some years later, the commander of the fort at Jemseg, Pierre de Joybert de Marson, bought foodstuffs (molasses, wheat, and flour) and other supplies (axes and tobacco) from the same source.[35]

The Acadian population on the Bay of Fundy practised fishing, but mainly for domestic consumption. There were also some who used fish as a medium of exchange in commercial operations. In the commercial fishery, European fishing vessels were gradually replaced by grantees, who took over the most productive fishing grounds. Nicolas Denys, for example, developed a number of sites at locations such as Miscou, St Peter's on Cape Breton, and Chedabucto. From the 1650s onwards, however, he had difficulty meeting the competition of New England vessels, which moved steadily into fishing areas off the Acadian coast and fiercely resisted any French attempts to dislodge them. Frequent attacks on Denys's fishing sites resulted from this rivalry. 'Caught, like the iron between the hammer and the anvil,' was how one historian described the Acadian situation *vis-à-vis* the commercial expansionism of New England.[36] During the unsettled period from 1654 to 1670, New England fishers and merchants had regularly pursued their activities on Acadian waters and territory. They continued to do so, practising a kind of free trade, despite French efforts to prohibit them, following the return of Acadia to France under the Treaty of Breda. Salem vessels fished off Cape Sable. Several Boston merchants, notably John Nelson, were active in trade all along the Acadian shoreline. The results were felt as far afield as Canada, since the high prices paid in Acadia for furs and the ready availability of English trade goods encouraged the routing of furs towards Acadia from the St Lawrence Valley.[37]

French officials were also drawn into this illegal trade. Henri Brunet of the French Compagnie du Nord, while in charge of developing the Acadian fishery, traded with the English during voyages in 1672, 1673, and 1674. Governor La Vallière attempted to maintain the appearance of French authority by selling permits to English fishers through the good offices of a Boston merchant.[38] His successor as governor, François-Marie Perrot, lost no time in forging close commercial links with New England and was alleged to have attempted to make himself 'the only merchant in Acadia.'[39] The reality in this part of North America was that European decisions and policies were taken to heart by those in the colonies only insofar as they were consistent with their own interests – which did not necessarily coincide with metropolitan goals. Outsiders looked on such attitudes with a jaundiced eye; one accused the Acadians of having 'virtually taken in with their first milk the air of independence with which they have become infected.' This judgment must be tempered by considering the comment of Robert Challes, an acute observer of Acadia in this era, that 'the colonists were forbidden all commerce with the English, but without any other provision to supply them with what they needed.'[40]

The socio-economic configuration of the colony was little affected by the transfer of seigneurialism to North America. Under the seigneurial system, the state granted land to seigneurs on condition that they promoted development by establishing settlers. Some fifty-five seigneuries were granted in Acadia, from the Gaspé in the north to the Penobscot River in the south. Few of the grantees showed any desire to develop their lands as they were expected to, and the large size of the land grants combined with lax enforcement by the metropolis to ensure that this state of affairs would continue. The few seigneuries that were populated, such as Beaubassin and Port Royal, were characterized by struggles between seigneurs and their tenants that indicate clearly that the former did not wield in practice the extensive authority attributed to them in theory.[41] The seigneurial system in Acadia simply did not fulfil its intended role as an instrument of leadership, stability, and social organization, and the Acadian censitaires had no incentive to discharge their own obligations towards their landlords.

Nor did the distance of Acadia from France, and its small population, provide incentive for French shipowning merchants to develop commercial relations with the Fundy communities. The scheme favoured in the early 1670s by Jean Talon, intendant of New France, for a triangular trade joining France, its North American colonies, and the French West Indies, was never fulfilled in Acadia because there was nobody there who was sufficiently 'substantial in business matters.'[42] The isolation of Acadia from other French territories reinforced in turn the colonists' links with New England. This north-south connection between nearby populations made itself felt in the formative years of Acadian culture and continued to exercise a strong influence. Even speech patterns were affected by Acadian contacts both with New England and with the Native population, as witness the use of phrases such as 'vous "too," ' and 'pas "yet,"'[43] and the adoption of Amerindian place names. The experience of numerous military attacks and the lack of certainty about the future tended to weaken any sense of loyalty the Acadians felt towards European authority. In their economic relations and cultural accommodations with their non-French neighbours, Acadians showed their adjustment to the context of their lives. The converse was their desire to keep a certain distance, and freedom of action, in their dealings with French officialdom. At the time of the Port Royal census of 1671, some inhabitants refused to give information regarding their age and how many children they had, or on their holdings of livestock.[44] Furthermore, the adoption of certain place names, such as Beaubassin (beautiful basin), Cocagne (land of milk and honey), and Paradis Terrestre (earthly paradise) showed a conscious appreciation of the colonists' material well-being and of their surroundings.

Among the Native populations, there developed comparable attitudes towards relations with non-Natives. Indigenous people retained their independence of thought and action and were never servile or passive supporters of French interests. Jean-Vincent d'Abbadie de Saint-Castin, a French military officer at Pentagoet, married Pidianske, daughter of a Penobscot chief, and devoted himself to maintaining the French presence in that area. In doing so, he maintained close contact with Native leaders, notably during the Abenaki-English war of 1675–8. Consequently, the area between the Penobscot and Kennebec rivers became a territory where the French exerted considerable influence. Saint-Castin built his habitation on the Bagaduce River – not far from the old fort at Pentagoet, which had been destroyed in the Dutch raid of 1674 – and it became an important population and trade centre. According to contemporary sources, Saint-Castin maintained trade relationships with the English, even though they were enemies of the Penobscot.[45] Also influential on relations between non-Natives and indigenous peoples were missionaries such as the Recollet Chrestien Le Clercq, who assisted in the development of a hieroglyphic system of Micmac written language. Le Clercq's writings and his narrative of his journey in January 1677 from Nepisiguit (Bathurst) to the residence of Richard Denys de Fronsac on the Miramichi bear witness to the testing circumstances of his life as a missionary.[46]

French colonial administrators, meanwhile, found difficulty in enforcing their authority in matters relating to the fishery and the fur trade. The problem was compounded by the location of administrative centres far from the principal Acadian communities. Grandfontaine established his capital – that is, his headquarters for the military defence of the colony – at Pentagoet, while Pierre de Joybert removed to Jemseg, on the St John River, following the Dutch attack of 1674. Matters were not helped either by the lack of intervention by the government of France or by the intermittent meddling of Quebec-based officials in Acadian affairs. Governor Frontenac of New France, by naming La Vallière governor in 1678, indicated his desire to involve himself in the administration of Acadia and thus to extend his power over the various components of the French Empire. All administrators in Acadia, however, whether through necessity or simply to enrich themselves, conducted trade with New England merchants. French merchants, in bypassing Acadia for the greater profits of the Canadian fur trade and the Newfoundland fishery, encouraged this state of affairs. Mathieu de Goutin, a French official who married an Acadian, Marie-Jeanne Thibodeau, made a pertinent observation in declaring that 'with the Bostoners, [we must] be extremely cautious.'[47]

Tensions also persisted in Newfoundland. In 1675, a census of the east coast of the island enumerated thirty English settlements, from Salvage and Bonavista in the north to Trepassy in the south. Of the settlements, twenty-four had fewer than five families, and eight of those counted only a single family. The small numbers derived from the fact that only a quarter of those enumerated were permanent residents, and only 12 per cent were women. The large proportion of men, and the absence of industries, led to high rates of alcohol consumption.[48] Both the French and the English populations in Newfoundland suffered reverses at the hands of the Dutch. Ferryland was raided by Dutch corsairs in 1673, and Plaisance in 1676. For the English inhabitants, however, the most critical threat came from England itself, in a series of government decisions that restricted the rights of the island residents. In 1671 settlement was forbidden within ten kilometres of the coast. The continuing pressure exerted by the West Country merchants culminated in an order for the deportation of the residents, and harassment reached its height when all the settlements between Cape Race and Cape Bonavista were pillaged by English seasonal fishermen in 1676 and again in 1678. Two residents, John Downing and William Hinton, attempted at this time to demonstrate to the English government that colonization represented order and stability, as well as a permanent obstacle to French expansion. In 1675, the report of John Berry, naval commander in Newfoundland, revealed in England the nature of the abuses that the residents had experienced. Even so, it would be many years before civil government was established. Yet, in spite of all these disturbances, the fishery was productive. Salt cod produced by the English in Newfoundland exceeded 220,000 quintals in a typical year during the 1670s. The number of people who overwintered in the English fishing harbours reached some 1,200 at this time and during the 1680s, although the majority were not colonists but employees of the 'planters,' who conducted fishing operations and in most cases had moved their families to Newfoundland. Of the employees, or 'servants,' some might eventually stay, but most would leave with whatever they had saved from their wages after as little as two or three seasons.[49]

French Newfoundland experienced a period of tranquillity under the governorship of La Poippe from 1670 to 1684. A list of inhabitants prepared by him in 1671 indicated the presence of twenty-nine men, twelve women, and thirty children, most of them originating from the Ile de Ré and from La Rochelle. Religious services were being provided by Recollets of the province of Saint-Denys, under the authority of the bishop of Quebec. The French fleet was approximately double the size of that of the English fishery – some 400 ships, with 10,000 men – and this caused enough concern among the English residents to prompt them to call for better military protection and the encouragement of further English colonization.[50]

The West Country merchants, it was true, continued to regard the presence of English colonists as a greater threat to their interests than any competition in the fishery from the French in Plaisance. But those who favoured colonization insisted that the French represented a profound challenge. If the French could not be expelled altogether, they argued, then at least their fishing should be regulated by the English by way of a system of cash levies. When he arrived at Plaisance in 1685, Governor Antoine Parat noted the presence of English families who served as intermediaries between the local population and New England merchants. The substitution of English for French merchants in the provisions trade was partly a result of the trading strategy of the French. By limiting the entry of essential products into the colony, French traders had created an artificial scarcity and forced up prices. The rise in the cost of living in turn created chronic indebtedness among the inhabitants, who became resentful of the metropolitan merchants. The entire situation, similar as it was to that of Acadia, worked against the era's characteristic mercantilist goal of encouraging trade to take place exclusively between the metropolitan power and its colonies. The French colony in Newfoundland owed its existence solely to the fishery, which, for certain French ports, was an important pursuit. Honfleur, for example, fitted out thirty-six ships for Newfoundland in 1687, employing 540 seamen. But this dependence on fishing did not encourage large-scale immigration to Newfoundland, most fishers preferring to work as labourers for a finite number of years. In 1687, the majority of the population of 256 at Plaisance consisted of employees of the twenty-five heads of families. The balance of the total of 640 French colonists in

Newfoundland lived in smaller groups on both sides of the Burin Peninsula and on the island of St Pierre.[51]

The funds provided by the French government were inadequate for the administration of the colony, and this prompted the administrators to take advantage of their positions to supplement their salaries, and thus to make up for their lack of earnings. Governor Parat, as well as becoming personally involved in the fishery, traded with English merchants and reserved for himself the best drying sites on the beach at Plaisance. Preoccupied with economic matters, he gave little attention to rendering the colony militarily defensible, despite receiving a reinforcement of twenty-five troops in 1687. Because there was neither a fort nor even a barracks, Parat was forced to lodge his soldiers with residents of Plaisance, and the soldiers had to turn to fishing in order to pay for their keep.[52]

The 1680s saw a number of noteworthy developments in Acadia. Following the Dutch attack of 1674, several families had left the Port Royal area to search for new lands and greater security: Jacques Bourgeois began the migration towards Beaubassin in the early 1670s. The first residents arrived in the vicinity of Les Mines (Minas) during the 1680s. The expansion of population to the north and east coasts of the Bay of Fundy from a single origin at Port Royal led to the creation of a sense of solidarity and a complex pattern of kinship ties that gave unity to the entire Acadian people. The new settlements continued the style of marshland agriculture already begun at Port Royal. Meanwhile, anxious to wrest from New England control the profits from the lucrative fisheries in Acadian waters, France made a large land grant to the Sedentary Fishery Company of Acadia. Formed by La Rochelle merchants, the company was also to enjoy a fishing monopoly. The principal ports among several established by the company were at Chedabucto – which accounted for fifty fishers in 1686 – and in the vicinity of Canso. The company encountered a variety of difficulties on the way to its final disappearance in 1702, including internal disputes, problems of capitalization, and English competition. Its effort to use force to compel respect for its rights and privileges was interpreted by New England commercial interests as an aggressive policy, and the reply came in the form of seizures of the company's vessels and attacks on its fishing ports.[53]

The colony of Acadia continued to depend on outside sources for its manufactured goods. At times when provisions were in short supply, these commodities, too, were sought from New Englanders. Such requests often did not have to be addressed far afield, for some Massachusetts merchants had stores nearby – notably at Port Rossignol and at Port Royal. Certain Acadians entered into trade not only as a means of obtaining necessary goods but also as a source of profit. Two inhabitants of Port Royal, Abraham Boudrot and Pierre Arsenault, were active in the New England trade, along with Jean de Saint-Aubin of Passamaquoddy, and – so it was alleged – Louis Petit, vicar general of Acadia, and his assistant, Abbé Geoffroy. These commercial transactions were characterized by insecurity on the part of the Acadians, who faced such difficulties as the theft or official seizure of their merchandise, not to mention constant indebtedness to their Massachusetts trading partners. As well as dealing with the capricious changes of attitude of their English neighbours, the Acadian traders had to enter into a relationship that was fundamentally unequal, with counterparts who took all the benefits of the trade for themselves, 'at the expense of Acadia.'[54]

The intendant of New France, Jacques de Meulles, made an extended visit to Acadia from October 1686 to July 1687, to make a survey of exploitable resources and to study the possibility of beginning a sedentary fishing establishment on the Bay of Fundy, along the same lines as the existing operations of the Sedentary Fishery Company on the Atlantic coastline. After touring Acadia, de Meulles expressed the opinion that, with adequate investment, the fisheries could serve in the future as the mainspring of the colonial economy.[55] What he failed to recognize was that New England interest groups would never give up their involvement in Acadia, unless faced with a large population, a healthy economic structure, and a military strength far beyond what the French Ministry of Marine was willing to provide. Yet in general, the Acadian people had adapted successfully to a physical environment that differed greatly from that of France, even though they did not have extensive technical knowledge in the areas of agricultural cultivation and livestock breeding. The abundance of land, and a varied diet that included adequate quantities of cereals and of the products of hunting and fishing limited the ravages of epidemics and of infant mortality. Indeed, the marshes produced enough grain to feed the Acadian population and still have a surplus for export.[56]

The foundation of the Acadians' phenomenal population growth was not immigration, but rather marriage within the community and a high birth rate. One French visitor, struck by the number of children he met, wrote about Acadian couples in the following verse: 'wedlock / Unites them both and they are free / To populate the World; which is / Moreover, that which they do best.'[57] Thus, the Acadian population, in which bachelorhood was virtually unknown and the normal marriage age was twenty years for a female and twenty-two for a male, grew at an annual rate of 4 per cent. During his stay in Acadia in 1686, de Meulles enumerated 583 inhabitants at Port Royal, 57 at Les Mines, and 127 at Beaubassin, of a total estimated population of 932. A census taken in 1687–8 by Gargas, a government clerk at Port Royal, counted fewer people in the major Fundy settlements, but provided detailed information on Native and non-Native inhabitants in areas such as Chedabucto, Port Rochelois, Jemseg, and Pentagoet.[58] Overall, the numbers doubled between 1671 and 1686, from 440 to more than 900. Yet, despite this rapid growth, the population of Acadia remained much smaller than those of neighbouring colonies. The number of Acadians in the late 1680s compared with more than 10,000 inhabitants in Canada and some 50,000 in Massachusetts.[59]

From April to June 1686, Acadia received another visitor from Canada, the bishop of Quebec, Monseigneur de Saint-Vallier. The bishop reported that there were several priests in the colony. Claude Moireau had arrived as a Recollet missionary in the St John Valley in 1675 and extended his ministry up and down the coastline, while Louis Petit had begun to live at Port Royal in 1676. With a member of a women's religious order, whose name is not known, Petit organized a school for both boys and girls. The Sedentary Fishery Company supported at Chedabucto two Penitent fathers from Normandy. The bishop of Quebec also noted the need for religious ministry in the new settlements on the Bay of Fundy, both of which received their first resident priests during the late 1680s. Louis Geoffroy, serving as missionary at Pentagoet in 1686, began to minister to the area of Les Mines in the following year. Claude Trouvé, who accompanied the bishop from Quebec, was assigned to Beaubassin. The Acadian population, Saint-Vallier reported, seemed well adapted to the environment and was using the region's resources effectively.[60]

Contrary to the assertion of the historical geographer Andrew Hill Clark, the evidence suggests that most nuclear families occupied a house of their own.[61] Housing was well adapted to the Acadian climate, which was more demanding than that of France. Archaeological research in the vicinity of Port Royal, at Belleisle, and at the Melanson settlement has revealed that houses were built of locally available materials such as wood, clay, and straw. The floor plan would include a large common space, partitioned sleeping areas, and a loft. The base of the hearth projected to the exterior of the house, thus offering to the farmyard animals some protection from the elements.[62] The Acadian settlements built around the Bay of Fundy, closely linked by blood and kinship ties, were also connected with the outside. Trade with the English colonists and day-to-day relations with the Native population opened the communities to various influences. The colonial wars tended to render less stable the relations between the colonists and the Native population, but at an individual level relations between Acadians and Native people were close and were strengthened by further intermarriage.[63] In general, the Acadians had adapted well to their physical and human environment. They had modified the landscape of the Fundy marshlands by their construction of dykes and other structures. They had forged a relationship – even though not an equal one – with their neighbours in Massachusetts, and also had intimate connections with Native inhabitants.

In some important aspects, the situation of the colonial establishments in Acadia and Newfoundland changed little during the period from 1650 to 1687. The lack of attention from the European parent countries did not encourage economic diversification. Acadia remained essentially an agricultural society, while Newfoundland's destiny was dominated by the fishery. The region's economic history of failing to yield profits led to a flight of capital and, in turn, forced those who were involved in trade to use barter as their method of operation. What little cash there was was quickly hoarded by inhabitants, whose custom was to 'bury it as soon as they get it.'[64] These economic weaknesses discouraged immigration, either of colonists or of rich individuals whose expertise and capital resources might have promoted some stabilization and expansion of the economy. Furthermore, the absence of institutions that could bring effective regulation of either the French or the English sector in Newfoundland further held back the process of settlement. The virtual isolation of Acadia from France forced the inhabitants to fall back on their own resources, and insofar as this meant illegal trade, showed again the weakness of administrative control. There were also elements of strength and unity within the colonial population, notably among the Acadians, whose communitarian spirit favoured cohesion and a firm sense of identity. This counteracted to some extent the influence of the centrifugal imperial forces. Yet the French and English settlements of the Atlantic coastline shared the same essential marginality. Dependent on the metropolis, the colonists suffered from the intolerance of their neighbours and from the influence of outsiders more powerful than they who wished to exploit the natural resources of the region and to treat it as a strategic era. By the late 1680s, Acadia and Newfoundland were colonies based on such weak foundations that their survival was not yet assured.

CHAPTER FIVE

1686–1720
Imperial Intrusions

JOHN G. REID

Visiting Acadia in 1686, the intendant of New France – Jacques de Meulles – was disappointed to find that the colony was 'si peu de chose.' To Louis-Armand de Lom d'Arce de Lahontan, third Baron Lahontan and a serving French officer in North America during the early 1690s, it seemed that '*Port-Royal*, the Capital or the only City of *Acadia*, is in effect no more than a little paultry Town.' For George Larkin, visiting St John's as an English official in 1701, it was the people of that settlement who drew attention: 'the Inhabitants and Planters of Newfoundland are a poor, indigent, and withall a profuse sort of people, that care not at what Rates they get into debt.'[1]

None of these perceptions was surprising. Since the establishment of the first colonial populations in the early seventeenth century, neither Acadia nor Newfoundland had developed as a successful colony by European standards. The ambitions of colonial promoters, and intermittently of the French government, to introduce a substantial colonial population to Acadia and develop a flourishing trade with France, had been frustrated. Although the fishery on the coasts of Newfoundland continued to be important to the English economy, there was still room for doubt as to whether permanent settlement of the island was necessary or desirable. The French settlements on Placentia Bay and around the Burin Peninsula were similarly characterized by a mixture of migratory and residential activity. By comparison with more populous colonies – such as Massachusetts, Virginia, Canada, or even Jamaica or the French Antilles – Acadia and Newfoundland might be valued for fish or for their strategic location, but hardly as jewels in any imperial crown.

For all that, the populations whom European visitors and officials so often disparaged were well established. The Native people, who represented a clear majority in Acadia and who may still have outnumbered the European permanent settlers in Newfoundland, could measure their residency in the region in multiple generations. By 1686, the Micmac may have been close to their nadir of some 2,000, the Maliseet-Passamaquoddy were probably less than 1,000, and the Penobscot Abenaki may have numbered rather more than 600. The Beothuk, whose number at the time of European contact has been estimated at 1,100, may until then have avoided substantial population loss through their unwillingness to associate with the settlers.[2] The colonists themselves, though small in numbers, had defied conventional European logic in their decision to live in the region. They had developed strategies for doing so successfully, frequently involving unorthodox economic links and sometimes kinship ties – such as those arising from Acadian-Native intermarriage, of from the presence of English settlers in French Plaisance – that crossed ethnic boundaries.[3] As communities, these peoples were used to exercising considerable autonomy. Between 1686 and 1720, however, the autonomy of both Native and non-Native residents would be put in jeopardy. During these years, dominated by war and by the threat of war, the imperial powers of France and Great Britain finally imposed their grip on Acadia/Nova Scotia and on Newfoundland. With increasing imperial intervention, the patronizing attentions of military and civil officials ceased to be a mere amusement or annoyance to the residents and became an active element in the shaping of their future.

Until the mid-1680s, both Newfoundland and Acadia were largely neglected by the European imperial powers. Influenced in part by the arguments of West Country merchants, who saw Newfoundland residents as competitors to the migratory fishery and accordingly resisted any recognition of the permanence of settlement, the English government had made no effort to establish a colonial administration in Newfoundland. 'We desire you ...' the commissioners of customs instructed New England governor Sir Edmund Andros in 1687, 'to give publique notice to all persons concerned within your Government, That the Newfoundland is not to be taken or accompted a plantation, being under no Government or other Regulation as all His Majesties Plantations are.'[4] France had regularly maintained governors in both Plaisance and Acadia, but had offered them little support. Nor had the governors necessarily been individuals of high prestige. Antoine Parat, for example, before he served as governor of Plaisance from 1685 to 1690, had been a fire-ship captain. In the late 1680s, in the context of an increasing recognition by European governments of the economic value and strategic significance of North America, this persistent neglect began – slowly – to change. Parat's successor in 1691 was a battle-hardened military officer – and a member of a noble family, by contrast with the commoner Parat – Jacques-François de Mombeton de Brouillan. Already, in 1687, a new governor had arrived in Acadia. Louis-Alexandre Des Friches de Meneval was another professional military officer, and he was equipped with a small military and naval force to be used in re-establishing the defences of the colony at the same time as its economy was weaned away from dependence on New England. These appointments evinced a new imperial approach. So did that of Andros, who, as governor and captain general of the newly established Dominion of New England, arrived in late 1686 to govern a territory that included most of New England and would briefly cover, from 1688, not only all of New England but also New York and the Jerseys.[5]

Paradoxically, in view of the increasing level of military preparedness in the northeastern coastal areas of North America at this time, 1686 was also the year of an attempt by France and England to reconcile their competing colonial interests in the Treaty of Whitehall. A product of the rapprochement between the two powers that had followed the accession of the Roman Catholic and pro-French James II to the throne of England in 1685, the treaty recognized the permanence of the French and English possessions in North America as they then existed. Even in the event of a future war between the two, there would continue to be 'true and firm peace and neutrality' between the colonial populations, although trading by the subjects of one power in the territory of the other was forbidden, as was inshore fishing on each other's coastlines. The treaty was a serious effort to reconcile imperial conflicts without resorting to expensive and destructive warfare, and it did bring about some slackening of tensions, notably in restraining French warships from seizing New England fishing vessels off the coasts of Acadia.[6] Nevertheless, it was questionable whether long-term reconciliation could be achieved, for the treaty did not establish agreed boundaries between French and English. The status of their respective territories in Newfoundland was unclear, and between Acadia and New England the boundary remained a matter of dispute. The English insisted that their territory extended northeastward along the coast to the modern Maine–New Brunswick border: the boundary, declared Sir Edmund Andros in 1688, 'hath always been and Deemed and knowne to be the River St Croix and a right Lyne from the head of that River to the River Canada.' The French, however, adhered to what Governor Meneval described as a 'tradition of the country' that the boundary was the St George River, just southwest of the Penobscot. That the disputed area included the home territory of the baron de Saint-Castin and his Abenaki kin meant that any English aggression would be firmly resisted, and a raid on Saint-Castin's house by Andros in the summer of 1688 significantly added to the risk of an outright conflict.[7]

There were other pressures that the Treaty of Whitehall did nothing to lessen. For the treaty to outlaw French–New England trading and to regulate the fisheries was easy enough to accomplish at a European bargaining table. To shape the behaviour of New Englanders and other colonists, however, was much more difficult. New England traders continued to frequent the ports of Plaisance and Port Royal, and Meneval confessed in 1689 that he was unable to exclude New England fishing vessels from the coasts of Acadia. A destructive raid on Chedabucto the previous year had already demonstrated that New England fishing interests were intolerant of French competition, even in Acadian waters. Thus, the Treaty of Whitehall could not prevent aggression by New Englanders who refused to be bound by its provisions, and New England ethnocentricism also succeeded by late 1688 in provoking a full-scale military conflict with the Abenaki.[8] During the late 1680s, despite the treaty, the possibility of a general conflict had become more rather than less threatening. The populations that were established in Acadia and Newfoundland, hardy as they were, were small enough that outright warfare would inevitably threaten their future persistence. For Native and non-Native alike, war would not only bring a direct military threat but would also jeopardize the strategies of coexistence that had emerged in the course of the seventeenth century.

When war came, its onset was sharp. England's declaration of war on France in May 1689 had been preceded by the so-called Glorious Revolution, in which James II had been deposed in favour of his daughter, Mary, and her Protestant and anti-French husband, William of Orange. Whatever modest safeguards the Treaty of Whitehall had provided were swept away, and the first year of war saw civilian populations disrupted by enemy raids in a number of areas. In August 1689, Abenaki forces captured the English fort and village at Pemaquid, between the Penobscot and Kennebec rivers. Although this seizure was part of the continuing war between the Abenaki and the English rather than of the conflict between French and English, the reports by French missionaries of the impressive military prowess of the Abenaki influenced the forging soon afterwards of a French-Abenaki alliance. In February 1690, a small English force – apparently an irregular one, drawn from the settlement of Ferryland and intent on plunder – attacked Plaisance and stayed there until April, imprisoning residents and destroying or seizing all the property they could find. The Recollet missionary Joseph Denys described to the French government in the following summer the sufferings of the 'thirty families exposed not only to the normal cruelty of the English, but also to the inhumanity of lawless renegades.' A similar experience was inflicted on the Acadians of Port Royal. Commanded by Sir William Phips, a New England expedition raided smaller French outposts from the Penobscot to Passamaquoddy Bay before descending on Port Royal on 9 May. Two days later, Meneval capitulated, and the victors – in violation of the terms of surrender – were then guilty, according to a group of French observers, of 'causing or allowing the pillage of most of the inhabitants, and the theft of their livestock and personal possessions.' After Phips's departure, an attack by warships from New York in June resulted in more destruction. According to the new French commander in Acadia, Joseph Robinau de Villebon, 'they had burned all the houses between the mouth of the river and the fort [at Port Royal], not having spared even the church; they had killed a number of the cattle, hanged two inhabitants, burning, with his house, the wife and children of one of them.'[9]

The raids of 1690 inaugurated a complex and difficult era in the relationships among Acadians, New Englanders, and French officialdom. After plundering Port Royal, Phips had required a number of Acadian residents to swear an oath of allegiance to William and Mary, and had appointed Charles La Tourasse, a sergeant in the defeated French garrison, as president of a council of Acadian residents that would supposedly govern in the English interest. La Tourasse soon reported this to Villebon, who established a new French military headquarters at Jemseg, on the St John River, in the summer of 1690. Villebon authorized La Tourasse to continue his ostensible functions as president, and reported to France three years later that 'since my coming into this country, he [La Tourasse] has carried out all my orders with the greatest exactitude.'[10] But the fragile connection with New England that La Tourasse provided was not enough to shield the Acadians from English military incursions for the duration of the war, while Villebon's frequent raids on New England, with Native allies, generated fear and resentment there. In 1696 a force of Indians and New Englanders under the command of Benjamin Church burned and pillaged the Acadian settlement of Beaubassin. Although trade continued between the Acadians and New England, and the government of Massachusetts maintained an intermittent but significant correspondence with Acadians who claimed to favour English rule, the relationship was a troubled one on both sides. Mistrust of the Acadians in New England culminated in late 1696 in a prohibition of all trade by the Massachusetts General Court, 'forasmuch as it is very evident, that both the French and Indian Enemy are relieved and succoured by the supplyes transmitted from hence unto Port Royal and other places.'[11] On the part of the Acadians, the relationship occasioned tortuous manoeuvring by individuals wishing to commend themselves to either the French or the New Englanders. Visiting the Minas settlements in 1694, one of Villebon's officials found the inhabitants divided as to whether to provide him with the food supplies he sought. In early 1696, Charles Melanson informed Governor Stoughton of the movements of French privateers, but pleaded that the correspondence be kept secret, 'for if it should be knowne it is death for me.' Meanwhile, his brother Pierre was acting as Villebon's 'captain of the coast,' and was responsible for informing the French of the whereabouts of English shipping.[12] The Acadian response to the difficult circumstances of the time had strong elements of pragmatism, but it was a pragmatism that was neither comfortable nor united.

Villebon was well aware of the Acadian dilemma, even if not of the lengths to which some Acadians would go to maintain relations with Boston. He accepted that the Acadian communities had no alternative but to trade with New England merchants, and on one occasion in April 1693 he hurriedly left Beaubassin when the approach of New England vessels was reported, 'that I might not be a witness to their trading.' Even the French government recognized that the Acadians' survival might depend on their ability 'to appear to be neutral.'[13] More generally, however, Villebon's mandate was unequivocal. From Jemseg, and then from the new headquarters established upriver at Fort Naxouat in 1691, the task of the commander and his force was to wage war on New England. This involved the encouragement and coordination of seagoing privateers such as the extraordinarily successful Pierre Maisonat, known as Baptiste. Villebon also continually maintained diplomatic contacts with Abenaki, Maliseet-Passamaquoddy, and Micmac leaders and sent French officers and soldiers with Native forces on overland raids deep into New England. The greatest French and Native success was undoubtedly the capture in 1696 of Fort William Henry, newly erected by the English at Pemaquid. The fort was induced to surrender when attacked not only by French troops but also by a substantial Abenaki force, including the baron de Saint-Castin, and a powerful naval squadron commanded by Pierre Le Moyne d'Iberville. Although Villebon had played a limited personal role in the expedition, which had been organized primarily by the governor of New France, the capture of the fort represented a noteworthy culmination of his aggressive efforts to take the war to New England. 'Sir, here is a delicate Country,' wrote Stephen Sewall of Salem to a London merchant later in 1696, 'to the Eastward of us deserted by the English, the ffrench and Indians haveing driven them away ...'[14]

The fall of Pemaquid had profound consequences. Not only was it the occasion of the retaliatory raid by Benjamin Church on Beaubassin, but it also freed d'Iberville to turn to Newfoundland. To this point, the war in Newfoundland had consisted of inconclusive naval raids by the English on Plaisance and by the French on Ferryland and St John's. D'Iberville's instructions were to cooperate with Brouillan in an effort to

expel the English entirely from Newfoundland. Despite initial disagreements between the two commanders, the attack was devastatingly successful. Brouillan and approximately 100 French troops of the Plaisance
garrison embarked on the warship *Profond* for Renews, while d'Iberville's force of 124 Canadians, Acadians, Micmacs, and Abenakis
marched overland to Ferryland. They met at Renews in mid-November,
and campaigned northwards to capture St John's at month's end. By
April 1697, every English settlement had been destroyed excepting only
Bonavista – which the French did not reach – and a stubborn group of
defenders on the tiny Carbonear Island. Relief for the English came only
when d'Iberville received instructions to proceed northwards to
attempt to reverse English naval successes in Hudson Bay. By this time,
surviving evidence suggests that well over 100 English had been killed,
many times that number captured, and almost 500 deported to England
or France.[15]

Had the French successes of 1696–7 led to a lasting conquest, their
strategic significance would have been profound. Certainly, the English
feared that their grip on Newfoundland had been decisively loosened.
On 21 January 1697, hearing of the capture of St John's, the Board of
Trade – since 1696, the English adminstrative body responsible for both
trade and colonies – informed William III simply that the French were
now 'Masters of the whole Island.'[16] When the English relief expedition
was ready in mid-April, its commanders – Capt. John Norris in command of the fleet, and Col. John Gibsone at the head of 2,000 troops –
expected a stern battle when they reached Newfoundland. First impressions on their arrival in June were of 'nothing but distruction and
Ruine,' especially on the south shore of the Avalon Peninsula: 'there is
not a living soule Left,' marvelled Gibsone, 'Yea not at Feryland which
was allwayes Look't upon, as I am told, to be the best harbour and the
pleasantest place in the Whole Island.' But it soon emerged that, with
d'Iberville long gone and Brouillan in Plaisance – soon to depart for an
extended stay in France – the military position was not as bleak as the
English had expected. On 10 June, Gibsone's regiment landed in the
undefended ruins of St John's, 'and in few days did Hutt themselv's.'
Thus, modestly, began the lengthy process of rebuilding English Newfoundland.[17]

In September 1697, England and its European allies signed with
France the Treaty of Ryswick. Influenced by the exhaustion of all the
belligerent powers, the peace had the flavour of a truce rather than a
lasting settlement, and it dealt with colonial affairs simply by restoring
the status quo ante bellum. Eight harsh and costly years of war had
ended inconclusively. Few contemporaries harboured the illusion that
peace had been lastingly secured, although in the meantime there was

an opportunity for recuperation and consolidation. In English Newfoundland, this meant restoring the fishery. During the years of war, the
migratory fishery from the west of England had suffered from the disruption of shipping on the Atlantic and from the pressing of seamen
into the Royal Navy. The disputes of 1696–7 had extended the crisis to
the resident fishery. With the peace, the West Country fishing ships
returned quickly and were augmented by larger numbers from other
ports, such as London, Liverpool, and Dublin. Gradually, the resident
population recovered, though many of the former residents did not
return, and the so-called Winter War thus proved to be a genuine watershed in Newfoundland's development. Yet, by 1698, Captain Norris
was able to report that there were forty-three settlements housing 284
planters, 1,894 servants, 176 women, and 186 children; of those people,
1,416 were 'designed to stay this year in the Country.' The government
sought to defend these settlements by building a new fort in St John's
and establishing a garrison.[18]

Unresolved, however, was the old question of how, if at all, to regulate
residence in Newfoundland. Masters of migratory fishing ships continued to complain about unfair competition from residents who monopo-
lized the best harbours, and found in Norris a sympathetic transmitter
of their views to London. In 1698, William Popple, secretary to the
Board of Trade, declared unequivocally to a correspondent that 'there
are no planters nor any manner of Government in that Island [New-
foundland] as there are in other Plantations, the trade thither being only
by fishing ships, and a few poor fishermen on the shore ...'[19] But the
truth was that a resident population was already re-established, and
that a case could be made that residence was necessary if only for effective defence. Hence the attempt of the government to strike a compromise in 1699, with the Act to Encourage the Trade of Newfoundland.
Usually known as the Act of William III, this legislation set aside all fishing rooms used by migratory ships since 1685 as public land, to be
reserved in perpetuity for such vessels. Settlement, however, was not
prevented elsewhere. The act was significant in recognizing the existence of settlement, while trying to limit it in the interests of the traditional ship fishery. In the absence of effective government structures,
however, its provisions could not be enforced. More and more permanent buildings sprang up on supposedly public land, many of them
owned by English merchants. In effect, the distinction between merchants and planters was being eroded, to be replaced by a more simply
class-based division between merchants and servants – with an intermediate category of smaller boatkeepers – who might be resident or
might not.[20]

French authorities also made efforts to intervene in Acadia. In this case, the imperial intent was to bring the colony more nearly into conformity with practices elsewhere in French North America by refurbishing the seigneurial system. A series of new seigneuries along the strait between the mainland and the Ile Saint-Jean (later known as the Northumberland Strait) had been granted in 1696 and 1697, though with little or no practical effect on settlement. Thus, in 1699, the French government embarked on a major effort to disentangle the confusion that existed over seigneurial land titles – many of which were either dormant or generally ignored – by sending a commissioner to Acadia to ensure that all relevant documents were sent to France for scrutiny. The investigation may have enabled some seigneurial claimants to make good their right to rent payments, chiefly in Port Royal, but in general the seigneurial system continued to be only marginally influential in Acadia.[21] Like the English government in Newfoundland, France had limited ability to shape formal structures in a colony that had its own societally determined patterns. Of more immediate concern to Acadians was the harvest failure that afflicted the colony in 1698 and re-emphasized Acadian dependence on Massachusetts. Villebon had been displeased to learn in September 1698 that a letter had reached the Massachusetts governor from the Port Royal inhabitants, 'to implore him to continue his protection of them, and to allow trade with them.' But just a few months later, he himself was requesting shipments of grain and other provisions from New England, 'our harvest failing the last yeare in severall places.' At the same time, the Acadian population continued to grow, and as the turn of the century approached, more and more land was being brought into cultivation. A census taken in 1701 gave a count of 1,200 Acadians on the isthmus and the peninsula. By this time, Pierre Thibaudeau and members of his family had moved from Port Royal to Shepody, in modern New Brunswick, and so had inaugurated yet another cluster of Acadian settlements here and on the Petitcodiac River.[22] Despite the famine, Acadian agriculture remained promising, in its potential production of grains and other crops.

For Native people the years of war had been costly, not only in terms of loss of life but also in disruption of the yearly harvest of resources. Nor did the Treaty of Ryswick, in which no Native representative had participated or acquiesced, remove all cause for suspicion or conflict between Native people and New England. As late as the spring of 1698, New York envoys reported that on a visit to Canada they had met 'a Jesuit coming from Acadia with ten or twelve Indians who told us that three weeks ago there had been a [Native] party going to war against New England.'[23] In general, however, there was little evidence of Native anxiety to prolong the war. On the borders of Acadia and New England, both English and French sought to use the years of peace to manoeuvre the Abenaki in ways favourable to their strategic interests. The French maintained trade relationships and, through Jesuit and other missionaries, religious contacts. The English, through the government of Massachusetts, gradually moved beyond the acute fear of and hostility towards the Abenaki that prevailed in New England in the immediate aftermath of war, towards a cautious policy of negotiation. A conference at Casco Bay in June 1701 brought professions of friendship between Abenaki leaders and Massachusetts commissioners, although not the kind of commitments the English sought: 'wee thank you,' the Abenaki declared, 'that you will give us notice of the likelyhood of a war between the french and the English, and we desire to Keep our selves free, and not to be under the Command of any party ...'[24] Native people throughout the northeast had more pressing needs than to be embroiled in European imperial conflicts. Disruption of hunting territories and shortage of game had to be dealt with by establishing new migration patterns, as in the case of the Micmac, who crossed the Cabot Strait more and more frequently to hunt in Newfoundland. The effects of trade and acculturation were also problematic, as an Abenaki elder made clear in 1701 in sternly declining the offer of the sieur de Villieu to set up an inland trading house. Speaking 'in the name of the entire nation,' reported the missionary Antoine Gaulin, the elder explained that 'I see my brothers, for example those of the St. John river, not praying any more because of drunkenness, and that the level of illegitimate births is such that we hardly know each other any more. Even my kindred on the Kennebec, since they have been trading with the English, have lost their senses and do not pray because they are always drunk.'[25] Native cultures were not damaged beyond repair, but responsible leaders knew that European conflicts could be dangerous distractions from more important matters.

Yet there were ample warnings that imperial disputes had not been settled by the treaty of 1697. French and English – in London, in Versailles, and in the respective colonial headquarters – continued to argue about the Acadia–New England boundary, and about the fishing rights that the New Englanders claimed in Acadian waters. The Kennebec, so the French government informed Villebon in 1698, was the boundary, and the governor must take measures 'to prevent the English from trading or fishing in our colonies, and the French from trading with the English settlements.' Predictably, Lieutenant-Governor Stoughton of Massachusetts emphasized in October 1698 'the fatal and irreparable hurt and damage' that would result from 'any concession to the French in their unjust and unreasonable pretentions now made.'[26] Even more threatening were developments in European international affairs. The ailing King Charles II of Spain finally died in late 1700, leaving the crown to Philip of Anjou, who now became Philip v. Philip was the grandson of Louis xiv of France, and the succession thus opened an era of alliance between France and Spain, as well as what was to France's enemies the alarming prospect that Philip might one day combine the crowns of the two powers.

Crisis turned in 1702 to a new war that would have many characteristics in common with the old. None of them boded well for resident populations, Native or non-Native. Once again, the clash between rival imperialisms would imply a deeper clash of values and interests. On the one hand were the long-established Native populations and the non-military cultures of the settler societies, their strategies of coexistence embodied in unorthodox economic and family liaisons. When the Micmac Marie-Thérèse married the Frenchman Claude Petitpas of Port Royal in 1686, or when Englishman Thomas Picque had married the Frenchwoman Anne Raymond at Plaisance some years earlier, they forged partnerships that epitomized the necessity for neighbouring peoples to coexist in a region where quarrels might damage or destroy them all. In contrast to such accommodations were the militarized, male-dominated élites that represented the empires. While the English and the French empires were not essentially military in character – political, administrative, and economic questions were fundamental to the workings of both the English Board of Trade and the French Ministry of Marine – the strategic importance of Acadia and Newfoundland had now been recognized, and it implied that in this region military considerations would frequently prevail.[27]

In imperial terms, the stakes were high. Acadia, with its geographical position close to New England, had proved devastatingly effective as a base for French and Native attacks. Newfoundland had been close to coming under French domination in early 1697, and if it had done so, French control of the Gulf of St Lawrence would have become absolute. For the residents, the stakes were also high. Native peoples had sustained considerable damage from earlier warfare and needed a period of recovery to avoid serious socio-economic and cultural decline. Settler populations in places such as Placentia, Ferryland, St John's, and Beaubassin had suffered not only economic disruption but also the destructive effects of attacks by land and sea. They too could ill afford to repeat the experience. The conflict between military and colonial cultures, in fact, had become evident in Acadia even before war began. Governor Brouillan, who arrived in the colony in 1701, lost no time in describing as 'mutineers' those Acadians who questioned his orders in such matters as labouring on a new road between Port Royal and the Minas settlements. The inhabitants, he reported to France, 'are so little accustomed to subjection that it seems to me that they live as true republicans, recognizing neither royal authority nor any structure of justice.' When informed of the possibility that Acadia might be given over economically to a French trading company, the Acadians had baulked, 'proclaiming stridently that they would rather come under English rule.'[28]

The war itself soon brought more than the peremptory demands of military officers. The response of Native people to its onset was varied. A significant number of Micmacs immediately put themselves at Brouillan's disposal, and he reported in late 1703 that he had 100 Native fighters at Port Royal. Hard-pressed by the decline of the fur trade, Micmac chiefs had even expressed interest in a proposal of Brouillan that they should be resettled in a sedentary community at 'Chequabenakady' (Shubenacadie). Less enamoured of the French alliance were the Abenaki. Courted for some years by New England governors and commissioners, Abenaki leaders declared in 1703 their intention 'to be as Neuters' in the French-English conflict. That they were brought in on the French side later that year owed more to New England's ultimately fear-inspired aggressiveness than to any great enthusiasm for the French cause.[29] Settler populations in Acadia and Newfoundland, on the other hand, had no effective refuge from involvement in the war. It was true that a short-lived mutiny of Acadian militia in the Minas region in 1703 produced declarations 'that they would give themselves over to the English if they presented themselves.' But when the English did arrive in the following year, it was in a manner that gave no scope for any such threat to be carried out. In the aftermath of the sacking of Deerfield, Massachusetts, by Canadian and Native forces in March 1704, Benjamin Church again led a raid on Acadia, laying waste the Minas and Beaubassin settlements. Governor Joseph Dudley of Massachusetts was cheerfully succinct in reporting to London: 'the forces and vessells I sent Eastward into Nova Scotia and L'Accadia are all returned with a good booty and have destroyed and burnt all the Coast ...' Such invasions were not the sole preserve of the English. In the early months of 1705, French and Abenaki forces made a difficult winter march from Plaisance to attack St John's. Although failing to take the fort, they burned much of the town and then went on to similar successes in the other settlements of the Avalon and on Conception Bay.[30]

Serious as their effects were on the residents, these raids were strategically inconclusive. Yet there was always the potential in this war for invasions that would have more lasting results. Paradoxically, trade continued between Massachusetts and Acadia. Though not as freely conducted as during the previous war, it was sufficient to cause a major scandal in Boston in 1706 when Samuel Vetch, a Scottish former military officer and now a merchant in Boston, was convicted with five others of conducting illegal trade with Acadians and Micmacs. There was evidence that Governor Joseph Dudley had been personally involved in the illegal trade, and while Vetch departed for London to apply – successfully, as matters turned out – for the overturning of his sentence, Dudley attempted to redeem his own reputation and advance the English cause by launching a seaborne attack on Port Royal.[31] In late May 1707, a New England fleet with some 1,300 soldiers and sailors arrived off Port Royal. Now governed by Daniel d'Auger de Subercase – Brouillan had died in 1705 – the town refused to surrender. The siege that followed was a farcical exercise. Confusion and indecision among the New England officers was aggravated by the success of Subercase's policy of harassing the invaders. The New Englanders withdrew in early June, only to be ordered back again with reinforcements in July. Having failed again, they returned to an unfriendly reception in Boston in August. Dudley blamed 'Wickedness and folley,' and 'the disorderly Temper of the fforces abroad,' and he concluded that a future attack would need the stiffening of British regular troops. With Samuel Vetch in London arguing for a speedy conquest of Acadia and its resettlement by Scots – the union of 1707 between England and Scotland made this a feasible proposal, at least in theory – the prospects of such assistance were not as dim as would have been true in the earlier years of the war.[32]

St John's was the next to experience an invasion. In the early hours of the morning of 21 December 1708 – on New Year's Day 1709 according to the Gregorian calendar of the French – the fort commanding the town was infiltrated by a force of some 160 from Plaisance and surrendered virtually without resistance. The governor of Plaisance, Philippe de Pastour de Costebelle, reported triumphantly that the affair had given to the French 'absolute control of the people and their goods throughout the part of this English colony where most of their strength is concentrated.' The joy was short-lived, however, as a delay in the arrival of reinforcements from France prompted Costebelle to order St John's evacuated in April. The commander of the expedition, Joseph de Mombeton de Brouillan – brother of the former governor, and usually known as Saint-Ovide – retreated reluctantly to Placentia, but not before destroying the fortifications of St John's and extracting a substantial ransom from inhabitants there and in nearby ports for sparing their fishing vessels and installations. The British garrison, with much of its ordnance and other munitions, was carried to imprisonment in Plaisance and then in Canada, while the inhabitants coped again with the destruction of their houses and a shortage of food. Again, the episode had fallen short of being a lasting conquest, but the vulnerability of British Newfoundland had been demonstrated anew.[33]

The narrow escape of St John's added to the case in favour of new British attacks on Port Royal and on Canada. Already, in 1708, Samuel Vetch had presented the Board of Trade with an elaborate plan to make the Queen of Great Britain 'sole and peaceable possessor of all the North Continent of America,' and the board had endorsed this goal. Plans for an attack on Canada in 1709 were abandoned when an expected British fleet failed to arrive in Boston, but in July 1710 a force of some 400 British marines disembarked under the command of Francis Nicholson, an officer with long experience in North America and a former lieutenant-governor of Virginia. The marines and approximately 1,500 New England troops attacked Port Royal. Against a force this large – and one more effectively led than in 1707 – Subercase could do little with his small, demoralized garrison and tumbledown fort, and on 2 October he and Nicholson agreed terms of surrender. The new union flag of Great Britain now flew over Port Royal, which was speedily renamed Annapolis Royal in honour of Queen Anne, and on 12 October 1710 Nicholson and his council of war proclaimed to all inhabitants of 'l'Acadie and Nova Scotia' that these were territories to which the British Crown had 'an undoubted right of inheritance as well as conquest.'[34] The proclamation disguised a host of uncertainties. It was easy enough to assert the British right to rule Nova Scotia, but in peace treaties signed in 1632, 1667, and 1697, English claims had been set aside. The same might happen again. There was also the question of whether Nicholson's forces, and then the 500-strong garrison left under the command of Vetch as the new governor of the colony, could hold on to the conquest.

There was no immediate prospect of a French counter-attack. The news of the Acadian conquest reached Canada only in December 1710, and in the following summer the St Lawrence colony had enough to do in preparing its defences against a British invasion fleet, which was eventually wrecked in a storm on its way upriver. In Plaisance, meanwhile, Costebelle reacted tersely to a suggestion by the missionary Antoine Gaulin that he send a relief force to Acadia: 'we are too far distant from one another for that. I have much ado to furnish an Indifferent Guard to the Different posts that I Employ. The few troops that we have are Extraordinaryly fatigued ...' But the Micmac were a different proposition, and they were soon reinforced by Abenaki dispatched from the Penobscot by Saint-Castin. This force of some 40 Abenakis – the number inflated to 150 by the anxious Vetch – inflicted defeat on a British detachment of 64 upriver from Annapolis Royal in the late spring of 1711, and the garrison spent the summer in a virtual state of siege at the hand of 'lurking Indians' who were sometimes imaginary and sometimes real.[35] Disease as well as Native resistance threatened the numbers and the morale of the troops, and Vetch was reduced by August

1712 to reporting to London 'allmost ... in Dispair,' and to making
gloomy predictions of a possible British abandonment of Nova Scotia.
For the Acadian inhabitants, the years immediately following the conquest were also difficult and dangerous. The terms of surrender of 1710
had provided that 'the Inhabitants within Cannon shot of the Fort of
Port Royall, shall Remain upon their Estates, with their Corn, Cattle,
and Furneture, During two Years, in Case they are not Desirous to go
before, The taking of the Oaths of Allegance and Fidility to her Sacred
Majesty of Great Brittain.' The clause offered only minimal guarantees
to the 500 or so Acadians deemed to fall under its terms, while leaving
the rest virtually with the status of prisoners. One officer of the garrison
– the French-speaking Paul Mascarene, whose personal origins were
French Huguenot – believed the initial British intentions were benevolent: 'as for those without the said capitulation it was left to Governor
Vetch to treat with them and use them like Friends till her Majestys
Pleasure should be further known.' Mascarene reported that he had
been received at the Minas settlements with 'Demonstrations of Joy,'
and described the choice by the Acadians there of deputies to represent
them in dealings with the garrison.[36] But these early expressions of a
wary desire for accommodation were misleading. From the beginning
there were some Acadians, especially at Annapolis Royal, who cooperated actively with the garrison. In some cases, the links were strengthened by marriage. By 1714, for example, Agathe de Saint-Etienne de La
Tour had married a British lieutenant and had also commenced a legal
claim to extensive Nova Scotia lands as a descendant of the early colonizer Charles de Saint-Etienne de La Tour.[37] Other Acadians, by contrast, signed a letter soon after the conquest appealing for help to
Governor Vaudreuil in Canada, and subsequent demands for cash levies from the Acadians outside the banlieue, and for labour on the fort by
those of Annapolis Royal, quickly produced further anger and alienation.[38]

In Newfoundland, too, the final years of the war were characterized
by difficulty and uncertainty. In Plaisance, shortages of food and essential supplies became acute as a British naval blockade intensified. Following the capture of St John's in 1708–9, British strategy had been
adjusted. Rather than undertake a costly counter-attack, the British
sought to cut off French communications. Plaisance thus experienced
severe privation, and its military functions were impeded not only by
lack of munitions but also by unrest among the underfed and unpaid
soldiery. In British Newfoundland, the residents sought to deal with
wartime disruption of the fisheries through economic diversification.
Trapping to the north of Bonavista – carried out in Newfoundland by
non-Native rather than Native people – increased from its modest

beginnings in the seventeenth century. Commercial sealing began early in the eighteenth, and by 1709 seal oil was being exported to the west of England. By 1705 St John's merchant James Campbell had an investment in 'a Salmon fishery' at Bonavista, conducted by a local resident, George Skeffington. The benefits of these initiatives, however, were outweighed by the beginning in 1711 of a serious and lengthy downturn in cod catches, owing to periodic changes in fish-migration patterns. The productivity of the fishery would remain depressed until well into the 1720s.[39] The rebuilding of St John's was slow to take place, and even by the end of 1710 the financial health of the town's economic pursuits was still affected by the size of the ransom payments made to the French in the previous year. The Board of Trade flirted briefly in 1710 with the notion of making Ferryland the chief military headquarters, at the expense of St John's – a prospect that called forth anxious protest from the west of England – and also fulminated against illegal trade in Newfoundland by New England vessels. On both points, the board was brusquely put right in the following year by Commodore Joseph Crowe, commanding the naval squadron in Newfoundland waters. St John's and not Ferryland, Crowe insisted, was 'the Metropolis of this Island.' He also defended the trade with New England, pointing out that 'the people are pretty Numerous, and would want in the winter Season both bread and Flower if not Supply'd from New England ...'[40] The British response to the fact that the provisions of the 1699 legislation were being widely ignored remained tentative and inconsistent.

In April 1712 the Board of Trade was asked for its opinion of the possibility that Great Britain might be confirmed in possession of Nova Scotia and all of Newfoundland, if France maintained fishing rights on the Newfoundland coast and also gained possession of Cape Breton. The board's reply was unequivocal. If the French retained fishing rights, 'the good end of our having Newfoundland restor'd to us will be defeated.' As for Cape Breton, 'that Island has always been esteem'd as part of Nova Scotia,' which, the board added, 'does comprehend all that the French call Accadie, and is bounded by the River St. Croix on the West by the Sea on the South and East, and by Canada River on the North and ought to be so describ'd for avoiding future disputes.' The advice was ignored on all counts. When the Treaty of Utrecht was signed in April 1713, France conceded all right of settlement in Newfoundland, including at this time St Pierre and Miquelon, but retained exclusive fishing rights on a coastline stretching from Cape Bonavista to the tip of the northern peninsula, and down on the west side some 125 miles as far as Point Riche. France also kept control of the islands in the Gulf of St Lawrence, notably Cape Breton and the Ile Saint-Jean (later Prince Edward Island). Although Britain acquired 'Nova Scotia otherwise known as Acadie, in its entirety,' this colony was defined only by reference to 'its ancient boundaries' – a conveniently high-sounding phrase that meant nothing, as there was no clearly understood notion of where those boundaries lay.[41] The Treaty of Utrecht, unlike that of Ryswick sixteen years before, did represent a serious effort to resolve international disputes in North America. Great Britain, in accordance with its strong showing in the European war, had made important gains in the northeast and in the Hudson Bay and Great Lakes regions. France, retaining Canada, along with a territorial presence in the Gulf and its Newfoundland fishing rights, had salvaged some hope of continuing as a significant North American power. Yet the treaty's ambiguities would lead to later quarrels, notably over the boundaries of Nova Scotia and marine jurisdiction on the Atlantic coasts. One thing was clear: that the settlement had been reached, as the war had been largely fought, on the basis of imperial and strategic exigencies. Neither the interests nor the wishes of the Native or non-Native inhabitants had received attention.

In France, Robert Challes – a government official with experience in Acadia – denounced the Treaty of Utrecht for the economic and strategic disadvantages that came with the loss of Acadia and Newfoundland, and suggested bitterly that it would have been better to give up French provinces such as Normandy, Brittany, or Aquitaine. In Britain, the cession of Newfoundland fishing rights to the French was sufficiently contentious to be cited among the grounds for the parliamentary impeachment in 1715 of the earl of Oxford, one of the treaty's architects.[42] The criticism of the treaty from both sides gives an indication of the virtually irreconcilable interests that were at stake. Together with the treaty's own ambiguities, those opposing interests posed a serious potential threat to the lasting maintenance of the peace. For the moment, though, the provisions agreed at Utrecht were carried into effect. The French evacuation of Plaisance was complete by the fall of 1714, except for a small number of residents who chose to accept the British allegiance and remain. The formal proclamation of the treaty there in May 1714 signalled the beginning of the British regime in Placentia, which was now placed under the jurisdiction of Nova Scotia. The change, along with the downturn in the inshore fishery, also led by 1715 to the beginning of English fishing on the Grand Banks.[43]

For Native people, the extension of British influence in Newfoundland had varied implications. The strategy of withdrawal that the Beothuk had adopted in the face of the seventeenth-century English presence meant that for them exchanges of territory between European powers had limited significance. 'They have no Commerce with the Indians, who are a Savage People, not as yet acquainted with the use of

Guns,' was the report of one British officer in 1720 on fur trappers at Bonavista. Native people, he added, were seen as far south as Bonavista only in the summer, and migrated north in canoes for the winter. In the context of the Beothuks' long-term struggle to deal with exclusion from natural resources and a shrinking land base, it was the entire phenomenon of European encroachment – and, later, that of the Micmac – that presented the major threat, rather than the respective positions of British and French. For the Micmac in Newfoundland, the French withdrawal was a setback. It meant the removal of a military ally and the extension of a British regime that did not even recognize the Micmac right to hunt on the island. Nevertheless, Micmac hunters were not deterred for long, if at all. In 1716, they were reported to be active in the area of Cape Ray, and by 1720 were trading furs to Newfoundland merchants. For British officials, the Micmac presence was disturbing, but it represented the continuation of a long-established and necessary hunting strategy.[44]

British Newfoundland at this time was a maelstrom of conflicting interests. To mediate effectively among them was more than the current administrative structures of fishing admirals, naval officers, and the small garrison at Placentia could ever hope to achieve. To establish a full civil government would be not only prohibitively expensive in view of the depressed state of the fishery but also of questionable feasibility as long as Newfoundland had a small and shifting population. By the end of 1718, the Board of Trade had decided, in effect, to throw up its hands in despair. In a lengthy report, it argued that Newfoundland's problems over the previous forty years represented 'an undeniable Argument, that it cannot flourish under the present Regulations.' The Newfoundland fishery, the board concluded, 'can never be revived or restored to its former flourishing State and Condition, until it be again wholly carried on by Fishing Ships, according to its Ancient Custom, and regulated by Laws agreeable thereunto'; the best means to this end 'would be to remove the Inhabitants or Planters to Nova Scotia, or to some other of Your Majesty's Plantations in America.'[45] The report, painstakingly constructed as it was, was a foolish one. The traditional ship fishery from the west of England was clearly in decline – not because of the presence of the residents, but because of falling yields and the cumulative effects of wartime disruption. Indeed, if the war had taught any strategic lesson regarding Newfoundland, it was that both residents and a garrison were needed if the fisheries were to be defended properly.

The French faced some of the same questions as they contemplated the development of Cape Breton Island – now known as Ile Royale – and of Ile Saint-Jean. In the French fishery, too, a balance had to be struck between residence and the interests of European-based merchants. The French answer, however, involved the deliberate recruitment of residents and the immediate creation of formal structures of government. Not that the French presence on either of the two islands was easily or quickly organized. A few Acadians had crossed to the Ile Saint-Jean in 1711, but they received no encouragement from the French government, which, even after 1713, preferred to concentrate on recruiting for Ile Royale. These first Acadian residents apparently left within a few years, and only in 1720 did a new group of colonists arrive at Port La Joie, on the later Charlottetown Harbour. From France came settlers recruited by the nobleman Louis-Hyacinthe Castel, comte de Saint-Pierre, for his newly founded Compagnie de l'Ile Saint-Jean. Saint-Pierre had received a grant of a number of Gulf islands, and in late 1720 his commander – Robert-David Gotteville de Belile – was reporting optimistically that he expected 250 to spend the first winter and that more Acadians were arriving each day. The economy, it was hoped, would flourish on the basis of the cod fishery in the Gulf, seal and walrus hunts, and trade with the French West Indies. How far these hopes would be fulfilled was not evident in 1720, though already competition with the larger economy of Ile Royale was proving difficult.[46] Ile Royale itself was slow to become securely established. In the summer of 1713, Saint-Ovide de Brouillan – the conqueror of St John's in 1708–9 – led a military expedition to explore the coasts of the island, and recommended that Havre l'Anglois be the headquarters of the new colony. There, on the site named Louisbourg, the first makeshift settlement was established. As yet, there was no certainty that Louisbourg would retain its pre-eminent status. Philippe de Pastour de Costebelle, the first governor – and the last of Plaisance – preferred a site farther northwest at Port Dauphin, on Baie Ste-Anne. Only in 1718 was Louisbourg irrevocably selected and construction begun on a new fort. Originally conceived as a small centre that would protect French fisheries, much as Plaisance had done previously, Louisbourg emerged as the location of a large fortress that would be intended not only as a centre for the fisheries but also as a safeguard for French communications, a base for privateers in time of war, and a bulwark of French control of the Gulf of St Lawrence.[47]

Louisbourg also developed quickly as a centre of the cod fishery and other trades. The nucleus of the new colony's population was from Plaisance, but other immigrants came from France and Canada. Over time, Louisbourg would also have a significant Black population, slave and free. Altough a number of individual Black residents and visitors can be identified from the earliest years of French Acadia, the numbers at Louisbourg were considerably larger: more than 100 Black slaves can be placed at Louisbourg, and the port was visited by many others serving as free or slave crew members of merchant or naval vessels.[48] Among the Acadiens, sixty-seven families accepted repeated French invitations to remove to Ile Royale. Central to the early fishing economy were the fishing proprietors who moved from Plaisance, who might employ two or three dozen fishers, and in turn would market their catch through merchants who also supplied – on credit to the proprietor – the necessary salt, gear, and other supplies. The proprietors had the advantage that many of them were married and had been long-term residents of Plaisance. Thus, they were likely to contribute to the growth and stabilization of population. The French approach contrasted with British indecision in the face of the same questions in Newfoundland and was further shown by the legal framework for landholding in Ile Royale, which gave a clear preference to the resident over the migratory fishery. By 1718 most of the proprietors held formally granted land on which their operations were based. The success of the Ile Royale cod fishery was soon evident. 'Within a few years of its foundation in 1713,' one historian has written, 'the new colony was producing and exporting stocks of cod worth about three times as much as Canada's beaver trade.'[49] But cod, while it was the only major product of Ile Royale, was not the only commodity in which the colony dealt. Ile Royale fish were marketed in France and the French West Indies. Imports from France included manufactured goods, wine, and textiles, while rum, sugar, and molasses came from the West Indies. These imports were partially re-exported to Canada, to New England, and to the Acadians in Nova Scotia, chiefly in return for agricultural produce. Coastal trade – as well as the transatlantic trade with France – was therefore essential to the economy of Ile Royale. Significantly, the Acadian heads of households who emigrated to Ile Royale – the largest group settling at Port Toulouse (the modern St Peter's) – included only three fishers out of the sixty-seven, while those described wholly or partly as navigators numbered twenty-three.[50]

For Acadians, the decision to remain in Nova Scotia or to remove to one of the two French islands was difficult and complex. The Treaty of Utrecht, to be sure, had resolved some of the uncertainties that had persisted since the conquest. While the relatively new Acadian settlements at Shepody and on the Petitcodiac and Memramcook rivers were in disputed territory – since France and Britain continued to argue over whether the 'ancient boundaries' of Acadia/Nova Scotia included only peninsular Nova Scotia and the isthmus or also the area later known as New Brunswick – all the major Acadian communities were now undoubtedly within Nova Scotia. The treaty guaranteed that Acadians would have a year to remove, if they wished, 'with all of their movable effects,' and that if they chose to remain they would have 'the exercise of the Roman Catholic religion insofar as the laws of Great Britain allow.' These terms were confirmed in a letter of Queen Anne to the governor of Nova Scotia in June 1713, in which the Acadians were also promised the right to sell their lands if they moved. At first sight, the position seemed simple enough. As at Plaisance, a French population was offered the opportunity to adjust to the terms of the treaty by moving to French territory, and it might seem natural that the majority – here, as at Plaisance – would accept. During 1714, officials from Ile Royale and religious missionaries visited the Acadians to urge them to move; by late in the year, Samuel Vetch was reporting to London that, of the approximately 2,500 Acadians, 'they have oblig'd themselves ... all to remove save two familys.'[51]

In reality, matters were more complex. The comparison with Plaisance was not exact, since the Acadians were more numerous and were largely an agricultural population. For the fishers of Plaisance, Ile Royale offered just as productive a base, and for those who were prepared to risk the displeasure of British and French authorities alike, there was still the possibility of making surreptitious voyages to Newfoundland for fishing or winter hunting. For the Acadians, whose wealth and well-being were tied closely to long-cultivated land, the prospect of removal was more disturbing. As early as September 1713, the missionary Felix Pain reported that Acadians of the Minas settlements were uneasy about leaving for new and possibly unproductive lands in Cape Breton.[52] Furthermore, the British – whose chief goal at Plaisance was to have the French residents removed from the fishing harbours and from the fishery itself as soon as possible – were ambivalent about the Acadian departure. Samuel Vetch was clearly opposed, on the ground that the loss of the Acadians would 'intirely Strip that Colony of ... Cattle of all sorts and reduce it to its primitive state.' Moreover, he argued in a report subsequently endorsed by the Board of Trade, the acquisition of the Acadians would dangerously strengthen Ile Royale.[53]

Vetch's fears were not realized. Although French officials offered assurances of land grants and provisions to the Acadians in Ile Royale, the Acadians remained, according to an exasperated Costebelle, 'uncertain and undecided.'[54] The sixty-seven families that did move were largely non-agricultural, and came disproportionately (forty-two, or 71.2 per cent) from the vicinity of Annapolis Royal. That area was not only the closest to the British garrison, with its potential to restrict illegal trade by Acadians, but was also a relatively crowded settlement where economic opportunities were less attractive for young males – and most of the emigrant household heads were under forty years of age – than elsewhere. Those who remained, wherever they were, had to pay a long-term price. It was measured in such terms as the narrowing availability of prospective spouses other than blood relations. With the ending of immigration from France and the small size of the British garrison at Annapolis Royal, marriages between cousins became increasingly common. Also evident was a decline in literacy, as the religious orders were now excluded from Nova Scotia. The parish priests who were still allowed access did not function as formal educators. Although in terms of population increase and agricultural production the Acadians now embarked on a thirty-five-year era of unprecedented expansion, the political basis of this prosperity was always tenuous.[55] Refusal to leave for Cape Breton did not mean that undisturbed continuation in Nova Scotia was assured.

In particular, British demands that Acadians take an oath of allegiance to the British Crown posed serious questions. To swear the oath meant to accept the possibility of being called to bear arms against French former compatriots and against the Micmac in any future war, in addition to compromising the Roman Catholic faith by giving personal allegiance to the head of the Church of England. Not to do so meant to be suspected of being – as a British officer commented when no Acadians could be persuaded to swear allegiance to the newly enthroned King George I in 1715 – 'a Pack of Notorious Villains in Generall and not to be Trusted if they had taken five thousand Oaths.'[56] Acadian groups attempted to compromise. From Minas in February 1718, community representatives wrote to Annapolis Royal to explain their difficulties and recall that 'when our ancestors were under English rule they were never asked to swear such oaths.' In the spring of 1720, 136 residents of the Annapolis Valley informed the newly arrived governor of Nova Scotia, Richard Philipps, that 'we can take no other oath than to be loyal to King George without being forced to take up arms against anybody, which we promise to keep faithfully and humbly implore you to accept.' Conversely, other Acadians wrote at the same time to Saint-Ovide, governor at Louisbourg, to declare their continued allegiance to France. Both British and French military officials looked ahead to the next war and calculated the advantages and dangers that might be represented by an Acadian population that had not sworn allegiance to Britain. Philipps despaired of 'making them English,' and saw them as 'Enemys in our Bosom,' while Governor Vaudreuil of New France expressed corresponding relish at the prospect of Nova Scotia's being retaken by the Acadians on behalf of France.[57]

The French had similar reasons for wishing to maintain contacts with the Micmac. They and other Native peoples, however, had an advantage that was denied to the Acadians: military power that demanded respect from both French and British, no matter how grudgingly it was given. French hopes of attracting large numbers of Micmacs to move to

Ile Royale were quickly dashed, although the establishment of a new religious mission at Antigonish in 1715 was a step towards defining a close relationship. Missionaries, while far from exercising control over Native people, were effective conduits for presents and for encouragement of pro-French attitudes. The British did not show corresponding diplomatic skill. As early as in 1713, a treaty of peace was signed at Portsmouth, New Hampshire, between New England and the Abenaki, but any lasting value that it might have had was soon undermined by the colonists' territorial expansion and failure to live up to the commercial terms of the treaty.[58] Philipps and his lieutenant-governor, John Doucett, were well aware of the British need to reach agreement with the Micmac and Maliseet-Passamaquoddy, but their requests for authorization to distribute gifts met only temporization and then unenthusiastic acquiescence in London. Philipps did manage to draw promises of friendship from Maliseet leaders at a conference on the St John River in the summer of 1720, and later in the year received carefully circumscribed assurance from the Passamaquoddy that 'as long as our Great King Louis of France is at peace, we shall be also.' Reporting to London on the meeting with the Maliseet, Philipps again requested that gifts be sent, and observed that he was out of pocket by some £150 through his own efforts to atone for the British government's neglect.[59] With the Micmac, the governor had less success. Not signatories to the Treaty of Utrecht, the Micmac were nevertheless deeply affected by its supposed giving over of their territory to their old British enemies. Threats against Annapolis Royal in 1713 and seizures of New England ships in 1715 were followed by a successful raid on the British fishing port of Canso in 1720 and the rifling of a New England sloop in the Minas Basin shortly afterwards by a Micmac group that had first demanded payment in return for licensing the vessel to trade on their territory. Philipps' angry demand that the Acadians of the Minas settlements act as intermediaries to find out the reasons for this last incident yielded more than he bargained for, in the form of a declaration from two of the participants in the name of the Micmac of the area: 'we are here to tell you that this land here that God has given us ... cannot be disputed by anyone ... We are masters, independent of all, and would have our country free.'[60]

Striking as this statement was, there was another side to the situation of the Micmac. During the summer of 1715, Micmacs in the Cape Sable area had seized a number of Massachusetts fishing vessels, declaring – as reported by two of the aggrieved merchants – that 'the Lands are theirs and they can make Warr and peace when they please ... '[61] Within weeks, however, all the vessels had been restored. Peter Capon, commissary to the garrison at Annapolis Royal, sailed in August to inquire what had happened. From Costebelle, at Louisbourg, Capon received little satisfaction. The governor disclaimed all French involvement, probably truthfully in this instance, although he and other French officials were not averse to encouraging privately the tensions between Micmac and British. Acadians at Pubnico blamed the ship seizures on rumours of the tensions currently building in Great Britain over the Jacobite challenge to the accession of George I, and the possibility that a war between France and Great Britain might result: 'the Indians,' they observed, 'resolved to begin first.' When the rumours had proved ill-founded, the ships had been released. Capon went on to hold meetings with Micmac leaders at Merliqueche (the later site of Lunenburg), Port Maltais (Port Medway), and Pubnico. At each stop, the Micmac were conciliatory. At Merliqueche, they coupled a renunciation of further ship seizures with the request 'that the ffishermen should not make them drunk, for they said Strong Liquors would make them kill their ffathers.' At Port Maltais, Micmac representatives proposed negotiations with the colonial governor the next year, 'and desired Articles then to be drawn relating to trade and other affairs at that Conference.' The request was repeated at Pubnico. The British apparently did not appreciate the significance of the Native proposal, for negotiations did not take place in 1716. Nevertheless, it indicated the continuing effort of the Micmac to deal both with the long-term problems posed by trade and acculturation, and with the new difficulties arising from the French withdrawal.[62] Weakened by acculturation, a declining population, and economic disruption stemming from the decline of the fur trade, the Micmac could make a case for a strategy of accommodation along the lines already pursued by the Abenaki. Whether this approach would prevail, or the alternative of asserting territorial control by direct harassment of the British, was not yet apparent by 1720. What was clear enough, however, was that both Acadians and Micmacs faced a dangerous and prolonged period of adjustment to the conditions prevailing after 1713.

By 1720, it was evident that the Treaty of Utrecht had not laid to rest the disputes between imperial powers that had been put to the test of war during the earlier years. Boundary disputes persisted. Whether at the level of dispute between French and British colonial officials in 1718 over which of the powers could rightly claim the St John Valley, or at negotiations held inconclusively in Paris in 1720 over the proper definition of Acadia's 'ancient boundaries,' disagreement was impossible to resolve.[63] To be sure, conflict resolution could still take place efficiently in specific cases. An apparently intractable dispute between French and New England fishers over the question of which nationality should control the fisheries around Canso led in 1718 to the pillaging there of

French ships and shore installations by a New England force. Yet the matter was soon resolved, partly by a decision by Governor Saint-Ovide to withdraw French claims to Canso, and also by an informal *modus vivendi* established by the fishers themselves, by which fishing in the area was shared between both nationalities. With this kind of arrangement capable of emerging from conflict, with Saint-Ovide's predecessor Costebelle willing in 1715 to suggest to Peter Capon the possibility of free trade between Ile Royale and Nova Scotia, and with Philipps' instructions in 1719 containing a clause in favour of British-Native intermarriage and offering incentives of cash and land to any British man or woman who married a Native person, it might have seemed that the pre-war days of unorthodox economic and personal liaisons had returned.[64]

Such an impression would have been entirely misleading. In one respect, genuine continuity might be traced. In 1720, as before 1690, New England fishing vessels were conspicuous in Nova Scotia waters, and Massachusetts merchants were prominent in trade. Costebelle's musings on free trade with Ile Royale, however, lacked substance. So did the British hopes for intermarriage with Native people. The Board of Trade might observe enviously that 'nothing has so much contributed to strengthen the hands of the French in those parts, as the Friendship they maintain, and the Intermarriages they make with the Indians,' but it was powerless to duplicate that relationship.[65] In reality, the years since 1690 had wrought fundamental changes in the situations of the peoples of Acadia and Newfoundland, and in the quality of the relationships among them. Even the relationship between Micmacs and Acadians was now showing signs of stress, as Acadians wrestled with the question of how close they could afford to come to a British regime to which the prevailing Micmac approach might still turn out to be one of total hostility.

For all the peoples of the region, the war years had demonstrated the capacity of imperial disputes to disrupt and endanger their ways of life, and the imperial pressures continued to be felt even after the Treaty of Utrecht. British Newfoundland, having experienced depopulation and resettlement as a result of the 'Winter War' of 1696–7, continued to suffer the uncertainties of British vacillation as to the economic and military arguments for and against the very presence of a permanent population. The civilian inhabitants of Ile Royale, many of whom had lived through the privations of war at Plaisance and had then embarked on a forced migration, enjoyed greater stability than did those of Newfoundland, but the economic and societal health of Ile Royale was still liable to be held hostage to the strategic importance of Louisbourg. The Acadians and the Native peoples, meanwhile, were the best able of all the inhabitants consciously to assert their autonomy, but their scope for doing so was lessened. The political culture of the Acadians, and the economic strength of their communities, led to a pragmatic search for ways of accommodating to British rule. At the same time, the Acadians' lack of military strength made them potentially vulnerable to pressures from either imperial power, and diminished the limited sphere within which their freedom of action could be maintained. The Micmac were beginning to face a similar reality, but for opposite reasons. Military power gave strength, but economic decline and cultural dislocation imposed potentially severe limitations. The Beothuk and Maliseet-Passamaquoddy, meanwhile, faced similar disruptions combined with lesser strategic importance. All the territories were more firmly under European imperial control by 1720 than in the past. All the peoples who lived there had already felt the effects of imperial struggles and were liable to do so again in the future. Their areas of autonomy, apparently so extensive prior to 1690, were now becoming circumscribed.

PART TWO
THE ENCOUNTER WITH IMPERIAL MILITARISM,
1720–1820

CHAPTER SIX

1720–1744
Cod, Louisbourg, and the Acadians

GEORGE RAWLYK

Imagine for a moment that a sophisticated satellite carrying a 'camera of perfect accuracy'[1] had been able to transmit, in the early 1720s and again in the early 1740s, detailed snapshots of Atlantic Canada. These pictures would show convincingly that the forces of geophysical continuity were far more significant and salient than those of historical and demographic change. For the entire 1720 to 1744 period, both the Atlantic Ocean and the Appalachian forests overwhelmed the seemingly insignificant human element, marginalizing it and also shaping virtually every aspect of its often-perilous existence.

In the early 1720s, Newfoundland had a summer population of approximately 6,000 Europeans, most of whom were from the English West Country and almost all of whom were involved in the fishery. The permanent population of the island, however, was only 1,000 Europeans, probably fewer than that number of Beothuks, and perhaps a few Micmacs. Two decades later, the permanent British Newfoundland population had grown by only a few hundred and that of the Beothuk had fallen considerably. There were also perhaps as many as a hundred permanent French residents. The number of British summer residents had grown to more than 10,000, and a substantial percentage of these were now Irish Roman Catholics.[2] On the French island colony of Ile Saint-Jean, present-day Prince Edward Island, there were, in the middle of the 1720s, an estimated 422 European settlers. Two decades later the European population was only approximately 550. The Micmac population on the island during these decades was never larger than a handful of families. On Cape Breton Island – Ile Royale, where the French were constructing at Louisbourg their 'Dunkirk of North America' – the total French civilian population on the island grew from some 2,500 in 1720 to more than 4,000 in the early 1740s. There were also, by the early

1740s, some 700 French soldiers. The number of Micmacs on the island in the 1720–44 period probably equalled the number on Ile Saint-Jean.[3]

The most significant population changes during the 1720 to 1744 period took place in Acadia/Nova Scotia, which had officially become a British colony in 1713. The Acadian population grew from approximately 2,500 in 1720 to more than 9,000 in the 1740s. There were also more than 200 British regular troops and a smaller number of permanent British settlers, located both at Annapolis Royal and at Canso. Despite variations in contemporary estimates, the number of Micmacs in peninsular Nova Scotia from 1720 to the 1740s probably remained at somewhat fewer than 2,000.[4] The maximum number of permanent European settlers in any one year in the Atlantic region, between 1720 and 1744 never exceeded 15,500. The population of the indigenous people in any one year probably never exceeded 4,000. It is not surprising, therefore, that the tiny, largely isolated, human population on the northeastern extremity of North America found itself vulnerable and powerless as it was ground between the millstones of French and English imperial rivalry.

If it had not been for 'the knob-headed, richly fat, and succulent codfish'[5] there would have been few European settlers in Newfoundland in the first half of the eighteenth century. In fact, the distribution of British fishing bases and settlements was little different in 1720 from what it had been in the 1670s. Nor was there any real difference in the functioning of the cod fishery. Between 1720 and the 1740s, however, the production from Newfoundland's cod fishery increased greatly from less then 100,000 quintals to almost half a million, and some of this phenomenal increase took place in new areas of settlement and exploitation, particularly on the southern shore and Placentia Bay.[6]

Two other important changes took place in the Newfoundland fishery during this period. First, there was the growing significance of the British Bank fishery. The traditional offshore fishery had yielded catches of about 150 quintals per boat since 1713, but the new Bank fishery averaged some 600 quintals. The second important change was the remarkable growth of Irish Roman Catholic involvement in the Newfoundland fishery. The Irish percentage of Newfoundland's permanent population and also of the summer fishermen increased dramatically after 1720. The Irish were leaving Ireland because of famine and unemployment and were drawn to Newfoundland because of cheap transportation and the promise of work. They were carried by the ships from Bristol into Conception Bay and by the vessels from Bideford and Barnstable to the southern Avalon and Placentia. By 1729, the Irish made up a substantial majority of the wintering population on the island. They were, in fact, so numerous 'that in many places there remains during the winter time nine of these Irish Roman Catholics to one Englishman.'[7] By the early 1730s, large numbers of Irish Roman Catholics were also being brought to Newfoundland in ships sailing from the south of Devon. According to Professor W. Gordon Handcock, 'by the end of the eighteenth century the southern Avalon had become the "Irish Shore."' Elsewhere, as at Trinity Bay, Bonavista Bay, Notre Dame Bay, and Fortune Bay, 'although Irish labour was employed ... only small and scattered Irish communities emerged compared to those which developed in the Avalon.'[8]

Despite the Irish influx into the Newfoundland fishery, the permanent population of the island grew remarkably slowly. The number edged up from approximately 1,000 permanent residents in 1720 to perhaps 1,200 in 1744. The summer population remained much larger, and grew from about 6,000 to a little more than 10,000 during the same period. It is not surprising that Grant Head has described these years as forming a crucial core of 'The Stable Half-Century.'[9] In so many respects the 1720 to 1744 period had far more in common with the seventeenth century than it did with the latter part of the eighteenth century.

The cod fishery and the fortress of Louisbourg shaped the essential contours of Ile Royale life between 1720 and 1744. So much has been written about the fortress that the fishery's essential significance has often gone unrecognized. Yet throughout the first half of the eighteenth century, because of its fishery, Ile Royale's 'combined import and export trade [was] equal in value to the trade of the larger colony of Canada.'[10] In fact, the evidence suggests that for much of the period Ile Royale's cod fishery was worth more to the French economy than the entire Canadian fur trade: three times as much, according to Christopher Moore. Moreover, the cod fishery contributed far more to the island's economy than it cost to build the fortifications of Louisbourg. The total cost of the fortifications was approximately four million livres, and the amount spent between 1720 and 1744 was less than the total value of any two years' cod production in the 1730s. Meanwhile, the percentage of fish caught and dried by Ile Royale residents gradually increased at the expense of the French migrant fishermen. In 1721, of the 125,600 quintals of cod produced, residents accounted for 62.1 per cent and French migrants for 37.9 per cent; in 1731, 77.1 per cent of the total 167,540 was produced by local residents, and in 1744, 80.1 per cent of the small total of 69,430 quintals.[11]

Between 1720 and 1744 the total Ile Royale population probably never exceeded 5,000 civilians and soldiers. In 1719 it was estimated at 2,012, growing to 4,618 by 1737. The civilian and military population of Louisbourg grew from 853 in 1719 to 1,963 by 1737, and thus made up approximately 40 per cent of the island's total.[12] Most of the island's population had come from Newfoundland, after the Treaty of Utrecht, and from France. Very few Acadians had been persuaded by the Ile Royale officials to leave Nova Scotia for the French island colony to the north.[13]

Even though the cod fishery dominated Ile Royale's economy, Louisbourg's important role as a commercial centre and an entrepôt for trade should not be underestimated. As B.A. Balcom points out, since contemporary navigational instruments could determine latitude but not longitude, seamen commonly sailed along a selected latitude until they reached landfall. Cape Breton's shared latitude with major French ports made Louisbourg a favoured destination for ships bound for North America. It was also useful in the trade between France and Quebec. 'By transhipping cargo at Louisbourg,' Balcom comments, 'vessels from France avoided the time consuming and potentially hazardous navigation of the St. Lawrence. Cargoes were efficiently carried from Louisbourg to Quebec in smaller vessels locally owned in the two ports.' French intercolonial trade again affected Louisbourg. 'Although,' in Balcom's words, 'this trade incorporated triangular patterns for movement of goods between France, the West Indies, and Ile Royale, individual ships, like their British counterparts, probably engaged in a "shuttle" service between two of these points. Louisbourg merchants extended this trade pattern to include transshipments to Acadia and New England as well as to Quebec.'[14] Another way to look at Louisbourg's role as an entrepôt is to ascertain the actual movement of ships to the island fortress town. Between 1733 and 1743, as many as 178 and never fewer than 94 vessels called annually. The largest number came from France or from New England and Nova Scotia, but significant numbers came from Canada and the West Indies: as many as 32 from the West Indies in 1743.[15] When tonnage of the ships is taken into account, the France-Louisbourg and Louisbourg–French West Indies trade becomes even more important, since the larger trading vessels involved accounted for approximately 75 per cent of the actual total tonnage.[16]

Louisbourg also served as a bastion of French power in the North Atlantic. Most of the construction of the fortress of Louisbourg took place under the direction of its first governor, Saint-Ovide de Brouillan, who served from 1717 to 1738. Although the fortifications of Louisbourg had not actually been planned by the famous French military engineer Vauban but by some of his faithful disciples, in most respects Louisbourg was indeed a 'ville fortifiée par Vauban.'[17] The fortress walls enclosed an area of less than 100 acres. On the landward side, the defences were dominated by three bastions of varying strength, while the narrow entrance to Louisbourg Harbour was defended by two seemingly powerful batteries. The Island Battery was located on a tiny island to the northeast of the fortress, and the Royal or Grand Battery was situated on the northeastern shore of the inner harbour about one mile by sea from both the town of Louisbourg and the Island Battery. The 116 cannon and mortars of these batteries made Louisbourg the most heavily fortified military base in North America.[18] They did not protect it effectively, however, from a land assault. The Royal Battery was dominated by a nearby hill, and the guns of the Island Battery could easily be silenced by a battery built at Lighthouse Point, to the immediate northeast. Furthermore, largely because the stones were inadequately dressed and laid and the mortar was made of unsuitable sea sand, the landward walls of the fortress as well as the Royal Battery were already in a dangerous state of disrepair in the early 1740s. And, in the later summer months of 1744, there were only 705 soldiers and some 900 civilians available for defence.

In sharp contrast to that of neighbouring Nova Scotia, Louisbourg society was characterized by its military and aristocratic pretensions. Social and class distinctions were the norm rather than the exception, and the military and commercial élite assiduously attempted to replicate the metropolitan society they had left behind in France. Consequently, in many respects Louisbourg had far more in common with Havana or Dunkirk than it did with the Acadian agricultural settlements in Nova Scotia.[19] With the outbreak of war in 1739 between Great Britain and Spain, the Louisbourg officials realized that hostilities would soon engulf them. They felt supremely confident, however, that, given Louisbourg's fortifications and cannon, together with the French Navy, and considering the dilapidated state of the English defences at Canso and Annapolis Royal, they were more than adequately protected from an Anglo-American attack. Moreover, the Louisbourg officials saw no good reason why neighbouring Nova Scotia should not be easily recaptured. For once, it seemed, the French had the military advantage in the region.

Ile Saint-Jean also had military significance in this period, but only as a minor outpost. It represented the northern settlement frontier for the Nova Scotia Acadians, although again on a small scale. Never having more than 500 permanent settlers at any time between 1720 and 1744, it was indeed a colony of marginal importance. French officials in 1719, 'frustrated in their efforts to attract Acadians to Ile Royale,' accepted an offer from Comte de Saint-Pierre to establish a company to encourage agriculture and fishing on Ile Saint-Jean.[20] It was hoped that the proprietary grant to Saint-Pierre would be the means whereby hundreds of Acadians and French settlers would transform Ile Saint-Jean into the breadbasket of Ile Royale. On 15 April 1720, three small vessels with 300 passengers, provisions, and supplies sailed from Rochefort for Ile Saint-Jean.

Deterred primarily by the strenuous effort involved in clearing the island's forests, few Acadians were, at first, attracted to Ile Saint-Jean. They were also suspicious of the demands that might be made on them by Saint-Pierre's company. By the autumn of 1724, the Saint-Pierre settlement experiment had failed, despite the expenditure of some '1,200,000 livres on the enterprise.'[21] Not all of the Saint-Pierre settlers, however, quit the island in 1724. A few Acadians and a few independent French fishermen persisted. In 1725, fearing possible inroads by New England into the Ile Saint-Jean fishery, Louisbourg officials proposed sending there a military detachment of some twenty-five troops. When the French troops finally arrived on Ile Saint-Jean in the spring of 1726, they discovered a small number of settlers in the Port La Joie area – where the Saint-Pierre company had concentrated its efforts. 'An eyewitness,' it has been observed, 'declared that the fields of wheat he saw at Port La Joie were equal to any he had seen in France, Spain, or Italy.'[22]

According to the first official census on the island, there were 297 agricultural settlers in 1728: 76 men, 51 women, 156 children, and 14 domestic servants. There were also 125 fishermen. By 1730, their numbers had grown to 325 agricultural settlers and 140 fishermen. The two major nuclei of settlement on Ile Saint-Jean were at St Peter's on the north shore and Port La Joie, near present-day Charlottetown. The 1735 census listed 432 agricultural settlers and 131 fishermen. Of the 432 agricultural settlers, 3 came from Spain, 15 from New France, 198 from Acadia, and 216 from France. There was little population growth on Ile Saint-Jean from 1735 to 1740. Forest fires and a plague of field mice encouraged a number of Acadians to return to Nova Scotia and discouraged Acadians from emigrating to the island. The early 1740s, however, witnessed the arrival of at least twenty-four Acadian families, a movement encouraged by the military commander on the island, the lieutenant de roi, Louis Duchambon. These settlers strengthened the Acadian bias of the population and the island's overall orientation towards Nova Scotia rather than Ile Royale.[23]

J.B. Brebner once perceptively observed that there were two Acadias: the one 'the Acadia of the international conflict, the other the land settled and developed by the Acadians.'[24] Acadia/Nova Scotia after 1720 continued to find itself a territorial pawn in the ongoing imperial struggle between the French and the English, during the 'phoney peace' that spanned the end of Queen Anne's War in 1713 and the outbreak of King George's War in 1744. This is, of course, one important side of the historical coin. But there is the other side as well – the remarkable growth and prosperity of the Acadian population during what Naomi Griffiths has aptly called their 'golden age.'[25]

Between 1720 and 1744 there was only one governor of Nova Scotia.

Col. Richard Philipps, a largely absentee administrator, resided in the colony only from 1720 to 1723 and from 1729 to 1731. Philipps was assisted until 1739 by successive lieutenant-governors, Capt. John Doucett and Maj. Lawrence Armstrong, and from 1740 by Maj. Paul Mascarene, who served in the capacity of president of the Council of Nova Scotia. Throughout the period, Annapolis Royal was dominated by the British military presence. In fact, because of the virtual absence of immigrants from New England and Britain, there were too few qualified civilians to fill the available places on the Council. Doucett and Mascarene were very effective administrators; Armstrong, on the other hand, was probably insane for much of the time between 1731 and 1739 when he governed the colony. 'Frequently Afflicted with Melancholy fitts,' Armstrong committed suicide on 17 December 1739 in Fort Anne, Annapolis Royal. He stabbed himself five times with his sword and died slowly in a pool of his own blood.[26]

When Governor Richard Philipps arrived in Nova Scotia early in 1720 he knew of the military and commercial threat represented by Louisbourg. The French military threat was most explicitly felt among the Acadian inhabitants and at the expanding Anglo-American fishing centre at Canso. Philipps carried with him firm instructions to invite the Acadians 'In the most friendly manner by Proclamation [and] other ways, as you shall think fit, to submit to your Government & Swear Allegiance to His Majesty, within the space of four months from the Date of Such Your Proclamation, upon which condition they shall enjoy the free Exercise of their Religion, and be protected in all their Civil & Religious Rights & Liberties so long as they shall behave themselves as becomes good subjects.' 'Shrewd, determined, and vigorous,' Philipps spent the entire summer of 1720 in 'negotiating the best possible understanding' with the Acadians to prevent their emigration to Ile Royale.[27] Philipps at first tried to pressure the Acadians to take an unqualified oath of allegiance to the British Crown. This the Acadians stubbornly refused to do, declaring that such a collective decision would result in immediate raids by French-incited Micmacs. Realizing that he possessed little real bargaining power, Philipps reluctantly accepted the reality of Acadian 'neutrality.' He turned his attention to Canso, where French-Micmac inroads were still producing unwanted instability; this, among other things, strengthened the Acadian resolve not to be overly sympathetic to the British occupiers.

Despite the fact that the British warship the *Squirrel* had, in the fall of 1718, captured at Canso a number of French ships, fish, and other goods valued by the French at 200,000 livres, the French fishermen had, by 1720, returned to try to establish their economic hammerlock over the region. A British naval officer visiting Canso reported in that year that

'When a ship of warr is not there or anything to hinder the French fishing amongst us then our fishing Vessels cannot take four fish when they
will take tenn.'[28] Resenting any kind of English presence at Canso, and
in all likelihood encouraged by their French allies, an undetermined
number of Micmacs on 8 August 1720 attacked some Massachusetts
fishermen in and around Canso, killing three and taking a number of
prisoners. 'Everything was pillaged,' one participant reported, 'fish,
goods, clothes, bedding and even pockets, the loss being said to amount
to £18,000 ...'[29] On hearing of the Micmac attack, Philipps decided to station three companies of his troops at Canso and to construct a small fort
there to protect his colony's most important commercial centre. He had
the support of the Massachusetts government and the bay colony's
influential fishing interests, who took a proprietorial attitude towards
the Canso fishery. The arrival of British troops discouraged further Micmac attacks in 1721 and encouraged the arrival of no fewer than eighty-
eight Massachusetts fishing schooners.[30]

Canso's new defensive strength and Philipps' military skill were both
tested in 1722 when the Nova Scotia Micmacs, together with some
Abenakis, began a major offensive against New England fishermen and
traders. During the summer of 1722, Natives captured eighteen trading
vessels in the Bay of Fundy and an additional eighteen New England
fishing schooners between Cape Sable and Canso.[31] An enraged Massachusetts General Court reacted by sending hundreds of troops into
northern and eastern Maine and by dispatching sixty men to the 'Coast
of Cape Sable to recover the Fishing Vessels.'[32] Before the Massachusetts
naval force could do anything of consequence about the eighteen captured Yankee fishing schooners, however, Philipps took the initiative at
Canso. 'By this time,' he carefully explained, 'we were in the middle of
the fishery and the harbour full of ships wayteing their loading, when
fresh advices came that the Indians were cruising upon the Banks with
the sloops they had taken assisted by the prisoners whom they compelled to serve as mariners.' To deal with what he was certain would be
an imminent Micmac naval assault, Philipps persuaded the remaining
Massachusetts fishermen to agree to the 'fitting and manning out two
sloops to protect the Fishery, and having reinforced each of them with a
detachment of the Garrison and an Officer, it had that good effect that in
three weeks time I retooke all the vessells and prisoners, except foure
which the N. England people poorly ransom'd.'[33]

The quick implementation of Philipps' plan by the New England fishermen was encouraged, without question, by the letter the governor
had received from the governor of Massachusetts, Samuel Shute. It con-
veyed 'a Declaration of Warr by that Government against the Indians'
and also a strong request that the Massachusetts fishermen should

enthusiastically support the war effort.[34] Massachusetts, without any prior consultation, had declared war on the Micmac. Nova Scotia, still considered by some Yankee merchants as the British northeastern appendage of Massachusetts, was thus dragged by its neighbouring British colony into what came to be known as Dummer's or Lovewell's War. The often-bloody frontier conflict continued until August 1726, when a formal peace treaty was agreed upon.[35] One of the clauses of the treaty stipulated that delegates 'from the tribes of Penobscott, Naridgwalk, St. John's, Cape Sable, and other tribes inhabiting within his majesty's said territories of Nova Scotia or Acadia, and New England' agreed to 'acknowledge his said majestie king George's Jurisdiction and Dominion over the territories of said province of Nova Scotia.'[36] The treaty of 1726 brought peace to Nova Scotia, and it certainly underlined not only Massachusetts' interest in Nova Scotia affairs but also the determination of British officials to bring the Native people in the northeast under their control.

The treaty of 1726 also ushered in a brief period of unprecedented prosperity for the Canso fishery. In 1729, there were an estimated 223 Massachusetts schooners at Canso with 1,118 men, who caught 51,749 quintals of cod. In 1732, however, there were only 80 schooners, 450 men, and 25,176 quintals of cod caught, and by 1737 the number of vessels had fallen to 65. In addition to the fishing schooners coming to Canso, there were nineteen Massachusetts whaling ships in 1735, ten in 1736, and ten again in 1737. The scarcity of whales off Canso, however, resulted in late 1737 in the whalers' decision to move their operations much farther north to 'Davis straits.' By 1737 Canso was a mere shadow of its former importance, and the onset of war between Spain and Britain in 1739 dealt it a fatal blow. The Massachusetts Canso fishermen, after 1739, were certain that once the long-anticipated war between France and Britain was declared, the Louisbourg French would immediately attack and capture Canso, and they understandably had little desire to lose whatever they possessed to the invading French.[37]

By the early months of 1744, the British government had come to the conclusion that 'there is no Fishery now at Canceu.'[38] Only a few fishermen, together with four incomplete companies of Governor Philipps' regiment, were left. These men, with their poverty-stricken families, and the small number of fishermen-settlers were housed in rickety shelters on the islands in the harbour and along the nearby rocky and inhospitable mainland. Canso's only defence work was now a weak blockhouse built of timber donated years before by grateful fishermen. In short, Canso was nothing more than a tiny, jerry-built British military outpost waiting to be captured.[39]

Throughout the 1720s and 1730s, the government of Nova Scotia was not blessed by an abundance of administrative talent. For example, Lawrence Armstrong, the lieutenant-governor for much of this period, was a 'brooding, moody man' whose 'mind was full of plans and suspicions and he was fated never to realize how irreconcilable with actual conditions, within and without Nova Scotia, his aspirations were.'[40] When he made his way to Annapolis in the autumn of 1726, he was determined to succeed, where Philipps had failed, in imposing an unqualified oath of allegiance on the Acadian inhabitants. In early October, he met with the Acadian deputies from the Annapolis region and presented them with this demand. After having the oath read to them in French, the deputies requested that 'a Clause whereby they might not be Obliged to Carry Arms might be Incerted.' At first, Armstrong stubbornly refused to consider the Acadian proposal. But when it seemed quite obvious, even to him, that the Acadian deputies would only sign a 'qualified oath of allegiance,' he agreed that the Acadian clause demanding military exemption might be written 'upon ye Margent of the french translation in order to get them over by Degrees.'[41] The pragmatic and tough-minded Acadians had won yet another battle against the British governing élite.

In the fall of 1727, on hearing of the death of George I and the accession of George II, Armstrong resolved again to impose an unqualified oath of allegiance on the entire Acadian population. As in the previous autumn, the Acadians agreed to consider such an oath only after it had been explicitly stated that they as 'French neuters' were exempt from bearing arms. On being informed of the Acadian 'neutrality' response, the Nova Scotia Council, encouraged by Armstrong, recommended in late November, 'that the Said Articles & Concessions are unwarrantable & dishonourable to His Majesty's authority & Government & Consequently Null & Void & that the Liut Governor of the province be desired not to Ratify and Confirm that Same.'[42] Armstrong's 'unqualified oath policy' had once again been unceremoniously rejected by the Acadians. Instead of British order there was Gallic chaos in the colony, and instead of Acadian submission there was a growing sense of Acadian confidence and assertiveness. By 1730, Philipps observed, the Acadians, 'Like Noah's progeny' were 'spreading themselves over the face of the Province.'[43] Once again he came to the province in an attempt to try to make the Acadians loyal British subjects. In one sense he seemed to succeed, but in another he failed abysmally.

Determined to win unconditionally where Armstrong had lost, Philipps began carefully, late in 1729, to woo the Acadians to the British side. At Annapolis he apparently persuaded 194 persons to swear 'on my faith as a Christian that I will be utterly loyal, and will truly obey His Majesty King George the second, whom I recognize as the sovereign lord of Acadia or Nova Scotia.'[44] Nothing about exempting the Annapolis Acadians from possible military service was added to the oath either in writing or verbally. They, having little fear of the Micmac and impressed by the Anglo-American economic and military suzerainty established over their region, were prepared to become British subjects. In September 1730, Philipps further reported that the oath had been subscribed to by all the Acadians of the colony. The evidence suggests, however, that in underscoring his success outside Annapolis Philipps was, in fact, not telling the whole truth. 'Almost certainly,' as J.B. Brebner has persuasively argued, Philipps succeeded in administering his oath 'only after considerable negotiation and by a solemn verbal promise that the *habitants* should never be called upon for military service.'[45] It is known, for example, that two Roman Catholic priests serving the 'Main Body of the Inhabitants up the Bay' prepared, on 25 April 1730, a certificate for the future use of the Acadians of the Minas region to the effect that the Nova Scotia governor had explicitly promised 'that he exempts them from bearing arms and fighting in war against the French and the Indians, and that the said inhabitants have only accepted allegiance and promised never to take up arms in the event of a war against the Kingdom of England and its Government.'[46] In fact, despite Philipps' assertion to the contrary, an unqualified oath of allegiance had been sworn only by the Annapolis Acadians, who made up approximately 25 per cent of the Acadian population in 1730. This situation certainly contained, as Naomi Griffiths has contended, 'everything necessary for a first class débâcle.'[47] The 'débâcle' would, in twenty-five years, take the form of the infamous 'Grand Dérangement.'

When Philipps sailed from Nova Scotia in 1731, never to return, he left the Acadians as they were entering their 'golden age'. The 1730s and 1740s would be years of unprecedented economic growth: remarkable population increase would be matched by expanded cultivation of the land and by the proliferation of cattle, sheep, pigs, and horses. Many Acadians were also involved in shipping produce and livestock to Louisbourg and New England. Others earned some or much of their livelihood from the fur trade and from fishing. The population of the Annapolis Royal region grew in real terms only from approximately 900 in 1730 to some 1,500 in 1748, but hundreds of people from this community, many of them young and recently married, emigrated to Minas, Pisiquid, and Cobequid, near present-day Truro, and also to Beaubassin. In 1737, there was a total of 6,958 Acadians living in the Bay of Fundy settlements, but by the late 1740s the number exceeded 9,000. The most significant growth was taking place in the Minas Basin, Cobequid, and Chignecto-Memramcook regions. The population of Beaubassin increased from 1,816 in 1737 to some 2,800 by the end of the

1740s.[48] Some outside observers were now beginning to see regional distinctions in the seemingly homogeneous Acadian population. The most pro-British region was found at and around Annapolis. Then there was the Minas-Cobequid heartland, and finally the Beaubassin-Chignecto western frontier. The Acadians in this latter region found themselves farthest from their English overlords, and they were often under considerable pressure from the Ile Royale French, and their Micmac allies. It is not surprising, therefore, that these Acadians were regarded as the most 'disloyal' Nova Scotians by the British authorities in Annapolis Royal. In a profound sense, of course, they were. And located between the two extremes, the pro-British and the pro-French, were the Minas-Cobequid Acadians – the quintessential 'neutral French.'[49]

J.B. Brebner once wrote that the Acadians 'were completely competent in a practical way; blessed in the possession of a fertile and easily worked land, and therefore not ridden by a passionate industry; lacking stimulation and criticism from abroad; and content to live for generations much as their fathers had done.'[50] Acadian society in the 1720 to 1744 period was, however, considerably more complex and richly textured than Brebner realized. The Acadians were not simple, bucolic peasants living in some kind of Nova Scotia Elysium. Because of the powerful influence exerted by the North American environment and also because no European power had succeeded in continuously establishing its power, they found themselves in a society that considerably relaxed many of the land-holding customs and social relationships that would have characterized late-seventeenth- and early-eighteenth-century France. Despite the existing vestiges of the seigneurial system, there was 'a general equality of rank.' The local elders, who became known as deputies during the British administration, reflected local opinion to those in authority and also relayed governmental proclamations and laws to their peers. In a very real sense, these deputies were the representatives of the Acadian people; though not formally elected, they were carefully chosen by the people to represent faithfully their interests. And the deputies would never commit their constituents to any policy without first asking them for their collective opinion. Always, the voice of the majority would prevail at these 'little Democratic Assemblies.'[51] Though not, in any way, an idealized egalitarian society, Acadian society – by contrast with Louisbourg and Canada – certainly lacked a formal social hierarchy.

The Acadians were very much people of the spoken rather than the written word. Theirs was an oral culture. They loved to gather together and to talk, to tell stories, to mimic their friends and their enemies, and to discuss a myriad of local and provincial issues. At these meetings, apparently, Acadian men often participated in short dramatic pieces during which the political and religious institutions of New England were savagely lampooned. Not only were many Acadians gifted mimics and devastating critics of neighbouring New England, but also a number possessed remarkable creative skills.[52] According to Rev. Andrew Brown, who studied the Acadian experience from his Halifax Presbyterian vantage-point in the 1780s and 1790s, 'In a country where everything was sung, many pieces both of familiar and serious poetry had been produced and the authors did not borrow, like those who wrote verses in the English colonies, the descriptions or the imagery taken from a state of nature and a form of society altogether different from their own.' The Acadian songs, poetry, and stories were passed from one generation to another and became the core of Acadian oral culture. 'Submitting to the impressions that were made on the imagination and the heart, they painted what they *saw*, and uttered what they felt.'[53] They also loved to dance, especially to violin music, and this too would help to 'relieve any last vestige of monotony in the colony.'[54]

The lack of hierarchy in Acadian life was further reflected in the way in which – according to Brown – with few exceptions 'the architecture and distribution of the family dwellings ... conformed to a single pattern.' Brown's description of Acadian housing, it should be noted, has been largely confirmed by recent archaeological work in the region. The chimney in 'the cabin of rough logs,' according to Brown, 'rose high in the east gable. There was a door near the centre of each side wall, and one in the west end of the house. Each side wall contained two neat windows of clear glass trimmed with some care.' 'The free space, in front of the fire' served as both 'a kitchen and a parlour.' There was also a 'shelf,' which 'exhibited many bright rows of pewter dishes, and a full assortment of wooden trenchers and horn spoons.' The wooden chests, 'which contained the cloathing of the household were well finished, and being covered with the shaggy hide of the moose or black bear served as seats for the family and its guests.' 'These seats' as one might have expected 'were generally crowded, every house swarming with inhabitants.'[55]

It is highly likely that the cramped conditions of the typical Acadian home, made even worse by the large numbers of people living under one roof, created a serious lack of privacy and the internalization of a great deal of anger. As a result, as was the case in Plymouth Colony to the south, some Acadians tended to direct their inner hostility and aggression at their neighbours in the form of verbal violence and litigiousness.[56]

Women played an extremely important role in the Acadian community. Like many New England rural women, they worked in the fields, planting and harvesting, and they must also have spent a great deal of time spinning and weaving, since 'the whole community was clothed in domestic manufactures, the exclusive product of female industry.' Men and women worked closely together during 'seasons of hardest labour ... in seed time and harvest,' but at all times 'each sex pursued the business of its respective department.' In such an economy, the roles of men and women were fully interdependent. The young men were solely responsible for building and repairing dykes.[57] Poultry raising and orchard cultivation, meanwhile, were regarded as the specific responsibility of women. The apple trees 'were planted in close rows; and in order to preserve the blossoms from the hoar frosts of the spring and the fruit from the high winds of autumn, a deep belt of willows furnished a firm screen.'[58] It has been observed that 'the orchard was an extension of the home; it was a work place, a place for schooling, social interaction and religious observance. Just as women organized and undertook the bulk of the work generated within the Acadian home, they oversaw the activities of the orchard. When a couple began a home of their own – meaning those who did not take over their parents' establishment – it was the duty of the wife to begin the orchard.'[59]

Although Acadian agricultural output may have lagged somewhat behind that of neighbouring New England, the Acadians, by the 1730s, had moved far beyond basic subsistence agriculture. Many Acadians had herds of up to 100 cattle. Moreover, it is known that at mid-century 'the department of Minas alone exported from eight to ten thousand bushels of wheat, and could deliver to the butcher no fewer than fifteen hundred head of fat cattle.'[60] The success of Acadian agriculture not only fuelled an expanding export trade but also provided the inhabitants with a great deal of food and a well-balanced diet. Meat and fish were staples, and winter storage techniques ensured that fruit and vegetables were always plentiful. A noteworthy feature of Acadian diet was its emphasis on milk products. According to one observer, 'at Breakfast, served up at an early hour, the assembled household feasted on pancakes, mixed with slices of fried pork, milk and water forming the beverage. When the hour of dinner arrived they sat down to a substantial meal ... of beans, pease, potherbs, toasted bread and a full allowance of beef or mutton ... supper was a lighter meal, consisting wholly of different preparations of milk in which cream was not spared.'[61]

Apple cider, made by the women, was often consumed, especially at special occasions that had religious significance, such as the processional feast of the spring, known as 'the return of the geese.' The spring festival was balanced by an autumn Thanksgiving celebration during which the Acadians collectively expressed their gratitude to the Almighty. Then, on New Year's Day, 'the men and boys of each family made the tour of the whole canton; entering every house, and embracing, in a spirit of unaffected kindness, every person it contained.' According to the ideal embodied in the celebration, 'all strife was composed, resentment forgotten and a new course of harmony and peace begun.'[62] This was a community revitalization ritual, and it must have helped to rebuild at least some broken relationships, especially those snapped by the litigiousness of so many Acadians.

Acadian society was certainly not priest-ridden; nor was it particularly devout in its Catholicism. 'Acadian Catholicism,' Naomi Griffiths has argued 'was a religion far less authoritarian then the Catholicism of New France.' With relatively few priests, laymen played a crucially important role in weekly worship, and this helped to give Acadian Catholicism its pragmatic shape. 'They practised their faith with a secular utility,' according to Griffiths, 'registering their baptisms, marriages and deaths.'[63] A certain tough-minded pragmatism seemed to characterize the Acadian response to all features of their existence – whether in the realms of agriculture, trade, religion, or their relations with the Micmac, the English, and the Louisbourg French. These overlapping layers of pragmatism, together with their growing economic prosperity in the post-1730 period, helped to shape an Acadian sense of identity – despite regional differences.

Acadian pragmatism would be sorely tested in 1744, when war broke out yet again between the British and the French. The French at Louisbourg first learned about the declaration of war on 3 May 1744, some three weeks before the news reached New England and Annapolis Royal. Jean-Baptiste-Louis Le Prévost Duquesnel, now governor of Ile Royale, was instructed to take the military initiative against Nova Scotia in order to protect Ile Royale's southern flank, and also in order to win over the Acadians to the French cause.[64] Duquesnel selected Capt. François Du Pont Duvivier to lead an attack on Canso. Duvivier had never before seen active military service, but was regarded as an excellent officer. He was familiar with the situation of the tiny British fort and settlement some sixty miles to the south of Louisbourg. On 23 May, a small flotilla of seventeen French ships, carrying 22 officers, 107 soldiers, and 212 sailors, left Louisbourg. In the early morning hours of the following day, Duvivier's force arrived in Canso Harbour. In preparation for a dawn landing on 24 May, the two French privateers in the flotilla began to bombard the Canso blockhouse. The first shot apparently sailed through the thin blockhouse walls, and almost immediately the British officers in command rushed out with a flag of truce, thinking 'it advisable to capitulate in time to obtain the better terms.' Of the 87 British soldiers at Canso 'one third was sick or lame' and most of the others were poorly armed and badly trained.[65]

With Canso captured, Duquesnel turned to the more difficult matter of attacking Annapolis Royal and taking back all of Nova Scotia/Acadia. Having few troops to spare for such an expedition, he instructed Abbé Le Loutre, the energetic Roman Catholic missionary to the Micmacs of Nova Scotia, to try to enlist some of his Indian parishioners.[66] It was hoped that a number of Acadians would join the Micmac invading army. However, most of the Acadians, even those residing in Beaubassin, were still determined to walk the knife-edge of neutrality, and, on 12 July 1744, Le Loutre, with only two Acadians and some 300 Micmacs, began an irregular siege of Annapolis Royal.

The town seemed to be ripe for a Micmac plucking. The commanding officer, the unusually able Paul Mascarene, had only 100 troops under his command. Thirty of them he considered to be 'utterly invalids,'[67] and the fort was in poor repair. But the Micmacs, after killing two British regulars and making one half-hearted foray against the fort, decided that the time was propitious to demand that Mascarene surrender. On 13 July, Mascarene coolly replied that he would 'defend this Fort until the last drop of blood.'[68] The Micmac invaders burned some of the remaining buildings located outside the fort, fired a few harmless volleys, and on 16 July retreated to Minas. Their unexpected retreat had been precipitated not by Mascarene's letter but by the arrival of 70 Massachusetts reinforcements on board the *Prince of Orange*. According to the *Pennsylvania Journal*, 'the Indians seeing the Hammocks in the Netting of the ship, took them for Indians; and being informed by a French woman that [it] had a great number of Mohawks on board, and had landed several hundreds of Men to cut them off, they ran into the Woods in such haste, that their Priest left his Crucifix and other religious Trinkets behind him.'[69]

Despite the retreat of Le Loutre's Micmac force, Duquesnel was still determined to eradicate the British military presence from Annapolis Royal. He decided to gamble on a combined land and sea assault led by the captor of Canso, Duvivier. On 29 July, Duvivier was sent to Minas, by way of the Chignecto region, with fifty regular soldiers and a small number of Micmacs. It was hoped that the invading force would be joined at Minas by Acadians and Maliseets from the St John River as well as by other Micmacs for a final push against Mascarene's fort. At Annapolis Royal the French-Micmac-Maliseet force was to be met by two large French warships, *Le Caribou* and *L'Ardent*.[70]

Duvivier's troops landed at Chignecto on 8 August, but did not arrive at Minas until two weeks later. In neither place were the Acadians enthusiastic. They were unwilling to provide supplies for the invaders, let alone fight for them. Finally Duvivier felt compelled to make explicit threatening demands, which did little to endear him to the Minas-

Cobequid Acadians. On 27 August, Duvivier therefore threatened that all supplies and draft animals 'must be brought to me at ten o'clock on Saturday morning at the french flag which I have had hoisted, and under which the deputies from each of the said parishes shall be assembled, to pledge fidelity for themselves and all the inhabitants of the neighbourhood who shall not be called away from the labours of the harvest.' He warned that 'those for whom the pledge of fidelity shall be given will be held responsible for said pledge, and those who contravene the present order shall be punished as rebellious subjects, and delivered into the hands of the savages as enemies of the state, as we cannot refuse the demand which the savages make for all those who will not submit themselves.'[71] Despite Duvivier's threats of Micmac reprisals, the Acadians of Minas refused to join the expedition; and they only reluctantly provided supplies.[72] Duvivier's bitter disappointment with the lack of Acadian support for the invasion was exacerbated by the fact that so few Micmacs had rushed to his banner. At the most, there could have been only 160 Micmacs, since Duvivier's total force numbered 280 men, 50 of them Louisbourg troops, and 70 Maliseets. Micmac support was relatively weak for two reasons: the French and the Micmacs had lost face by their previous failure to capture Annapolis Royal, and Le Loutre took no part in the second expedition.

On 30 August, Duvivier finally led his men out of Minas, convinced that the local priest, Father Miniac, had done everything in his power 'to cause the wreck of the enterprise.'[73] On 8 September, the invading force attacked the British fort 'under the cover of some hedges and fences, with Colours flying.' A week later, after a number of disorganized and desultory 'night attacks,' Duvivier boldly demanded that Mascarene surrender. He declared that he expected naval reinforcements, and suggested the drawing up of preliminaries to a capitulation that would come into force when the French ships sailed into Annapolis Basin. In the intervening period a truce was to be carefully administered and observed.[74]

Mascarene was disappointed to discover that most of his officers were 'very ready to accept of the proposal, the dread of being made prisoners of warr having no small influence with most.' Duvivier's terms were reluctantly accepted by Mascarene, and all eyes turned seawards. But by 23 September, realizing that the French ships were not coming and the truce was only benefiting the British, Duvivier cancelled the 'truce.' The British troops, now numbering more than 250 men, including 53 additional reinforcements who had arrived from Boston in the late summer, received news of Duvivier's decision with 'three cheerful Huzzas.' They found the renewed French-Indian nightly forays 'more and more contemptible.'[75]

On 26 September, two vessels were sighted in the basin, and the invaders and the besieged strained their eyes to see the colours of the armed brigantine and sloop. As the two ships edged closer to the shore, jubilation swept through the British fort – the vessels were from Boston, carrying a force of fifty Pigwackets and much-needed supplies. As Duvivier sadly noted in his journal, 'the British yelled out many hurrahs ... They were singing and enjoying themselves thoroughly, they probably spent the whole night drinking.' The morale of the invaders had been shattered once again by the timely arrival of reinforcements from Massachusetts. On 2 October, a disillusioned Duvivier received orders from Louisbourg to lift the siege since 'The King's vessels were not coming.'[76] Three days later the retreat to Minas began. This retreat, however, was not the end to the Duvivier expedition against Annapolis Royal. Duvivier's urgent request for naval assistance had struck a responsive chord with the new governor of Ile Royale, Louis Du Pont Duchambon, who had replaced Duquesnel on the latter's death on 9 October. Duchambon, not realizing that his predecessor had ordered Duvivier to lift the Annapolis Royal siege, sent two privateers to the fort. The French ships arrived off Annapolis in the evening of 25 October, some three weeks after the Duvivier force had left the region.[77] If these two vessels had arrived a month earlier, it is highly unlikely that Annapolis Royal would have remained in British hands. However, instead of assisting in a successful land-sea assault on Nova Scotia's capital, the men on the two ships returned disappointed to Louisbourg.

The two Annapolis Royal expeditions provided convincing proof that the Acadians were indeed committed 'neutrals.' The expeditions also revealed that Louisbourg was of limited military value as an offensive base against Nova Scotia without reliable seapower and the at least tacit support of large numbers of Acadians. And, of course, it was clear that without military assistance from Massachusetts, Annapolis Royal was virtually useless as a military base. In 1744, Massachusetts had saved Annapolis Royal twice; Louisbourg had failed twice to capture the fort. What would 1745 bring, as the expansionist vision of the governor of Massachusetts, William Shirley, confronted the military realities of Louisbourg – the 'French Gibraltar of North America' – as well as the harsh geophysical realities of Atlantic Canada?

CHAPTER SEVEN

1744–1763
Colonial Wars and Aboriginal Peoples

STEPHEN E. PATTERSON

The period from 1744 to 1763 in Atlantic Canada was a time of war and dramatic events, beginning with the unprecedented attack of 5,000 New England militiamen on France's jewel in the gulf, Fort Louisbourg. Supported by a Royal Navy fleet of six ships of the line and five frigates, the raw colonials laid siege to the fort during May and June 1745, and after seven weeks of heavy bombardment, the French, outnumbered ten to one, capitulated. From this first fall of Louisbourg to the final collapse of French power in North America in 1763, the history of the Atlantic region can appear as a sideshow to the main event, the great imperial struggle between Britain and France. They fought two wars in this period: the War of the Austrian Succession, 1744–8, concluded by the Treaty of Aix-la-Chapelle, which restored territories in the region to the status quo ante bellum; and the Seven Years' War, 1756–63, actually begun in North America in 1754 and concluded by the famous Treaty of Paris, which surrendered to Britain all French possessions in North America, the tiny islands of St Pierre and Miquelon excepted. Viewing the region's history as a fragment of a global conflict, however, or even as an extension of the history of New England, another possible approach, provides only an exterior perspective, one that is necessarily distorted. Viewed from the inside, the region's history in this time had its own distinctive shape, moulded by the circumstances of time and place. It was indeed a time of conflict, conflict that was more or less continuous rather than confined neatly to the periods of declared war; and it was also a three-cornered struggle – among British, French, and Native people. The Native involvement provided the continuity from 1744 to 1760 and 1761, when the Micmac, Maliseet, and Passamaquoddy signed their respective treaties of submission and peace with the victorious British, two full years before France and Britain agreed to the Peace of Paris. Understanding the region's history in this time requires some attention to the Native people, for in many ways their role was central – indeed, more critical than in any subsequent period – and until it is understood, little sense can be made of any of the other historical events of the time, including the massive expulsion of the Acadians.

Unfortunately, the Native people are mostly seen through the eyes of Europeans, who left the only written documents that survive; these are replete with European biases and perhaps false assumptions. But a careful sifting and winnowing permits at least a tentative historical view of Native culture at mid-eighteenth century. It was a culture in the advanced stages of adaptation, influenced chiefly by the French. At the very most, there were 3,000 Natives in the region, not counting the Beothuk of Newfoundland. The Micmac were the most numerous, with perhaps not quite 2,000 spread throughout present Nova Scotia and eastern New Brunswick as far as the Gaspé; the Maliseet of the St John Valley numbered fewer than 1,000; and the closely related Passamaquoddy, whose territory spread from the St Croix Valley to Mount Desert Island, may have numbered no more than 100.[1] Tools, diet, clothing, language, religion, organization, and day-to-day behaviour all showed signs of change as the century progressed, especially in time of war. The Micmac acquired the skills to sail European vessels; diet frequently included European-style baked bread, domestically raised meat, and garden vegetables (grown by Acadians and Québécois); and European fabrics and clothing became the favoured trading goods when barter was possible. Many Natives could speak or at least understand French and had chosen French names (many adopting at first one French name to go with an a Native name, and then by mid-century adopting two French names, with a man's first name becoming the family name of his children). Most had been converted to Roman Catholicism by a network of French priests that reached into almost every corner of the region by mid-century. Native government was in a state of flux, shifting from the apparently loose and decentralized forms of the past into larger councils, probably influenced by the concentrations of warriors for military purposes and by the annual summer pilgrimage of Catholic Micmacs to Chapel Island on Cape Breton. War added its own twists by splitting some bands, altering their seasonal migrations, geographically redistributing the Native population, and creating rivalries among the bands as their leaders sought to redefine their roles and their relationship with the Europeans.

In part, at least, these changes were the direct result of French policy. From the late seventeenth century, the French had formed a relatively tight and effective network of alliances among the Native peoples within the territories they claimed, and by the 1720s they had made a system of it.[2] A defensive barrier of Native allies provided a useful buffer zone that effectively prevented the penetration of English-speaking settlers northward and, in the case of Acadia, northeastward. The British in New York responded with their own alliance system, which was built around the famous Iroquois Confederacy and its extensive alliance network known as the Covenant Chain.[3] There was a difference, however: the British relied on the Iroquois to provide the infrastructure of their alliance system; the French, in contrast, used a vigorous program of trade, religious conversion, and acculturation to draw together a tighter system of allies who, while never subservient or ready to sacrifice Native for French interests, usually cooperated with the French by providing scouts and warriors and accepting French direction in time of war.[4] It was this network into which the Micmac, Maliseet, and Passamaquoddy Indians of old Acadia were drawn. During the 1744–8 war, they served as couriers between Acadia and Quebec, disrupted the English dry fishery on Nova Scotia's east coast, fought under French command at Grand Pré and Port La Joie (opposite present-day Charlottetown), and scouted the frontier as far west as New York. 'The dread of these Indians,' according to French officials, is what kept the English from settling Nova Scotia. While provisioning the Natives was expensive, the French claimed it was worth it since the Micmac, 'of all the nations, are the most faithful to us.'[5]

The French and the British ended their war in 1748, but the peace terms that they agreed on changed very little in the region. New Englanders who had spent their blood and treasure taking Louisbourg were offended that the fortress went back to the French in exchange for Madras, no more than a pawn, it seemed, in an inscrutable chess game. But the British attempted to make amends by reimbursing them and by establishing a new role for Nova Scotia: policy makers in London decided that the Acadian population should be counterbalanced with English and foreign Protestant immigrants and that a new heavily fortified town should be erected beside the excellent harbour at Chebucto 'as a counterweight [to Louisbourg] and as a protection for New England and her trade.'[6] To accomplish this, the British sought to make Nova Scotia a self-sufficient colony, capable of feeding itself, of developing its exploitable resources, and of managing its internal government.

The founding of Halifax marked the beginning of the new policy. It would be the capital, and was, for a time – with the exception of the original British headquarters, Annapolis, and some military outposts – just about all there was to British Nova Scotia. In June 1749, Governor Edward Cornwallis, an experienced army officer, and 2,500 settlers sailed into the protected waters of Chebucto and began building Halifax on its spruce-lined shores. An indispensable participant was the New Englander Charles Morris, a surveyor, who with John Brewse laid out the city and was rewarded with the position of chief surveyor of lands and membership in the governor's Council. The latter, made up of military men and a handful of functionaries, served with the governor as both the government and the highest court in the province for the first few years, following the pattern of the early royal government of Virginia. Fear of Native attacks led the government to concentrate first on building fortifications around the settlement, while the ravages of winter created the need for a hospital and then an orphanage. Soldiers, sailors, and merchants made Halifax very much a man's world in its first years, but women and children also shared in the struggle with the climate and rough conditions.

While many settlers sought the first ship out once their bounties and government provisions were gone, the hardiest remained, and the town soon began to acquire the cultural institutions that could sustain it. Clergy and teachers from the Society for the Propagation of the Gospel supervised the building of the first Anglican church, St Paul's, and established the first school. The large number of New England merchants and other settlers who arrived to collect military supply contracts and to exploit the exportable resources and the new markets quickly created the need for a second church. St Matthew's was a Congregationalist church in the New England Puritan tradition, commonly called Mather's Church. In the opinion of William Tutty, first rector of St Paul's, the early problems of the town arose from conflict between the English and New England segments of the population. As the town matured, however, the leaders of the two groups gradually united as a commercial élite tied by common economic and political interests. Joshua Mauger, an English merchant who began as victualler to the Royal Navy, became the first great merchant and shipowner. He shipped fish and lumber to the West Indies in exchange for rum, molasses, and sugar, and then, with John Fillis, a New Englander, built the first rum distilleries. New Englanders such as Malachy Salter, Benjamin and Joseph Gerrish, and Benjamin Green prospered from general trade, government contracts, or patronage appointments. With the addition of Michael Francklin and John Butler, Mauger's principal agents after he left the province in 1760, these Halifax merchants became the province's first power élite, the political rivals of successive colonial governors.[7] Obstacles, however, stood in the way of the attempt to make Halifax more than a Navy and garrison town dependent on British financing, and these included the rival ambitions of France in the region and a perceived threat from the Native people.

Before Cornwallis could achieve his objective of peopling Nova Scotia with English and foreign Protestants, he needed peace with the province's Natives. His first chance came when representatives of the Maliseet, Passamaquoddy, and a single band of Micmac from Chignecto arrived in Halifax in the summer of 1749 and expressed their willingness to stop fighting now that the French and English had settled on terms. They agreed to renew an earlier treaty, drafted in Boston in 1725, which was now redrafted as the Treaty of 1749 and which other Maliseet and Passamaquoddy leaders also soon ratified at a meeting arranged at the mouth of the St John River.[8] But the treaty failed to establish a general peace. Within days, Cornwallis received a letter from Micmacs of Cape Breton and Antigonish claiming that the British were occupying Micmac land and that they would 'make neither alliance or peace with you.' The letter was written for them by their religious leader, Father Maillard, the founder of the Holy Family Mission on Chapel Island.[9] Almost simultaneously, reports arrived of a Native attack on a British ship at Chignecto, an attack attributed by the Council to the influence of another French priest, Abbé Le Loutre, whose presence there they assumed was 'on purpose to excite them [the Natives] to war.'[10] Whatever the source of their information, the British correctly read French intentions. Only shortly before, Le Loutre had written to the minister of marine in France: 'As we cannot openly oppose the English ventures, I think that we cannot do better than to incite the Indians to continue warring on the English; my plan is to persuade the Indians to send word to the English that they will not permit new settlements to be made in Acadia ... I shall do my best to make it look to the English as if this plan comes from the Indians and that I have no part in it.'[11] He obviously failed in covering up his own role, but both the incidents at Chignecto and Maillard's letter appeared to be consistent with Le Loutre's plan. When subsequently the British received information that Micmac raiders had seized a number of sailing vessels, captured English prisoners, and killed workers at a sawmill near Halifax, the governor and Council angrily replied with a proclamation ordering British subjects to 'destroy the savage commonly called Micmacs wherever they are found.'[12]

These were harsh measures, but the British soon came to believe that, despite the Treaty of Aix-la-Chapelle, the French intended to continue warfare through their Native allies and that French priests formed in effect a fifth column working among the Natives of Nova Scotia. How the British gained their information they never fully revealed, but British traders frequented Louisbourg, and British authorities regularly intercepted letters from Louisbourg and Quebec to Le Loutre and others. Eventually, when the French began to fortify themselves at the Isthmus of Chignecto, the British had spies who kept them informed.

Moreover, documents from the French side, including a lengthy autobiography by Le Loutre himself, show conclusively that there was substance to British fears and beliefs.[13]

The British believed that they were at war, loosely called 'the Indian War' at the time but which historians have since referred to as the Micmac War or the Anglo-Micmac War.[14] Since there was no general treaty with the Micmac in 1749, it was in effect a continuation of the war that had begun in 1744, and it continued through the 1750s, blending into the Seven Years' War. Despite several British attempts to bring this war with the Natives to a close by treaty, first in 1749 and then again in 1752 and 1753, the conflict continued in Nova Scotia until 1760, when a series of treaties with all the various Micmac bands finally brought peace. As for the Maliseet, the British at first seemed willing to overlook evidence that they were being drawn back into active support of the French; the British badly wanted the treaty they had with these Natives to work, and therefore both the Maliseet and the Passamaquoddy were conspicuously exempted from the Proclamation of 1749. It was the Micmac alone who were to be destroyed. But as time passed, the British realized that the Maliseet were indeed actively supporting the French, for which the British again blamed French missionaries. Although British officials were bound by treaty to consider the French friendly, what followed in Nova Scotia was at best a half peace. Diplomatic and military niceties were observed, both sides bending over backwards to deal with the other with effusive and thus not always credible politeness. But all the while, French civil and military officials both in Quebec and at Louisbourg directed the missionaries, and the missionaries directed 'their Indians,' in hostile actions against the British, and the British knew it. It was war, even if it masqueraded as peace.

Moreover, it was a war that even the French could not at all times contain. The Micmac, and especially some bands among them, were independent-minded. They had their own strategies, the object of which was to survive in a land now filling with European intruders; and while at times these strategies were congruent with French plans, at others it seemed in the Micmac interest to strike a course that neither French officials nor missionaries would approve. Never quite sure what they were dealing with, Nova Scotia's governors throughout this period looked constantly for opportunities to treat with the Natives, hoping for both peace and an acceptance of British sovereignty. But at the same time they maintained a defensive posture and took the necessary steps to protect such tiny and scattered British settlements as there were. The approach was essentially a military one: not surprisingly, since the governors from 1749 to 1760 – Cornwallis, Hopson, and Lawrence – were not only civil administrators but also active officers of the British Army.

The Micmac War and the semi-peace with the French were both complicated by a profound disagreement between Britain and France over the legal boundaries of Nova Scotia. In 1713, the French had surrendered Acadia 'according to its ancient boundaries' with the exception of Ile Royale and Ile Saint-Jean. The British believed that they had won all the territory of present Nova Scotia, New Brunswick, and any French claims to Maine, although the boundaries between Acadia and Quebec in the north and Maine in the west necessarily remained vague. Yet the French acted as if they had not surrendered as much as the British thought. They continued to come and go through parts of the old Acadia without challenge, a freedom made possible by the general British neglect of Nova Scotia from 1713 to the late 1740s. Once the British moved into Halifax, the French recognized at once the threat it represented to their domination of the Gulf of St Lawrence; they also feared that the British would in future use the St John Valley as a corridor through which to attack Quebec City itself. They therefore officially challenged the boundaries of 1713 and began insisting that they had surrendered only the peninsular part of Nova Scotia, a claim which they asserted physically by building a small earthenworks fortress, Fort Beauséjour, on the Isthmus of Chignecto. Since this in itself could be seen as an act of war, they simultaneously agreed with the British to establish a boundaries commission, which, as it turned out, spent five years in Paris poring over maps to no avail.[15]

The Beauséjour scheme became much more than a frontier defence of Quebec; it quickly became a solution for France of another long-standing concern, namely British control of the approximately 8,000 Acadians who lived within Nova Scotia in coastal settlements around Minas Basin, near the mouth of the Annapolis River, or scattered in various other places. The plan was to encourage all Acadians to remove behind the Missaguash River at Chignecto or to Ile Saint-Jean where they would re-establish agricultural communities, gain self-sufficiency, and at the same time help in the defence of the French claims. Acadia would revive with an instant population while the British would be deprived of hard-working and productive farmers.

Acadians who had previously tried to keep out of the power struggle between Britain and France now found themselves an official target of French policy. Making matters worse, these external pressures on Acadian communities coincided with internal ones similar to those being experienced by long-settled New England communities to the south. Populations were rapidly rising. At the last official census in 1736, there were 6,000 Acadians; by 1752, varying estimates suggest from 10,000 to 15,000 throughout the region. More to the point, in Nova Scotia after 1749, British policy was to prevent expansion of Acadian communities onto uncleared land, placing enormous pressure on young prospective farmers, whose only choice was to move away. They easily fell in with French plans for the region. A few went to Cape Breton, although most who moved there quickly left its sparse soil behind; substantially more went to the Chignecto area; and the largest numbers went to Ile Saint-Jean, swelling its population from a few hundred in 1749 to more than 5,000 by early 1755. One reasonable estimate is that one-third of the Acadians made at least one move in this pre-expulsion period.[16] Demographic pressures thus played into French policy while the French had men on the spot ready to exploit the opportunity. One of the chief of these was the missionary Abbé Jean-Louis Le Loutre, who later claimed credit for both the plan and its implementation.

Le Loutre had come first to Cape Breton in 1737 from the Paris-based Séminaire des Missions Etrangères, and from there he was sent into Nova Scotia to minister to the Micmac. The British during these years did not object to this, recognizing that the Micmac had become Catholics and hoping that as Christians they would be peaceable. Le Loutre chose Shubenacadie as his headquarters and erected a church and presbytery there.[17] From this central location, ideally situated to make the best use of the inland water routes that cut across the province from Minas Basin to the Atlantic, Le Loutre travelled widely to visit Micmacs who, as he himself explained, 'lived in scattered communities widely separated from each other.' In 1744, when war broke out between Britain and France, Governor Duquesnel at Louisbourg sent orders to Le Loutre 'that the Indians were to declare war against the English and that he must accompany them as chaplain in all their expeditions.' This he did, both before and after Louisbourg was captured, with the particular order to use Micmacs to block any supply of the British from Acadian farmlands.[18]

When the war ended, Le Loutre returned to Louisbourg, once more in French hands, where he received fresh instructions to remove his headquarters from Shubenacadie to Beauséjour and to take with him 'the Indians from Chigabenakady and the other tribes dependent on it as far away as Cape Sable, as they were too near Halifax.' Le Loutre was never precise about how many Micmacs he controlled, but it is clear that he had a large following, which he called 'my Indians'; several families of them removed with him to Beauséjour, held a council in which they 'decided to oppose the unjust invasions of the English,' sent necklaces to the Maliseet 'to induce them to break the treaty which they had made with the English,' and fought off two English vessels that had arrived in Beaubassin to look things over. As Le Loutre explained it, this is why, immediately afterwards, the British 'declared war on the Indians.' And it was his interpretation that it was this declaration rather than the earlier Micmac actions that brought on general hostilities, an interpretation diametrically opposite to the British view and at odds with his own earlier recommendation that the French 'incite the Indians to continue warring on the English.' He wrote: 'On receipt of this news all the Indians went on the warpath, and, everywhere they rose in arms and resumed acts of hostility.' His own role, he explained, was to urge the Micmac to treat their prisoners with humanity, but also 'to uphold their rights and their claims to their lands, their hunting areas and their fishing of which the English wished to gain control.' Le Loutre's conflicting remarks make it difficult to determine whether the Micmac resort to open warfare at this point was a French or a Micmac strategy, whether it was a response to French incitement, the British declaration, or some other reason. Whatever the case, the Micmac decision to fight served French purposes as well as their own. Moreover, the Micmac invitation to the Maliseet to join them soon worked; they too, it seems, accepted Le Loutre's direction, for when winter approached 'the Missionary [he wrote of himself in the third person] dismissed the Malecites until spring time and retained only his own Indians.'[19]

The larger purpose was to settle Acadians north of the Missaguash, and this soon became apparent to the British; in fact, Cornwallis knew that Le Loutre went to Cobequid (now Truro and neighbouring area) to persuade Acadians to move behind Beauséjour, and was even threatening them with Native massacre if they did not obey him. From a reconnaissance party sent to Chignecto under Maj. Charles Lawrence, he learned that the French had already located a company of regular troops there and that 1,000 Acadians were dispersed in the Memramcook-Petitcodiac-Shepody area, all of them claiming that this was the territory of the King of France. Cornwallis countered by planning a British fort and a small settlement on the isthmus, both to match the French threat and to protect the province 'during an Indian War.'[20]

Accordingly, in August of 1750, Cornwallis sent troops under Lawrence's command to erect a fort within sight of Beauséjour. Their landing at Chignecto was systematically and vigorously opposed, but British numbers prevailed in the end. They erected Fort Lawrence on the high ground east of the Missaguash, reconnoitered the low marshlands that separated the two sides, and skirmished with the French along the river.[21] In one famous incident, British captain Edward Howe, meeting under a flag of truce with French officers to effect a prisoner exchange, was shot down from the French positions, purportedly by Natives, although the facts of the killing were never settled with any certainty.[22] For almost five years, the uneasy standoff between British and French at Chignecto was to continue, while Micmac raids and skirmishes around the British settlement became so common that the governor gave up trying to report them all. However, the governor was certain, on the basis of the seizure of French vessels and the interception of their letters, that the French in Quebec were constantly supplying arms, ammunition, and provisions to the Micmac, so directly in violation of the Treaty of Aix-la-Chapelle, said Cornwallis, 'that I own it astonishes me.'[23]

For another year, French-supported Micmac hostilities continued unabated before a lull indicated the chance for peace. In May 1751, a well organized body of about sixty Native warriors swooped down on the tiny British settlement at Dartmouth, across the harbour from Halifax, catching the small garrison and most of the inhabitants in their beds, killing eight, and capturing several others. The British thereafter referred to it as the Dartmouth Massacre, and it convinced Cornwallis that it would be dangerous and foolhardy to attempt new settlements away from the immediate vicinity of Halifax until the threat to their security could be removed.[24] In the late summer of 1751, however, Cornwallis received news that gave him hope of a peace with the Native tribes. The governments of New England regularly held conferences with the Abenaki of Maine, and Nova Scotia was usually represented there by Paul Mascarene, who had negotiated the first treaty with representatives of Nova Scotia tribes in 1725. Since not all the tribes were present in 1751 when commissioners gathered at Fort George on Casco Bay, negotiations were less than complete, but among those who showed up were eight Maliseets. One of them, Mascarene reported, was a chief named Monsarrett who 'promised to go to Halifax with some deputies from his tribe to treat of peace with Your Excellency and to bring the Micquemacques in, and in the meantime to cease all acts of hostility.'

For the next several months, British optimism increased. Natives failed to arrive to make peace, but they avoided hostile acts. By the summer of 1752, just before taking his leave of the governorship, Cornwallis, hoping to set the stage for a formal peace treaty, issued a proclamation repealing his earlier injunction against the Micmac.[25] His successor, Peregrine Thomas Hopson, maintained the initiative by seeking out Micmac leaders who might come in and negotiate a peace. He soon found such a person in Jean-Baptiste Cope, chief of a small band on the eastern shore, who, encouraged by presents, arrived in Halifax in September 1752.[26] While he could speak only for the 90 persons in his own band, Cope promised to sign a treaty and to bring in as many other Micmac chiefs as he could to do likewise. It turned out that Cope could not attract any other Micmac leaders, but in November he and several other members of his band formally signed a treaty that Governor Hopson and his Council intended should be a model for treaties to be signed with all the other Micmac people. A printed proclamation spread the word widely that 'the Chibenaccadie [Shubenacadie] Tribe of Mick Mack Indians, Inhabiting the Eastern Coast of this Province' had signed a treaty. Hopson was delighted, although most of the remaining 2,000 or so Micmac people rejected Cope's action as the work of a renegade.[27]

Until April 1753, all Hopson's information suggested that his peace overtures were working. The Micmac remained quiet during the winter following the signing of Cope's treaty, and on 12 April, Glaude Gisigash, 'an Indian who stiles himself Governor of La Heve,' came into Halifax to seek similar terms. But within days, Micmac intentions became ambiguous. First, two English settlers paddled into Halifax Harbour in an Indian canoe, the survivors, so they swore in an affidavit, of a group of four that had been attacked by Micmacs along the eastern shore. Their two colleagues had been murdered, they said, but they had eventually escaped after killing six of their captors and taking their scalps to prove it. Second, Cope's son, Joseph, arrived in Halifax with the news that the Micmac were divided on the issue of peace – a fact that seemed to make sense of the attack just reported – and that, for their own safety, Cope and Gisigash wished to remove to the Halifax vicinity with their people and therefore requested that a vessel be sent to bring in their provisions. The council agreed, and a ten-man sloop sailed for the eastern shore. Only one survivor of the crew ever returned. He was Anthony Casteel, an Acadian in the British employ as an interpreter, who reported that the crew had met Jean-Baptiste Cope as planned, but that Cope and his band had turned on them, seizing and killing all except him because he was French. After a harrowing journey that took him to Micmac encampments and eventually to Louisbourg, where he was interviewed by the French governor and by Abbé Le Loutre, he was released with strict warnings to the British that treaties with the Micmac would not be tolerated and that British forts were doomed.[28] Hopson's treaty-making efforts, so it seemed, had failed.

Episodes such as this convinced Governor Hopson that 'what we call an Indian War here is no other than a pretense for the French to commit hostilities upon his Majesty's subjects.' The evidence, however, suggests that French influence was not as absolute as the British believed. In fact the Micmac were divided among themselves; some worked much more closely with the French than others did, and even those who did so may well have had their own objectives, which were simply congruent with French goals. Still, the French were well informed about Micmac activities in general and tried their best to turn them to their own advantage. Clearly they often succeeded. French sources reveal that Cope's treaty angered many Micmacs, that Cope and Gisigash subsequently dismissed the treaty as only a trick to get British presents, and that under threats from fellow Micmacs, Cope had agreed to the plan to lure a vessel out of Halifax to the eastern shore where its crew would be killed in revenge for the six Micmacs lost earlier. Cope's request for a British vessel, in short, was a hoax. Governor Hopson acknowledged in his official letters that his treaty had failed to bring about peace. He would try again with the Cape Sable Micmacs later that fall, but for now his conclusion was that 'very little progress can be made in the service I have the honour to be employed in, until the French flag is removed out of this province.' Only then would the Native people lose their ability to disturb the British and 'make proper submissions to His Majesty's government and live under it in peace and quietness.'[29]

The need to come to terms with the Micmac was crucial if Governor Hopson were to get on with his principal task of settling Nova Scotia. German and Swiss Protestants from the Rhineland, poor 'Palatines' recruited by an English agent, John Dick of Rotterdam, were drawn to Nova Scotia by promises of free land and the British government's undertaking to pay their passage. At first, in order to repay the government, they worked in Halifax where the demand for construction labour was great; but many then remained almost three years, awaiting a time when they could safely plant a new community. Early plans had been to settle them at Musquodoboit Harbour, and surveys had actually been carried out there in 1752. But the continuing fear of Native attack led Hopson to fix on a site on the other side of Halifax, on the south shore at a place the Micmac and French called Mirligueche, but the British renamed Lunenburg. The German Protestants were part of a long-planned scheme to counterbalance the large Acadian population of Nova Scotia at a time when English migrants, it seemed, preferred to go to the better-established English colonies to the south. The arrival of the Germans and the necessity of feeding and housing them until they could be settled had contributed to the pressure on Nova Scotia governors to get a peace treaty with the Micmac. Yet even in the spring of 1753, Hopson was receiving warnings from the little fort at Pisiquid [Windsor] that as many as 300 Natives nearby were prepared 'to oppose the Settlement of Merlegash and intend to begin their March there as soon as they have information when the Settlers are to Sail.'[30]

Despite this alarming news, Hopson was determined to establish the town of Lunenburg, which was already partially laid out by surveyors. In June a flotilla of vessels from New England arrived to remove 1,450 foreign Protestants and some Halifax craftsmen the short journey down the coast. Supervised by Charles Lawrence, who eventually replaced Hopson as governor, and protected by several ships of the British Navy and about 160 regular soldiers, the German settlers occupied their designated town lots and began constructing houses, while surveyors set out a town common as well as garden plots and thirty-acre farm lots for each head of household and single man. It was an enormous undertaking. There was a good deal of cohesion provided by language and religion (most were German Lutherans) and by the sensible official decision to assign civil and militia leadership roles to Germans, but this was mixed with apprehension about Natives and grumbling about the hard work. There was also a three-year accumulation of grievances and a growing belief that someone was withholding the building materials and provisions that had been promised them by the government. By December, anger suddenly turned into an armed insurrection. It took a prolonged civil trial and the stern hand of the British military to restore peace in the community, which, within a couple of years, finally began to settle into the fishing and farming economy that was to sustain it.[31]

While the British tried their hand at treaty-making and settling foreign Protestants, the French were busy with their own plans for resettling Acadians in order to strengthen their hold on Chignecto and on the area now known as New Brunswick. This project, as Abbé Le Loutre explained in his autobiography, had reached a critical point in the summer of 1752. There were by then more than 2,000 settlers, an incredible shortage of provisions, and great marshlands near Beauséjour that needed draining and dyking if the Acadians were to practise their particular type of agriculture and thus become self-sufficient. As a result, Le Loutre left Beauséjour in August 1752 and travelled, by way of Quebec and Louisbourg, to France where he asked the highest authorities for 50,000 livres to pay for the massive draining and dyking project he had in mind. Le Loutre succeeded, but it was June 1753 before he was back at Louisbourg. When he then learned about the Treaty of 1752, he was enraged. Cope was not the head of the Shubenacadie but the 'tail,' he claimed, and if the British wanted to deal with these Natives,they should have done so through him.[32] Le Loutre doubtless exaggerated his influence with the Micmac, but it is noteworthy that the signing of Cope's treaty and the curious lull in Micmac militancy coincided with his absence from the country, and the revival of hostilities accompanied his return.

By midsummer of 1753, Le Loutre was back at Beauséjour with 300 Micmac families encamped nearby. French accounts for August show that Le Loutre paid out '1800 argent de L'Acadie' to Micmacs in payment for '18 scalps which they took from the English in different incursions that they have made on their establishments during the last months.' But just then, after several years of surrogate warfare marked by regular reports from French officials that Micmacs were both constantly harassing the English and being supplied with arms and provisions by the French, French Native policy took a new turn. The larger interests of France at this point dictated that there not be full-scale war with Britain before the French were ready, leading Governor Duquesne of New France to write to his military commander at Beauséjour in July 1753 that he was 'prohibiting the Killing of the English,' and 'if therefore, the Indians in your district ask for permission to do so, tell them that I have forbidden you to do so.' Duquesne acknowledged that the French did not have, nor could they have, absolute control over what the Micmac did: 'As the Micmac have gone on the warpath against the English, you can scarcely prevent their striking at distant places in the spirit of vengeance.' But both he and the French at Beauséjour knew that the construction of dykes and the completion of the fortress, essential before the ultimate removal of Acadians behind the Missaguash, required a peaceful environment. Given the strained relations already existing between Britain and France, it was going to be a race against time for the French to complete their project before war broke out. Meanwhile, Le Loutre, the recognized man in charge, had Duquesne's unqualified backing: 'I cannot do otherwise than approve the efforts of the Abbé Le Loutre to have the uncultivated land occupied. No one is more capable than he is [to oversee this project] and to encourage the inhabitants to undertake a solid settlement.'[33]

The French idea of keeping the Natives quiet for the time being actually benefited both the French and the English. Le Loutre's followers worked tirelessly building dykes, *aboiteaux*, and roads at Chignecto, while his emissaries applied pressure on Acadians at Minas and elsewhere to accept Le Loutre's authority and remove from British soil to French.[34] The new British governor at Halifax, Charles Lawrence, meanwhile perceived that the Native threat was diminished, providing an opportunity to expand and secure British settlements. In June he granted a 20,000-acre plot to some of the principal people in Halifax for a new settlement at Musquodoboit, while British troops explored the Shubenacadie Valley, the occupation of which, the governor reasoned, would tighten the security of both Dartmouth and Halifax against future Native attack.[35]

Even though fear of Native hostility continued to govern British policy in Nova Scotia, official minds were not closed to the possibility of peaceful accommodation. Despite the collapse of peace on the eastern shore, the British did not formally renounce the Treaty of 1752 until 1756, and meanwhile they had two encounters with the Micmac suggesting that some Natives were clearly under French control and others were not. The British concluded that their policy must take account of this. In November 1753, two representatives of the Cape Sable Micmac arrived in Halifax, sent on from Lunenburg where they had first presented a message of peace to the British commander. The Cape Sables were a small band of about sixty persons who lived on the south shore. Their spokesmen convinced the governor and Council that they were not taking part in the general hostilities, and their band was therefore given winter provisions to hold their friendship. The second encounter, however, raised sceptical eyebrows, because Abbé Le Loutre attempted to serve as an intermediary. Through a British officer at Fort Lawrence, Le Loutre sent the message that the Natives wished to make proposals 'towards establishing a General and lasting Peace.' The council dealt with the request in July 1754, and agreed that the Natives 'or anybody on their behalf might come here with great security to make their proposals and that nothing should be wanting on our part to establish a general peace.'[36]

British doubts may well have grown out of what they were observing at Chignecto. Here, in the summer of 1754, Le Loutre's amazing engineering feats manifested themselves on the great sweeping marshlands of the isthmus; he now had in his workforce and within a forty-eight-hour marching radius about 1,400 to 1,500 Acadian men. Nearby at Baie Verte there was a summer encampment of about 400 Natives that would have been one of the largest concentrations of Native people in the Atlantic region at that time. Altogether, he had a substantial fighting force capable of defending itself against anything the Nova Scotia government might have mustered at that time. But Le Loutre's construction work was still incomplete; he needed time, and perhaps even more he needed to extend his influence among the Micmac people and to demonstrate to them that French interests and their own interests coincided. Such circumstances explain Le Loutre's willingness to draft the Micmacs' letter to the British, even while opening to question its provenance and purpose. It proposed, in a nutshell, that a substantial portion of Nova Scotia should be recognized by the British as Micmac territory. It would run from the isthmus to Minas, then to Cobequid and Shubenacadie, including Le Loutre's old mission, across to Musquodoboit, then along the eastern shore to Canso, and finally through the strait (or Fronsac) along the north shore and back to Baie Verte. For a people who lived by hunting and fishing, argued Le Loutre, this was a reasonable demand, and doubtless the Micmac thought so too, given the reports that were coming in to them at Baie Verte about British expansion into their former hunting grounds. Le Loutre's letter to the British was transparent where it served his purpose, but in fact utterly silent on one crucial point. The land proposal would have the effect of creating a Native buffer state between a rather truncated British Nova Scotia and a French Acadia occupying all of present-day New Brunswick, Prince Edward Island, and Cape Breton. Moreover the proposal would leave the British with precisely the small area that French boundary commissioners in Paris were at that very time claiming was the only land surrendered by France in the Treaty of Utrecht in 1713. The Nova Scotia Council interpreted the proposal as a strategic manoeuvre on Le Loutre's part reflecting French objectives, and they rejected it as 'too insolent and absurd to be answered through the Author.' However, if the Micmac were at all serious about making peace, they could come into Halifax 'where they will be treated with on reasonable conditions.'[37]

In February 1755 the Micmac replied by sending as their emissary a Micmac named Paul Laurent, who had for a time lived in captivity in Boston and could speak English. Laurent's message was that a peace treaty depended on a land grant similar to the one outlined in the Le Loutre letter, and while he was not empowered to negotiate this, he asked for a written reply 'indicating the Quantity of Land that they would allow them, if they thought what was required was too much.' While the Council rejected the proposed land cession as 'unreasonable,' it was quite willing to set aside a tract of land 'for your hunting, fishing, etc. as shall be abundantly sufficient for you and what we make no doubt you, yourselves, will like and approve.' Moreover, the Council extended this offer by letter to all 'the different Tribes of the Mickmack Indians,' assuring them that the concept of setting aside lands for Native occupancy was acceptable provided it was negotiated within the framework of a general peace treaty sanctioned by all the Micmac chiefs together, a condition that clearly reflected British disillusionment with past experience.[38]

Before anything could come of peace negotiations, fighting broke out between British and French in the distant trans-Appalachian west; by 1755, Nova Scotia was drawn into the conflict, followed within another year by most of Europe and the Americas. Armed conflict quickly destroyed whatever distinctions there were between French and Native objectives in the region, as the British lumped both groups together as the common enemy. Moreover, the British had now become deeply suspicious of the Acadians, many of whom had participated directly in France's design to create a new Acadia, or at least had indirectly lent their support, raising troublesome questions about their neutrality once war began.

By the summer of 1754, British officials had become alarmed by the out-migration of Acadians from Nova Scotia. The impact on the major population centres of the Minas Basin area, with the exception of Minas itself, was enormous. Almost the entire community of Cobequid, about 1,000 persons, and a very large part of Pisiquid, several hundred, removed to Ile Saint-Jean over a three-year period. More than 2,000 others moved to Chignecto and the Shepody Basin area, although by 1754 some of these wanted to return to the richer farmlands they had left behind. These mass movements created problems at both ends of the migration. Without civil courts to act as moderators, those who remained behind fell into acrimonious disputes about land boundaries and ownership. In the new areas, the time-consuming tasks of clearing forestalled planting and the quick achievement of self-sufficiency, forcing a continuing dependence on the old settlements. Minas Basin communities willingly responded to the call for basic foodstuffs; the breadbasket of the region, they raised wheat and other grains, produced flour in no fewer than eleven mills, and sustained herds of several thousand head of cattle, sheep, and hogs. Regular cattle droves made their way over a road from Cobequid to Tatamagouche for the supply of Beauséjour, Louisbourg, and settlements on Ile Saint-Jean. Other exports went by sea from Minas Basin to Beaubassin or to the mouth of the St John River, carried in Acadian vessels by Acadian middlemen. The new economy was characterized by poverty and deprivation in many new settlements and a contrasting wealth for the most enterprising in the old.[39]

This period of rapid social and economic change among Acadians, however, quickly created political problems that Acadians did not anticipate and that many did not fully understand. The British had not only made it difficult for young Acadians to expand into new agricultural lands; they also opposed Acadian emigration into French territory, knowing that it would eventually strengthen French power in the region. The Halifax government attempted to prevent it by developing an elaborate passport system that virtually forbade the free movement of Acadians into and out of the province. For the most part, the prohibition was unenforceable. Secondly, Halifax attempted to control trade by enforcing imperial acts that forbade trade in enumerated goods with foreign countries or colonies. Thirdly, their war with the Micmac led the British to interpret Acadian supply of Native people as a belligerent act. These developments combined to convince the British that the Acadians were not, as they professed, maintaining political neutrality; migrants were helping the French to establish themselves illegally at Beauséjour, food exports supported what amounted to the revival of a new French Acadia, and Acadian provisioning of the Native allies of the French made possible a protracted conflict that stood squarely in the way of British ambitions to establish new Protestant communities.[40]

Were the Acadians still neutrals by 1754? There is certainly no easy answer to this question. Circumstances were changing the definition of neutrality. There were many Acadians who in all good conscience claimed that they were scrupulously neutral, meaning that they would not take up arms for or against either British or French. What is more, they denied that they were sending foodstuffs to the French. But this was true only in the narrow sense that most individuals were not themselves exporting produce; in their changed economy, middlemen were in fact buying up all the agricultural surplus of the region and shipping it directly to the French. By 1754, the British reported that no Acadian produce was reaching the Halifax market. In fact, when British merchants attempted to buy directly from Acadians, they were refused. In the fall of 1754, Acadians who had regularly supplied the small British fort at Pisiquid with winter firewood refused to supply it. Halifax ordered the arrest of a handful of Acadian middlemen and a priest whom they suspected of preaching defiance. Then they took the drastic step of passing a new Corn Law, forbidding Acadian exports until the Halifax market had been supplied, while a governor's proclamation warned shippers of heavy penalties should they attempt to export grain without the governor's permission.[41] How Acadians disposed of surplus food was in effect becoming a test of loyalty, establishing the framework for a new moral economy in which the British and Acadians were clearly not in agreement. For Acadians, sending food to distant relatives was perfectly consistent with social and cultural traditions in which family was central, and it was far from a political act. But for British officials, mostly military, Acadian behaviour was interpreted in strategic terms; they understood that conflict requires logistical support and that food supply was a critical controlling factor in the power struggle in which they were involved.

To make matters even worse for the Acadians, the British devised a war plan for Nova Scotia that focused on cutting off the food supply to the two principal French forts in the region, Beauséjour and Louisbourg.[42] This would require not only siege tactics but also attention to the source of supply. The French at Beauséjour were taken almost completely by surprise on the morning of 2 June 1755, when forty British vessels of various sizes anchored in a cove just out of sight of the fort and began disembarking 2,000 British regulars and New England militiamen under Robert Monckton, all of whom marched up towards Fort Lawrence unresisted. The French commander, Vergor, immediately called in the Acadian and Native men in the vicinity to augment his puny garrison of 165, burnt Acadian buildings that might fall into British hands, and sent pleas for reinforcements to Louisbourg and the mouth of the St John River. After several days of skirmishing with casualties on both sides, the British moved in heavy guns and began firing large shells and bombs, eventually scoring a direct hit on a casemate that killed several French officers and a British prisoner. Vergor's key men argued about what to do; one account reported that 'M. l'Abbe de Laloutre vehemently proclaimed that it was far better to be buried in the

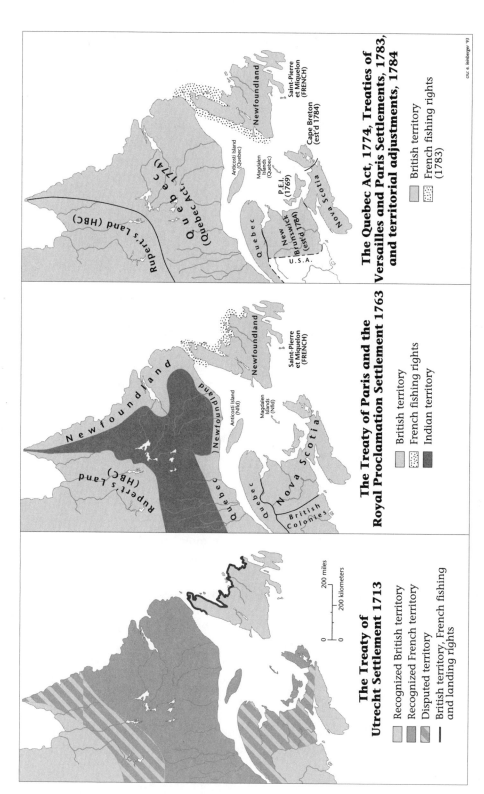

**The Treaty of
Utrecht Settlement 1713**

Recognized British territory

Recognized French territory

Disputed territory

British territory, French fishing
and landing rights

200 miles

200 kilometers

**The Treaty of Paris and the
Royal Proclamation Settlement 1763**

Newfoundland

Rupert's Land (HBC)

Quebec

Newfoundland (Newfoundland)

Quebec

Nova Scotia

British Colonies

Anticosti Island (Nfld)

Magdalen Islands (Nfld)

Newfoundland

Saint-Pierre et Miquelon (FRENCH)

British territory

French fishing rights

Indian territory

**The Quebec Act, 1774, Treaties of
Versailles and Paris Settlements, 1783,
and territorial adjustments, 1784**

Rupert's Land (HBC)

Quebec (Quebec Act, 1774)

Quebec

New Brunswick (est'd 1784)

Nova Scotia

Quebec

U.S.A.

Anticosti Island (Quebec)

Magdalen Islands (Quebec)

P.E.I. (1769)

Cape Breton (est'd 1784)

Newfoundland

Saint-Pierre et Miquelon (FRENCH)

British territory

French fishing rights (1783)

csc e. leinberger '93

Political-territorial claims in northeastern America, 1713–84

Fort than to surrender it.' But Vergor, knowing by now that they would not be reinforced, saw the hopelessness of their situation and sent envoys to the British with articles of capitulation. A surprised Monckton promptly agreed to the surrender, with conditions that paroled the French garrison to Louisbourg and pardoned the Acadians for their participation. Within days, the French likewise surrendered Fort Gaspereaux near Baie Verte and abandoned their fort at the mouth of the St John River to a small British force.[43] Le Loutre disappeared from Beauséjour before the British entered, his dream of a new Acadian homeland under the flag of France dashed forever. But what seemed like a complete British victory was far from that: there were no terms with the Micmac and the Maliseet, who remained to threaten British power at Chignecto as throughout Nova Scotia, and who continued to work closely with the still-intact network of French priests. And Louisbourg still loomed as a far more powerful threat than Beauséjour, strengthened, as it was believed, by the supply of Acadian foodstuffs.

The British answer was to destroy the base of supply by deporting the Acadians. The Council in Halifax justified the policy on the grounds of widespread refusal of Acadians to swear an unqualified oath of allegiance to the British king. In reaching their decision, they swept aside Acadian petitions that professed loyalty or neutrality or that promised a complete surrendering of arms.[44] Critical to the British decision was the availability of several hundred New England militiamen fresh from the Beauséjour victory who might oversee the process of expulsion. Col. John Winslow of Massachusetts commanded about 500 troops in the largest operation at Minas, or Grand Pré, where Acadian farmers and their families were rounded up and told that, for their failure to take the oath, their homes and farms were confiscated and they must board waiting ships with only the personal possessions they could carry. For the Acadians, the deportations (there were eventually several spread over the duration of the war) brought untold hardships. Not only were they torn from lands that they had tilled over several generations, but families were split up and hundreds died from the ordeal. In the fall of 1755, about 2,000 people were removed from Minas and another 1,100 from Annapolis to be spread out along the Atlantic coast from Massachusetts to Georgia. Several hundred others escaped by fleeing into the woods and hiding in places like the eastern and northern shores of present-day New Brunswick that were beyond the effective limits of British administration in Nova Scotia, or by removing to Ile Royale or Ile Saint-Jean. The French regular officer Boishébert established a headquarters on the Miramichi River from which he helped Acadians escape to Quebec, while rallying others to maintain an armed resistance at Chignecto. Several hundred remained in the Petitcodiac-Memramcook area until finally routed in 1758.[45] Others were kept as prisoners in the Halifax area until new legislation in 1764 again offered freedom to all who would take an oath of allegiance. Remarkably, the Acadian revival began almost at once. Freed prisoners soon joined returning refugees in re-establishing Acadian communities in scattered locations ranging from the southern tip of Nova Scotia to the Bay of Chaleur.

The expulsion of the Acadians remains a controversial subject for historians, who have argued, among other things, that it was an expression of New England imperialism, a greedy wish for Acadian lands, or the policy of vindictive British military men like Charles Lawrence.[46] While most historians conclude that the deportation was cruel and unnecessary, a balanced account must take note of the circumstances or the context in which the deportation occurred. It took place in a time of war, a bitter war between inveterate enemies for whom possession of Nova Scotia had become symbolic of their power and prestige in the international world. Moreover, for British Nova Scotians, this was not a new war. Rather, it appeared as a continuation of the violent resistance that had met the attempts of the British since the 1740s to build Halifax and enlarge their settlements in Nova Scotia, a war with Micmac and Maliseet that had been, in all but name, as British officials believed, a war with France. Unfortunately for the Acadians, the British had come to see them as willing accomplices in this contest. After 1713, the British had moved carefully to win over the Acadians of Nova Scotia to become faithful subjects of the British Crown. They expected oaths of allegiance to Britain but, in their numerical weakness, settled for the promise of neutrality in the event of war between Britain and France. Even in the war that ended in 1748, despite scattered evidence to the contrary, the official British position was that most Acadians had maintained their neutrality. But it was now three generations since Nova Scotia had become British, and the British believed they had the right to expect more than neutrality, especially when they experienced what they believed were flagrant abuses. Governor Lawrence believed that he had solid evidence that Acadians had provided both the French and the Native people with 'intelligence, Quarters, provisions, and assistance in annoying the Government' during the 'Indian War'; the movement of nearly 2,000 Acadians to Le Loutre's settlements and their assistance in building dykes and fortifications beyond the Missaguash seemed far from a neutral act; and the simple fact that 'three Hundred of Them were actually found in Arms in the French Fort at Beauséjour when it surrendered' was the last straw.[47]

The expulsion of the Acadians was an act of war taken by a military governor for military reasons. While the normal practice in eighteenth-century warfare was to respect the civilian population and to confine military conflict to the battlefield (and even there to observe widely accepted rules of civilized behaviour), experience had already changed the rules in Nova Scotia. The 'Indian War' had done much to create the condition of total war; British civilians had not been spared, and as Lawrence saw it, Acadian civilians had provided intelligence, sanctuary, and logistical support.[48] But the question remains, was it necessary for military reasons for Lawrence to take so drastic a step? The facts must here speak for themselves. If the object was to undermine France's ability to defend its interests in the region so that the British might remove French power completely, nothing could have been more effective or disruptive than the expulsion.

The French had, in fact, created a monstrous problem for themselves: even in time of peace, or of the quasi-peace from 1749 to 1755, the great fortress of Louisbourg had trouble feeding itself and the growing number of people who were dependent on it. Supplies from France were inadequate. Louisbourg relied on provisions from Quebec and Acadia and on legal and illegal shipments from the British colonies.[49] The French themselves added to their problem with the huge Acadian resettlement program; until crops grew on reclaimed land of the Tantramar marshes and in the fertile soils of Ile Saint-Jean, France had to feed not only its garrisons but a sizable civilian population as well. Add to this the facts that the lives of hundreds of normally self-sufficient Native people had been completely disrupted by their service to the French cause and that these Natives also needed regular supplies of food and ammunition, and one can quickly see how fragile was the underlying economic support for the French presence. Recognizing the problem, in 1753 and 1754 Le Loutre temporarily stopped pressing Acadians at Minas to evacuate to his new settlements. Instead, he encouraged them to grow more grain, which they did in record quantities sufficient to support the large French, Acadian, and Native population otherwise occupied in the service of France. Yet the growing of bumper grain crops at Minas was meant to be only a temporary expedient; the French themselves were planning the complete evacuation of the Acadians in this area just as soon as their new lands were secure and under cultivation.[50] In fact, through Le Loutre's efforts, a new French priest, Henri Daudin, was specifically sent out from France to work in the Minas and Annapolis Valley region, ostensibly as a parish priest but covertly as the agent of France, to convince Acadians that they must prepare to evacuate to Le Loutre's settlements.[51] The expulsion completely disrupted this plan and destroyed the only substantial prop there was to France's broader scheme to undermine British power in Nova Scotia; it was a military step of profound consequence. At one stroke, the expulsion not only deprived France of its only ready supply of produce in the region, but also magnified the supply problem, as the hundreds of Acadians scattered about the region in hiding appealed directly to Louisbourg for help, particularly for food. The former dependence of the Native people on the Acadians and on Beauséjour also became immediately apparent: 'We already see the hardship that the Indians suffer on the frontiers of Acadia because of the visits they make here,' wrote Louisbourg's highest officials. 'They seem zealous and ready to serve the king, but we cannot employ them without feeding them, and we beg of you to procure for us enough foodstuffs to be able to do it.' What they asked was only the beginning. The supply problem plagued the French for the rest of the war,[52] they never resolved it, and maybe more than any other single factor – including the massive assault that eventually forced the surrender of Louisbourg – the supply problem spelled doom to French power in the region.

The expulsion of the Acadians, however cruel for the victims, made sense to British officers in simple military terms, as much sense as it made later for the retreating Russians to burn their own lands before Napoleon's dreadful invasion, or for General Sherman to destroy everything in his path as his unchallenged army drove its powerful way across Georgia in the American Civil War. Total war has its own perverse logic, which Lawrence, with his military background, understood probably as well as anyone did in the eighteenth century. He could not have foreseen how completely incapable of solving the problem the French at Louisbourg would be, but he fully believed that the expulsion robbed them of both the means and the incentive to wage war: 'it furnishes us with a large quantity of good Lands ready for immediate Cultivation, renders it difficult for the Indians, who cannot as formerly be supply'd with provisions and Intelligence, to make incursions upon our Settlers, and I believe the French will not now be so Sanguine in their hopes of possessing a province that they have hitherto looked upon as ready Peopled for them the moment they could get the better of the English.'[53]

While the expulsion seriously undermined French fighting ability, it did not diminish their determination nor that of their Native allies. By the spring of 1756, Governor Lawrence had reports from all parts of the province littering his desk detailing the hit-and-run incursions of Micmac and Maliseet warriors. With this information now before them, governor and Council agreed to a new proclamation. Notwithstanding the Treaty of 1752, it read, 'the Indians have of late, in a most treacherous and cruel manner killed and carried away divers of his Majesty's Subjects in different parts of the Province.' The officers and subjects of the British Crown in Nova Scotia were therefore commanded 'to annoy, distress, take and destroy the Indians inhabiting different parts of this province, wherever they are found,' and a reward was offered for prisoners or scalps.[54] Effectively, the proclamation represented the abandonment by the British of their treaty-making policy on the grounds (as the proclamation asserted) that the Micmac themselves had violated earlier treaties and professions of their peaceful intentions. While the Micmac would have put a different construction on events, there is no doubt they believed themselves to be at war. French correspondence from Louisbourg at this time confirms clearly that the Micmac in general were most active in scouting and raiding, in guarding the passages between Nova Scotia and Ile Royale or at Chignecto under Boishébert, or in spying and guerrilla-style attacks in the Halifax area. French officials bragged that their Native allies 'always had some success,' but it is clear from Louisbourg account books that the French paid for the help they got. By late 1756, supplies were regularly dispensed to 700 Natives, while from 1756 to the fall of Louisbourg in 1758 the accounts show regular payments of scalp money, including notably one payment to Baptiste Cope.[55] Indeed, not only were Micmac and Maliseet warriors now essential to the defence of Ile Royale, they had emerged by this time as the most effective offensive force in the region and the most reliable source of intelligence for the French.

British strategy now called for large-scale assaults on Louisbourg and Crown Point in 1758, to be followed by a coordinated two-pronged attack on the heartland of French Canada, first at Quebec City and then at Montreal. The object was the virtual elimination of French power in America. The French could not have known all this, but their intelligence provided broad hints of what was to come and by the summer of 1757 they began their own build-up of military resources on Ile Royale and laid plans for the disposition of their Native and Acadian allies in the event of a full-scale attack on Louisbourg.[56] When the attack came it was overwhelming. An enormous British fleet under Admiral Edward Boscawen anchored in Gabarus Bay just south of Louisbourg in early June 1758, carrying a fighting force of 13,000 men commanded by General Jeffery, Lord Amherst. The defenders – French regulars, militia, Acadians, and Natives – numbered fewer than 4,000. The British increased their prospects by unorthodoxly attacking the relatively undefended rear of the fortress. When they also took key positions beside the harbour, mounted artillery, and bombarded the few French warships there and then the fort itself, Governor Drucour recognized the futility of further bloodshed and surrendered on 27 July, including in his capitulation Ile Saint-Jean and the French garrison there. Within a few months, French regulars had been shipped off as prisoners, replaced by a small British garrison under Edward Whitmore (with the title of 'Governor'), while the Native people who had been so carefully recruited, provisioned, trained, and deployed had dispersed (fleeing, in fact, with Father Maillard before the inevitable surrender had occurred). Two years later, the British levelled the structure to its foundations so that it would never again tempt its builders back.[57] While the taking of Louisbourg was in a sense a dress rehearsal for the ultimate British attacks on Quebec City and Montreal, it was more than this. It marked the end of French power in the region, closing an era stretching back to 1603, and leaving France's Native allies and the remaining Acadians to fend for themselves.

As they had done in the past, however, Micmac and Maliseet warriors continued to carry the war to the British, even when their principal support had been removed, and they did this by returning to the guerrilla tactics they had employed so effectively at the high tide of the Micmac War in the early 1750s. Even though Governor Lawrence advertised in New England newspapers in 1758 that Nova Scotia was now open for settlement, incursions by Micmacs and Acadians in the Minas and Pisiquid areas effectively prevented it until 1760. Micmac raiders were also attacking British vessels along the coast. It was bad enough to lose civilians as close to the capital as Dartmouth, lamented Governor Lawrence, but 'what is still more extraordinary they have now commenced a War upon us by Sea, and in one Month have taken ten Coasters between this Place [meaning Halifax] and Louisbourg in spite of every measure Mr. Whitmore and I could concert for the Protection of the Coast.'[58]

The continuation of Native warfare, however, was based on a belief that the power of France would be reasserted in the region as it had been in the past; when word reached France's Native allies in the region that Quebec itself had fallen, the will to fight rapidly evaporated. A key element in the Native collapse as a fighting force was the complete removal of their logistical support; without the French to supply them with arms and ammunition and the Acadians or Louisbourg to feed them, they suddenly found themselves in the same desperate misery as the scattered groups of Acadians. Dire need and the recognition that their Acadian neighbours were in even more destitute condition forced them to capitulate wherever they could find British troops. The Maliseet were the first to do so (at Fort Frederic at the mouth of the St John River in November 1759) and they, like the other tribes that followed, were told to send representatives to Halifax to sign formal treaties with the governor and Council.[59]

Representatives of the Maliseet and Passamaquoddy tribes arrived in Halifax in February 1760, and the terms negotiated with them became a model for the several subsequent treaties with the Micmac. Because there were so many bands of the Micmac and they could not all be assembled without great difficulty, the Council decided to treat with the bands separately as their spokesmen came in, a process that took more than eighteen months.[60] A short-lived feature of all these treaties was the establishment of a trading system through government-operated truckhouses where prices were fixed according to a schedule agreed to by the Natives themselves. But enormous government losses, perhaps made worse by an unscrupulous Indian commissary in charge of the operation, brought a hasty end to the truckhouse system by 1764. By this time, all the Nova Scotia Natives had signed treaties with the government, and imperial policy regulated trading practices and required fair dealing with Natives everywhere in North America.[61] For the Natives of what became New Brunswick, there would be later treaties in 1778 and 1779, signed after momentary lapses of loyalty during the American Revolution. But for all the others, the treaties of 1760–1 became the benchmark treaties governing Native–non-Native relations in the region thereafter. According to the official record of the treaty-signing ceremony in Halifax in June 1761, the chief of the Cape Breton Micmacs declared: 'As long as the Sun and Moon shall endure, as long as the Earth on which I dwell shall exist in the same State you this day see it, so long will I be your friend and Ally, submitting myself to the Laws of your Government, faithful and obedient to the Crown.'[62] Whether the translator got the chief's words precisely or not, he accurately captured their portent: the long, disruptive years of war were at an end. The collapse of French power and of the French-Native alliance represented a pivotal point in the history of the Atlantic region and, for the British, both the fulfilment of their strategy and a vindication of their 'total war' approach.

While overshadowed by war, the roots of a new society were already taking firm hold in Nova Scotia, where, among the civilian population, non-military concerns had already begun to force change. For example, dissatisfied with the early court system in which men with no professional qualifications dispensed a rather uneven and, in the view of some, biased justice, the Halifax merchant élite demanded and got reform. New England-born and London-educated Jonathan Belcher was appointed the first chief justice, and the court system was reorganized. Then the same Halifax power-brokers demanded a legislature, as required by the governor's instructions, and after winning the support of the Board of Trade, they succeeded in forcing the first Nova Scotia elections and the establishment of a legislature in 1758. From their new power base in the Assembly, the merchant élite at first played a cautious political role, but when Governor Lawrence suddenly died in 1760 and was replaced by Jonathan Belcher – an event that coincided with the end of war in the province – the potential for struggle between rival views of government quickly turned into reality. Belcher was conservative, imperial-minded, and committed to the application of British law in the colonies; the merchants' priority was to protect their own interests. Angered first by the governor's refusal to approve excise laws that would have favoured local distilleries, and then by his determination to remove the protection of the debtors' act that limited the actions of foreign creditors in Nova Scotia courts, key assemblymen organized a boycott of the Assembly during the winter of 1761–2, thus preventing a quorum. While the Board of Trade supported Belcher and ordered the boycotters dismissed, it eventually came under heavy pressure from Joshua Mauger, now the Assembly's agent in London, pressure that led the board to replace Belcher and reinstate the dissident assemblymen. Nova Scotia politics had come of age.[63]

Emerging also from the shadows of war was the framework of a new society, shaped, however tentatively, by British institutions, and characterized by the plural mix of English, German, Scottish, Irish, and New England settlers. Thousands of new immigrants, most of them from New England, arrived in the period from 1759 to 1762 to settle in new communities along the south shore at Yarmouth, Barrington, and Liverpool, or in the Annapolis Valley, at Annapolis and Granville, or at the Minas end in Horton, Cornwallis, and East and West Falmouth townships. Smaller groups went to Maugerville in the St John Valley or to the Chignecto communities of Sackville, Cumberland, and Amherst. They were pushed out of the older towns of eastern Massachusetts, Rhode Island, and Connecticut by land shortages and dwindling economic opportunities and pulled to Nova Scotia by Governor Lawrence's exaggerated proclamations in 1758 and 1759 offering 100,000 acres of cleared or already productive farmland. Lawrence assured prospective settlers that danger from the French and the Native peoples had been removed, and conscious of the New England traditions of Puritan congregationalism and representative institutions, he promised religious liberty and a familiar style of government.

Thus encouraged to think of Nova Scotia as an extension of New England, the Planters, as they were called, brought their New England ways with them, and in their correspondence, travel, and eventually their trade reinforced the already strong links between the two regions. While settlement patterns varied from one township to another, they generally followed the New England model, with town lots around a village common and an equitable division of marshland, woodland, and cultivable upland. Grantees almost immediately began exchanging their plots to consolidate larger self-contained farms or to raise cash. Fishing or farming occupied almost everyone, although it was to take several years before the Planters advanced beyond the initial stage of dependence on government rations to a subsistence level and finally to the surplus production of livestock and grain for the Halifax and Boston markets.[64] At the census of 1766, there were 11,272 'Freeholders and Inhabitants' in the province, to which the surveyor general added an additional 2,050 made up of Native people, Acadians, and itinerant fishermen, an underestimate that revealed how vague authorities remained about the existence and whereabouts of people who did not fit the established mould.[65] Yet while the Planters now represented the majority, they entered into the political mainstream only gradually, preoccupied as they were with building, clearing, and cultivating. It would take time before they penetrated the oligarchical men's club that effectively controlled Nova Scotia politics.

Meanwhile, before Britain and France came to terms at Paris in 1763, there was one last martial hand to be played out in the Atlantic colonies, this time in Newfoundland. From the time of the Treaty of Utrecht, French fishermen had enjoyed fishing rights and drying privileges along the northern and western shores of Newfoundland, or the French Shore as it was known. They were often engaged in bitter rivalry with English fisherman on the Grand Banks. Limited in their options once they had surrendered Montreal, the French looked for ways of harassing the British wherever damage might be done, and the minister of marine decided on a limited naval and military disruption of the Grand Banks fishermen followed by an assault on the lightly defended Fort William at St John's, from where, it was thought, French and Irish fishermen along the French Shore might be recruited for an armed French return to Cape Breton. The plan was ambitious yet plausible, and in 1762 six vessels of various sizes carrying 750 soldiers were put under the command of Charles-Henri d'Arsac de Ternay and set sail for Newfoundland. Everything went as planned, including the taking of the fort and the destruction of 460 fishing vessels, all within a few days in the month of June. The British, however, reacted firmly and swiftly; within weeks a strong fleet with 1,500 men collected from New York, Halifax, and Louisbourg arrived off St John's Harbour. The lucky de Ternay escaped capture or destruction by slipping out of St John's Harbour in a dense fog, abandoning his little army to face the inevitable. Aboard the British fleet was Newfoundland's next governor, Hugh Palliser, who in his subsequent tenure vigorously policed the French Shore and quickly re-established the rights of English fishermen to fish there, while maintaining the treaty rights of the French to do likewise.[66]

When news that the French had taken St John's reached Nova Scotia, it had an immediate galvanizing impact on both Acadians and Natives, who, as the British observed, began gathering in large numbers at various points throughout the province and behaving in a confident and 'insolent' fashion. Officials were especially alarmed when Natives concentrated close to the two principal towns in the province, Halifax and Lunenburg, where there were also large groups of Acadian 'prisoners,' people who had surrendered at various times during the war and who were allowed a relative freedom to come and go in the Halifax area under parole. The association of Acadians with Natives provoked a nasty reaction even at the highest level, where it was assumed that intermarriage and previous close associations, together with an undiminished loyalty to France among the Acadians, would forever prevent a fully peaceful accommodation of Natives to a British Nova Scotia. The government therefore tried yet another expulsion, an attempt to ship Acadians from the Halifax area to Boston that aborted when the government of Massachusetts refused them permission to land and sent them back where they had come from.[67]

Following the collapse of French power in America, the Micmac and Maliseet struggled to fill the void in their culture and in their lives. They shortly established contact with St Pierre and Miquelon, hoping for French presents and, even more urgently, for a lifeline for their Catholic faith. For a short time these contacts alarmed Nova Scotia and Newfoundland governors sufficiently to provoke the use of military means to curtail them. Moreover, the British continued to fear the political influence of French priests. In due course, however, they relented and allowed priests whom they believed they could trust to minister throughout Nova Scotia. The Micmac themselves continued their summer pilgrimage to Cape Breton, meeting at either Chapel Island or Ile Madame, in part to celebrate their Catholic faith and in part to discuss common concerns.[68] The cultural and political impact of years of contact with the French still shaped their behaviour and would continue to do so for some time to come.

The increased contact with the French islands near Newfoundland may also have led to another accidental collision of peoples; for although Micmacs certainly travelled to Newfoundland in earlier times, they resumed hunting there in 1763, and the increased contact now led them into direct competition with the already dwindling Beothuk, who were forced from the coastal resorts into the interior with its scanty food supply. One theory suggests that warlike Micmacs directly attacked the Beothuk and were largely responsible for their demise.[69] But what seems more probable is that the Beothuk disappearance was the end of a chain reaction that began during the unsettled years of the mid-eighteenth century in Nova Scotia and ended in Newfoundland in the early nineteenth century, a cause-and-effect link that had to do with an increasingly scarce food supply and the erosion of customary food-gathering practices. The hunting-and-gathering lifestyles of Micmac and Maliseet had been completely disrupted by war, their dependence on French and Acadian food supplies having made possible their abandonment or near-abandonment of seasonal hunting; their changed distribution across the region and their tendency to gather in larger groups prefigured disaster when they attempted to return to their traditional lifestyles after the war. Other factors included the lure of British towns where rum could be obtained, the continuance of an ill-conceived program of government presents reinforcing the earlier dependence, and the obvious competition for limited game among an increased planter population. Those Native people who attempted to combine hunting and fishing with their new activities quickly ran out of game, and the disappearance of the moose populations in many areas was to have a horrible impact on an already undernourished society. Consequently, some Micmac hunters, increasingly in touch with southern Newfoundland, turned to hunting there, and in so doing pushed aside the numerically weaker Beothuk and left them without the means of survival. It was a chain reaction that nobody had planned and nobody understood.

The historical lesson, if there are any such to be drawn, is that it is difficult to separate victims from villains. The wiser conclusion may be the historically certain one that the turmoil of the period from 1744 to 1763 radically altered the lives of almost all the area's inhabitants, and the ferocity of the conflict left the principal groups relatively isolated from one another. While the region, given the plural society developing in it, badly needed a cultural or intellectual framework based on accommodation and toleration, neither the materials nor the creative intelligence had yet emerged to forge it. At this stage there were three solitudes – British, Acadian, and Native – and for the time being they would all go their separate ways. The British, of course, dominated, their political forms and cultural institutions essentially defining the mainstream of the Atlantic provinces' history thereafter, although there were Newfoundland fishermen, Halifax merchants, foreign Protestants, New England Planters, and various British military units offering variations on the theme. Remarkably, the Acadians survived, enduring their uprooting and dispersal to return to the south shore, or to Memramcook and Shediac, or to tiny communities hidden away in the far northeast. It was the Native people who suffered the most profound alteration in their lives and cultures, and the change had little to do with whether the English or the French emerged victorious in war, for the balance that had once permitted the coexistence of separate and autonomous European and Native cultures had by now been ineluctably tilted. The war was simply another in a long series of cultural interactions altering the Native lifestyle, and now the rapid influx of non-Native settlers ensured a massive impact on the environment. Some Natives soon chose to adapt more fully to European ways by settling down on small plots of land, for which they received grants or licences of the same sort that were provided to the Planters or the later Loyalists. Eventually, larger tracts were reserved for various bands, forerunners of official reserves established throughout the region in the early nineteenth century. But while some Natives settled down to accept the sedentary European life-style, others remained hunter-gatherers until well into the nineteenth century, visible reminders that history is both change and continuity, and culture like putty in the hands of the gods.

CHAPTER EIGHT

1763–1783

Resettlement and Rebellion

J.M. BUMSTED

The years between 1763 and 1783 formed a period formally demarcated by two international peace treaties, both signed at Paris and each commonly called 'the Treaty of Paris.' The first ended the Seven Years' War and signalled the end of a French imperial presence in North America. The second, only twenty years later, ended the War of the American Rebellion and established the United States of America as an independent republic on the continent. For the Atlantic region of North America, both treaties were extremely significant, and the changes that they brought about were profound. Not only did imperial policy strongly affect the Atlantic region in the years 1763–83, but the region seemed unable to generate its own development, always appearing to be at the mercy of external stimuli – French, British, or eventually American – for its prosperity and growth.

The peace treaty of 1763 reflected for the most part negotiations conducted throughout the preceding year.[1] It contained few surprises. In Article IV, France surrendered Acadia, Cape Breton, and all the St Lawrence islands and coasts (including Ile Saint-Jean) 'without restriction.' Since that same article provided a number of guarantees for the inhabitants of Canada, including liberty of religion and the right to depart their homeland, and a subsequent article explicitly extended these stipulations to the French inhabitants of the Mississippi, such protection apparently had not been extended to the remaining Acadian inhabitants of the eastern region. In concessions not unexpected but controversial at the time and for years thereafter, the British allowed the French to renew the fishing rights granted to them in 1713 by the Treaty of Utrecht, rights that in effect meant that they could land and dry fish on much of the coast of Newfoundland westward from Cape Bonavista and south to Point Riche. The British also ceded the islands of St Pierre

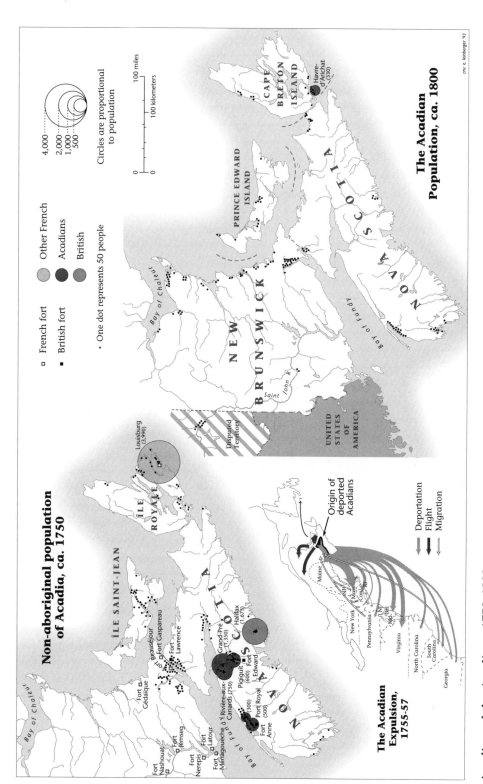

Non-aboriginal population of Acadia, ca. 1750

Bay of Chaleur

ÎLE SAINT-JEAN

Fort Nashouat

Fort Jemseg

Fort Nerepis

Fort Latour

Fort Gédaique

Beauséjour

Fort Gaspareau

Fort Lawrence

ÎLE ROYALE

Louisburg (3,990)

Fort

Ménagoueche

Riviére-aux-Canards (750)

Grand-Pré (1,350)

Pigiguit (600)

Fort Edward

(300)

Port Royal (300)

Fort Anne

Bay of Fundy

NOVA SCOTIA

Halifax (1,675)

□ French fort

■ British fort

· One dot represents 50 people

Other French

Acadians

British

Circles are proportional to population

4,000

2,000

1,000

500

100 miles

100 kilometers

The Acadian Expulsion, 1755–57

Origin of deported Acadians

Deportation

Flight

Migration

Maine

N.H.

Mass.

Conn.

R.I.

New York

N.J.

Md.

Pennsylvania

Virginia

North Carolina

South Carolina

Georgia

UNITED STATES OF AMERICA

Disputed Territory

NEW BRUNSWICK

Saint John R.

Bay of Chaleur

PRINCE EDWARD ISLAND

Bay of Fundy

NOVA SCOTIA

CAPE BRETON ISLAND

Havre-d'Arichat (330)

The Acadian Population, ca. 1800

cnc e. leinberger '93

Acadia and the Acadians, 1750–1800

and Miquelon as an unfortified 'shelter to the French fishermen.' These provisions formed part of a wide-reaching treaty, which, except for the eastern fishing concessions, effectively eliminated the French from North America. In a complicated arrangement, Spanish Florida went to Britain, and Louisiana west of the Mississippi was transferred to Spain. Many in Great Britain had argued that the French ought to have surrendered much more territory around the world, but there could be few complaints about the North American settlement, which the government of George III made the justification of the peace treaty.[2]

At the same time, the British really had no firm plans for any of the territory they had acquired in North America. The principal reason for eliminating the French had been to provide security for the American colonies to the south. Other motives, such as protecting the fisheries or securing Nova Scotia, were distinctly subordinate. Instead of plans, what Britain had for its newly obtained Atlantic property was little more than a series of assumptions that would have to be knitted together into a policy. No concessions had been made at Paris to existing inhabitants, either French or Native peoples, and their interests would not dominate policy making for the lower provinces. Settlement of both new and old territory in the region would be permitted, provided it was done by private entrepreneurs who made no demands upon the public purse. The settlement subsidies for the New England Planters who had been brought to Nova Scotia, part of the package of expenses involved in defending that province after 1749, had been ended in 1762 and were not to be repeated. The earlier colonization of Halifax, as well as the Yankee migration, had proved far more costly than the British government had anticipated, and both programs seemed to demonstrate that subsidized settlement did not work. Private settlement after 1763 would be based chiefly upon more traditional European notions of landholding, involving large landlords and subordinate tenants.

The imperial authorities made their first attempt at overall North American policy after the Treaty of Paris in the well-known Proclamation of 7 October 1763.[3] Four new governments were organized out of the new acquisitions: Quebec, East and West Florida, and Grenada. Quebec was reduced to the St Lawrence settlements, and Newfoundland was given the fishing islands in the Gulf of St Lawrence as well as Labrador. Nova Scotia acquired Ile Saint-Jean (anglicized to the Island of St John) and Ile Royale (renamed Cape Breton Island). Military men who had served in North America were entitled to apply for wilderness land grants, ranging from 50 acres for privates to 5,000 acres for field officers, 'without fee or reward.' No settlement was to take place beyond the coastal Appalachian Mountains, where territory was to be reserved to the Native people. The movement of American pioneers north and south into the newly acquired territories was to be encouraged, and the governments of the new colonies were required to make land grants upon moderate terms to any applicants. The new colonies were also to be given elected assemblies modelled upon those in the older colonies, as soon as possible.

Perhaps significantly, many of the proclamation's clauses dealing with Native people did not extend to the Atlantic region. The region was, however, included in the declaration 'that the several Nations or Tribes of Indians with whom We are connected, and who live under our Protection, should not be molested or disturbed in the Possession of such Parts of Our Dominions and Territories as ... are reserved to them, or any of them, as their Hunting Grounds' and in the provison that any lands not 'ceded to or purchased by Us as aforesaid, are reserved to the said Indians.' The proclamation also suggested that the government had a monopoly over land negotiations with the Indians. It insisted that 'no private Person' could purchase land previously 'reserved' to Native people. Such purchases could be made only at public meetings called 'by the Governor or Commander in Chief of our Colony.' The proclamation may thus have sought to prevent private land deals between speculators and unrepresentative Native people, but it also seemed to indicate that land was reserved to Native people only until the Europeans had need of it, at which point the state could renegotiate the agreement. The aboriginal clauses of the proclamation, particularly, have been subject to a variety of interpretations and litigation.[4]

Between 1763 and 1775, the Atlantic region became a marginal part of a larger continental empire that caused its British masters increasing anxiety. Insofar as the British government concentrated its attention on imperial matters, it was constantly forced to focus on the complaints and demands of the American colonists to the south. The British did permit the creation of another formal colony on the Island of St John in 1769, but made clear that the Island, like its other possessions, would have to be self-financing. While the Atlantic territories were not completely neglected by the imperial administrators, little public money was invested in the region, and no evidence existed of any development policy beyond reliance upon private entrepreneurs, of whom the Island of St John proprietors were only the most notorious. The British government permitted the granting of millions of acres of wilderness in Nova Scotia and the Island of St John to large landed proprietors, many of whom intended (and some even attempted) to recreate European estates in America.

The period between 1763 and 1776 also witnessed another round of British emigration to North America, one that picked up in volume during the critical years of escalating crisis from 1773 to 1776, existing almost as a counterpoint to the worsening political situation. For the first time in its history, the entire Atlantic region was part of an unsubsidized movement of people from Britain to North America, a migration that refused to cease until open warfare made both the transatlantic passage and subsequent resettlement too risky. Precise figures of the numbers in this emigration are not available, although the British government's official data for 1773–6, which showed 9,364 emigrants to British North America travelling on 402 different vessels, seriously understated the total.[5] Whatever the numbers, the available data, which do not include Ireland, suggest that there were really two emigrations: one of single indentured servants (chiefly to the southern colonies), and another of families to the northern regions, including the Atlantic area. The major origins of the new immigrants were in London, Yorkshire, and the Scottish Highlands and Lowlands.

Because so much of the Atlantic region's historiography for this period has been shaped by the fascination of scholars with the breakup of the British Empire, the political crisis has been accorded undue importance in the years between 1763 and 1775. It plainly influenced the classic treatment of the largest colony in the region – John Bartlet Brebner's *The Neutral Yankees of Nova Scotia* – which concentrated upon the problems of the American settlers who had come to Nova Scotia before 1762 and largely neglected the new round of British settlement and its implications.[6] Contemporaries did not realize that the political conflict would result in fissure and open warfare, and historians ought not to anticipate events. Freed from the preoccupations of Brebner, one can see that Nova Scotia and the Island of St John, as well as Newfoundland, were beginning to develop in some very interesting, non-American, ways before 1775.

The elimination of France from North America had not been total in 1763, since as we have seen the French were allowed to carry on a migratory fishery. But the sedentary fisheries at Gaspé and Cape Breton were seriously disrupted, and markets expanded for Newfoundland. The years between 1763 and 1775 were good ones for Newfoundland, as evidenced by a substantial population increase to 12,000 in the winter and 24,000 in the summer. Males in Newfoundland fell basically into only three occupational categories: merchant, boatkeeper, and servant. Merchants kept stores and supplied the fishery; boatkeepers were those who owned the equipment used in the inshore fishery, and were either winterers or summerers; servants (or labourers), disproportionately Irish, were the most numerous group, doing the actual work of fishing and curing.[7]

The structure of the Newfoundland population remained unbalanced, containing only a small proportion of women and children. Such age and gender skewing was not uncommon in recently settled frontier populations in North America, although Newfoundland had ostensibly been developing for nearly 200 years. Newfoundland's total population contained only 10 per cent women and 25 per cent children in the winter, with lower figures of 5 per cent and 15 per cent in the summer, whereas a normal American distribution would have been 25 per cent adult males, 25 per cent adult females, and 50 per cent children. The percentage of males in the western fur trade was even higher – nearly 100 per cent among the Europeans – but here European relationships with females of Native and mixed blood were common, and large mixed families the western norm. In Newfoundland there were few Native people, with the Beothuk rapidly declining in numbers and withdrawn to the interior of the island, hidden from the European population, which clung to the coasts. The opportunity for normal family life was therefore quite restricted in Newfoundland.

Newfoundland had a substantial non-English and non-Protestant population, which was, nevertheless, British (rather than American) in origin. Close to 50 per cent of the wintering population was of relatively recent Irish origin. The Irish influx worried the local authorities. One observer noted of the Irish that a 'Great part ... could not get Employ in the fishery, being oblig'd to wander and walk from place to place, unemploy'd the whole Summer.' Governor Hugh Palliser used the contemporary code-words by which the Irish were discussed without being specifically mentioned when he commented in the late 1760s that the island was 'crouded with Poor Idle and the most disorderly People, who are neither good Fishermen nor Seamen or if they were so, are of no service to England as Seamen they never going there and out of reach, are a nuesance to this Country, being all dealers in Liquor more than Fish to the great Increase of Idleness, Debauchery and every kind of Excess and Vice amongst the Fishermen and others.'[8] Certainly in Newfoundland, as everywhere else in North America where life was hard, the consumption of intoxicating beverages was high. Better wages and the absence of normal family life in Newfoundland probably made the consumption even higher.

In Nova Scotia, the artificial prosperity produced by imperial expenditures on both civilian and military business came to a grinding halt in 1762. The colony had acquired a provincial assembly in 1758; from the perspective of the imperial authorities, this event marked not only political but fiscal maturity, since only a colony with an assembly could raise its own taxes. Like most elective bodies, the Nova Scotia Assembly was considerably more proficient at spending money than at raising it through taxes. It was hampered by two features of the hitherto heavily subsidized nature of Nova Scotia development. One was the gulf between Halifax and the Nova Scotia back-country. The colony's élite resided in Halifax. They not only failed to understand the remainder of the province, but insisted on controlling it politically and economically. Members of the élite – like other similar élites of the era – were interested in acquiring land for speculative purposes and in advancing their own standards of living, but not in constructive public policy. The second factor was the sheer fragility of the Nova Scotia economy once subsidies were removed. The colony may have been relatively rich in natural resources, a fact that led to occasional successes of exploitation by individual entrepreneurs, but it did not have an integrated commercial system. Much commerce was in the hands of New Englanders, who had no reason to encourage Nova Scotia as a rival. There were few autonomous trading connections with potential markets in Newfoundland and the Caribbean. Nova Scotia desperately needed to free itself from New England.

The Yankee Planters attracted to Nova Scotia between 1758 and 1762 – between 7,000 and 8,000 in number – came from land-hungry districts of southern New England.[9] Most were drawn by the promise of the fertile lands vacated by the Acadians, although others came to gain access to the rich fishing grounds of the Nova Scotia coast. Both agricultural and fishing communities were established, the former mainly in the Annapolis Valley, along the Chignecto Peninsula, and on the St John River, the latter along the southwestern coast of the colony. The Annapolis townships had been founded with the same procedures of land allocation and form of local government that migrating New Englanders had been using successfully for more than a century. Unfortunately, the Halifax government did not take kindly to Yankee institutions of democratic local government and worked actively to suppress them, preferring instead a more traditional European political structure modelled on Virginia's system.

Most importantly, the vast majority of the new arrivals to Nova Scotia were very short on capital. Had they possessed substantial financial resources, they would probably never have responded with such alacrity to Nova Scotia's offers, preferring instead to buy land in their own region or to settle in interior parts of northern New England. The drawing power of Nova Scotia went beyond already-developed free land, although Acadian land was a powerful lure. The province had also offered subsidized transportation and assistance in resettlement. The whole process had been a ready-made recipe for successful recruiting mainly among less prosperous New Englanders. In theory there was nothing wrong with repeopling Nova Scotia through a policy of subsidization, but the process meant that those without capital were attracted. Furthermore, the subsidy schemes became part of an artificial wartime prosperity that would be followed by an inevitable depression when war ended. The newcomers quickly discovered that Nova Scotia was not a bargain. Successful Planter settlement would demand not only usable land, but also a market for agricultural surplus. The first could be seized from the Acadians, but the second would require time to develop. In the meantime, Nova Scotia in the 1760s became known as 'Nova Scarcity,' and many of the recent arrivals returned to their homes in New England.

The communities of the south and west coasts of Nova Scotia – like those in Newfoundland and unlike those in the Annapolis Valley – contained few families and were dominated by single men. Many fishing ports tended to fill up in the summer fishing season with men who would return home to New England for the winter, as Simeon Perkins did in Liverpool for many years before eventually settling down in Nova Scotia on a year-round basis.[10] Whether engaged in farming or fishing, the Anglo-American villages of Nova Scotia were characterized by a continual turnover of population, well in excess of 50 per cent within ten years of first arrival. Contemporaries might have explained these high transiency rates in terms of the instability of the Nova Scotia economy of the 1760s and the itinerant traditions of the fishery, but such turnover was common to all pre-industrial communities in England and agricultural settlements in British North America. By and large, the mobile were the less successful members of local society – often the young, but including a core of permanent transients of all ages. Whether mobility was the cause or consequence of failure is still not clear.

One characteristic of the Planter communities, particularly in the agrarian districts, was an initial allocation to any settler of small parcels of land (upland, meadow, town lot) within a township rather than a single contiguous holding. This deliberate attempt at giving each settler an equal start, as well as encouraging village formation, proved unavailing. Farmers scattered across the landscape rather than huddling together, and there was much buying and selling of land to consolidate holdings. For these Planters, freehold tenure was regarded as essential.[11] Significantly, consolidation did not become officially recognized until 1767, for until that date the provincial authorities refused to permit individual ownership of land within township grants, so as to discourage traditions of freehold in Nova Scotia.

The Planter landholding patterns, particularly the insistence on equitably allocated small freeholdings, were not necessarily characteristic of either Nova Scotia or the Atlantic region as a whole. From the outset of the settlement of lands formerly belonging to Acadians, some individuals had intended to recreate European estates based on traditional land-lord-tenant relationships and even slavery. The Anglo-Irish Henry Denny Denson, for example, established 'Mount Denson' in a community just outside Windsor, an estate that in 1770 had a number of tenants and black slaves residing upon it. The Swiss-born mercenary J.F.W. Des-Barres had an even larger estate at neighbouring Castle Frederick and, unlike Denson, was prepared to become a landlord in many parts of the province.[12] Both Mount Denson and Castle Frederick came to be managed by the concubines of their owners. In the St John Valley, the Canada Company – founded in 1764 among officers of the Montreal garrison – acquired 400,000 acres in five townships, as well as an island in Passamaquoddy Bay. The company intended a full range of activity, from the fishery to timbering to the creation of agricultural estates, and it did expend some money before it ceased operation in 1767 and allowed its land to revert to its sixty-eight individual proprietors.[13] In any event, those who after 1763 received government largesse in the form of land grants would tend to follow two patterns. Either they would merely add their undeveloped grants to their portfolios, quietly waiting for settlement by others to raise the value of the land, or they would engage in development themselves, frequently expecting to settle tenants rather than to sell land to newcomers.

Acadians, meanwhile, were still recovering from the effects of the deportations that had taken place in 1755, 1758, and intermittently to 1762. Not all the Acadian population had been eliminated. Some had retreated inland from their villages, and others had gone to remote districts, such as the Magdalen Islands. The French had attempted to relocate those Acadians who made their way to France, but without much success. Many Acadians responded to the post-1763 British policy of permitting resettlement provided that unconditional oaths of allegiance were taken by small groups inhabiting remote areas. Others were attracted by the explicit recruiting practices of merchants, often Channel Islanders, such as the Robin family, who took over the traditional French fishery in the Gaspé and St Lawrence districts.[14] While some Acadians relocated along the traditional dykelands, many avoided their former lands and potential trouble by settling (without proper land title) in unpopulated sections of the region, such as St Mary's Bay in western Nova Scotia, Cheticamp in Cape Breton, Malpeque in the Island of St John, and the northwestern and northeastern sections of what is now New Brunswick.

Some of those Acadians resettling on tidal lands did so as tenants on the estates of J.F.W. DesBarres, who specialized in acquiring land near rivers and marshes in Nova Scotia. Few Acadians had proper land titles to their holdings, and many were consequently forced into the fishery, an occupation that had previously not been common in Acadian communities. Acadians were one of the groups severely underreported in census returns, partly because the census-takers did not regard them as important and partly because the Acadians tended to reside away from the main centres of population, so that much effort was required to enumerate them. A 1767 census in Nova Scotia listed 1,265 Acadians – 650 in Nova Scotia proper, 271 in Cape Breton, 197 on the Island of St John, and 147 in the 'north section' of the mainland (later New Brunswick). The figures for the north section were particularly suspect, but the totals suggest the trend of the post-1763 period. By the turn of the century, there were more than 8,000 Acadians living in the region.[15]

The early development of the Island of St John well illustrates British policy in the Atlantic region after the Treaty of Paris.[16] When military officers and merchants familiar with the region began pressing the British authorities for land on the Island, the authorities were certain that any settlement had not only to pay its own way, but to avoid draining the mother country of precious resources, including manpower. Within these constraints, the government's attitude was liberal. The Board of Trade, responsible for policy recommendations to the Privy Council, rejected a series of proposals from a syndicate headed by the earl of Egmont for colonization of the Island of St John through a complex series of feudal obligations. The board instead ordered the Island surveyed into 20,000-acre townships, and awarded them in 1767 to a list of proprietors that included most of Egmont's original partners.

The proprietors in the region in this period were all required to pay an annual quitrent to the Crown for their land. On the Island of St John, they were expected to pay quite substantial quitrents, but were able to take advantage of an attempted grab of the Island's government by greedy Nova Scotians to argue for a separate colony. This request was granted in 1768 on the condition that the government be financed completely out of quitrent revenue and not become a burden on Great Britain. The proprietors were less successful in meeting the requirements for settlement, however, which called for the establishment of one settler for every 200 acres of land grant within ten years, all of whom were to be either foreign Protestants born in Europe outside the British Isles, or North Americans. These unfulfillable terms ultimately became a built-in excuse for inaction.

Although the Island of St John would not serve as a model for the reintroduction of feudal tenures into British North America, it did offer an alternative social vision to that of the Planter settlements of Nova Scotia: a European-style hierarchical society. Indeed, the terms of grants on the Island were quite similar to those in the millions of acres of land granted in Nova Scotia in the post-war and post-Yankee period. The major difference between the Island grants and those in Nova Scotia was that quitrents were higher, most Island proprietors did pay them, and a number did attempt to settle their properties. The land grants made between 1763 and 1775 did not insist that the land included had to be maintained as a large estate and could not be sold in small parcels as freehold. The Board of Trade may well have thought that those granted land would become land developers rather than estate managers. But the provisions for quitrents and the requirements of settlement did suggest individuals or companies with a fair degree of capital. Were such grantees to invest in this remote and undeveloped corner of British North America, they were not likely to do so merely as land promoters, but as men with strong social intentions as well.

Much of the active investment and involvement by land grantees in settlement before 1775 was by those who sought to create North American estates replicating those in the Old World. Not surprisingly, such men linked their activities to the burgeoning interest in immigration to North America on the part of those from the various constituent parts of the British Isles, although such settlers did not technically fulfil the terms of their grants. On the Island of St John, the lord baron of Scotland, Sir James Montgomery, actually brought Highland settlers under indenture (long-term labour contracts) to establish a flax farm in 1770.[17] A major Highland tacksman, John MacDonald of Glenaladale, led a party of Highland Catholics to the Island in 1772, his intention being to recreate a traditional Highland estate on the Hillsborough River. 'Our Method is to give them by lease for ever a certain number of Acres, such as they can manage easily, they paying us a small yearly Quitrent out of it, & furnishing themselves all necessarys & Passage, only that we must direct & assist them to carry it on,' he wrote to a kinsman.[18] Lieutenant-Governor Thomas Desbrisay, an Anglo-Irishman, recruited tenants in Ireland until ordered to stop by Lord Hillsborough, the colonial secretary; it was on Hillsborough's Irish estates that Desbrisay had been most active.[19] A Quaker merchant named Robert Clark brought out Londoners to New London, intending a religious Utopia on the exposed north shore of the Island.[20] By 1775, there were 1,500 inhabitants on the Island of St John. Few were either foreign Protestants or Americans. Most had been recruited by proprietors in Ireland, Scotland, and England, with the intention of settling them on landed estates under long leaseholds rather than providing them with freehold property.

The extent of settlement and active proprietorial investment on the Island of St John was considerably greater than the British authorities had any real right to expect, given the way in which proprietors had originally been selected. The Island was one of the few jurisdictions in the Empire where substantial amounts of quitrents were ever paid.[21]

Unfortunately, the Island required not just considerable proprietorial involvement and investment, but total commitment. The salaries of its office-holders depended on a 100 per cent collection of the quitrents every year, and those officials were not happy with arrearages. The Island convened a legislative assembly before there was sufficient population to warrant one, chiefly in order to pass legislation directed against quitrent shortfalls. Moreover, Island officers were, with the exception of Governor Walter Patterson (who held a part of one lot), not proprietors themselves. Inevitably the resident office-holders would gang up against the absentee proprietors, with the stakes being most of the vacant land on the Island.

Intentions of establishing a tenantry were not confined to the Island of St John. William Owen, a retired naval officer, attempted in 1770 to settle Campobello Island with thirty-eight indentured servants, retaining title to the land as 'lord of the soil or principal proprietary.'[22] DesBarres was active in establishing tenant farmers in many parts of Nova Scotia: at Falmouth, at Tatamagouche, at Minudie, at Maccan-Nappan, and at Memramcook-Petitcodiac.[23] The Canada Company and its proprietors settled tenants at Gagetown and Burton. Because the immigration from Britain to the region had not yet become a flood when the warfare of the American Rebellion halted it, no clear trend about landholding had been established. It was true that one of the few active land companies granted land in the 1760s, the Philadelphia Company, was prepared to sell land around Pictou to any arriving settlers at 'five pounds sterling for every hundred acres payable two years after their arrival,' attracting the famous immigrants of the *Hector* to their grant in 1773.[24] It was also true that some of the immigrants of the 1770s, particularly those from Yorkshire, had sufficient capital to purchase freehold farms, often improved ones, from restless New Englanders.[25] But not all the new arrivals had capital, and not all intended to pioneer in the wilderness. 'Some,' reported Governor Francis Legge to the British authorities, 'come to purchase, others perhaps, to become Tenants & some to Labour.'[26]

Exact figures for the number of immigrants arriving in the region before 1775, or for their origins, do not exist. What is clear, however, is that by the time of the rebellion the New England component of the population remained dominant in only a few sections of Nova Scotia and was probably no longer a majority even in that province. According to a detailed census as early as 1767, Nova Scotia contained 6,913 Americans (i.e., English-speaking individuals born in North America, most but not all of them Yankees), 912 English, 2,165 Irish, 173 Scotch, 1,936 Germans, and 1,265 Acadians, giving the Americans a bare 51.7 per cent of the total population apart from Blacks and Native people.[27] Since the

New England townships were the best recorded and other groups like Acadians significantly underreported, even in 1767 the New Englanders were probably not a majority. By 1775 a fair proportion of the earlier Planters had returned to New England before the outbreak of warfare, and virtually no new ones from that part of the world replaced them. On the other hand, between 1767 and 1775, perhaps in excess of 2,000 British immigrants, about equally divided between English and Scots, had arrived in the province. The vast majority of the population of the Island of St John was Scottish in origin, although there were also some settlers from England and Ireland among the 1,500 to 2,000 new arrivals on the Island. Newfoundland was equally divided between those of Irish and English origin, and never contained any substantial number of Americans.

On the eve of the American Rebellion, two collateral trends were at work in the Atlantic region, particularly in Nova Scotia and the Island of St John. One of these trends was a substantial decline in the proportion of those of American origin in the total population of the region, with a corresponding reduction in the Yankee social and cultural impact. The other trend was a significant increase in the number of those large landholders attempting to establish European rather than American conditions of land tenure, with a corresponding potential impact upon cultural and social conditions. Neither of these trends would be allowed to work themselves out naturally, because of the eruption of the American Rebellion. In a curious irony, the American separation from the British Empire assured that what remained to Britain in the Maritime region would retain American characteristics and features.

The beginning of open warfare between the American colonists and the British government in April 1775 inaugurated North America's first civil war. Every inhabitant would eventually be forced to choose sides, either for the Continental Congress or for the British Crown. For the inhabitants of the northernmost colonies, those decisions of loyalty would be made against the background of military conflict and economic isolation, often privation. The effects of the American Rebellion upon the region were mixed and often unintentional in nature. Colonization was not so much ended as reoriented away from immigration from Europe to migration within British North America. Not only did Loyalists arrive in large numbers after 1782, but the existing inhabitants of the region tended to retreat to the larger centres where they could be better protected and might enjoy some of the military largesse of the British government. The development of trade and commerce was once again replaced by government subsidy as the principal economic engine of the region.

Although the revolutionaries mounted a military invasion of Canada as part of their overall strategy for winning their independence, neither the Congress nor George Washington's general staff had any serious interest in the Atlantic region, partly because of the British Navy and partly because of the uncertain sentiments of the local population. Only the Planter districts of Nova Scotia were likely to have any affinity with the American position. The Island of St John had been settled almost entirely from the British Isles, and its largest single population group consisted of Highland Scots, who were loyal to the Crown no matter where in North America they landed. As for Newfoundland, its population was unpoliticized and unfamiliar with the issues under agitation. The only newspaper in the entire region was published in Halifax, and outside that town it was extremely difficult to obtain sufficient regular and detailed information to understand and appreciate what was happening in the external world. Before 1775, the Americans had indicated little interest in involving the northernmost colonies in their quarrel with the mother country.[28]

Too much has probably been made of the immediate conflict of loyalty in the Atlantic region. It was a conflict that affected only a minority of the population and only in some sections of Nova Scotia. The former New Englanders may have wanted 'to be neuter,' since, as the inhabitants of Yarmouth explained to the Nova Scotia Council in December of 1775: 'We were almost all of us born in New England, we have Fathers, Brothers & Sisters in that country; divided be-twixt natural affection to our nearest relations, and good Faith and Friendship to our King and Country, we want to know, if we may be permitted at this time to live in a peaceable State, as we look on that to be the only situation in which we with our Wives and Children, can be in any tolerable degree safe.'[29] But the authorities understandably rejected this petition, and there is little reason to assume that neutrality would have preserved the Planter population from the depredations of privateers. Although a good deal of pro-American sentiment was voiced in parts of Nova Scotia in 1775, there was little evidence of armed defiance of authority. Many Yankees who had not already done so returned to New England. Others, like Simeon Perkins – who was a magistrate at Liverpool – carried on their duties, chafing under reports that the residents of his village had 'been represented to the Government as a lawless and rebellious people.'[30] He agreed to attend the assembly meeting at Halifax in October 1775 to confute these charges.

Apart from privateering, direct military activity did not begin until the summer of 1776, initiated by enthusiastic rebels from the Maine district of Massachusetts Bay and a number of former Nova Scotians resident in Maine. The American commander-in-chief, George Washington, was not persuaded that Nova Scotia had given much evidence of serious sympathy for the American cause.[31] Nevertheless, Massachusetts-born Jonathan Eddy, long resident on the Isthmus of Chignecto, recruited a small invading force in 1776, including twenty-seven settlers from Maugerville (a Yankee community on the St John River) and strengthened by a few Acadians. The invaders arrived in August in small boats and without artillery. They managed to find about 100 locals to join their 'army,' and they then attempted to besiege Fort Cumberland. The British quickly sent reinforcements, and the invaders equally swiftly withdrew. Most of those involved were granted amnesty by the Nova Scotia authorities, although some Nova Scotians (including the Acadians) left for the United States, probably permanently. The Fort Cumberland attack was the closest anyone in the region came to actual invasion.

The absence of invading armies did not mean that inhabitants of the region were spared wartime anxiety. The chief instrument of American aggression was the privateer, a legalized pirate operating in times of war in coastal waters under letters of marque. Almost any vessel could be fitted up with guns and its crew armed to the teeth. Smaller commercial vessels could not protect themselves against such armed aggressors. But the privateers also attacked defenceless coastal communities when frustrated by their inability to find more profitable victims at sea. Few places in the Atlantic region escaped unscathed, either at sea or from local looting by privateers.

The best place to catch a glimpse of the effect of privateering on a coastal community is in the pages of Simeon Perkins' diary, a chronicle of day-by-day events in the southwestern village of Liverpool, Nova Scotia. The diary recorded regular offshore activity by privateers, although the village itself was initially spared because of the presence of a British frigate in the harbour through the winter of 1775–6. On 13 September 1776, Perkins noted that 'my brother, Capt. Mason, and Mr. Gideon White are all taken by American privateers. That there is a great number upon the shore, and that they have taken near 20 sail about the Head of the Cape.'[32] A month later he recorded 'the fourth loss I have met with by my countrymen, and are altogether so heavy upon me I do not know how to go on with much more business.'[33] Liverpool managed to avoid an open confrontation with a privateer until April of 1778, when an American captain anchored his sloop in the harbour and offered not to attack his target in return for a £100 ransom. The sloop then left, but soon returned.

Perkins wrote:

I immediately alarmed the people from one end of the street to the other, and mustered about 15 under arms. The sloop came in with Drum and fife going, and whuzzaing, etc. They anchored a little above the Bar, and sent a boat on board Mr. Gorham's schooner, and Mr. Hopkins schr. I gave orders not to speak to them or fire upon, except they offered to come on shore to rob the stores, etc. If they made any such attempt to engage them. They searched the two schrs. mentioned, and returned on board ye Privateer, and hove up their anchor, and went off after daylight.

Perkins, who was a magistrate, was understandably 'mutch fatigued' by the whole business. The need for constant vigilance over several years doubtless wore down everyone in the community. Far from being the romantic figure of popular fantasy, the privateer specialized in intimidation and was in most respects little different from a pirate. From the standpoint of defenceless communities, privateers were little more than professional thugs and gangsters. While a few got rich, most did not. Little of the fruits of victory reached the common seaman, who often suffered the brunt of defeat. Privateering captains recruited young men on the strength of adventure and profits. The song 'Barrett's Privateers,' by the Canadian folk-singer Stan Rogers, does a good job of capturing the unpleasant realities of privateering existence.[34]

The toll taken by civil wars extends even to the marginal areas isolated from the operations of the regular armies and navies. During the American Rebellion the Atlantic region was one of those nasty marginal areas. John Brebner referred to the conflict's 'exhausting, nerve-racking forms – privateering, counter-privateering, the establishment and destruction of privateer bases, and the uncertain business of rival bidding for the friendship of Indians near the Maine boundary.'[35] Brebner appreciated that the real sufferers were the people of the outports, but did not attempt to document this insight at length. The privateers were the guerrilla fighters of the northeast. In a region where almost the entire population lived in or near communities on the sea, where both communications and economic transactions depended entirely upon coastal shipping, the privateers were a totally disruptive influence.

Although many Nova Scotians had openly sympathized with the Americans at the outset of the war, others had from the first joined the inhabitants of the Island of St John and of Newfoundland in enlisting in British military units: the regular army, the militia, and the navy. Some may have been 'pressed' into service, particularly in the navy; Simeon Perkins records many reports of press gangs in operation on the south coast of Nova Scotia. In any case, a number of regiments and naval vessels recruited in the region, particularly in Newfoundland, where a predominantly young and male population was equally attractive to recruiters and press gangs. Moreover, as the war went on, the number of inhabitants sympathetic to the rebels declined precipitously. This was caused partly by the migration back to the States of those most committed to the rebel cause, partly by increasing British military strength in the region, and partly by resentment at destructive American behaviour. In a civil war, guerrilla raiding and looting forays do not make friends among the civilian population affected. When the British came to investigate the situation in the St John Valley in 1783, prior to the settlement of the Loyalists, that former hotbed of American sentiment and centre of American guerrilla activity contained few inhabitants willing to admit to revolutionary sympathy. In one tract, fully a quarter of the population (including many Acadians) had assisted the British cause in one way or another, and only 5 per cent were open American sympathizers. Most claimed to have taken no sides, merely attempting to get on with their lives as best they could.[36]

While the resettlement of Loyalist refugees and disbanded soldiers after 1782 would complete the process of re-emphasizing freehold tenure in the Atlantic region, the trend towards large European-style landlords and tenant farmers – which had become apparent in the years before 1775 – was also checked by the wartime disruption of communication and economic development. A European landholding style was difficult to maintain in North America at the best of times. Honest and competent estate managers were always in short supply, and wartime conditions brought out the worst instincts in employees, who came to feel that they deserved some rewards for their suffering. Some landlords attempted to deal with the problem by putting trusted females in charge of their operations. Many women doubtless ran farms and business enterprises for long periods during the wartime disruptions, and the work of Mary Cannon and Helen MacDonald offers some insight into both the process and the problems.

Mary Cannon (1751–1827) joined J.F.W. DesBarres as housekeeper and mistress at Castle Frederick in 1764, bearing him five daughters and a son out of wedlock. When DesBarres returned to England on the eve of the American Rebellion in 1774, he left Mary (or 'Polly,' as she was known) in charge of his Nova Scotia estates, and in 1776 he formally appointed her his agent and attorney. Her domain was vast and her problems many. Tenants often refused to pay rent or paid it in kind for which there was no market. Arrangements with tenants that appeared advantageous to the landlord when made would prove disastrous over the long haul, particularly if constant inflation was not taken into account. Later, DesBarres and Mary engaged in complex litigation over her administration, but there is no reason to doubt her assertion in one court document that DesBarres might well have lost his Nova Scotia lands during the war 'had it not been for Defendant's unremitted exertions.'[37]

Another woman left to manage an estate during the war – and beyond – was Helen (Nelly) MacDonald of Glenaladale. She had accompanied her brothers to the Island of St John in 1772, where they had attempted to organize an estate of Highland Scots at Scotchfort. Short of money, the MacDonald brothers left the Island for military service in 1775, leaving Nelly in control until her brother John returned in 1792. Her seventeen-year stewardship was not an easy one. She had to operate the family farm, which included more than ninety head of cattle, as well as to deal with the tenants and an acquisitive Island government. In the 1780s she even had a house built for her brother, according to his written specifications. In return John occasionally sent her remittances of money and luxury goods, in one instance eight pairs of shoes, two to three yards of lasting, patterns, and two pairs of galoshes. He also offered advice and, occasionally, what amounted to orders.[38]

In 1795 John MacDonald insisted in a lengthy letter to J.F.W. Des-Barres that landholders in both Britain and America needed to manage their own holdings. 'Tell me if you Know a Proprietor living in England,' he challenged DesBarres, 'that has ever been able to hold an Estate in America.' He added, 'It is true a good Agent may do it all. At the same time, how many do you know capable of so acting & susceptible of the trust?'[39] In the end, neither Mary Cannon nor Nelly Mac-Donald had proved totally satisfactory agents. But they had both been expected to do the impossible, managing estates over long periods of time with little financial assistance or instruction from the landholders. What happened in the hands of less competent and less loyal administrators could be far more disastrous.

Millions of acres of land in Nova Scotia (which, it must be remembered, still included what would become the colonies of New Brunswick and Cape Breton) and the Island of St John had been handed away in the 1760s, mainly to absentee land speculators. The vast majority of the grantees in Nova Scotia had made no effort to fulfil the terms of their grants nor paid any quitrents, and when land was needed for the Loyalists in the 1780s it was possible to recover it by relatively uncontroversial if occasionally time-consuming legal proceedings of escheat in the courts of the province.[40] The situation on the Island of St John was considerably different. Here the legal procedure to be employed was not escheat (the forfeiture of property to the Crown for failure to fulfil terms of granting) but distraint (the seizure and sale of land to the highest bidder to satisfy arrears, in this case of quitrent). Most Island landholders had paid some quitrents, although all fell behind in their payments during the war.[41]

Instead of consulting with the British authorities, the Island government in 1781 chose unilaterally to proceed with distraint against delinquent landholders. Island officials were owed salary arrears, had suffered from isolation during the war, and clearly thought themselves more worthy landowners than the absentees. More than half the Island was distrained and a large number of lots put up for auction late in 1781, most of which ended up at bargain prices in the hands of Governor Walter Patterson. When the proprietors learned of this action early in 1782, they rallied behind John MacDonald – now lobbying on their behalf in London – in protest against it. In 1783 the British government agreed with the proprietors that the distraint proceedings and subsequent auction had been precipitous, and as much as ordered Patterson to reverse them. At this point no one in London realized the extent to which legal form had not been observed or that Patterson was the main beneficiary of the sales. Only MacDonald suspected, correctly, that Patterson would ignore the explicit instructions of the colonial secretary over the remainder of his tenure. Instead of reversing the sales, Patterson attempted to entrench them into Island landholding in ways that could not be undone, thus adding a new dimension to the tangled land question of the Island of St John.

In most places, land grabbing was a less serious problem than loss of essential supplies. Until the later years of the war, the shipping lanes of the Atlantic region were so dangerous that normal commercial activity was gravely disrupted. All vessels were at risk, but the larger and more valuable the cargo, the more attractive it was to the voracious privateer. European merchants virtually stopped shipping to the region. Shortages of food and supplies occurred almost everywhere, but were most severely felt in places where there was no immediate agricultural surplus upon which to rely. No place was more affected than Newfoundland, which relied upon open commerce for its very existence, although the Island of St John experienced many shortages as well.[42]

American privateers were more dangerous on the Banks than they were in and around the harbours, where local fishermen were less exposed. The result was the virtual collapse of the offshore fishery, a development that ought to have worked to the benefit of the inshore residents – but did not. The Americans had supplied most of the foodstuffs consumed by fishermen, who normally had not time, inclination, or land to produce their own food supplies. Privateers also generally reduced commercial activity, including shipment of fish to North America and Europe. With the drying up of supplies of imported foodstuffs, famine and malnutrition became common, particularly in isolated outports. In a search for food, Newfoundland increased substantially the amount of land under cultivation between 1775 and 1781, and it also increased its traffic with its neighbouring colonies.

Absence of markets, isolation, military anxiety, and the limitations of subsistence agriculture (a bad harvest was a real disaster when food could not be imported from elsewhere) all combined with the attractions of the larger seaports to depopulate the countryside. Towns like Halifax, Charlottetown, and St John's acted like a magnet to draw people to them. These larger communities provided some sense of security against the ubiquitous privateers, but the same British military presence that protected the inhabitants also meant a subsidized level of expenditure that created booming economies. The presence of the British Navy in St John's and Halifax was hardly a surprise, since both ports had long histories as strategic naval centres. More difficult to explain was a substantial garrison of six companies (augmented by Hessians) at Charlottetown, costing the British government more than £12,000 pounds per annum by 1780. But the acting governor of the Island had operated on the assumption that the British would honour any expenditures made for military reasons, whether or not they had been properly authorized, and he parlayed an early privateering raid on Charlottetown into a substantial defence force.[43]

Military garrisons easily consumed the productive capacities of local agriculture, raising food prices and causing further shortages in the process. Garrisons required housing, and a major construction activity in Halifax and Charlottetown during the war was the building of barracks. The salaries of the troops also worked into the economy, chiefly in the form of the consumption of alcoholic beverages at the countless public (and private) houses set up to cater to the military thirst. Thus, while most of the outports and back-country districts suffered throughout the war, the major seaports enjoyed a subsidized prosperity that had been quite unknown in the preceding years of peace.

Prosperity was not without its price, particularly for the poor and those on fixed incomes, for rampant inflation was one of its consequences. Capt. John MacDonald in 1776 insisted of his fellow officers at Halifax that 'those only were benefited who could afford the prodigious prices; the remainder were supplied by fresh fish only, which might be had anywhere.'[44] One British official in Halifax later complained that his salary could 'not maintain my Horses, pay my servants' wages, and find my House in fuel.' Similar comments were made by residents of Charlottetown and St John's. If those on substantial official salaries were unhappy with prices, the plight of the poor can only be imagined. Military garrisons always meant dependants, of course, many of whom lived on the edges of poverty. What was significant was that despite the obvious problems for those on the margins, the back-country population continued to defect to the larger ports. By war's end and before the Loyalist migration, Halifax, Charlottetown, and St John's contained more than half the population of the region and of their respective districts.

Undoubtedly, the best known and most heavily studied development of the wartime years in the Atlantic region has been the religious revival usually known as the 'Great Awakening.'[45] In late March 1775 a young twenty-six-year-old Nova Scotian named Henry Alline, who had long been 'groaning under a load of guilt and darkness, praying and crying continually for mercy,' finally experienced the 'redeeming love' of God. He felt, in the language of the time, converted. For nearly a year thereafter, during the most uncertain months of the outbreak of the American Rebellion in New England, Alline wrestled with the question of whether to heed an inner call to preach the gospel. He broke free from a New England upbringing on the first anniversary of the battles of Lexington and Concord, finding a spiritual reassurance that rejected tradition and emphasized the individual's own inner feelings.

Like most of those who would be affected by his preaching, Henry Alline had been born in New England and had come to Nova Scotia as part of the Planter migration of the early 1760s. Like his contemporaries, many of whom had come from those districts of New England most heavily influenced by the religious revivals of the 1740s known in those parts also as the 'Great Awakening,' Alline had long sought spiritual assurance, without much success. He found himself shut off from most opportunities to assume leadership and develop his natural intellectual gifts, partly by Nova Scotia circumstances and partly by responsibilities he felt towards his aging parents. Frustration was probably well entrenched in the younger generation of the Yankee population of Nova Scotia long before the outbreak of conflict forced them to decide their loyalties.

While his evangelical techniques were the standard ones of eighteenth-century revivalism, Alline's message was unconventional and at least potentially radical. Instinctively, he concentrated his efforts on those elements of the Nova Scotia population most likely to be receptive: those of New England background living in exposed back-country settlements, for whom religious assurance might provide a deliverance from confusion and anxiety. Eschewing traditional New England beliefs heavily dependent on idea of predestination, Alline taught that everyone could be saved, for God is Love. The preacher was not particularly interested in institutions. Although he founded several ephemeral churches, he detested a 'hireling ministry' and insisted that financial support for a clergy was a purely voluntary matter. Uninterested in personal possessions – his effects at his death consisted of 'a horse and sleigh, his apparel, and about twelve dollars in money' – Alline was also hostile to materialism in others, notably in the booming urban environments of the region. While not all his listeners would have found such asceticism appealing, its anti-urbanism struck some respondent chords. So did Alline's insistence that all humankind was equal in the sight of God and his vision of the existence of salvation in a better world for those who had experienced the 'new birth.'

Alline confined his preaching ambit to the Annapolis Valley until after 1779, gradually expanding his territory thereafter to the communities and islands of Nova Scotia's south shore, then to the Island of St John and the up-country part of the territory that would become New Brunswick in 1782. He died of tuberculosis in New Hampshire in 1784, at the beginning of a proposed preaching tour of the northern American states. Few of Alline's peculiar doctrines or idiosyncratic views on church government survived him, although he wrote a large number of hymns, which were published mainly after his death. As a hymn-writer Alline expressed in simple language the concerns of his pioneering contemporaries.[46] He was perhaps most important as a symbol of a disoriented generation of Yankee settlers, although he also set in motion an evangelical impulse that characterized the region for many decades.

Joining Alline on the evangelical trail almost from the outset was Methodist William Black, one of the Yorkshire arrivals of the 1770s.[47] The Methodists were strongest at the outset in the Chignecto Isthmus, on the Island of St John (where Benjamin Chappell, a former lay preacher associated with the Wesley brothers and now working as a carpenter and wheelwright, provided much support), and in Newfoundland (where Church of England missionary Laurence Coughlan had defected to Methodism by 1770).[48] While the Baptists became the principal heirs of evangelism among the New Englanders first inspired by Henry Alline, the Methodists flourished among recent British immigrants and in the back-country districts where there was little or no religious competition.

The evangelical pietism begun in the region by Henry Alline, William Black, and Laurence Coughlan would eventually have flourished even if such outstanding early leaders had not existed, since it was a continental rather than a regional phenomenon. Its early beginnings, however, had both short- and long-range consequences. In the short run, evangelism provided religious solace and experience for a rural generation – particularly during the disruptive years of warfare – that would otherwise have had little spiritual assistance in surviving difficult times. More highly institutionalized churches, such as the Church of England, had neither an interest in helping nor the ability to do so. In the long run, this early success of the evangelicals would distinctly limit the appeal of mainstream Protestantism, again especially in the back-country districts. At the same time, it should be emphasized that the fascination of scholars (including this writer) with Henry Alline and the Great Awakening, like the emphasis on the Yankee settlers in Nova Scotia of the early 1760s, has created an imbalance in our understanding of this period, both in general and in religious terms.

The American Rebellion – because of its guerrilla warfare – represented the last period in which the authorities in the Atlantic region took the Native population at all seriously. The Micmac and Abenaki, both Roman Catholic in religious persuasion, had been traditional allies of the French in the warfare before 1763, and the British had not done much to win them over after the French removal. Nor had they done much to resolve long-standing aboriginal claims to the land of the region, claims that were continually reasserted in one form or another. In Cape Breton, Micmacs protested the surveys of Samuel Holland and discussed with him the possibility of land 'granted them by His Majesty for the Conveniency of Hunting in which they might not be molested by any European Settlers.'[49] On the St John River, Maliseet warriors refused to allow Yankee settlers to survey above Grimross, claiming the land for themselves. In 1768 one group of Maliseet were given 704 acres of land on the St John River 'forever,' the grant fundamentally un-European in that the Natives were not allowed to sell it. The relative lack of settlement of wilderness land before 1775 prevented the British failure to extinguish most Native claims from becoming a major problem.

Not surprisingly, the Native people assumed more importance after the outbreak of fighting. The Massachusetts authorities were quite prepared to encourage the 'eastern Indians' to rise in righteous indignation against oppressive British policy, although the Continental Congress would have been contented enough with Native neutrality, a position considerably less expensive to maintain. Most of the Micmac found a policy of neutrality attractive, particularly since they were understandably confused by the problem of sorting out right and wrong in a war between 'Father & Son.' The situation became further confused when the French in 1778 entered the war on the American side; but by this time the British had clear military superiority over most of the region and were able to ignore the Natives. This refusal to take them seriously carried over into the post-war settlement. As L.F.S. Upton has observed of the Loyalist colonization, 'in all the flood of correspondence concerning the details of that great migration, there is not one word about the Indians who would be dispossessed by the new settlers.'[50]

More generally, in a recently settled (and resettled) region of relatively sparse population, shifts in the origins of newcomers could swiftly alter the nature of the society and culture. The Maritime colonies formed just such a volatile region, and the arrival of the Loyalists provided just such a rapid shift. After the Planter influx to Nova Scotia of the early 1760s, the bulk of new immigration and settlement had been European in origin, and sociocultural trends had begun running against the Americans. The Loyalists rapidly snapped matters back in a North American direction.

As a full-scale civil war, the American Rebellion was bound to produce some Americans who would be forced into exile. In fact, the proportion of exiles to total population from this 'Revolution' would exceed that of the French Revolution of 1789 or the Russian Revolution of 1917 or the Cuban Revolution of 1959. Perhaps as many as half a million White Americans (20 per cent of the White population) supported the British cause, and more than 50,000 went into exile.[51] The British had also encouraged both free and slave Blacks to oppose the Americans, and had forced the Native people along the northern and southern frontiers (although not the 'Eastern Indians' of the Atlantic region) to choose sides. While in most Loyalist families the political decisions were made by the males, there were also substantial numbers of independent Loyalist women, often widows. Of the 3,225 Loyalists who presented claims for compensation to the British government after the war, 468 (or nearly 15 per cent) were women.[52]

From the outset of hostilities between Britain and its colonies, some Americans had been forced into exile.[53] Initially known as 'Tories,' the refugees soon acquired the more positive label of 'Loyalists.' In the early years of conflict, most Americans who fled the United States for political reasons were members of the colonial élite. Often office-holders who had supported the British, they were sufficiently prominent to be singled out by the rebels for harassment and proscription. Many of these early exiles went to Britain, but there was a constant trickle into Halifax and Nova Scotia as well. Later in the war, as the British finally encouraged supporters to organize militarily and attempted to find popular backing within the American population, larger numbers of people were branded with the Loyalist mark.

The British lost the military struggle in 1781 when Lord Cornwallis surrendered at Yorktown. They then turned to attempting to extricate themselves from a lost cause at minimal cost by negotiating a peace treaty with the United States. While negotiations dragged on in Europe, Loyalist refugees and soldiers were drawn to New York, the major centre of British authority and military power on the eastern seaboard. New York had already become the wartime home of thousands of pro-

British supporters, and it now attracted even more. The Loyalists waited anxiously for word about the outcome of the peace negotiations. In the meantime, agents fanned out across Britain's remaining American possessions, investigating land and political conditions for potential exiles. Not all eyes turned to the Atlantic region, but many agents were active there over the summer of 1782. By the autumn it had become clear that the revolutionaries were not likely to be magnanimous in victory towards those who had opposed them. Sir Guy Carleton in New York began arranging for the movement of large bodies of Loyalists to Nova Scotia, where Governor John Parr had been warned to reserve as much land as possible for their settlement. Providing land for thousands of newcomers was no easy matter, since so much of the land would have to be escheated back to the Crown. The Island of St John, Cape Breton, and Newfoundland had no land readily available, however, and were not destinations for the primary migrations of 1782 and 1783.

On 22 September 1782, Carleton sketched out a policy for Loyalist relocation, emphasizing that land grants were to be 'considered as well founded Claims of Justice rather than of mere Favor, to be made in freehold tenure without fees or quitrents.' He expected that families would receive 600 acres and single men 300 acres, and promised tools from New York stores. Nova Scotia would be required to make available additional assistance.[54] Loyalist settlement policy, therefore, would see a return to the principle of relatively small plots of land held in freehold tenure, as well as to subsidization. Carleton initially overlooked the soldiers in various provincial regiments recruited in America to fight the rebels, and this oversight was pointed out to him in a memorial from the regimental officers early in 1783, demanding land grants and subsidies parallel to those extended to civilians. These claims were readily accepted, and the ultimate cost of Loyalist resettlement made the earlier expenditures on colonizing Nova Scotia appear puny. The major migration of Loyalist refugees to the Atlantic region took place in 1783, with troop transport ships bringing thousands of newcomers to the region. There were two principal destinations in the spring of 1783: the mouth of the St John River and Port Roseway (later Shelburne), on the southwest shore of Nova Scotia. Two instant towns sprang up, as the transports disgorged their passengers.[55]

The 'spring fleets' brought civilian refugees to the region, and they were joined later in the year by the Loyalist soldiers and their families, as well as by merchants attracted by the promise of good trading connections within the rebuilding empire. The disbanded soldiers, including those in units stationed in the region and discharged there – such as the King's Rangers or the St John's Volunteers on the Island of St John –

scattered around the region, with battalions often staying together under the leadership of former officers, although in less significant concentrations than the civilian refugees. Nova Scotia (including the northern section to be hived off as New Brunswick in 1784) was the destination for more than 30,000 Loyalists and disbanded soldiers, but about 1,000 newcomers each went to the Island of St John and Cape Breton after examining their initial locations and finding them wanting.[56]

The Loyalists represented a fair cross-section of the population of the American colonies from which they were drawn. Most were not well-to-do; a full 92 per cent of those settling in what became New Brunswick made no attempt to recover compensation from the British government for their losses. Those who did claim compensation, by and large the Loyalist élite, both male and female, were far more likely to have been born outside the American colonies than the average Loyalist, who was American-born. The compensated were also more likely to have been engaged in commerce or the professions than the typical Loyalist, although even among the compensated, farmers represented a majority. Among both compensated and uncompensated, the middle colonies of New York, New Jersey, and Pennsylvania were overrepresented, reflecting the fact that much of the movement to the Atlantic region originated in New York City. Southern Loyalists tended to move south, into Florida and the Caribbean area, although a considerable contingent did make their way north. Even within the ranks of those compensated, 41.8 per cent asked for less than £500 for their losses.[57]

Although most of the Loyalists were literate and many skilled at some occupation, the number of university graduates was relatively small, proportionally even smaller than in the American States. While there were doubtless many adherents of the Church of England among the new arrivals, the religious preferences of the Loyalists were spread across the full spectrum of Protestantism and often seemed inclined towards various pietistic sects. In age, the Loyalists tended to be in their mid- to late thirties. Many of those granted land were disbanded soldiers who had no families, but most of the refugees brought wives, children, and even Black slaves with them. The typical Loyalist, therefore, was probably little different in most respects from the American settler the region might under other circumstances have hoped to attract. Where the Loyalist may have been different from the ordinary American colonist was in the strength of his or her commitment to the British Crown and British institutions, and in the force of his or her hostility to the new republic in the United States.

Two special groups among the Loyalist arrivals deserve separate mention: women and Blacks. Women have often become lost in the Loyalist crowd, leaving relatively few documents behind for later historians to analyse. A substantial proportion of those who presented claims to the British government after the war, however, were women. These women claimants offer one window into the world of the female Loyalist. A detailed analysis of their claims by one American scholar indicates that they represented the larger cross-section of American society that is now recognized as typical of the Loyalists. They came from all regions and all social classes. The vast majority did not work outside the home, and they had a very limited understanding of the total financial operations of their families. Almost all the claimants who did work were urban dwellers, their occupations quite varied.[58] By definition, Loyalist women made claims only if no man existed in the family, and such women found life extremely difficult, being conscious both of their femininity and of its limitations. The adjective they most commonly used to describe themselves was 'helpless,' and many commented on being 'left friendless in a strange Country.' These women were almost wholly domestic in their lives, but without any positive sense of there being a pedestal for wives and mothers. Many had probably not – unlike the males – been able to make a conscious, autonomous decision for king and country.

The other special subgroup among the Atlantic Loyalists was the Blacks. Guy Carleton had to fight hard to protect Blacks claiming sanctuary under various British proclamations regarding slaves, and more than 3,000 departing freed Blacks represented some 10 per cent of the total number of Loyalists removing to Nova Scotia from New York City. They joined a population of some 500 Blacks, slave and free, who had already constituted a small but significant group in British Nova Scotia since 1749.[59] The Black Loyalists operated in Nova Scotia under considerable disadvantages, most ending up without land or with only very limited amounts. Thus, of the more than 3,000 freed Blacks transported to Nova Scotia, only about one-third received any land grants at all, at an average size of less than twelve acres per grant. They also suffered from other disadvantages, ranging from denial of the franchise to harsher treatment before the courts. Not all the Blacks brought to the region were freed, however, for some unknown number came with refugee Loyalists as slaves. No colony in the region abolished slavery through legislation, and it was gradually eliminated only through court extension of British precedents in the nineteenth century.[60] Religion provided both solace and cohesion for these people, particularly the 'new light' of Henry Alline and of the Black Baptist preacher David George.

The Loyalists provided the region with a much-needed infusion of people and money – at least outside Newfoundland – for the British government gave them land, supplied them, and compensated at least an élite minority for their losses. Assessing their impact is difficult. Certainly, in the short run, the Loyalists returned landholding patterns in the region to small freeholding; few Americans were ever prepared to become tenants. They also helped assure that American speech patterns and cultural values would survive, particularly as they gradually merged with the earlier Planters.[61] In the long run, the pensions for lost civilian offices and half-pay awards to former military officers, both inheritable by widows, were paid by the British for half a century. They constituted not only a major item of cash injected into the region's economy, but also helped to preserve an old élite beyond its usefulness.[62]

CHAPTER NINE

1783–1800
Loyalist Arrival, Acadian Return, Imperial Reform

ANN GORMAN CONDON

What can one say of the year 1783 in Atlantic Canada? That it marked a watershed? That history repeated itself in its peculiarly heartless way? That once again the ordinary life of the Atlantic peoples was deranged by outside events utterly beyond their control?

Two cataclysmic events in the year 1783 changed Atlantic Canada forever. The first was the Treaty of Paris, which separated America from the British Empire. For the people of Atlantic Canada this rupture was unnatural and ominous. Long-established networks of trade, treasured sources of religious inspiration, and intimate bonds of kinship and community were suddenly severed. The second, simultaneous event was the influx of perhaps 35,000 Loyalists into the region. The sheer numbers and power of these newcomers made a transformation of existing patterns inescapable. Nova Scotia felt the impact of the Loyalist arrival most keenly – the original province was divided in three, a more comprehensive system of local government and religious establishment was put in place, and the Loyalist grandees were catapulted into power. The islands of St John and Newfoundland were less immediately affected, yet over time they too would seek the kind of colonial self-government that the Loyalists had brought from America.

Responses to these events varied with the status of the inhabitants. Predictably, the New England Planters fiercely resisted both the new trade regulations and the Loyalist bid for power, while somehow managing to take financial advantage of both. The Native peoples and Acadians, the oldest but now the most vulnerable groups in the region, were more evasive. Presumably these minorities felt an anxiety close to despair at the sight of thousands more English settlers pouring into their region, bringing with them more British troops and a more penetrating government. Yet armed resistance was simply not an option for either group. Moving farther away from established areas of settlement was the most they could do to limit the damage.

Despite the fears aroused by this massive new population, the Loyalists came to Atlantic Canada as exiles, not as conquerors. They too had known persecution, war, defeat, and deportation. Certainly, by the time of their arrival in 1783, their instincts were profoundly peaceful. Like all exiles, they had an obsessive need to restore order and security to their lives, and so they would pursue land, status, and power relentlessly. Yet they felt neither hostile to, nor even very curious about, the existing population. This indifference would produce a pragmatic attitude of 'live and let live,' a viewpoint that boded well for relations among the various peoples of the region.

The worrisome terms of the Treaty of Paris would be offset by greater British commitment. The solemn promises to aid the Loyalists produced capital investment, trade protection, and military establishments on a scale never before experienced in the region. Ten years later, another revolution, this time in France, extended and deepened British involvement in British North America and enabled the Loyalists to realize some of their fondest cultural objectives. For the first time, the Atlantic colonies became the beneficiaries rather than the victims of global war.

Thus the period 1783–1800 was an era of profound, if limited, change. The region had more cohesion in 1800 than in 1783, but not much. Tiny clusters of people continued to live in isolated pockets of settlement, separated from each other by vast waterways, dense forests, and a forbidding climate. Social conflict and suspicion among groups persisted, and for the ordinary inhabitant life continued to be a lonely, back-breaking struggle with a rich but exhausting natural environment. Personal failure and despair were common, especially among Loyalists whose hopes went unfulfilled, and among the Native peoples, whose hopes were diminished.

Nonetheless, it was also a time of new opportunity and new autonomy. The grandest development was the rise of a real public life in Halifax, fuelled by wartime commerce and the presence of a military garrison headed by the Duke of Kent. Less conspicuous but highly significant for the long term was the appearance of strong new local forces: tenant resistance in Charlottetown, courts of local justice in Newfoundland, the first Acadian participation in the common defence, Catholic toleration throughout the region, and the growth of dissenting churches along the St John River and in peninsular Nova Scotia. By 1800 the Atlantic colonies were more populous, more socially integrated, and more prosperous than in 1783. The benefits generated by these halcyon times were, however, spread unevenly – so much depended on who you were and where you lived. To understand this transforming process requires, first, a description of the Loyalist migration, and then a survey of its impact on the disparate peoples of the region.

Looked at from the perspective of the late twentieth century, it is clear that the Loyalists were the first mass movement of political refugees in modern history. The world has witnessed many such movements since that time, but before 1783 only the exodus of 9,000 Puritans from England to Massachusetts Bay in the 1630s resembles the Loyalist migration in terms of both diversity of people and enduring political impact. The Loyalists' status as political exiles distinguished their experience in Atlantic Canada in several ways. First, and perhaps most obviously, the Loyalist influx was quite different from ordinary patterns of immigration and settlement. Typically, immigrant communities in colonial North America began with few people; often they suffered severe setbacks in the form of starvation, disease, and wars with Native peoples, and usually two or three generations of painstaking effort were required to establish stability and prosperity. By contrast, the Atlantic region received a sudden, massive burst of perhaps 35,000 political refugees in the short space of three years. Internally this movement was far better organized than most immigrant ventures, and externally it was supported by the imperial government to an extent unknown to ordinary, non-political movements.[1]

Even more important, the experience of war, persecution, and exile meant that the Loyalists came to Atlantic Canada with a political agenda. To be sure, like all newcomers, they wanted wealth and opportunity. But unlike most immigrants, they also wanted to reshape society to reflect the values for which they had suffered expulsion from America and to assuage their nostalgia for their old homeland.[2] At the same time, although bound together by this common cause, the Loyalist movement included an exceptionally broad range of people and circumstances, a diversity that made it less cohesive than typical immigrant groups. The cross-section of ages, races, religious affiliations, places of origin, and personal skills contained within Loyalist ranks constituted an unusually complex social mix. While such élite groups as the military officers, Anglican clerics, Crown lawyers, and wealthy merchants tried to act as spokesmen for the entire movement, they were proportionately few in number and their leadership was not always accepted by the rank and file. The overwhelming mass of Loyalists were ordinary folk – farmers, small traders in the outports, skilled craftsmen in the cities, some fishermen, and some ex-slaves. The vast majority were born in the old Thirteen Colonies, although Loyalist ranks also included many natives of Scotland and Ireland and small but tightly organized groups of French Huguenots and Dutch and German religious minorities.[3]

Most of the 35,000 Loyalists who resettled in Atlantic Canada left by ship from New York City under the protection of Sir Guy Carleton and the British headquarters staff. Quite understandably, most moved north in conjunction with family or friends so that they would have a support network in the wilderness. Thus military comrades, religious associates, and neighbourhood groups clung to each other and resettled together. This intricate pattern of migration provided an important source of stability and solace in the Loyalists' new homes; at the same time, subgroup ties often prevented the Loyalists from acting in concert and sometimes led to sharp internal rivalries.

Although every effort was made by the British government to ease the resettlement process, the Loyalists proved to be an anxious, quarrelsome lot. They bombarded Carleton with petitions and demands for special treatment before they left. Once they arrived in Nova Scotia, they turned on each other and the officials who tried to help them. The general discontent was fanned by the fact that all but the wealthiest had to spend the first year or two huddled in tent cities, or ramshackle huts, or church basements. A race riot at Shelburne and a violent election in Saint John were the worst, but not the only, eruptions of Loyalist anger.

This great migration nearly doubled the population of the Atlantic region and profoundly altered its life. The changes that occurred, however, can only be understood within the context of British imperial policy. For while the Loyalists were often the agents of change between 1783 and 1800, it was British power and British goals that determined the actual direction and extent of change.

Over and above Britain's promises to the Loyalists, the mere fact of American independence meant that Great Britain had to pay more attention to its Atlantic colonies. Before 1783, the region had been on the periphery of empire, valued for its fish and strategic location, but in no way as complex or economically dynamic as the original Thirteen Colonies. Except for the garrison city of Halifax, the British had made no effort to govern the little settlements along the coastline and in the interior. They were perceived as mere 'marches,' frontiers on the rim of more settled colonies, without a separate identity or recognizable culture. After 1783, however, the Atlantic colonies were central to British ambitions in North America. They had the greatest number of English-speaking inhabitants. They were closest by sea to England itself and to the vital sugar colonies in the West Indies. They offered the best chance of undermining the American republic by taking over the supply trade to British bases in Newfoundland and the Caribbean. Most important of all, the sea lanes and harbours of Atlantic Canada were needed for British naval power. For all these reasons, the Empire could not, in theory at least, govern the remaining colonies offhandedly any more. The fisheries, the navy, the boundary, the enlarged population, all cried out for new policies and firm direction.[4]

Unfortunately, the loss of America had sapped Britain's political energy. There were suggestions, of course, on both the right and the left. Lord Sheffield and the navy wanted a tightening of the Navigation System and much firmer government in the colonies, while Lord Shelburne and the merchant community felt that Britain's highest priority should be recapturing the American trade. Besieged by such contradictory advice, Lord Sydney, the colonial secretary, repeatedly chose the line of least resistance. No serious discussion of the implications of American independence or the needs of the Atlantic colonies took place in the 1780s. Instead major political changes were made, new institutions created, and new men thrust into power on a piecemeal basis in response to political pressure.[5]

The case of Newfoundland is instructive. By 1783 Newfoundland was in fact, if not in law, a colony of settlement. Nearly 12,000 people lived there year round. St John's now had a resident community of merchants who were building substantial houses and demanding luxuries. Henceforth the resident fishery would outnumber the migratory force sent out from England. Yet the imperial government proved exceedingly reluctant to recognize this fundamental change in the island's status. Thus, the Treaty of Paris ending the American war permitted New Englanders to continue their long participation in the Newfoundland fishery, including the right to fish inshore and dry their catch on land. It also permitted France to maintain its exclusive fishing rights on Newfoundland's north shore. Both these concessions demonstrated that Britain still clung to the fiction that Newfoundland was simply a fishing base, not a permanent settlement.[6]

Fortunately the British could not entirely ignore the inhumane conditions on the island. During the American war, naval officials and Anglican missionaries had sent home harrowing reports about the lack of food and the desperation of the population. As a result, two major new initiatives were undertaken. First, Catholic toleration on the island was declared in 1784, and the first 'legal' priest, Rev. James O'Donnell, arrived in St John's to minister openly to the growing Irish-Catholic population. Secondly, the Board of Trade began an inquiry into the island's commerce in order to understand the causes of the wartime famine. As a result of the board's findings, for the first time in Newfoundland's history the interests of the resident population were placed above those of the West Country merchants. The merchants' long monopoly of island trade was declared unnecessary, and permission was granted for the continued importation of food and provisions from the United States. This judgment marked a major breakthrough for the resident population, for although the board did not endorse settlement, it clearly accepted responsibility for the needs of the settlers.

It was a beginning, but that is all. Some merchants built elegant houses in St John's and enjoyed imported luxuries, but for most residents life was strictly utilitarian. Neither the colony nor the port town had any legal way to raise taxes, meaning that after 200 years there were still 'no roads, no public hospital, no postal service, no newspapers, few jails, courthouses, schools, or churches.' Men were not even legally entitled to own land, and this of course discouraged food production and any impulse towards improvement. Nonetheless, the growth of a resident population did mean more permanence and more individual enterprise. Furtively, residents began to enclose pieces of land, especially those with dwellings or storehouses. In the 1790s the governors tried to protect the fishermen against merchant greed by setting down market regulations and establishing a Committee for the Relief of the Poor. Such measures, although never enough, doubtless helped many to survive the desperate winter of 1798–9. The face of St John's itself began to change as it slowly established its dominance over the island. It became, for one thing, a predominately Irish town and included many more women and children. The forest, moreover, had been pushed back, and a 'clutter of stages, flakes, boats, ships, warehouses, dwellings, vegetable patches, wandering cattle, and snaking trails' gave unmistakable evidence of permanent settlement. Rudimentary courts of civil justice were set up in response to the demands of the local merchants. Yet, on the whole, British neglect continued. As late as 1789 the new colonial secretary, William Grenville, could declare: 'Newfoundland is in no respect a British colony and is never so considered by our laws.'[7]

British treatment of the other major islands in the Atlantic region followed a similar pattern. Officials in London would yield to strong colonial pressure from either the Loyalists, the Society for the Propagation of the Gospel (SPG), or the shipowners, and would even make major structural changes. Yet, as the colonists learned, occasional British intervention did not imply a continuing interest in their development. The most bizarre example occurred in Cape Breton, when Abraham Cuyler convinced Lord Sydney that he could attract 5,000 Quebec Loyalists to the fortress island if it was given a separate provincial government. In 1784, the colonial authorities agreed. Cape Breton was separated from Nova Scotia; the brilliant cartographer J.F.W. DesBarres was sent out as lieutenant-governor, and Ranna Cossit, a Connecticut Loyalist, became the Anglican missionary in Sydney. To his dismay, poor Cuyler could convince only 140 Loyalists to leave Quebec with him, and although 300 more drifted in over time, the colony suffered from extreme isolation and almost non-stop controversy. Desbarres's high-handed methods forced his recall in 1787. Cossit's missionary zeal was so provocative that Bishop Charles Inglis had to transfer the fiery cleric elsewhere, lest his flock be tempted to become 'Methodists, Catholics or infidels.' Both the Acadian and Micmac inhabitants kept clear of the seat of government at Sydney, which early visitors described as a dismal 'Town ... of about 50 Hovels ... [with] not the smallest trace of Industry as the Inhabitants live by selling rum to the soldiers.'[8]

The situation on the Island of St John presented an even thornier problem for the British. The dispute between its buccaneer governor, Walter Patterson, and the absentee proprietors grew worse in the 1780s. Patterson warmly encouraged Loyalists to settle on the Island in hopes that they would shore up his political base and enable him to profit from his illegal auction of proprietary land. Fewer than 800 Loyalists came, however, for the questionable validity of these titles, as well as the governor's unabashed profiteering, gave the Island an unsavoury reputation. Loyalists who did come included both soldiers and civilians, but they were mainly middle-aged, single men, with the result that Loyalist settlement on the Island proved unstable, as many tended to drift off their lands and sell their provisions for rum.[9]

The Colonial Office was properly incensed at the confusion over land titles, but it proved unable to cut through the contradictory claims of the proprietors and the local resident 'squatters,' and politics on the Island moved inexorably towards deadlock. Although Lord Sydney did recall Patterson in 1786 and replace him with the Loyalist military hero Edmund Fanning, Patterson's refusal to vacate his post for more than a year simply deepened the prevailing discord. By the end of the decade, the astute Fanning had consolidated his power. Unfortunately, he tended to use it to advance his own interests rather than to address the broader needs of the Island and its people. As a result, by 1790 much of the land on the Island was jointly claimed by resident squatters and absentee proprietors in a conflict that began to seem irresolvable. Nonetheless, the Island was beginning to produce food for export, mainly for Newfoundland, and to fulfil its role as an agricultural heartland. The dispute over land titles would, however, delay Island development for decades, for few Loyalist or English immigrants were willing to become tenants. Only the Highland Scots and the Irish, peoples less attached culturally to English forms of land tenure, would choose the Island's lush acreage so long as it remained under the proprietorship.

On the mainland, by contrast, Great Britain made decisive, far-reaching changes. Here Loyalist numbers, Loyalist ambitions, and Loyalist ideology exerted their maximum force. The 35,000 refugees who descended on both sides of the Bay of Fundy doubled the population of peninsular Nova Scotia and increased the number of settlers north of the bay by nearly five times. Their determination to become dominant in their new homes was clear even before they arrived. While still in New York, various Loyalist leaders began agitating to get special land grants and official posts that would ensure their control of the new settlements. The most notorious example of their ambitions was the Petition of 55, in which several well-known Loyalist merchants, lawyers, and clergymen asked the British government to grant them 5,000-acre estates in Nova Scotia 'considering our several characters and our former situations in life.'[10]

The creation of the province of New Brunswick was the greatest political triumph of this Loyalist élite. Nearly 15,000 soldiers and refugees had chosen to resettle north of the Fundy, particularly around the mouth of the St John River and up its fertile river valley. Although the Loyalists were of disparate origins – the majority came from the middle colonies of New York, New Jersey, and Pennsylvania, while many of their leaders were from Massachusetts or Connecticut – the long years they had spent together in wartime New York permitted them to join forces and plan a common future. As a result, they were conspicuously well organized as they moved north. Their leaders knew each other, and they easily forged alliances with the most important settlers in the area, especially the merchant William Hazen and the group of Maine timber merchants who had resettled across the Penobscot Bay in St Andrews at the end of the war in order to remain within the British Navigation System. Furthermore, these Loyalists had powerful friends in London and used them to conduct an intricate, transatlantic campaign to convince the British government to partition Nova Scotia and create a new, predominantly Loyalist province north of the Fundy. Edward Winslow, an imaginative Massachusetts Loyalist, masterminded this campaign. Naturally Governor John Parr and his Halifax government protested, as in fact did many of the people already living along the St John. But the Loyalists were not to be denied. In June 1784 the province of New Brunswick was established with the significant motto 'Spem Reduxit' – 'Hope Restored.'

The creation of New Brunswick could certainly be justified in terms of both geography and population. In actuality, however, English officials seem to have yielded to this aggressive coalition out of ennui and a desperate need to find posts for the horde of Loyalist office-seekers clustered in London. Thus every post in New Brunswick went to a Loyalist leader, and Thomas Carleton, the brother of Sir Guy, became its first governor. With almost military dispatch, Carleton and his Loyalist advisers worked to fulfil their aristocratic dream that New Brunswick would become 'the most gentlemanlike' society in North America. Land grants were vacated to make room for thousands of Loyalist settlers;

local government was organized along county lines to avoid the more democratic town model of New England; and most significant of all, the seat of government was moved seventy miles up river to 'Frederick's Town.' Carleton and most of his advisers wanted their province to be a stable agricultural society led by a landholding gentry and firmly protected by British troops. The commercial hustle of Saint John and its proximity to the American border must be held firmly in check.

New Brunswick's first election showed both the limits of this policy and the firm determination of the leadership. Although most of the outports and rural areas supported the government, Saint John simply erupted. An angry coalition of common soldiers and civilian refugees waged a bitter campaign in the newspapers and taverns of the city, denouncing the government candidates, the Petition of 55, élite favouritism, and above all the failure of government to get people securely on their lands. A riot during the actual polling gave Carleton the excuse he needed to call in the troops. Order was restored, the rioters were thrown in jail, and stiff regulations were enacted to prevent further popular demonstrations. Yet rank-and-file Loyalists were not subdued by these authoritarian measures. Much as they respected the principle of leadership and the British connection, they automatically assumed that, as good colonial subjects, they would run their own local affairs and enjoy a government responsive to their needs.[11] From its very inception, therefore, a sharp tension existed in New Brunswick between the official leadership, appointed and paid by London, and the popularly chosen representatives of the people. Nor, as Carleton learned to his dismay, would the imperial government intervene to prop up authoritarian rule. When the governor incorporated the City of Saint John in 1785 to tighten his control, he received a sharp reprimand from Lord Sydney. Tampering with voting procedures clearly frightened the colonial secretary. There must be no repeat of the American troubles.

For the moment, prosperity and the challenge of settling the wilderness permitted Carleton to ride out the storm. Once the people were settled on their own lands, the new province enjoyed remarkable growth for almost a decade. A thousand houses sprang up in Saint John, mills dotted the river-banks, lands were laboriously cleared and cultivated, shipbuilding began, and merchants resumed their overseas trade. There were occasional amusements – militia days, neighbourhood frolics, military balls, even a visiting theatre troupe. The wilderness was still everywhere, but enough progress had been made to keep alive the dream that New Brunswick could one day become 'the envy of the American states.'[12]

No such Loyalist sweep was possible in peninsular Nova Scotia, but here too their impact was considerable. Nearly 19,000 refugees poured into its harbours and valleys. Most were civilians, although their numbers included almost 1,000 provincial soldiers from the Carolinas and Georgia, as well as 2,000 disbanded British soldiers and their families. These Loyalists were less unified than the New Brunswick groups and more commercial in their outlook. The greatest number chose to settle either at Shelburne, whose sweeping harbour inspired dreams of capturing the great supply trade to the West Indies, or around the well established port of Halifax. The balance settled in small clusters along both the Atlantic and Fundy shores.[13]

These Loyalists did resemble the New Brunswickers, however, in their political ambitions. The difference was that in Nova Scotia Governor John Parr and his Halifax supporters were firmly entrenched, completely controlling the Council, the judiciary, the customs officers, and even, until the Loyalists arrived, the House of Assembly. Furthermore, the Parr government was assured of strong support from Lord Sydney. Faced with this impregnable but unfriendly government, some Loyalist leaders did a remarkable thing – they went into opposition! From 1786 onwards, they used their seats in the House of Assembly to challenge the domination of Parr and the old Halifax establishment. They attacked the qualifications of the judiciary, going so far as to impeach two judges of the Supreme Court, and they joined forces with other groups to reduce the executive powers of government. Parr, of course, was outraged and bitterly accused the Loyalists of introducing 'levelling Republican principles' into his community. The governor managed to hold his ground until his death in 1792. Then the appointment of Sir John Wentworth, probably the ablest politician the Loyalists ever produced, placed the patronage of Nova Scotia in hands that would consistently favour persons with strong Loyalist credentials.[14]

Although the conflict between Parr and the Loyalist Assembly leaders was nothing more than a familiar battle between the ins and the outs, this brief period of Loyalist opposition did produce one important result in Nova Scotia. The Loyalists drew on their American experience to strengthen the House of Assembly. They insisted that the House should control its own membership and proceedings, refused to permit government officers to sit in the House, and even gained for the Assembly complete control of revenue bills by 1791. While not all their initiatives were successful, the Loyalists' constitutional awareness served to reduce the prerogative powers of government and increase popular control.

In addition to the spur they gave to political life, the Loyalists added notably to economic activity in Nova Scotia. Land values soared in response to the new settlers. Ads in the Halifax newspapers took up more space and featured more luxury goods. The number of merchants in Halifax doubled, as did the demand for labour and the sales of rum. Shelburne's history was even more spectacular. Virtually overnight, this tent city became an international seaport, supporting three newspapers, elegant Georgian houses, and a growing supply trade to the West Indies. As the years wore on, however, the reality of Nova Scotia's soil and topography reversed original expectations. Loyalist farmers discovered that the lands available to them were barely fertile, and it was all a family could do to grow enough food for itself, with no surplus for sale or export. The great forests were almost impossible to penetrate once the most accessible trees were cut, and the poor state of the few roads hindered the woodsman from getting his sticks to the mills. Merchants who had so optimistically invested their capital in ships and trading ventures found they lacked sufficient supplies to keep up a steady commerce. As the economic limits of Nova Scotia became apparent, some Loyalists dug in and accepted the slow growth of frontier communities. Others began to look elsewhere. Returning to the United States or making a new start in Upper Canada appealed to many White Loyalists. For many free Black Loyalists, resettling in a colony of their own in British West Africa proved almost irresistible. Eventually more than half the Loyalists who came to Nova Scotia would move on.[15]

These massive changes in the population and government of the Atlantic colonies were accompanied by equally strong imperial initiatives in the economic sphere. The region benefited from more British investment and more British commitment. Every male Loyalist received a free land grant, scaled according to his family size and military service, plus tools and provisions for up to three years. These supplies were usually purchased on the spot, to the benefit of local merchants, farmers, and fishermen. In addition, officers of the provincial regiments all received half-pay for life, and their widows got a portion of this amount. A few Loyalists also received either capital grants or pensions as compensation for their property losses.[16]

A second form of imperial support was the civil and military establishments of the region. After 1783 the number of officials, judges, and Anglican missionaries multiplied, as did the British soldiers and sailors stationed in regional garrisons and ports. Their salaries, offices, dwellings, parade grounds, ammunition, and churches were all paid for by the British Treasury. The continuing injection of so much outside capital enormously strengthened the material resources of the region, and at times saved some inhabitants from starvation.

Finally, after a strenuous debate between those who wished to continue trading with the United States and stalwart defenders of the Navigation System, the Empire decided in 1783 to give the British North American colonies a monopoly of the valuable supply trade to the British West Indies. American traders were specifically prohibited from the islands, and the merchants of the region rejoiced at news of the ban, feeling sure that this guaranteed market would provide a solid foundation for their commerce and shipbuilding. While true in theory, in reality the new settlements proved unable to produce enough surplus goods for export to meet market demand. Even worse, the Atlantic colonies found they had to admit American foodstuffs into their own communities to meet their local needs, so that the Empire's determination to enforce the Navigation Laws only produced smuggling and evasion. An unhealthy compromise developed whereby American goods, including lumber, were carried on British bottoms into both the Atlantic colonies and the West Indies. This failure of policy ravaged the capital as well as the hopes of merchants and entrepreneurs. Shelburne suffered the most, but trade and shipbuilding also dried up in Halifax, Saint John, and St Andrews, owing to the inherent limitations of a frontier economy.[17]

Despite the disappointments, these imperial economic measures gave a tremendous stimulus to commercial activity and urban life, permitting the region to retain much of the new population acquired in 1783 and to develop, in Halifax particularly, specialized forms of trade and lavish consumption patterns. Clearly, however, the benefits of this imperial bounty were not spread evenly through the population. The Loyalists were the obvious winners, especially those who received compensation for their losses or those who had access to official patronage. Established merchants and farmers with capital benefited more than pioneers. Port cities did better than hinterlands, and English-speaking inhabitants better than cultural minorities. Doubtless the increased level of prosperity helped all, but there was a clear hierarchy to the pattern of imperial generosity.

The uneven effects of imperial policy were more pronounced in the religious sphere. The Anglican church was legally established in the individual colonies; each had one or more SPG missionaries, and a determined effort was made by the Anglican bishop, Charles Inglis, to extend the influence of the church and to erect legal barriers against other forms of Protestantism.[18] In every way available to them, Inglis and his clerics tried to build a 'respectable' community in their new homes. They founded colleges in both New Brunswick and Nova Scotia shortly after their arrival. Major public events – military displays, public funerals, official fast days, and even theatre performances – were accompanied by rituals or sermons. Their goal was to unite the community around principles of deference, civility, and respect for public order – all the qualities that the frontier militated against.[19] In particular, Inglis wished to discourage evangelical religion, with its hostility to ritual and its wholehearted embrace of emotional expression. Perhaps the most revealing aspect of this Anglican policy was its warm tolerance of both the Presbyterian and the Catholic faiths – religions known for their disciplined memberships and stern theologies – and its use of every legal means available to discourage the evangelical sects. The problem was, of course, that the sects were numerous and politically shrewd – the last people in the region to accept discrimination passively.[20]

Perhaps the greatest disappointment of the Loyalist generation was its limited success in fostering education. The need for educational institutions was felt keenly by all English-speaking inhabitants, as their frequent petitions to government amply attest. As early as 1785, the New Brunswick Loyalists drafted a charter for a college in Fredericton, but their request for royal support was denied. Because the local Assembly insisted that common schools must be funded before advanced institutions for the élite, nothing was done before 1800. Nova Scotia was luckier, receiving a royal subsidy of £1,000 in 1791 to launch King's College at Windsor under the strict Anglican rules devised by Bishop Inglis. Otherwise, grammar schools at Saint John and Halifax, an academy at Fredericton, and numerous short-lived private educational ventures were all the region could afford before 1800. The dearth of schools produced great anxiety everywhere in the region among adults who tied their hopes for their settlements and their children's future to educational opportunities.[21]

As part of their constant effort to reproduce the more ordered world they had once known, the Loyalists introduced new forms and new standards of cultural achievement in many fields. Public and domestic architecture, the decorative arts, personal dress, and civic ceremonies were all enriched, but the greatest Loyalist cultural contribution was the spur given to intellectual life. 'We had no reading rooms – no lectures – no social gatherings for mental improvement ... no libraries,' moaned one Loyalist recalling his arrival in Halifax. As exiles, the Loyalists felt a particularly keen need to keep in touch with the larger world on both sides of the Atlantic, so that newspapers, reading societies, and subscriptions to foreign periodicals began to flourish in both Nova Scotia and New Brunswick. The most significant development was the publication beginning in 1789, of *The Nova Scotia Magazine*, the first literary journal in the Atlantic colonies. Begun by the classical scholar William Cochrane and supported enthusiastically by the Loyalist élite, the journal was remarkably broad in its coverage. Excerpts from the latest British and American magazines, novels, and philosophical works appeared side by side with local poetry and learned discussions of the region's history, natural science, and agricultural development. The ambitions of the editors, however, could not be sustained financially, and *The Nova Scotia Magazine* ceased publication in 1792. Nevertheless, its intellectual standards and comprehensive coverage set an inspiring precedent for all future ventures.[22]

Surprisingly, for many inhabitants, the arrival of the Loyalists and the new imperial policies did not immediately change their pattern of life. Day-to-day existence continued to be shaped by geography, climate, and the cultural habits of their particular heritage. As always, the centrifugal impulses of the land's dramatic contours prevailed. Forests, sea, and rocks dispersed settlement, mainly into the river valleys and along the coasts. Whether native Micmacs or incoming Loyalists, like-minded people gathered together in these clearings and set up communities that reflected their values and somehow produced the food, clothing, and shelter needed to live. Some of these settlements, the port towns for example, developed considerable material wealth and a dynamic commercial relationship with the outside world, while others like the Acadians were mainly inward-looking, without the financial resources or the cultural incentive to reach beyond their settlements. Yet even the simplest communities could enjoy a comfortable day-to-day existence, thanks to the natural abundance of the Atlantic region in the eighteenth century. Patrick Campbell, a Scottish traveller to the region, reported with astonishment on the quantities of fish in the rivers and bays and on the ability of the land and forests to provide food and fuel.[23]

There were advantages and disadvantages to this fragmented pattern of settlement. Geography clearly lent itself to the diverse character of the population. Most cultural groups – Acadians, New England Planters, Lunenburg Germans, Scottish Highlanders, Quaker Loyalists – could stake out a space and live out their lives free from outside interference. This clearly lessened intergroup tensions and permitted the inherited customs of each group – its language, religion, architecture, foodways, and dress – to remain central to its members' lives. At the same time, fragmentation discouraged communication among groups and acted as a brake on economic or political momentum. As a result, regional development lacked underlying unity and can best be understood by examining individual groups and categories of people, some of whom benefited from the new order, while others suffered severe setbacks or continued on oblivious of the larger world.

Although they were loath to admit it, the New England Planters benefited almost as much as the Loyalists from the new population and the new money. Land values simply soared in Cornwallis, Horton, Maugerville, and the Annapolis Valley after 1783, and the Planters were well placed to meet the almost insatiable demand of the refugees and the British garrisons for food, meat, and fuel. Planter merchants in Saint John and Halifax did equally well, expanding their businesses and the variety of goods for sale.[24]

Despite the profits that they derived from the new order, most Planters were highly censorious of the Loyalist newcomers on both political and religious grounds. Men like James Simonds in New Brunswick or Richard John Uniacke in Nova Scotia fiercely resented Loyalist slurs on their patriotism and Loyalist pretensions to power. Though outmanned and outgunned in both the region and in London, Planter communities consistently resisted the Loyalist drive to reshape the region. In New Brunswick, Sunbury County was the heart of the opposition, especially after the arrival in 1789 of James Glenie, a hard-driving, acerbically brilliant Scot, whose mast contracts gave him independent connections to imperial power. Glenie harboured an ancient grudge against Lieutenant-Governor Thomas Carleton, and supported by the Maugerville farmers and masting crews, he challenged the Fredericton élite's dominance. Glenie and his Planter phalanx were often supported by Loyalist merchants in the coastal areas, thus deepening the split between the military-agricultural establishment in Fredericton and the more commercial forces in the outlying areas. 'Our gentlemen have all become potato farmers,' moaned Edward Winslow, 'and our shoemakers are preparing to legislate.'[25]

Religious divisions between Planter and Loyalist were sharper and more durable. As New England Congregationalism slowly disintegrated in the region, many Planters joined Baptist or Methodist churches, evangelical sects whose enthusiasm was viewed with deep suspicion by Bishop Charles Inglis. Yet aside from reserving to Church of England clergy the right to perform the marriage ceremony, Inglis could do little to impede the growth of the sects. Tithes were not collected in the Atlantic colonies, and there were no religious tests for public office after 1783, so that a high degree of religious toleration prevailed in the region regardless of the wishes of government officials. The settlers themselves seemed indifferent to these doctrinal distinctions. The ordinary English-speaking inhabitants – whether Loyalist or Planter, Black or White – flocked indiscriminately to these various expressions of Protestant Christianity, so eager were they to receive religious consolation. Thus, although all religions expanded in the Atlantic region during this period, they did not produce a unifying bond among its peoples.[26]

The region's French-speaking population, the Acadians, had a far different experience in the late eighteenth century. Like the Loyalists, the Acadians had endured persecution and exile, but they had no benign imperial government to help them rebuild their lives. Some did not make it, succumbing to disease or privation along the way. Others settled successfully into new locations, particularly in Louisiana where the hospitable French environment would permit the formation of a distinctive Cajun community. An indeterminate number made their way back, slowly and tentatively, once legal permission to return was granted in 1764. Since their original homes were now taken over by thousands of New England settlers and European immigrants, the returning Acadians were forced to resettle in less fertile, more remote areas: on the western tip of the Nova Scotia peninsula around St Mary's Bay, up the St John River and around the Bay of Chaleur, or in the tiny outports of present-day Prince Edward Island and Cape Breton. Most of these new settlements achieved permanence, but when the Loyalists arrived in the 1780s, the Acadians on the St John River were forced to pull up stakes and move again, this time to the Madawaska region. Even Edward Winslow considered this second dispossession unjust.

The Acadians were now a vulnerable minority, neither British nor Protestant nor supported any longer by powerful Micmac allies. Their only interest in government was to acquire secure title to their lands and freedom to practise their Catholic religion. In New Brunswick, Thomas Carleton was quite willing to meet these needs in return for Acadian participation in the militia. It was a good compromise. By the 1790s a rising birth rate among the Madawaska families suggests they had recovered their ability to thrive in a simple, rural existence.[27] In Nova Scotia, government indifference to their needs created much anxiety among the Acadians over land titles and Loyalist neighbours who eyed their lands acquisitively. Nonetheless, the Acadians of Nova Scotia also succeeded in re-establishing a viable way of life. Education took place within the family and consisted mainly of instruction in the ancient truths of Catholicism plus the basic skills needed for adult life. According to Scottish antiquarian Rev. Andrew Brown, they would gather together in the evenings to re-tell their experiences, preserving orally deeply emotional memories of such things as the 'golden age' before the Expulsion, the terrors of the Deportation period, the quaint personalities they had met on their travels in Boston or Philadelphia, and the harrowing saga of their return home. Their isolation and their folkways enabled the Acadians to achieve their foremost goal of cultural preservation. By 1800, the Acadian population of Nova Scotia numbered almost 8,000, a total close to the numbers resident on the peninsula before the Deportation, and a remarkable tribute to their resilience as a people.[28]

If Loyalists, Planters, and Acadians improved their situations at least marginally during the period 1783–1800, the opposite was true of the Black and Native peoples in the region. The 3,000 Black Loyalists who arrived in 1783 had won their freedom during the American Revolution by escaping to British lines. They had been given firm promises of land, assistance, and protection in beginning a new life of freedom in British-held territory. The fate of these people is both tragic and heroic. Technically, the British government redeemed its promises. The Black Loyalists were settled in Nova Scotia and New Brunswick, given land, rations, tools, and the chance to begin a new life. Practically, however, the details of this policy reveal a heartbreaking pattern of discrimination. Britain had promised freedom, but it had never promised equality. The Black Loyalists were settled in separate areas, on smaller plots of remote, often uncultivable land. Their share of provisions and tools was substantially less – sometimes only a third as much as the Whites received – although their hunger and their need were surely as great. Their freedom was recognized in law, but they did not get the right to vote or sit on juries or fish in the Saint John Harbour, and they were punished more severely for crimes than Whites. They could attend White churches and White schools, but they had to sit in segregated sections. They could form their own churches – which they did with remarkable enthusiasm – but the attempt of the Black Methodist preacher Boston King to baptize a White couple touched off a riot.[29]

In short, the free Black Loyalists were British subjects, but legal and social barriers consigned them to the periphery, the margins of civilized life. Some Loyalist leaders, such as Lieutenant-Governor John Wentworth or the humanitarian lawyer Ward Chipman, did try to help them develop a self-sufficient way of life, but most Blacks were far too vulnerable and inexperienced to cope with both White contempt and the northern wilderness. Nothing in their previous life as slaves had prepared them to be independent farmers or free citizens, and many drifted into tenantry or into the port towns, where they worked as servants or day labourers.

One remarkable man rebelled. His name was Thomas Peters, a sergeant in the Black Pioneers who had fled from slavery in North Carolina. Peters would not accept the unequal treatment given to his family and friends. He spent six years petitioning local government for decent land and then, tired of waiting, went to England to lay his grievances before the imperial government. He discovered in London a group of English reformers promoting a 'back to Africa' scheme, seeking to establish in West Africa a free, Black colony for the relief of the many distressed Black people within the British Empire. Peters enthusiastically embraced this idea, and the British government agreed to underwrite the passage of all Black residents of Nova Scotia and New Brunswick who wanted to go.[30]

This migration led to the beginning of Sierra Leone, the first permanent British settlement colony in Africa and a powerful source of African nationalism in the nineteenth and twentieth centuries. More than 1,100 Blacks left Atlantic Canada in 1792 to resettle in Freetown on the

West African coast. They brought with them from their experience in North America a strong sense of their separate identity, a conviction that land ownership was indispensable to personal liberty, and an enduring race consciousness. They were joined in 1800 by some 550 Maroons, descendants of Black slaves who had escaped from the old Spanish regime in Jamaica two centuries earlier and had been deported to Halifax by British authorities in 1796 following an outbreak of hostilities in the previous year. The Maroons maintained the cohesiveness of their communities for four years, until they were again deported – this time to Sierra Leone – at the request of a British government worried about the cost of subsidies to support their establishment in Nova Scotia.[31] The unfortunate side-effect of these exoduses was that those Blacks who remained in the Atlantic colonies were left in a weakened position. With most of their leaders now gone to Sierra Leone, the community slipped farther into semi-slavery, a social underclass working for Whites, with few rights and less hope, except that offered by their families and their own churches.

The problem with the Native peoples was less one of discrimination than of cultural clash. The sheer numbers of Loyalists who flooded into the region disrupted the pattern of seasonal migration so vital to the traditional Native way of life. In Nova Scotia, the Loyalists took all the good land, while on the island colonies no lands were reserved for either Micmacs or Beothuks, reducing their chances for survival. The vast acreage of New Brunswick provided enough living space for all, but the Loyalists seized the most favoured spots on the coastlines and river-fronts, and the provincial government diminished the bands' legal position by whittling away at their reserve lands and restricting them to licences of occupation, rather than the free grants enjoyed by the non-Native population. The worst blow, however, was the collapse of the old economic equilibrium based on the exchange of furs for trade goods. Trade in furs could no longer support the needs of the Native population, while their dependence on European goods – ammunition, food, medicine, and clothing – had increased. Some groups developed new economic activities, such as the sale of moose meat, porpoise, and other food items, as well as of axe handles, barrels, baskets, and similar wood products. Others, particularly the Maliseets on the St John River, made sporadic shows of force to protest non-Native encroachment. Although the non-Native population lived in constant fear of guerrilla attacks or uprisings, their governments proved insensitive to the survival needs of the bands, viewing their determination to preserve their traditional way of life with contempt and their demand for a resumption of the traditional system of presents as mere begging. The solution, those in authority agreed, was assimilation. The Native peoples must be taught to adapt to the Europeans' way of life, to agriculture, Protestantism, and British civilization.[32]

In a remarkable example of paternalism, an Anglican missionary project called the New England Company was transferred from Massachusetts to New Brunswick in 1785. Eight mission schools were set up, and £800 sterling invested each year in hopes of inducing the local Micmacs and Maliseets to settle down and become good farmers and good churchgoing subjects. The Natives fiercely rejected these efforts to domesticate them – to turn them into women, as they said – although their need for presents and government aid did force them to permit some of their children to go to the mission schools. The only real enthusiasts for the project were local Whites, who sought to siphon off company funds to educate their own children and to use the Native students as a form of cheap labour. Misuse and abuse became so serious that by 1800 half of the local directors were threatening to resign in protest.[33]

Scottish penetration of the region began quite gradually. Ever since the founding of Halifax in 1749, there had always been some Lowland Scots in the region engaged in mercantile activity. In the years after 1770, small numbers of Scots migrated from the Highlands to lands bordering the Gulf of St Lawrence. One of the largest early groups arrived at Pictou on the *Hector* in 1773. These people had left Scotland in order to escape the forces of overpopulation and industrialization that threatened to destroy their ancient, pastoral way of life. They first settled around Pictou and Antigonish. Most were farmers, but a fair number of tradesmen and skilled craftsmen also came, and their ranks were swelled after the American Revolution by disbanded Highland soldiers from the British regiments. Thanks to its proximity to Halifax, Pictou quickly developed into a commercial centre and supported several merchants. Most of the first generation of migrants, however, chose to continue on as farmers and began the slow, grinding routine of clearing land, cutting timber, and depending for food and shelter on their day-to-day exertions.

These Scots brought their religious differences with them. Roman Catholics chose either Cape Breton or the Island of St John for settlement, while Presbyterians favoured the Nova Scotia mainland. With the arrival of Rev. James MacGregor in 1786, Pictou became the centre for Presbyterianism in Nova Scotia. The great creative contribution of Presbyterianism to the culture of the Atlantic colonies would begin just after the turn of the century, with the arrival of Thomas McCulloch and his profound sense of educational mission.[34]

Catholic Highlanders converged first on Antigonish and Cape Breton

Island, and then in the 1790s a new wave settled on the Island of St John. Contracts arranged beforehand with the Island's proprietors assured the immigrants of sufficient land. They moved in family or community groups, bringing with them some capital in the form of savings and 'a deserving young clergyman full of zeal,' Father Angus MacEachern. Such carefully laid plans enabled these Highlanders to achieve their goal of maintaining their Catholic faith and Gaelic language. It also made them an unusually cohesive group of settlers who used their isolation to recreate their cherished culture. By 1800 nearly 10,000 Highlanders had emigrated to the Maritimes.[35]

The ratio of men to women in all these groups cannot be specified, although there was a serious sexual imbalance in Newfoundland and among some groups of Loyalist veterans. Patrick Campbell tells of soldiers on the Nashwaak River complaining to him of the dearth of women for their young men. 'They begged of me to recommend some hundreds of them to come, and that they should all get husbands, or masters, before they should be three weeks in the country.'[36] The centrality of women to economic hopes on the frontier or in the wilderness was plainly evident. Most undertakings were family enterprises, where men and women worked in partnership, and where a solitary individual, male or female, was severely handicapped. Yet the importance of women to community stability and to all economic tasks did not produce any increase in their status or autonomy. Women were prohibited by custom from active participation in public life. Any wealth they possessed was controlled by their fathers while they were young and their husbands thereafter. Marriage was the only attractive choice for adult life, and paternalistic norms confined wives to the domestic sphere and compliance with their husbands' choices. The historian Beatrice Ross Buzek has suggested that Loyalist women were caught as well in a 'double bind.' Like the men, they were forced to give up homes and family as a result of the American Revolution, but they carried the additional psychological burden of knowing that the decision to become a Loyalist had been imposed by the men without consultation, a situation that could add to the bitterness and heartache of exile. The few surviving documents on Loyalist women present an ambiguous portrait. Jonathan Odell's several poetic tributes to his wife, Anne, or Edward Winslow's sly, flirtatious letters to his Mary, suggest that war, exile, and the 'shipwreck' of their fortunes did not diminish the bonds of affection between these Loyalist couples. By contrast, Beverley Robinson, Jr, bellowed like a military martinet in letters reminding his wife of her obligation to serve him, and Amos Botsford turned his spouse out of the house, destitute, as punishment for an adulterous affair. Even under the best circumstances, virtually all Loyalist women lost that network of mothers, sisters, and friends that was so important to colonial women during childbirth and other personal challenges, but that could not accompany them north into exile.[37]

Among Acadian women, by contrast, the experience of deportation, exile and return seemed, if possible, to strengthen their importance. While there was a long-standing sexual division of labour in their communities – with men responsible for hunting and fishing, and women for cloth-making and food preparation – Acadian women had always been respected partners in the management of work and the organization of family and community. After the Deportation, Acadians' commitment to their families and to retaining their historic ways of life became more compelling, while socially they became more isolated. The old, expansive kinship networks and practice of intermarriage with Micmac or English people were not renewed, as they seemed to prefer 'an almost inviolate Separation from all other classes of People.'[38]

The changing economic roles of Micmac and Maliseet women produced a net loss of status during this period. Most of the goods once manufactured by Native men and women working together had been gradually replaced by European products, especially weapons, blankets, cooking utensils, clothing, and food. While these new European goods unquestionably made the men more efficient at hunting and fishing, they radically altered the contribution of women to daily life and made them more dependent. The Native women continued to work, of course, and constantly searched for new ways to meet the increased need for cash by producing handicrafts for market and selling berries, fruits, and small fowl from door to door. None of these activities, however, restored their old economic partnership with the men of their band. As well, Micmac and Maliseet women, like their non-Native sisters, were severely restricted in their right to hold property and in the kinds of jobs open to them. All wage labour and work requiring technical skills, even farming, were reserved for men, thus confining Native women's opportunities to domestic work, handicraft sales, and occasional prostitution.[39]

Overall, the record suggests that so long as women conformed to the standards of their community, they would be protected. For example, when the Loyalist military officer David Fanning was convicted of rape, he was banished from New Brunswick forever, to his great economic distress. Challenging community norms, however, could produce real difficulty for women. Young Rebecca Byles felt a natural resentment when her brother went off to Paris, while she was confined to the 'necessity of immediately going into the kitchen to tye up a pudding.' Byles read England's new generation of female authors with sharp attention and declared mockingly: 'in a few years I expect to see Women fill the most important offices Church and State ...' It took repeated readings of Dr John Gregory's *A Father's Advice to His Daughters* to reconcile this high-spirited young woman to the necessity of confining her life to the private domestic sphere. She eventually succumbed to the 'rage for matrimony' that prevailed among the Loyalist exiles in Halifax, and clearly found both marriage and motherhood rewarding. In her final years, Byles became a rigid conservative, condemning public tracts on women's rights and her own daughter's embrace of evangelical religion.[40]

Like Byles, young Mary Bradley knew the risks women ran in challenging convention, but she persevered in her determination to play a public role. The daughter of Maugerville farmers, Mary experienced intense religious feelings early in her life and spoke out with spiritual fervour in her church, to the dismay of the Congregational elders. She married at eighteen and clearly wanted to be a good wife, taking great pride in the money that her weaving added to the family income and supporting her husband's effort to run a grocery store in Saint John. Yet her need to express her spiritual convictions publicly was a constant source of tension. After her first husband's death in 1816, a second marriage produced a more sympathetic partner, and Mary devoted the remainder of her life to the spread of Wesleyan Methodism, a rare example of female success in an assertive public role.[41]

Left alone, the Atlantic provinces would doubtless have continued to develop slowly and unevenly. Certainly by the year 1790 the Empire had terminated any active interest in the region. The Jay Treaty, which opened the West Indian trade to the Americans, was signed without any attempt to consult those affected in the region, and the only new imperial policy was a restriction placed in 1790 on all the Atlantic colonies forbidding any further grants of land. Unexpectedly, a new world war reversed this trend. In 1793 Great Britain and a coalition of European powers declared war on the government of revolutionary France. To protect its North American colonies against certain French aggression, the Empire sent ships, troops, and thousands of pounds sterling to the Atlantic region. Privateers were commissioned, the militia called up, cannon and arms distributed along the coastlines, new presents authorized for the Native bands, and even a public salary of £70 per annum offered to the Catholic priest ministering to the Acadians. And all paid for by His Majesty's government! In 1794 alone, £4,597 sterling crossed the Atlantic to cover the costs of massive preparations against a rumoured French invasion.[42]

The threat was real, although it never materialized. Instead, the wartime boom enabled Halifax, especially its clique of Loyalist officials and Scots merchants, to begin building a distinguished public life for their city. Lieutenant-Governor John Wentworth sponsored balls, theatre performances, and elaborate military ceremonies to inspire patriotism and satisfy the élite's love of ritual. The arrival of the Duke of Kent to command the garrison, in company with his beautiful mistress, Mme St Laurent, heightened both the level of British support and the festive rounds. Before the decade was out, the House of Assembly had voted funds for a sumptuous governor's mansion and a beautifully proportioned building for the provincial legislature. The Duke crowned these new public monuments by commissioning a stunning octagonal Clock Tower on Citadel Hill to ensure, so it was said, that his troops appeared on time.

The major beneficiaries of this extraordinary boom were the merchants of Halifax and, to a lesser extent, those in Saint John, St Andrews, and St John's. The war enabled Halifax to fulfil its long dream of becoming the main supply base for the British West Indies and the entrepôt for goods travelling between the Atlantic ports, Montreal, and Scotland. Although there were some Loyalist participants, the merchants involved were mainly Lowland Scots who had dominated the trade of the Atlantic region for thirty years or more. They were a distinctive group, tightly knit and compulsively hard-working. The key to their success rested on the elaborate web of connections they maintained with other Scottish firms and that gave them access to credit, up-to-date market information, and reliable agents in distant ports. Moreover, the traditional, fierce Scottish resentment of British trade restrictions favouring London and Bristol made these merchants past masters in the arts of smuggling and evasion. As a result, although their legitimate trade in fish, ships, and timber was undeniably profitable, these cargoes also served as masks for equally lucrative exchanges of illicit American and European goods.[43]

New Brunswick's trade revolved around shipbuilding and timber. Although the great boom period would not occur until after the turn of the century, significant foundations were laid in the 1790s. Most startling was the entrepreneurship of Jonathan Scott, who built twenty-seven vessels in Saint John between 1797 and 1801 by bringing out from Scotland the nucleus of crews and such materials as nails, copper and iron spikes, and anchors. This transfer of technology and craftsmen not only increased the level of skill and the quality of Saint John's ships, but also introduced local merchants to the advantages of large-scale operations. As a sideline, it also encouraged a local furniture industry, for the Scottish craftsmen immediately appreciated the potential for transforming local black birch trees and the mahogany readily available from the Caribbean into pieces of exceptionally high quality.[44]

Vessels returning to Atlantic Canada brought an ever-increasing variety of goods to the traders and shopkeepers of the region – the tailors, clockmakers, goldsmiths and silversmiths, hairdressers, and coffee-house keepers who catered to all with money to spend. Advertisements in the *Nova Scotia Royal Gazette* grew bigger in size and in the diversity of goods offered, as the boom rolled on. Luxury goods in particular became more conspicuous. Ostrich feathers, pearl dentifrices, exotic spices, pianofortes, and violet-scented hair powder were some of the items 'received from London' to embellish the glittering social life presided over by the Duke, Sir John, and their guests.

Perhaps no place was affected more by the war than Newfoundland. Just before hostilities broke out, the island suffered severe depression and near famine conditions as a result of the glut of fish on the European market. The war not only inaugurated a new boom, but permanently changed the life of the colony. The two most conspicuous changes were the consolidation of the resident fishery, which by 1800 was responsible for 95 per cent of the island's exports, and the emergence of St John's as the dominant commercial centre of the island. True to its ancient policy, and prodded by ever-greedy English merchants, the Empire continued to resist giving the island a proper colonial government. It did, in 1792, appoint a chief justice for Newfoundland, one John Reeves, but only required that he reside on the island during two summer months. In fact, Reeves's winters in England probably helped the colonists more than his summer tours, for he became a warm advocate of the need for more government on the island. Newfoundland, Reeves declared, 'is no longer a place resorted to only by mere fishermen who ... caught their fish and at the close of the season returned to the mother country.' Rather, he insisted, it 'has been peopled behind your back.' Reeves's pleas were echoed by the growing community of resident merchants, who organized a Society of Merchants in 1800 and began to demand more public institutions. Reform would not begin until after the turn of the century, but the boom of the 1790s made it almost inevitable. Whether it would benefit the local fisherman was another question. Undeniably, he was now more self-sufficient in terms of food and housing. But for the average fisherman, the local merchant had simply replaced the English merchant as his supplier, and the need for advance credit to finance his gear and provisions meant that the chronic problems of debt and dependency would continue to plague his existence.[45]

The wartime boom seemed to skip over the smaller island colonies entirely. Cape Breton lost its British garrison, a major source of cash for the colony, and the fortress island felt more neglected than ever by its distant rulers. The Island of St John got a new name – Prince Edward Island – in honour of the Duke of Kent, but angry land disputes continued to wrack its public life. The cry for escheat became more strident as the century came to a close, and local opponents of the government began to suggest reannexation to Nova Scotia. None of these protests resolved the land issue or dislodged the powerful Fanning. Paradoxically, the Island would enter the new century with a young and growing population and a rising record of food production, but with a pervasive feeling of political grievance.[46]

A final effect of the war was the spur it gave to local cultural life and feelings of British patriotism. Unfortunately, the war began too late to save *The Nova Scotia Magazine*, the one outlet for local poets and writers. Nonetheless, the royal endowment of King's College, Windsor, gave solid hope of a rising generation trained in the arts and sciences. In the interim, the newspapers in Halifax, Saint John, and Charlottetown did their weekly best to keep their publics in touch with the world. The war and the French Revolution were easily the most popular topics, and reports inevitably had a heavy political bias. News from France concentrated on the worst atrocities of the Reign of Terror, while selections from the English press featured English military victories and lovingly detailed accounts of the King's health. By far the most popular author of the period was William Cobbett, the British Tory radical. Writing under the pen name of 'Peter Porcupine,' Cobbett issued brilliant, outrageously funny tirades against the tyranny of France and the excesses of republican America. Naturally, the faithful British subjects of the Atlantic colonies loved it. All the regional newspapers carried Cobbett's columns, and when he visited Halifax in 1800 he was feted at a public banquet by Sir John Wentworth.[47]

In these and other ways the wars of the French Revolution strengthened the ties of the Atlantic people to the Empire and contributed to the growth of civic life. One of the most unexpected but important results of the war was the arrival of priests from revolutionary France to begin a new mission to the Acadian people. Superbly educated and rigidly conservative in matters of personal morals, men like Père Sigogne were received by the Acadians with mixed feelings of gratitude at having their own resident priests and grave concern over clerical disapproval of their easygoing ways. Over time, however, the French priests would assist the Acadians to take their proper place in the public life of the region, just as the Loyalists had earlier raised the level of public leadership and public consciousness.[48]

By 1800, the Planters, the Loyalists, the Scottish merchants, and the Highland farmers were all settled comfortably into their individual niches. And the continuing possibility of a French invasion made government much more responsive to the Acadian, Micmac, and Maliseet minorities. Yet a persistent, deepening fissure lay below this surface calm. Atlantic Canada was now split into two sets of people with widely divergent approaches to life. On one side were the dominant, mainly British settlers with their firm commitment to the Empire, their Protestant faiths, and their aggressive commercial outlook. On the other side stood several discrete minorities who valued communal bonds more strongly than economic success, who mainly adhered to the Roman Catholic faith, and who had no voice whatsoever in the direction of public affairs. This basic social contradiction would increasingly preoccupy public attention in the years ahead. The contribution of the late eighteenth century to that future was to give the region stable local government, the rudiments of educational and legal institutions, and an expanding, skilled population that approached the 90,000 mark by 1800. The challenge for succeeding generations would be to realize the promise of these assets by developing a public life that included all of its people and rewarded their allegiance.

CHAPTER TEN

1800–1810
Turning the Century

GRAEME WYNN

Nova Scotia's Government House is the Atlantic region's most gracious and enduring monument to the first decade of the nineteenth century. Described at the ceremonial laying of the cornerstone in September 1800 as a symbol of 'the increasing Prosperity of this infant colony,' the building was a steady drain on colonial finances through the next several years. Erected by local craftsmen using colonial materials, according to plans derived from *A Series of Original Designs for Country Seats* published in London in 1795, Government House stood in spacious grounds on the outskirts of the city. In the eyes of its master-builder it was a triumph of skill and taste, 'equalled by few, [and] perhaps exceeded by none in the Western Hemisphere.' To countless contemporaries it reflected the political and cultural ties that bound colony and mother country, reinforced the social order, and served as an emblem of 'the loyalty and attachment of ... [Nova Scotians] to the best of Sovereigns.'[1] But Government House was also a monument to colonial achievement and a statement about what Nova Scotia might become. By confirming the success of Loyalist John Wentworth's governorship, it suggested that the tribulations of the past were being left behind and bespoke confidence in the future. In a sense it epitomized the transitional character of the decade in which it was built.

Because time is a continuum and most change is gradual, it is easy to exaggerate the significance of those common milestones of history's path, decades and centuries. In many respects, however, the years between 1800 and 1810 were pivotal ones. In broad terms, at least, the development of the Atlantic region in the 1790s is most intelligible within the framework of eighteenth-century events and policies. By the second decade of the nineteenth century, patterns of settlement, social organization, economic development, and political behaviour in all five

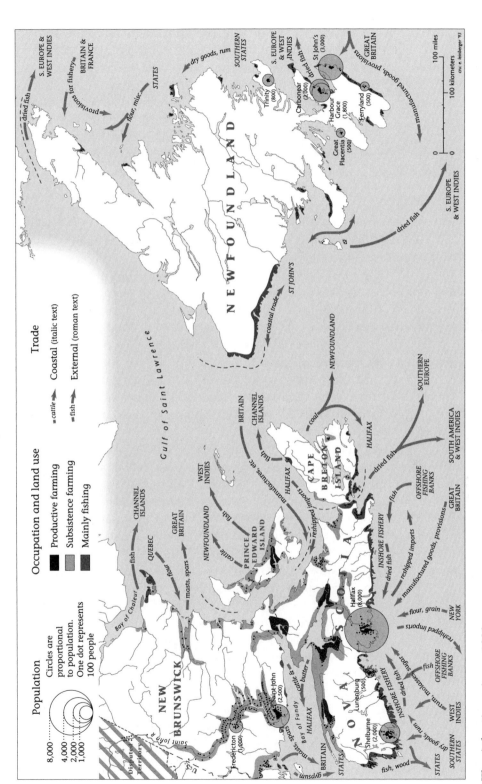

The Atlantic region c. 1800

colonies require a different grid of interpretation. Consider the four 'maritime' colonies. Late in the eighteenth century, most of their residents were 'Planters' or Loyalists from the colonies to the south; economies sputtered; and American and West Indian ports attracted most of their relatively trifling trade. Little more than a decade later, colonial wood was the basis of a vigorous transatlantic commerce; a rising tide of British immigrants had begun to swell the population of the colonies; and vibrant local markets had produced a 'general improvement in the appearance of the peasantry, as well as in the comfort of their dwellings and in the number and value of their stock.'[2] So too in Newfoundland, this was a period of remarkable change. In 1790, it was still feasible to see that colony much as it had been regarded for decades, as a great ship moored off the Grand Banks for the convenience of the fishery. By 1810 it was impossible to do so: the island was clearly a settlement colony rather than a distant summer camp for European fishermen.

These pointed contrasts suggest the broad trends of change that differentiated the Atlantic region of the eighteenth century from that of the nineteenth; they are a reminder that it is necessary to look forward as well as backward to understand this turn-of-the-century decade, and that one must seek pattern in the complexity of the past. Yet they drain much of the vitality from the story of people struggling with their circumstances that forms the vital core of history. They are no substitute for close analyses of lives lived and places made in this corner of the New World.

In 1800, the five Atlantic colonies were a poorly integrated amalgam of families and small communities. Approximately 100,000 people lived in the region, but they were widely scattered along rocky, forbidding coastlines and narrow, heavily forested valleys. Here and there the pattern of hard-scrabble existence imposed by the effort to squeeze a living from thin soils and the unforgiving sea was broken by clusters of settlement in more fertile and extensive pockets of land, and by the concentration of people in modest urban places; but few had had time or chance to prosper in this harsh and fragmented domain. Although successful merchants and office-holders in Halifax, Saint John, and St John's owned sizeable fortunes, they were a small fraction of those who lived in these cities of 8,000, 2,500, and 3,000. Shelburne, the only other town with more than 1,000 people, was in decline. Fredericton, Charlottetown, and Sydney were capital villages, with populations of approximately 750, 500, and 200. A modest two-storey province hall was under construction amid the 130 or so houses dotted across the rich and delightful 'sheep pasture' that bordered the St John River some ninety miles from its mouth, but Sydney, laid out on an ambitious classical-revival plan in 1785, had more deserted than inhabited houses and several grandiloquently named streets frequented only by cattle. In Charlottetown, seventy houses – 'many of them very indifferent' – stood in large lots scattered across a regular grid of wide, muddy streets, and the church was the only public building.[3] For all the lustre that Edward, Duke of Kent and commander-in-chief of British forces in North America, added to Halifax society, the pomp and ceremony of colonial administration, and the ostentatious behaviour of the leading citizens of the region, who consumed fine claret and imported their clothes from first-rate milliners in London, there can be no mistaking the fact that arduous toil, utilitarian furnishings, and homespun were the common lot of most of the region's people. On this score, at least, the splendour of Nova Scotia's Government House masked rather than revealed the character of the period; few of the region's inhabitants shared the wealth, privilege, and power that it embodied.

Along the Atlantic front of the region, from Fogo to Cape Fourchu, and here and there around the Gulf of St Lawrence from Cheticamp to the Gaspé, fishermen and their families occupied isolated coastal settlements. The products, for the most part, of migration streams that linked particular source areas to specific destinations, the majority of these settlements were dominated by a single ethnic group. Ireland and the English West Country had provided most of the people of Newfoundland's outports; in Cape Breton, Acadians were pre-eminent; on Nova Scotia's south shore, the majority had come from New England; only in parts of the Gulf, where the fishery engaged Canadians, Acadians, English, Irish, and Channel Islanders, were ethnic patterns thoroughly mixed. Most of the fishing settlements were tiny. Trinity, among the largest, had approximately 100 houses and 800 residents scattered about the several small coves of its commodious harbour.[4] Stakes, sheds, and flakes (on which fish were dried) dominated the waterfronts of these settlements. Among and around them, small dwellings, a few ramshackle outbuildings, a scatter of rough fields, and several small kitchen gardens hugged the beach, with scant regard for geometrical order. Typically, families kept a couple of cattle and a pig or two; a few had a handful of sheep. In settlement after settlement, at least three-quarters of all families made their living from the sea; many were indebted to the merchants who took their catch; few indeed were rich in material things. By and large they were a 'very hardy People', who – noted one contemporary – 'chiefly Live on Fish and Pork with what Potatoes they may grow.'[5]

If farm families – who made up the majority of the 'maritime' colonies' 80,000 or so people – fared better, on average, than those in the fishing settlements, their circumstances varied enormously in detail. In some places the contrasts were striking: large, productive farms lay adjacent to ill-tended smallholdings; substantial, graceful houses next to dark and draughty cabins. But generally (and notwithstanding the capital, energy, and vision of their occupants), the development of substantial farms depended upon the availability of markets for their surplus produce, and these were scarce. Through much of the region, then, most farms were correspondingly modest. With approximately ten cleared acres, half a dozen cattle, a horse, and perhaps a few sheep, they could provide a meagre and rather uncertain subsistence for a small family. Slightly larger properties might allow their occupants a few small luxuries, but farm families often found it necessary to supplement the small, sporadic surpluses of their fields and barns with returns, in cash or kind, for various kinds of work, from domestic service to day labour, or from weaving to shoemaking. Some of these modest farms included comfortable dwellings (many built with the help of military half-pay or the returns of local office), but few of them had more than twenty acres under cultivation. Whether they turned a dozen cattle and twenty or thirty sheep onto well-fenced fields or practised the rudimentary agriculture of pioneers, their occupants applied their hands to a wide variety of tasks and were linked to other settlers in their immediate vicinities by an intricate web of contractual arrangements and social obligations. Few had regular and significant economic connections beyond these cells of local life, although the commercial interests of storekeepers and mill-owners scattered through the countryside ensured that these were never more than partially closed economies.

This pattern was broken decisively in only a few places where rich soils, relatively long-established settlement, and access to the urban populations of Halifax and Saint John gave farming a more commercial orientation. Still, American flour and other imported provisions were stiff competition for local producers in these markets – as they were in St John's – and, in the main, farmers on the Bay of Fundy marshlands, along the lower reaches of the St John Valley, and in Lunenberg provided livestock, hay, and vegetables to their urban neighbours.[6]

Standing at the threshold of the nineteenth century, many Nova Scotians were confident that better times were ahead. The embodiment of the militia, work on the defences, and the presence of British naval vessels in Halifax had put coin in circulation during the 1790s. The prosperity of the capital had begun to percolate into other parts of the colony. Even the difficulties of overland communication were being addressed. Several thousand pounds were allocated to road building each year. There was talk of joining the Bay of Fundy with the Atlantic by constructing a canal from Bedford Basin to the Shubenacadie River. And military officers considered extending to New Brunswick the line of semaphore stations that linked Halifax and Annapolis.

Reflecting the extent to which optimism had become an item of faith among the colonial élite, in March 1800 the rector of St Paul's, Halifax, gave shape to the buoyant mood from his pulpit. Addressing many of the principal inhabitants of the town, Rev. Robert Stanser chose his text from the Old Testament and likened the colony to the land of Deuteronomy, to which God had promised 'the rain ... in his due season,' that his people 'mayest gather in' their corn and wine and oil. Laborious and monotonous though his preaching was said to be, Stanser's message was clear.[7] According to the Book of Moses, the Lord's people entered a territory that was 'not as the land of Egypt,' from whence they had come, a place where they 'sowedst ... seed, and wateredst it with [their] foot as a garden of herbs,' but the eyes of the Lord were always upon it. Its hills and valleys were blessed with the rain of heaven, and to its diligent and faithful inhabitants God had promised 'grass in thy fields for thy cattle, that thou mayest eat and be full.' The parallel was clear. Beyond the great and terrible wilderness through which Moses had led his people lay the promised land of milk and honey. For all the hardships and difficulties of recent years, Nova Scotians could look forward to better times ahead.

Similar optimism surfaced in New Brunswick only a few months later, although that colony was a backwater by contrast with Nova Scotia. Lacking the strategic importance of its neighbour, it had lost troops to Halifax and the West Indies with the resumption of war between England and France in the 1790s, and with the troops had gone their salaries and their contracts for fuel and provisions. The colony's population of approximately 26,000 was barely two-thirds of that in the peninsula across the Bay of Fundy: its annual revenue hardly amounted to a tenth of its larger counterpart's. Late in the 1790s, Loyalist dreams for the colony appeared to be in tatters. Edward Winslow expressed something of the frustration of many of his fellow leaders when he discerned their society 'gradually sinking into a sort of lethargy,' and lamented the exodus from the province.[8] But a quickening of provincial life was evident by 1800. The boundary settlement of 1798, which confirmed the northern branch of the Schoodiac River as the western limit of British territory identified in the Treaty of Paris, dispelled the uncertainty associated with American claims that the Magaguadavic River was the St Croix referred to in the agreement of 1783.[9] Shipbuilding and commerce expanded, and with the coming of peace between England and France, the *Royal Gazette* of 1 December 1801 anticipated that New Brunswick's *'wilderness'* would soon *'blossom as the rose.'*

Lieutenant-Governor Wentworth's plans to produce an illustrated history of the lower colonies, mooted early in 1801, were thoroughly in keeping with these anticipations of a new dawn. Hoping to change his colony's austere reputation, Wentworth envisaged production of a promotional volume by local residents William Sabatier and George Isham Parkyns. Sabatier was a wealthy merchant, the author of a treatise on poverty, and Parkyns a skilful English water-colourist who had come to the colony the year before.[10] With its image refurbished, hoped Wentworth, the region would attract new settlers, its rich resources would be developed, and a growing trade would bring economic independence.

Although nothing came of Wentworth's 'history,' the changes it was intended to promote were soon under way, driven by economic and political developments beyond the region. With the peace of 1801, migration from the British Isles quickened.[11] Year after year, a few families and small groups of English artisans, farmers, and labourers, dislocated by the transformation of their country into the world's first industrial nation, took ship for the colonies. From the hinterlands of Poole, Dartmouth, and a handful of other West Country fishing ports, where the serge-cloth trade was in difficulty, small but increasing numbers of men and women followed old-established lines of commercial connection to the outports of eastern Newfoundland. Ireland also contributed to the rising population of that colony. Again, most of the newcomers came from a particular corner of the country – the southeastern counties of Wexford, Waterford, and Tipperary, which had long been involved in provisioning the Newfoundland trade and where a declining domestic textile industry spelled hardship for many. Harbingers of a far more substantial exodus from England and Ireland in the decades that followed, these movements helped raise the number of Newfoundland residents from fewer than 19,000 at the turn of the century to 25,000 by 1810. They also added people, skills, and capital to the economies and societies of Nova Scotia and New Brunswick and provided those who had remained in the home countries with new sources of information about eastern British North America.[12]

Yet these migrations were less significant than the flow of migrants from Scotland to the Maritimes. Late in the eighteenth century, the precepts and practices of improved agriculture – among them land enclosure, thorough ploughing, summer fallowing, crop rotation, and sheep herding – had begun to remake traditional patterns of economy and society in the Highlands. By 1800, many crofters in the kelping townships of the Western Islands were in difficult circumstances after several years of bad harvests and rising rents.[13] Regimental recruiting sergeants no longer scoured the glens, and letters from earlier Scottish migrants to North America told of their successes in the new world. Between 1801 and 1803, more than 7,000 Scots sailed for British North America. Almost a quarter came ashore in Prince Edward Island, and slightly more than half landed in Nova Scotia, most of them in Pictou. Some established themselves as merchants in the major towns of the region, but the majority settled on the eastern perimeter of the Gulf of St Lawrence and began to develop farms and communities in this thinly settled region.[14] Although efforts to create employment in the Highlands and new regulations governing conditions on emigrant ships slowed the exodus in 1803, they did not halt it. Within seven or eight years, at least 1,500 more Scots reached Prince Edward Island. Others came to Cape Breton and eastern Nova Scotia.

Set down in 'the boundless forests of America,' many of these newcomers from old and closely settled lands surely felt the childlike helplessness attributed to them by Thomas Douglas, Earl of Selkirk, in his important contribution to the early-nineteenth-century debate over emigration from Scotland, *Observations on the Present State of the Highlands*.[15] Arguing, in opposition to those who would restrict the exodus of Scots, that 'the habits and inclinations' of dispossessed tenants were more likely to be satisfied by settlement in the New World than by factory labour, Selkirk was far from blind to the difficulties that immigrants might face in such settings. Every time they left their huts they were 'exposed to the danger of being bewildered and lost.' Accidents were common; winters were severe; and countless new details about preparing and cultivating the land had to be learned. These realities led Selkirk to argue for careful planning of new settlements. He also recognized that immigrants had to adapt to new circumstances. At base, however, he was convinced that emigration would allow Highlanders to cling to their traditional pastoral and independent way of life.

To illustrate what was possible, Selkirk described his own settlement of 800 Scots in Prince Edward Island in 1803. Coming late in the evening to the encampment established on disembarkation a few days before, Selkirk saw that each family had a large fire near the conical 'wigwams' (of poles covered with spruce boughs) that they had erected in a former Acadian clearing dotted with thickets of young trees. People milled about and 'confused heaps of baggage were every where piled together beside ... [the] wild habitations.' A month or so later, most settlers were on their own land, despite a contagious fever that ran through the camp in late August. Generally, four or five families 'built their houses in a little knot together,' and similar hamlets lay less than a mile away. By this means, the spirit of 'emulation was kept alive'; settlers worked together, shared experience, lifted the spirits of those who grew despondent, and cast out 'the terrors which the woods were calculated to inspire.' Although 'their first trials of the axe were awkward, they improved rapidly.' Soon, rough log cabins, fifteen or eighteen feet long and ten to fourteen feet wide, chinked with moss and clay and roofed with bark and thatch, housed the new arrivals. A year later there were about two acres of cultivated land for every 'able working hand' in each hamlet; potatoes had yielded in abundance; there had been a small harvest of various grains; and fish, taken from several boats built by the settlers, supplemented the produce of the fields. Zealous industry and 'the pride of landed property,' wrote Selkirk, had allowed these people to secure a considerable degree of independence in short order. For all that, conditions in Orwell Bay, as in most other new settlements, were far from easy. Some families had failed to gather a 'crop adequate to their own supply,' and all lived in primitive conditions. 'Their houses,' admitted Selkirk, 'were, indeed, extremely rude, and such as, perhaps, few other European settlers would have been satisfied with.' Yet here, as elsewhere, improvements came with time. Tighter, neater log houses, with shingle roofs and wooden (rather than dirt) floors were built within a few years; the treed horizon was pushed back; stumps and stones were removed from fields. Success was never assured, but most knew something of it. By 1810, the newcomers' efforts had left their mark on the regional landscape: along many valleys and coastal inlets, modest (and even occasionally substantial) farms had been carved from forests unbroken a decade before.

In trade and commerce, the picture was less of a piece. According to mercantile theorists, Britain's truncated late-eighteenth-century empire was to be as self-contained as that developed before 1775. Foreign vessels would be excluded from imperial trade. Britain would meet colonial needs for manufactured goods. Supplies for the West Indies and hemp and masts for the navy would come from the northern colonies rather than New England, New York, and Philadelphia. With a pivotal position in the Atlantic trading triangle added to their strategic location on the northeastern foreland of the continent, the lower colonies would become the entrepôt of British North America. But harsh reality quickly riddled this grand design. The colonies could neither feed themselves nor supply the West Indies. American grain, livestock, and lumber were allowed into Nova Scotia and New Brunswick in the 1780s; Americans provisioned the West Indies and took their rum, sugar, and molasses; and American fishermen – entitled to come ashore on unsettled parts of the British North American coast – conducted a lively contraband trade with colonial residents. In the 1790s, such trade as there was between British North America and the West Indies declined appreciably.[16] Privateers harassed colonial shipping, and American tonnage entering the British Caribbean islands climbed thirteenfold. By 1804, colonial merchants were protesting their plight, and local officials were sombre about the prospects of further trade with the sugar islands.

In truth, conditions were not as black as colonial officials perceived them. Despite the efforts of George Leonard, superintendent of trade and fisheries at Canso, to drive American smugglers from the Gulf of St Lawrence after 1786, and the extension of his authority to all the coasts of the Maritime colonies in 1797, contraband trade flourished.[17] Much of it occurred among the islands of Passamaquoddy Bay, scattered on both sides of the international boundary. Little vessels from small harbours on the Bay of Fundy exchanged grindstones and gypsum for republican manufactures and more exotic goods. At the turn of the century, about 30,000 tons of gypsum crossed the boundary, almost half of it over the narrow passage between Campobello and Moose Island. By 1810, the trade had tripled in volume. Minor officials appointed to stop the illicit commerce turned a blind eye to it, and many provincial households enjoyed its products if not its profits.[18]

Other cracks in the dyke of imperial self-sufficiency were equally troublesome to colonial administrators and pleasing to the population at large. St Pierre and Miquelon provided a convenient base for the unofficial movement of goods into Newfoundland, and the long, remote coast of Labrador, frequented by thousands of American fishermen each summer, was almost impossible to patrol effectively. Merchants in Halifax alleged that most of the East India goods consumed in Nova Scotia came ashore from fishing vessels. According to Loyalist Ward Chipman, all the silver coin in New Brunswick had been 'carried to the United States to pay for contraband articles.'[19] So, too, Newfoundland procured much of its molasses illegally and circuitously from the French West Indies through the United States. In an attempt to staunch the flow, Britain annexed the coast of Labrador to Newfoundland in 1809. But opportunities to smuggle, and popular demand for contraband goods remained high. So the dark trade continued, and a frustrated Attorney General Uniacke conceded, 'that in the opinion of too many among us, it is a crime to support the fair trader by repressing smuggling ... we are surrounded by ... unprincipled men who are one day British subjects and the next citizens of the United States, as it best suits their interests.'[20]

Through the early years of the century, colonial merchants and British shipowners lobbied to plug these and other leaks in the imperial trading system. From Halifax, a committee with William Sabatier at its head submitted memorial after memorial to the Board of Trade lamenting American access to the West Indies. Similar petitions came from New Brunswick.[21] At the same time, Lord Sheffield orchestrated an English campaign in support of the Navigation Laws. Pointing to the same broad end – the maintenance of a closed mercantilist empire – the two crusades quickly became intertwined. Sheffield appended colonial petitions to his pamphlets in support of the old colonial system, and the *Fredericton Telegraph* published his defence of the Navigation System in serial form.[22] In 1806, the New Brunswick Assembly voted funds to have the Earl's portrait hung in Province Hall. But these efforts won little ground. British policy was shaped by wartime needs and powerful West Indian interests. Regulations that restricted American commerce with the islands were readily circumvented. Spanish and French privateers took their toll on colonial shipping. And an attempt to reduce illegal imports of fruit, wine, oil, and salt from the Mediterranean via the United States, by allowing British North American vessels limited rights to carry these goods across the Atlantic without calling at a British port, was undermined by the weight of Crown duties that Americans did not have to bear. Through 1807, the region's much-remarked potential as an Atlantic entrepôt remained unfulfilled.

Within months, however, New Englanders were commenting on the rising wealth, strength, and importance of their northern neighbours; 'every paper from the British provinces,' reported the *Boston Gazette* in June 1808, 'exhibits numerous clearances for the West Indies and Europe loaded with provisions and lumber of all kinds.'[23] In essence, the change was attributable to Napoleon and Jefferson. In 1807, the latest in an escalating series of trade blockades implemented by England and France closed much of Europe to neutral commerce. As scores of American vessels were seized by the belligerents, a press gang from HMS *Leopard* removed four men from the American frigate *Chesapeake* off Virginia. In the furor that followed, Thomas Jefferson forbade American vessels to leave harbour and required foreign vessels to depart in ballast. Haligonians rejoiced as Bostonians lamented the decay of their trade and a fleet 'fallen ... prey / To Jefferson, worms, and Embargo.'[24] With colonial ports open to American vessels by gubernatorial proclamation, dissident Yankees evaded their government's restrictions on trade to carry lumber, flour, and other provisions to Halifax, Shelburne, Saint John, and St Andrews and return with British manufactures and Caribbean produce. The Americans replaced their general embargo with a more specific set of restrictions on commercial intercourse with Britain and France in March 1809 and initiated several subsequent twists in trade policy, but these little affected the big picture. Until 1812 the Atlantic region prospered at the pivot of convoy sailings between the United Kingdom and the Caribbean. Nova Scotia exports to the West Indies doubled; imports were up threefold. In New Brunswick imports from and exports to the sugar islands grew twofold between 1810 and 1811. Public revenues increased, and the profits of trade invigorated local and regional economies.

At the same time, a rapid increase in colonial exports of masts, spars, and other wood products stimulated regional economic growth. This was also due to geopolitics. By closing most northern-European ports to

British ships, Napoleon's continental blockade all but choked off England's vital supply of naval and domestic timber. In the two years after 1807, British imports of European wood were down to a third of pre-blockade quantities. Reserves were depleted and prices soared. In these circumstances, the costs of shipping bulky timber across the stormy Atlantic were no longer prohibitive, and old doubts about the quality of North American wood were quickly cast aside. Between 1805 and 1809, British North American wood exports increased tenfold, and then doubled again within the next decade. From Pictou and Prince Edward Island, from the Miramichi and Saint John (as well as from the St Lawrence), a rapidly expanding fleet plied the Atlantic, carrying wood eastbound and British manufactures (as well as a swelling tide of immigrants) on their return voyages.[25] For New Brunswick, in particular, the new trade was a boon. Between 1805 and 1812, the colony's square-timber exports increased almost twentyfold. British firms invested capital in the industry. Wages rose. Americans were drawn across the border. Towns flourished. Resolute anti-republican though he was, even the erudite Edward Winslow found it necessary to fall back upon that oft-used American expression 'progressing' to describe the transformed state of his colony.[26]

After a decade of decline, Newfoundland trade also expanded rapidly in the early nineteenth century. Competition from Norway, new duties on dried fish, and war with France drove British cod production from the island down precipitously after 1790. More than 750,000 quintals in 1791, it was less than 250,000 quintals ten years later. At the same time, the proportion of the catch taken by British-based fishing vessels and independent migratory fishermen (known as by-boat men) fell sharply. In 1800, these groups accounted for little more than 15 per cent of the total, less than one-third of the fraction they claimed through the 1770s and 1780s. By the turn of the century, the traditional migratory fishery was all but over. Barely 30 vessels made the annual crossing to fish Newfoundland waters; twelve or fifteen years before, well over 300 had done so.[27] Massive adjustments were necessary in the face of such changes. In addition, supplies grew more costly as the price paid for fish declined, and in many parts of the colony conditions were difficult indeed by 1800. In response, residents attempted to 'wring more from the ... resource base' by expanding the seal fishery and moving each summer to the productive cod-fishing grounds of the northeast coast, where women toiled at splitting and curing the catch 'even in advanced pregnancy.' Without new markets, however, many feared that the cod fisheries would not survive.[28]

With American merchants pre-eminent in the West Indies trade, and New England fishermen increasingly aggressive competitors for northern cod – they sent as many as 1,800 vessels to the Gulf, Labrador, and Banks fisheries, and complaints about their readiness to fish on the sabbath were legion – alternative markets were not easy to find. In the two years of peace after 1801, sack ships took their cargoes directly to the Mediterranean. When this trade declined on the resumption of war – and regardless of the Navigation Laws – considerable quantities of Newfoundland fish reached southern Europe through New York and Boston. Then growth was sustained by the American embargo, which opened the substantial West Indian market to Newfoundland (and Nova Scotia) suppliers. At the same time, lower tariffs on Newfoundland cod, and improvements in the North Atlantic convoy system increased sales in Iberia. By 1810, well over 500,000 quintals of fish went to market from the British coasts of Newfoundland.

As the British migratory fishery declined, mercantile control of the industry shifted from the English ports of Dartmouth, Exeter, and Poole to St John's. Soon after 1800, several merchants from St John's joined together to promote their commercial interests and to seek constitutional government in the colony. By 1810, their city was the hub of island trade. Some 700 houses stood along the irregular lanes and paths that ran back from a waterfront crowded with wharves and stores. Hundreds of vessels visited the harbour each year. Some were coastal traders, which extended the hinterland of the metropolis by delivering fish from the outports and ferrying immigrants and supplies to them. Others brought goods from around the North Atlantic and carried away substantially more than half the cod produced on the island. Many of the traditional fishing rooms around the harbour, legally reserved for the use of migratory fishermen, had been taken over by residents of the town. Here and there, squatters cultivated land despite regulations against settlement. In the face of these and other anomalies created by the transition of Newfoundland from fishing station to settlement colony, merchants and other leading residents of the town joined the recently arrived Scottish surgeon William Carson in a campaign for change. Although the better part of a decade would pass before British officials responded to their demands by appointing a full-time resident governor, in 1810 it was quite clear that Newfoundland was no longer an uninhabited, uncultivated outpost of the fishery.

For the Native people of the Atlantic region, these years of population growth and economic expansion brought little but further marginalization. Their situation was cheerless enough at the beginning of the decade. Even in the eighteenth century, White settlement had seriously disrupted the Micmacs' access to the resources upon which they depended. White hunters killed enormous numbers of moose for their skins; settlers' clearing fires destroyed the slow-growing moss on which the caribou fed; according to Titus Smith, who knew the interior of Nova Scotia as well as anyone, even beaver were scarce. And – despite earlier guarantees of Natives' access to their traditional hunting territories – the expansion of settlement along shores and streams had proceeded regardless of Native interests in the fisheries. Occasional gifts and parsimonious allocations of relief failed to alleviate the causes of Native distress. Nor did half-hearted efforts to 'rehabilitate the rising Generation' of Micmacs by encouraging them to farm have much success: they have, noted a sympathetic Titus Smith, 'as strong a prejudice against our way of living as we can have against theirs.'[29]

Still, imperial and colonial authorities baulked at providing Native people with land or financial support enough to ease their poverty and reliance on the sale of baskets, quill boxes, axe handles, butter tubs, and berries to White settlers. In their view, charity simply encouraged laziness and dissolution. When the Nova Scotia government recognized the plight of its Micmac inhabitants in 1800, and voted £350 for the 'rescue of our wretched fellow creatures,' it was with the clear intent of converting them from Native to White ways. Some of the 'best disposed' Natives would be given farms in hope that their developing self-sufficiency would be an example to others; parents would be encouraged to send their children to live with White families 'to learn our domestic arts'; and women would be instructed in spinning and knitting. But not even this purposeful initiative was sustained. No lands were surveyed, and financial support for the plan quickly disappeared.[30] Only the renewed threat of Anglo-American war brought Native people back to official attention, and this interest was purely pragmatic in its concern to ensure their neutrality in case of conflict.

In New Brunswick, several Micmac bands responded to White encroachments on their traditional resources by petitioning for areas of their own. Early in the nineteenth century, reserves ranging in size from 240 to some 51,000 acres were allocated to groups on the Miramichi, Restigouche, Tabusintac, and Buctouche rivers. But these tracts were by no means inviolate. Several were substantially reduced in size (sometimes by sales made by Natives), and White settlers encroached on others with impunity. The situation of Prince Edward Island's Native people was even more tenuous. With the entire colony in the hands of the proprietors, the government was unable to respond to Micmac requests for land with access to water. A handful of families squatted on Lennox Island, where they were encouraged to begin farming by the missionary Abbé de Calonne, but the majority of their fellows struggled to survive in Abegweit, hunting and fishing as they could, and maintaining close ties with the Natives of northern New Brunswick and Cape Breton.[31]

In all, there were probably no more than 3,000 Micmac people in the region in 1810. Scattered and suffering though they were, they clung to their migratory ways and retained a strong sense of their distinctiveness. The Catholic church's hope of centralizing its missionary activities in Native farm villages around the shrines to St Ann on Chapel Island in Lake Bras d'Or, Lennox Island, and Burnt Church on the Miramichi went unrealized. And the lofty benevolent ideals behind the Native school established by the Anglican church at Sussex Vale, New Brunswick, were equally ineffective in persuading the region's Native people to abandon their past. Closed in 1804 – after failing, its critics said, to convert a single Native child in seven years – the school was reopened two years later. Now Natives were encouraged to give their children up for apprenticeship to a White family at any age between birth and sixteen. In return, they received an annual gift of cloth and a small cash allowance each week. White families who took Native apprentices received £20 a year to feed and clothe their charges until they reached the age of twenty-one, to instruct them in the Protestant religion, and to ensure that they received 'proper schooling.' These arrangements, which separated Native children from their families in the belief that parental influences were largely responsible for the school's earlier failures, were sadly open to corruption. Micmac boys, and especially girls, were exposed to exploitation and abuse. In practice, apprentices were little more than cheap servants, and their indentures provided a significant cash leaven for those White families who took one, or more; Oliver Arnold, the director of the school, had six, who brought him £120 a year.[32] Yet relatively few Micmacs endured these appalling circumstances. Most remained largely beyond the reach of colonial law and on the very periphery of regional life. Unable to communicate in their own language with local officials or, with a single exception, the handful of Catholic missionaries who worked among them, they were, observed Lord Dalhousie in 1817, 'little better than outcasts of society.'[33]

Set apart from the majority by language, as well as by deep-seated British suspicion of the French, Acadians were another maligned and misunderstood fraction of the region's early-nineteenth-century population. Drafting some notes on the early history of New Brunswick in 1804, Edward Winslow described the Acadians resident in the colony twenty years before as an 'improvident and slovenly race.' Although he recognized that after suffering expulsion in 1755 many of them had been 'removed again from their possessions and obliged to seek situations more remote' by the coming of the Loyalists, he believed that they had been more than adequately compensated by grants of land in Madawaska and elsewhere, and resented the fact that they had 'never been really conciliated' to English authority.[34] Most, in fact, lived in isolated, inward-looking communities, largely beyond the direction of colonial officials and the influence of English-speaking society.

Lt. Col. Joseph Gubbins captured something of this separation when he journeyed into the Acadian settlements along the Northumberland Strait as inspecting field officer of the New Brunswick Militia in 1813. He described a coast so little known 'even at the seat of government' that he was unable to obtain 'certain intelligence' as to the existence of roads in the direction that he wished to travel. Arriving at Grand Digue, near Shediac, by boat, he was met by 'a numerous assembly of the ladys of the neighbourhood, who were in the full dress of the Norman mode as it was perhaps a century before.' Several days later Gubbins received the impression that the Acadians of Escuminac 'were in utter ignorance of what was going on in the world ... [and] had not even heard of Bonaparte or of the war with France for so many years ...'[35]

At the turn of the century, there were some 8,000 Acadians in the region; by 1810 the population of their widely scattered settlements may have exceeded 10,000. Approximately 1,500 of the 4,000 Acadians in Nova Scotia and Cape Breton in 1803 lived near Canso; there were 1,000 at Saint Mary's Bay, 500 in the vicinity of Chezzetcook near Halifax, and some 400 in each of the Tusket and Cheticamp areas. Most of New Brunswick's 3,750 Acadians lived in small coastal settlements strung along the eastern and northern edges of the province and isolated both from one another and the main centres of colonial administration and commerce: slightly more than 1,100 occupied the Memramcook-Petitcodiac area; there were another 900 between Shediac and Richibucto; 300 more between Richibucto and Tracadie; and 900 between Tracadie and Restigouche. On the upper reaches of the St John River, Madawaska had fewer than 500. In Prince Edward Island, the 687 Acadians recorded by Monsignor Denaut were divided among Malpeque Bay, Rustico, and Fortune Bay.[36]

In most of these places, Acadians lived in strikingly modest material circumstances. 'They content themselves,' said Gubbins, 'with the absolute necessaries of life.' At one stop his party was offered 'the best fare the place afforded' – 'some milk and slices of salt cod fish, which is here used as a substitute for bread until the potatoes ... [are] fit to dig.' At Caraquet, early in 1800, missionary René-Pierre Joyer found famine as well as poverty. 'Potatoes ... the daily bread in this country,' he wrote, 'have almost entirely disappeared ... and to make matters worse, almost no eels were caught ... even though they are the chief supplement to this daily bread.' Far away in Tusket, eighteenth months later, Titus Smith learned of 'a French Village below here where the People live entirely upon Eels & Potatoes. One of the most able of them assured me that most of the French Families did not use 4 Pounds of Flour in a year.

They keep Sheep enough to make their own Clothing, & the Meat and Butter which they sell supplies them with the little money they need.'[37] Houses were spare and tiny; with dimensions of ten feet by twelve feet, the priest's dwelling in Tracadie barely matched the size of most rooms in modern houses.[38] For Gubbins and other English-speaking commentators, all this was evidence that the Acadians were 'bad farmers' virtually devoid of enterprise and industry. But hard as conditions in these settlements often were, they were no measure of indolence. In general, the region's Acadians revealed a good deal of resourcefulness and self-reliance in coping with the marginal environments that were their common lot. When the missionary Abbé Champion bequeathed his furniture and money to the poor of Cheticamp in 1809, the inhabitants of the parish asked his successor to use the money for the church, 'there being no one among them reduced to begging.'[39]

As Catholics, Acadians had few legal and political rights in the turn-of-the-century colonies. In Nova Scotia, Catholics who wished to hold property or establish schools had to swear allegiance to the British Crown, deny the spiritual authority of the Pope, and renounce the doctrine of transubstantiation. In general, Catholics were allowed neither to vote nor to hold public office.[40] In such circumstances, missionary priests (whose numbers were augmented by the arrival of a dozen refugees from the civil constitution of the clergy in post-revolutionary France) played large roles among the scattered residents of 'divided, uncohesive' Acadia. All were called upon to deal with a range of civil questions, from administering wills to resolving disputes. The energetic Abbé Jean-Mandé Sigogne even went so far as to establish a code of conduct and procedures for settling disagreements among his parishioners in St Mary's Bay. Outlined in twenty-eight articles, this quasi-legal system required the inhabitants to elect four respected elders as judges, sought 'the maintenance of good morals' and 'justice based on charity', and bound the richer members of the community to ensure that their poorer brethren received religious instruction and the rudiments of education.[41]

Among the 85 or 90 per cent of the region's people who were neither Native nor Acadian, lives and material circumstances varied enormously. Reflecting their origins in several parts of Britain, Europe, and North America, members of this diverse majority bore the marks of different traditions. Occupying several markedly different environments, they pursued a wide range of strategies to feed and clothe themselves. They worshipped in diverse ways, clung to discrete memories, anticipated different futures, and participated to varying degrees in the political affairs of their colonies. Because some settled with kin and others alone, because some were powerful and others weak, because some prospered and others starved, the social geographies of their settlements were almost infinitely complex.

The single most obvious cleavage – in political outlook, religious affairs, and economic interests (perhaps even in *mentalité*) – was between the seats of colonial authority and their outlying districts, between colonial officials and their associates on the one hand, and the rank and file of the population on the other. In more formal terms this was a division between 'court' and 'country.' At base, such a categorization acknowledges that the attitudes and interests of those who enshrined and promoted the power and privilege of British institutions were essentially different from those of most colonials, whose concerns were primarily local. It points, in short, to a simple yet generally rather sharp divide between 'official' and 'unofficial' culture in the region.[42] Yet this distinction should not be overdrawn. In the fluid social and political environments of the early-nineteenth-century colonies, factional interests and alignments were ever-changing; they were a kaleidoscope of associations that swirled about the court-country divide, not a rigid set of allegiances.

For all that, the fundamental fissure between court and country appeared, time and again. In trade, for example, the interests of important city merchants were often at odds with those in outlying settlements. In the 1790s, outport residents protested the substantial fees levied by Naval Office deputies and the requirement that all vessels leaving Nova Scotia acquire papers for the voyage in the capital. 'It Seems,' observed Simeon Perkins in Liverpool, 'that the Current is aginst us in Halifax ...'[43] A few years later, commercial men in Halifax and St John's, heavily committed to trading under the Navigation Laws, campaigned vigorously against the contraband traffic conducted in small vessels sailing from scattered harbours beyond effective surveillance. Not only was this trade illegal; it eroded the profits of metropolitan merchants and undermined their influence in the hinterland by loosening the credit-dependence of outport traders and their customers. In 1806 and 1807, the clash of interests focused on efforts to encourage the Nova Scotia fishery. Spokesmen for the outports sought a bounty of fifteen shillings per ton on all fish exports; their opponents argued for a premium of one shilling per quintal (twenty shillings a ton) on shipments to Britain and the British colonies – an arrangement that would have eliminated many small (outport) traders with links to New England from government largesse.

In politics, court and country factions characteristically found voice in the appointed councils and elected assemblies of the colonies. The general situation was well summarized by Judge Alexander Croke (whose background generally led him to equate 'Government' with imperial power). Commenting on the political state of Nova Scotia in 1809, he observed that the Assembly was 'comprised largely of farmers ... suspicious of Government, jealous of their rights and strongly retentative of the public purse. While the Council, mainly of His Majesty's officers was always disposed to second the view of Government.'[44]

As the Nova Scotia economy expanded in the late 1790s, Halifax merchants (who dominated the Council) sought reduced customs duties, while assemblymen wanted to increase government expenditures in their constituencies. Quickly, the control of appropriations and appointments became a flashpoint. Led by William Tonge, the Assembly opposed construction of Government House; a year later, in 1800, they attempted to increase the impost on imported wine. When Tonge and his associates in the 'country' party, James Fulton of Londonderry (in the Colchester district) and Edward Mortimer of Pictou, took three of four seats in Halifax County in 1799, Wentworth fulminated at Tonge's efforts to 'disturb the Peace and Harmony of the Country, by the tricks, falsehoods and follys used in popular elections.' Through debate and tactical manoeuvre, the prorogation and dissolution of the Assembly, and the governor's rejection of Tonge's election as speaker of the House in 1806, the battle between Council and Assembly continued until Sir George Prevost replaced Wentworth as lieutenant-governor in 1808 and engaged Tonge in an expedition to the West Indies, where he remained. Despite the provocative actions of Alexander Croke during Prevost's absence through the first quarter of 1809, Prevost succeeded in smoothing relations between Council and Assembly through the remainder of the decade.[45]

In New Brunswick, members of the Council and Assembly had been at loggerheads in the mid-1790s over the necessity and costs of constructing a legislature and court house in Fredericton. Early in the nineteenth century, Lieutenant-Governor Thomas Carleton and his Council clashed with the Assembly again, this time over the appointment and payment of the clerk to the House. Carleton nominated Dugald Campbell; the Assembly wanted Samuel Denny Street. A dubious, short-term compromise gave Street the work and Campbell the remuneration of the clerk, but the legislature was soon dissolved. This only carried the debate into the streets in a vigorous pamphlet war that culminated with the appearance in the *Saint John Gazette* of a satirical poem, 'Creon,' depicting the governor's supporters as selfish and irresponsible. Still, the election went to the governor's friends; Samuel Denny Street, author of 'Creon,' and many of his supporters lost their seats; and Gabriel Ludlow, who assumed control of the colony with Carleton's departure for England, presided over a period of amicable relations between Assembly and Council.[46]

In Prince Edward Island, too, 'Democratical' and 'Aristocratical' interests, as Lieutenant-Governor DesBarres described them, confronted each other through the first decade of the nineteenth century. Here access to land was the central issue. A campaign for escheat of those proprietorial lots on which settlement conditions had not been met had begun in 1796. When DesBarres succeeded Edmund Fanning at the head of the Island's administration in 1805, he found himself standing between 'two contending parties.' One was comprised of 'men of slender property, leaseholders of small plantations unadorned with education ... [determined] to move heaven and earth for obtaining an universal partitiobonheur of their landlords.' The other was a cabal of large proprietors. The struggle between them intensified with the emergence, in 1806, of the Society of Loyal Electors. Under the leadership of J.B. Palmer, they sought 'the introduction of upright, independent men ... into the House of Assembly with a view of counteracting a dangerous influence ... possessed by ... [those] engaged in monstrous speculation in land.' Thus threatened, powerful absentee proprietors took their concerns to the colonial secretary in England, and succeeded in having DesBarres dismissed and Palmer removed from public office in 1812.[47]

Together, these conflicts have often been seen as significant reform movements, as important flexings of political muscle by a colonial rank and file intent on challenging British authority over the colonies and determined to wrest local rights from royal officials. 'Court' interests certainly argued as much. They denounced their opponents as fools and Jacobins and their views as tending towards 'the subversion of all government of Church and State.' According to Edward Winslow, James Glenie and other members of the New Brunswick Assembly in 1797 were 'fellows ... who three years agoe did not know that Magna Charta was not a Great Pudding.' J.B. Palmer was described as 'an adventurer of infamous character ... who in many instances acted the part of an absolute swindler,' and prepared his followers to 'welcome an invasion of the Republican Americans.' And Wentworth, convinced that Tonge had generated 'improper zeal and animosity' among the electorate by establishing 'corresponding societies, Clubs and Committees professing reform,' reflected darkly that such organizations should be 'discouraged and vigorously suppressed': 'It is not eno' that people are happy prosperous and well disposed. The fallen Angels, Milton tells us were so in Heaven. Yet Satan introduced corresponding societies, I believe, and dissensions and Evil soon followed.'[48]

In truth the political clashes of these years were far less transcendant. James Glenie, William Tonge, and James Bardin Palmer were, undoubtedly, the foci of diverse dissident interests in their colonies, and in the most general of terms their supporters shared a distrust of officialdom, were concerned to promote the rights of elected assemblies, and objected to the dominance of economic and political affairs by the few. But neither these three men nor those who joined them in opposition demonstrated great consistency of allegiance or principle. In education and social background, Glenie, Tonge, and Palmer were probably closer to court than country circles: Glenie was a brilliant mathematician, Tonge came from one of the most prominent families in Nova Scotia, and Palmer was a Dublin lawyer. Each held appointments from the Crown, and Palmer, who was very close to DesBarres, took a seat on the Island Council in 1809. All, indeed, appear to have been propelled by self-interest and personal animosities as much as by ideological conviction. Similarly, those who rallied behind their rhetorical skills and forceful personalities are more accurately seen as loose coalitions of interest than as defenders of a coherent sociopolitical position. Their alliances were built on a sense of exclusion from power or influence, by reason of geography, nationality, tradition, belief, wealth, office, favour, or other cause.

Among these factors, none divided residents of the Atlantic region along court-country lines as pervasively or as consistently as religion. Anglicanism was the official church of the colonies, but its adherents were a minority of colonial residents. Even among the Protestant population, dissenters – Presbyterians, Congregationalists, Baptists, Wesleyan Methodists, New Lights, Lutherans – held numerical sway in many settlements and were a serious challenge to Anglican hegemony in others. Still, Anglican leaders clung to their privileges and espoused intrinsically conservative social, political, and doctrinal ideas.

Taking their timbre from their spiritual leader in Halifax, Anglicans envisaged their church as an instrument for promoting loyalty to the Empire. For Bishop Charles Inglis, government and religion were the pillars on which society rested and by which it was upheld; 'remove these,' he observed, 'and the fabric sinks into ruin.' Indeed the American and French revolutions seemed to have demonstrated as much. 'Whoever is sincerely religious towards God, from principle and conscience,' believed Inglis, 'will also ... be loyal to his earthly Sovereign, obedient to the laws, and faithful to the government which God hath placed over him.'[49] Inglis had no doubt that sincerity in religion implied adherence to the traditional practices of Anglicanism. A reticent man who deplored fanatical conduct and public displays of emotion, he was quick to associate religious dissent with political disloyalty. Most of his ministers, scattered in small settlements across the colonies, likewise failed to appreciate the appeal of evangelical religion among relatively poor and isolated settlers, resisted modifications of church doctrine, and were quick to disparage their rivals.

Reports from Anglican clergymen to the Society for the Propagation of the Gospel, and letters between them and Inglis, were replete with critical and defensive assessments of the dissenting evangelical population, and especially that part of it influenced by the New Light doctrines of Henry Alline. They were 'deluded creatures,' led into 'pious frenzy' by illiterate rambling preachers' and 'powerful ranters.' They 'seem[ed] to think nothing essential to religion but extraordinary effusions of Spirit, proved by faintings, screams, delirium & convulsions.' At one revival meeting in Annapolis, reported the local Anglican minister, 'ignorant men, women, & even children under twelve years of age, were employed to pray & exhort, calling aloud, Lord Jesus come down & shake these dry bones. Groanings, screamings, roarings, tremblings, & faintings immediately ensue, with a falling down & rolling upon the floor, both sexes together ...' After years of confronting the inroads of these 'upstart enthusiasts' and 'self appointed Teachers' upon his flock, Inglis observed resignedly, but revealingly, 'The Church of X[t] is by no means what these people seem to suppose it – it is not a tumultuous disorderly & unorganized multitude. On the contrary, it is a regular, well-formed Society.'[50]

During the first decade of the nineteenth century, the main challenge to this 'well-formed society' came – in Anglican and official eyes – from those areas of Nova Scotia and New Brunswick in which the eighteenth-century New Light movement had been strongest.[51] In reaction to the antinomian (free will) turn taken by some of Alline's followers (known to contemporaries as New Dispensationalists) in the early 1790s, a small handful of Allinite disciples sought to restore order and discipline to a movement in which the doctrine of individual illumination had led some to 'great irregularities' and 'extravagancies.' Within a few months, their wish 'to appear as respectable' brought them into association with the Baptist church of New England. By 1799, the region's 'Second Great Awakening' was well under way. Predictably, Inglis described it as 'an enthusiastic and dangerous spirit' whose leaders were 'engaged in a general plan of total revolution in religion and civil government'; his only comfort was in the hope that the new religious stir would prove 'too violent ... to be lasting.' Like many a similar episode, the progress of this Second Great Awakening was enormously complex. Here it ran up against doctrinal objections, there against the established strength of other denominations. But it clearly reached a spiritual and emotional peak in the years after 1806, when Baptist missionaries from Maine travelled through the region and hundreds of people were reported caught up in 'a wonderful moving of the power of God.'[52]

By 1810 the essential shape and longer-term implications of what Nova Scotians sometimes called their 'Great Reformation' were clear. In

the broadest perspective, it was part of a wider North American movement. But it grew from the particular circumstances of turn-of-the-century life in the Bay of Fundy region, and it had important local
consequences. Less an explicit country challenge to established religion
than a direct consequence of post-revolutionary turmoil and the
religious enthusiasm generated by Henry Alline, it served to revitalize
those whose ecstatic eighteenth-century conversions had given way to
'spiritual stupor.'[53] Yet precisely because the Awakening was a localized
phenomenon, it served to underline the distinctiveness of life in many
of the region's out-settlements. It also fostered the transition of sect into
church. By the War of 1812, most Baptist leaders in Nova Scotia, at least,
had set Alline's heterodox 'Spirit of Liberty' aside in favour of Calvinist
orthodoxy and a church based on closed communion. Although many
ordinary people clung to Allinite traditions for the remainder of their
lives, 'Yankee order' had begun 'to neutralize New Light spontaneity.'
Support for orthodox Allinism was localized and marginalized. In New
Brunswick, by contrast, the 'anti-formal, unsacramental and mystical'
spirit of Henry Alline retained a considerable foothold, antinomian
communities persisted, and radical evangelicalism gained ground.[54] In
the 1830s, an anti-Calvinist Free Baptist movement would build on
these foundations.

In almost all the communities in which the revival fire took hold,
women and children were prominent in 'telling the Goodness of God'
and in exhorting their friends and relatives to bear witness. They
became in a sense the moral and spiritual leaders of their communities.
Perhaps, indeed, they found in the excitement of revival meetings the
'psychological and social space' necessary to discard – if but temporarily – traditional roles of subservience and deference. But whether this
reversal of status had any significant consequences for individual and
family life in the region remains a moot point. By its very nature, such
paradoxical, aberrant behaviour may ultimately have underlined the
virtues of the status quo. Certainly, and in related vein, it has been
argued that because Alline's emphasis upon the importance of personal
salvation became the evangelical norm among Maritime Baptists, they
did not seek to realize 'impossible dreams' on earth. Their New Jerusa-
lem would be built in heaven, and they were correspondingly little
interested in developing instruments of worldly reform.[55]

Thus divided along several axes, the Atlantic region of 1810 was an
extraordinarily fragmented realm, a territory of many particularisms
that spilled beyond the administrative and cognitive grasp of colonial
officials, just as it today eludes the comprehensive understanding of historians. Yet it is clear that through the length and breadth of the region,
the first decade of the nineteenth century was a significant watershed in

the settling of people into place, the development of local economies, and the shaping of colonial societies. The disorder and ferment associated with the coming of the Loyalists had been largely overcome. Newcomers were swelling colonial numbers and providing the essential infrastructure for future growth. Small, tenuous settlements had grown into substantial communities. Roads, extended and improved, facilitated links between them. There were new prospects for trade; and the fruits of prosperity, if not universal, were being tasted by some. Although many settlers remained remote from the administrative power of colonial government, and the challenge of furthering the economic, social, and political integration of each of the colonies was still considerable, Nova Scotia, New Brunswick, Prince Edward Island, Cape Breton, and Newfoundland were all fairly embarked on the course that would carry them through the next several decades. Moreover, economic and political differences between residents of the out-settlements and the colonies' major towns, and the doctrinal rivalry among Baptists, New Lights, Methodists, Anglicans, and others had encouraged many of the region's people to assess and reassess their perceptions of themselves and their world.[56] In the process, they had begun to develop a firmer sense both of their own identities and of the distinctive places that they were helping to create. Incomplete though they were, the symbolic associations of Wentworth's Government House were by no means inappropriate.

CHAPTER ELEVEN

1810–1820
War and Peace

D.A. SUTHERLAND

On Saturday, 28 August 1819, at Rollo Bay in King's County, Prince Edward Island, a murder occurred. The victim, Edward Abell, was estate agent for Lord James Townshend, one of the colony's leading landlords. That morning, Abell had come to the home of Richard Pearce, a tenant farmer who had fallen £5 into arrears in payment of rents owing to Townshend. Abell insisted that payment be made and in cash, an almost impossible demand, given the acute scarcity of coins and paper money in this frontier economy. When the hard-pressed debtor failed in desperate attempts to raise the requested money from among his neighbours, Abell ordered the sheriff's bailiff to seize Pearce's handsome black riding horse as compensation for the amount owing. At that point, Pearce came out of his house with a musket and bayonet. Lunging at Abell, he stabbed him twice. The second blow, which penetrated the victim's intestines, proved lethal. News that an obscure farmer had killed someone representing the Island establishment sent shock waves through the colonial capital, Charlottetown. The authorities there posted a reward of £20 for the capture of Pearce. It was never collected. Concealed by his fellow tenants, Pearce evaded his pursuers and eventually escaped to the mainland, to begin life over again, presumably in a place where freehold tenure prevailed.[1]

The murder became part of Island folklore, thanks to its involvement with the later emergence of sustained tenant agitation against the landlord regime that the colony had inherited from the eighteenth century. As successor to the ill-fated Abell, Lord Townshend chose William Cooper. Within a decade, Cooper turned renegade by becoming leader of the 'escheaters,' a rural protest movement dedicated to the breakup of all the Island's large estates.[2] The confrontation between Abell and Pearce is also important, however, for what it tells us about the character of events in the coastal colonies of British America through the second decade of the nineteenth century. This was an era of major upheaval, highlighted by the transition from war to peace and from prosperity to adversity. Ecstasy and despair became so mingled in the public mind as to create an atmosphere of sustained crisis, infused with an undercurrent of violence. Thus the events at Rollo Bay that summer day in 1819 belong to the mainstream, rather than to the margins, of the regional experience.

The period began amid escalating tension. Through 1811 and into 1812, as hostilities in Europe moved ever closer to global warfare, it became increasingly difficult for the United States to maintain its rights as a neutral against French and British aggression. Pressured also by expansionist interests in Congress, the administration of President James Madison struggled against mounting odds to secure the republic's merchant marine, as well as extend America's western frontiers. Finally, on 18 June 1812, frustrated by British resistance to its efforts and convinced that no other options were available, Washington declared war on the United Kingdom.[3]

Halifax learned of this ominous development when HMS *Belvidera* staggered into port after being mauled by an American naval squadron. The outrage provoked among Nova Scotia's Tory-Loyalist ruling class by this American attack was expressed by Bishop Charles Inglis, who observed that the U.S. politicians had allowed themselves to become the 'dupes of Bonaparte' and were now acting in a manner 'more criminal than in their late rebellion.'[4] Among the common people of the region, fear prevailed over anger, especially once scores of American privateers entered local waters to raid merchant shipping, loot the fisheries, and even attack isolated coastal communities. Panic became pervasive, as Quebec's Roman Catholic bishop, Joseph-Octave Plessis, discovered on visiting the Cheticamp area of Cape Breton. Approaching the shore in an unknown vessel, Plessis was astounded to see the people fleeing into the woods. One man, convinced that American privateers were about to land, went to the extreme of burning his home to prevent it from falling into enemy hands.[5]

Through these early months of the war, the strategists in Washington seriously considered invading across the New England frontier, so as to drive the British back into Halifax and ultimately seize that strategic naval base. Fearful that they would become a prime target for the American war effort, the colonial authorities rushed to fortify their major harbours and transform the local militia into an effective fighting force. In the front line colonies of Nova Scotia and New Brunswick, the legislatures met in emergency session to vote war supplies. Simultaneously, emissaries went out to the Native peoples of the region to offer gifts in exchange for promises of military support should an American army of invasion arrive.[6] Initially, the odds seemed to be overwhelmingly in Washington's favour. Stripped of resources by the demands in the European theatre of war, neither the Royal Navy nor the British Army could mount an effective defence against a determined American military drive into the coastal colonies of British America. Moreover, the British lacked the will to fight, preferring to try to end the war with diplomacy built around concessions on issues of concern to the United States. This passivity derived, in part, from a fear that, even if the enemy did not invade, the Maritimes and Newfoundland were still doomed. Most of the region remained heavily dependent on imports of foodstuffs from the United States. So long as Napoleon ruled on the European continent, alternative supplies could not easily be brought across the Atlantic. Thus, simply by imposing an economic blockade, Washington apparently could secure the colonies' rapid capitulation.[7]

This bleak scenario was never realized, essentially because the Madison administration found it impossible to wage total warfare against the British presence in North America. Although Yankee shipping interests were willing to go to war as privateers, they and many of their neighbours proved reluctant to proceed further as belligerents. In particular, the New England heartland of Massachusetts opted to resist much of Washington's military program. Fear and opportunism, mingled with a regional pride that verged on secessionism, prompted the authorities in Boston and nearby capitals to refuse to call out the state militia. They then threatened insurrection if the federal government tried to coerce New England into a commitment to full-scale hostilities. Though infuriated, Washington lacked the legal, political, and especially military capacity to impose its will on the northeast. Madison and his advisers were obliged to restructure their war strategy. Instead of striking simultaneously into both the Maritimes and the Canadas, American land forces would have to concentrate their efforts on the Great Lakes and St Lawrence sector of British North America. In effect, Yankee obstreperousness had created a military shield behind which the coastal colonies could take refuge.[8]

By the late summer of 1812, rumours that New England was moving towards a policy of qualified neutrality began filtering through to the authorities in places such as Halifax. Sir John Sherbrooke, lieutenant-governor of Nova Scotia, sought to exploit this situation by issuing a proclamation offering to abstain from attacks on the American frontier if settlers in those areas made a reciprocal commitment. Even more important was his decision to begin issuing licences to vessels willing to engage in trade between Halifax and New England. By acting in this manner, without prior consultation with London, Sherbrooke exposed himself to severe criticism, but he argued that quick and unilateral action had been essential to avert shortages of supply that might well cripple the entire British war effort in America. Sherbrooke's pragmatic outlook was shared by Lieutenant-Governor George Smyth of New Brunswick, who quickly followed suit with licences authorizing trade between St Andrews and nearby ports in the United States.[9]

Attracted by strong demand and high prices, New England merchants proved eager to evade U.S. custom-house officials and to use British licences to pour provisions into the Maritimes. On their return journey, the small coastal vessels engaged in this traffic carried large volumes of European manufactures and Caribbean produce, which, because they were scarce, could be sold into the American market at a large profit. By the beginning of 1813, this two-way commercial shuttle had become so extensive as to eliminate the threat of famine in the seaboard colonies. Abundance rather than scarcity rapidly came to be a dominant feature of the war. Moreover, this officially sanctioned smuggling operation proved highly lucrative. Wholesale merchants in entrepôt centres such as Halifax grew rich, now that the main flow of trade between Britain and the United States passed through their warehouses. Under these conditions, making money soon took priority over preparations for defence. Most militiamen were demobilized, and the small resident contingent of British regulars was left to help in the defence of Canada. For the next two years the people of the Maritimes and Newfoundland had only naval activity to remind them that they still lived in a theatre of war.

Conventional wisdom suggests that the war at sea during this Anglo-American conflict was dominated by colonial privateers. Legends have grown up around the activities of vessels such as the *Liverpool Packet*, which, in thirty months, with five cannon and a crew of forty-five, captured more than two score enemy craft, worth $1.5 million. Such exploits proved alluring to contemporaries as well as to posterity. Early in the war, Maritime merchants rushed to muster the capital, crews, vessels, and commissions required for privateering. All told, Nova Scotia and New Brunswick sent to sea some forty of these private war ships. Although outnumbered ten to one by American privateers, the *Liverpool Packet* and her kind captured an impressive number of enemy vessels. Disposed of through Admiralty Court proceedings, these prizes became a source of significant profit, particularly for men like Enos Collins, who owned a small fleet of privateers.[10]

Care must be taken, however, to avoid distorting the motivation and military significance of Maritime privateers. It is sometimes suggested that these vessels were crewed by pure patriots whose heroic endeavours crippled the American merchant marine. In reality, however, naval vessels rather than privateers accounted for the lion's share of prizes taken in the North Atlantic. Moreover, coastal blockade rather than mid-ocean capture was what really drove the American merchant marine off the high seas. Thus in strategic terms, Maritime privateers were of only incidental importance to the war effort. It must also be noted that colonial privateers went to sea more in search of profit than for patriotic glory. The last thing they wanted was to get involved in bloody and expensive encounters with enemy warships or privateers. Self-interest rooted in profit-and-loss calculations prompted Maritime privateers to concentrate on the pursuit of small, lightly crewed, and unarmed merchantmen. These were then captured, not by bombardment and boarding, but usually through bluff and persuasion. More privateers died from disease and shipwreck than from enemy action. Because it was essentially an entrepreneurial venture, privateering flourished only briefly at the beginning of hostilities. As lucrative prizes became scarce, largely because of competition from the Royal Navy, vessels like the *Liverpool Packet* were ever more likely to be redeployed. Owners preferred the prosaic profits obtained through trade to the romance of military combat, especially if the latter was not likely to yield large and immediate rewards.[11]

Misrepresentation of the war at sea may owe something to the fact that at first the Royal Navy did badly, losing a celebrated series of single-ship encounters to enemy naval vessels. Gradually, however, reinforcements arrived to shift the balance of naval power in favour of the British. A symbolic turning point in the naval war came in June 1813, when HMS *Shannon* defeated and captured the USS *Chesapeake* in a confrontation off Boston Harbour. The arrival of the two vessels at Halifax set off ecstatic rejoicing. Patriotic pride grew steadily over the next few months as the Royal Navy succeeded in imposing a blockade on the entire American coast south of Boston. By November 1813, virtually the whole American commercial and military fleet lay bottled up in harbour. The only exception consisted of the small craft that participated in the licensed shuttle between New England and the Maritimes. Permission for this trade eventually had been granted by the authorities in London, since it had the practical advantage of ensuring continued access to American sources of supply, something deemed to be essential for the success of the British war effort, both in North America and Europe.[12]

Newfoundland was a major beneficiary of this contradictory blend of Anglo-American hostility and accommodation. During an earlier stage in the revolutionary-Napoleonic wars, the migratory fishery based in England's West Country had collapsed. That precipitated a major expansion of Newfoundland's sedentary fishery, leading to rapid growth of the island's year-round resident population. By the time war erupted with the United States, these settlers produced more than 90 per cent of the cod exported from Newfoundland. Though efficient as fish killers, Newfoundlanders remained acutely dependent on imports of foodstuffs, most of which came from what, in 1812, abruptly became enemy territory. Alarm gripped both merchants and fishermen, resulting in an enormous jump in the price of provisions. By year's end, however, American privateers were in retreat from Newfoundland waters. Supplies forwarded through Maritime ports had begun to arrive in sufficient volume to alleviate fears of winter hunger. From this point through to the end of hostilities, Newfoundland enjoyed an uninterrupted economic boom. Strong demand and minimal foreign competition in the island's traditional Mediterranean markets for cod combined to create what would thereafter be regarded as a moment of glory for the Newfoundland fishery. A sign of the times was provided by the clerks of St John's, who spent their Sundays taking target practice at champagne bottles lined up on the wharves of their employers.[13]

The economic bustle that prevailed across the region at the height of the War of 1812 found most dramatic expression in the three major population centres, the ports of St John's, Halifax, and Saint John. They all grew in size, through migration mainly from the surrounding rural hinterland but also from abroad. At Saint John, as many as 1,000 carpenters arrived every year from the United States to work in the local shipyards. Other newcomers went into general construction work where, in the period 1812–14, 'more houses, stores, wharves and other buildings were erected ... than in any other two years before.'[14] In Halifax, the single largest employer was the Crown, which built up the workforce at the naval dockyard to some 1,600 men. At St John's, immigration from Ireland rose sixfold, as young men ran the risk of transatlantic migration to earn the phenomenal wages being paid in the fishery.[15]

Some of the gain was consumed by inflation. Rents in Saint John, for example, rose 40 per cent. Certain government officials and others on fixed incomes complained of a fall in their standard of living. A few people may have moved to the countryside in an effort to reduce expenses, but most urban dwellers preferred to stay put and adapt to changing circumstances. In the case of skilled artisans, that meant organizing to form embryonic unions, which then became instruments for collective bargaining designed to drive up wages. Meanwhile, those who persisted in agriculture became increasingly market-oriented, seeking to raise ever-larger surpluses for sale into nearby urban markets or to the growing workforce employed in the fishery and forest sectors of the regional economy. The general scarcity of labour meant that more and more workers were paid in cash rather than in goods or credit. The resulting trend towards ever-expanding consumer purchasing power was one of the most positive effects of war on the regional economy.[16]

The major beneficiaries of wartime prosperity were found among the élite of colonial society. Chief among the winners was probably Richard John Uniacke, attorney general of Nova Scotia. The fees he earned in wartime, while serving as advocate general of Halifax's Vice-Admiralty Court, became the major source of his £50,000 fortune.[17] Privateering and speculation in prize goods played a role in making several merchants rich, but military contracts and general wholesaling activities were even more important as avenues for capital accumulation. The mainstream of colonial entrepreneurship in wartime was represented by the career of Patrick Morris of St John's. Arriving in Newfoundland from Ireland in 1805 at age twenty-eight, Morris went to work as a merchant's clerk. By 1811 he had gone out on his own, importing provisions such as pork, butter, and bread from the Old Country and sending back payment in the form of dried cod and fish oil. Thriving as a wholesaler, Morris began to diversify. In 1814 he bought an ocean-going ship, the first of what quickly grew to be a three-vessel fleet. By the end of the war, Morris had established himself as a man of property, with aspirations to rise into the ranks of the St John's business élite. His counterparts could be found in scores across the region.

The extent to which the rewards of wartime prosperity trickled down to the common people of the Atlantic colonies is difficult to ascertain. One benefit they derived involved increased activity by government. Surging imports generated a major rise of custom-house receipts. Abundant revenue encouraged local officials to spend as never before on public works, bounties for agriculture and the fisheries, and school construction.[18] Bustle in both the public and private sectors of the colonial economy fostered relatively full employment and high wages and likely made life a bit easier for the labouring poor. Moreover, while few ordinary seamen who shipped out as privateers got much prize money, it was an enterprise that at least briefly, put a bonus in their pocket. Confirmation that war had a positive impact on the lives of ordinary colonists is provided ironically by Rev. Thomas McCulloch. Writing to the Halifax press early in the 1820s, this Pictou Presbyterian cleric repeatedly attacked the materialism that he saw as being a negative legacy of the recent period of war. Similarly, a blunt Lord Dalhousie observed in 1819 that hard times at least had the virtue of weaning people away from their wartime habit of eating 'beef steaks at breakfast, dinner & supper.'[19]

While prosperity prevailed, few people worried about the character flaws that might result from having too much money to spend. Of much greater concern was the question of what would happen to people's standard of living once the war came to an end. One major indication that hostilities might soon cease came in May 1814, when it was learned that Napoleon had been overthrown, following the collapse of his invasion of Russia. The news provoked major rejoicing; in Saint John, for example, the citizenry lit up their houses and massed in a downtown square to eat roast oxen.[20] Delight soon turned to worry, however, as the Royal Navy took advantage of victory in Europe to become ever more aggressive in America. One by-product of this shift in military fortunes was an increase in press gang activity. Hungry for extra manpower, Royal Navy captains began raiding the waterfront of ports such as Halifax, often in arrogant defiance of local authorities.[21] Far more ominous from the perspective of colonial merchants was the navy's extension of its blockade to include the coast of New England. That meant it became impossible to persist with the licensed trade that had developed into a mainstay of colonial prosperity.

A major confrontation between military and civilian notions over how the war should be prosecuted never materialized, thanks to developments that came during July 1814. That month, British forces easily succeeded in occupying the northeastern coast of Maine. The area above the Penobscot immediately emerged as the focal point for a massive smuggling operation. Merchants from places such as St Andrews, Saint John, and Halifax moved into Castine and transformed it into a forward base for the continuation of their trade with New England. Hundreds of wagons and scores of small coasters moved in and out of Castine, evading the Royal Navy and American custom-house authorities with equal finesse. In effect, the Castine base provided a substitute for the use of licences. Significantly, in this last stage of the war, the terms of trade moved ever more in favour of the colonists, as the value of what they sold exceeded the cost of what they bought. Americans made up the difference by paying out in hard cash, a commodity traditionally in short supply in the underdeveloped British-American economy.[22]

The mood prevailing across the colonies late in the war was summed up by a letter that appeared in Halifax's *Acadian Recorder*, in the summer of 1814. The anonymous author boasted: 'Happy state of Nova Scotia! Amongst all this tumult we have lived in peace and security; invaded only by a numerous host of American doubloons and dollars.'[23] When hostilities ended in 1815, however, many were as pessimistic as the merchant John Young. Writing from Halifax to his son, who was running a branch of the family firm at Castine, Young moaned, 'The rejoicings of humanity are checked in my bosom by the whispers of self interest as I know not what new direction trade may take ... This peace has blasted all our prospects.'[24]

Throughout the last months of the war, the legislatures and business leaders of the Atlantic colonies had continually petitioned London for assurances that their interests would be protected during negotiations leading to peace. Spokesmen for coastal British America placed particular emphasis on the need to exclude foreign fishermen from the inshore waters of their region. They also insisted that American merchants must be denied direct access to markets in the British West Indies. Their third priority involved continuation of the tariffs, introduced during the struggle against Napoleon, which gave colonial timber protection from foreign competition in the British market. Finally, pressure was exerted to have the Castine area of Maine made permanently a part of New Brunswick.[25]

Thanks to support received from metropolitan business interests, the colonists largely succeeded in getting what they wanted, at least in the short run. The terms of peace agreed to with France and the United States reflected the extent to which the war had ended as a British victory. While willing to retreat from northeastern Maine, the British generally proved to be tough bargainers. The only major concessions to former enemies involved the fisheries. French and American fishermen secured a qualified renewal of their rights to operate on a migratory basis along certain shores in Newfoundland and Labrador. The French also regained title to St Pierre and Miquelon. Otherwise, however, British diplomats successfully resisted pressure, especially from the Americans, for access to colonial resources and markets. The new order emerging in the aftermath of war appeared to be one where British policy makers had opted to persist with the old mercantilist ideal of building the British Empire into a largely self-contained economic unit.

Military victory, coming in association with a reiteration of traditional assumptions about the need for close integration of the colonial and metropolitan economies, brought relief to some in the Maritimes and Newfoundland. The various lieutenant-governors were quick to make optimistic predictions about what the future would bring. But their confidence rested on a shaky foundation. During twenty years of almost continual warfare, coastal British America had enjoyed a strategic importance that made it attractive for large-scale infusions of capital and labour. There were good reasons to fear, however, that in peacetime the region might well sink into relative irrelevance. If that happened, could this small and still highly undeveloped community avoid a descent into crisis? That was a question of preoccupying importance for most colonists as they confronted the transition from war to peace.[26]

At this watershed in its history, the region held no more than 200,000 people, and few of them had been resident for more than one generation. The bulk of the population lived in isolated oases of settlement scattered amid vast stretches of forest. For example, one visitor to Prince Edward Island in 1820 described the place as being 'one entire forest of wood.' In 1815 stage coaches had begun to run out of Halifax, and a year later steamboat service was inaugurated on the St John River. But, typically, roads were little better than bridle paths, where a man and horse would be lucky to proceed at a pace of three miles an hour. Dependence on water for transportation and communication meant that settlement tended to hug the ocean and river front. Overall, the Maritimes and Newfoundland remained locked in frontier backwardness, exhibiting an appearance and character comparable to what had prevailed in New England a century earlier.[27]

Each of the urban concentrations of Saint John, Halifax, and St John's held a population of about 10,000. European visitors have left a generally negative impression of what these towns had to offer. Lord Dalhousie, for example, regarded Halifax as little better than a shantytown, a place dominated in summer by dust and stench and in winter by 'mountains of snow and sheets of ice.'[28] Here and there expressions of refinement broke through the prevailing squalor and disorder. In Halifax work was progressing on construction of a magnificent stone palace designed to house the legislature and the courts of Nova Scotia. Eventually £52,000 of the profits of war would be spent on the erection of this embodiment of colonial ambition.[29] The Nova Scotia capital also offered such expressions of high culture as theatrical and musical performances. But often these facilities had only a transient presence, and even then existed more because of the patronage provided by officers of the imperial garrison than thanks to any genuine commitment to refinement on the part of colonial civilians. Dalhousie found it significant that the Nova Scotia capital possessed not a single bookstore.[30]

Cultural barrenness was not offset by the virtues of equality and harmony. The towns of this frontier era had a social structure that was decidedly hierarchical. Wealth and power were concentrated among a few leading families, and only a small minority enjoyed what could be called middle-class comfort and respectability. The lives of most people were steeped in poverty, insecurity, conflict, and exploitation, a reality underscored by the conditions that prevailed at the jail in Halifax. There debtors were left to freeze to death in winter, or, if they had money, were coerced by the jailor into spending most of it in scenes of 'riot and drunkenness.' Theft was a capital offence, and the hangings that often brought judicial proceedings to a climax were public events attended by people who regarded death as a source of grisly humour.[31] At the opposite extreme of urban society stood Richard John Uniacke, whose newly accumulated wealth enabled him to acquire an 11,000-acre country estate, complete with formal gardens and a mansion house that boasted stoves in every room, mahogany furniture, carpets, oil paintings, a library, a billiards room, and a bevy of servants. Such refinement failed, however, to offer perfect protection from the turmoil of the times. In 1819, Uniacke's son went on trial for his life, after a duelling incident that ended in the killing of a Halifax merchant, William Bowie. Because he was a Uniacke, however, and also because duelling still possessed an aura of legitimacy among the gentry, the young man was acquitted. The incident did little injury to his career. Within months after the duel, Uniacke, Jr, became procurer general of the Vice-Admiralty Court, president of Halifax's Charitable Irish Society, and member of the House of Assembly for Cape Breton County. Clearly, the social norms that then prevailed gave overwhelming advantages to those at the top of the colonial ruling class.[32]

Out in the countryside, once they proceeded beyond such rare bastions of gentility as Mount Uniacke, visitors encountered a landscape and social structure dominated by underdevelopment. Where older settlements existed they might display 'neat common houses' occupied by people who could be said to have possessed 'frugality and comfort.' But those remained very much an exception. Most farm communities consisted of crude huts and fields broken by stumps and rocks. Conditions were even more primitive in the fishing outports. Rural society largely lacked schools and churches, or, if found, they were little better than what Bishop Plessis encountered at Port Hood, Cape Breton. Upon entering St Cuthbert's Chapel, the touring prelate discovered the building to consist of 'thirty pieces of square timber ... supporting badly assembled rafters, the ensemble covered with cross boards ... with a half foot opening between one board and another, so that rain, wind and snow could come in without obstacle.' Squeezed inside a tiny room of about forty square feet packed with adults and children, the Bishop tried to conduct mass, shouting to be heard over a cacophony of 'babbling and bawling.' Under foot, dogs howled; outside, cows grazed in the unfenced cemetery; all the while rain drummed down on the ship's tarpaulin that had been slung over the broken roof so that his eminence could at least remain dry.[33]

Bad as these facilities were, they offered better than could be found across much of the region, as can be seen by examining the correspondence of Rev. Angus B. MacEachern, who served as missionary priest to the Catholics of Prince Edward Island and Cape Breton. Writing in 1815, MacEachern noted: 'If a clergyman can hear the confession of his people once a year in even a cursory way, he does a great deal.' The challenges of the frontier left MacEachern exhausted and increasingly overwhelmed. Worst of all, many settlers seemed content to slip into religious indifference. On occasion he had to threaten denial of the sacraments to compel observation of the sabbath. MacEachern feared that poverty, illiteracy, and a general lack of institutional discipline might well plunge his flock into enduring superstition and immorality.[34]

Lord Dalhousie, who became lieutenant-governor of Nova Scotia in 1816, was equally appalled by the character of the rural population. A man of strong Tory persuasion, Dalhousie thought that freehold tenure, which prevailed outside Prince Edward Island, fostered a dangerous levelling mentality. In his words, 'Every man ... is laird here, & the classes of the community known in England as Tenantry and peasantry do not exist in these provinces.' Restrictive land-granting policies could partially remedy the situation, but Dalhousie worried that even then popular attitudes and behaviour were likely to subvert the social hierarchy he yearned to build. Passing through Wilmot Township, in Nova Scotia's Annapolis Valley, Dalhousie observed: 'I see no symptom of industry; extreme lazy & bad farming, & the lower orders ill clothed, poor & have no idea of civility; they stood & stared at us as we passed with the utmost American impudence.' Nor were the leaders any better. Coming to the farm of assemblyman Shubael Dimock, the lieutenant governor was shocked to see this pillar of local society 'at home without a coat or waistcoat, just in the dress of a labouring man.'[35]

The image of egalitarian achievement created by these comments is contradicted by other passages found in the Dalhousie journals. For example, while journeying in the Guysborough district of eastern Nova Scotia, an area settled thirty years earlier by Loyalists, the lieutenant-governor observed that 'utmost poverty appears in every hut; they subsist entirely by fishing and their small potatoe [sic] gardens.' Here he encountered what once had been a gentleman, a person who could converse in Latin and Greek but who was so much in economic distress as to be obliged to wear 'a hat in rags ... sewed together with rope yarns, a shirt of flannel, red & yellow pieces patched ... old soldier's pantaloons & no shoes.' In such communities, the few who did have wealth and power, even though they might dress as commoners, exercised enormous influence over their neighbours. This Dalhousie glimpsed when he visited Parrsboro, where the entire community was 'under the rule & control of Mr Ratchford who is everything – keeping a shop for every sort of supply; the whole population is individually indebted to him; selling his goods at enormous profit he makes money on those that pay their accounts, and of those that do not he takes mortgages on their lands.'[36] A similar situation existed among the Acadians in Nova Scotia's Pubnico district. There a visitor reported that the local justice of the peace, a man who 'scarcely knew enough to sign his name,' dominated his countrymen to the point where they 'were as much afraid of him as if he had been the King of England.' [37]

Stratification of experience was also found among the women of the region. One extreme consisted of the comfortable and cosmopolitan little enclave occupied by the wives and daughters of the colonial ruling class. For example, Christian, Countess of Dalhousie, experienced a continual round of receptions, balls, and outings in and around Halifax during her husband's vice-regal tenure in Nova Scotia. Amiable, intelligent, and curious, she served as a patron of literature and the arts while simultaneously dabbling in botany, geology, and chemistry.[38]

At the other extreme were women such as Mary Campbell, a Halifax prostitute murdered in the autumn of 1818, and Maria Rider, sent to the Nova Scotia Bridewell for six months after being convicted of arson. Situated in between were a host of women of middling circumstances, many of whom were remarkably self-assertive. The Halifax press regularly carried advertisements from women working as private schoolteachers, milliners, and boarding-house keepers. Women also acted on the public stage and appear to have been co-proprietors of touring theatre companies. Out in the countryside, Lord Dalhousie encountered their kindred spirits, such as the wife of a Cumberland County settler who boasted that she 'could chop wood and use the hatchet as well as any man.' Again, near Arichat on Cape Breton Island, the lieutenant-governor caught up with a boatload of Acadian women. 'They were,' he reported, 'rowing and singing very gaily, dressed altogether in the old French taste with coloured handkerchiefs tied in turbans very becoming around the head. The men being all absent on the fisheries, the women do all the harvest and home work at this season.'[39]

Overall, the Atlantic colonies emerged from the Napoleonic wars in a vulnerable condition. With few residents and largely undeveloped resources, the region faced enormous challenges, not the least of which involved rapid military demobilization. Reductions in the size of the army and naval establishment had a major impact on places such as Halifax. Particularly devastating was loss of the dockyard, which moved to Bermuda in 1819. As a result, this once bustling enterprise deteriorated into a scene of inertia. Here and elsewhere, departure of the soldiers and sailors brought a drastic curtailment of military spending, on everything from rum to beef. Business slowed, prices fell, and unemployment rose, as the colonial economy struggled to do without the stimulus of war.[40] In the long run, even greater damage derived from the way in which peace facilitated a return to normal patterns of trade between Europe and the United States. Freed from both naval blockade and the harassment of privateers, merchant vessels once again proceeded directly, for example, from Liverpool to New York. Ports such as Saint John and Halifax lost their status as transshipment points. Soon their wharves and warehouses lay more or less idle. Local merchants who had once grown rich by acting as middlemen for the trade of the whole North Atlantic now had to scramble for profit in a depressed colonial backwater.[41]

Hard times were made all the harder by the fact that the colonies were caught up in a growing international economic recession. Deflation, falling investment, and soaring import duties in Europe had negative ramifications in areas such as coastal British America. Demand for colonial exports, especially fish, went into a slump. Importers, traditionally dependent on extended lines of credit, now found themselves under heavy pressure to meet curtailed deadlines for payment. Meanwhile, goods such as textiles and hardware began to be dumped into local markets through the use of commission agents and auctioneers.[42] Shrinking profits combined with increased competition to decimate the wholesaler fraternity in colonial entrepôts. From there, adversity spread out through the rural hinterland, proceeding by way of country storekeepers and outport 'planters' to the mass of primary producers. An early symptom of the onset of crisis involved the disappearance of actual cash. Reserves of gold and silver increasingly had to be shipped out to pay for imports, mainly foodstuffs, which the region still depended upon. By 1818, the situation had deteriorated to the point where one Nova Scotia legislator was prompted to observe: 'A man ... may travel from Cape Sable to Pictou, and not find a dollar in his way.'[43]

Other afflictions also haunted the colonists as they struggled to come to terms with the transition from war to peace. In 1816 the region suffered through such protracted frosts that this went down as the year 'without a summer.' Woodsworkers were obliged to wear mittens in June, and crops rotted in the fields for lack of sunshine. At the same time, mice and hurricanes further ravaged the countryside, to such a degree that famine conditions appeared in places. Then came fire, especially at St John's, where a conflagration left one-fifth of the population homeless late in 1817, at the onset of winter. Law and order broke down as armed gangs took to roaming the streets in search of shelter and food. Several of the Newfoundland outports, deprived of their usual sources of supply from St John's, faced mass starvation. Visiting ships resorted to the extreme of using gunfire to prevent settler expropriation of their stores of food and drink.[44]

As if this was not bad enough, coastal British America found itself subjected to hostile pressure from outside economic interests. Immediately after hostilities ceased, American fishermen began encroaching on the inshore waters of the Maritimes. Rioting erupted at Grand Manan and elsewhere, as residents attempted to enforce the law that required foreigners to operate beyond the three-mile limit. Similarly, on the Newfoundland coast, colonists who had moved into the old French Shore fought to prevent migratory French fishermen from competing for cod. And almost everywhere Yankee smugglers hovered along the coast, running in contraband and taking away staples, much to the annoyance of both tax collectors and local business interests. Challenges also emerged overseas, notably in the Mediterranean markets favoured by Newfoundland fish exporters. There Scandinavian entrepreneurs developed into major rivals.[45] Most ominous of all, at least from a Maritime perspective, was the refusal of American merchants to accept their post-war exclusion from British Caribbean markets. In 1818, the u.s. Congress embarked on a sustained program of port closure designed to prevent American goods from being shipped to the West Indies by way of British America.[46]

These foreign actions provoked a sustained chorus of complaint from colonial leaders, who insisted that London should intervene to safeguard the peace settlement. Initially, it seemed that assistance would be forthcoming. The Royal Navy provided strengthened coastal patrols, and colonial legislation was approved that imposed draconian penalties on those who persisted in smuggling. As well, Halifax and Saint John were set up as 'free ports' under an arrangement designed to subvert American embargo regulations.[47] Gradually, however, London began to edge away from vigorous defence of colonial interests. British America's inability to achieve rapid economic growth, hostile pressure from Caribbean planters, and above all metropolitan recognition of the overriding importance of trade with the Americans made it all too tempting to accommodate rather than antagonize the foreigner. At first this was portrayed as a short-term tactical manoeuvre. Over time, however, it became ever more apparent that London had embarked on a long-term strategic realignment, leading from mercantilism towards free trade.

Amid what was generally a scene of gloom and paranoia, the colonists at least could look to one relatively bright spot in their overall post-war economic scene. It was found in the timber-producing area of the Maritimes, which stretched across New Brunswick, into Prince Edward Island, and along Nova Scotia's Northumberland Strait coast. British demand for colonial forest products held up relatively well after 1815. Thus, districts that depended primarily on production and export of square timber to the metropolitan market were spared the worst effects of the onset of peace. Nowhere was this better seen than in New Brunswick's Miramichi Valley. Endowed with a heavy forest cover, rendered easily accessible by an extensive array of main and branch rivers, this territory developed rapidly as capital and entrepreneurship, mainly from Britain, arrived in strength. By the early 1820s the Miramichi had acquired a network of towns, mills, and shipyards that together made it one of the most dynamic components of the regional economy.[48]

In peacetime, the growing numbers of vessels engaged in the timber trade found themselves short of paying cargo to move westbound across the Atlantic. Rather than proceed in ballast, they offered cheap fares to those in the British Isles seeking passage to America. Accommodations were primitive in the extreme, and the voyage exposed passengers to an often fatal combination of brutality, disease, hunger, and shipwreck. Nevertheless, starting early in the post-war period, thousands of British people began to flock on board ships bound for the Maritimes. Pushed by economic crisis at home and pulled by promises of free Crown land in the colonies, they poured into eastern British America. By 1819 these new arrivals were becoming a major presence throughout much of the coastline bordering the Gulf of St Lawrence.[49]

The first wave of post-war immigrants, made up largely of small farmers and rural artisans from Scotland and Ireland, were relatively well off and skilled by comparison with those who came later. Most persisted in the Maritimes to become an instrument for steadily diluting the region's Anglo-Protestant character. Their first months in the country, however, were often difficult. Exhausted by their travels, short of ready cash, and unfamiliar with wilderness conditions, British immigrants frequently had to beg for food and shelter. The growing welfare problem this created quickly became a focal point of controversy. Although eager for the cheap labour supplied by the immigrants, colonists resented the newcomers' temporary lack of self-sufficiency. As the economy worsened, fears deepened within the host population that the new arrivals would become chronic paupers whose presence would forever cripple prospects for development.[50]

The accelerating slide into crisis experienced by both Newfoundland and the Maritimes after 1815 generated a variety of responses. Some people simply despaired and left. In the case of ordinary folk, that generally meant departing for the United States. Those of a higher station, especially if they had been born in the British Isles, migrated back across the Atlantic. The loss of these people, whose numbers can only be guessed at, deprived the region of much-needed skilled labour, capital and entrepreneurship.[51] The vast majority of colonists, however, opted to hang on in the hope that conditions eventually would improve. In the interim, they scrambled for survival, often resorting to measures that did little but accentuate the prevailing atmosphere of disarray and anxiety. For example, in the depressed little community of Shelburne, Nova Scotia, merchant Gideon White threatened his debtors with arrest and imprisonment. Writing to his son in November 1818, he observed: 'I am truly in a fever. I have sued twenty persons and shall fifty more in

April.'[52] It is doubtful that such court action achieved anything other than to make White a figure of fear and hate among his hard-pressed neighbours.

Responsibility for guiding eastern British America through this traumatic episode in its history lay, first of all, with the small group of officials resident in the capital of each colony. Although ultimately responsible to the Colonial Office for their actions, these men usually enjoyed a large degree of autonomy from imperial interference when dealing with day-to-day problems. Except in Newfoundland and Cape Breton, which had yet to acquire representative government, the power to make and enforce laws was distributed among the lieutenant-governor, an advisory group of executive councillors, the upper house of the legislature (most of whose members also served on the Council), and the legislature's lower house, the Assembly. Of these, only the assemblymen were elected to office. All the rest obtained their positions through appointment and enjoyed almost complete security of tenure. Complemented by appointed justices of the peace (and, in Saint John, with elected municipal officials), this regime was held together by a complex blend of tradition, class, and ideology. Elitist in character and conservative in outlook, colonial government was nevertheless prone to internal disarray. Conflict usually arose out of nothing more profound than personal rivalries, particularly those associated with the distribution of patronage. But occasionally debate erupted over matters that touched on issues of public policy and involved clashes between major interest groups within the community. A survey of governmental affairs across the region during the period of transition from peace to war reveals that this latter phenomenon was occurring with increasing frequency.[53]

In Newfoundland, Lieutenant-Governor Francis Pickmore, upon taking office in 1817, 'literally worked himself to death,' as he struggled to avert mass starvation. The depth of the crisis had been sufficient to persuade Pickmore to make a major break with tradition by becoming the first governor to winter over on the island. His death came at St John's in February 1818.[54] Such sacrifice was only partially appreciated by the local inhabitants. More and more, the business and professional élite of St John's was coming to believe that the community needed not only dedicated officials but also fundamental changes in the structure of government. An elected assembly, freehold land title, and the other components of full colonial status had come to be their central objective. Constitutional reform, it was hoped, would give the island the means to raise new revenue, embark on a major public works program, and, above all, promote economic diversification, so that Newfoundland might become less dependent on the vagaries of the cod and seal fisheries. Agitators like Dr William Carson insisted that the migratory fishery, based in England's West Country, had suffered a final collapse during the Napoleonic wars. The dramatic growth in permanent settlement that had occurred in wartime meant for people like Carson the emergence of a 'new' Newfoundland. Here, he argued, was a society that was every day becoming more like its counterparts on the mainland. Accordingly, it needed and deserved all the institutional infrastructure of a true colony, in order to cope with the challenges of peace.[55] This demand, above all for 'representative government' (that is, an elected assembly), would be resisted, but it could not be eradicated. The rhetoric of reform, spawned by immediate post-Napoleonic adversity, was destined to persist.

In 1819 two incidents occurred that dramatically underscored Carson's thesis that Newfoundland needed a revised political order. Both involved considerable violence. In March of that year, deep in the island's interior, near Red Indian Lake, a group of settlers on a mission to recover what they regarded as stolen property encountered a small party of Beothuks. A fight ensued that climaxed in the murder of Nonosbawsut, the aboriginal chief, and the capture of his wife, Demasduwit.[56] The incident proved disastrous for the Beothuk, who lost what appears to have been their last formidable leader. It also drove home the point that the authorities at St John's lacked the capacity to maintain law and order on the frontier. The regime could do little better in older areas of settlement. Also in 1819, two Conception Bay fishermen defied the authority of the local courts over payment of a business debt. Local magistrates responded by calling in the military. Seized and convicted before what amounted to a court martial, both men were lashed as if they had been naval deserters and had all their property confiscated.[57] This raw demonstration of power immediately became controversial. Upon learning what had taken place, Carson and his associates insisted that ordinary Newfoundlanders were being denied their civil rights, especially if they happened to be Roman Catholic, as were the two fishermen involved in this incident. Over the next decade, a growing number of island residents became convinced that economic and social change was creating an imperative need for political innovation in Newfoundland.[58]

A comparable situation developed after the war in the island colony of Cape Breton. There the government had become embroiled in a debilitating conflict over its constitutional status. Led by Richard Gibbons, Jr, a former official in the island administration, a faction based in Sydney began arguing that duties could not be levied on imports, since the laws that sanctioned such taxes had not been passed by any elected Cape Breton legislature. Using the cry of 'no taxation without representation,' Gibbons and his associates demanded that the colony be granted an elected assembly. This simmering dispute came to a climax in 1816, when Cape Breton's chief justice declared that duties could not be charged on the rum imported for sale to local coal miners. The decision deprived the administration of its main source of income. In desperation, the authorities appealed to London for assistance. Puzzled as to what should be done for this long overlooked colony, the Colonial Office sought advice from the newly appointed lieutenant-governor, George R. Ainslie. He replied in no uncertain terms, damning the group around Gibbons as so many 'rogues' and alleging that Cape Bretoners collectively lacked the money and education required to make an assembly work properly. Such comments harmonized with London's post-war pursuit of economy measures. Accordingly it was decided, in 1820, to reverse the initiative of 1784 and reunite Cape Breton with Nova Scotia. Outside Sydney the announcement was greeted with indifference, although in time the neglect and exploitation associated with renewed Halifax rule would foster secessionist sentiments across much of Cape Breton.[59]

Prince Edward Island also became embroiled in partisan debate during the second decade of the nineteenth century. Within months of taking office in 1813, Lieutenant-Governor Charles D. Smith had antagonized 'virtually every important interest group on the Island.' Described as being 'arrogant, quick tempered and vindictive,' as well as paranoid and prone to nepotism, Smith went to the extreme of surrounding his residence with troops to guard against the imagined threat of assassination.[60] For three and half years, he refused to call the Assembly into session, lest it become a sounding board for dissatisfied public opinion. In 1817, when the legislature finally did convene, debate immediately erupted over the failure of most landlords to pay the annual quitrents they owed to the Crown. The lack of such payments was depriving the Island treasury of substantial revenues needed for everything from payment of official salaries to road and bridge construction. As justification for their behaviour, the landlords, mostly speaking through their local agents, insisted that their good intentions had been sabotaged by the recent war. Hostilities, they argued, had made it difficult to develop or even derive any revenue from their real-estate holdings. The landlords followed up with threats to withhold future investment from the colony unless released from the obligation of paying back taxes. That argument provoked the reply that perhaps Prince Edward Island would be better off, particularly in terms of attracting immigrants, if some or all of the landlords were dispossessed and their property parcelled out to small-scale freeholders.[61]

This dispute, which involved the core of the imperial government's long-standing development strategy for the Island, grew all the more intense when Lieutenant-Governor Smith intervened against the land-lords. Acting on his own initiative, mainly in an effort to secure his own salary, Smith announced that two estates on which large arrears of quitrents were owing were to be repossessed by the Crown. Escheat proceedings duly took place, and Smith moved on to take the even more provocative step of breaking the properties up and letting them out on leases that in effect amounted to freehold grants. The initiative earned Smith a brief measure of popularity among settlers, but Island landlords were outraged, seeing his actions as the beginning of what could develop into a sustained assault on their vested interests. Propri-etors resident in Britain put enormous pressure on the imperial govern-ment, demanding that it intervene against further expropriations. Conservative-minded imperial officials, reluctant to tamper with poli-cies inherited from the eighteenth century, sympathized with the land-lords. Smith was ordered to desist from meddling with the structure of the land-distribution system. He complied, but the local legislature proved harder to discipline. Riddled by factional disputes and under pressure to do something to remedy hard times, frustrated assembly-men turned on Lieutenant-Governor Smith. Demands for Smith's impeachment generated counter-attacks, in which Smith told the Colo-nial Office that the colony was on the threshold of insurrection.[62] Per-haps it was mere coincidence that these were the conditions prevailing when Richard Pearce stabbed Edward Abell. It is tempting, however, to speculate that the fatal confrontation between these two derived, at least in part, from the tension then growing in Island society between landlord and tenant.

New Brunswick politics proceeded at a somewhat more relaxed pace, thanks largely to the vitality of the forest-industry trade, which secured the colony against the worst effects of post-war economic dislocation. Nevertheless conflict did erupt in 1818, following Lieutenant-Governor George Stracey Smyth's decision to assert his authority over the timber trade. Eager to obtain an additional source of revenue and dismayed by the growth of what amounted to free-for-all exploitation of the colony's most valuable resource, the Fredericton administration imposed new regulatory taxes on those cutting trees on Crown land.[63] The move was immediately challenged by New Brunswick's powerful timber interests, who argued that Smyth's fees would drive up the price of wood and thereby compromise their ability to sell into the British market. They also claimed that the taxes would subvert the constitution by giving the executive a large income over which the legislature had no control. Called in to arbitrate, the London authorities endorsed Smyth's reforms, most likely because they offered a means of reducing colonial calls on the imperial treasury. That decision, which came in 1819, inaugurated what has been termed 'a revolution in the commerce and politics of the province.'[64] Now firmly established as Britain's chief source of supply for wood products, New Brunswick proceeded into the 1820s with a regime destined to become ever more polarized between factions fighting for control of the tax revenue generated by the highly lucrative timber trade.

Political wrangling also prevailed in post-war Nova Scotia. On leaving the colony in 1820 to become governor general of British North America, Lord Dalhousie sullenly rejected the congratulatory sword and star offered to him by the local legislature. In Dalhousie's opinion the gift was nothing more than an exercise in hypocrisy. Recently, his authority had been repeatedly challenged by the House of Assembly, a body led by a speaker, Simon Bradstreet Robie, whom Dalhousie described as 'an ill-tempered crab, deeply tinctured in Yankee principles.'[65] By the beginning of the 1820s, good feelings were very much on the wane in Nova Scotia, as various interests struggled for ascendancy.

Religion provided one major source of contention. As in other jurisdictions, Nova Scotia's Roman Catholic minority was becoming ever more assertive. In 1817 the Catholics acquired their first bishop, and three years later a cornerstone was laid for St Mary's cathedral church, located in the heart of Halifax. Such encroachments on Protestant ascendancy struck many as being a dangerous innovation. One high official went so far as to describe Roman Catholicism as an 'evil' threat to peace, order, and good government.[66] That antagonism derived largely from the fact that a high percentage of the region's expanding Catholic population was of Irish and Highland Scottish extraction. Thus the colony's growing denominational pluralism was being compounded by ever-greater ethnic diversity. This trend away from eighteenth-century norms received explicit expression in 1820, when Laurence Kavanagh, a Roman Catholic, won election to the Nova Scotia Assembly as a member for Cape Breton County. He had to wait three years to take his seat, while debate raged over the propriety of abandoning the principle of reserving high public office exclusively for Protestants.[67] Traditionalists became all the more alarmed when Protestant Dissenters joined Roman Catholics in attacks on custom in the area of relations between church and state. Although not fully established in law, Nova Scotia's Church of England did enjoy a privileged relationship with government. The Anglican bishop usually sat on the colony's executive and legislative councils. As well, every lieutenant-governor and most high officials in the colonial administration were practising members of the Church of England. Sunday service at St Paul's or St George's church in Halifax was presided over by an urban gentry to a far greater extent than in any neighbouring assembly of Presbyterians, Methodists, or Baptists. These

Protestant sects had long been tolerated; at the same time, however, they were expected to be deferential.[68]

That convention was beginning to disintegrate. Emboldened by growing numbers and strengthened clerical leadership, Nova Scotia religious Dissenters began demanding equality before the law. An early expression of this campaign for change involved the matters of marriage and education. Non-Anglican ministers insisted that they too should have the right to conduct weddings, using licences issued by the lieutenant-governor. They also wanted access to government funds for the schools then being set up to promote mass literacy. Spokesmen for the Anglican hierarchy opposed all encroachments on their privileged position within the colonial power structure, insisting that the Church of England alone could be relied upon as a bulwark in support of the British connection.[69] Such arguments, rooted in counter-revolutionary enthusiasm, were to become increasingly obsolete as memories of the American and French upheavals faded. Moreover, it did not help the Tories' position that they were being challenged at a time when Nova Scotia Anglicans were suffering a crisis of leadership. Bishop Charles Inglis had been unwell through much of his last years in office and Robert Stanser, who succeeded Inglis, took up residence in England. Meanwhile key Church of England institutions, notably the University of King's College, had gone into decline. When Lord Dalhousie visited what then was still Nova Scotia's sole institution of higher education, he found it to have a leaking roof, fewer than a dozen students and a faculty of two who refused to talk to one another.[70] Such disarray operated to the advantage of Nova Scotia's Dissenters in the immediate post-war period. Working through allies in the Assembly, they established the precedent of having public funds provided for new interdenominational institutions, notably Halifax's Royal Acadian School and Pictou County's Pictou Academy.[71] Despite his own reactionary political inclinations, Lieutenant-Governor Dalhousie contributed to the assault on the Church of England's ascendancy. Using the custom-house duties collected during the war at Castine, Dalhousie founded a new institution of higher education, independent of Anglican authority, in the Nova Scotia capital. Although Dalhousie College remained stillborn through the next quarter century, its creation underscored the way in which the post-war era was coming to be characterized by the emergence of new ideals.[72]

It would be a mistake, however, to assume that colonists were preoccupied with denominational affairs. Most people paid far greater attention to issues relating to economic development. High priority was assigned to the question of how best to utilize the immigrants who were beginning to flood into eastern British America. The first major group to arrive were some 2,000 Black Americans who had fled from slavery to take refuge with British forces during their wartime invasion of Maryland and attack on Washington. Four hundred of these people resettled in New Brunswick, but most came to Halifax. Although welcomed during the war as a source of cheap labour, once peace brought mass employment to the Nova Scotia capital these immigrants came to be viewed as an undesirable nuisance. The Black refugees themselves agitated to be given land that they could develop as freeholders. In response, the authorities sponsored a program of rural resettlement in the districts of Preston and Hammonds Plains, a few miles outside Halifax.[73]

Lord Dalhousie visited these communities in 1816, just as they were taking shape and expressed delight over the volume of land cleared and the rate of house construction. The Black pioneers struck him as being 'industrious, sober & deserving of every encouragement.'[74] Unfortunately, the positive promise of that first year was not fulfilled. Hit hard by crop failures, the settlers required extended government rations. Over the decade, their efforts to achieve self-sufficiency were crippled by low agricultural prices and a lack of demand for their labour in Halifax. Continued requests by Black settlers for welfare roused Dalhousie's ire, and his earlier sympathy gave way to a retreat into hostile racial stereotyping. Black spokesmen offered a different interpretation of what had gone wrong. As they saw it, their work would always be compromised so long as Black settlers were forced to make do with land that had little agricultural potential and was parcelled out, in ten-acre lots, to occupiers who ranked more as tenants than as freeholders. But adversity did not extinguish pride, as was revealed by an 1818 incident when a Black family outside Dartmouth drove off their land three armed White trespassers, commenting, 'we are not in the [United] States, and we can now do as we like'.[75]

Similar problems characterized government dealings with Nova Scotia's aboriginal population. After the war, as the pressure of White settlement grew, the colony's Micmac people became ever more insistent that land should be set aside for their exclusive use. Starting in 1819, the Halifax authorities responded by laying out a series of 1,000-acre 'reserves,' at sites frequented by the still largely migratory Native population. This initiative embodied a large element of paternalism. Suspicious that the Micmac would act irresponsibly if given freehold title, the Crown declared that it would hold the land in trust for the Natives. That trusteeship, however, was discharged in a negligent manner. Above all, those in power became notorious for neglecting to block White encroachment on reserve property. This failure of official policy with respect to the colony's Native people owed much to the coming of peace. After 1815, aboriginal leaders ceased to be regarded as an interest group that had to be accommodated for the sake of military security. Thus, while Lord Dalhousie might praise them as being an 'extraordinary race of humans,' he followed with comments implying that he believed Atlantic Canada's first people to be doomed to extinction.[76]

The Micmac and Maliseet ultimately avoided annihilation, but the Beothuk of Newfoundland were less fortunate. Efforts by the authorities in St John's to communicate with local aboriginals led to the capture of Demasduwit in 1819, but the woman died of tuberculosis before she could be used as an agent of contact. The military expedition that returned her body to the Exploits River area in the winter of 1820 found evidence showing that some Natives still were alive in Newfoundland's interior, but their numbers had dwindled to the point where they could not long survive as a people.[77]

Continued dependence on government assistance was not a phenomenon limited to the region's Black and aboriginal populations. The soldier settlements launched after the war in the western interior of Nova Scotia quickly became notorious as expensive failures. Lord Dalhousie made every effort to shore up these frontier communities, but ultimately was obliged to say that once government rations ran out, two-thirds of the soldier pioneers would likely take flight.[78] Similarly, the Welsh immigrants who ventured into Shelburne County and up the St John River of New Brunswick left a record of hardship and defeat, and many fled the forest to wander as beggars in the streets of towns like Fredericton.[79] Having discovered that large-scale immigration was seriously flawed as a strategy for achieving rapid economic development, colonial leaders put ever greater emphasis on exploring other means of alleviating hard times. Repression of the working poor proved appealing, especially at a time when similar measures were being employed by the metropolitan government. Nova Scotia's legislature outlawed labour-union activity and also established new facilities for incarcerating such nuisance elements as beggars, runaway apprentices, and 'stubborn servants.' Similarly, attempts were made to stamp out smuggling and outlaw sales by auction, both being seen as a threat to legitimate business practice. A strong lobby also emerged, especially among farmers and craftsmen, for tariffs that would protect colonial producers against both foreign and British competition. On a more positive note, demands were made for increased spending on public works, especially for road and bridge construction. Many thought that priority should be given to increasing the money supply, either by creating private banks or by having the local government issue its own paper currency. In addition, it was suggested that abolition of debtor imprisonment would encourage risk taking and curb the number of people fleeing to the United States.

For the most part, however, talk did not translate into effective action, since what appealed to one group antagonized some other faction. Judging by the situation in Nova Scotia, geographic and class alignments prevailed in the discussion over how best to cope with the rigours of peace. Halifax's merchant and bureaucratic élite, entrenched in the appointed upper house of the legislature, repeatedly clashed with the farmers and outport traders who dominated the elected Assembly. Legislative debate, echoed by a war of words in the weekly press, revolved around the question of whether innovation would remedy or aggravate the problems of the day. For example, advocates of protective tariffs were challenged by the argument that new duties would simply drive up the cost of living and increase smuggling activity. Similarly, proponents of an easy-money policy were told that such measures would merely accelerate the flight of hard currency from the colony. In the end, not much of anything was decided, both because of a lack of agreement within the colonial élite and also because the imperial government threatened to veto any legislation that appeared innovative.[80]

On occasion women were singled out for attention by those seeking to chart a course for the future. For example, Thomas McCulloch's letters to the Halifax press repeatedly insisted that females had become an obstacle to the practice of thrift, sobriety, and hard work. Their alleged infatuation with fine clothes, gossip, and frivolity were portrayed as devices that led men astray. McCulloch particularly singled out for censure behaviour that hinted at promiscuity. Thus he fiercely denounced 'bundling,' the tradition that allowed unmarried young couples to cuddle together in bed, while fully clothed. Among Reverend McCulloch's other targets were evangelical women who dared to assume a leadership role in the promotion of organized religion. Females, McCulloch insisted, should confine themselves to the domestic sphere, even when that meant submitting to physical abuse. The very fact that authority figures saw fit to issue such misanthropic diatribes could be taken as a sign that women in early-nineteenth-century Nova Scotia refused to remain passive and deferential. As McCulloch himself put it, in many a colonial household, the wife had 'got into the trousers.'[81]

The extent to which a reform consciousness emerged out of these bitter exchanges over remedies for hard times is difficult to discern. A new distrust of those with wealth and power began to assert itself, however, especially in written form. For example, in 1818 the Halifax press reported, after an election in Kings County, that a defeated candidate had accused his opponents of being 'worshippers of the GREAT, who would sell you and your interests for a good dinner.'[82] A year later, William Wilkie, an obscure Halifax shopkeeper, dared to write a pamphlet that proclaimed: 'We are governed by a set of drivellers, from whom we can expect no remedy, but in *poison*, no relief but in *death*.' Wilkie's strong language derived from his belief that the entire apparatus of government was steeped in corruption and incompetence. Such overt expression of political alienation, coming from the growing number of printing presses that were available to those with grievances to express, represented a provocative change.[83] Wilkie's extremist behaviour, as well as his lack of social connections, made him a likely target for counter-attack. As occurred in Upper Canada in the case of the rabble-rousing Robert Gourlay, those in power in Nova Scotia opted to squelch this shrill voice of protest. Tried and convicted on a charge of seditious libel, Wilkie went to jail. Nevertheless, other expressions of dissent were tolerated, including that of John Young, the merchant who had greeted the coming of peace with such foreboding. Young's pessimism proved prophetic. By 1818 his business had failed, leaving him with little to do other than write, under the pseudonym 'Agricola,' a series of letters to the press, urging Nova Scotia farmers to improve their lot by emulating the example of their modernizing counterparts in Scotland. Though dismissed by some as merely a pompous opportunist likely to stir up trouble, Young won the support of a fellow Scot, Lord Dalhousie himself. As a result, Young got access to government funds, which were used to subsidize a network of agricultural societies throughout Nova Scotia's hinterland. Within a decade, the contacts and expectations fostered by Young's initiative were contributing to a major destabilization of Nova Scotia public affairs.[84]

The career of John Young is indicative of what life was like in the coastal colonies during the second decade of the nineteenth century. Circumstances varied widely according to the factors of place, class, race, and gender, but all colonists shared the basic contradiction of moving through war to peace and of enjoying a brief measure of prosperity, only to have it slip away during the onset of adversity. Contemporaries may have concluded that this era amounted to little more than the proverbial 'one step forward' followed by 'one step back.' In truth, however, this was not a period of inertia. It possessed a basic momentum, the nature of which was illustrated by that confrontation between those two combatants at Rollo Bay in 1819. Edward Abell epitomized those conservative forces in colonial society that were attempting to build a future within a framework of institutions and ideals inherited from the eighteenth century. Richard Pearce, perhaps unwittingly, embodied those who sought to repudiate that inheritance and replace it with structures that were more pluralistic and open to change. Their particular encounter ended in violent futility. Abell died and Pearce fled into exile. This lack of a clear cut winner and loser reflected the character of the century's second decade. War and peace left a legacy of ambiguity. As of 1820, traditional forces remained in the ascendant, but their hold had begun to weaken and would erode further as all sections of colonial society persisted in the paramount quest for an escape from hard times.

PART THREE
THE CONSOLIDATION OF COLONIAL SOCIETY,
1820–1867

CHAPTER TWELVE

The 1820s

Peace, Privilege, and the Promise of Progress

JUDITH FINGARD

The 1820s was the first decade undisturbed by a British war in almost a century. As usual, peace was a mixed blessing for the Atlantic colonies, where war had always produced much-needed contracts for merchants, markets for primary producers, and jobs for wage labourers. In the wake of peacetime contraction on military expenditure, the loss of customary markets for fish through the rise of European protectionism and American competition, and unplanned immigration, the four colonies felt disruption and anxiety that varied only in degree as a result of differences in staple exports, locational factors, and local ambitions. Recovery was uneven, reform was erratic, leadership was fragmented. At the same time the region was subjected to various competing, but not always incompatible, influences from within and without: evangelical reform and reform favoured by political economists; traditional Tory paternalism and emergent liberal individualism.

Extremes in everyday life were everywhere apparent. The élites lived in comfort in each colony, in a style as closely modelled on metropolitan standards as conditions would allow. New communities, as well as isolated ones, struggled to overcome poverty, disease, and illiteracy. Relatively recent improvements like steamboats and stagecoaches were available in only a few locations, and most travel was at the mercy of the vagaries of wind and fog or the inconvenience of mud and forest. The landscapes and seascapes were dangerously beautiful, ranging even in midsummer from the raging forest fires of the New Brunswick interior, where in 1826 the mercury climbed to the high nineties Fahrenheit day after day and the accompanying drought destroyed the season's prospects, to the spectacular icebergs off the eastern coast of Newfoundland, a constant threat to the boats anxiously putting to sea each day to fish for cod. Dotted across the region were occasional signs of development, the much-vaunted progress of the nineteenth century: water-powered mills, shipyards, schools. The decade was kind to a lucky minority; it meant unremitting toil and frequent reverses for the majority. It delivered thousands from misery in the British Isles; it had catastrophic meaning for one whole portion of humanity in Newfoundland.[1]

One of the few rewards that peace between Britain and France bestowed on the colonies was their share of Napoleonic war heroes sent out as governors. Despite such an unlikely apprenticeship, the four most prominent 'veteran' governors of the decade were relatively popular, humane, and constructive administrators: James Kempt in Nova Scotia (1820–8), Howard Douglas in New Brunswick (1824–31), John Ready in Prince Edward Island (1824–31), and Thomas Cochrane in Newfoundland (1825–34). Still the leading officials in the colonies and subject only to the scrutiny of the distant British government, particularly the Colonial Office and the Treasury, their main virtue was their sponsorship of projects and reforms, paid for out of local revenues, that accorded with the preferences of the people. They thereby secured the goodwill of the local politicians and temporarily postponed conflict between the appointed executive and the elected Assembly, except in Newfoundland, where representative government was still a goal rather than a reality.[2]

The key to Kempt's success in Nova Scotia was his ability to maintain a mutually beneficial working relationship with the speaker of the Assembly. As the leader of the popular branch of the government, the speaker was the leading politician of the pre-reform era in each colony with representative government. Kempt also avoided constitutional controversy by deliberately refusing to follow British instructions relating to the negotiation of a civil list. The imperial authorities wanted to transfer to the Assembly the salaries of colonial officials, hitherto provided by British taxpayers through a parliamentary grant. In return for a permanent civil list – one, that is, which did not reduce the established salaries – the British government was willing to allow the Assembly to appropriate Crown revenues that had traditionally been controlled by the lieutenant-governor and his appointed executive. Since these did not amount to much in Nova Scotia, they did not provide the same basis for conflict as in resource-rich New Brunswick and the Canadas.[3] This is not to suggest that Kempt's administration was completely devoid of constitutional change and political conflict. One of his first duties was to oversee the administrative re-annexation of the Island of Cape Breton to mainland Nova Scotia in 1820. Cape Bretoners were rewarded with two Assembly seats. Although this measure facilitated a more constructive development policy for Cape Breton, it also brought the island within the orbit of Halifax, to the latter's benefit and to the disgust of the persistent Cape Breton separatists.[4]

The dominant political issue of the decade was not, however, either constitutional or economic. Rather, it was the social issue of what religious denominations had the right to train the new generation of professionals needed to direct the future of the colony. By 1820 Nova Scotia had the makings of three institutions of post-secondary education, each with a different philosophy and competing sponsors. The oldest, King's College at Windsor, remained until the end of the decade the only degree-granting institution in the Atlantic region. It also remained until 1829 an exclusively Anglican college because of the religious tests required of degree candidates. It was both a theological and a classical college but, given the religious allegiances of the population, was unlikely to appeal to more than a quarter of the potential clientele. In John Inglis, its premier alumnus and bishop of the diocese of Nova Scotia (officially by 1825, but unofficially since the turn of the nineteenth century), King's had a steadfast champion. Unfortunately, Inglis was not the final authority when it came to the character of the college. That privilege had been given, since its first charter in 1803, to the Archbishop of Canterbury, a British high churchman who did not choose to understand the multiconfessional nature of colonial society. Twice during the late 1810s and mid-1820s he prevented liberalization of the statutes and the union of King's with the second of the three institutions, Dalhousie College. The failure of these initiatives was a major impetus to the development of the plethora of small denominational colleges characteristic of Nova Scotia ever since.[5]

Conceived by Lieutenant-Governor Dalhousie, chartered in 1818, and promoted by Kempt, Dalhousie College remained a concept on paper throughout the 1820s. It was intended to be non-denominational and modelled on the University of Edinburgh. Its urban setting was expected to overcome some of the disadvantages suffered by King's. Since Lord Dalhousie was a kirkman, the college acquired a Presbyterian aura of the established variety. The third player in the trio was Pictou Academy, a secondary or grammar school established by the talented and irascible Thomas McCulloch, a Presbyterian clergyman of one of the two eighteenth-century secessionist branches of the Scottish church. He was at one and the same time the school's greatest strength and its greatest weakness. His scientific interests meant that the curriculum of Pictou Academy offered a real alternative to that of King's College. On the other hand, he was as interested in converting the institution into a sectarian theological college as he was in providing a secular education.[6]

The whole matter of higher education became politicized when the colleges turned to the legislature for funding. King's enjoyed a permanent grant; Pictou was never able to acquire more than an annual grant and could not even be sure of that. Historians once thought that Bishop John Inglis used his influence to prevent the conversion of the academy into a government-supported, degree-granting college, but more recent research has persuasively argued that McCulloch lost his campaign because he would not cooperate with the kirkmen, whose numbers and influence were increasing in the post-war period. By the end of the 1820s, however, the supporters of Pictou Academy blamed their inability to secure permanent funding and control their own board on the Anglican-dominated colonial executive, a resentment that contributed to their transformation into 'Pictou scribblers' – critical journalists – and advocates of political reform. With substantial support in the Nova Scotia Assembly for McCulloch's institution, the Pictou Academy question became a focus for the struggle over the supply bills. Seven times between 1825 and 1830 the Council rejected bills initiated by the assembly for the support of the academy, a telling example of the constitutional crisis building between the elected and appointed branches of government.

Such socioreligious inspirations for dissatisfaction with the status quo were lacking in New Brunswick, the second most populous colony, where the élite, composed largely of Anglican Loyalist stock, was more homogeneous. Beneficial but controversial new directions in social and economic life were introduced during the early 1820s under Lieutenant-Governor Smyth. As a result, he 'bore the opprobrium; Douglas enjoyed the advantages.'[7] Indeed, Lieutenant-Governor Howard Douglas proved to be the right man in the right place at the right time. The colonial timber boom, which had survived the readmission of Baltic timber to Britain, created a harmonious mood that shaped the political outlook. Like Kempt, Douglas had a facility for maintaining constructive relations with the speaker of the Assembly, and his political astuteness was one of the reasons he has been described as 'the most popular of New Brunswick's colonial governors.'[8] On such revenue issues as the responsibility for paying customs officers, which the Assembly resisted, Douglas proved to be an ally. However, he shared Kempt's concern for the unpredictable transfer of the civil list to the colony, a concern that must have been not a little self-interested, given the possible impact on his salary and prestige.

The one really serious political problem during the decade was the introduction to the colony of a virtually independent commissioner of Crown lands, whose duty it was to care for the colony's prime timber resources. Commissioner Thomas Baillie spent most of his career at odds with the resident landowners and local timber interests. Douglas

supported the colonists against Baillie, though his reasons were different from theirs: he naturally resented a powerful rival, and he saw the
Crown funds that Baillie controlled as the necessary bargaining chip for
obtaining a permanent civil list from the Assembly. Apart from the colonists' mounting frustration over Baillie's unprecedented exercise of
power, the political scene in New Brunswick was quiet, the populace
being well pleased with Douglas's development policies, which centred
on improvements in transportation and education, and his leadership
abilities, which he demonstrated so favourably in fighting the devastating Miramichi fire of 1825 and in relieving its victims. Douglas also
oversaw the chartering of King's College in Fredericton, initiated by his
predecessor. In 1829 the college opened as a more broadly based Anglican institution than its counterpart at Windsor.[9]

Prince Edward Island had its *bête noire*, analogous to New Brunswick's commissioner of Crown lands, in the guise of another imperial
official, the receiver general of quitrents. With the support of Lieutenant-Governor Smith, John Edward Carmichael, who married one of
Smith's daughters, tried in 1822–3 to collect land taxes owed since 1816,
though not in fact paid at all since 1800. Some Islanders defiantly
refused to pay, using as one of their perennial justifications the long-
standing failure to collect quitrents in neighbouring Nova Scotia; but in
1823 Carmichael launched legal proceedings against a number of resident proprietors and tenants. Many of the latter were forced to travel to
Charlottetown in midwinter to sell their meagre possessions to pay the
arrears. The subsequent popular outcry and Smith's high-handed reaction led to Smith's recall. He was succeeded in 1824 by the far more
genial Col. John Ready. Ready reinstated the Assembly, which Smith
had refused to convene since 1820. Although conflict between the
Assembly and the Council over the supply bills ensued, Lieutenant-
Governor Ready sided with the Assembly against both the Council and
the Colonial Office. He eventually won over the Colonial Office and
reshaped the Council into a more cooperative body. Without any Crown
lands, local revenues in Prince Edward Island, known as the 'permanent' revenue, consisted largely of import duties on liquor. Ready
adopted a similar policy to Douglas by supporting the appropriation of
the revenues for the benefit of the colonists, through agricultural
improvements, road building, and education, 'until there was a school
house in almost every community.'[10] Most importantly, he abandoned
the attempt to collect quitrents, supporting the position of the proprietors; and John Stewart, who had been dismissed by Smith to make way
for Carmichael, was now resurrected as a reluctant receiver general.[11]

Since it lagged far behind the Maritime colonies in constitutional
development, Newfoundland was long overdue for reform by the

1820s. Charles Hamilton, the last of the admiral governors, was in actual fact the first administrator to spend the whole year on the island. His term of office between 1818 and 1824 saw the abolition of the corporal punishment previously meted out by the surrogate courts and the initiation of serious discussion about political reform. In 1825 his successor, Thomas Cochrane, a young naval captain, brought expensive tastes and reformist enthusiasm to the position of the first truly resident governor. Gradually Newfoundlanders were edging towards a degree of recognized local control, which went beyond appointed grand juries with opportunities to recommend but no real power. Introduced in 1826 as a result of British legislation of 1824 were a circuit court system to replace the surrogates and a governor's advisory council of five men, 'an embryonic form of constitutional government.'[12] The pace of constitutional change was influenced by Cochrane's authority and prestige. He was not in favour of admitting Newfoundlanders to the privileges and responsibilities of the franchise without careful preparation. Since he held strong negative views about the capacity of Newfoundlanders for representative government, he agreed with the 1824 legislation that the starting point for electoral political experience should be at the municipal, not the colonial, level. But from the 12,000 inhabitants of St John's he was unable to secure cooperation. Worried that St John's would exert too much power in an island Assembly, Cochrane opposed the constitutional demands of such reformers as Patrick Morris and William Carson, men who believed that representative government was the panacea for Newfoundland's post-war economic ills. Despite, or perhaps because of, his conservative views on political change, Cochrane was remembered by late-nineteenth-century observers, who experienced the subsequent sectarian and sectional strife generated by democratic politics, as 'the best Governor ever sent to Newfoundland.'[13]

The military peace of the 1820s not only bequeathed war heroes to the colonies as governors, it also unleashed a flow of humble folk from the British Isles. Although most immigrants made their way to the Atlantic region of their own volition, Britain's new breed of social planners began to advocate emigration as a remedy for domestic population explosion, pauperization, and agrarian unrest. They concluded that surplus population could be directed overseas to relieve the mother country of a dangerous burden, while contributing to the development of the colonies as markets for manufactured goods and sources of raw materials. This major reversal of British policy (until this time, emigration had been viewed as a loss of national strength) affected the Atlantic region less than other settlement colonies. But the push from Britain combined with the pull to British North America did result in significant augmentations of population. Nova Scotia, for example, attracted more immigrants between 1826 and 1831 than in any other five-year period since the 1780s. Population figures cannot be conclusively compared in the 1820s except to confirm that the population of Nova Scotia was the largest and, at 123,000 in 1827, was about twice the size of Newfoundland's, 40 per cent more than New Brunswick's and five times that of Prince Edward Island.[14]

Historians agree that there was a qualitative difference between the folk who arrived in the first half of the decade and those who arrived in the second half. This analysis can be applied to Scottish immigration to Cape Breton and Irish immigration to New Brunswick. The Scottish immigrants to Cape Breton in the early 1820s were victims of the decline of the kelp industry, but they had more resources and initiative than similarly affected immigrants who were propelled from their crofters' cottages after 1825 in the wake of the complete collapse of the kelp industry and the impact of the Highland clearances.[15] Many of the Irish arriving in New Brunswick were *en route* to the United States. Those newcomers who stayed in the colony were equally divided between Protestants and Catholics in the first half of the decade but predominantly Catholic in the second half. While the timber trade was responsible for the increasingly cheaper passages, British attempts to control the notorious trade in immigrants by means of the Passenger Acts also contributed to the quality of Irish immigration. Tight regulations passed in 1823 reduced the influx, especially in 1824 and 1825, but the temporary lifting of the restrictions in 1827 unleashed a flood of poor immigrants to New Brunswick and the other colonies. Local response to immigration was determined by the negative perceptions of newcomers and the problems that poor and diseased arrivals created.[16] Temporary hospitals were organized in both Saint John and Halifax in the summer of 1827 to separate the typhus- and smallpox-afflicted immigrants from the resident population, an epidemic from which St John's and many of the smaller communities also suffered.[17]

The subsequent behaviour of immigrants was undoubtedly determined as much by the locations in which they settled and the jobs in which they were employed as by ethnicity. The timber trade in the relatively undeveloped Miramichi area, for example, produced greater instability and disorder among Irish immigrants in the 1820s than did the unskilled and semi-skilled urban employment in Saint John. The problems in northern New Brunswick necessitated the stationing of troops at Chatham and Newcastle from 1822 to 1830 'for the purpose of quelling the numerous Riots and disturbances that arise among the lower order of Irish Emigrants.'[18] Leadership was also important in shaping the character of immigrant communities. The Scottish settlers of St Ann's, Cape Breton, were subjected to a veritable theocracy under the watchful eye of the rigid, dour, and puritanical Reverend Norman McLeod, and were effectively cowed and cooperative as a result.[19]

The immigrants were also caught in the midst of debates over schemes for colonization current in government circles in London. In the 1820s, the principal exponent of uniform policies to replace the plethora of approaches across the settlement regions of the British Empire was R.J. Wilmot Horton, parliamentary under-secretary at the Colonial Office until 1828. One of his most important initiatives was in the realm of colonial land reform and included Nova Scotia and New Brunswick. The Crown land policies were revised in 1827 to eliminate free grants and substitute instead two alternative systems of land occupation: ownership through purchase at public auction for settlers of means, and rental of land on the basis of the payment of an annual fee for poorer immigrants. These regulations remained in force until 1829 in New Brunswick and 1831 in Nova Scotia, when sale became the only approved method of alienating Crown land. The new policies had little effect in Nova Scotia, where most good land and all readily accessible acreage had already been converted to private ownership or occupation. Those settlers who could not afford the new arrangements joined those who despaired of the quality available and increasingly resorted to squatting on Crown and Native lands. In New Brunswick, however, the timber-rich tracts of Crown land, amounting to some ten million acres, encouraged speculation, especially by non-resident investors, whose interest lay not in the marginal agricultural potential of the land but in the stands of timber with which it was so well endowed.[20]

The neglect of agriculture in favour of the timber trade, the fishery, and commercial ventures became a serious cause of post-war concern within the colonies, where local pundits somewhat unrealistically believed the future to be an agrarian one. Agrarian spokesmen used their predominance in the Nova Scotia Assembly to defeat merchant-inspired initiatives such as fish bounties in the first half of the decade. Even urbanites were interested in agricultural reform, a movement in which Nova Scotia led the way. Sparked by the new-found enthusiasm of John Young ('Agricola'), a Central Board of Agriculture was established. Until its demise in 1826, it encouraged the formation of numerous local agricultural societies and fostered new farming techniques, improved animal breeds and seeds, and competition for enhanced performance. A combination of Young's erratic control and his patronizing approach to provincial farmers, together with the reorientation of colonial interest towards commerce with the beginnings of freer trade in 1825, helped to undermine the agricultural movement. More importantly, the average farmer felt no need to undertake scientific farming when he had ample land and readily available alternative ways of supplementing his living in the woods and on the sea.[21]

In the meantime, Nova Scotians were joined in the enthusiasm for agricultural improvement by New Brunswickers and Prince Edward Islanders. As a rapidly developing field for immigration, New Brunswick offered the opportunity for wedding agricultural reform to the development of a local settlement policy, which was lamentably lacking. The initiatives of Howard Douglas and of combined immigration and agricultural societies to assist new immigrants to settle on the land made some headway in the 1820s but did not result in a systematic local policy. Established settlers, like the Acadians of northeastern New Brunswick, raised produce to supply the large contingent of timber workers, but even they had already become pre-eminently fishermen and were inevitably attracted to timbering as a supplementary livelihood. In the case of Prince Edward Island, the lieutenant-governor's patronage was again key in promoting agricultural reform in the form of an agricultural society suggested by John Ready in 1827.[22]

While agrarian idealists and gentlemen farmers dabbled in agriculture, and governors promoted agricultural improvement, a less influential but upwardly mobile segment of society organized to promote schooling, fair play, and piety. These controversial activities often led to criticism of the existing order, especially its exclusiveness. The attack on privilege, most clearly represented by interrelated, wealthy Anglicans holding key salaried executive and judicial positions and exerting the power of an oligarchy, took many different forms during the decade. On some issues, such as the basic civil rights of all well-to-do White males, both establishment figures and the up-and-comers could agree. One infringement of rights that troubled both parties concerned the political disabilities of Catholics, whose position was still determined by the British Test Acts. Most colonial Catholics were Irish, which in the pre-famine period was not necessarily a disadvantage in itself. In Nova Scotia, a number of upwardly mobile Irishmen had successfully acquired enough wealth and influence to command respect among the colonial patricians. The first Catholic to sit in the Nova Scotia Assembly in 1823 was Irish, and the colonial legislature confirmed the political rights of Laurence Kavanagh and his co-religionists by passing an act that abolished Catholic disabilities in 1827, two years before the similar British legislation of 1829. The parliamentary emancipation act forced the other colonies, which lagged behind Nova Scotia in their fair treatment of Catholics, to conform to the new equality in 1830.[23]

Problems that generally pitted the oligarchy against the majority were created by the lack of equality between Anglicans and the other denominations: Presbyterians, Methodists, Baptists, Catholics. The college question and other denominational issues, such as the right to marry by licence and the right of congregations to hold property and to benefit from lands reserved for the support of clergy and schoolteachers, engendered considerable ill feeling because of Anglican monopolistic practices. Opposing points of view produced many conflicts, even within denominations, and sometimes reflected the enduring contrast between New World democracy and Old World autocracy or, increasingly, the irrelevance of Old World divisiveness. The prime example of such a polarity occurred within the established Church of England itself, when the congregation of St Paul's church in Halifax split over the choice of a new rector in 1824. The resolution of this appointment had far-reaching effects for the province, since many of the losers in the contest, who were both upholders of congregational rights and evangelicals, left the Anglican church and threw in their lot with the hitherto marginalized Baptists, who were becoming respectable and stable enough to offer a real Nova Scotia alternative to fractious, uncompromising Anglicanism. In 1829 the Nova Scotia Baptists reinforced the denominational character of higher education with the opening of Horton Academy, the precursor of Acadia University.[24]

At the same time, British evangelical influences produced concern for the colonial poor, including immigrants, widows and orphans, the rural destitute, the urban unemployed, indigenous people, and Afro-colonials. Based largely on the kind of inspiration that had destroyed the British slave trade and created missionary societies to convert the 'heathen,' evangelicals who turned their concern for the salvation of souls to the Atlantic colonies recognized as the steps to godliness not only piety, morality, and temperance, but also literacy and self-help. Translated into practice this meant more missionaries, more schools, more to read, more systematic social welfare, and more debate about social issues. The activities of the 1820s were part of a continuum; although some of the initiatives belong to the decade, others were well under way by that time. These movements had a number of common characteristics: the organizing mechanism of the voluntary society; the emergence of women as collectors, sponsors, and society organizers in their own right; the long-term trend towards anti-Catholicism; the familiarity with contemporary social theories, ranging from utilitarianism to Malthusianism; and, above all, the prevalence of self-interest as the basis of social policy.[25]

Of the existing evangelical organizations that had the widest effect during the decade, the most significant was probably the Bible Society. Branches of the British and Foreign Bible Society, which attracted the support of Presbyterians, Methodists, Baptists, Anglicans, and Lutherans, could be found in all English- and Gaelic-speaking centres of population in the region by the early 1820s. While the society suffered a decline later in the decade, local branches were instrumental in promoting reading through distribution of the Scriptures, and the education of children through enthusiasm for Sunday schools and other forms of organized learning. In a rapidly developing area like the Miramichi, women played a key role in sustaining such social ventures. Although Bible Society supporters included many Anglicans, the church establishment tried to counter evangelical influences and promote official Anglicanism through a revival of the much older Society for Promoting Christian Knowledge, in which church women again played a key role. Of new evangelical-inspired initiatives during the 1820s which were launched in Britain by Bible Society stalwarts for the Atlantic region, two of particular note were the long-lived Newfoundland School Society and the relatively short-lived Glasgow Colonial Society.[26]

The Newfoundland School Society of 1823 was the brainchild of Samuel Codner, a West Country fish merchant who lived in St John's between 1801 and 1811 and continued to be involved in the Newfoundland fishery until 1844. Moved by the illiteracy and lack of educational opportunity of the fisherfolk of Newfoundland and by his own evangelical convictions as one of the fortunate, he interested similarly inclined members of the Church of England in supporting his venture. A popular project in London's Exeter Hall, the hotbed of public evangelical activity for Protestants, the new society also secured the support of the British government through the interest of leading Tory politicians Lord Liverpool and Lord Bathurst. The support took the form of free grants of land on which to build schools, free passages to the colony for teachers, and advice to the governor to promote the project locally. The first Newfoundland School Society school, which opened in St John's in 1824, resembled the earlier semi-charity organizations such as the Royal Acadian School in Halifax (established 1813) and the Anglican National Schools in both Halifax (1816) and Saint John (1819). Branch schools very quickly spread throughout the Avalon Peninsula and provided the only formal educational facilities in many communities. By the end of the decade, twenty-eight schools had been opened under the society's auspices.[27] Both the Newfoundland schools and charity or semi-charity schools sponsored by mainland school societies in all the major towns and villages of the region adopted the monitorial (Madras) system, which encouraged rigid rote learning at the same time as it established, through the use of pupil-monitors, the earliest instances of accessible teacher training for colonial youth. The school societies also strengthened the interest in Sunday schools, night schools, and worker education and led to the establishment of organizations for their promotion and regulation.[28]

The Glasgow Colonial Society had a more limited objective. It was established by evangelical clergymen in 1825 to provide Presbyterian missionaries for Scottish immigrants in British North America. The first two petitions for aid came from Richibucto, New Brunswick, and Preston and Dartmouth, Nova Scotia. By 1833 the society had sent five ministers to the Maritimes, despite the resolute opposition of the local Presbyterians, who viewed it as an unnecessary, foreign interloper once they realized that the society would not support locally trained clergymen. Active among the members of the society was Isabella Gordon Mackay, whose initial philanthropy resulted in the dispatch of libraries to Scottish settlements in Nova Scotia during a decade that marked the inception of public libraries. Mackay's enthusiasm culminated in 1831 with her establishment of the Edinburgh Ladies' Association, with the specific aim of evangelizing the settlers of Cape Breton.[29]

Another interest of the evangelicals was in ameliorating the condition of the poor, as they put it. This did not mean that they advocated far-reaching reforms to eliminate poverty. They subscribed to the philosophy that poverty was a given and not a curable condition in society. Nonetheless, they did believe in the principle of Christian stewardship, which recognized the responsibility of those blessed with worldly goods to relieve the misfortunes of the less fortunate. Given the widespread economic reverses that occurred in the period following the Napoleonic wars, distress – which was by no means confined to indigents but reached into artisanal, professional, and mercantile homes – commanded widespread attention. Sometimes whole communities needed relief, such as the new community of St Ann's in Cape Breton in 1820 and, repeatedly, the struggling Black refugee communities.[30] Where voluntary efforts most commonly came into play were in the urban areas. Here individual failure was usually the most severe, and the number of waifs and strays attracted from surrounding rural areas accumulated. The acute distress experienced in Halifax as a result of post-war commercial recession led to the formation of the Halifax Poor Man's Friend Society (HPMFS) in 1820. Organized largely for winter relief and therefore catering to the hordes of both local and transient unemployed, especially from Newfoundland, this group of concerned citizens tried systematic investigation as a way of determining need. Only when the problem became so great that mass relief in the form of soup kitchens was introduced did a simmering debate come to a boil among Halifax's political economists about indiscriminate relief as an encouragement to indigence. The HPMFS disbanded by 1827, after the economy improved and full employment returned, but it is notable as one of the earliest winter-relief organizations, which became the common nineteenth-century response to seasonal unemployment.[31] The

1820s also saw debate over the workhouse principle (which meant confining relief to public institutions) a decade before the final institutionalization of a similar principle in England in the form of the new Poor Law of 1834. As a result of the seasonality of work and widespread poverty, the decade also witnessed the first attempts to establish savings banks for the working class, an apparently successful venture in Saint John at Sir Howard Douglas's instigation.[32]

Another type of distress that focused the attention of evangelicals and others in the 1820s was the fate of the Black and Native people of the region. On the fringes of Saint John, Black refugees from the War of 1812 were denied equal rights to land ownership with Whites and forced into wage labour in the city. Once in the city, the children came to the attention of the governor, who made some effort in the 1820s to provide them with schooling. Interest in the welfare of Blacks and aboriginal people relied too much, however, on the whims of particular individuals in this period for such efforts to have any lasting effects. In New Brunswick, the schools for Blacks in Saint John and Fredericton closed in the thirties after the departure of humanitarian administrators such as Smyth and Douglas. Walter Bromley was another individual, albeit a good deal less influential than a governor, whose activities in Nova Scotia and New Brunswick led to a number of attempts to refashion Micmac and Maliseet society more humanely than had previously been attempted. Bromley's revelations of the treatment endured by the Native people of Sussex Vale at the hands of the local agents of the New England Company suggested for the first time that exploitation of Natives could not be tolerated. More promising were the Native settlements in northern New Brunswick and at Bear River, Nova Scotia, where the leading proponents of amelioration secured the cooperation of French Catholic priests, like Abbé Sigogne, and the Natives were not subjected to the 'assistance' of rapacious Whites.[33]

At the same time, interest in native peoples emerged too late to save the Beothuk of Newfoundland. Expeditions to try to capture some of these mysterious people in the early 1820s only increased the already irreversible rate of mortality and hastened their demise. When Bishop John Inglis met Shawnadithit at Exploits Bay in 1827, three years after her capture with her mother and sister (who had since died), he decided that a determined effort should be made to find her remaining people. The task fell to William Epps Cormack, the Newfoundlander who had been the first White man to cross the island in 1822. Cormack established the Beothuk (Beothic) Institution, with the aims of communicating with and civilizing the Beothuk and of training Shawnadithit as the necessary interpreter. Neither goal was possible: Shawnadithit proved to be the last known surviving Beothuk, a survival that lasted only until 1829, when she succumbed to tuberculosis at the age of twenty-three.[34]

The case of the Beothuk Institution highlights an additional influence that was emerging in the region in the 1820s. Curiosity about the nature of Native peoples was linked to a concern for the region's past, a concern that resulted in the fostering of a sense of history and, for at least a small number of well-educated, articulate colonists, in the effort to define a local identity. Evangelical interest in the Native people was based ultimately on saving their souls; historical interest on saving their culture as an artifact of the past, a concern that did little, if anything, to preserve the life of the Beothuks. In the Maritimes, the Native population was large enough that there was no immediate chance of extinction, but the attitude of the settlers was certainly based on the perception that extinction was inevitable, that 'the period is not remote, when the very name of this once free and powerful people will be blotted out from the enrolment of the living.'[35] Fortunately, though ironically, the policies that were designed to ease the Maritime aborigines into oblivion had the positive effect of providing sufficient relief to enable them gradually to resume population growth and thereby ensure their own survival.[36]

The cultural awakening, of which historical interest in the region's native peoples by the region's first- and second-generation White residents formed a part, encompassed a range of intellectual and literary activity by a talented array of residents of both American and British origins, as well as new educational opportunities for people of all ages. Sons of Planters and Loyalists were the first generation to be educated locally and to tie their prospects to colonial progress in the age of improvement. Thomas Chandler Haliburton became Nova Scotia's first published native-born historian; Peter Fisher, New Brunswick's first locally raised historian. Joseph Howe wrote for public consumption about his own province on the basis of firsthand experience and became an arbiter of local literary talent in his role as newspaper editor. These young men benefited from the facilities available through printing presses, which were plentiful enough by the 1820s to reduce the cost of printing and make newspapers, journals, and books available to a broader stratum of society than ever before. In the development of the press, Nova Scotia took the lead, but examples of critical debate in the pages of newspapers also occurred in the 1820s in the other three colonies, where the proliferation of newspapers encouraged the kind of competition essential to the development of public discourse on a range of economic, political, and social issues. British immigrants also contributed to public debate. John Young's letters of Agricola were followed by Thomas McCulloch's Stepsure letters, both Scottish perspectives on an agrarian future tinged with moral rectitude and didactic fervour. John

MacGregor wrote about all the British North American colonies but particularly Prince Edward Island, which he knew best. All these writers helped to reinforce the agrarian ideal through their endorsement of the 'intelligent, hardworking, progressive, yeoman farmer.'[37]

In respect to agriculture and other development issues, one common feature that shaped public debate by the second half of the decade, at least outside Newfoundland, was a note of economic optimism. For Nova Scotia, one of the colonies hardest hit by the post-war depression, the period between 1825 and 1832 was marked by rejuvenating peacetime prosperity. In the early twenties, the readmission of the Americans to the West Indies trade and their refusal to recognize colonial free ports hampered both Halifax's accustomed role as an entrepôt and Nova Scotia–West Indies trade, which was still the basis of the economy. Conditions in the West Indies also deteriorated. The crisis in the sugar markets and the effects of the abolition of the slave trade were further complications. In essence, Nova Scotia suffered two fundamental economic problems: metropolitan failure of Halifax, which, for largely geographical reasons, lacked a readily accessible hinterland, and a traditional reliance on the declining institution of slavery for determining staple production and trading networks. The post-war failure of the West Indies trade, coupled with the reduction of military, naval, and dockyard business, remained serious impediments until 1825, when William Huskisson, president of the British Board of Trade, announced a less restrictive imperial trade policy, which would admit the colonies to markets and carrying trades hitherto closed to them. The impetus to development in Nova Scotia was impressive. Annual rates of shipbuilding tonnage tripled between the first and second halves of the decade, and wages for common labourers increased by 12 to 25 per cent. At the same time, new financial institutions were introduced, beginning in 1825 with the establishment of the Halifax Banking Company.[38]

The colony benefited from expansion in both local and foreign investment. Halifax merchants, finally freed of total reliance on the West Indies trade, ventured into iron mining (albeit unsuccessfully), into the whale, seal, and Banks fisheries, steamboat operations (in the harbour and the St Lawrence), and, with British help, the Shubenacadie Canal Company, with the intention of providing a water link between Halifax Harbour and the Bay of Fundy where the rival Saint John dominated. The British share of investment in the canal company amounted to almost half the capital.[39] The most significant British investment resulted from the bizarre acquisition in 1826–7 of the colony's coal mines under a thirty-six-year monopolistic lease, by the London jewellers Rundell, Bridge and Rundell. This unlikely investor took over the lease as payment for the Duke of York's debts, and established the General Mining Association (GMA), a company with rights to virtually all the province's mineral resources. Notwithstanding the fears of the local business community that this non-resident company would prevent rather than facilitate the development of the province's coal, the GMA 'exceeded all expectations with a very aggressive approach to modernization.'[40] The company introduced new technology and skilled miners to Nova Scotia's coalfields, including state-of-the-art steam-driven mining equipment and, in 1830, the region's first railway line, from pithead to dock in Pictou. Despite the industrial potential that existed, the company's aim remained a purely commercial one, that of extracting the coal and selling it to American seaboard markets.

Even with new forms of investment, the traditional West Indies trade continued as the backbone of the Nova Scotia economy, producing most of the merchant wealth and, through this commerce, the bulk of the income of the province. Perhaps because of the failure of local suppliers to meet the demand, trade rather than home production lay at the heart of the shipping economy. Merchants had to import one-quarter of the cod that they exported to the British Caribbean. While the 1820s boom may have been one of the 'false starts' of Nova Scotia's colonial economy, the revival of trade and the introduction of new and more diversified investment created an exceedingly buoyant mood within the business community by the late 1820s. To contemporaries, the future prospects for both Halifax and the province looked very bright indeed.

In terms of growth, development, and investment, however, the 1820s belonged to New Brunswick. Although the first few years of the decade saw a fall in prices and an increase in business failures as a result of the reduction in the colonial preference for timber, recovery had occurred by 1824. The mid-decade marked the high point in the export of square timber that reinforced the faith in colonial protectionism. Given the perceived advantages of mercantilism to the development of the colony's timber resources, Huskisson's reforms were not popular in New Brunswick. Nor was British land policy. Crown land was the great natural resource of timber-rich New Brunswick, a staple that contributed three-quarters of the colony's export revenues. The effective enforcement of timber duties and other fees relating to timbering began in earnest in 1824 with the appointment of Thomas Baillie as commissioner of Crown lands. By far the most controversial New Brunswick resident of his generation, Baillie was determined to make the timber policy work. He was initially limited to regulatory measures that resulted in the zealous accumulation of revenue. The adoption of a land-sales policy by the British government in 1829, as part of an integrated colonization scheme designed for the land-rich settlement colonies, gave Baillie a chance to be creative. He favoured selling timber land to large-scale entrepreneurs and encouraged foreign investment, an approach that deeply alienated the resident population, who had always considered Crown land to be common land and part of their birthright. Until Baillie acquired this new measure of power, Lieutenant-Governor Douglas had been able to hold the commissioner's ambitions in check. Now the scene was set for a united attack by both the Assembly and the Council on the unpopular commissioner. Baillie's only local allies were the great merchants of Saint John, who benefited from the commercial rather than the harvesting aspects of the timber trade. In the 1820s and 1830s, however, the health of the New Brunswick economy was much more dependent on that of Britain, to which it was inextricably tied through good years and lean, than on the machinations of Commissioner Baillie.[41]

The central element in the colony's development was the economy of Saint John. It was healthy through the 1820s, since the timber trade was not subjected to the same post-war problems as the fishery and the West Indies carrying trade. Indeed, as the major export centre for timber, rivalled only briefly in the 1830s by the Miramichi, Saint John and its hinterland on both sides of the Bay of Fundy also became the shipbuilding centre of the region. Although the vessels in the 1820s were small and somewhat indifferent in quality, shipbuilders acquired valuable experience in the artisanal skills necessary for sustaining a successful shipbuilding industry. Saint John also had significant import functions that benefited from the increase of population within its easily accessible river and bay hinterland regions. As the leading urban-mercantile centre in the region and the only one to enjoy elected civic government, Saint John was the first to establish corporate institutions for finance, insurance, resource development, and trade. In the wake of the establishment in 1820 of the region's first bank, the Bank of New Brunswick, the favourable economic conditions of the mid-1820s led to the formation of the Marine Insurance Company, the Saint John Water Company, and the Labrador Fishing Association. Although few leading merchants, the wealthiest group of entrepreneurs in the city, either diversified into industrial enterprises or supported the artisans who did, the manufacturing sector of Saint John's economy also acquired a promising dynamism in the 1820s as a result of the emergence of successful master workmen and the producer ideology they promoted.[42]

In contrast, Newfoundland's economy was badly hit by post-war conditions. The decrease in the demand for fish was largely determined by protectionist policies in Spain and poverty and civil war in Portugal. Even when Italy and Brazil became important alternative markets, the net effect of the continuously low fish prices for Newfoundlanders was 'a falling standard of living, near-starvation in certain places, and political and socio-economic confrontation.'[43] Although the hold of the West

Country fishing interests had been broken, the resident fishermen had to contend with what they perceived to be crippling American and French competition in Newfoundland waters, as well as the crisis in the traditional export markets and the success of Scandinavian fishermen in capturing new European markets. During the first half of the decade the problem of resulting seasonal poverty continued to be addressed by out-migration. When Kempt complained about the influx to Halifax from St John's, Charles Hamilton replied 'that a very considerable number of the people who are employed in the fisheries of this Island are unable to obtain employment here in the Winter and are necessitated to remove elsewhere,' but promised to discourage them from choosing Nova Scotia as a destination.[44] Cochrane adopted the more utilitarian approach of the political economists by putting the seasonally unemployed fishermen to work on road building. However, these policies were but palliatives. Far more important to the Newfoundland economy was the development after 1815 of the Labrador and seal fisheries, which supplemented the inshore production of salt cod.

Fishing and coastal trading were also important economic activities in Prince Edward Island, where farmers needed to supplement their planting and harvesting with other activities in order to make a livelihood. Like New Brunswickers, Islanders combined harvesting the forests with shipping timber, and thereby developed skills as shipbuilders. Diversity of activity in the 1820s affected all manner of men, from the precarious wage earners and subsistence producers normally associated with occupational pluralism to the emergent entrepreneurs of the age of sail. James Peake, who immigrated to Charlottetown in 1823, became one of the more substantial jacks-of-all-trades on the Island: shipowner, import merchant, retail shopkeeper, ship broker, ship chandler and outfitter, and moneylender.[45]

With some of the colonies enjoying a renewed prosperity by the late 1820s, the character of everyday life took on a more stable and civilized appearance in a wider variety of towns and villages. In Truro, for example, an agricultural township that benefited from being part of Saint John's hinterland, farming families could now afford to send their sons to night school and diversify into such commercial activities as milling, shopkeeping, shipbuilding, and shipowning. Although the common medium of exchange was still barter, Truro's strategic location gave it access to a hinterland and some hard currency in the form of road money voted by the Assembly for building and maintaining an essential transportation network. Economic diversification was accompanied by greater specialization of labour, more denominational points of view, and a more stratified social structure in a community that was in the process of making the transition from rural to urban.[46]

Nonetheless, maturing communities still experienced influences more often associated with pioneer life, such as the religious revivals that occurred in Yarmouth township in 1827–8 and Prince Edward Island under Donald McDonald, beginning in 1828.[47] Modernity was a feature singularly lacking in most communities. Rural settlers in the backwoods of New Brunswick, the highlands of Cape Breton, and the outports of Newfoundland and eastern Nova Scotia endured the harsh and relentless poverty associated with a bare and primitive subsistence livelihood. In Conception Bay, Bishop Inglis found that the short fishing season required the full-time labour of the whole family in production: 'every man, woman and child must be engaged and often by night as well as by day.' In Yarmouth County he identified the occupational pluralism so characteristic of rural Nova Scotia when he recorded: 'the country populous, the farms small, and not very well tilled, and most of the farmers engaged in fishing also.'[48] When eking out a living from marginal lands and tempestuous waters failed them, the menfolk and boys provided the cheap labour for employment on public works, in the woods and mines, and in the burgeoning marine industries.

Female labour was the most pluralistic of all. Not only were women and girls engaged, alongside their fathers, brothers, and husbands, in harvesting the land and the sea for both commerce and subsistence; they also made the labour of their menfolk possible through the maintenance of the household – gardening, cooking, preserving, cleaning, washing, healing, sewing, knitting, weaving, and dairy and poultry production. Wives also contributed to the labour force through their reproductive activities of bearing and raising the next generation. They felt especially blessed if they delivered live children and survived the experience of childbirth. In the emergent town of Truro, the average age of women at marriage in the 1820s was 21.4 years, and the first ten or twelve years of married life were characterized by births at two- or three-year intervals, with somewhat longer spacing thereafter. For couples married in the 1820s the average number of children was 6.6, a birth rate that was gradually declining.[49]

The social life of most women consisted largely of visiting neighbours and relatives. On the Miramichi, additional female activities outside the home were virtually impossible because of the total preoccupation with large, young families. With a modicum of leisure, acquired either through middle age or a comfortable station in life, some women of the 1820s pursued voluntary activities in their churches and their communities. These extra-familial interests were largely spiritual, moral, and charitable. They involved teaching Sunday school, organizing the first charitable bazaars as fund-raisers for the relief of the poor, and forming the first female societies for the collective pursuit of good works, both charitable and religious. Although public opinion was divided on the appropriateness of such activities for women, a widely subscribed viewpoint was expressed by the editor of the *Novascotian* in 1826, when he noticed the Methodist Female Benevolent Society, the members of which spent the best part of a day a week in making up clothing for distribution among the poor. 'This is indeed an admirable field of female exertion. Woman is sent upon this earth, with all the milder qualities of our nature, unquestionably to smooth down the asperities of life ... Charity, among them, is not so much a matter of calculation, as of feeling ... in its exercise they yield not to the stirring impulse of the mind, but to the sympathies of the soul.'[50]

Occasionally, women were provided with opportunities to challenge the social constructions of gender that devalued their intellectual abilities while applauding their emotional sensitivity. A few wives of wealthy or prominent men, either in widowhood or during their partner's absence, are known to have acted as surrogate estate managers or merchants. In order to arrange more effectively their relations with men, improve the raising of their children, and contribute to society through female organizations, women needed access to better educational facilities, according to 'Mary ———' of Pictou. Writing in the press in 1826, she appears as an early advocate of women's rights. Despite their limited educational opportunities, women operated private-venture schools that sometimes secured church or state subsidies. In 1829, for example, three of the five elementary teachers receiving government assistance in Truro were female.[51]

Many of the new opportunities available to women as activists and entrepreneurs arose because of the demands of a rapidly changing society nurtured by British influences. In terms of population growth, this was a significant decade, and much of the increase was the result of immigration from Britain. While the settlers of the 1820s were not a monolithic group, many of them came in groups much larger than families, after experiencing severe problems in Britain. On his way along the coast by water, John Inglis personally observed the arrival of one of these human cargoes at Ship Harbour in the Gut of Canso. He saw 'a ship landing 360 passengers from one of the Orkneys, where they had left only 3 families. Unable to pay their rents, their landlord had forgiven them for several years, and their finding no prospect of improvement he proposed to supply them with a passage to Cape Breton and three months provision. This they gladly accepted and their Island is now a sheep walk.'[52]

Along with the immigrants came social and religious ideas and organizations that were again stamped with the British imprint, especially the evangelical and the political economistic. Another import vital to a poor region was capital. Some of it was for traditional activities and from long-known sources, like the Channel Island fish merchants who controlled the Cape Breton and New Brunswick fisheries, and the Church of England, which subsidized clergymen and teachers throughout the region. Others were the legacy of the Napoleonic wars, like the timber firm of Gilmour, Rankin. Still others like the General Mining Association, were totally new and strengthened monopolistic control. Often in conjunction with capital, but also for specifically public purposes within Britain itself, came new policies relating to major resources like fish, coal, timber, and trade. They demonstrated graphically the region's dependence on British diplomacy, British domestic conditions, and British commerce. In the wider British scheme of things, however, the four colonies remained peripheral dots on the map of empire.

CHAPTER THIRTEEN

The 1830s

Adapting Their Institutions
to Their Desires

ROSEMARY E. OMMER

By the 1830s, the seaboard colonies of British North America were beginning to mature. The emergent colonial society of which W.S. Mac-Nutt has written was in the process of becoming self-aware.[1] In the Colonial Office, the old *modus vivendi* of securing the Empire by working with visiting colonial élites and domestic interest groups was on the wane, and the 'web of vested interests stretched across the Atlantic' was wearing thin.[2] In the colonies, assemblies and executives quarrelled over fiscal control and the structure of the government as they wrestled with where decisions about colonial development should be taken and how that development should be paid for.[3] Related to this debate was the problem of opposing philosophies of development: were the colonies to be shaped by imperial requirements or by indigenous imperatives? And could a solution be found that would not result in the kind of separation that had destroyed the first British Empire? The question, in essence, was how and when to loosen the imperial apron strings that bound the maturing colonies to the mother country.

The maturation process was both political and economic in nature. The international economic context in which the old colonial staple trades had been fostered was altering of necessity as industrialization created new trades and required new ways of organizing old ones. Board of Trade president William Huskisson's reforms, started formally in 1825 and designed to produce the kind of trade liberalization that would be advantageous to a developed manufacturing nation, were a recognition of the changing world order. They were also a threat to the old staples interests in the colonies, where mercantile élites in the timber trade, the fish trade, and the related carrying trade with the British West Indies feared the loss of protected markets. By contrast, those who sought to develop agriculture and local markets for agricultural produce, or who dreamed of substituting domestic manufacturing for British imports, sought a different and indigenous form of protectionism, one that would encourage economic diversification. The signs of growing domestic self-direction were everywhere: in emerging banking and transportation structures, urban development, and the establishment of educational, religious, welfare, and other social institutions. Even protests against imperial landholding practices, whether against large grants of timberland in New Brunswick to speculators, the large estates of the Prince Edward Island proprietors, or apparent refusals to encourage agriculture in Newfoundland, were formulated in terms of the need to develop colonial resources for colonial purposes.

After 1815, the numbers of people migrating to the Atlantic colonies had risen steadily. By 1838, Nova Scotia had a population of 202,500,[4] New Brunswick would reach 154,000 by decade's end,[5] Prince Edward Island had 32,000 by 1833,[6] and the permanent population of Newfoundland (a minimum figure that excluded the large number of temporary settlers and migrants in the fishery) doubled between 1815 and 1830 to 40,000.[7]

After 1815, some of the colonial immigrants were military personnel or gentry, literate and relatively well-to-do, and the majority possessed at least some resources. But starting in the late 1820s and increasingly in the 1830s there was heavy immigration of another kind: poor and illiterate Irish, English, and Scots fleeing industrial dislocations and distressful conditions in the United Kingdom. In New Brunswick, where the ballast factor in the large vessels of the timber trade encouraged passengers as freight on the westward voyage, immigration was heavily Irish: 60 per cent of all immigrants between 1815 and 1865. Irish and West Country people were also migrating to Newfoundland throughout these years as a labour supply into the fishery, some as transients and some as year-round residents, arriving on the provision ships from places like Waterford, Teignmouth, and Dartmouth.[8] The other predominant ethnic migration of the period was that of the Scots from the Highlands and Hebridean islands. Some of these sailed in timber vessels, but many left from bays and sea lochs in family or community groups, as part of an ongoing process of chain migration that had started with the exodus of relatively well-to-do tacksmen around the turn of the century, as the last vestiges of the clan system were wiped out by improving landlords. By the mid-1820s, the Highland migration was changing in scale and nature, as the collapse of the kelp industry brought eviction to thousands of small-scale tenant farmers. At least 10,000 Highlanders emigrated to Cape Breton alone between 1827 and 1832, and there were also migrant streams settling the north and east coasts of Prince Edward Island and the Northumberland Strait shore of

Nova Scotia.[9] Victims of eviction from traditional lands at home, they dreamed of security of tenure in the New World and were often prepared to keep moving until they could find it. As the decade wore on, however, migration continued without respite, and cheap land became more and more scarce. At the beginning of the decade, most of the land along the coasts or beside the good waterways had already been settled, and while large tracts of the hinterland remained Crown land – as much as two-thirds of New Brunswick, for example – they were less accessible and increasingly expensive. On Prince Edward Island, where landlords 'controlled 90 percent or more of the colony's acreage and two thirds of the population were tenants or squatters ... [while] six families controlled more than a third of the colony's lands,' insecurity of tenure was particularly problematic, and unrest among tenant farmers was a feature of the decade.[10]

Until 1827, Crown lands had been granted free except for a nominal quitrent of about one farthing per acre that was rarely paid, although attempts were made to collect it in the early 1830s. In 1827, however, the British government overhauled the land-granting system, and in the 1830s land was sold at public auction at a minimum (or 'upset') price. By raising the cost of settlement and discouraging settlers from expanding their holdings, this policy hindered the future growth of the colony, as Moses Perley argued in his condemnation of the Crown Lands Office in New Brunswick for restricting, not encouraging, settlement.[11] Immigrants who settled the colonial backlands because the front (coastal or river) lots were taken up often lacked the means of sustaining themselves, since the rear lands were of poorer quality and costly to farm. If they could not afford to purchase better land, or improve the backland, they either squatted there or occupied Native lands (a problem Perley was faced with in New Brunswick in later years) in default of any other option. As the 1830s progressed, more and more Scottish and Irish immigrants were paupers or displaced farmers although there were still some small farmers with limited capital, tradesmen and artisans among them. Thomas Baillie, the New Brunswick commissioner of Crown lands, observed in 1832 that many of the Irish were very poor indeed; and the same comment could have been made of the Scots.[12] Squatters were commonplace in some areas – up to 20,000 in Cape Breton Island by 1837 – and impoverished migrants often became a burden on the treasury, as the statistics for poor relief across all four colonies demonstrate. The problem was particularly acute in Newfoundland, where the fish markets had collapsed. Some officials and businessmen in the Maritime colonies attempted to provide agricultural implements, start-up seed, and the like for newly arrived immigrants, and there were also private emigration companies that built such requirements into their planning, but the process was haphazard and insecure. Indeed, Nova Scotia found it necessary in 1833 to pass an act to protect indigent people who might be unjustly removed from their chosen location by officials seeking to allocate them to townships where they could be supported by local taxation.[13]

One part of the problem was that the United Kingdom, intent on providing an alternative life for the flotsam and jetsam of the industrial and agricultural revolutions, had failed to create a balanced policy that would provide both a tolerable emigration voyage and initial support for migrants once they had reached the colonial shore of their choice. In the face of considerable opposition to any state 'interference' in commercial affairs, the Passenger Act of 1828 had been not only 'an unambitious measure' in terms of legal protection for migrants, but also a toothless one, since it made no provision for enforcement. Consequently, as emigration to British North America swelled to massive proportions in 1831–2, abuses continued apace. Conditions were appalling: overcrowding, foul drinking water, inadequate provisions (in terms of both quantity and quality), a complete lack of medical support, and the disease consequent upon such conditions were made even worse by the subjection of passengers to various kinds of fraud and extortion before boarding the vessel and throughout the voyage. Vessels were often unseaworthy, the incidence of shipwrecks was rising, and no compensation was available to those who survived only to be stranded ashore with the whole process to be gone through again, this time without money or possessions. Moreover, those who made it across the Atlantic had no guarantee of being landed at the right place and often arrived seriously ill and penniless. There were severe cholera outbreaks on board emigrant vessels as well as in several ports of arrival, in 1832 and again in 1834. Even opponents to legislative interference were reluctantly compelled to agree that 'it was the state's duty to see that vessels were seaworthy, provisions sufficient and contracts fair.' In 1833, the first emigration officer was appointed at Liverpool (the port of embarkation with the worst record of abuse), and in 1835 a new Passenger Act was passed. However, since it 'compromised unintelligently between humanitarian instinct and free trade persuasion,' it also produced little improvement in conditions. Not until the creation of the Colonial Land and Emigration Commission in 1840 was any real protection established.[14]

Ironically, many of the emigrants themselves opposed government regulation, since it raised the cost of the transatlantic passage. After all, part of the attraction of the Atlantic region to the increasing migrant stream pouring out of Britain was that there was no head tax on immigrants until 1832, and even then it was only half what it was in the

United States. As a result, as many as 50 per cent of the migrants, many of them young, single men, came to places like Saint John or Halifax, planning to proceed from there to New England; the complaint was often heard that only the paupers stayed behind.[15] Indeed, emigration was already a feature of the four colonies, even as immigration swelled, and there was also a continuing relocation of settlers within the colonies after their initial arrival. This kind of mobility, sometimes across considerable distances, meant that life in the Miramichi or Lunenburg or Prince Edward Island was not an unknown quantity for people in Newfoundland, for example. It would be erroneous to think of the colonies' rural populations as existing in separate solitudes.

By the 1830s there were three distinct layers of agricultural society: relatively prosperous farmers who had inherited good land from the earliest settlers; later arrivals who had sufficient means to purchase the increasingly expensive remaining good land; and recent settlers whose survival depended on eking out a meagre existence in the backlands.[16] These fitted inside a broader geographical classification of settlement zones that incorporated the fishers who also 'farmed ten or twelve acres and kept a handful of cattle,' the backland settlers who made a living from farming supplemented by seasonal forest work, and in between the majority, who 'occupied more productive farms that together comprised a substantial portion of the ... core farming zone.'[17] Much the same could be said of Prince Edward Island, where by 1833 there was still little improvement beyond the coastline, with the exception of the Hillsborough River area: a total of 95,000 improved acres in all, or one-fifth of the Island, although there were exports (not yet very substantial) of oats, potatoes, wheat, and barley to Nova Scotia by 1832. Indeed, as late as 1837, the Island would have had a seriously adverse balance of trade had it not been for shipbuilding revenues, which more or less balanced the colony's books.[18]

In Newfoundland, there was no agriculture; indeed there was no settlement beyond the coastal zone, and the fishery was the sole productive occupation of that colony. But even in the three Maritime colonies, the extensive growth in agriculture was most often a result of increasing population, rather than of an overall increase in per-capita productivity, except in the richest of the older settled areas, such as the Fundy Basin.[19] In all places, successful farms relied on family labour and the mutual help of neighbours. Mixed farming was common. Depending on local conditions, the production of oats, barley, rye, potatoes, and some wheat and flax was combined with animal husbandry (sheep and cattle), while berrying, moose hunting, and partridge shooting supplemented the family diet.[20] Away from the coast and the river banks, farming was still most often an exercise in breaking open new land and attempting to survive on what it produced. In this respect, the 'wasteful' practices of peasant farmers like the Highland Scots (who ignored crop rotations and farmed continuously, thereby saving improved land from the rapid encroachment of weeds and saplings) need to be re-evaluated: they were arguably a practical response to primitive and difficult conditions. The Maritime colonies' farmland was not like that in the United Kingdom, and the newly developed wisdom of the British agricultural revolution was often inappropriate (as well as extremely expensive) in this new setting.[21] While agricultural societies were on the rise, they tended to be an élite phenomenon, and their real impact was much less significant than has previously been suggested.

In the Atlantic coastal communities, the fisheries, of course, predominated. Fish is a difficult staple to exploit, since it is both mobile and a free-access resource (it cannot be 'fenced in'), and in the 1830s, as today, the deep-sea fishery was prosecuted in international waters by the fleets of several nations. In the Atlantic colonies, the principal focus was on the inshore fishery, since only coastal waters had been protected from the exploitation of New England fleets by the terms of the 1818 Fisheries Convention. From 1818 on, the Georgian and Grand Banks fisheries were vigorously prosecuted by both the New Englanders and the French, with very substantial support from their governments in the form of bounties.[22] Nova Scotia and Newfoundland pleaded for similar imperial bounties to support their local fleets, but to no avail. Throughout the 1830s some Nova Scotia communities experimented with sending their vessels into waters that the French and the New Englanders had been fishing virtually exclusively; but it would be mid-century before Nova Scotians regularly included the local Banks on their trips to Labrador, and the 1870s before the bounty legislation would be created that was needed to ensure real success. In the meantime, Nova Scotia's Banks fleet remained technologically backward. In Newfoundland, without imperial support, the Banks fleet shrank to about eight vessels, and over the next four decades the fishery there was reduced to an inshore operation.[23]

The inshore fishery, wherever prosecuted, was controlled by merchant capital, even when most fishers were not hired directly to work for a merchant but were ostensibly independent, as in Newfoundland, Cape Breton, the Bay of Chaleur and probably also southern Nova Scotia.[24] The merchants owned the ocean-going vessels that took the fish to market and returned with supplies, which were then traded (or bartered) for fish, with the books being balanced at the end of the fishing season. The merchant thus carried the financial risks of the fishery – such as poor fishing seasons, market gluts, and/or falling prices – in exchange for a guaranteed supply of product. This arrangement made sense in the capital-scarce economy of the time, but it was open to abuse, since the merchant set both the price paid for fish and that charged for supplies in the company store: this 'truck system' usually resulted in a significant reduction in the earning power of fishers.

The Channel Island merchants dominated the fisheries of the Gulf of St Lawrence, the West Country and Water Street merchants those of Newfoundland. The Newfoundland fishery was a complex affair. The sole staple of the colony, since the late eighteenth century it had been in the throes of evolving into a de facto resident fishery, which in 1830 had not yet gained official metropolitan sanction. The major outports of the colonies, where the production of cod took place, combined the functions of production, processing, importation, exportation, distribution, and mercantile control. Smaller villages or fishing 'stations' fed into this system. Together, these communities operated as the bases for an essentially sea-oriented industry; land was important only insofar as it gave access to marine resources and (sometimes) allowed fishers the means of growing a few meagre subsistence crops.

In the 1830s, fish prices in the European markets reached the bottom of a downward trend that had started in the aftermath of the Napoleonic wars. In the Maritime colonies, this resulted in a tightening of merchant credit – the normal response to such cyclical downturns – while structural shifts in international fish markets also produced some adjustment in the industry. The 1830 reciprocity agreement between the United Kingdom and the United States, for example, let Nova Scotia and New Brunswick vessels call at American ports *en route* to the West Indies, and between 1830 and 1840 the growing American market began to supplement the traditional very substantial British West Indies market (important for Nova Scotia) as well as the Brazilian and Mediterranean markets (important for the Gulf of St Lawrence). The Maritimes' fisheries also developed a strong market in the foreign West Indies in this decade. In Newfoundland, however, continuing poor prices for fish were exacerbated by tariff changes in the crucial European markets (particularly that of Spain), a circumstance that created a major crisis in the essentially single-staple economy.[25]

Unlike that of the Maritimes, the Newfoundland fishery was enmeshed in a complex web of legislation that had been created to protect the old migratory fishery, rather than the evolving resident one.[26] Moreover, the return of the Treaty Shore (or French Shore) to the French fishery after 1815 had restricted the scope of the Newfoundland fishery; the Banks fishery had gone into serious decline; and marine diversification into the seal and Labrador fisheries, while extremely successful in the 1830s, had been unable to pick up all the slack. The collapse of fish prices, in turn, led to contraction in both the merchant and the resident 'planter' fisheries. Newfoundland planters were independent fish producers who used family labour supplemented by the hiring of servants on wages when necessary, and who purchased their supplies from merchants and sold their fish to them. As falling fish prices, more expensive supplies, and a consequent tightening of merchant credit worked their way down the system, many of the servants were stranded on the coast without employment, supplies, or wages. Planter insolvency rose, and merchants increasingly protested the legislation (Palliser's Act of 1775) that required them to pay servants' wages for insolvent planters on their books. By mid-decade the colony was experiencing severe difficulties in supporting its growing population, and winter relief was being given by the government.[27] The crisis enabled the merchants to argue that the emerging settler economy was clearly not sustainable, while reformers like Patrick Morris and William Carson contended that the colony required diversification into agriculture, but that a cabal of merchants in the legislature was inhibiting local development in order to perpetuate the mercantile stranglehold on the fishery. In fact, more and more fish merchants got out of fish production, limiting themselves to supplying a resident household fishery in the outports, while increasing numbers of discouraged well-to-do planters left the colony. This loss of a potential 'gentry class' benefited the Maritime colonies: the Nova Scotia Council judged these migrants 'the only acceptable newcomers,' who settled there 'without any expense or burthen to the government or the Country.'[28]

The successful staple of the decade was timber. In 1831, the British North American trade in timber employed 2,000 ships and 25,000 sailors per annum in a carrying trade that was entirely British. Timber was a seductive staple for government officials, merchants, and settlers alike. In boom times it promised high revenues for the state, rapid high returns for the capitalist, and, for the labourer, a 'quick buck' in the woods – although that was more often than not promptly taken back in the company store, which charged a 35 to 40 per cent mark-up on imported goods. Moreover, from the point of view of those concerned with company profits or colonial revenues or both, the opportunity had to be seized while it lasted, for in 1831 a bill to end the British duties on Baltic timber failed by a narrow margin and from then on fear of the loss of the protected British timber market was a constant of the trade. The upswing started at the beginning of the decade. In 1830, Thomas Baillie sold, with the approval of the Colonial Office and as part of a deliberate policy to raise additional revenues from the Crown lands, £60,000 worth of timberland in New Brunswick. Much of it went to American entrepreneurs, who bought via New Brunswick go-betweens, paying in instalments and often not completing their payments. Many of the old timber interests were infuriated by the increased price of Crown land, and the House of Assembly argued bitterly about the control of the increased revenues. Mill manufacturing of spruce deals (sawn fir or pine timbers) had been growing since the 1820s – an important develop-ment, since it involved local processing and hence increased the value of timber exports. By 1834, the complex of ports around Saint John was exporting 50 per cent of the value of its prime timber in this form, and by 1835 sawmills were on the increase, a few of them steam-operated. Investment increased, coming from the United Kingdom and the United States into such places as the southwest Miramichi, and encouraged by Thomas Baillie, who believed in the need for rapid, capital-intensive development of the staple while the markets lasted. He therefore sup-ported major capitalists if they were willing to risk heavy investment in building mills to process timber, since in the long term such mills had the greatest development potential.[29]

Timber for shipbuilding was part of the trade. By the 1830s, the begin-nings of what is now referred to as 'Atlantic Canada's age of sail' could be discerned, as vessels were constructed in the colonies and sent across the Atlantic for sale in the British marketplace (the so-called 'transfer trade') or used for coasting and fishing in the colonies. There was a degree of local specialization: coastal, fishing, and West Indian trading vessels predominated in Nova Scotia and Newfoundland and transfer trade vessels in New Brunswick, while Prince Edward Island built for those markets and also for timber-scarce Newfoundland.[30] In major urban centres, but also on beaches scattered all around the coasts, slip-ways were constructed and wooden sailing vessels built, although few shipowners had as yet made the strategic shift to operating their own vessels within the burgeoning worldwide carrying trade that was a fea-ture of the new industrial age. Regionally owned and operated vessels were still, for the most part, vessels under 200 tons that sailed the coastal waters southwards as far as the West Indies and northwards to Labrador, carrying fish or colonial goods or prosecuting the various fisheries. The region's shipbuilding was still, in other words, basically rooted in its own staple sectors.

There was one other resource, in its infancy in the 1830s, that was a portent of things to come – coal, the quintessential industrial staple, which had remained virtually undeveloped until 1828, when the Brit-ish-directed General Mining Association (GMA) had been given sole rights to all mines and mineral resources in Nova Scotia. The GMA used the best British industrial practice of the day, including steam engines, railroads (the GMA was operating a steam locomotive by 1839 – there was only one other in British North America, at La Prairie), and an iron foundry. The company imported skilled labour from Britain, housed its employees close to the pits, and provided them with that dubious blessing, the company store. Coal exports rose throughout the decade, especially after 1833 when the export tax was removed and while the American tariff was still relatively low.[31] But, while the company covered its production costs, it did no more than that. Indeed, it is entirely possible that the policy of establishing a large British owned company was ill-advised, since 'widely distributed local control ... would have likely increased the degree of industrialization,' giving local entrepreneurs 'both an investment opportunity and a cheap source of energy for their businesses.'[32]

In theory, export-based staple economies should generate economic diversification and, ultimately, self-sufficiency through the operation of three kinds of linkage formation. Forward linkages involve the increased processing of the staple in the colony before export, as, for example, was the case with deals in the timber trade. Backward linkages are the local development of the manufacture of inputs into the staple industry – nets and barrels, for example, in the fishery. And final-demand linkages are those industries that develop to service the producers of the staple – in essence, consumer goods and services. If linkage formation is satisfactory, and if the state encourages the appropriate socio-economic infrastructures (particularly in finance and education), then over time import substitution in many producer and consumer goods will occur, with the result that the staple sector is no longer the sole, or even principal, generator of wealth.

By the 1830s, the forward linkages from timber were quite strong, and they grew increasingly better as the decade drew on. Everywhere shipbuilding (itself a forward linkage from timber) was developing and creating its own potential spin-offs, although their extent and durability remained to be seen. In agriculture, flour and grist mills were on the increase, but further processing was still slight and import substitution in agriculture not very developed. In the fisheries, there was even less diversification around the staple base, and given the technology of the day, little could be hoped for.

In newly developing areas, backward linkages in the form of transportation are crucial. Both land and sea transportation were developed in the Atlantic colonies, the latter to facilitate trade, the former to allow access to fresh stands of timber. In the fishery, of course, marine transport did nothing to open up hinterlands, although where it was combined with local shipbuilding some basis for diversification existed. But in Gaspé and Cape Breton, where the Jersey Island merchants ran the inshore fishery, local vessel construction actually decreased, having been transposed back to Jersey itself.[33] More serious, perhaps, was the stultification of even simple manufacturing such as the production of nets, gear, cooperage, and cordage for the fishery. The Jersey and New-foundland merchants imported these as exchange goods in the barter system that operated at the company store. Fortunately, in the larger ports and on the Nova Scotia and Newfoundland southern shores, where American vessels traded regularly in bait and supplies, there was less opportunity for fish merchants to maintain a stranglehold on the local economy.[34]

The real difficulty in terms of linkage formation, regardless of staple, lay in the generation of final-demand linkages. An externally focused trade with the mother country tended to foster concentration on enhancing metropolitan connections rather than creating domestic consumption, while use of credit systems in the colonial staple trades also inhibited the creation of final demand. The fundamental problem was the chronic shortage of specie that afflicted the region throughout this period.[35] In the Atlantic colonies, there does not appear to have been at this time any perception of the population as a potential consumer market, and sentiments of concern about the labouring poor seem to have been expressed in terms of morality rather than of their potential contribution as consumers to the regional economy. The avowed purpose of the Halifax Savings Bank, for example, when it was created in 1832 as a working-class bank, was (at one level) to reduce the public debt and (at another) to teach people to be provident. Of course, the chronic shortage of coinage in North America until the mid-nineteenth century exacerbated the problem, creating strains and stresses not only in the financial (banking and other) systems of the rapidly expanding international economy, but also all along the chains of credit that stretched from the British Isles across the oceans, through (and beyond) the ports of the empire, and ultimately into the outports, mines, farms, and logging camps of the Atlantic region. The problem was one of payment of debt and of returns on investment, since bills of exchange, treasury notes, or loan certificates could provide a short-term lubrication of the system but ultimately had to be redeemable, a requirement difficult to meet in a specie-scarce economy. Specie shortage made truck an effective means of exchange from the point of view of merchant and settler alike. In the timber trade, the fishery, and the coal mines, the worker's account at the company store was the common mode of payment, but mark-ups on goods were sufficiently high effectively to reduce real wages and hence stifle final demand. The little evidence that exists for agriculture suggests that final demand was growing in the better-established farming regions but was very slight in the newer ones, because of the existence of truck systems or the poverty of some areas.

One other important aspect of the economy of the four colonies was the informal economy, based on household production, local barter of surplus (which should be thought of as de facto import substitution on a very small scale), and occupational pluralism. This was a common-place of rural areas throughout the four colonies, and was an ideal way of dealing with marginal and seasonal resources, since a variety of occu-pations could be woven together into an annual round of activities, any one of which on its own would not have been viable but which, taken together, provided more security. The informal economy was a vital underpinning to the colonial economy, subsidizing merchants' wage costs, since they did not have to pay to keep labourers year round in areas where the formal (commercial) economy was heavily seasonal.[36]

In staple economies, the ports are the principal foci of initial develop-ment, based on import/export and warehousing functions but diversi-fying, over time, beyond that. In the 1830s, the colonial entrepôts of Halifax, Saint John, and (to a degree) Charlottetown and St John's were exporting staples and importing manufactured goods and foodstuffs from Britain and the United States, while other smaller urban centres (such as Fredericton) operated as administrative centres or serviced local areas. Halifax, the military headquarters for the region, served as the main port of entry not only for Nova Scotia but also for parts of the Gulf of St Lawrence. The Halifax peninsula alone contained 14,439 peo-ple in 1827 and the whole district another 10,546, but in 1831 depression slowed the rate of growth, which remained sluggish for the rest of the decade. Nonetheless, the city exhibited many of the signs of a rising metropolis: it could boast a steamboat ferry, increasingly good road communications with the rest of the province, and a burgeoning com-mercial life based, by 1830, not only on trade but also on a rising domes-tic consumer demand for the kinds of non-basic goods booksellers, silversmiths, and the like had to offer.[37]

Trade generated landward transportation systems as well as ship-ping, and the Nova Scotia road system was well developed by 1830. Road links between Halifax and the Pictou/Truro and Windsor/Annap-olis areas had been established a decade earlier, funded by a combina-tion of public subscription, private capital, and toll charges; the year 1830 saw the highest amount spent between 1820 and 1840 on Nova Scotia roads – a total of £25,000.[38] Stagecoach and even steamer services had been established in the colony by the thirties, including the forerun-ner of a regular transatlantic mail steamship service. However, if Hali-fax were to function as the principal entrepôt of the Atlantic colonies in the face of a burgeoning timber-rich New Brunswick hinterland and the rapidly expanding port of Saint John, it had to attempt to capture the trade of the Fundy Basin by building a waterway across the peninsula to carry bulky goods cheaply. A Nova Scotia version of canal mania thus developed around the building of the Shubenacadie Canal: a sadly mistimed commercial venture, for the railway age was about to start. By 1835, Joseph Howe was arguing that a railroad would be a much better idea, but the government proceded to buy out the ailing canal company. The canal would finally open in 1861 and make a modest profit until 1870, but (not surprisingly) a similar plan for the Ishmus of Chignecto never got beyond the planning stage.

Emerging throughout British North America at this time was a conflict between domestic manufacturers (in whose hands lay the potential for an industrial future) and the established commercial order, and there were hints of it, too, in Saint John and Halifax.[39] In Halifax, conflict between commercial and manufacturing interests was an ongoing affair, full of accusations from shopkeepers of 'arbitrary and discriminatory ... exercise of power' and demands for subsidies for local manufacturing. By 1839, the establishment of a broadly based (and cooperatively named) Society for the Encouragement of Trade and Manufactures spoke to an emerging compromise that achieved tariff protection for local manufacturing while allowing special exemptions for fishery supplies.[40] In Saint John, New Brunswick, the health of the resource sector was paramount.[41] The city, which had been a mere thirty-year-old village of 5,000 souls in 1815 had, by 1840, outstripped Halifax to become the largest city on the Atlantic seaboard, with 20,000 residents within its boundaries. The timber trade, of course, had generated this rapid growth through widespread commercial diversification, but there was also considerable spin-off potential for the establishment of manufacturing. In the 1830s, however, the 'great merchants' of the city fought tooth and nail to preserve the pre-eminence of the imperial commercial system that was so vital to the city's entrepôt function. To this end, they fostered the development only of that range of enterprises that either assured supplies of timber (production) or enhanced the carrying trade (marketing). Thus, resource processing was encouraged, especially mill operations for the timber trade, related energy sources (both coal and water) were explored, supporting infrastructure in such forms as marine and fire insurance and banking services were started, and transportation in the form of canals and railroads was either created or planned in this decade. Since the 'great merchants' of the city were well represented at all levels of the government, it is not surprising that local non-staple manufacturing remained very limited until mid-century, having few connections to the commercial system of the timber trade and being seen therefore as 'marginal to the basic structure of the economy.'[42]

Across the Atlantic colonial world, however, older élites were being challenged by business people, artisans, and an increasingly vocal labouring class.[43] Entrepreneurial success was becoming a passport to social status, and in towns and cities everywhere a *petite bourgeoisie* in which artisans and small merchants were important can be identified; although, in what was still essentially a pre- or proto-industrial economy, class formation (as that is currently understood) had yet to develop. Paternalism was the order of the day, and the Mechanics' Institutes, the first of which was established in Halifax in 1831 to be followed by many more throughout the decade, reflected the belief of the middle and upper levels of society that the labouring classes could and should 'better' themselves through education directed to the acquisition of appropriate skills and appropriate attitudes.[44] A desire for the improvement of society in general and of the lower classes in particular pervaded the decade, and social-welfare issues became matters for concern: prison reform, for example, started at this time (although the Bridewell prison in Halifax remained in dreadful condition until the 1840s), and legislation to stabilize the rather erratic annual handling of poor relief was under way by decade's end. The Halifax Poor Asylum continued to have a high mortality rate – one in ten in 1839 – but there was by then an attempt under way to teach inmates of the Orphan Asylum a trade, an initiative that would help to remedy matters in the future. When cholera struck Halifax in 1834, the 284 deaths that occurred in the first six weeks produced renewed efforts, not only to have emigration conditions at source in Britain improved, but also to have dispensaries opened in Nova Scotia and public health boards created.[45] Temperance societies were another manifestation of this improving spirit, their avowed purpose being to 'change, to improve and to guarantee the morality of society,' since intemperance 'placed in jeopardy the salvation, security and prosperity of the individual, the family and the community.'[46]

The evangelical movement, now drawing strength from the growing entrepreneurial ranks of society as well as from the agricultural, seafaring, and labouring elements, was also interested in social reform and self-improvement, underlining the movement of the dissenting churches out of their previous isolation. The formation of educational institutions was part of this 'outward manifestation of inward change,' and so was the heightened interest in temperance and foreign missions. At the same time, despite the desire to educate, anti-intellectualism persisted among older evangelicals, and the trenchant warning of the dying Baptist minister Harris Harding that he did not 'object to the Latin and Greek, and Hebrew, but let them be placed at the *feet* of Jesus, and not inscribed, as by Pilate, over his head' still had its adherents until the end of the decade, and much later. The times were changing, however. Disruption in the Anglican communion in Halifax, and later in Saint John, brought believers with formal education to the Baptist ranks. Since they did not wish to lose their young people, their need for an educated clergy and laity became compelling. These new forces combined with developing attitudes of the rural Baptist leadership to propel the Baptists rapidly towards involvement in educational endeavours. A Baptist secondary school was opened in Fredericton in 1836, offering education similar to that provided at Horton Academy since 1828, with the important exception that in Fredericton boys and girls were to be educated on equal terms. The school failed to secure funding from the Council, however, as that body saw it as a threat to Anglican control of education in the colony.[47]

In post-secondary education, serious denominational restrictions hampered access to higher education for many students. At King's College in Windsor, and Dalhousie College in Halifax (restructured in 1838), the faculty were drawn exclusively from the Church of England and the Church of Scotland respectively, giving a strong denominational bias to both institutions.[48] In response to this exclusivity and to provide an alternative to an institution (Dalhousie) located in 'sinful' Halifax, the Baptists in 1838 founded at Horton their own institution of higher learning, Queen's (later Acadia) College, which immediately became the largest post-secondary institution in the colony. In spite of efforts by some members of the legislature to control the spread of denominational colleges, the Roman Catholics and the Methodists would follow suit early in the next decade. Approaches to education echoed social distinctions. The Church of England leaned towards classical knowledge; the Presbyterians, under the influence of Scottish learning, stressed science and mathematics; the Methodists and Baptists worked for the diffusion of elementary education, 'underlining the Baptist shift from a powerful anti-intellectual force to one of the foremost advocates of universal education to be found in the Maritime colonies.'[49] Distinctions were not made solely along class lines; for example, education for Blacks was kept separate when, in 1835, a school for Black students was founded in Halifax. Nonetheless, improvement was under way; in 1836 security for teachers' salaries was being investigated, and plans were soon being laid for the establishment of an institution for the training of teachers.[50]

For the Catholics, the 1830s were a time to establish themselves. The quintessential missionary priest of the decade was Angus Bernard MacEachern, who had started his colonial mission days in 1790 as the only priest on Prince Edward Island. In 1829, aged sixty-nine years, he was appointed titular bishop of Rosen, with his see at Charlottetown and jurisdiction over the Island, the Magdalen Islands, and New Brunswick. In 1831, MacEachern set up a seminary on the site of his old Island family farm at St Andrew's, and he died four years later, still journeying across the Island to minister to his scattered flock. Cape Breton, which had been under MacEachern in earlier years, became part of the Nova Scotia Vicariate Apostolic (not a full diocese until 1842) under Bishop William Fraser, another Scot, while Bishop William Dollard (an Irishman) held the New Brunswick see, and Bishop Michael Anthony Fleming (also Irish) that of Newfoundland. Each appointment reflected, to some degree, the ethnic distribution of Catholics in the various jurisdictions, although the Acadians were not represented at this time, despite pleading from Quebec to Rome in 1836, after MacEachern's death.[51] In Cape Breton, the work of Rev. James MacGregor did for Highlanders of the Presbyterian persuasion what MacEachern had done for the Catholics, and in much the same way: through hard journeying, dedication, and a facility with the Gaelic tongue.

Everywhere throughout the decade there were strong links between education, religion, and ethnicity, emphasizing the general desire for improvement. A literate population meant a society in good standing, even if the practicalities of dealing with the complex ethnic, social, and religious issues of the day challenged any easy élite assumptions about how a respectable colonial society should be constituted. For the most part, however, ethnic and religious divisions were still dormant,[52] although in Newfoundland different perspectives on the problems that beset the colony were increasingly expressed in a bitter factionalism that fed on ethnic and religious differences. Nonetheless, at the community level, especially in Conception Bay and St John's, where Protestant English and Catholic Irish lived cheek by jowl, factions could, if the issues were sufficiently crucial and universal, submerge their differences in a demonstration of some kind of class consciousness in those proto-industrial occupations the seal and cod fisheries.[53] Likewise, on Prince Edward Island, protests over escheat (the struggle to secure ownership of the land for those who actually worked it) bonded potentially divisive elements together, as established tenant farmers joined forces with large numbers of immigrant Highland Scots and Irish who had fled insecurity of tenure in the Old World.[54]

Indeed, there were many factors at work in the colonies that created a sense of community and played formative roles in bonding people together to craft a new society in this comparatively new land. The spread of information, through roving libraries, newspapers, pamphlets, community meetings, and the like, meant that ideas of how society should be ordered, debates about future political structures for the region, and knowledge of what was happening in Britain were all accessible, not only to urban dwellers, but in the countryside as well. Literature about the colonies (especially Nova Scotia) flourished, written by such eminent persons as Joseph Howe (*Western and Eastern Rambles*) or Thomas McCulloch, an advocate of educational and political reform whose character Stepsure was portrayed as having a hoe in one hand and a Bible in the other.[55] It would be incorrect to think of the ordinary people of the colonies as always illiterate or ill-informed. Whether one speaks of the tenant farmer in Prince Edward Island or the merchant-middleman in the New Brunswick timber trade, the political reformers or churchmen of all four colonies, or the immigrants from Scotland and Ireland, there seems to have been a sense that community spheres were building, either in contradistinction to those that had unravelled in the Old World or in an attempt to recreate them for a variety of purposes, under new conditions and personnel, in this new society. So, for example, William Cooper (on the one hand) might aspire to create a New World order in which 'common people might gain real power over their lives' on the Island, or Patrick Morris (on the other) might hope to establish agriculture, and himself as a member of a New World landed gentry, in Newfoundland.[56]

Such visions, even when conflicting, spoke to a society that was moving beyond pure localism. People aspired to a new and better polity, and the *sine qua non* of the ability to achieve that was political power. Not surprisingly, therefore, political structures were themselves undergoing significant change in the 1830s as the colonies sought to craft appropriate institutional structures in the face of a variety of still unreconciled aspirations. In New Brunswick, the Assembly was at odds over a variety of issues with the unpopular, Anglican-dominated, and Fredericton-based Council, which combined both executive and legislative functions and was dominated by the commissioner of Crown lands and surveyor general, Thomas Baillie. Baillie's rigorous enforcement of the timber regulations generated large returns from the sale of Crown lands, so that the executive had at its disposal rapidly expanding casual and territorial revenues. These provided the executive with an effective fiscal buffer that allowed the Council to govern without much concern for the wishes of the Assembly. Baillie's attempts to attract outside capital for development purposes made him enemies among the timber merchants and added fuel to the grievances against him. Consequently, when Sir Archibald Campbell, the lieutenant-governor, acting on instructions from the Colonial Office to divide the Council into two bodies, gave Baillie the senior position in an executive of five (instead of twelve) and refused to appoint leading members of the House of Assembly, the stage was set for a constitutional confrontation in which the arrogant and high-handed Baillie would be a central figure.

The Assembly, predictably, was dissatisfied with Campbell's efforts and, in 1833 and again in 1836, sent a delegation to London to negotiate a solution that hinged on the Assembly's getting hold of the large casual and territorial revenues in return for a permanent civil list. Lord Glenelg, colonial secretary from 1835 to 1839, was impressed with the negotiators and – against the backdrop of a mounting crisis in the Canadas that would lead to rebellion – was satisfied. The Assembly then passed a civil-list bill, but Campbell – a man of military background and a determined upholder of the status quo – refused consent, offering his resignation if his judgment proved unacceptable to the Colonial Office. It did, and Campbell was replaced by Sir John Harvey, who negotiated a settlement containing three essential elements. First, Baillie was shunted aside and his Crown-lands policies abandoned, thus pacifying the timber merchants who wanted easier access to Crown lands. Second, an administration – which had the support of the House since it was effectively led by Charles Simonds, the speaker of the Assembly – was installed: an action that gained Harvey the applause of the Colonial Office. Third, in return for a permanent civil list, the Assembly was given control of the casual and territorial revenues, which were distributed through the appropriations committee of the House and channelled into local improvements and local patronage. Expenditures on Crown lands were reduced and urban and rural developments undertaken. In the ensuing years, Harvey introduced other social, economic, and legal reforms, including improvements in education, communications, and agriculture. In fact, in Harvey's years in office, the political situation in New Brunswick changed from one guided by self-interested and often interrelated élite factions who dominated an unresponsive Council, to one in which the colonial executive discharged its responsibility to the elected representatives of the people in such a way as to provide a solid basis on which to build in the future.[57]

In Nova Scotia, despite somewhat parallel political manoeuvrings, there were also some key differences, among them the much smaller amounts of money involved. As was the case in New Brunswick, Nova Scotia already had control of the distribution of locally generated revenues, which were similarly used for local development; but the casual and territorial revenues were of less significance and would have been virtually absorbed by the cost of a permanent civil list. Although the ostensible issue was finance, the real conflict was over the composition of the Council of Twelve, which, as in New Brunswick, exercised both executive and legislative authority and was composed of a small group of interrelated, predominantly Anglican civil servants and merchants resident in Halifax. Thus, to some degree, there was a capital-versus-hinterland bias to the conflict, although there were also reformers within the Halifax élite. Initially, Lieutenant-Governor Sir Colin Campbell was able to contain the discontent. But by mid-decade a broadly based reform movement had emerged under the leadership of the mercurial Joseph Howe, whose self-conducted defence against a charge of libel (the result of a series of accusations he directed at magistrates and police in Halifax on their misuse of public funds) had resulted in his becoming a public champion of the principles of free speech, a free press, and a responsible legislature. Howe and the reformers won the election of 1836 and pressed for radical changes in the constitution. Along with demanding repeal of the militia act and control over the casual and territorial revenues, the reformers passed a resolution in favour of an elected legislative council. The Colonial Office, burdened with the crisis in the Canadas, was again sympathetic. But Sir Colin Campbell, like Sir Archibald Campbell in New Brunswick, was unwilling to go far enough to conciliate the reformers: he thought Lord Durham's recommendation of responsible government 'absurd,' and so he too was removed from office, while the Colonial Office sought another official who might find a way to implement the reforms that were becoming, by now, inevitable.[58]

On Prince Edward Island, although constitutional reform was also under way in the 1830s, the central issue was the thorny question of escheat. With immigration expanding rapidly, colonial property was increasing in value and land speculation had become profitable. Many landowners, including absentee proprietors, were therefore desirous of holding onto their lands until they could get good returns for them on a rising land market. In the meantime, they insisted on short leases and high rents that were payable only in hard currency and without reward for improvement or any release from arrears. With the emancipation of the Catholics, however, many Highland tenants became able to vote and hence to protest politically; and so, when William Cooper (a resident farmer and former land agent) was elected in 1831, escheat was placed 'at center stage.'[59] In 1832, the Assembly under the new lieutenant-governor, Sir Aretas William Young, appointed a special committee of the House of Assembly to investigate the number of townships liable to escheat because of non-fulfilment of the conditions of the original grants and to report thereafter to a Court of Escheat that Young was to establish. In 1833, he attempted to get the Colonial Office to approve a land-assessment bill, designed by the Assembly to provide a new basis for tax assessment that would force proprietors to dispose of undeveloped property and generate land revenues for local development. But the Colonial Office, concerned about the dangerous precedent involved, refused to confirm the act or to condone escheat.

In 1834, a sufficient number of radicals were elected to the Assembly to form the Escheat Party, led by William Cooper. In 1835 Young died, and in 1836 Sir John Harvey took over. Mindful of the unrest that similar circumstances had produced in Ireland (which he had just left), Harvey sought a solution that would alleviate the ills of the landowning system without challenging inalienable property rights. In 1836, tenants threatened to withhold rents, petitioning again for a Court of Escheat. Harvey found the terms 'treasonable,' but sought a compromise that might take the wind out of the Escheators' sails: longer leases, a rent based on actual agricultural production, and the remittance of arrears for the impecunious. At the same time, he sought to improve the justice and education systems. In 1837, just prior to his transfer to New Brunswick, he suggested that a limited form of escheat would probably have to be established, but his successor, Lieutenant-Governor Charles FitzRoy, 'scion of one of the great aristocratic families of England,' found this impossible to champion. FitzRoy, however, was conscious of the obligations to tenantry that came with the rights of property, and he also sought adjustments of the situation, such as the sale of property to tenants. In 1838, another election was held and eighteen out of the twenty-four seats in the Assembly went to the Escheat Party. Cooper was elected speaker of the House and sent to London to plead for total escheat, but Lord John Russell, now colonial secretary, would not see him, writing instead to FitzRoy refusing a Court of Escheat or the Crown takeover of proprietorial lands. The fruits of a decade of struggle appeared to have been lost.[60]

While Nova Scotia and New Brunswick searched for a new kind of colonial status and Prince Edward Island faced demands for radical change, in Newfoundland the drive to reform centred on the slow transition from fishery to colony. The old form of government was clearly inadequate in a de facto settled colony. Reformers like Carson and Morris argued that, in hard times, a measure of control of one's own destiny would allow the kind of sympathetic and informed response to economic crisis that did not seem to be forthcoming from a distant Colonial Office. In particular, they sought the establishment of officially sanctioned settlement that would allow the colony to develop its (untested) agricultural potential and solve the ongoing provisions crisis.[61] In 1832, Newfoundland was finally granted representative government, bringing the colony in line with the Maritimes. But the crisis worsened, and relief in the form of roads work, supplies of seed potatoes, or minimal provisions had to be expanded. The reformers (now Liberals) continued to press for agricultural expansion; they also had a new villain in their sights – Chief Justice Henry John Boulton, an ultra-conservative appointee who was also president of the Council and whose mandate was to update the antiquated and inappropriate legislation of the colony. Boulton was a disaster, inflexible and unable to cast his legislative improvements in terms that would not offend the various political, religious, and ethnic factions of the day. When he refused to revive the 1824 extension of Palliser's Act after it lapsed in 1832, for example, he was accused of being in league with the fish merchants. Although actually acting out of a recognition (which received considerable support from all classes of society round the bays) that the old act was a leftover from the migratory fishery, he made his case in rigid legal formulations that sounded oppressive even when they were not.[62] As the debate raged, it became entangled with religious and ethnic factionalism, since Governor Cochrane, and his successor, Governor Prescott, had appointed Conservative Anglican merchants to the government, while many of the Liberals were Irish and Catholic. The archbishop, Michael Anthony Fleming, was also politically active in the debate. He sought to consolidate Catholic power in the colony, hoping that political pressure from the church would be as successful in Newfoundland as it had been for Catholic emancipation in Ireland and reading the ongoing politico-legal battles in terms of religious, ethnic, and economic bias in the legislature. At decade's end, nothing had been resolved; factionalism was rampant, the economy seriously crippled, and the colony's ability to govern itself increasingly doubtful.[63]

Nonetheless, the drive to political power, even in Newfoundland, although necessarily cast within the constraints of an unusual history of imperial resource control and a vulnerable marine economy, spoke to the belief that policies based on colonies' sensitivity to their own problems had a better chance of succeeding than did imperial fiats. Imperial experience across the Empire may have provided the Colonial Office and its officials with broader vision, but such vision was necessarily framed within the requirements of larger imperial concerns. On the other hand, while the assemblies were better placed to identify the real developmental needs of their economies from close at hand, they also ran the risk of being naïve, parochial, or even self-serving. By the late 1830s it had begun to be apparent that steering between the Scylla of imperial insensitivity to local requirements and the Charybdis of domestic myopia (or, worse still, greed) would be no easy task.

In a theoretically ideal staples world, of course, the sequencing of events would have been orderly. The timing and nature of population growth, and its distribution, would have been such that the export-led colonial economy would have slowly rooted, and government structures would have developed in line with the increasing complexity of the evolving society, providing or encouraging appropriate educational, social, and financial services as required. In due course, thresholds for widespread consumer and producer demand would have been reached, generating domestic manufacturing and diversification around the staple base. In phase with this, the export-led commercial economy would have slowly diminished in importance as import-substitution accelerated. Naturally, not all of this would have happened in the 1830s, but the important question is this: given the population, resource bases, and relative location in the trading world of the Atlantic colonies at that time, how favourable to future development were the political, economic, and social foundations that were being laid in that decade? It is a dangerous question, because it can be misinterpreted as an invitation to designate failure and ascribe blame, but an important one, because it deals, not in deterministic teleologies, but in realistic assessments of what was desired and what was possible. It can only be partially answered at this time. As things stood in the temporary hothouse conditions of a booming timber and shipbuilding trade in New Brunswick and Prince Edward Island, in the volatile trading economy of Nova Scotia, and in the conditions of paralysis engendered by economic collapse in Newfoundland, it was often not clear what was best or even what was possible. For trade, regulation was a handicap rather than a blessing; for developing agriculture and potential manufacturing, tariff protection was essential but, for consumers, too expensive. The various staple sectors of the colonies were too fragmented, the population base too thinly scattered, and financial infrastructures still too immature for integration and diversification to take place. Moreover, both the Colonial Office and colonial governments knew they were in an age of transition the political outcome of which might be inevitable but the manner of arriving thereto was not.

In short, the evolutionary flexibilities of a slowly maturing staples economy were not to be forthcoming. Nor, of course, were they looked for by the actors of the day. Without modern theories to influence their choices for good or ill, and without enough time passed to garner the hindsights that might have allowed them to comprehend the economic implications and effects of the Industrial Revolution and a changing world economic order, the people of the region, in their various ways and at their various levels of influence, were involved in putting together their new society. Indeed, it is the hallmark of the 1830s that this was the decade in which the debate began to be shaped at all levels of society about who the ruling class should be, what its role might become in the context of an emerging colonial community, and how power should be exercised in order to promote economic prosperity, political responsibility, and social well-being. In 1830, the issue had been when and how to untie the imperial apron strings. Ten years later, with that process essentially under way, the focus of debate had shifted to the manner in which the Atlantic colonies would shape their future development. The sense of hopefulness that pervades some of the history of the decade stems from the fact that the conflicting visions of the region's future were still sufficiently blurred to allow the hope that such dreams and aspirations might actually be attainable. All that would change in the forties.

CHAPTER FOURTEEN

The 1840s
Decade of Tribulation

T.W. ACHESON

Decades, like people, tend to be personalized by those who have had to live with them. The 1830s had been a period of optimism and excitement. The economy had moved in roller-coaster fashion, but there were more heights than depths and the ride had been exhilarating. Settlement and population growth followed this expansionary trend, and even the political conflicts of the decade had an optimistic quality to them. The 1840s, by contrast, were years of economic depression and social and political uncertainty. There was change, but the change was frequently the product of forced accommodations to circumstances beyond the control of the people and institutions of the British North Atlantic colonies. The dominant motif of the decade was anxiety, as the 1840s saw a narrowing of opportunity both for newcomers and for the native-born who came to maturity in this difficult time. Many fled the region, and the anxieties of those who remained were reflected in a growing unwillingness to acquiesce in the moral authority of the traditional leaders of society.

The principal cause of this widespread social and economic dislocation was the decision of the British government to dismantle its old colonial commercial policies and move into an era of free trade. The policies of protection for colonial produce and shipping had provided the umbrella under which the staples industries of British North America had flourished. These policies had been designed to provide the motherland with a secure supply of timber and fish and ships and sailors, and also to keep the benefits of trade – the profits from freight – within the Empire and to keep British treasure at home. By mid-century, however, Britain was the wealthiest and the most economically advanced nation on the face of the earth, and political power was gradually passing into the hands of an urban-based business élite of economic liberals who emphasized efficiency, cheapness, and material benefit over national self-sufficiency, security, and the landed interest. The fate of the old system was finally sealed when a Conservative government, headed by Sir Robert Peel, decided to move to deregulation and free trade.

Protection for colonial produce was very costly to the British consumer. The protection on colonial timber, the commodity of greatest concern to people in the Maritime colonies, amounted to about 80 per cent of the cost price of the timber in 1840. Foreign timber paid a tariff of forty-one shillings a load, colonial timber only nine shillings. The costs of protecting colonial timber amounted to millions of pounds sterling each year and provoked growing resentment. The government responded to that resentment when Peel's 1842 budget reduced the duty on foreign timber from forty to twenty-five shillings a load and effectively eliminated it on colonial timber. More gradual cuts from 1846 reduced the duty on foreign timber and lumber to seven shillings sixpence and ten shillings, respectively, by 1851. In 1849, the government completed the destruction of the old colonial system by repealing the Navigation Acts, which had given colonial shipping an advantage over American shipping in the transportation of goods into British possessions.[1]

This sharp change in commercial policy on the part of the imperial government produced enormous dislocation in the North Atlantic colonies. No colony escaped its influence, although New Brunswick, as the principal exporter of timber and deals, was especially vulnerable. Its timber exports fell by 50 per cent between 1840 and 1842, and while they rose sharply in 1845 and 1846 as producers rushed to get their output to England in anticipation of further tariff cuts, the resulting glut of timber on the British market drove prices sharply down and combined with further tariff reductions to create a falling demand for colonial timber for the rest of the decade.[2] The smaller Nova Scotia timber industry experienced a similar decline. Even more badly hit was the Nova Scotia carrying trade with the British West Indies, for the West Indies sugar staple was as adversely affected as the colonial timber trade. Since much of Nova Scotia's seagoing commerce had been based on purchasing fish, meat, and grain from the other colonies and from the northeastern United States and carrying them for sale in the West Indies, most of this re-export trade was eliminated in the 1840s.

The carrying trade of all the colonies suffered during the decade. The earnings generated by freights and by wages of sailors and masters were significant elements in the colonial economy, and the shipbuilding industry was one of the most dynamic sectors in the regional economy in 1840. Most Maritime-built vessels were eventually sold on the British market – in the 1840s vessels built in the Maritimes comprised nearly 30 per cent of the tonnage added to the Liverpool registry – and together with freight earnings made possible the large-scale importation of goods that added so much to the quality and standard of living of the colonists. A short-term decline in the shipbuilding industry followed the decline of the shipping and timber industries in the early 1840s. Prices for New Brunswick and Prince Edward Island vessels fell from an average of £7 a ton in the late 1830s to less than £4 in 1844. Since colonists no longer had the resources to pay for any but the most essential goods, imports fell dramatically. And since most of the revenues of all colonial governments were generated by the collection of import duties, public revenues collapsed, reducing the incomes of those employed in the small public sector of the colonial economy and limiting the services they could provide to the destitute, the elderly, and the sick.[3] The one exception to this picture of decline was Newfoundland. Markets for Newfoundland saltfish traditionally were found in southern Europe, notably Portugal, Spain, and Italy, and secondarily in the British West Indies. These markets generally held up in the 1840s, and Newfoundland enjoyed a degree of modest prosperity compared with the other colonies.[4]

The essentially export-oriented economies of those colonies had developed within the framework of an integrated imperial structure organized by the British metropolis. The system had provided many material benefits to the colonists. True, the colonial economic and political élite of great merchants and public officials had prospered to a far greater degree than had the ordinary folk of the colonies. Nonetheless, material prosperity had been more equitably distributed than in most other parts of the Empire, notably in those areas employing servile labour. Moreover, large-scale water-borne commerce traditionally has been the breeding place of modern capitalism. Despite the persistence of some relatively self-sufficient rural communities, the colonial economies by 1840 were highly specialized. Most people were dependent upon complex, capital-intensive commercial networks.

The most characteristic form of this capitalism was an omnipresent chain of debt that linked the great commercial firms of Great Britain to the major colonial wholesalers and shippers, and through them to the modest colonial general merchants and retailers, down to the common colonial farmers, fishermen, and lumbermen of the countryside and the artisans and labourers of the towns.[5] The grant of credit to a customer at any stage along the chain both provided the debtor with an opportunity to better himself and placed him in jeopardy in the event of an unsuccessful season. Inevitably, the debtor became a client of his creditor, dependent on his goodwill to remain out of debtor's prison. Disaster could strike at any part of the chain. Bankruptcy was not the prerogative of the small property owner. Commercial collapse often began when a major commercial firm failed and its creditors in turn pursued the debtors of their debtor. By means of the chain of credit, a capital of many millions of dollars could be dispersed over thousands of debtors. Most of the capital was held in promissory notes of the debtor, and those might be carried in various forms for years. Every season provided a new opportunity for large numbers of people to gamble on the export markets for timber, fish, and ships, and every season brought the same possibilities of failure.

Seasonal successes and failures had been an ongoing process for generations before 1840. The 1839–41 seasons had been among the best in living memory, but persistent rumours concerning the proposed changes in the mercantilist system created a commercial panic in the autumn of 1841. Prices for timber and fish fell, and eventually merchants simply would not purchase at any price. Producers could not dispose of their surplus and could not acquire the credits or currency to pay down their debts. Dozens of merchants, both large and small, were forced to take refuge in the Bankruptcy Acts. As the commercial decline continued over the winter of 1841–2, they were joined by hundreds more. The crisis slowly made its way down the social ladder. In the towns, hundreds of master craftsmen and small manufacturers who were dependent on the local markets provided in large part by the seagoing trades were driven to the wall, many facing bankruptcy and debtor's prison, all of them turning their journeymen and apprentices out into the streets with neither jobs nor prospects. The greatest difficulties were faced by the urban poor, a group that included the families of day labourers, female-headed households, servants, and those too infirm to support themselves. These were people whose entire efforts were at the best of times devoted to securing a bare subsistence.

Winters were always a period of privation as wages fell, fuel costs rose, and many spent months on the dole.[6] In the terrible winter of 1841–2, many thousands desperately overstrained the shrinking institutional resources of the Maritime towns. Perhaps 20 per cent of the population of the city of Saint John were on outdoor or indoor relief through at least part of that winter, dependent on the overseer of the poor and the private charity of churches and individuals. The usual spring commercial revival did not occur in 1842, and a process of de-urbanization began as thousands abandoned the wage economy of the towns for what they hoped was the greater security of the more self-sufficient countryside. Hundreds of Saint John artisans banded themselves into associations and, with their families, founded farming communities in the upper reaches of the Kennebecasis; hundreds more abandoned the colony altogether and sought a better future in New England.[7]

Urban poverty was always more desperate than rural, but the people of the countryside could no more escape the effects of the depression than could those of the town. While townspeople sometimes fled to the farms, often just a step or two ahead of the constables, those already there also keenly felt the onslaught of depression. The saving virtue of a farm seemed to be that it could become a largely self-contained ark capable of supplying the basic food and fuel needs of the farm family and insulating it against the hunger and cold that could threaten all but the most prosperous town dweller. By and large, rural freeholders could more easily survive, but not even the most self-sufficient farmer escaped the 1841–3 depression. Virtually every farmer, farmer-lumberman, and farmer-fisherman had a trading relationship with at least one or two merchants. As the bankruptcy and devastation moved down the great chain of debt in 1841–2, rural dwellers were increasingly caught up in it.

Both lumbering and fishing were usually based on the truck system, where the producer received advances in goods from a merchant's store in return for selling the timber or fish to the merchant at the season's end. Often this system of advance and payment continued without a break for years. In other cases, usually involving more prosperous farmers, producers received large advances in goods or cash to enable them to hire several men and prosecute the timber-cutting operations as self-employed operators. Sometimes these operations were carried on in partnership with the merchant, but the farmer's share of the capital was usually borrowed from the merchant, normally on the security of a mortgage on the farmer's land. When the collapse occurred, the merchants, under pressure from their creditors, often put pressure on the farmers to redeem their notes and pay their mortgages. If the merchants went into bankruptcy, their creditors, usually wholesalers outside the country or the colony, without personal knowledge of the farmers involved, sent in the bailiffs to collect the debts. The poorer farmers might be jailed for debt; the more prosperous lost everything they owned. The devalued farms of bankrupt farmers were often sold at public auctions or through private transactions by the creditors to immigrants. The situation was most difficult in the major timber centres. New Brunswick farmers were hardest hit. At Doaktown in the upper Miramichi Valley, nearly half the pioneer families that had settled the area forty years earlier were forced to abandon their homesteads. A number of men and women in their sixties and seventies whose farms were mortgaged to Chatham and Newcastle merchants lost everything. Most moved to the new pioneer settlements of Aroostook, Maine, and their farms were sold to Irish immigrants.[8]

The worst of the crisis of the first depression was over by 1843.

Exports of wood products rose sharply in the next few years. Those colonial merchants, shipbuilders, farmers, and labourers who had managed to survive the worst of the Great Depression enjoyed a short-lived prosperity. The shipbuilding industry recovered and continued to expand for the rest of the decade. But, between 1846 and 1849, the colonial economy was rocked by a second, albeit less severe, commercial depression. It was less severe because, much to everybody's surprise, the colonial wood and shipping industries managed to survive the movement to free trade, although prices fell and so too did much of the profit traditionally taken from these industries. By the end of the 1840s, British consumers paid about 10 per cent less for their timber than they had at the beginning. The colonial timber industry could not compete at this price and went on to virtual extinction in the 1850s; but the lumber industry was able to overcome the disability, and by 1850 most colonial timber was being shipped to Britain as deals. Processing the raw timber allowed colonial producers to sell the same weight of wood for more than twice the price in the British market.

New technology revolutionized the structure of the woods industry, as the number and capacity of sawmills in the colonies rose sharply in the 1840s. All sawmills required significant water-power and a considerable investment of capital, and they were owned by men with more capital than that possessed by the most prosperous farmers. The largest and most efficient sawmills began to employ steam engines, which were very costly indeed. Throughout the 1840s, profits and opportunities in the woods industries narrowed, and control came to be vested in the hands of a smaller and wealthier cadre of prosperous lumbermen and lumbermen-merchants than had been the case earlier in the century.[9] The colonial shipbuilding industry, one of the principal domestic markets for lumber, grew rapidly in the late 1840s. Maritime-built vessels accounted for about a third of all the tonnage added to the Liverpool ship registry in 1846, most of it coming from New Brunswick.[10] By 1850, a leaner, less profitable, but more efficient and technologically superior wood-products industry was emerging in the British North Atlantic colonies.

The second depression was much more a rural than a town phenomenon. The decline in the total quantity of timber harvested in the colonies during the late 1840s created depressed conditions in the rural areas of the Maritimes. Another serious problem was crop failure. The farmers of the region, like those of Ireland and of Prussia, lived on the potato. The potato was a humble food. Most were consumed on the farm and rarely entered into commerce; hence they were little valued by merchants or by those who commented on the prosperity of the colonies. Yet it was a most nutritious food and easily grown in every part of the

Atlantic colonies, even in the outports of Newfoundland. In a good year New Brunswick farmers produced fourteen bushels and Nova Scotia farmers harvested seven bushels for every man, woman, and child in the colony. It was a basic dietary staple of every farm, and because it was so common it was sold for next to nothing in the colonial towns. Potatoes and fish provided a nutritionally rich and almost inexhaustible supply of very cheap food and made possible an acceptable standard of living in rural and urban areas alike. In 1846 and 1847, in North America as in Europe, the potato crops failed. The failure did not produce the starvation that occurred in Ireland and Germany, because alternate food sources were available, but it did cause hardship in the rural areas. Larger farmers lost a cash staple that they could sell in the West Indies and in the lumber camps. Many marginal farmers lost that margin and were forced off their lands. In the towns food prices rose, and the poor could find no substitute for the ubiquitous potato.

Because of its role as the principal Maritime producer of timber, New Brunswick suffered the greatest human and material consequences of the 1840s depressions, but Nova Scotia and Prince Edward Island were badly hurt as well. By 1850, most of Nova Scotia's trade with the West Indies had disappeared and the Nova Scotia timber industry was decimated. There were, however, profound differences in the structure of the colonial trading patterns. New Brunswick trade was characterized by its high degree of specialization. Nearly 90 per cent of exports consisted of timber, deals, and ships, most of it sold on the British market. By contrast, the external markets for Nova Scotia and Prince Edward Island staples were much more diverse and balanced. Their principal exports were fish, agricultural produce, timber, deals, and ships. This produce was sold to other colonies and to the West Indies, the United Kingdom, and the United States. By far the most important markets for both colonies were each other and New Brunswick. The interdependence of the three economies is clearly evident in the 1840s trading patterns. The engine that had powered the expansion of this trade in the 1830s had been the New Brunswick timber industry and the demands it created for food for men and animals. The decline of that industry after 1841 was reflected in the fall of intercolonial trade. The value of Nova Scotia's intercolonial trade fell from £405,000 (nearly 40 per cent of all exports) in 1840 to only £96,000 (18 per cent of exports) in 1848.

By 1850, external trade was a considerably less significant element in the economies of all the Atlantic colonies than it had been ten years earlier. The American market was somewhat more important, and the British, intercolonial, and West Indies markets much less significant than they had been in the previous decade. Living standards had almost certainly fallen. Imports of manufactured consumer goods had fallen dramatically, and town and country people alike were eating less wheat flour, buying less imported cloth, and either doing without many commodities or using local produce. Wages fell and opportunities for advancement, whether on farms or in business, became more limited. Under the circumstances, many people made the decision to seek their fortunes elsewhere. The theme of the emigration of productive people, of abandoned town houses and abandoned farms, was a common one in the 1840s and one that reflected an important reality. Driven by desire for greater gain, or by despair, or by fear of debtor's prison, thousands made their way to the United States or, occasionally, to Canada.

The problems of commercial adjustment and economic depression were compounded by the difficulties of dealing with the effects of the Irish potato famine. Constant sea communication by timber ships and fishing vessels had brought large numbers of Irish people to all four Atlantic colonies before 1840. A majority of the early settlers in the Maritimes were probably northern Irish Protestants, most of whom settled as farmers in the rural areas. As the century wore on, Irish migration became increasingly Catholic and a disproportionate number settled in the towns, where they constituted the largest part of the urban labour force. The Irish brought with them their distinctive institutions, such as the St Patrick's Society, the Orange Order, and the Sons of Erin, as well as the experience of a long history of ethnic and social mistrust. Usually, they came in extended families, and they sometimes formed group settlements in the rural areas and distinctive ghettos in the towns. Even by 1840 they were the largest immigrant group in New Brunswick and Newfoundland and were second only to the Scots in Nova Scotia and Prince Edward Island. Most early Irish arrivals came with a little capital and a few skills and integrated readily into the expanding labour market. Yet Ireland itself remained overpopulated, and its eight million people were heavily dependent upon the potato crop. Crop failures occurred three times in the 1840s, the worst, in 1846, resulting in the terrible famine year of 1847. Perhaps a million people eventually died from the effects of the hunger and the diseases that became endemic among those whose immune systems were seriously weakened by malnutrition. The famine migration began in 1844 and reached its peak in 1847. Millions left, either on their own or thrust out by landlords or municipal agencies attempting to lift the burden of feeding the indigents. Tens of thousands arrived in the major ports of the Atlantic colonies, bringing with them their destitution and their disease. At Saint John the largest port in the region, more than 14,000 arrived in 1847. They were quarantined on Partridge Island, where more than a thousand eventually died.

Colonial authorities were at first anxious, then increasingly horrified, at the carnage that faced them. Since the arrivals were all British subjects, the colonies could not refuse to admit them. Yet clearly many of the newcomers were so old or so disabled that they must become permanent public charges in a system where all welfare costs were borne by the residents of the parish.[11] The refugees who arrived during the second depression could do little more than compete for the already diminishing pool of wage-labour jobs available for the unskilled. The result was to drive down even farther the already shrinking wages of the labouring poor of the region's ports. The newcomers, however, had even less of a stake in the community than did the thousands of native-born colonists who were leaving, and as soon as they were able to accumulate enough resources to take ship for Boston, many moved on, usually within a year or two of their arrival. The pre-famine Irish continued to constitute the great majority of the permanent Irish population of the region, except in Newfoundland.[12]

The arrival of the famine Irish fuelled growing ethnoreligious tensions, particularly in the towns of New Brunswick and Newfoundland, and in Halifax, where the greatest concentrations of Irish were found. At first these tensions were created by the universal misunderstandings that often arise between natives and newcomers in any society. Many of the early Irish were highly respectable people who resented both the monopoly of political power and natural resources the natives seemed to possess, and the discrimination the Irish seemed to face. But the Irish themselves were divied by centuries-old tensions centred on ethnicity, religion, and class. The depressions and the consequent competition for jobs exacerbated these tensions. Most of the Irish newcomers in the 1840s were Catholic and poor. Most Irish settlement was in New Brunswick and Newfoundland. In Newfoundland the overwhelming majority of Irish emigrants were Catholics, who comprised the largest part of the population. In New Brunswick, by contrast, Catholic and Protestant Irish were rather equally divided.

The most difficult situation developed in the St John Valley of New Brunswick, which contained the greatest concentration of Irish in the Maritimes. Here a majority of the Irish were Protestant, although that proportion had probably been in decline since the mid-1830s. The unity of the Irish community began to come apart in the early 1840s in the face of a growing Catholic presence. The situation was exacerbated when the deepening depression of 1841–4 financially crippled the city government of Saint John, which was finally put into bankruptcy by its creditors. Irish Protestants and perhaps some native-born Protestants turned to the Orange Order, the characteristic instrument of the Protestant ascendancy in Ireland, to prevent what was perceived as a potential Catholic take-over of the colony. The order grew rapidly during the decade, and confrontations between the two groups occurred in the towns. As early as 1841 and 1842 the poorest group of Irish Catholic labourers, concentrated in the tenements of York Point in Saint John, effectively sealed off their quarter of the city and successfully defied the authority of the Common Council, the only popularly elected municipal government in the region, and one controlled by its Irish freemen. Between 1841 and 1849 virtually every Irish feast day (notably St Patrick's Day and the anniversary of the Battle of the Boyne) was the occasion for significant disturbances in Woodstock, Fredericton, and Saint John, in which order was restored only by the use of militia or British troops. Each confrontation was more deadly than the one before. The violence culminated in the great Saint John riot of 1849 when hundreds of Orangemen from the countryside joined hundreds from the city in an invasion of York Point. As the Loyalist minority hid in their basements, the assailants battled with guns, swords, and paving stones in the narrow streets of the ghetto. Hundreds were injured and at least a dozen died. The smell of tribalism abounded. Critics of popular sovereignty almost succeeded in having the civic charter revoked. As it was, control of the city police was taken from the Common Council and vested in a magistrate appointed by the lieutenant-governor.[13]

Similar problems were experienced in Prince Edward Island and Newfoundland. Communal disturbances on the Island usually occurred during elections. On the first of March 1847 a by-election was held at Belfast, Prince Edward Island. Most of the resident Tories of the constituency were Scottish Presbyterians. To bolster their position, the reform leaders imported a large number of Irish Catholics. The resulting riot, in which hundreds of men did battle, resulted in three deaths.[14] Irish ethnic violence was so common a feature of Newfoundland life by 1840 that British administrators viewed the colony as a kind of 'wild east' of the North American empire, a place that communal tensions made almost ungovernable. At the Conception Bay by-election in 1840, two Irish-Catholic candidates, one having the support of the clergy, opposed each other. Rioting at Carbonear grew day by day until, on the concluding of the poll, 8 December, seven people were shot and a magistrate had his skull fractured. It required a hundred soldiers from St John's to restore order.[15]

The growth and persistence of communal violence in the 1840s suggests both the tenuous and undigested nature of colonial society at midcentury and the ease with which the major concerns and traditions of the mother country were brought into the colonies by immigrants. In some very important ways there were no colonial societies even by the late 1840s. Geography, history, and culture all conspired against their development. Authority within the colonies was exercised by the state, but this state was the creature of Great Britain. Its ideal was the ideal of a hierarchical community led by gentlemen under the moral leadership of a state church, but this ideal had been under attack throughout most of the nineteenth century. For one thing the model was English, and most colonists were not English either by nativity or by tradition.

The institutions that most faithfully reflected the world-views of most colonists were the churches, and despite considerable effort, a majority – in some areas a very large majority – of the population had always refused to conform to the Church of England. The Anglican church was strong in the cities and very strong among the cultivated and politically influential classes, but it never held the support of more than a minority of the freeholders and artisanal and labouring classes of the countryside and towns. Much of this failure reflected the patterns of settlement. The Annapolis Valley had been settled by New England Congregationalists, most of whom eventually became Baptists. The north shore of Nova Scotia and much of Prince Edward Island were enclaves of Scots Presbyterians. A distinctive Scottish-Catholic community had developed in eastern Nova Scotia. The south shore of the Avalon Peninsula and many of the ports became centres of Irish Catholicism. And hovering on the Anglican flanks were the Wesleyan Methodists, always willing to draw converts into their search for perfectionism. In most areas of the region these other religious traditions provided the basis and sensibility for the local culture. All of them believed the Church of England had been given an unfair advantage by the government, which provided grants for Anglican buildings, maintained an Anglican monopoly of higher education, and ensured that the incumbents in most public positions would be Anglican. To add to Anglican problems, while a large proportion of Irish Protestants, particularly those of Orange background, were Anglican, they were 'low' Anglicans. During the 1840s the colonies were strongly influenced by the 'high' Anglican movement that was becoming more popular in England. The first Anglican bishop of New Brunswick, John Medley, was one of the new tractarians, much to the displeasure of the Anglican evangelicals, who rejected the exclusiveness and ecclesiastical authority claimed by the high-church party. The tractarians attempted to introduce many medieval practices and architectural forms into the life of the church in their search for a deeper spirituality. Using the authority of his office, Medley introduced many of these practices into New Brunswick, seriously dividing the church in the process.[16]

With its emphasis upon the necessity of personal change and its denial of ecclesiastical authority, evangelicalism made great strides at mid-century, particularly among the Baptists, Methodists, and Free Presbyterians. The Baptists were most successful in their efforts at making converts in New Brunswick and Nova Scotia, as were the Methodists in Newfoundland. As they grew in numbers and in confidence, the Protestant Dissenters and the Catholics became increasingly insistent that the Anglicans share the public offices and favours they enjoyed through the prerogative power of the lieutenant-governor. Some of the most bitter public debates were waged over the issue of the colleges. If a religious tradition was to provide public leaders it must have the institution in which to train an élite. Anglicanism already held this privileged position, and one by one the other traditions moved to create their own publicly funded educational institutions. Most started with academies, which soon developed into colleges. In 1838 the Baptists had acquired a charter for what would become Acadia University. In 1841 the Irish Catholics of Halifax chartered Saint Mary's, and in 1843 the Methodists established Mount Allison in New Brunswick.

While most colleges admitted students from all denominations, the academies inculcated the values and practices of their founding religious traditions. Able young people from moderately prosperous families within the communion were sent to these institutions, and eventually they became associated with the prominent families of the communion and provided part of a powerful network of identity. The fierceness of the debate and the power of religious identity is reflected in the 1840s in the creation of political parties in Nova Scotia. When the great reformer Joseph Howe attacked the notion of public support for Acadia in 1842 ('if we are to have a pope I would as soon have one at Rome as Horton'), the Conservative leader J.W. Johnston, a former Anglican evangelical who had converted to the Baptists, was able to lead most of the Baptist community into the Conservative Party in alliance with their traditional rivals, the Anglicans.[17] Waging war on the Baptists became a politically costly undertaking in New Brunswick and Nova Scotia, where by the 1840s the Baptists were the most rapidly growing evangelical tradition. The movement derived from the Calvinist New England Congregationalists of Nova Scotia, most of whom were drawn into a closed Baptist order by 1800, as well as from the influence of the late-eighteenth-century evangelist Henry Alline in the frontier settlements of New Brunswick. Originally viewed as an outcast and disreputable sect by the establishment, the regular Baptists became increasingly respectable and prosperous, expanding from their Nova Scotia bastion into the valleys of the St John and Petitcodiac. In New Brunswick, they were joined in the 1830s by the Free Christian disciples of Alline. By 1861, they comprised nearly one-fifth of the population of Nova Scotia and nearly one-quarter of that of New Brunswick.[18]

The 1840s also saw the emergence of a dynamic Roman Catholic church, whose leaders, inspired by a new ultramontane zeal, were determined to establish the primacy of the authority of the church.

Apart from the Scottish-Catholic settlements in Prince Edward Island and Antigonish, the Catholic presence in the region had been limited and uninfluential. Large-scale Irish migration occurred after 1820, but most Catholic parishes in the 1830s looked surprisingly like their Protestant neighbours. Many of the early Irish and Scottish Catholics were prosperous people who built and owned their churches, participated in Protestant services, intermarried with Protestants, and showed an unsettling tendency to challenge even the authority of the church when called to submit to its discipline. The missionary bishops of the 1840s worked to create a community that was distinctively Catholic. Unlike his more conciliatory predecessors, Newfoundland's Bishop Michael Fleming repeatedly challenged both the Anglican-dominated political establishment and the social élite of his own communion. Although he was an Irish nationalist who supported the repeal of the union of Ireland and England, Fleming's major concern was to create Catholic schools, ensure equality for Catholics, and clearly establish the paramount authority of the bishop within the Catholic community.[19] In New Brunswick, Bishop William Dollard eventually forced the Catholic social élite to submit to his authority and then negotiated with the government as the leader of a powerful religious community. Dollard named the Catholics who would be appointed as county and parish magistrates, and he was able to persuade the government to create the institutions necessary to fashion a Catholic community. The traditional parish élites lost their ownership of church property and their control over their priests.

The bishops were able to achieve a high degree of centralized control of their parishes by utilizing the prejudices of the poorer Irish-Catholic labourers arriving in the 1830s and 1840s, and by 1850 they had succeeded in stemming the integration of Catholics into the dominant Protestant communities that surrounded them. Their efforts were now bent to proselytizing the larger community and to the creation of a Catholic social order with institutions that paralleled but did not connect with those of the larger society. Inevitably, these communities would also be Irish, in the case of New Brunswick, Halifax, and Newfoundland, and Scottish in the case of Prince Edward island and eastern Nova Scotia. Although there were communities of Acadian Catholics in all the Maritime colonies, but especially New Brunswick, in the 1840s these were small, scattered, and uninfluential. They were in effect a double minority, possessing neither political nor religious influence.

Given the strength of religious traditions in the cultural life of the region, it is not surprising that the developing colonial educational systems were often shaped by them. The 1843 Newfoundland Education Act provided for separate Protestant and Catholic school boards in each district, all supported from public funds. The only teacher training in Nova Scotia was done at the Church of Scotland's Boulardarie School. Non-denominational teacher-training facilities were found only in New Brunswick, where the Fredericton and Saint John normal schools were established by the province in 1847 and 1848.[20]

Of the half million people who lived in the four Atlantic colonies in 1840, about one person in eight lived in the port cities of St John's, Saint John, or Halifax. Another one in eight lived in a dozen towns like Fredericton, Charlottetown, and Pictou. The overwhelming majority were found in the countryside or in the tiny settlement clusters that characterized the outports of Newfoundland and the rural villages that often consisted of little more than a general store. Even rural communities, however, were surprisingly diversified. Most contained professionals, artisans, and labourers capable of providing a variety of services and products for the people of the locality. Indeed, outside the cities, much of the commercial activity was carried on as barter and often involved quite complicated exchanges of goods and services.

Except in Newfoundland, where the fishery reigned supreme, most people lived on farms and derived a substantial part of their living from the produce of those farms. The term 'farmer' described a great range of social statuses and economic levels. Location, soil quality, size, capital assets, and personal qualities all determined the place a family occupied in the rural hierarchy. 'Farms' in 1840 ranged in value from £50 for a pioneer lot to £2,000 for the best-stocked interval land in a good location. Most farm families did not produce enough from their farms to provide a good standard of material well-being. Social critics of the period argued that farms were not as productive as they might be because farmers and farmers' sons were lured into non-farming activities. In fact, most rural labour moved rationally to receive the highest return for their time. Farm labourers in New Brunswick could make £20 a year and board in the 1840s. By contrast, a lumberman could earn £3.13.0 and board a month. Sailors and lumbermen shared common experiences and common expectations: they were generally the sons of farmers, fishermen, and craftsmen; they left home to work for good wages and opportunity; and they usually started work as young men and gave it up in early middle age.[21]

Towns normally provided still other opportunities. Although the towns failed in the early 1840s and wages fell significantly, skilled carpenters could make £2 a week when work was available, and if they were willing to follow work from place to place – and this was a common practice – they could normally enjoy a respectable livelihood and the expectation of eventually owning their own shop. In the town as in the country, the unskilled day labourers faced the bleakest future.

Forced to live in a developed market economy, they found their lot precarious at the best of times; in the depressions they often became a public charge, supported on outdoor relief and in church soup kitchens. The great majority of labourers present in 1840 were not living in the region by the end of the decade.

Opportunities for men narrowed in the 1840s; those for women, never extensive, became even more restrictive. Most adult women in 1840 were farm wives. Rural women married younger than their town counterparts and on average gave birth to more children. There were sharp demographic differences between areas of older and newer settlement. In frontier communities like Restigouche County in northern New Brunswick, males over sixteen outnumbered females by more than two to one. Young unmarried women gravitated to the towns in far greater numbers than men, since there were more opportunities there than in the countryside. Menial tasks, such as those performed by seamstresses and laundresses, provided employment. For those with some capital, the option of running a boarding-house or tavern was available. The most common women's work was that of live-in servant, a job that paid about £12 a year and board.[22] Women in the fifteen-to-thirty age group sometimes outnumbered men in the towns and cities by a ratio of three to two. In both urban and rural areas, respectable women could find careers as common school teachers, particularly after women were admitted to the New Brunswick Normal School in 1849.[23]

For most women, life revolved around the family, and their status and prospects were closely linked to those of their fathers. With marriage came the responsibility for a household. Farm women normally kept the dairy and made butter, cheese, and cloth. Irish and Acadian farm women often worked in the fields. In both rural and urban families, unmarried women frequently remained at home permanently and were sometimes provided for in their fathers' wills. Unlike their Canadian counterparts, Nova Scotia and New Brunswick women were able to escape from the worst kinds of marriages. The divorce laws of these colonies, enacted in 1758 and 1791, permitted divorce in a number of circumstances. Although their political rights were severely restricted, women from evangelical families were beginning to play a public role as proponents for legislation to restrict the sale of liquor.[24] A further reflection of the impact of depression was public concern over the growing incidence of infanticide. The penalties for concealment were extended by Nova Scotia and New Brunswick to include persons other than the mothers. The same colonies also extended the penalties for abortion. Before 1849, abortion performed before quickening did not fall under the criminal code; between 1849 and 1851 abortion at any point in a pregnancy became a criminal act.[25]

The 1840s were not kind to linguistic and racial minorities, who generally lived apart from the mainstream communities of the Atlantic colonies. The largest of these minorities was the Acadians, who were concentrated in several groupings in the three Maritime colonies. Their largest settlement was in the prosperous agricultural district of the Kent-Westmorland area of southeastern New Brunswick, where Acadians were sufficiently influential that in 1846 they were able to elect one of their own, Amand Landry, a Westmorland farmer, to the New Brunswick House of Assembly. They also had some modest success in participating in the public school system. In Nova Scotia, the 1841 Schools Act even permitted French-language schools a share of public monies. But these were small gains. Attempts to establish an Acadian college at Barachois failed. When the Roman Catholic diocese of New Brunswick was created in 1842, the francophone clergy failed to secure the appointment of a francophone bishop. Oddly enough, the most significant contribution to the Acadian cause in the 1840s was made by a Maine poet, Henry Wadsworth Longfellow, whose romantic tragedy *Evangeline* immortalized the Acadian Deportation throughout the English-speaking world. *Evangeline* was an immediate commercial success, passing through five editions in the year following its publication in 1847. It was translated into French in 1853, became known in Acadia in the 1860s, and contributed to the rise of the Acadian national movement.[26]

The impact of the depressions was even more severely felt among the non-European peoples of the region. Perhaps 3 per cent of the population of Nova Scotia and 2 per cent of that of New Brunswick was Black or aboriginal in 1840. The impact of the depression was most evident among Blacks in New Brunswick, who were concentrated in the urban centres. Despite a high birth rate, the number of Blacks in New Brunswick fell by nearly 40 per cent in the decade; Saint John lost 80 per cent of its Black population. The aboriginal population of New Brunswick and Nova Scotia declined equally dramatically, largely as a result of the devastation caused by disease. The 1,425 Micmacs of Nova Scotia, scattered in small groups across the colony, possessed about 22,000 acres of reserves in 1842; the 1,377 Micmacs and Maliseets of New Brunswick held 66,000 acres. Most Micmacs subsisted by hunting, selling crafts, and casual labour, although the Digby band prospered by hunting porpoises and making oil from the flesh.[27] The experience of the Native population of the two colonies was remarkably similar. Native leaders petitioned the Colonial Office for help, and the occasional sympathetic governor, like Sir William Colebrooke in New Brunswick, attempted to help them with proclamations ordering squatters off Native lands, and through attempts to persuade the colonial governments to provide welfare payments.

In its efforts to extricate itself from its larger North American responsibilities, the British government proved willing to support any colonial
proposal that would provide a final solution to the problems of the
aboriginal peoples. The suggestion offered by sympathetic colonists,
notably Joseph Howe in Nova Scotia and Moses Perley in New Brunswick, was to convert the Native reserves into European villages in
which each family would own land for agriculture and wood, and common grazing land would be provided. Each village would have a
school. Chiefs would retain some social position as militia captains.
Support would be given to assist Native families to acquire tools and
stock for farming. To finance these programs, all reserve lands not
needed for agriculture would be sold and the income invested in an
Indian fund. Indian acts were passed by both colonies, and Howe and
Perley were appointed commissioners to supervise the programs. Howe
succeeded in placing a number of families on 100-acre farms in the mid-
1840s, but most farms were wiped out in the potato blight, which, combined with an outbreak of diseases, reduced the Natives of Cape Breton
to starvation by 1850. The experiment was no more successful in New
Brunswick. By 1846, Perley realized that squatters were not being
ejected and that the auction sales of lands not needed for Native agriculture were raising little money; but his demands that the policy stop
were rejected by the Executive Council and resulted in his dismissal.[28]
Given the lack of interest of colonial assemblies in their welfare, Natives
were unlikely to view with enthusiasm colonial demands for greater
self-government.

Central to the study of the political culture and institutions of British
North America in the 1840s, has been the question of responsible government. In 1840, the members of the executive councils in British North
America were selected by the governor (with the consent of the Colonial
Office) and held office at the governor's pleasure; by 1850 in Canada,
Nova Scotia, and New Brunswick, the councils could hold office only
with the consent of the legislative assemblies of those colonies. Historians have traditionally viewed the 1840s as the great constitutional
watershed of the colonial era. The Canadian experience was seen as the
model for this transition, and the Maritime colonies were judged in
terms of their emulation of the Canadian experience. Coming out of the
Rebellion of 1837 and the Durham Report, Canadian responsible government was seen as a liberating experience finally accomplished when
the British government acceded to the popular will and permitted a
party of reformers to take control of the government. That party, with
power to initiate all money bills, now became master of the Assembly
and of the state.

The Canadian experience had produced relatively strong opposing groups of political parties, and Canadian reformers argued that it was not enough for the government to have the support of a majority of the members of the Assembly; the Executive Council must consist of the heads of all the leading departments of state and of members of a single party. Moreover, in the United Province of Canada after 1841, the power to initiate money bills – that is, to determine how tax money would be spent – rested with the government, a circumstance that increased the patronage under the control of the party in power, promoted cabinet solidarity, and soon accelerated the evolution of parties. The idea and implications of colonial responsible government, however, had not been fully worked out in the 1840s. All that seemed to be required for responsible government was for the Executive Council to have the support of a majority of Assembly members for their major policy initiatives.

In Nova Scotia, as in the other British American colonies, there was a tradition of antagonism between the social establishment centred on the capital and a number of interests that did not share in the benefits the state could confer. These might be called traditions of court and country, the former representing the more genteel, more urban, and usually Anglican interest, often holding office or influence because of family or birth; the latter, like the New England Baptists of the Annapolis Valley or the Scots Presbyterians of the north shore, often feeling alienated because of their social status or their economic position or simply their lack of influence with those who counted. During the 1830s, Joseph Howe had managed to focus the feelings of frustration and inferiority of the latter group, and by 1840 he had so much support in the Assembly that it passed a resolution calling for the removal of the lieutenant-governor. The man sent to Nova Scotia to achieve some workable arrangement was the new governor general of Canada, Lord Sydenham. His compromise was to form a government that would contain representatives of most major groups in the Assembly. This 'all party' government would emphasize the unity of the community and avoid the bitterness of a partisan system. In effect, the lieutenant-governor would play the roles of prime minister and monarch. Sydenham arrived in Nova Scotia in 1841 in an attempt to implement his system there and persuaded the moderate conservatives, led by J.W. Johnston, and the moderate reformers, led by Howe, to cooperate in the Assembly. The government was reorganized, and the new Executive Council included four reformers and five conservatives. This government managed the province until 1843, when Howe led three of the four reformers out of the coalition. The division of the government began over the question of Acadia University. Johnston was responsible for acquiring a charter for the Baptist university in 1842, but the following year Howe supported a proposal to strip the sectarian institutions of their funding and devote the money to the support of a single colonial university. Johnston retorted with an attack on the 'godless' reformers, and on Johnston's advice the lieutenant-governor, Lord Falkland, dissolved the Assembly. The 1843 election splintered the religious communities of the province, with the Baptists and Anglicans giving strong support to Johnston and his allies.[29] At the conclusion of the election, Falkland called Johnston's conservative brother-in-law to the Executive Council. Arguing that this was an unacceptable act of favouritism, the reformers left the government. By this point, however, Johnston had accepted the principle that the government could not survive without the support of a majority of the Assembly. In the ensuing debate in early 1844, his government was sustained by a slim majority.[30]

Free from the restraints of government, Howe indulged in a merciless campaign of ridicule against the lieutenant-governor and the members of the Executive Council. Johnston was able to hold power between 1844 and 1846, but the personal bitterness that inflamed public life in this period created strong party loyalties. Johnston's adept use of patronage to reward his followers drove the reformers (now commonly called Liberals) wild. Increasingly, those who did not support the Liberals were forced into the position of being partisan Tories. Party discipline became more and more important as the two evenly matched groups fought out their battles on the floor of the Assembly.

When the British Whigs came to power in 1846, the controversial Falkland was replaced by the conciliatory Sir John Harvey, who had successfully served as governor of Prince Edward Island, New Brunswick, and Newfoundland. Harvey confidently expected he could restore Sydenham's form of non-partisan responsible government in Nova Scotia. He failed. By 1846, no Liberal would consider any reconciliation with Johnston's administration. By 1846, too, the new British government had already begun to dismantle the imperial commercial system; the move to colonial self-government seemed inevitable and would relieve the British government of a number of responsibilities. In his famous dispatch of 31 March 1847, the secretary of state for the colonies, the third Earl Grey, directed Harvey to follow the advice of any party that had a majority in the Assembly.

The Assembly was dissolved in August 1847 and dissolution was followed by an unusually partisan election fought on the issues of patronage, Crown lands, salaries of officials, and religion. Catholic and Free Presbyterians rallied to the Liberals, and the support of Irish Catholics in Halifax assured a Liberal victory in the city. The Liberals now demanded all the spoils of victory. Grey wanted them to settle for majority control of the Executive Council; they insisted that all the Council and all the heads of government departments must be Liberals.

In the end, London conceded everything. Over the opposition of the Colonial Office, the provincial secretary (a senior civil servant who had held office for thirty-five years) was dismissed without pension. So too was the provincial treasurer. So too were more than 100 local magistrates who ran the county and parish administrations. They were replaced by 300 Liberal appointees.[31] Under pressure from the new government, the Colonial Office surrendered control of the Crown lands in return for an annual civil list, as they had in New Brunswick a decade earlier. W.S. MacNutt has argued that the shift in 1847–8 represented the triumph of a 'British system of party government over the more disorderly and antiquated American methods that had long been jealously guarded.'[32] The shift was even more extensive than that. With the growing strength of party discipline, the centre of political power moved from both the lieutenant-governor and the Assembly into the hands of the Executive Council, although so long as the government lacked the power to initiate money bills this transition would remain incomplete.

Professor MacNutt's description of the pre-1847 Nova Scotia government exactly describes the situation in New Brunswick throughout the 1840s. In New Brunswick, as in the other colonies, there had long existed divisions between 'court' and 'country,' but the centre of political conflict had been the vast revenues generated by the sale of Crown lands. The surrender of the Crown lands to the Assembly in 1837 meant that most important financial decisions were not made in the Executive Council but in the Appropriations Committee of the Assembly, where one representative from each county gathered to distribute most of the provincial revenue. The major concerns of the country representatives were for roads and other local public works, both to facilitate development and to provide some cash employment for hundreds and even thousands of farmers and urban labourers. Since these vital decisions were not taken by the government but by county representatives in the Assembly, the divisions between the Executive and the Assembly were muted, particularly under the mildly populist administration of Sir John Harvey, who included the most popular leaders in the Assembly in his Executive Council. There were men of reform temperament in the Assembly and even groups of assemblymen representing common interests, but in the main, members voted as individuals on each separate issue. Never in the 1840s was any faction able to control the votes of a significant body of legislators drawn from several counties consistently enough to be described as a party.

After Harvey was removed in 1841 for his failure to take a sufficiently belligerent attitude towards the United States in the Aroostook border dispute, his successor, Sir William Colebrooke, included three prominent assemblymen in his Council who could normally command the support of the Assembly. Like Falkland in Nova Scotia, Colebrooke had the misfortune to govern through much of the worst of the depression, and his attempts to cut expenditures on public works in the face of falling revenues created devastation in both rural and urban communities and fuelled bitter resentment of the imperial administration.[33] Divisions based on class, religion, ethnicity, and section emerged in the face of the commercial crisis. These were played out on the floor of the legislature. A producers' group of farmers, artisans, and manufacturers organized the Provincial Association in 1843 and fought successfully for colonial tariffs to protect New Brunswick products from the implications of British free-trade policies. The growing body of evangelical Dissenters demonstrated increasing impatience with the privileges of the Anglican establishment. The unpopularity of the Anglican establishment was reflected in the Assembly's determination to support the Methodist institution at Sackville and in the decision to end the Anglican monopoly of power at King's College, Fredericton, in 1845. The resentment against the official classes was reflected in populist demands for reducing the salaries of officers of the Crown and for efficiency and puritan simplicity in government. In the streets of the towns, Irish Protestants fought Irish Catholics, to the horror of most respectable native-born Protestants. All these influences were present in the 1843 and 1846 elections. While traditionalists kept control of the Assembly, Colebrooke found it expedient to reorganize his Executive Council in 1843 to include Lemuel Allan Wilmot, a protectionist, an opponent of Orangeism, a native-born Methodist, and one of the few proponents of responsible government in the Assembly. When Colebrook appointed his son-in-law as provincial secretary in 1844, Wilmot resigned on the principle that the office must go to a member of the Assembly. Wilmot's motion that the appointment was unconstitutional was barely defeated on a 18–15 vote in the Assembly. Although the Liberals were strengthened in the 1846 election, the traditionalists retained a clear majority. Protectionists forced modifications of the free-trade proposals of the colonial secretary by raising colonial tariffs against both British and foreign produce.[34]

Colebrooke's successor in 1848 was Sir Edmund Head. Faced with the British government's 1847 decision to concede responsible government, Head reconstituted the Executive Council so that it was composed of two Liberals, including Wilmot, and six traditionalists, including three permanent office-holders and two members of the Legislative Council. This hybrid Council had the support of the Assembly, which agreed to accept the principle of responsible government. Members of the Assembly would not, however, agree to surrender their right to initiate expenditures of public funds. The Assembly remained a brokerage where the needs of the various interests of the colony were mediated and the Executive Council only an embryonic cabinet dominated by no single party.

The political development of Prince Edward Island proceeded very differently from that of Nova Scotia and New Brunswick. The proprietorial system of the Island not only reduced most of the population to a tenantry but meant that no government possessed Crown lands for revenue or development. In a colony where at least two-thirds of farmers were tenants, the land issue dominated public life and provided the basis for a class-based party system. After 1838, the Assembly was controlled by the Escheat Party, which in 1839 prepared an act to confiscate all unsettled lands. That act was defeated in the Legislative Council, which was controlled by the representatives of the proprietors. The lieutenant-governor, Sir Charles FitzRoy, then unsuccessfully attempted to resolve the deadlock by having the British government lend the colonial government £200,000, which could be used to buy out the proprietors. In 1840, the Land Purchase Bill, under which the estates of those proprietors who had not fulfilled their obligations would be purchased and resold to the tenantry, was also rejected by the Legislative Council. Finally, in frustration, the Assembly in 1841 condemned the proprietors, the British government, and the Executive and Legislative councils of Prince Edward Island. It was a futile act and resulted in the refusal of the colonial secretary to consider any proposal to buy out the proprietors. Short of rebellion, the Escheat Party had no other role to fulfil.[35]

In November 1841, a new lieutenant-governor, Sir Henry Vere Huntley, was sent to the Island. Huntley supported the conservative establishment of the colony and, in the aftermath of the failure of the Escheaters, succeeded in winning a major victory in the general election of 1842. The establishment was controlled by a small group of interrelated patricians centred on the great officers of the Crown and a few proprietors, or their agents and merchants, who controlled the Legislative and Executive councils. Shortly after his victory, Huntley quarrelled with this élite over his salary. The governor's relationship with conservative speaker of the Assembly and executive councillor Joseph Pope was particularly unpleasant. Huntley disagreed with the spending policies of the Assembly and criticized them in public addresses. When Pope retaliated by attacking Huntley's behaviour in 1846, Huntley suspended him from the Executive Council.[36] In an abrupt about-face, Huntley abandoned the conservatives and threw his support behind a group of moderate reformers. The nature of the reform movement changed in the years following the 1842 defeat. While a body of radical Escheaters advocated change by violent means if necessary, most reformers accepted the view that change would have to be brought about gradually. Under the leadership of George Coles, a prosperous farmer-businessman, and Edward Whelan, the Irish publisher of *The Palladium* and the *Morning News*, gaining control of the Island's government through responsible government became their primary goal.

In the 1846 election, the Escheaters and reformers greatly increased their strength in the Assembly. They then demanded control of the Executive Council. Their enthusiastic ally, Huntley, appointed Coles to the Council in April 1847. As the sole reformer in the heartland of the traditional élite, Coles was very out of place. A compromise position was brought forward by a moderate conservative, John Longworth, who proposed that the Assembly should have the right to name four of the nine executive councillors. This position received considerable support in 1847, but became increasingly untenable as the reform position on responsible government hardened in the late 1840s.[37] The growing confrontation ended when the Colonial Office, at the request of the compact and over the objections of the Assembly, recalled Huntley. His successor followed the Colonial Office instructions not to grant responsible government. Coles, alone and isolated, resigned from the Executive Council in 1848. So long as the salaries of the Island's executive officers were paid out of a grant voted by the British Parliament, the Assembly had little bargaining power, but in 1849, as part of its dismantling of the imperial system, the Colonial Office cut the parliamentary grant to the Island and asked the colony to assume the cost of the civil list. The Assembly refused unless at least four members from the majority party in the Assembly were appointed to the Executive Council. Conditional responsible government – in that the Island government was specifically denied the authority to interfere with the rights of private property – was finally granted in 1851.

Representative government in Newfoundland was less than a decade old in 1840, and the intervening period had been marked by bitter class, ethnic, and religious strife. The major division was between the Irish Catholics, under Bishop Fleming and John Kent, and the English Anglicans, who included virtually the entire mercantile, office-holding and professional élite of the colony. The complete dependence of the island on the fishery and the extraordinary influence of the merchant intermediaries in that trade created a society that was much more highly polarized than any other in the region. The considerable social and geographic distance between the commercial and administrative centre of St John's and the scattered fishing outports created a strong court-country tradition that added to other tensions. Such marked social distinctions produced a breeding ground for strong partisan sensibilities. Reformers drew the support of the great majority of the Irish Catholics of the colony and the fervent support of their bishop. They also had the support of the Protestant Dissenters – mostly Methodists – from the outports. Since the population was quite evenly balanced between Catholics and Protestants, this alliance generally ensured a reform majority in the Assembly. In areas where Catholic and Protestant reformers were found together, the tradition was to alternate Assembly membership between the two groups. In the early 1840s, however, Catholic leaders showed less of a willingness to share these offices, and the reform party in the Assembly increasingly became a Catholic party.[38]

By 1840, the bitterness within the Assembly and the stalemate between the Assembly and the Legislative Council reached the point where the lieutenant-governor, Capt. Henry Prescott, refused to summon the Assembly and, following a series of violent confrontations in 1840, refused to call an election. Instead he carried on a personal government operating on warrants issued without the authority of the Assembly. In the autumn of 1841, the British government suspended the constitution and decided to embark upon a constitutional experiment. In the 1842 Newfoundland Bill, the new legislature consisted of a single body containing twenty-five members, fifteen of whom were elected and ten appointed by the lieutenant-governor. The lieutenant-governor was also given power to initiate financial measures in the legislature. Responsibility for making the new constitution work was given to the new governor, Sir John Harvey, that capable, supple Whig who had managed to bring peace to New Brunswick during his previous term. Harvey worked carefully to conciliate the various interests in the colony. Although an Anglican, he actively courted the Catholic bishop and the Protestant Dissenters. He persuaded Bishop Fleming to withdraw from politics in return for a promise to allow Catholics a share in power and in patronage. He shared available school funds among Catholics, Anglicans, and Protestant Dissenters. He tried but failed, in the face of Anglican opposition, to secure public support for all church construction and for non-sectarian higher education. He encouraged the creation of a Newfoundland yeomanry and contributed to the development of a third political force composed of native-born small merchants and clerks. Harvey supported the Natives Society and a culture based on the twin pillars of Newfoundland respectability and allegiance to the British constitution. His Executive Council was composed of Protestants and Catholics, reformers and conservatives. He even had considerable support among the merchant élite, whose economic policies he espoused.[39] Under Harvey's direction, the new system brought a measure of political stability to the colony. It was made possible, however, only by the fact that between 1841 and 1846 Newfoundland, unlike the other Atlantic colonies, enjoyed a period of relative prosperity.[40]

Harvey's Newfoundland sojourn was only a tranquil break in an otherwise tempestuous period. The Newfoundland Act expired in 1846, and the Liberals, demanding responsible government, opposed its renewal. Harvey's term expired; a great fire destroyed two-thirds of the city of St John's; and the potato blight began. Harvey's last act was to recommend a return to the 1832 constitution but without the grant of responsible government. The older constitution was re-established in 1847, but despite the demands of the Liberals, responsible government was not considered for another decade. The popular element in the state could control supply, but government remained in the hands of the governor and through him the Colonial Office in London.

The grant of responsible government to Nova Scotia and New Brunswick in the 1840s was a logical and perhaps necessary part of the devolution of imperial responsibilities between 1842 and 1849. Outside Newfoundland, public demands for it seem to have arisen from a growing sense of frustration and abandonment as the commercial impact of the British 'betrayal' of the loyal colonies became more and more evident. The feelings of betrayal and the searching for an economic alternative are evident in the discussions over railways. The railway was the new technological god that spelled progress and improvement to mid-nineteenth-century minds. Railway construction would stimulate the stalled colonial economies; railway links would revolutionize the trade of the region and open up the hitherto inaccessible resources of land and timber and coal. Nova Scotia and New Brunswick first moved in this direction in 1846, the year of the British decision to abandon imperial preference. The legislatures of the two colonies petitioned the Queen to construct a railway between Halifax and Quebec. A study undertaken for the British government recommended that the line be constructed along the north shore of New Brunswick as far as possible from the American border, since even after the Webster-Ashburton Treaty of 1842 resolved the Maine–New Brunswick boundary dispute, the British continued to distrust the United States. But such a route was far from the populous centres of the colony in the St John Valley. Construction costs were estimated at £3 million. The report was presented in 1848 at the bottom of the second depression. The legislators demanded that the British government bear these costs in compensation for their commercial abandonment of the colonies. London declined. In Nova Scotia, the new Liberal government of Uniacke and Howe persuaded the legislature to pledge £330,000 of public money to construct the line between Windsor and Halifax. In New Brunswick, the Assembly divided sectionally between a line along the north shore or one from Saint John to Shediac, although guarantees to the competing proposals rivalled those of Nova Scotia in terms of capital costs.[41]

The feelings of betrayal in Nova Scotia and New Brunswick were supplemented by the very real concern to find alternative markets for colonial produce. As the value of exports and imports plunged, as agricultural failure continued, as emigration of the native-born rose, as social violence increased, and as the burden of providing for the famine refugees grew heavier, colonial leaders sought a new destiny. In desperation many of the most loyal elements of the population repudiated the British views that had been central to their sense of national identity. In Saint John, as in Canada, there were calls for annexation to the United States, although most spokesmen drew back from a solution as radical as this.

Representatives of Canada, New Brunswick, and Nova Scotia met in Halifax to seek a solution to their common problems. The problem from the Maritimes' view was that, after 1849, their ports would be open to American ships and American produce, but Maritime vessels could not carry on the American coasting trade and American produce continued to be protected. The solution was mutual reciprocity with the United States. New Brunswick was prepared to offer its fisheries to the Americans to achieve this. Nova Scotia would not make this concession. The meeting came to nothing. In the end, even the Canadians would not enter a free-trade agreement with the Maritime colonies, on the grounds that Maritime manufactures would drive Canadian manufacturers to the wall. Even Prince Edward Island would not sanction free intercolonial trade. By 1850, the only accommodation reached was a free-trade agreement between New Brunswick and Nova Scotia. So ended the decade of the 1840s in the North Atlantic colonies of Great Britain. The anxiety and uncertainty that had characterized the decade for most colonists continued as a persistent concern to the end. The larger colonies had achieved a large degree of local self-control, but the cost had been an end to the economic security that the paternalism of the old empire had assured.

CHAPTER FIFTEEN

The 1850s
Maturity and Reform

IAN ROSS ROBERTSON

The 1850s was the decade in which the three remaining Atlantic colonies won responsible government, and it marked the high tide of reform movements within the region. Reformers, despite significant blind spots, had much to be proud of: extension of the franchise, increases in educational opportunities, removal of denominational privilege, and the tackling of such long-standing problems as the Prince Edward Island land question. The economies of the Maritime colonies were also attaining their full dimensions of development in the pre-Confederation period. The middle decades of the nineteenth century have often been referred to as a 'golden age' for the Maritimes, and by quantifiable measures the region was indeed reaching new peaks. One indicator was substantially increased population. Between 1851 and 1861 population grew 19.5 per cent in Nova Scotia to 330,900 and 30 per cent in New Brunswick to 252,000; between 1848 and 1861 (there was no Prince Edward Island census for 1851) Prince Edward Island experienced 29.2 per cent growth for a new total of 80,900.[1] The two mainland colonies were beginning to look inland to the continent with their increasing commitments to railway development. If any decade in Maritime history qualified as a 'golden age,' it was the 1850s; and Newfoundland shared in some of the trends.

Growth in shipowning was especially impressive. As Eric W. Sager and Lewis R. Fischer have observed, 'In the three decades after 1850, the fleets of the Atlantic provinces grew rapidly and almost continuously.'[2] The carrying capacity of ships was on the increase: during the 1850s in eight major ports the total tonnage on registry of ships under 250 tons rose slowly, while the registered tonnage of ships with greater capacity more than doubled. Improved construction brought the average life of a vessel in the six leading Nova Scotia and New Brunswick ports to 12.1

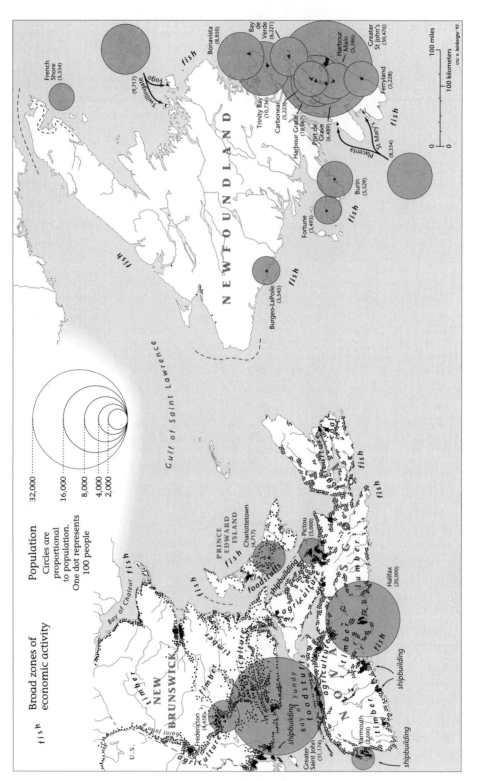

The Atlantic region c. 1850

Population

Circles are proportional to population. One dot represents 100 people

32,000
16,000
8,000
4,000
2,000

Broad zones of economic activity

fish

NEW BRUNSWICK

Greater Saint John (31,174)
Fredericton (4,458)

U.S.

Bay of Chaleur   fish

timber

agriculture

Bay of Fundy   foodstuffs   shipbuilding

Yarmouth (2,600)

shipbuilding

PRINCE EDWARD ISLAND
Charlottetown (4,717)

fish

foodstuffs

shipbuilding

Pictou (3,000)

NOVA SCOTIA

agriculture

timber   lumber

Halifax (20,000)

fish

shipbuilding

agriculture

Gulf of Saint Lawrence

NEWFOUNDLAND

fish

fish

Burgeo-LaPoile (3,545)

fish

Fortune (3,493)

Burin (5,529)

fish

Placenta (8,334)

St Mary's

Ferryland (5,228)

fish

Greater St John's (30,476)

Harbour Main (5,386)

Port de Grave (6,489)

Harbour Grace (10,867)

Carbonear (5,223)

Trinity Bay (10,736)

Bay de Verde (6,221)

Bonavista (8,850)

fish

Twillingate (9,717)

Fogo

French Shore (3,334)

fish

100 miles
100 kilometers

0

eric e. leinberger '93

years, a dramatic 17.5 per cent advance over the 10.3-year average for ships built in the 1840s.[3] Longer life and greater sizes meant more passages, more and larger cargoes carried, and increased profitability.

The boom in shipowning during the third quarter of the nineteenth century was based on an already well-established regional ship*building* industry. In some cases, the owners were the shipbuilders themselves, but most new tonnage in the seven leading Maritime ports (Charlottetown, Halifax, Miramichi, Pictou, Saint John, Windsor, and Yarmouth) was registered by persons identified as 'merchants.' Typically, the merchant-shipowner was the head of a family business concern who found that owning his own tonnage was both a competitive advantage in his ordinary commercial dealings (procuring imports, exporting staples, and transporting commodities between major colonial ports and outports) and profitable in itself. He frequently had practical experience at sea and knew exactly what he wanted in a vessel; hence, especially after mid-century, ships were often built on contract to local merchant-shipowners.[4]

Although the shipbuilding industry fluctuated with the business cycle, the sale of ships was a significant source of export earnings. The United Kingdom was a particularly important market: of all new tonnage registered during the 1850s in Saint John and Charlottetown, 76 per cent and 70 per cent, respectively, would eventually be transferred to Great Britain and Ireland. Together, Saint John and Charlottetown accounted for 70.5 per cent of the tonnage relocated from the seven principal Maritime ports to the United Kingdom.[5] The average age of Nova Scotia and New Brunswick ships at the time of sale was 4.1 years, and thus the owners tended to get significant use out of them before selling. In Prince Edward Island, the pattern was different: the average age at time of sale was only 1.97 years, a fact that, combined with the high proportion of Island vessels sold (81.2 per cent when non-United Kingdom destinations are included), resulted in a negative annual growth rate of tonnage on registry at Charlottetown from 1850 through 1859.[6]

Of the Maritime colonies, Nova Scotia had the most diversified economy, with shipbuilding, shipping services, fishing, and coal mining all forming solid sectors of the economy. Shipowning was particularly important, and throughout the decade Nova Scotia, with several significant shipowning ports, had far more tonnage than New Brunswick and Prince Edward Island combined, and more than twice as many ships on register.[7] Agriculture was the weak link in the Nova Scotia economy, and in fact the colony had lacked self-sufficiency in food since the expulsion of the Acadians in the 1750s. According to Julian Gwyn and Fazley Siddiq, farmers were in economic decline during the final decades of the colonial era, despite more than a generation of preaching on the need for improvement in agricultural technique. Research by other scholars reinforces the image of pervasive rural poverty and indicates that, at least in eastern Nova Scotia, where Gwyn and Siddiq describe the decrease in wealth among farmers as 'disastrous,' farmers often counteracted the insufficient productivity of their holdings by selling their labour-power, primarily but not exclusively in agriculture, the timber trade, and shipyards. Gwyn and Siddiq emphasize the poverty of many other Nova Scotians, especially fishermen, in the middle decades of the nineteenth century, and also argue that the benefits of expanded economic opportunities in the final decades of the colonial era accrued largely to the élite, especially in the area of Halifax. In fact, they contend that the 1851–71 era witnessed a significant increase in the concentration of wealth in the hands of the richest 5 per cent of the population and, overall, 'a clear trend towards greater inequality.'[8]

Nevertheless, Nova Scotia exports grew through most of the decade, almost tripling between 1850 and 1857. After the international depression that commenced in 1857, there was a decrease, but even in 1860 exports were approximately 2.5 times the value they had been in 1850. New Brunswick's economic situation was much less secure. The decline in total New Brunswick export values began after 1854, and the level of that year would not be reached again until 1866; in forest products, the former mainstay of the economy, the descent was especially dramatic, and in 1860 the value of forestry exports stood at approximately 66 per cent of the 1854 level. Timber prices reached a post-1830s peak in 1853 and followed an unrelenting downward path for the rest of the decade.[9] In contrast, Prince Edward Island's trading figures gave much cause for optimism at the end of the decade. The annual growth rate of visible exports for the period 1850–9 was 11.5 per cent, and in both 1850 and 1860 the Island was a net exporter when sales of ships are counted.[10] Moreover, the colony was becoming proportionally less dependent on ship sales, for in the years 1850, 1855, and 1860, these accounted for approximately 52, 31, and 20 per cent of exports, respectively.[11]

One reason for the diversification of Island exports in the second half of the 1850s was the Reciprocity Treaty of 1854, by which the United States and the British North American colonies agreed to free exchange of natural products. The increasing importance of the United States for the Maritimes is apparent from comparisons of exports going there in 1853, the year before the treaty, and in 1860. The overall percentage increase in Maritime exports to the United States was 82.3, but the proportional impact varied enormously from colony to colony.[12] One way of measuring the *growth in relative dependence on the American market* is to take the difference in percentage of exports destined for the United

States for the period 1853–60 as a proportion of the 1853 percentage; or, to put it another way, taking the 1853 percentage in each colony as 100, what level of increase does the 1860 percentage represent? For Nova Scotia, the proportional increase was 30.6 per cent (from 25.8 to 33.7 per cent), for Prince Edward Island 83.9 (from 21.1 to 38.8 per cent), and for struggling New Brunswick 137.7 (from 11.4 to 27.1 per cent).[13] Looking at the Maritime colonies from this perspective, New Brunswick may have been the likeliest to infer that still greater links with the United States would be its best hope for the future – particularly since it was the only one with a negative annual growth rate of exports (to all destinations) for the decade.[14]

Saint John was the largest city in the region, despite its lack of the built-in advantages of being a colonial capital. In fact, within British North America as a whole, only Montreal and Quebec City had larger populations in 1851 than the 31,174 of Saint John and Portland.[15] Positioned at the mouth of the St John River, the city dominated the commerce of the river valley, its tributaries, and the Bay of Fundy counties of both New Brunswick and Nova Scotia. T.W. Acheson estimates that its hinterland had more than 300,000 inhabitants – more than one-half of the entire population of the mainland colonies – by the end of the 1850s. Saint John was the biggest shipbuilding centre in the Maritime region and one of the leading shipowning ports in the world. It also contained a number of artisan-oriented manufacturing industries and, at the 1861 census, of 4,000 artisans in Saint John and Portland, 3,000 were in non-shipbuilding trades. In the second half of the 1850s there appeared to be a trend away from reliance on shipbuilding: the total new tonnage built was 21.1 per cent less than in the first half.[16] Having originated as an offshoot of the timber trade, Saint John's shipbuilding industry was beginning to show signs of a parallel decline.

Halifax was no match for Saint John economically. It was never a major shipbuilding centre, and over the period for which we have comparable figures on shipowning, it had less than one-third of Saint John's tonnage on registry. Its shipping was primarily involved in fishing, the coastal trades, the West Indies trades, and the business of 'commission merchant,' taking and filling orders for specific goods in Nova Scotia and elsewhere.[17] Halifax did not dominate the Nova Scotia hinterland, and partially this reflected the tyranny of location: built in 1749 for the strategic importance of its harbours, it lacked a productive adjacent agricultural hinterland and had no other exploitable resources nearby. For this reason or others, the city was not destined to make its mark through leading the industrialization of its province. There seemed to be a conservatism among its moneyed class. Writer Thomas Chandler Haliburton had criticized the relative lack of Haligonian hustle – using

Saint John as a regional counter-example of enterprise – many years earlier, but in the 1850s the same case could be made. Native Nova Scotian Abraham Gesner went to New York to find business backing for making kerosene into a mass-production commodity. Among the reasons, as well as an adverse result in a New Brunswick lawsuit, was lack of interest among Halifax capitalists.[18]

Halifax conservatism relative to Saint John showed in other ways: for example, trade unions had been virtually outlawed in Nova Scotia from 1816 until 1851, three years after the reformers took office, and in 1864 a conservative government would pass legislation all but outlawing strikes. In contrast, at mid-century industrial Saint John was the trade-union capital of the British North American colonies. No fewer than thirteen unions and more than 2,000 workers participated in a public procession in 1853. The success, aggressiveness, and public visibility of the movement in Saint John were unparalleled elsewhere. Centred at the waterfront, the union movement thrived on the wealth of the shipbuilding industry; the demonstrators in 1853 included shipwrights from sixteen different shipyards. Builders anxious to keep the shipyards working were willing to bargain with unions and pay good wages. The union movement even had spectacular success in organizing a relatively unskilled group, the longshoremen. Effective organization of this group in nineteenth-century British North America was unusual; Halifax longshoremen, for example, did not enjoy the success of their Saint John counterparts. Part of the explanation lies in the more specialized work performed in Saint John, for specialization provides a greater opportunity to organize. But the Nova Scotia capital also was not a shipbuilding centre on the scale of Saint John and therefore lacked a manufacturing base in which a vigorous trade-union movement might be grounded.[19]

Both mainland colonies were actively engaged in the construction of railway lines in the 1850s. The reform government of Nova Scotia commenced railway construction in 1853; it did so under public ownership, in large measure because of Joseph Howe's commitment to the policy and his willingness to defend it in the face of strong opposition. The immediate objectives were to link Halifax to Windsor, on the Bay of Fundy, and to Truro, from which a branch line could be built to Pictou. In New Brunswick, construction of a railway connecting Saint John and the Northumberland Strait – the European and North American Railway, a name symbolizing its grandiose hopes – began at the end of 1854. Construction on another New Brunswick railway, aiming to join St Andrews and Woodstock, had commenced in 1847 and continued intermittently for a decade before the first stretch of thirty-four miles was opened. The building of two unrelated lines pointing in different directions revealed the regional divisions within the colony.[20]

The new Maritime railway lines of the 1850s were constructed in the context of hopes for realization of a much larger project, a rail link to the Province of Canada often referred to as 'an intercolonial railway.' The rationale was commercial, for business interests in the Maritimes wanted an overland connection between their major ports and the continental interior to complement their ocean-going trade. The St Andrews–Woodstock line was a reduced version of what was to have been the first intercolonial rail link and was built along part of the projected path; but a territorial dispute with the United States had stalled the grander plan, and in 1842 the awarding to the Americans of territory through which the line was to pass had, along with other considerations, rendered it unfeasible. The British government commissioned a survey of potential routes in the late 1840s, and Gene Allen has argued that its insistence then on a terminus in Nova Scotia, which was never reversed, was 'the single most important decision about the route.' He points out that 'a railway that reached [Halifax] via Saint John or St Andrews would be longer than a central line through New Brunswick and about as long as one near the Gulf [of St Lawrence]. Many subsequent claims on behalf of a so-called "short" line to Saint John ignored this basic fact.' Acceptance of a British veto over the route was the price of an imperial loan guarantee that would reduce interest costs sufficiently to enable the colonies to build twelve miles of railway for the same annual cost as seven if relying only on colonial credit. Regional differences over the route to take to Halifax and the division of costs meant that the broader plan was not realized during the 1850s; a breakdown in negotiations in 1852 led directly to the commencement of work on local lines. The divergence over sharing costs was crucial. In arguing for British participation in the financing, colonists often made their case on military and political grounds; but the primary motive of Maritime businessmen and politicians was economic, and many wanted an intercolonial railway that would also link up, via a second line, with the United States to tap American as well as Canadian trade.[21]

Construction of the local lines certainly did not mean that Nova Scotia and New Brunswick were turning their backs on the idea of an intercolonial railway, and indeed these early lines whetted the appetites of areas not touched by the rails. Since the financial resources of the two colonies, and particularly those of New Brunswick, were stretched by the end of the 1850s, the intercolonial project represented the best way to realize these hopes. Taken as a group, Maritime railway schemes, realized and unrealized, demonstrate that the economic and political strategists of the region were not wedded exclusively to oceanic wood, wind, and sail technologies but were anxious to profit from the emerging industrial revolution and were committing themselves to the most modern land-based transportation technology of the period, the railway. One vital mineral resource of the early industrial era was coal, and in 1858 Nova Scotia, with an abundance of coal, terminated the virtual monopoly of the British-owned General Mining Association over the minerals of the colony, thus asserting its vital stake in its own economic development.

In politics during the decade, reform movements were able to focus their energies on efforts to put their panaceas into practice after long years of agitation. The reform parties of New Brunswick and Prince Edward Island – and also Newfoundland – came to power for the first time in the 1850s and remained there for most of the decade, although in Nova Scotia and Prince Edward Island they eventually foundered on disputes revolving around sectarianism. In New Brunswick, the conservatives were able to profit in 1856 from an ill-fated attempt to ban alcohol, but the reformers returned to office a year later. As the decade closed, reformers remained in power or were about to return to power in all colonies except Prince Edward Island. In Nova Scotia the conservatives hung on to office until the Assembly met early in 1860, despite the victory of the reformers at the election of 12 May 1859.[22]

Nova Scotia may have had the most moderate reform movement of the era. In 1851, the legislature repealed the law banning trade unions, revoked the 1758 statute that had made the Church of England the established church of the colony, and withdrew the preferential grant from King's College. In fact, although both measures regarding Anglicanism were important symbolically, the Anglican bishop of Nova Scotia, Hibbert Binney, had told the lieutenant-governor that church establishment had been 'practically ignored,' and therefore disestablishment would make little difference; and King's continued to receive funds at the same level as other denominational colleges.[23] Once Nova Scotians had responsible government, life in most respects could go on much as before.

The Nova Scotia of the 1850s was a relatively prosperous and sophisticated colony. Its economic diversity made it less vulnerable than New Brunswick and Newfoundland to cyclical fluctuations in international commodity markets and to changing economic patterns. This relative economic stability led to a sense of security that in turn nurtured self-confidence and faith in the future, at least among the comparatively privileged. Higher education had proceeded more rapidly in Nova Scotia than elsewhere in the region; by the 1850s the colony had five institutions of higher learning: King's, Dalhousie, Acadia, Saint Mary's, and St Francis Xavier. In Haliburton, Nova Scotia also had the only literary figure in all the British North American colonies to attain an international reputation. A born-and-bred member of the local élite who had an ambiguous and somewhat uneasy relationship with the rest of the colonial community, he had brought recognition to his native colony with his satiric works focusing on local themes and, while many might have been reluctant to admit it, had fuelled local pride. Haliburton – a thorough local patriot – had been inspired to broach local topics in a literary way by another Nova Scotia writer who has since become recognized as the founder of English-Canadian literature, Thomas McCulloch. Although he died seven years before mid-century, McCulloch's exceptional legacy endured not only in literature but in education, respect for learning, and pride in local achievement. One of his students at the Pictou Academy, J. William Dawson, became the first superintendent of Nova Scotia schools in 1850 and gained an international reputation as a geological researcher. In 1855, Dawson was appointed principal of McGill University in Montreal, where he would be the longest-serving and most important chief academic officer in the history of the institution.[24]

Several other individual Nova Scotians emerged as figures with claims to international renown in the 1850s. Gesner invented kerosene, which would become the standard lighting fuel in homes around the developed world. William Fenwick Williams won fame through his gallant but unsuccessful defence of the Turkish town of Kars in 1855 during the Crimean War. Two years later, in the course of the Indian Mutiny, William Hall became the first Black and the first member of the Royal Navy to win the Victoria Cross for bravery. Those three, all born in the Annapolis Valley, joined Haliburton, Dawson, Howe, Enos Collins, and Samuel Cunard as native Nova Scotians who could match the best of what British North America and indeed the English-speaking world as a whole could offer. There was an intense sense of local pride in Nova Scotia in the 1850s, and by 1854 this consciousness of local achievement had resulted in a provincial exhibition displaying the products of local industry, agriculture, and the arts. The exhibitors numbered 1,260, and the exhibits 3,010. In 1857, a resolution moved by Howe, then in opposition, and seconded by Premier J.W. Johnston, led to the appointment of a provincial archivist; no other province would appoint such an officer until 1903.[25]

Yet deep divisions in Nova Scotia society became politically visible during the Crimean War. That struggle evoked ardent declarations and symbolic gestures of loyalty among many colonials, but some Roman Catholics of Irish origin were obviously disaffected from the British war effort because of their hostility to British rule in Ireland; the Halifax *Catholic* newspaper even attributed British military reverses to divine retribution. Conflicting views over the relationship of Ireland and England combined with the question of loyalty in wartime to result in a series of denominational and ethnic disputes that led to the breakup of the reform government in 1857, and the conservatives entered office under the leadership of Johnston. In the election campaign of 1859 the liberals called the government 'Romo-Johnstonites' and the latter replied with the term 'Proscriptionists.' Even Howe, in private correspondence, argued the need 'to control the Papists in this country.'[26] Politically, it was an inglorious end to Nova Scotia's final complete decade as an autonomous British colony.

Just as the timber trade and its offshoot, shipbuilding, had moulded the trade-union movement in Saint John, it had given the political development of New Brunswick a peculiar twist. Responsible government had come in a series of at least three stages: 1837 (effective power of the purse), 1848 (the principle of ministerial responsibility), and 1854 (the testing of the principle that brought to power the first undiluted reform ministry). Different historians emphasize different dates; yet there is no doubt that the process was distinctive to New Brunswick and cannot be explained without reference to the influence of the timber trade.[27] The political parties that emerged proved somewhat unorthodox and unusually fragile by British North American standards.

The major political controversy in New Brunswick during the middle years of the decade concerned legislation prohibiting the manufacture and sale of alcoholic beverages. Society had a raw edge in New Brunswick, a fact that could be traced in part to the influence of the mores of the timber trade. Those who doubt the connections should ponder the example of Peter Mitchell, shipbuilder, lawyer, and lumber entrepreneur in the Miramichi area, who 'carried a pistol for protection and quantities of rum for his supporters' when contesting the election of 1856 in opposition to prohibition.[28] The excessive drinking associated in the popular mind with the trade, and the violence that sometimes resulted, had been factors leading to the prohibitionist campaign, which has been described as the first mass movement in New Brunswick history, a social mobilization that cut across the sex, class, ethnic, and religious lines in the colony. Broader, more universal considerations had also played a role in creating fertile ground for the movement. Samuel Leonard Tilley, the politician most closely associated with this cause, had in early life witnessed personally the results of an especially bloody murder of a parent by a drunken spouse wielding a butcher's knife. In 1855 a majority of assemblymen passed a prohibitory law originating in a private member's bill that Tilley, the provincial secretary, had introduced. The lieutenant-governor, John Manners-Sutton, thought the legislation unwise, and by the following year disruption of provincial revenues and flagrant violations of the law prompted him to schedule a new general election on his own initiative; this led to the resignation of his constitutional advisers. The conservative government that took over triumphed at the polls despite being abused by their opponents as 'Rummies,' and repealed the legislation. In 1857 a new election returned to office the reformers (called 'Smashers' by the 'Rummies'); they took their revenge on the errant governor by ignoring him as much as possible and doing what they could to harass him.[29]

According to C.M. Wallace, the government formed in 1854 and led by Charles Fisher 'ranks with the best in the history of the province.' Politicians who distrusted privilege, in their first year in office they repealed church establishment; and in 1859, after much deliberation, they converted the Anglican King's College in Fredericton into the non-sectarian University of New Brunswick. They also reduced the powers of the Legislative Council, broadened the franchise, and introduced the ballot. The previous decade had featured large-scale violence between gangs linked to rival timber entrepreneurs, and also lethal ethnoreligious rioting on a major scale in Saint John in 1849.[30] These elements in New Brunswick politics became much less pronounced in the 1850s, and one is tempted to refer to a political maturing. Yet politics remained highly regionalized, reflecting the fragmented nature of the colony, whose Fundy shore and 'north shore'[31] had little contact with each other; the partisan divisions were never as clear as elsewhere in the Atlantic region, a fact that probably made it easier for Manners-Sutton to execute his putsch against the reformers in 1856. Party struggles had been confused by the unique impact of the timber trade and the prohibition battle, and ideological linkages to party names were less significant than elsewhere. The regionalism of New Brunswick made it difficult to govern as a coherent whole and had ethnic dimensions that deepened the divisions and made accommodation even more difficult.

Politics had purpose in Prince Edward Island in the 1850s, but a logic entirely distinct from that of public life on the mainland. In 1851 the reform party of George Coles and Edward Whelan took office with a program of democratization centred on the land question. Most of the Island remained in the grip of leasehold tenure, with the majority of large landlords residing in Great Britain. The prime beneficiaries of the system were the local agents of the absentees. In many cases the overseas owners chose agents because of their prominence on the Island, in the hope that at least they would exercise influence to protect their employers from the predatory behaviour of the colonial élite. This strategy did not often work, since the absentee proprietors were usually unable to find agents who combined sufficient competence, trustworthiness, and dedication. Some owners gave up and sold out to their agents; in the 1850s examples of such absentees were the Mann family in the United States and Sir George Seymour in England, who sold their lands to their agents, James C. Pope and James Yeo, Sr. Two overseas proprietors who showed no inclination to sell were Lady Cecilia Georgiana Fane and Maria Matilda Fanning, unmarried females who exhibited much intelligence and force of character. With their Island properties, Fane and Fanning – residing in London and Bath – probably wielded more power than any women in the region.

The reform party was committed to abolition of leasehold tenure. It faced the opposition of more than the absentees, since the agents were at least as opposed to abolition as were their employers; in the event of extinguishment of proprietary titles through purchase, the owners would be compensated, but the agents would lose a lucrative source of income and – although they would never volunteer this motive – unimpeded access to timber valuable for shipbuilding on their employers' lands. Both Pope and Yeo were major shipbuilders, and much evidence suggests that they took their timber at will where they found it. The resident owners, some of whom had been agents, were also unsympathetic to abolition. Nothing in the record suggests that resident owners enjoyed better relations with tenants and squatters than did absentees. Indeed, in 1851 the only recorded premeditated shooting of a person involving the land question occurred when individuals thought to be aggrieved tenants ambushed and wounded a resident owner known for short leases, high rents, and willingness to evict.[32]

The reformers approached the problems of the Island with the most far-reaching agenda of any reform government in the region. In 1852 they passed a Free Education Act that provided for payment of the entire salaries of district schoolteachers by the colonial treasury. The immediate result was a dramatic increase in the number of children attending school. The Island was the first in the Maritime region to take this measure, preceding Nova Scotia by twelve years and New Brunswick by nineteen. Coles stated that the colony was 'the first place in the British dominions, in which a complete system of free education was established.'[33] The only plausible explanation for such an initiative in an overwhelmingly rural colony is the unique circumstances created by the land question, which placed exceptional emphasis upon written contracts. Since settlement often preceded – by years – any formal arrangement with the legal owner of the land, the act of attorning, or acknowledging the title of the landlord by accepting a lease, was absolutely crucial, especially since it was irrevocable. Once an occupier of land had attorned, the conditions of his holding the land had been set for as long as 999 years. Without basic literacy, it was impossible for the settler even to be certain of the nature of the document confronting him. Popular access to basic, primary-level education was a means to redress in part the imbalance in power between the landowners, who had legal title to most of the Island, and the working settlers. A farmer gaining access to public lands in Nova Scotia or New Brunswick, a lumberer committing himself to a season in the woods, a fisherman going out to exploit a common resource after incurring a debt for supplies – none of these encountered even an approximate parallel to the Island settler who was being told that he must attorn.[34]

Measures like the Free Education Act and extension of the franchise to virtually all adult males in 1853 could be termed indirect approaches to the land question. Extending the franchise would strengthen the hand of the reformers in dealing with the landlords, a fact recognized by their opponents. One of the final wishes of the reactionary lieutenant-governor Sir Donald Campbell in 1850, when he realized that a political deadlock was likely to end in the granting of responsible government, was that the effects of the constitutional change be tempered by an imperial statute that would restrict the franchise so as to curtail any impulse towards radicalism.[35] When the local conservative leader, Edward Palmer, argued against extending the elective franchise in 1853, he explicitly 'took his stand against the Bill on the ground that it will give a political ascendancy to men destitute of property over those who possessed it.'[36] In the same speech, Palmer used the raising of funds for the free-education system as an example of how the unpropertied could use the franchise to victimize the propertied. That perspective illustrated the class consciousness that gave Prince Edward Island politics a hard edge not found elsewhere in British North America in the 1850s.

The reformers also attacked the land system more directly. They pursued a dual policy. One thrust emphasized ameliorative measures to reduce the insecurity and arbitrariness to which the working of the system might expose the land occupier and to make leasehold tenure less financially attractive to the owners through taxation. These received short shrift from the Colonial Office, where landlords and their allies found a sympathetic hearing the tenants could never hope for. The second major thrust of the reformers' land policy was the Land Purchase Act of 1853, which authorized the government to make large-scale purchases of land, on a voluntary basis, for resale to the occupiers. The voluntary element was necessary for acceptance by London; but it also left the Island reformers at the mercy of landlords, who, as a group, were not interested in selling. The only major purchase in the 1850s was of the Worrell estate, a property owned by a bachelor in his eighties who had given up on the Island in 1848, after more than forty years as a resident landlord, and moved to London. In a classic case of exploitation of a non-resident by his representatives, William H. Pope and others purchased the estate in 1854 and rapidly flipped it to the local government at an immense profit.[37] The deal also humiliated the reformers, who had little choice about accepting the proposal of the former Worrell trustees, for no other large estate was on the market. Although Islanders had had a vigorous reform government for most of the decade, they had to face the fact that in the 1850s the perennial land question had defied solution. The number of leaseholders was still increasing. Only a minority of land occupiers were freeholders, and no one seemed to have an answer to the problem.

At the end of the decade, Island politics took a new direction. Ill-grounded Protestant fears that the Bible would be banned from the schools inflamed sectarian feeling and cost the reformers much support among the majority Protestant population. By 1859, following two elections in less than a year, Palmer's conservatives were able to form an all-Protestant government. They had succeeded in replacing class with 'religion and education' as the focus of political debate. Yet, after capitalizing on Protestant fears, often expressed in virulently anti-Roman Catholic terms, they took no drastic action. Their solution amounted to a legal guarantee of the permissive daily non-sectarian Bible reading that had been tolerated in the past; but the Bible would not be read unless parents in individual school districts requested it. The only real change they made was to establish a provincial college, Prince of Wales College, in 1860. It replaced the grammar school known as the Central Academy, which had been at the apex of the Island's public educational system since 1836, and to the chagrin of militant Protestants who had voted for the conservatives and 'the open Bible,' it continued the academy's tradition of having no place whatever for religion.[38] Despite the verbal excesses of politics surrounding religion and education on the Island in the dying years of the 1850s, there was little or no actual violence. The shooting of the resident landlord was a relatively isolated incident of violence in the 1850s and was not linked directly to political strife as such. In summary, the Island polity was becoming more mature, with a greater level of civility limited aggression to verbiage.

The reform movements of the region in the 1850s had limitations. These were particularly apparent with respect to cultural minorities and women. The European-descended majority studiously ignored the problems and plight of the Black and Micmac minorities. Both groups remained marginalized through the 1850s; responsible government did not include an agenda of change for them. The Acadians were also in poorer-than-average circumstances, and relatively removed from the mainstream, although there were signs of future improvement for them.

The Micmacs were present in each Maritime colony, but everywhere they formed much less than 1 per cent of the population. In Nova Scotia, as elsewhere, the ostensible aim of settler society was to assimilate them into European ways through making farmers out of them. For this to work, they would have to be given security on their lands. This meant paying for surveys and then challenging and expelling non-Amerindian squatters or trespassers. The White population and officials in Nova Scotia were not sufficiently committed to Micmac rights to take such measures, and the result was a long succession of White encroachments on Amerindian lands. Yet, ironically, when Nova Scotia participated in the Great Exhibition in London in 1851, the colonial government fell back on the crafts of its Micmac inhabitants in seeking something truly distinctive about their society to display to the world. Canoes, paddles, moccasins, and other such items were welcome when they could be used to make an impression abroad; but the people who created the artifacts received little consideration from colonial society. The passage in 1859 of a new statute on reserve lands that purported to stabilize the landholdings of the Nova Scotia Micmacs in fact changed little.[39] The Amerindians of New Brunswick, including Maliseets as well as Micmacs, were generally ignored, although there were isolated sympathizers among the majority population. The story of the Prince Edward Island Micmacs, numbering approximately 300, was that of the mainland provinces on a smaller scale.

Yet the culture survived. Micmacs continued to speak their own language, to pass on their own traditions and folklore, and to produce beautiful works of folk art. Micmac women specialized in porcupine quillwork on birch-bark, a genre they developed almost exclusively for sale or trade, and by the 1850s it had found an international market. The art of the Micmac, which Ruth Holmes Whitehead has dubbed 'post-contact-traditional,'[40] was certainly not derivative, and indicated that the people themselves had not been assimilated. Over time it incorporated some elements from the settlers' world, including new dyes or such motifs as the Prince of Wales's feathers, which appear on commemorative work prepared for the occasion of his visit in 1860. Even the Micmac's attempt to establish a place as artists in the European-centred world encountered obstacles. Whitehead reports that 'Some time prior to 1854, the importing of quillwork and other Indian crafts had become lucrative enough to be taxed by Great Britain.'[41] Whether the British motive was revenue or protection or both, the effect on the Micmac could only have been negative. Despite barriers and the cross-cultural tradition of artistic poverty, Micmac quillworkers could earn substantial incomes. In 1857, Mary Christianne Morris (née Paul) of Halifax provided her niece with a wedding reception that included wine and cake for a large crowd and dancing to flute and violin music. Micmac men were known especially as skilled woodworkers, and they applied their abilities as coopers, furniture makers, wharf builders, ship's carpenters, and builders of small boats, as well as making their own tools. In 1853 the scholarly Silas Rand began his mission to the Micmac; although religious in ultimate purpose, the endeavour involved an intensification of his remarkable efforts to understand and to document their life-ways. He did not believe they were fated to fade away.[42]

Nova Scotians of African descent had been present in significant numbers since the Loyalist migrations of the 1780s; but, deprived of equal opportunities to become self-sustaining and often isolated geographically from the rest of society, they could be pardoned for wondering whether they were wanted. They were in fact a tiny minority – between 1 and 2 per cent of the total population – with little possibility of exerting political influence. Yet in 1854 there was concrete evidence of increasing institutional self-sufficiency among Black Nova Scotians: Richard Preston, a clergyman long known for his anti-slavery activities, founded the African Baptist Association, a union of twelve Baptist churches. In the words of James W. St G. Walker, it provided 'a regular link for communications and it assisted in the preservation of doctrines and styles of worship which distinguished the blacks from white Baptists in the Maritimes.'[43]

The other two Maritime provinces had smaller Black populations, but the pattern of restricted opportunity and discriminatory treatment was the same. Black New Brunswickers formed less than 1 per cent of the population, although modest numbers of escaped slaves from the United States entered the colony in the 1840s and 1850s. One was Robert J. Patterson, a native of Virginia, who left Boston after the Fugitive Slave Act of 1850 made it easier for slave owners to recapture former slaves. He arrived in Saint John in 1852, participated in anti-slavery demonstrations over a period of years, and in 1859 opened a dining establishment that became the most popular in the city. Despite Patterson's success story, New Brunswick was not always hospitable to Blacks; the first of each sex to graduate from provincial institutions of higher learning would have to leave to find suitable employment.[44]

Black Prince Edward Islanders probably never numbered more than 200, and the largest concentration was in a very specific part of Charlottetown known as the Bog. The area was racially mixed, and its children attended a school for the poor of all origins known as the Bog School. Established under Anglican auspices in 1848, it had the same teacher for its entire fifty-five years of existence, Sarah Harvie. The school was successful, and for a small community, the Bog produced its share of high achievers. One child born in 1852, George Godfrey, would go on to become the American Black heavyweight champion boxer by 1883; a standard boxing authority has written that John L. Sullivan, the White champion, refused to fight him. Defying stereotypes about boxers, Godfrey, known in the ring as 'Old Chocolate,' was a financial success who held a large amount of property in Massachusetts, his adopted home.[45]

The Acadians were a larger minority than the Blacks and the Micmac in Nova Scotia (although still less than 10 per cent of the population) and were partly insulated by language from the majority society. A full century after the expulsion, the Acadians still showed marks of their collective trauma. Their communities were remote from the centres of power and did not have much economic potential. Their educational facilities lagged behind most of the rest of the colony; the available books were often written in English; and the provincial authorities seemed to have less interest in the educational progress of Acadian areas at the end of the decade than at the beginning. Acadians did not control their institutions: they were usually represented in the assembly by non-Acadians, and in 1853 Hubert Girroir became the first Nova Scotia Acadian to be ordained priest in the nineteenth century. The more positive interpretation of the relative isolation of the Acadian areas in this period emphasizes the self-contained quality of their lives and the way in which this 'independence' made cultural retention possible.[46] Nonetheless, poverty, in large part attributable to the marginal areas where they had settled after the expulsion, was a significant feature of Acadian life.

New Brunswick Acadians, comprising some 15 per cent of the population, were too large a portion of the population to be left out of account completely. Yet, as in Nova Scotia, they were relatively poor and often located in areas distant from the centres of economic and political power, and were unable to play a major role in directing the colony in the 1850s. Amand Landry, the first Acadian member to win election to the Assembly, had not done so until 1846, ten years after the first two Acadians were elected in Nova Scotia. Landry was in the Assembly for part of the 1850s, and appears to have been the only Acadian political figure of importance in the decade. Nonetheless, there were signs of awakening: in 1854, Rev. François-Xavier-Stanislas Lafrance established Collège Saint-Thomas at Memramcook 'to provide the Acadians with their own élite of priests, merchants, doctors, lawyers, and even judges.'[47] The college, undermined by lack of funds and episcopal support, lasted only eight years. Yet it had had ninety-five students at the end of its first year, an important indication that what novelist Antonine Maillet has called '[le] siècle de silence' for the Acadians was drawing to a close.[48]

On Prince Edward Island the Acadians were usually perceived by the colonists as a linguistic minority within a religious minority. The Acadians were much less numerous than the Catholics of Scottish and Irish origin, and in fact clergy of Scottish ancestry dominated the Catholic community and its institutions. In 1852 the Acadians received distinctive recognition within the school system of the Island – their teachers were exempted from the usual licensing procedure, but were paid less than English-language teachers. Two years later, Stanislaus Perry, a nephew of Sylvain Perrey, the Island's first Acadian priest, became the first Acadian elected to the local Assembly. According to folklorist Georges Arsenault, with Perry's election the Island Acadian community 'began to move out of its century-old isolation and to open up to the English-speaking world that surrounded it.'[49]

The identity and distinctive history of the Acadians were also becoming better known outside the region. In the 1840s H.W. Longfellow had published his poem *Evangeline*, and by 1853 a French translation appeared in London. Six years later a French historian, François-Edme Rameau de Saint-Père, published a historical work on the Acadians. Rameau visited Acadia in 1860 and maintained contact with Acadian leaders for decades; his emphasis was on renewing Acadian contact with France. As Acadians slowly emerged from their isolation, their tragic history as a people was attracting international attention that would help them define their identity.

None of the cultural minorities mentioned – Amerindian, Black, or Acadian – pressed reformers of the 1850s hard on issues of equality. Indeed the reformers could show another, reactionary face, as they did when equality between the sexes was at issue. The most obvious example was removal in 1851 of voting rights from propertied women in Nova Scotia by ostensible reformers. In fact, the decade was studded with instances of legislated unequal treatment of the sexes. The egalitarianism of the Prince Edward Island Free Education Act of 1852, one of the rationales of which was to equalize access to education between districts of differing economic circumstances, did not include sex-blind salary scales. Women were to be paid at a lower rate. New Brunswick legislation in the same year restored the differential payment for male and female teachers that had been abandoned in 1837.[50]

In the disfranchising of females, Nova Scotia had been preceded by Prince Edward Island in 1836 and by New Brunswick in 1843.[51] Perhaps it was simply coincidence, but on 13 January of the same year that New Brunswick women lost the possibility of the vote, Charles Simonds had been found guilty on five counts of raping his married housekeeper. His sentence is not known, yet it did not prevent his remaining an executive councillor and being elected speaker of the Assembly twice in the 1850s – a fact that surely reveals something about contemporary sensibilities regarding sexual assault of social subordinates.[52] Deprived of the vote, women had their best official access to the legislature through the petitioning process. Female use of petitions in the New Brunswick counties of Albert, Charlotte, and Sunbury indicates that, although women petitioned less than men, they did so in significant numbers and there was no challenge of their right to do so. The disfranchised women of New Brunswick appear to have played a major role in petitioning the legislature for prohibition, and *not* to have played a comparable role in supporting repeal; indeed, it was 'the moral issue' that mobilized New Brunswick women to petition as never before.[53]

During the decade there was significant change in the legal framework surrounding sexuality and marriage. In 1852 Prince Edward Island passed a seduction act allowing a seduced female to sue in her own right; the usual legislation in British North America dealing with sexual activity outside marriage required that any suit for expenses, damages, distress, dishonour, loss of services, or whatever be brought by the head of the family. Unfortunately for women's rights, a judicial decision effectively nullified the change two years later.[54] With respect to marriage, in 1857 Nova Scotia became the only British North American colony prior to Confederation to allow legal divorce on the ground of cruelty. According to Constance Backhouse, the divorce laws in all three Maritime provinces, which she describes as 'apparently "gender-neutral,"' were relatively relaxed in comparison with those of England and the other British North American colonies even before 1857.[55]

The purpose of the divorce reform was to allow termination of intolerable marital situations. The broader question of deliverance from a life of underpaid or unpaid toil within patriarchal confines remained. For *men* of humble origin, education might provide an escape from manual toil, and to an extent education offered opportunity to women also. Yet there were real limits to the educational possibilities open to them within the region. Although they could be admitted to many secondary institutions, including the normal, or teacher-training, schools that operated in all three Maritime colonies by 1856, no colleges accepted them. Access to advanced institutions would require leaving and going to the United States, and for most women, regardless of personal potential, ethnicity, or social class, the prospect of such an opportunity was impossibly remote. No institution within the region would graduate a female with a university degree until 1875, although it should be noted that the Atlantic colonies were not unusual within the British Empire in their exclusion of women: that female graduate in 1875 would be the first from *any* university within the Empire.

If women turned their education to use as teachers, they faced restrictions imposed by the 'gender ideology' that interpreted their suitability in terms of their innate nurturing qualities as women rather than their professional attainments. Although women were acceptable as teachers of the younger students, the higher, more intellectually demanding levels of education required male teachers; and the small number of well-paying supervisory or bureaucratic jobs would be reserved for males.[56] This was part of a broader intellectual position on the relative roles of men and women that a Halifax audience heard articulated by Rev. Robert Sedgewick, a Protestant clergyman, in 1856. His topic was the doctrine of 'separate spheres' for men and women. Removing the right to vote was consistent with this ideological position, which assigned the private, domestic realm to women while reserving the public for men. Sedgewick's address consisted of a vigorous assault, spiced with ridicule, on arguments for changing the relationship between the sexes, and a strong affirmation that 'The sphere of woman is home and whatever is co-relative with home in the social economy.'[57] Although not opposed to educating women sufficiently to enable them to engage in drawing-room conversation, his axiom was that 'woman is the complement of man,' and as examples of 'ologies' that *all* women should know he gave 'washology,' 'bakeology,' 'darnology,' etc. Three modern scholars have described his words as 'a prescriptive injunction designed to keep women from following in the footsteps of their more radical sisters in the United States where "women's rights" in the public sphere had become a lively topic of debate.'[58] The Atlantic region was not self-contained intellectually, and this fact cut both ways: some women from the region were already attending institutions elsewhere that were open to them, some of these returned with a personal commitment to female education,[59] and defenders of patriarchy, also aware of the broader currents of change within the North Atlantic world, were ready to do battle.

Typically, the pattern of a female's life and her tasks were determined by the status and occupation of the male upon whom she was dependent. If he was a sea captain, it was possible that she would be travelling with him; if he was a fisherman, she would be the 'skipper of the shore crew'; if he was a farmer, she would be performing her share of the farm labour; and always, if conjugally attached, she had an expected role in reproduction. The majority of people lived in rural areas, which usually centred on agriculture, and although there has not been much formal study of the agrarian family economy in the region during the middle of the nineteenth century, it is virtually certain that the realm of women's labour extended outside the actual houses where they prepared meals, maintained the household, cared for children, and made clothes. When possible, they would be expected to help with work in the fields and barns; in popular thinking, their major contribution to the family economy was probably to bear and raise as many children as possible in order to enlarge the family labour pool and ensure a secure old age. Unmarried female relatives often assisted a mother or, in the event of a mother's death, fulfilled most of her responsibilities in terms of household management.[60]

It is doubtful whether the status of most women – dependency within a patriarchal world – was improving in the 1850s. The legal changes concerning seduction in one colony and divorce in another directly affected only small numbers. If alternative employment outside the rural household was available for young females, it was likely to be some variety of servant work: low in status and low in pecuniary reward. Some women attained enough education to become district schoolteachers. By the 1850s close to one-half of New Brunswick teachers were female. For some reason - perhaps there were fewer opportunities in resource industries for young males – the proportion of female teachers in contemporary Nova Scotia was significantly smaller, although it rose rapidly over the course of the decade.[61] But in economic terms this did not represent great advancement. Janet Guildford has estimated that the remuneration of a female teacher in Nova Scotia approximated that of a domestic servant,[62] and since higher institutions denied admission to females, the probability that they could rise within the teaching profession or use it as a stepping-stone to something better, as men did frequently, was slight. Labouring opportunities other than personal service were not numerous for women. Prostitution was one option. The number of sex workers in the region as a whole cannot be determined, but within Halifax alone they could be counted in scores, if not hundreds.[63] In most cases, the best a woman of the era could hope for was marriage to a man with the means to guarantee her a pedestal from which to supervise other, subordinate women of the household.

The general situation of Newfoundland women appears to have been similar to that of Maritime women. As well as working inside the house, they bore most of the responsibility for the garden and berry picking, the latter being a major part of food gathering in Newfoundland. Women frequently also played an essential role in the fishery. The colony depended on the export of saltfish, or salted dried codfish, and it was often women who processed on shore the fish that men caught. This has led one sociologist to comment that the sexual 'separate spheres' in the Newfoundland fishing village should be understood as 'the fishery at sea' versus 'the fishery on shore' rather than the conventional 'public' versus 'private' dichotomy. The share of women in the skilled work of the fishery, she points out, meant 'considerable economic leverage' within the family.[64]

Newfoundland was dissimilar from the Maritimes in many respects, from the structure of the economy to the political culture to the ethnic mix to the lack of development of higher education. In the first place, there was the overwhelming economic importance of saltfish exports; the only other significant source of visible export income was the seal harvest, whose products represented, on average, 24 per cent of the total from 1850 to 1859. Sealing functioned as a vital adjunct to one branch of the cod fishery, known as the Labrador fishery, which was migratory and dominated by fishermen from the St John's–Conception Bay–Trinity Bay area; without the sealing link, it would have been uneconomic. In terms of employment, the best year for sealing was 1857, when 370 ships and 13,600 men participated in the industry. Shannon Ryan has written that 'The Newfoundland economy probably owed its survival after 1815 to the development of the Labrador and seal fisheries.'[65]

Aside from the importance of cod and seals, the Newfoundland economy of the 1850s was different in the exceptional reliance of the Newfoundland-registered fleet on builders elsewhere. Ships built in Newfoundland were ordinarily small and intended for coastal voyages and support of the fishery; during most of the nineteenth century the colony was a net importer of shipping tonnage. The typical vessel was the schooner, which averaged a mere forty-three tons and was almost always locally built, but in the 1850s other rigs, particularly brigantines and brigs, carried the majority of registered shipping tonnage. Most of these other ships, usually several times larger than the schooners, had been built in Nova Scotia or Prince Edward Island. What accounted for the local investment in brigs and brigantines? Some were used in the seal hunt, but that occupied only a small part of each year. Sager has found a strong correlation between increased saltfish exports to Brazil and the acquisition of the larger vessels. Other evidence also suggests that, when not on sealing voyages, the ships were engaged in external trade, and by the 1850s St John's-registered vessels appear to have carried a greater proportion of Newfoundland's external trade 'than at any other time in the nineteenth century.' Sager has also found an exact correlation between reduced exports to Brazil and the West Indies in the next decade and disinvestment in brigs and brigantines. But for a period in the 1840s and 1850s Newfoundland, although dependent on other colonies for the supply of ships, apparently developed a significant ocean-going fleet, which had the potential to challenge external domination of its carrying trade. To a limited extent, then, the 1850s may be seen as a Newfoundland version of a 'golden age of sail,' with the attendant benefits in terms of capital, incomes, and employment. Afterwards, the seal harvest, the Labrador fishery, registration of non-schooners, and average vessel size declined sharply.[66]

For Newfoundland the 1850s were pivotal in several respects. Its people had long been treated by London as incapable of self-government, and although responsible government was conceded in principle to the mainland colonies in the 1840s and to Prince Edward Island in 1851, Newfoundland had to wait. As a consequence, ministerial responsibility became the dominant political issue in the colony during the first half of the 1850s. The struggle was prolonged, intense, and bitter.

The leader in the struggle for responsible government was a youthful Roman Catholic Prince Edward Islander of Irish extraction, Philip Francis Little, who had moved to Newfoundland to practise law in 1844 at the age of twenty. In 1850, with the support of the new Irish-born Roman Catholic bishop, John Thomas Mullock, he won a by-election over a Protestant reformer. But the decisive event confirming Little as leader of the reformers was the public reading in 1852 of a letter from Mullock to 'Dear Mr. Little' denouncing the local government as 'vile' for supporting a dispatch from the Colonial Office describing the Assembly's request for responsible government as 'premature.'[67] After an election in 1855, Little became Newfoundland's first premier under the new system. His cabinet included four Roman Catholics and two Protestants representing Catholic constituencies. The inclusion of Protestants was prudent since, after having been a minority, they had become a decisive majority. The reformers were particularly successful in attracting support from the Wesleyans, who constituted almost one-third of the Protestants by the mid-1850s.[68]

One of the issues Little had to face as premier was the British attempt in 1857 to strengthen its diplomatic *rapprochement* with France after the Crimean War by means of a convention defining French rights to use of the west coast for fishing and curing purposes. The existence of these rights and the ancillary right to freedom from encroachment by permanent non-French settlements on the treaty coastline had already placed inhabitants of those communities in a legal no man's land – an irritating reminder of the long generations during which the island had been regarded as a mere convenience for the migratory fishery. In the words of W.S. MacNutt, the convention 'granted to France effective ownership of the waters surrounding the northern arm of Newfoundland. It deprived the colony of effective sovereignty over great stretches of the coastline and made inoperative many acts of its legislature.'[69]

The French Shore controversy, as it was known, was one of the few public questions on which virtually all Newfoundlanders could agree, and Little led a chorus of patriotic indignation against the draft convention. The other colonies gave a travelling Newfoundland delegation a sympathetic hearing, and the Colonial Office conceded the principle that no change would be made without Newfoundland's consent. The victory was dramatic proof that the island's inhabitants could now gain the ear of Downing Street, and that their fellow colonists would raise their voices in support. The demonstration of solidarity over this issue may have been a factor influencing Newfoundland to send delegates to Quebec in 1864.[70]

Self-determination was the unifying theme in the struggles over responsible government and the French Shore, and that was a theme with resonance in the other colonies. But the political culture of Newfoundland was unique within the Atlantic region. One lieutenant-governor, Sir Alexander Bannerman, concluded that Newfoundland reformers were so obsessed with gaining partisan advantage and so inclined towards the use of patronage that they were unfit to hold office. Given the nature of political polarization in Newfoundland, the distaste of Bannerman, a Protestant Scot, for the local reformers might be interpreted as stemming from anti-Irish or anti-Roman Catholic prejudice. Yet this is not credible to anyone familiar with his record in Prince Edward Island. There Bannerman had been friendly with a reform party whose electoral bulwark was the large Roman Catholic minority. When evidence of Orangeism appeared on the Island, he issued a proclamation condemning it; his view of Newfoundland reformers cannot be attributed to ethnic or religious bias.[71] In fact, public life in the Newfoundland of the 1850s did have a communal bitterness and a level of consistent, direct clerical intervention in politics that was not matched in the Maritimes. Much of this difference in political culture can be traced to the Irish-born Michael Anthony Fleming, bishop from 1830 to 1850. Although Mullock, Fleming's successor, ceased public boycotts and excommunications and reversed the policy of barring Newfoundlanders from the priesthood, the first native Newfoundlander was not ordained priest until 1856, and in 1858 Mullock secured the suspension of a legislative councillor who criticized him; the suspended legislator was never reinstated. Like Fleming, Mullock thought of the Liberal Party as the 'Catholic Party,' and his subordinate clergy continued to act as election managers through the 1850s. In the words of Frederick Jones, he 'was by 1860 the most important politician in Newfoundland.'[72] This clericalism at the centre of Newfoundland politics was a decisive factor separating the political cultures of Newfoundland and the other three colonies in the region.

The unique dependence of Newfoundland on the cod fishery also set the island apart from the Maritime colonies. The migratory fishery had never recovered from the long Napoleonic wars, and the harvesting of the resource had passed permanently under the control of the colonists;[73] but although the West Country fishermen left, West Country firms remained, supplying the resident fishermen from fixed premises in the outports, taking fish in exchange, and marketing the fish overseas for specie. Over time, a rival commercial structure took shape, focused in St John's, whose wholesalers supplied small merchants and traders in the outports. The Newfoundland-controlled structure gradually gained the upper hand over the West Country firms. In some cases, the small outport traders were itinerant, in effect willing to go to the fishermen rather than obliging them to transport their products to the warehouses owned by West Country firms. The St John's firms also had more elasticity built into their commercial structure. The prices and catches of cod fluctuated from year to year. In good times more traders linked to St John's would become active, reducing the profit margin for all involved. But in poorer times, when prices were low, the itinerant traders would withdraw and perhaps turn to fishing; the West Country-based firms with their fixed premises would then be faced with fishermen wanting them to purchase their fish. Thus even market fluctuations played into the hands of the St John's firms in their contest with the West Country merchants.

Within the cod fishery, there was relentlessly increasing economic pressure on all players. The basic facts were quite simple. The population was increasing more rapidly than the earning capacity of the economy. It is not easy to measure population growth in Newfoundland over the 1850s, because there was only one census during the decade. But between 1845 and 1857 the number of inhabitants increased 29.1 per cent and between 1857 and 1869 another 17.9 per cent, for an overall increase of 52.2 per cent in the twenty-four years from 1845 to 1869. The population stood at 124,300 in 1857. With such growth in mouths to feed, a continuing reliance on the export staple of cod, and a steadily declining percentage of market share in a world where cod consumption was increasing, the colony was in the throes of a long-term crisis that would stretch into the twentieth century. When combined with relative price stability, stagnant sales and growing numbers of people dependent upon those sales had drastic implications for all aspects of life in Newfoundland: the incidence of poverty, the demand for poor relief, and the state of public finance were simply the most obvious. In this atmosphere of increasing economic pressure, the St John's firms had an advantage over the overseas branches of the West Country firms in maintaining the solvency of their operations, since they were able to exercise much closer supervision over operations than their competitors an ocean away who had to rely on agents.[74] In fact, by the 1850s the commerce of the island was increasingly centralized in St John's. The overall health of the cod fishery might be in decline, but control from the colonial capital became tighter and tighter. The paradox of tightening control within a stagnating economy would be a continuing feature of Newfoundland history for many decades. The resident élite, although successful in wresting commercial hegemony from the West Countrymen, had few other causes for self-congratulation. They would prove incapable of modernizing the fishery or effectively diversifying the economy.

In some respects Newfoundland in the 1850s appeared to be evolving into a colony more similar to the others. Responsible government had been attained, politics seemed less violent than in earlier decades, and there was reason for optimism in the acknowledgment by Britain that the French Shore was a matter of vital and legitimate interest to the inhabitants of the island. Yet the seeds of disaster were already apparent in the prolonged crisis within the fishery. One measure of the worsening economic situation is the fact that per-capita exports of saltfish, the colony's staple, after declining from 29.2 quintals to 11.5 in the twenty-one years from 1815 to 1836, and remaining fairly stable for the next twenty-one years, would drop from 11.2 in 1857 to 6.0 in 1869.[75] Newfoundland existed largely in isolation from the other colonies, and its history moved according to its own distinctive pace and rhythms.

A focus on local identities should not obscure common features and parallels. Each colony was locally self-governing by 1855, and in two – Newfoundland and Prince Edward Island – much energy was expended on attempting to free local development from the control of outsiders beyond the sea, be they landlords or merchants; to a lesser degree, Nova Scotia shared in this struggle, as is evident in the decision to terminate the monopoly of the General Mining Association. In each colony the political culture was resolutely British, and the reformers remained committed to the monarchical, parliamentary consensus of the era, although the Irish issue caused deep bitterness. The most numerous group in the region with different traditions, the Acadians, was dispersed and lacked the means for united action. In terms of language spoken, English was becoming dominant within all ethnic groups other than the Amerindians and the Acadians. A Scottish Gaelic monthly magazine in Antigonish commenced publication in 1851, and in the next year the publisher replaced it with a weekly partly in Gaelic but also partly in English because, as he confessed, 'Gaelic is drawing back every day.'[76] His newspaper, the *Casket*, reflected this retreat: the Gaelic content diminished until, by 1857, it had almost disappeared.[77] In Lunenburg County, the Lutheran church changed its language of service from German to English in 1860.[78]

No Atlantic colony in this decade was immune from ethnic and religious factionalism. Yet the apparent decline in political violence from previous decades indicated a greater maturity and civility, at least in the three Maritime colonies. The new initiatives in higher education reflected the sense of progress and refinement; once again Newfoundland did not participate in this trend. Being able to provide local opportunities for higher education was a mark of higher expectations and increasing self-confidence and self-reliance, as was greater willingness to spend money on matters not related directly to material progress and public order, such as roads, judges, jails, and insane asylums. Most people of the region remained rural, although there were urban concentrations in each colony. The degree of internal metropolitan-hinterland integration varied greatly from colony to colony, and there was no indication of an emerging dominant regional metropolis that could concentrate capital and entrepreneurship in such a way as to provide effective counterweights to Canadian cities within the future confederation. On the other hand, the region had a still-successful shipbuilding industry and harboured a thriving shipowning business; and while fortunes were being made in ocean-oriented activities, the mainland colonies were positioning themselves to link the industrial interior of the continent with the Atlantic Ocean through the construction of railways.

Since the initial settlement of the Atlantic region by European peoples, it has almost always been, in terms of political and economic power, a marginal part of a greater whole. In the 1850s the region (or its parts) came closer to being self-directing. The term 'golden age' may be a survival from another historiographical era, and may obscure either 'danger signs' that contemporaries failed to notice or anxieties of the same people about being left behind economically by the United States; but it is also a partial description of reality. This was a time when it had not yet been determined that the region would once again be subordinated by outside powers and relegated to secondary status.

CHAPTER SIXTEEN

The 1860s
An End and a Beginning

PHILLIP A. BUCKNER

In 1867, a Nova Scotia anti-Confederate pamphleteer decried his province's union with Canada. 'Few countries in the world,' he argued, 'are more favourably situated whether as regards political freedom, geographical position or the extent and variety of their natural resources ...' Yet 'the system of self government which has produced all this prosperity ... is to be thrown aside and the doubtful experiment thrust upon her of a political union with the other Provinces' in which she 'must submit to the rule of a larger and it is to be feared not too kindly population.'[1] This attitude was widely held throughout the Atlantic colonies and explains the lack of enthusiasm with which the people of the region embraced a scheme of union that seemed primarily designed to benefit the United Province of Canada. Except in Newfoundland, the pro-Confederates ultimately carried the day. But it is one of the ironies of history that those who lose a contemporary debate may win a posthumous victory in the hearts and minds of future generations. During the recession of the 1880s, there was a resurgence of anti-Confederation sentiment, and although this discontent flagged during the boom years of the early twentieth century, the theme of a lost 'golden age' before Confederation was resurrected in the 1920s as the regional industrial economy collapsed. In *The True Story of Confederation*, Alexander T. Paterson proclaimed that 'time has more than justified practically every point raised in opposition to Confederation by Maritime Anti-Confederates. Confederation has been for the Maritimes one of the worst commercial disasters ever experienced by an Anglo-Saxon country.'[2] Paterson's views were vigorously contested by professional economic historians, but many Maritimers continue to believe to the present 'that the provinces sacrificed their economic potential by entering the union with Canada in the 1860s and 1870s.'[3]

Since these arguments rest upon a speculative comparison of what might have been with what is, there can never be a definitive answer to the question of whether the Maritimes took the wrong path in the forked road. Yet even if, in retrospect, the foundations of the prosperity that underlay this 'golden age' appear somewhat shaky, contemporaries might be forgiven for not fully anticipating the changes that were about to overtake them. After passing through the bleak 1840s, the region had entered a period of substantial if cyclical growth in the 1850s, and this had persisted into the 1860s.[4] No single factor explains the rapid development during these decades. The 1854 Reciprocity Treaty with the United States allowing for the free exchange of natural products accelerated the pace of development, but probably only slightly, just as the abrogation of the treaty by the United States in 1866 was only marginally responsible for the slower growth in the latter part of the decade.[5] Much more important were the substantial spillover effects of the American Civil War, effects that artificially increased the demand for the natural resources of the Maritimes. Yet even without the stimulus of war there would probably have been a general increase in Maritime exports to both the United States and Britain.

The shipbuilding and shipping industries fuelled the regional economy. Indeed, the romantic image of wooden ships and the 'iron men' who sailed upon them came later to symbolize to many Maritimers the 'golden age' of the region. To be sure, the significance of shipbuilding and shipping has been questioned by a number of historians. Peter McClelland has insisted that in New Brunswick, even at its height between 1850 and 1875, the shipbuilding industry employed a mere 2.3 per cent of the labour force and contributed only 2.6 per cent of the estimated gross national product of the province. As for shipowning, it 'succeeded only in creating assets rapidly becoming technologically obsolete.'[6] This negative assessment is overstated. Impossible as it is to quantify exactly the contribution of the shipping and shipbuilding industries to the regional economy, the most recent study has concluded that 'given the size of fleets built and owned there, and given that these colonies were major shipowning societies in terms of tonnage built and owned per capita, the idea that these industries were minor contributors to provincial output, profits and wages is not credible.'[7] Nevertheless, it was becoming apparent by the 1860s that wooden shipbuilding was an industry with a limited future and that wooden ships represented a risky enterprise both for the capitalists who owned them and for the seamen who sailed on them. Even during the prosperous years of the industry, regional capitalists sought to balance their seaward investments with landward investments in banks and insurance companies, and the ships that sailed from Atlantic-Canadian ports carried a declining proportion of Atlantic-Canadian sailors.

The most vehement opposition to Confederation would come from merchants, such as the Killams of Yarmouth, whose fortunes were most closely tied to wooden shipowning and whose communities had few other resources to develop. The vast majority of Maritimers, however, earned their livelihood not from seafaring but from exploiting the natural resources of the region. Regardless of the party to which they belonged or their attitude towards Confederation, politicians based their development strategies upon the need to open up what were believed to be the untapped resources of their colony. They saw population growth as the key to future prosperity. All three of the Maritime colonies evolved landward programs of development (as did Newfoundland in the decades after it rejected Confederation), and the general, even enthusiastic, acceptance of these programs by the majority of the colonial electorates 'demonstrates the fallacy of the notion that for nineteenth century Maritimers, the "world was an oceanic one."'[8] Arguably, Maritimers did not see themselves as having a seaward destiny until after the age of wooden ships had ended and the mythology of a romantic age of sail emerged as an invented tradition.

Many young Maritimers certainly went to sea for a time, just as they sometimes engaged in lumbering or sought temporary employment as labourers in the urban centres of the region or on public works. Similarly, many Maritime women accepted employment in domestic service, worked in the small manufacturing plants of the region, or even travelled to New England in search of temporary employment. For most, however, their ultimate goal was the possession of a family farm. The most significant economic activity in the Maritimes, as in Canada, was agriculture. Critics of the timber trade, the advocates of 'scientific' agriculture, and the overly enthusiastic promoters of immigration to the region have all contributed to the image of Maritime farmers as backward. This criticism ignores the reality of life in an area where much of the soil was unsuitable for cultivation and where a cool, moist climate limited agricultural potential. Maritime farmers did not neglect agriculture in order to pursue the timber trade; more frequently they engaged in the timber trade so that they could afford to operate marginal farms. Most Maritime farmers did not join agricultural societies because they knew that the kind of investment that scientific agriculture called for would not be rewarded with commensurate gains in productivity,[9] and they did not concentrate on growing wheat, despite the lamentations of Canadian visitors, because moisture and a short growing season made wheat a risky crop. As T.W. Acheson argues, the vast majority of New Brunswick farmers were 'rational men and women who engaged in those rural economic activities which produced the highest return for their efforts.' They turned to those crops that were most reliable, such as hay, oats, buckwheat, potatoes, and roots, and emphasized the production of livestock, dairy products, meat, and wool. The region was not self-sufficient in agriculture, and much of the production was for subsistence; but by the time of Confederation virtually every area of potentially productive soil was under cultivation, and the region's agriculturalists were 'at least as efficient and productive as were farmers in other jurisdictions having similar geographic circumstances.'[10]

Although, by the 1860s, the limits of agricultural expansion had probably been reached, this was not apparent to contemporaries, including the anti-Confederates, who insisted that 'as grounds for emigration [sic], many unsettled portions of these provinces are as tempting to the settler as the prairies of the West.'[11] Like their contemporaries in Canada and the United States, Maritimers accepted as axiomatic that agriculture was the backbone upon which a stable and prosperous economy should be built. Much of the growth of the 1850s and early 1860s had been fuelled by population growth, and Maritimers did not believe theirs was an overpopulated region. Indeed, during the 1860s, the population of the Maritimes grew at a rate comparable with that of the United Province of Canada. Between 1861 and 1871, the population of Nova Scotia grew by 17.2 per cent from 331,000 to 388,000, of New Brunswick by 13.5 per cent from 252,000 to 286,000, and of Prince Edward Island by 17.5 per cent from 80,000 to 94,000. Even Newfoundland showed growth, increasing from 124,000 to 146,000 between 1857 and 1869, although it received fewer immigrants than the other colonies and depended more upon natural increase. Its comparatively sluggish growth was seen as a reflection of its overdependence on the fisheries, and there were cries even here for more emphasis on agricultural development.

Maritimers and Newfoundlanders also believed that their colonies possessed vast, untapped mineral resources. After the abolition of the General Mining Association's monopoly in 1858, fourteen new coal mines were opened in Cape Breton alone by 1865. In 1866 there were 3,043 men and boys employed in coal mining throughout Nova Scotia. More than 80 per cent of coal production in 1865 went to the United States, although the abrogation of reciprocity ended this period of rapid growth and left the coal operators apprehensive about the future.[12] Gold mining underwent an even more rapid rise and fall. Gold was discovered in the impoverished eastern shore of Nova Scotia between Ship Harbour and Musquodoboit in 1860, and between 1862 and 1871 some 192, 772 ounces were mined by a labour force averaging 700 a year. But production peaked in 1867, and by 1871 it had fallen by 30 per cent.[13] The other provinces experienced little real development in the mining sector, although there was a brief flurry of activity in Albert County, New Brunswick, where a unique sixteen-foot vein of solidified asphalt, named Albertite, was discovered. More than 100 men, twenty-two horses, and four steam engines were employed at the site in the early 1860s, but output fell sharply after 1869.[14] Nonetheless, the widespread belief that the resources were there was encouraged by regional geologists and the provincial governments that employed them.

Few Maritimers doubted that their provinces also had the potential for industrial development. By 1860, New Brunswickers were extensively engaged not only in processing timber but also in an ever-wider range of manufacturing activity; the 1871 per-capita output of manufacturing in the province rivalled that of Ontario and Quebec. Nearly half the output was produced in and around Saint John, which contained about 15 per cent of the provincial population. More than 4,000 artisans worked in the city. Foundry and shoe- and boot-making already exceeded the shipbuilding industry in terms of value of output, and even these activities were overshadowed by the clothing trades, which employed 1,033 people, 828 of them women.[15] The Nova Scotia economy was more closely tied to the production of staple commodities and to staple processing. In 1861, sawmilling and shipbuilding accounted for just over 60 per cent of the total value of manufacturing. There were some grist mills and tanneries, as well as a little brewing and distilling, but the largest industrial enterprise was the iron works at Londonderry, which annually turned out $40,000 worth of products. Few manufacturers employed more than ten men. Since most of the grist mills produced for a local market, and the sawmills dotted around the coastline shipped their products directly to foreign markets, urban centres were slow to develop. By 1871 only 17 per cent of Nova Scotians lived in places of 1,000 people or more. Although Halifax accounted for more than half the colony's output, manufacturing activity absorbed only about 22 per cent of the city's labour force in 1861. The city was essentially a commercial entrepôt, handling about three-quarters of the colony's imports and about two-thirds of its exports. Even so, in Nova Scotia as a whole, manufacturing production more than doubled during the 1860s.[16] Even Prince Edward Island sought to promote balanced growth by encouraging home manufacturing.[17]

Above all, the people of the region sought to escape from the boom-and-bust syndrome that had characterized the regional economy since the collapse of the old mercantile system in the 1840s. Although most Maritimers saw no dichotomy between the promotion of manufacturing and the encouragement of staples production for external markets, little real growth was anticipated in the staples industries. After the protection given to colonial timber on the British market came to an end in 1860, there was considerable fluctuation in the demand for Maritime timber in British and American markets. In New Brunswick, where timber continued to form the bulk of the colony's exports, anxious timber merchants sought to diversify their investments. In any event, the era when the great merchants involved in the exporting of timber could prevent legislation designed to encourage manufacturing had already passed. They were able to delay until the 1870s a substantial increase in the ridiculously low rates of stumpage for cutting timber on Crown land, but there was mounting pressure for higher rates in order to increase public revenues and to slow down the destruction of the forests.[18] Similarly, the Atlantic fisheries, which suffered from a series of poor harvests throughout the 1860s, were given virtually no financial encouragement by any of the colonial governments of this period, not even in Newfoundland, where fish was virtually the only export. Although temporary relief was given to fishermen, it was viewed as a distasteful reflection of the fact that there were too many fishermen chasing too few fish.[19] No one in the Atlantic provinces doubted the importance of the British market, and few welcomed the end of free entry of the region's natural resources into the American market, although there was disagreement over whether it would be easier to renegotiate reciprocity within or outside Confederation. But few of the region's political leaders seriously believed that continued growth and economic stability could be achieved without a diversification of their colonies' economies.

During the decade before Confederation, all three of the Maritime colonies set out to attain this goal through development policies that involved borrowing heavily on the British money market. The primary instrument of development was the construction of railways. In New Brunswick, the European and North American Railway, brought under public control in 1856, was intended to be the first of a series of railways criss-crossing the province and linking it with Nova Scotia, Maine, and Canada.[20] The strain of financing the E & NA proved too much for the province, however, and between 1861 and 1865 the railway generated only $89,533, while interest on the railway bonds absorbed $1,437,862. Debt servicing cost 37.6 per cent of all public expenditures after 1860. One of the arguments in favour of Confederation in New Brunswick was not only that it would result in an Intercolonial Railway linking the British North American colonies but also that it would relieve the province of the burden of debt servicing that prevented the completion of other desirable projects, such as the Western Extension from Saint John to the Maine border. Certainly, Tilley did not see Confederation as putting an end to provincial railway-building programs. Early in 1864, his government passed the Railway Facility Act, promising a $10,000-per-mile subsidy to any private company willing to construct certain specific routes. In June 1867, the government of New Brunswick took $300,000 in stock in the Western Extension and granted it the $10,000-per-mile subsidy.

Nova Scotia began its railway program with the construction of a line from Halifax to Windsor. Although officially completed in 1858, it also continued to require additional expenditures every year until 1864, when the next major railway – the Pictou Extension – was begun. These projects stretched Nova Scotia's credit to its limit and added weight to the pro-Confederate argument that without union there would be no further railways. In both Nova Scotia and New Brunswick, the scope of government activities could not now be expanded without the imposition of direct taxation or substantial increases in customs duties, neither of which would have been acceptable to the provincial electorate. Prince Edward Island had not yet reached that point. It had also increased its public indebtedness and, like the other two Maritime provinces, had steadily increased the per-capita income raised through customs duties, but the money was directed towards purchasing land from the landlords for resale on easy terms to the tenants. Prince Edward Islanders were as enthusiastic about railways as other Maritimers, but the land problem hindered railway construction. 'To make the proprietors' land more valuable by your public capital drawn partly from the tenants' would not be just, R.P. Haythorne declared in 1871, as he vainly sought to hold back the pressure for railway development on the Island.[21]

In retrospect, it is easy to cast scorn upon development programs that promised far more than they delivered and even to dismiss them as little more than another strategy for buying votes. Yet it is time to move away from the notion that public finance during this period was simply a mechanism for the distribution of spoils and the government merely 'a robust little corporation for private aggrandizement of its members and the incidental conduct of public affairs.'[22] The politicians of the pre-Confederation Maritimes did consider the long-term interests of their provinces. Undeniably, their policies unleashed sectional tensions, since they tended to give disproportionate benefits to those communities through which the railways passed. But the lines that the governments of Nova Scotia and New Brunswick built first were the ones that made most commercial sense, and it was intended that eventually railways would extend across the whole province. If there was disagreement over railway building it was over the priorities to be followed. The railways were not seen as conflicting with the existing commercial policies of the colonies but as complementary to them. While railways did not live up to the exaggerated hopes of their promoters, the very large sums of money imported for railway construction contributed to economic growth and to the widespread prosperity that marked this period.

Inevitably, the benefits of this prosperity were unevenly distributed. Those who benefited least were the Native people of the region. Although reserves had been set aside for them, the land was usually in the less desirable locations and discouraged any successful transition to agriculture. Confined to reserves that were too small to support a hunting culture, many became dependent on public and private charity. Native men worked as guides and engaged in marginal trapping, while Native women made and hawked handicrafts, particularly baskets and moccasins, from door to door. Many were reduced to begging for the survival of their families, like the woman who appealed to Juliana Ewing in Fredericton in 1868: 'she says "Sister, my baby very ill. Give me 2 or 3 cents" which I do.'[23] New Brunswick had decided in 1844 to sell reserved land in order to raise money for an Indian fund, but despite the sale of 16 per cent of the 66,096 acres by 1867, only £2,853.10.0 was generated for the Indian fund, never enough to meet even the immediate needs of the Natives for relief, let alone provide them with schools or other forms of assistance. In Nova Scotia, the government decided to allow squatters to purchase the land while providing for Natives by putting the money into an Indian fund, but by 1866 only $1,531 had been collected.[24] On Prince Edward Island, there was no reserved land to be sold. The Assembly proved particularly niggardly, voting £30 for Native people in 1862, nothing in 1863, and a mere £10 in 1864, although in 1865 Theophilus Stewart, one of the Island's two Indian commissioners, raised sufficient money in London to purchase Lennox Island as a reserve. When the federal government took over responsibility for Indian affairs in 1867, the deputy superintendent general of Indian affairs called for 'a philanthropic effort' to bring the Maritime Natives 'up at least to the standard of the more advanced Indians of Ontario and Quebec.'[25] Ironically, the 150 or so Micmacs in Newfoundland, whose numbers remained fairly constant during most of the nineteenth century, benefited from the underdevelopment of the interior of the colony. They continued to live by hunting and trapping, as their eighteenth-century forebears had done, although by the 1860s most of them had abandoned wigwams for houses and dressed essentially as Europeans. They also sold wood to local fishermen and acted as guides for the geologists, surveyors, and sportsmen who began to show a growing interest in the resources of the interior. Even the Labrador Inuit could not avoid integration into a European trading network, although here it was one controlled by the Moravian missionaries.[26]

Blacks benefited more than the Native peoples from the economic growth of the period, but still suffered from a legacy of discrimination and prejudice. The majority of the region's Blacks had been hived off on small plots of marginal land, in areas like Guysborough County in Nova Scotia or Loch Lomond just outside Saint John. Many of them drifted to the cities, the men to find casual labour, the women to work as domestic servants. Not surprisingly Blacks were frequently found among the urban underclass and ended up in court more often than Whites.[27] Over time they tended to form small, residentially segregated communities. In 1860 one 'owner of a lot of land situate [sic] at Africville' petitioned for aid for the 'Nine Families of Colour' residing in what would eventually become the major Black community in Halifax.[28] But although most Blacks remained poor, there were a growing number of seafaring, marine-related trades open to Black males in the larger urban centres, and the Black communities were strengthened by a small but steady flow of sailors from Bermuda and the West Indies, preachers from American Black churches, and until the Civil War, runaway slaves. These immigrants frequently provided the leadership in establishing segregated, voluntary institutions for their communities. In Halifax these came to include a mutual benefit society, a militia company, two fraternal lodges, a temperance society, and at least one labour-based organization. The most important of the Black institutions were undoubtedly the various African Baptist and African Methodist Episcopal churches. By 1861 the United African Baptist Association, founded by Richard Preston in 1854, had fifteen churches with 443 members in Halifax and along the south shore of Nova Scotia. The Black churches not only provided a variety of welfare and educational services for their members, but also community leaders who increasingly challenged the racial barriers that hindered Black advancement, particularly in areas like education and employment. At least at this stage, Black leaders had not yet abandoned their belief that there was a place for them in Maritime society, although growing residential segregation and the hardening of racial attitudes among the region's White population would erode this optimism in the later nineteenth century.[29]

Neither Natives nor Blacks could much influence the political decisions that affected them. For the Acadians, however, the decade would see the beginnings of a political struggle for recognition. Inevitably, the leadership came from New Brunswick, where Acadians formed just over 15 per cent of the population at the time of Confederation. The Acadians were concentrated in the less fertile northern part of the province, where agriculture was also handicapped by severe winters. Many Acadians therefore engaged in subsistence farming, often combined with timbering. Others entered the fisheries, which remained under the control of the Jersey merchants, particularly the Robins. Few Acadians were prosperous, but the élite, although small, was growing, and Acadians had begun to play a role in politics at the parish level.[30] Much of the leadership in Acadian society was provided by Roman Catholic priests from Quebec. The church operated convent and parish schools, and in 1864 it established the Collège Saint-Joseph, which was incorporated as a university and given a provincial grant in 1868. From Saint-Joseph would graduate the children of the Acadian élite, like Pierre-Amand Landry, who became the first Acadian admitted to the New Brunswick bar in 1870.[31] The founding in 1867 of *Le moniteur acadien*, the first French-language newspaper, also helped to accelerate the politicization of the Acadians. Acadian nationalism, however, would not emerge as full-blown force until the 1870s. Even then it remained an élite movement that concentrated on symbolic issues of limited concern to the vast majority of the Acadian population, who continued to live in a subsistence economy at a standard well below that of most English-speaking New Brunswickers.

It was not only cultural minorities that suffered from an inherently inegalitarian social structure. The myth that the rural population lived in a series of stable communities in which life was harsh but in which there was a rough equality of status has been exploded by a number of recent studies. In agricultural communities, the size and productivity of farms varied widely and so did the standard of living of those who toiled in the fields. Given the wide disparity in the agricultural capacity of the land, the date at which settlement occurred was critical in deciding who would acquire the most productive farms, and the gap between wealthier and poorer farmers was likely to widen over time. By the 1860s, every community had a class of backland farmers whose land could not provide them with an adequate standard of living and who were compelled to supplement their incomes by off-farm labour. The men might perform casual labour for their wealthier neighbours or travel farther afield to find employment. The women added to the family income by weaving cloth or performing other chores for neighbours, while their daughters were compelled to enter the service of others. One study estimates that in Nova Scotia farming communities perhaps 20 per cent of the population operated holdings sufficiently profitable to supply all their needs, provided most of the produce that went to market, and regularly employed their neighbours as farmhands or servants. At the other extreme were about a third of the farm households that generated less than half of their own subsistence requirements and depended upon off-farm labour for their very survival. In bad times they faced the threat of starvation, or at least malnutrition, which rendered them more vulnerable to disease and a lower life expectancy. In between the extremes were those who enjoyed a 'modest competence,' whose farms usually produced small surpluses, and who could by reciprocal exchange survive the periodic failure of crops or a collapse of commercial markets.[32]

It is possible that economic disparities were less pronounced in communities with access to a common property resource, such as the fisheries. But such communities were also more vulnerable to the vagaries of nature and fluctuations in market demand, and the operation of the truck system frequently meant that what they shared was poverty. During most of the 1860s the fisheries were the least prosperous sector of the regional economy. Indeed, by opening the inshore waters to American fishermen, the Reciprocity Treaty of 1854 may have offset whatever advantage there was in securing access to the American market. Part of the difficulty was a steady increase in the number of fishermen, and by the late 1860s, all along the coast of Nova Scotia, there was a steady decline in the quantities of fish taken in proportion to the number of men and vessels engaged in the shore fishery. One reason for this decline was the destruction of river spawning grounds that provided a source of natural food for migrating schools of cod and mackerel, and the Canadian government's efforts to protect the spawning grounds through the Fishery Act of 1868 provided little immediate relief. Because of a series of poor catches, Maritime fishermen were forced to move farther afield to compete with Newfoundland fishermen off the Labrador coast. The Newfoundland government responded by imposing duties on imported fishing supplies, while individual Newfoundlanders protested by acts of vandalism and even violence against their Nova Scotia competitors.[33] This reaction was hardly surprising. Many Maritime fishermen could ride out hard times because they were able to combine fishing with farming, and while they were at sea their wives cultivated the farm. But in most Newfoundland outports there was limited demand for casual labour, and even subsistence farming was extremely difficult. The collapse of the seal fishery in the 1860s compounded these difficulties, and mass starvation was avoided only through the distribution of relief by the government. Relief payments constituted a severe drain on the provincial treasury, and in 1864 the government sought to raise the money by local assessment, but this unpopular measure was soon abandoned. When a series of natural disasters resulted in island-wide destitution in 1866 and 1867, the government confined relief to the sick, the infirm, and destitute widows and orphans, a policy that contributed to its defeat in 1869 and led to the restoration of relief to able-bodied men in 1870.[34]

The gap between rich and poor was no less pronounced in the urban centres of the region. During the prosperous late 1850s and early 1860s, many merchants accumulated significant fortunes. In Halifax, the symbol of that wealth was Granville Street, which, after being levelled by a fire, was rebuilt in the early 1860s. The business core of Halifax was transformed from a mainly wooden district to 'a predominantly stone and brick quarter of new, large and fashionable buildings.' The 1860s also saw the construction of increasingly grandiose homes for the wealthy businessmen of the city, such as the 'commodious and well-built Brick Houses' that a contractor offered for sale in 1864, complete with 'Bathrooms fitted with pipes for hot and cold water; Water closets, &c.'[35] In the same city, many families lived in 'one room for all purposes, and in some of these, not over 14 foot square, eight, nine or ten persons of both sexes and all ages are huddled together.'[36] All the larger commercial centres of the region faced the problem of dealing with a large number of helpless and destitute people, and the ranks of the poor were swelled through immigration and seasonal unemployment.[37] For them the 'golden age' was certainly more myth than reality.

Class tensions undoubtedly increased in the 1860s, but they were muted by the structure of the largely pre-industrial economy. There were friendly societies and craft unions in the larger urban centres, particularly in trades connected with shipping and construction; but the artisan population was small and scattered, and artisans tended to identify their interests with the mercantile and professional élites. Both groups subscribed to an ideology that emphasized liberal political values, self-improvement, and the pursuit of economic growth. Class conflict, if such it can be called, tended to take the form of a struggle to broaden the franchise or introduce more popular control over the institutions of government. Class division was expressed as a debate over the terms upon which access to resources should be granted or the appropriate form of economic development to be pursued. Regardless of the nature of the franchise, the transients and the propertyless had little political power, and politics remained essentially a struggle between members of the mercantile and professional élites.[38] Economic self-interest was a major determinant of their voting behaviour, but of at least equal significance – and frequently intertwined – were ethnic origin and religious affiliation. During the middle decades of the nineteenth century there was a rapid expansion of evangelical Protestantism throughout British North America. In all the colonies, the evangelicals joined in alliances committed to introduce religious instruction into the schools, uphold the sanctity of the sabbath, encourage temperance, and prevent the spread of Catholicism. Inevitably the evangelicals clashed with the increasingly well-organized Catholics, whose numbers had been swelled in the urban areas by the influx of famine Irish during these same decades.

The extent to which class interest, ethnic loyalty, or religious commitment dictated the nature of politics varied from colony to colony. In New Brunswick the reformers, or 'Smashers,' remained the dominant party throughout the early 1860s. The conservatives had only the support of the well-entrenched but generally unpopular Anglican and Presbyterian establishment. The reformers had been forced to abandon prohibition, but their stand on temperance still ensured them the support of most evangelical Protestants. Many women, although they could not vote, were 'great allies' of the party and participated in political activities.[39] The reformers also enjoyed widespread support among Catholics, despite growing tension over the structure of the school system and Protestant fears over what appeared to be the increasing influence of Catholics in the government. In 1861, Samuel Leonard Tilley, an evangelical Anglican and the owner of a large drugstore in Saint John, emerged as the dominant figure in the party, shoving aside such rivals as Albert J. Smith and replacing Charles Fisher as premier when the latter was caught in a Crown land scandal.[40] Although an evangelical, Tilley and his supporters sought to 'put aside this "No Popery" cry!' and viewed with scorn the 'unscrupulous' efforts of Orange extremists who claimed that his government 'had knuckled to the Catholics by putting out a *green Postage Stamp*!!'[41] But the politicization of the substantial Irish-Catholic population of the colony, symbolized by the election of Timothy Warren Anglin to the Assembly in 1861 as an independent liberal, made it increasingly difficult for Tilley to retain Catholic support or to ignore the demands of the militant evangelicals for a reorganization of the education system that would put an end to denominational schools.[42] Partly for this reason, Tilley emphasized his party's commitment to a development program that had broad popular support.

In Nova Scotia, the conservatives were more successful in appealing for popular support by dropping the property qualification for the franchise, by forming an alliance with the Catholics, and by abandoning their opposition to the development program originally put forward by the reformers. Although the reformers returned to power in 1860, they took office at a time of shrinking revenues and so could not raise the funds for further railway development or reach an agreement with the Canadian government for the construction of the Intercolonial. They also faced 'the most determined opposition' of the Catholic population,[43] who were incensed by the efforts of the reformers to restore a property qualification for the franchise. The latter measure was blocked by the conservative-dominated Legislative Council and was an important issue in the 1863 election, which saw the reformers under the leadership of Joseph Howe virtually annihilated. The architect of the conservative victory was Charles Tupper, an Amherst doctor and businessman, who replaced James William Johnston, a fellow Baptist, as premier in May 1864. Like Tilley, Tupper was under pressure to reform the educational system, and in the school bills of 1864 and 1866 he created a system of public schools supported by general assessment. He sought to mollify the evangelicals by allowing Bible reading and prayer in the schools, while assuring Catholics that any religious instruction would be of a non-sectarian nature and that his bills would not prevent the continuing existence of Catholic schools in those parts of the province where there was a substantial Catholic population.[44] Tupper's compromise did not satisfy Catholic archbishop Thomas Connolly, and the spectre of direct taxation aroused widespread discontent. Yet Tupper undoubtedly hoped that the development policies of his government, which were unaffordable if money had to be found for schools, were sufficiently popular to stave off defeat on this issue.

In Prince Edward Island, since the introduction of what was effectively universal male suffrage in the 1850s, the conservatives had been on the defensive. They could not embark upon a policy of economic development as long as the land question was unresolved, and since their leaders were proprietors or land agents, they were not prepared to outbid the reformers in promising a radical solution to that problem. In 1859 and again in 1863 they were returned to power by appealing to the Protestant majority and by raising the spectre of Catholic aggression,[45] but the land issue would not go away. To buy time, the conservatives created a land commission in 1860; its report in 1862 recommended either an imperial guarantee of £100,000 to allow continued purchases from proprietors on a voluntary basis or compulsory conversion to freehold tenure by allowing tenants to buy their land at a price to be set by arbitration. The government passed enabling legislation for these measures, but the imperial government refused its assent. In 1864, the conservatives therefore passed a bill enabling tenants to purchase their holdings, but at a price most tenants considered exorbitant. Between 1864 and 1868 only forty-five tenants took advantage of the act. Out of frustration, many tenants turned to the Tenant League, which encouraged them to refuse to pay rents. During 1864 and 1865, the league spread across the Island, but it collapsed when the government used troops to enforce rent collection. Although the league failed in its objectives, it did convince many proprietors that the system was doomed, and in 1866 the huge Cunard estate, representing about 20 per cent of the Island, was sold to the government. Thereafter, at least one significant estate was purchased each year, and only a handful of die-hard proprietors refused to sell until forced to do so after Prince Edward Island's entry into Confederation in 1873.[46] The discontent aroused among the tenantry by the use of troops against the league and divisions among the conservatives over Confederation resulted in the return of a reform government in 1867 and again in 1870. The refusal of liberal Protestants to agree to a grant for St Dunstan's College, however, led to the defection of a number of Catholics and the formation of a new Catholic-Protestant conservative alliance.[47] The new government was dominated by men like James and William Pope who were in favour of Confederation, particularly if it would give them the resources to purchase the remaining proprietorial estates and embark upon the same kind of development projects as the Tilley and Tupper administrations. In the event, the conservatives did not bother to wait for Confederation but began to build a railway that ultimately drove the Island into near-bankruptcy and made Confederation all the more desirable.

In Newfoundland, sectarian bitterness went even deeper. According to the census of 1857, Protestants, of mainly English descent, formed 54 per cent of the population, while the Catholics, overwhelmingly Irish, had fallen to 46 per cent. Except in Conception Bay and St John's, there was little mingling between the two groups, but there was abundant potential for conflict.[48] Since the winning of responsible government in 1855, Newfoundland had been governed by a predominantly Catholic reform party, which gradually became more sectarian in character and lost the support of the Methodists and some liberal Catholics. Moreover, it was a party marked by disunity because of conflict between the Catholic bishop, John T. Mullock, and the Catholic premier, John Kent. In 1861 the governor, Sir Alexander Bannerman, dismissed Kent, and the result was a serious election riot between rival groups of Catholics in Conception Bay and the subsequent siege of the Colonial Building by discontented members of Kent's party. When troops fired at a crowd on Water Street, three were killed and twenty wounded. The riots persuaded both Mullock and Bishop Edward Feild of the Church of England to withdraw from political activity. Although the conservatives won the election by carrying all the Protestant constituencies, they offered cabinet positions to a number of Catholic politicians and in 1865 persuaded two of the leading Catholic liberals, John Kent and Ambrose Shea, to join the government of Frederic Carter. Thus began an era of power-sharing between Catholics and Protestants that resulted in a roughly proportional distribution of all government patronage. This escape from sectarian politics prevented Newfoundland from becoming a 'Transatlantic Ulster,' but it also hindered the development of reform. Because there were no municipal institutions on the island, the dominance of St John's was reinforced. Almost all the MLAs came from St John's, many of them elected by acclamation. Schools, roads, ferries, street lighting, wharf building, and all local services were financed from St John's and run by centrally appointed boards under the control of the

MLAs. Poor-relief funds were also distributed as patronage. The result was that 'for the most part, politics was a St John's pastime, and its players used the bays as their occasional arena.'[49]

During the 1860s the political climate of the four Atlantic colonies was altered irrevocably by the issue of Confederation. Because of the speed with which the union was constructed and the central role played by the government of the United Province of Canada, it is easy to assume that Confederation was a measure imposed upon the region by forces extraneous to it. What this interpretation minimizes is the ease with which Maritimers allowed themselves to be devoured by the Canadian wolf. Union of the British North American provinces was hardly a new idea in the 1860s, and there was a very large body of potential support for the measure. When Charles Lindsey toured the region in 1860, he reported optimistically that 'everywhere I have found a general feeling in favour of an Union of the Provinces.'[50] The vast majority of Maritimers were committed to the British connection, and like most Canadians, they envied the rapid growth of the American republic but were frightened by the implications of its increasing power and by the obvious desire of Great Britain to withdraw its protective umbrella. The growing certainty of a northern victory in the American Civil War and the increasing desire of Britain to limit its responsibilities for the defence of British North America inevitably revived discussion of the idea of a colonial union.

Many obstacles stood in the way of translating inchoate sentiment into a measure of practical politics. Although Tupper saw the advantages of union, he felt that 'it rests with Canada, as the largest and most important of the Provinces to take the first step.'[51] In this sense the formation of the Great Coalition in the United Province of Canada in 1864 was the critical event on the road to Confederation. The timing was propitious. The three Maritime governments had agreed to meet at Charlottetown in September 1864 in order to discuss Maritime Union. Since Maritime Union held out few tangible benefits, and the surrender of provincial autonomy had little popular appeal, the Maritime delegates at Charlottetown were persuaded by a delegation from Canada to shelve the idea and to endorse in principle a plan for the federal union of British North America. At the Quebec Conference in October 1864, the details were hammered out in remarkably short time. In part, the relative unanimity shown by the Fathers of Confederation reflected their homogeneity. Drawn from the political élites of the colonies, they drew upon a common ideological tradition, and their disagreements were over means, not ends. Moreover, the delegates from the Atlantic colonies again revealed the extent of their desire for union by allowing the Canadians to set the agenda and by agreeing to union on what were essentially Canadian terms. They had few illusions about the room they had for manoeuvre in the face of Canadian solidarity. Charles Tupper admitted that the gradual withdrawal of Britain made the subordination of the Maritimes to Canada inevitable and accepted that the goal of the Maritime delegates must be to gain the best terms of union that they could.

At Charlottetown it had been agreed that the union would be federal rather than legislative, but the Canadian resolutions called for greater centralization than many people in the Atlantic colonies wanted. Tupper and Tilley, like many of the delegates, would have preferred a legislative to a federal union, but they recognized that such a measure would be unacceptable to their electorates. When Tilley returned to New Brunswick, he insisted that only five of the fifty-nine acts passed by the New Brunswick legislature in the previous session would be found *ultra vires* of the provincial government under the proposed division of power and that the only power to be surrendered to Ottawa would be control over the Post Office.[52] It is easy to assume that such statements were calculated to deceive, but Tilley and his colleagues may indeed have believed that what they were creating was a government whose primary function was not to supersede the existing colonial governments but to take on new responsibilities that those governments were incapable of performing. If the Maritime Fathers of Confederation can be condemned, it should be for agreeing to a series of financial agreements that would leave the provinces with insufficient resources to carry out their remaining responsibilities. Once again this decision reflected the desire of the Maritime leaders to reach an agreement even if it meant bowing to Canadian terms. A potentially serious confrontation over the level of subsidies to be given to the provincial governments was avoided when Tupper came up with a formula that deliberately underestimated the needs of the Nova Scotia government in order to arrive at a figure – an annual grant of eighty cents per capita – acceptable to the Canadians. This decision ensured that the Maritime provincial governments would be left with wholly inadequate resources, while the government of Ontario would have an annual surplus. The roots of future regional disparity lay in creating a series of provinces with equal responsibilities but vastly unequal resources.

Much of the debate at Quebec focused on the structure of the new federal parliament. There was a general consensus that the House of Commons would have to be elected on the basis of representation by population, although the Prince Edward Island delegates remained angry that they would have only five members in the House. A solution to this impasse could have been found by enlarging the size of the House so that Prince Edward Island would be entitled to six members, but the Canadians were wedded to keeping the House as small as possible, and once again they carried the day. In the debate over the composition of the Senate, the Maritime delegates also showed their eagerness to reach an agreement acceptable to the Canadians. Instead of pushing for equal provincial representation, they accepted the principle of sectional equality. After a bitter debate, both the Canadas and the whole of the Maritimes were each given twenty-four senators, with an additional four senators for Newfoundland. But the decision that senators would be appointed for life by the federal government ensured that the Senate would have no moral authority to challenge the governing party in the House of Commons and limited its effectiveness as the guardian of regional interests.

It is hardly surprising that when the delegates returned home they were faced with widespread and vehement opposition to the Quebec Resolutions. Part of that opposition came from those who would have found fault with any scheme of union, but the ranks of the anti-Confederates were swelled by the general unpopularity of the Quebec Resolutions. One of the reasons why the men who gathered together at Quebec had been able to hammer out a constitution in such a short time was that they were not democrats. Indeed, they were determined to erect barriers against the democratic excesses that, in their minds, had led to the collapse of the American constitution and resulted in the American Civil War. For this reason they limited the size of the House of Commons so that it would remain manageable by the colonial élites and created an ultra-conservative second chamber to curtail the powers of the popularly elected Commons. Almost all the Maritime delegates shared these anti-democratic and anti-majoritarian goals, and so did many of the anti-Confederate leaders. But there was also a strong populist dimension to the anti-Confederate movement, a widespread feeling that what the Quebec Resolutions would establish was a remote and distant government that would be unresponsive to public opinion.

Such fears were expressed everywhere in British North America; but those Canadians who were suspicious of the centralizing tendencies of the Quebec Resolutions could at least comfort themselves with the fact that the new constitution would liberate the two Canadas from the union of 1841 and restore to each section control over its own affairs. Moreover, in new House of Commons, Ontario would have the largest bloc of members and could foresee the day when it might have a clear majority. Quebec, at least in the minds of the Bleu leadership, had sufficient strength to protect its vital interests. It was the Atlantic provinces that were being asked to make a leap of faith by surrendering their existing provincial autonomy in return for participation in a government that must inevitably be dominated by Canadian interests. Those

Maritimers who had assisted in drafting the Quebec scheme knew it would be unpopular. A few, most notably George Coles, Edward Palmer, and A.A. Macdonald of Prince Edward Island, abandoned their support for the union and placed themselves at the head of the rapidly mounting opposition to the measure. Even Tilley and Tupper dissembled by holding out the hope that the Quebec Resolutions could be modified in London. But the pro-Confederates were astute politicians. They knew that the Great Coalition was fragile, that its manoeuvring space was limited by the anti-Confederate feeling aroused by the Rouges in Lower Canada, and that accordingly 'it is the Quebec scheme & little else we can hope to have secured.'[53]

The strength of the anti-Confederate movement in the Maritimes was that it could appeal both to those whom Peter Waite describes in Canada West as the 'ultras,' who opposed Confederation on any terms, and the 'critics,' who disliked the Quebec Resolutions although they were not against Confederation *per se*.[54] Economic issues were inevitably central to this debate. Throughout the region there was a fear that Confederation would bring higher taxes without a commensurate increase in benefits. In fact, the only immediate advantage that Confederation held out was the Intercolonial Railway, and since it would only benefit those communities through which it passed, Tilley was in no hurry to have the route settled upon before Confederation was accomplished. In Nova Scotia it was clearer where the railway would run and consequently who would benefit from its construction, a fact that partly explains why enthusiasm for Confederation was less pronounced in the southwestern part of the province. But one should not overemphasize the political significance of the Intercolonial, since the long-term economic benefits of integration with Canada were far from certain.

Historians have vigorously debated and reinterpreted the Confederation question. In the late 1960s, Del Muise suggested that the conflict over Confederation in Nova Scotia was between those opposed to integration because they were committed to the old, maritime economy of 'wood, wind and sail' and the more progressive members of the provincial élite who sought to make the transition to continental integration and an industrial economy based on coal and railroads. Muise's interpretive framework was particularly convincing in explaining why pro-Confederates like Tupper, who came from areas with coal resources and the potential for industrialization, were prepared to accept Confederation even on the basis of the unpalatable Quebec Resolutions and why there was so much opposition to Confederation from those committed to shipping and shipbuilding, who saw little future for their industry in a continental economy. But any attempt to divide the whole region into anti- and pro-Confederates on the basis of their commitment to an economy of 'wood, wind and sail' or to industrialization is too deterministic. By the 1860s there was a growing desire to participate in an evolving industrial economy in the urban centres and larger towns of Nova Scotia and New Brunswick, but those involved in manufacturing in both colonies were divided over the value of Confederation.[55] Indeed, one of the arguments of the anti-Confederates was that union with Canada would hinder the growth of local industry by introducing Canadian competition. Even in those communities committed to shipping and shipbuilding, public opinion was deeply divided. It can hardly be denied that much of the support for Confederation came from those who equated union with material progress and modernization. Yet it does not follow that all the proponents of Confederation were on the side of progress, while all their opponents were opposed to such changes. Progressives and reactionaries could be found on both sides.

Years ago, Alfred G. Bailey suggested that in New Brunswick there were strong ethnic and religious overtones to the struggle.[56] Traditionally, historians have emphasized the growing independence of the colonies after the grant of responsible government, but these were also decades of increasing anglicization, as British immigrants flooded in and as the élites sought to emulate the social patterns of the mother country. The Quebec Resolutions appear to have been most strongly supported by the British-born, less enthusiastically endorsed by the native-born, and viewed with the greatest suspicion by cultural minorities who were far from enamoured of British and imperial models, like the Acadians and many Irish Catholics. Of course, no group was monolithic in its response to Confederation. Many anti-Confederates, like R.D. Wilmot of New Brunswick and Joseph Howe of Nova Scotia, criticized the Quebec Resolutions precisely because they did not adhere to strictly British models or out of fear that Confederation would lead inevitably to separation from the Empire. Imperial support for the proposed constitution was an important factor in persuading many of the colonists, including many of those initially opposed to the Quebec Resolutions, that Confederation was, if not desirable, at least inescapable.

The struggle between the pros and the antis was first seriously joined in New Brunswick, where Tilley was pushed by Lieutenant-Governor Arthur Hamilton Gordon into an election. Tilley criss-crossed the province in the winter of 1864–5 in a heroic but vain effort to sell the merits of the Quebec Resolutions. The mood of the province was best expressed by Albert J. Smith of Westmorland County, the leader of a diverse but widespread coalition of anti-Confederates, who 'emphatically urged his audiences to ponder the old proverb, which warns us "to let well enough alone."' He predicted that under the proposed constitution New Brunswick would became 'a mere municipality' and that 'in a few years we shall be at the feet of Canada – Upper Canada – who will exercise control not only over Lower Canada but also over us.'[57] In the election of March 1865, the antis carried at least 60 per cent of the popular vote and thirty of the forty-one seats in the Assembly. Yet the new government, headed by Smith, was a curious collection of all those who opposed the Quebec Resolutions and contained within its midst a number of men who might better be described as critics rather than as diehard opponents of Confederation. The Saint John *Weekly Telegraph* predicted that 'it cannot hang together and must fall to pieces of its own weight.'[58] Smith was also unlucky. By the time he assumed office the economy of the province had entered a downturn, and the government found itself with a rapidly depleted treasury. Moreover, shortly after the election the U.S. government gave notice that it intended to abrogate the Reciprocity Treaty in 1866, and Smith's efforts to renegotiate an agreement directly with Washington came to naught. Smith also found himself under increasing pressure from the British government to reconsider Confederation. So weak was Smith's government that he was coerced by Gordon into agreeing to support Confederation if the terms could be improved, and in April 1866 he resigned despite his party's nominal majority in the Assembly. In the June election the pro-Confederates won a majority as sweeping as the one by which they had been defeated the previous year. Recognizing that 'it was too firm an adherence to the Quebec Scheme which [had] made the defeat of the Confederation party at the March elections so disastrous and complete,'[59] the Unionists held out hope of substantial alterations in the scheme after the principle of union was accepted. They also raised the bogey of the Fenians, militant Irish nationalists who were amassed along the American border and who assisted the Confederates by making the loyalty cry more credible. Without the Fenians, the Unionist majority might have been smaller, but the pro-Confederates believed – probably correctly – that they would still have carried the day. Only in areas with an Irish-Catholic or Acadian majority, particularly the latter, did the antis show any real strength in 1866.[60]

In Nova Scotia, a widespread but diverse coalition was also formed to oppose Confederation. Joseph Howe emerged as its leader, and he attacked the Quebec Resolutions in terms very similar to those used by Smith. Tupper marked time, while the British government exerted pressure on the colony. This policy gradually began to pay dividends, as some of those who had opposed Confederation, including William Annand, the leader of the Liberal Party, indicated their support for union if the terms could be modified. On 10 April 1866, Tupper finally moved a resolution expressing the Assembly's support for Confederation and authorizing delegates to be sent to arrange with the imperial government 'a scheme of Union which will effectively assure just provisions for the rights and interests of the Province.'[61] In reality, both Tupper and Tilley were only too well aware there was no possibility that the Quebec Resolutions could be altered substantially. At the London Conference, in December 1866, few changes were made. Since only two of the Maritime colonies had indicated their assent for union, each was given twelve Senate seats, and minor adjustments were made to the financial arrangements for the provinces. Archbishop Connolly of Nova Scotia, who had assisted Tupper by openly supporting Confederation, sought to include in the act of Union a clause guaranteeing Catholics the right to separate schools, but, as worded, the provision inserted in the act applied only to Quebec and Ontario. At least one of the Nova Scotia delegates, W.A. Henry, wished to see the Maritimes given more weight in the Senate and the provinces more power, but his was a voice in the wilderness, and the terms embodied in law as the British North America Act were essentially those worked out at Quebec.

Because of the important role played by the British government, it is tempting to see Confederation as a measure imposed on the colonists against their will. But government pressure could not have been effective if the majority of the provincial leadership in both Nova Scotia and New Brunswick had not been convinced that Confederation, even on the basis of the Quebec Resolutions, was unavoidable. Undoubtedly imperial enthusiasm helped to convert the more conservative groups in colonial society. Imperial interference, however, was a weapon that had to be used cautiously, since it could provoke an adverse colonial reaction. Allies like the haughty and unpopular Gordon were a mixed blessing to the Confederate cause, and it is possible that the pro-Confederates won their victory in New Brunswick in 1866 despite, not because of, Gordon's intervention in provincial politics. In fact, even without imperial support there was a potential majority for union, on slightly improved terms. Anti-Confederate sentiment may have been marginally stronger in Nova Scotia than in New Brunswick, but the delayed victory of the antis at the polls in 1867, after Confederation was a *fait accompli*, was roughly of the same dimensions as in New Brunswick in 1865 and was distorted by the anger that many Nova Scotians, including many pro-Confederates, felt at the undemocratic way in which they had been forced into the union. If an election had been held earlier, an anti-Confederate administration would undoubtedly have come to power, but it would have suffered from the same internal tensions and been subject to the same pressures as the Smith government in New Brunswick and quite likely would have suffered the same fate.

Prince Edward Island chose not to enter Confederation in this decade, but even on the Island there was considerable potential support for union. After the Charlottetown Conference, the majority of the Island's newspapers came out in favour of union upon 'reasonable' terms, and at Quebec none of the delegates opposed the principle of federation. But the other delegates at Quebec refused to respond sympathetically to any of the Island's concerns. Even James C. Pope, although declaring that 'in the abstract I have always admitted the *principle* of union,' complained that 'the Quebec Conference did not do justice to our little Island.' The terms offered to the Island did not recognize its peculiar financial position with a very low debt and few sources of potential revenues, ignored the fact that it would not benefit from the building of the Intercolonial and was unlikely to develop a strong manufacturing sector, refused to assist in settling the land problem, and left the colony virtually powerless in the proposed federal parliament. The colonial Assembly rejected these degrading terms, and the entire notion of entering Confederation, by passing a 'no terms' resolution, introduced by Pope. Yet even Pope accepted that if the other colonies formed a union 'with us it would eventually be a necessity.'[62] The Islanders, unable to renegotiate Reciprocity on their own and eager for an infusion of capital to resolve the land question, did not abandon negotiations with Canada. The formation in 1870 of a coalition government, dominated by conservatives sympathetic to Confederation and headed by James Pope, accelerated the process, as did the financial crisis generated by the building of the Island railway after 1870. But the number of MLAs prepared to accept Confederation if the terms were improved was growing steadily even before the Island approached insolvency. Its entry was delayed only until 1873, when the Canadian government offered terms very similar to what had been refused at Quebec.

Only Newfoundland was able to resist the lure of continental integration. Unlike the other Atlantic provinces, it had no immediate reason for entering a union. Newfoundland had limited trading links with the mainland and little likelihood of developing them. It had few concerns over defence and would not benefit from the building of the Intercolonial. Its revenues consistently exceeded its expenditures, and it could borrow money in London at lower rates than any of the other colonies. Newfoundland was not represented at the Charlottetown Conference, and in Quebec its informal delegation of two – Frederic Carter, the speaker of the House of Assembly, and Ambrose Shea, leader of the opposition – played a relatively minor part in the deliberations. In the initial debate in the Newfoundland Assembly in 1864, eighteen members spoke against union and twenty-one spoke in favour, but many of the latter indicated strong reservations about the Quebec Resolutions. Outside the legislature, there was clear opposition from the leading merchants of St John's and Conception Bay and from the Roman Catholic population of the colony, and Confederation was not made an issue in the election of 1865. The victorious Conservative government contained a number of pro-Confederates, including Carter, who became premier, and Ambrose Shea and his brother, but it was not united on the issue. Gradually the attitude of many of the merchants underwent a change. Because of a series of poor catches of cod, the local economy entered a severe depression, and Confederation seemed to offer a reduction in the cost of the local government and the chance of economic recovery. Like the other colonies, Newfoundland was aware of the support of the imperial government for Confederation. In 1869, the Assembly even passed draft terms of union, and Newfoundland entered into negotiations with Canada and received just about everything it requested, including a special annual grant of $175,000 for surrendering its Crown lands, an agreement ensuring that no export tax would be levied on Newfoundland fish, and a promise that the Dominion Militia Act would be modified so that Newfoundlanders need not fear having to serve in Canada.[63]

These terms, however, proved insufficient to convince the people of Newfoundland that union was to their advantage. During the summer of 1869, economic conditions improved because of a reasonable seal fishery and an abundant cod harvest. The opposition, led by one of the colony's leading merchants, Charles Fox Bennett, launched a vigorous and highly effective campaign against Confederation. The most vehement opposition came from the Catholic minority. Overwhelmingly Irish in background, they viewed Confederation as a colonial version of the infamous Act of Union that had brought Ireland under English domination. When Ambrose Shea, one of the few Catholic candidates to support Confederation, attempted to campaign in a Catholic constituency, he was treated as a traitor: 'at Paradise he was advised not to land; at Oderin he was sent on his way with flags at half mast and three groans; at Placentia he was met by priest and people bearing pots of pitch and bags of feathers, and the moaning of cow bells.'[64] Every constituency with a Catholic majority returned an anti-Confederate candidate, but even in the Protestant outports there was a considerable dislike for Confederation. The final result saw the antis carry twenty-one out of the thirty seats in the Assembly. The scale of the antis' victory must be attributed to the adroit campaigning of Bennett, who played upon the fears and the patriotism of his fellow Newfoundlanders; and it is easy to conclude that in the election of 1869 Newfoundlanders succumbed to emotion rather than reason. But as Frederick Jones has recently pointed out, 'there was a very good case against Confederation in 1869 and it should be given due weight even though it was urged emotionally and not too scrupulously by a master of the art of propaganda.'[65]

The decisions of Prince Edward Island and Newfoundland to reject Confederation in the late 1860s were undoubtedly influenced by evidence of continuing resentment in the colonies that had entered. In 1867, Tupper was the only pro-Confederate elected from the nineteen federal constituencies in Nova Scotia, and he did not enter the cabinet until 1870. The provincial election was equally decisive, with thirty-six of the thirty-eight seats going to anti-Confederates. Sir John A. Macdonald sought to appease the Nova Scotians by eliminating the tariff on grain, adjusting the sugar duties to favour Maritime refineries, and removing the tonnage duties that were considered a nuisance by shippers. Even by the end of the 1868 session, a number of Nova Scotians elected as antis were supporting the government on a regular basis. Moreover, as it became clear that the imperial government was not going to allow Nova Scotia to withdraw from Confederation, Joseph Howe and a number of the moderate antis shifted their ground from demanding repeal to asking for better terms. The most pressing issue was financial. After one year of Confederation, Ontario had a budget surplus of $1 million, while Nova Scotia had a deficit of $100,000 and the prospect of a further cut in provincial revenues because its provincial debt was higher than anticipated. As Howe pointed out, the formula devised at Quebec was fundamentally unjust because it merely totalled the liabilities of a province without making any allowance for the earning power of the assets assumed by the federal government. Much of the debt in the Maritimes had been incurred for the construction of government-owned and -operated railways that would return a regular dividend to the government, whereas the Canadian debt had been incurred by grants to private railway companies. The Canadian minister of finance agreed in 1869 to concessions that changed little but were sufficient to mollify Howe, who entered the cabinet and thus 'broke the back of anti-ism in Nova Scotia.' By the end of 1869, twelve of the eighteen antis elected in 1867 were supporting the Macdonald government.[66] The provincial administration continued to push, largely in vain, for further changes in the financial arrangements that left them with little more than the resources to meet current expenditures. Out of despair, a few of the most vehement anti-Confederates advocated annexation to the United States.[67]

Although none of the fifteen members returned from New Brunswick in the federal election of 1867 supported repeal, fewer than half were elected as supporters of the government. Moreover, the majority of New Brunswick members opposed the decision, made partly to appease Quebec, to build the Intercolonial through the sparsely populated north shore route, protested against the tariff increases of 1867 and 1870, and fought against the 1870 election bill, which abandoned vote by secret ballot. The apparent success of Nova Scotians in securing better financial terms for their province led New Brunswickers to demand 'equal justice,'[68] but Ottawa, under pressure from the Ontario members, refused to reopen negotiations. The New Brunswick government, as in Nova Scotia, found itself in a financial strait-jacket that left it unable to provide the services the people of the province demanded. A few New Brunswickers also dallied with annexationism.

One reason for continuing Maritime discontent was that New Brunswick and Nova Scotia were weakly represented in Ottawa during the first few years after Confederation. While Maritimers received four of the thirteen places in the cabinet in 1867, only Tilley, as minister of customs, and Peter Mitchell, as minister of marine and fisheries, were given important positions. Mitchell was the most successful in bringing a Maritime perspective to bear on policy making, perhaps because there had been no pre-Confederation fisheries department in the United Province of Canada. Virtually all the other major departments were simply staffed by the existing Canadian bureaucracy. Where the federal department absorbed a Maritime department, a Canadian was placed at the head and the Maritimers were given subordinate positions. Since the majority of Maritime MPs remained independent of the government and patronage was distributed on the basis of party loyalty, the Maritimes would continue to receive an inadequate share of federal appointments until integrated into a party system evolved in the United Province of Canada. Much of the legislation during this period also reflected Maritime weakness in the corridors of power. In almost every instance where uniformity seemed desirable, it was the Canadian model that was followed. At the end of the decade, the finance minister, Sir Francis Hincks, deemed it 'exceedingly desirable to have a uniform system for the whole Dominion' and introduced banking legislation that imposed much stricter requirements on Maritime banks than any of the Maritime governments had thought necessary or desirable.[69] To many Maritimers it seemed clear that what had been sold to them as a union on equal terms was really an annexation of the weaker by the stronger.

Years ago, George Rawlyk wrote a famous article on the paranoid style of regional protest movements,[70] but there was little that was paranoid about the feelings of disappointment and powerlessness experienced by most Maritimers in the immediate post-Confederation era. The next decade would bring some sense of reconciliation, as Maritimers were integrated into the Canadian political system and Tilley and Tupper assumed positions of prominence where they could ensure that the national policies of the federal government did not ignore the Maritimes. Yet, at the provincial level, there remained a sense of anger, particularly among Nova Scotians, who could not 'forget the manner in which Nova Scotia was forced into the union.'[71] For the most part this discontent took the form of a vigorous assertion of provincial rights. As the Maritime provincial governments came to grips with the implica- tions of the financial terms established in the 1860s, terms that left them unable to provide a level of services comparable to those that could be afforded by the larger and more prosperous provinces, the provincial agitation focused on the need for increased subsidies. Maritime jurists and politicians would also play a role in pushing for increased provin- cial power and a more decentralized federal system in the latter part of the nineteenth century.

Ironically, in the twentieth century, decentralization served only to widen regional disparities, since the Maritime provinces lacked the means to provide their citizens with the same range of public services and welfare programs as the wealthier provinces. Moreover, changes in federal political structures saw the Maritimes steadily reduced in their proportional representation in the House of Commons, while the Senate degenerated into political impotence except when motivated by parti- san considerations. The collapse of the Maritime industrial sector and the widening gap in living standards in the twentieth century cannot be ascribed solely to the inadequacy of federal policies, but it is hardly sur- prising that many Maritimers would begin to see the period before Con- federation as a 'golden age' and the Maritime anti-Confederates as perceptive critics of the Confederation scheme. Yet the example of New- foundland, which eventually drifted into bankruptcy because it could not afford the long-run costs of independence and joined the union in 1949 because it could not provide its citizens with the standard of living of Canadians, serves, as David Alexander once noted, to remind us that for the Maritimes there may not have been a viable alternative to Con- federation, which at least provided the region with a 'shabby dignity.'[72] Moreover, it is not entirely fair to judge the pro-Confederates of the 1860s by such standards. The 'golden age' after all was not so golden, and the supporters of Confederation were forced to make hard choices at a time when the world they knew was being turned upside down. In the end, they struggled for Confederation because they saw no other option if the Maritimes were to avoid annexation to the United States, to retain their traditional ties with Britain, and to develop a more diversi- fied economy less vulnerable to the whims of external markets. And in all of these goals, at least for the short term, they were successful.

Notes

CHAPTER 1 Early Societies: Sequences of Change

1 Douglas R. Grant, 'Recent Coastal Submergence of the Maritime Provinces, Canada,' *Canadian Journal of Earth Sciences* 7: 2 (1970), 676–89

2 Brian M. Fagan, *People of the Earth* (Boston 1989), 202–3, 209–21

3 James A. Tuck, 'A Summary of Atlantic Canada Prehistory,' *Canadian Archaeology Association* Bulletin 7 (Ottawa 1975), 122–44

4 George F. MacDonald, 'Debert: A Palaeo-Indian Site in Central Nova Scotia,' *National Museum of Man, Anthropology Papers 16* (Ottawa 1968), 53, 120

5 Harold W. Borns, 'Possible Palaeo-Indian Migration Routes in Northeastern North America,' *Maine Archaeology Society,* Bulletin 11, no. 1 (1971), 33–39

6 Richard M. Gramly, 'Eleven Thousand Years in Maine,' *Archaeology* 34: 6 (1981), 32–9

7 K.O. Emery and R.L. Edwards, 'Archaeological Potential of the Atlantic Continental Shelf,' *American Antiquity* 31 (Washington 1966), 736–7

8 Tuck, 'A Summary,' 122–44; Priscilla Renouf, 'A Late Palaeo-Indian and Early Archaic Sequence in Southern Labrador,' *Man in the Northeast* 13 (1977), 35–44; Stephen Loring, 'Palaeo-Indian Hunters and the Champlain Sea: A Presumed Association,' *Man in the Northeast* 19 (1980), 15–42

9 James A. Tuck and Robert McGhee, 'Archaic Cultures in the Strait of Belle Isle Region, Labrador,' *Arctic Anthropology* 12: 2 (Madison 1975), 76–91

10 Richard A. Doyle, Nathan D. Hamilton, James B. Petersen, and David Sanger, 'Late Palaeo-Indian Remains from Maine and Their Correlations in Northeast Prehistory,' *Archaeology of Eastern North America* 13 (1985), 1–33

11 David L. Keenlyside, 'Late Palaeo-Indian Evidence from the Southern Gulf of St. Lawrence,' *Archaeology of Eastern North America* 13 (1985), 79–92; Robert McGhee and James A. Tuck, 'An Archaic Sequence from the Strait of Belle

Isle, Labrador,' *National Museum of Man Mercury Series* 34 (Ottawa 1975)

12 James A. Tuck, *Maritime Provinces Prehistory* (Ottawa 1984), 14–17

13 James A. Tuck, 'The Northeastern Maritime Continuum: 8000 Years of Cultural Development in the Far Northeast,' *Arctic Anthropology* 12: 2 (1975), 139–47; Bruce J. Bourque, 'Comments on the Late Archaic Populations of Central Maine: The View from Turner Farm,' *Arctic Anthropology* 12: 2 (1975), 35–45; William A. Fitzhugh, 'Introduction,' *Arctic Anthropology* 12: 2 (1975), 1–6

14 David Sanger, 'Culture Change as an Adaptive process in the Maine-Maritime Region,' *Arctic Anthropology* 12: 2 (1975), 60–75

15 David Sanger, 'Cow Point: An Archaic Cemetery in New Brunswick,' *National Museum of Man Mercury Series* 12 (Ottawa 1973)

16 James A. Tuck, 'Ancient People of Port au Choix: The Excavation of an Archaic Indian Cemetery in Newfoundland,' *Newfoundland Social and Economic Studies* 17 (St John's 1976), 93–7

17 James A. Tuck, *Newfoundland and Labrador Prehistory* (Ottawa 1976), 16–60

18 Robert McGhee, *The Burial at L'Anse-Amour* (Ottawa 1976)

19 Tuck, *Newfoundland and Labrador Prehistory,* 48

20 Tuck, 'Ancient People,' 111, 118; Bourque, 'Comments on the Late Archaic,' 35–45

21 James V. Wright, 'The Shield Archaic,' *National Museum of Canada, Publications in Archaeology* 3 (Ottawa 1972), 67; David Sanger, 'Deadman's Pool – A Tobique Complex Site in Northern New Brunswick,' *Man in the Northeast* 2 (1971), 5–22

22 William J. Ritchie, 'A Typology and Nomenclature for New York Projectile Points,' *New York State Museum and Science Service Bulletin* 384 (New York 1971), 53

23 Bruce J. Bourque, 'The Turner Farm Site: A Preliminary Report,' *Man in the Northeast* 11 (1976), 21–30; Sanger, 'Culture Change,' 60–75; Christopher L. Borstel, 'Archaeological Investigations at the Young Site, Alton, Maine,' *Maine Historical Preservation Commission Occasional Publications in Maine Archaeology* 2 (Augusta 1982)

24 William N. Irving, 'Punyik Point and the Arctic Small Tool Tradition' (PHD diss., University of Wisconsin 1964)

25 Tuck, *Newfoundland and Labrador Prehistory,* 86

26 Robert McGhee, *Canadian Arctic Prehistory* (Ottawa 1978), 70; Tuck, *Newfoundland and Labrador Prehistory,* 96

27 A.S. Ingstad, *The Discovery of a Norse Settlement in America* (New York 1977); Birgitta Wallace, 'L'Anse aux Meadows: Gateway to Vinland,' *Acta Archaeologica* 6 (1991), 166–97; J.V. Wright, V.K. Prest, and J.-S. Vincent, 'Cultural Sequences, 8000–4000 BC,' in R. Cole Harris, ed., and Geoffrey J. Matthews, cartographer/designer, *Historical Atlas of Canada I: From the Beginning to 1800* (Toronto 1987), pl. 16

28 Bruce J. Bourque and Stephen Cox, 'Maine State Museum Excavations at the Goddard Site,' *Man in the Northeast* 8 (1981), 112–30; Robert McGhee, 'Contact between Native North Americans and the medieval Norse: A Review of the Evidence,' *American Antiquity* 49: 1 (1984), 4–26; Thomas H. McGovern, 'The Archaeology of the Norse North Atlantic,' *Annual Review of Anthropology* 19 (1990), 331–51

29 McGhee, *Canadian Arctic Prehistory,* 79

30 Peter Schledermann, 'The Thule Tradition in Northern Labrador' (MA thesis, Memorial University of Newfoundland nd); Tuck, *Newfoundland and Labrador Prehistory,* 118

31 James A. Tuck, 'The Prehistory of Newfoundland and Labrador,' *Canada's Visual History,* National Film Board of Canada 67 (Ottawa 1984), 6

32 Christopher J. Turnbull, 'The Augustine Site: A Mound from the Maritimes,' *Archaeology of Eastern North America* 4 (1976), 50–61

33 Stephen A. Davis, 'Excavations at Whites Lake, 1987,' in 'Archaeology in Nova Scotia 1987 and 1988,' Curatorial Report no. 69 (Halifax 1991), 57–68

34 Bernard G. Hoffman, 'Historical Ethnography of the Micmac of the 16th and 17th Centuries' (PHD diss., University of California 1955); David Christianson, 'The Use of Subsistence Strategy Descriptions in Determining Wabanaki Residence Location,' *Journal of Anthropology at McMaster* 5: 1 (1979), 81–122

35 Bruce J. Bourque, 'Aboriginal Settlement and Subsistence of the Maine Coast,' *Man in the Northeast* 6 (1973), 3–20; David Sanger, 'Maritime Adaptations in the Gulf of Maine,' *Archaeology of Eastern North America* 16 (1988), 81–100; Stephen A. Davis, 'Teacher's Cove,' *New Brunswick Archaeology,* ser. 1, no. 1 (Fredericton 1978)

36 Ronald J. Nash and Virginia P. Miller, 'Model Building and the Case of the Micmac Economy,' *Man in the Northeast* 34 (1987), 49; David V. Burley, 'Proto-Historic Ecological Effects of the Fur Trade on Micmac Culture in Northeastern New Brunswick,' *Ethnohistory* 23 (1983), 203–16

37 Frances L. Stewart, 'Seasonal Movements of Indians in Acadia as Evidenced by Historical Documents and Vertebrate Faunal Remains from Archaeological Sites,' *Man in the Northeast* 38 (1989), 74

CHAPTER 2 The Sixteenth Century: Aboriginal Peoples and European Contact

1 By far the best survey of early European exploration and exploitation in the Atlantic provinces is David B. Quinn, *North America from Earliest Discovery to First Settlements: The Norse Voyages to 1612* (New York 1977).

2 David B. Quinn, ed., *Sources for the Ethnography of Northeastern North America to 1611* (Ottawa 1981), 11–12

3 W.C. Sturtevant, 'The First Inuit Depiction by Europeans,' *Etudes/Inuit Studies* 4: 1–2 (1980), 47–50

4 James A. Tuck and Robert Grenier, 'A 16th Century Basque Whaling Station in Labrador,' *Scientific American* 245:5 (Nov. 1981), 180–90; Selma Barkham, 'The Documentary Evidence for Basque Whaling Ships in the Strait of Belle Isle,' in George M. Story, ed., *Early European Settlement and Exploitation in Atlantic Canada* (St John's 1982), 53–96; James A. Tuck and Robert Grenier, *Red Bay, Labrador: World Whaling Capital*, A.D. *1550–1600* (St John's 1989), 8–15

5 Susan A. Kaplan, 'European Goods and Socio-economic Change in Early Labrador Inuit Society,' in William W. Fitzhugh, ed., *Cultures in Contact: The Impact of European Contacts on Native American Cultural Institutions, A.D. 1000–1800* (Washington 1985), 56

6 Selma Barkham, 'A Note on the Strait of Belle Isle during the Period of Basque Contact with Indians and Inuit,' *Etudes/Inuit Studies* 4:1–2 (1980), 51–8; J. Mailhot, J.-P. Simard, and S. Vincent, 'On est toujours l'Esquimau de quelqu'un,' *Etudes/Inuit Studies* 4:1–2 (1980), 59–76; C.A. Martijn, 'The "Esquimaux" in the 17th and 18th Century Cartography of the Gulf of St. Lawrence: A Preliminary Discussion,' *Etudes/Inuit Studies* 4:1–2 (1980), 77–104

7 Barkham, 'A Note on the Strait,' 54–7. There is a considerable debate about the number, nature, and even existence of Inuit groups in the strait in the sixteenth century, summarized in J.G. Taylor, 'The Inuit of Southern Quebec-Labrador: Reviewing the Evidence,' *Etudes/Inuit Studies* 4:1–2 (1980), 185–93, and C.A. Martijn, 'The Inuit of Southern Quebec-Labrador: A Rejoinder to J. Garth Taylor,' *Etudes/Inuit Studies* 4:1–2 (1980), 194–8.

8 H.P. Biggar, ed., *The Works of Samuel De Champlain*, 6 vols (Toronto 1922–36), v:168

9 F.A. Aldrich, 'The Resource Funnel of the Strait of Belle Isle,' paper delivered at the International Symposium on Early European Settlement and Exploitation in Atlantic Canada, St John's, 27–30 Oct. 1979

10 This essay focuses on those Montagnais who lived along the Quebec lower north shore from approximately just west of the Saguenay River to southern Labrador. This is in many ways a matter of convenience, since the Naskapi in northern Quebec-Labrador, and the East Cree in the region between Caniaupiscau Lake and James Bay spoke similar dialects of the same language and exchanged people, objects and ideas. See Edward S. Rogers and Eleanor Leacock, 'Montagnais-Naskapi,' in June Helm, ed., *Subarctic*, vol. 6 of the *Handbook of North American Indians* (Washington 1981), 169–89.

11 William W. Fitzhugh, 'Winter Cover 4 and the Point Revenge Occupation of the Central Labrador Coast,' *Arctic Anthropology* 15:2 (1978), 146–74; Stephen Loring, 'Keeping Things Whole: Nearly Two Thousand Years of Indian (Innu) Occupation in Northern Labrador,' in C.S. 'Paddy' Reid, ed., *Boreal Forest and Sub-Arctic Archaeology*, Ontario Archaeological Society,

Occasional Publications of the London Chapter, 6 (London, Ont. 1988), 157–81; Douglas Robbins, 'Regards archéologiques sur les Béothuks de Terre-neuve,' *Recherches Amérindiennes au Québec* 19:2–3 (Autumn 1989), 21–32

12 Eleanor Leacock, 'The Montagnais-Naskapi Band,' in David Damas, ed., *Contributions to Anthropology: Band Societies* (Ottawa 1969), 1–17

13 Eleanor Leacock, 'Seventeenth-Century Montagnais Social Relations and Values,' in Helm, ed., *Subarctic*, 190–5

14 Toby Morantz, '"Gift-Offerings to Their Own Importance and Superiority": Fur Trade Relations, 1700–1940,' in William Cowan, ed., *Papers of the Nineteenth Algonquian Conference* (Ottawa 1988), 134–5

15 Leacock, 'Montagnais Social Relations,' 191. The relative autonomy of women was apparently not extended to young unmarried women and those without children, who 'took no part in the management of affairs, and were treated like children.' Reuben Gold Thwaites, ed., *The Jesuit Relations and Allied Documents*, 73 vols (Cleveland 1896–1901), VII:89

16 *Jesuit Relations*, V:133; VI:235; VII:175

17 Leacock, 'Montagnais Social Relations,' 192–3

18 *Jesuit Relations*, V:27–31, 51–5; VI:239, 247

19 Bernard G. Hoffman, 'Account of a Voyage Conducted in 1529 to the New World, Africa, Madagascar, and Sumatra, Translated from the Italian, with Notes and Comments,' *Ethnohistory* 10:1 (Winter 1963), 14. The arguments for the ethnic identities of these and other early-sixteenth-century Native groups in the region have been analysed in Charles A. Martijn, 'The Iroquoian Presence in the Estuary and Gulf of the Saint Lawrence River Valley: A Re-evaluation,' *Man in the Northeast* 40 (Fall 1990), 45–63.

20 H.P. Biggar, ed., *The Voyages of Jacques Cartier* (Ottawa 1924), 22–3

21 Ralph Pastore, 'The Collapse of the Beothuk World,' *Acadiensis* 19:1 (Autumn 1989), 59–64

22 Biggar, ed., *Voyages of Cartier*, 76

23 Martijn, 'Iroquoian Presence,' 50–2

24 H.P. Biggar, ed., *A Collection of Documents Relating to Jacques Cartier and the Sieur de Roberval* (Ottawa 1930), 462–3

25 Bruce G. Trigger, *Natives and Newcomers: Canada's `Heroic Age' Reconsidered* (Kingston and Montreal 1985), 133–5

26 Ibid., 144–8. Trigger also suggests that the westernmost St Lawrence Iroquoians might have been attacked and absorbed by the Huron before the arrival of Europeans, and the historic St Lawrence Iroquoians at Hochelaga (Montreal) and Stadacona (Quebec City) might have been weakened by internal conflict, climatic change, European disease, and attacks from the Micmacs in the St Lawrence estuary, prior to their destruction by the Iroquois.

27 Laurier Turgeon, 'Pour redécouvrir notre 16e siècle: les pêches à Terreneuve

d'après les archives notariales de Bordeaux,' *Revue d'histoire de l'Amérique française* 39:4 (Spring 1986), 523–49; L. Turgeon and E. Picot-Bermond, 'Pêcheurs basques et la traite de la fourrure dans le Saint-Laurent au XVIe siècle,' in B.G. Trigger, T. Morantz, and L. Dechêne, eds, *Le castor fait tout: Selected Papers of the Fifth North American Fur Trade Conference, 1985* (Montreal 1987), 14-24; Martijn, 'Iroquoian Presence,' 58

28 Peter Bakker, 'Basque Pidgin Vocabulary in European-Algonquian Trade Contacts,' in Cowan, ed., *Papers of the Nineteenth Algonquian Conference*, 7–15
29 *Jesuit Relations*, VIII:29
30 Richard Whitbourne, 'A Discourse and Discovery of New-Found-Land,' in Gillian T. Cell, ed., *Newfoundland Discovered: English Attempts at Colonization, 1610–1630* (London 1982), 117
31 Trigger, *Natives and Newcomers*, 135–6, 141
32 Biggar, ed., *Works of Champlain*, II:171
33 Shaun Austin, 'Cape Cove Beach (DhAi-5, 6, 7), Newfoundland Prehistoric Cultures' (MA thesis, Memorial University of Newfoundland 1981); Clifford O. Evans, 'Frenchman's Island Site (C1A1-1) Preliminary Field Report,' in Jane S. Thomson and Callum Thomson, eds, *Archaeology in Newfoundland and Labrador, 1981* (St John's 1982), 210–25; Gerald Penney, 'Prehistory of the Southwest Coast of Newfoundland' (MA thesis, Memorial University of Newfoundland 1985); Douglas Robbins, 'Stock Cove, Trinity Bay: The Dorset Eskimo Occupation of Newfoundland from a Southeastern Perspective' (MA thesis, Memorial University of Newfoundland 1985); David M. Simpson, 'Prehistoric Archaeology of the Port au Port Peninsula, Western Newfoundland' (MA thesis, Memorial University of Newfoundland 1986). Until more archaeological work is done, estimates of Beothuk population at the time of European contact must remain, at best, informed guesses; however, given the pattern of repeated human extinctions in Newfoundland's prehistory, the estimated size of the prehistoric caribou herd, and the relative scarcity of Little Passage sites, it is difficult to believe that there would have been more than 500 to 1,000 Beothuks in 1492.
34 Quinn, ed., *Sources*, 13–14
35 Hoffman, 'Account of a Voyage,' 14. Charles Martijn believes that the Native people on Newfoundland's south coast referred to were Micmacs. Martijn, 'An Eastern Micmac Domain of Islands,' in William Cowan, ed., *Actes du Vingtième Congrès des Algonquinistes* (Ottawa 1989), 213
36 Biggar, ed., *Voyages of Cartier*, 7; Ruth Holmes Whitehead, 'I Have Lived Here since the World Began: Atlantic Coast Artistic Traditions,' in *The Spirit Sings: Artistic Traditions of Canada's First Peoples* (Toronto 1987), 31
37 'John Guy's Journal of a Voyage to Trinity Bay,' in Cell, ed., *Newfoundland Discovered*, 71–6; Trigger, *Natives and Newcomers*, 136. Etienne Bellenger is reported to have brought back 'A kynde of liquide muske or sivet taken out of the Bevers stones' from his 1583 expedition to the Maritimes. D.B. Quinn,

'The Voyage of Etienne Bellenger to the Maritimes in 1583: A New Document,' *Canadian Historical Review* 43 (1962), 341

38 James P. Howley, *The Beothucks or Red Indians* (Toronto 1974), 50–1; George Best's account of the Frobisher voyages (1576–8) described somewhat similar behaviour on the part of the Inuit. Walter A. Kenyon, *Tokens of Possession: The Northern Voyages of Martin Frobisher* (Toronto 1975), 51

39 Ralph T. Pastore, 'Fishermen, Furriers, and Beothuks: The Economy of Extinction,' *Man in the Northeast* 33 (Spring 1987), 47–62, and Pastore, 'Collapse of the Beothuk World'

40 Vincent O. Erickson, 'Maliseet-Passamaquoddy,' in Bruce G. Trigger, ed., *Northeast*, vol. 15 of the *Handbook of North American Indians* (Washington 1978), 123

41 Bruce J. Bourque, 'Ethnicity on the Maritime Peninsula, 1600–1759,' *Ethnohistory* 36:3 (Summer 1989), 257

42 James A. Tuck, *Maritime Provinces Prehistory* (Ottawa 1984), 42–85; Martijn, 'Eastern Micmac Domain of Islands,' 212

43 David B. Quinn, *New American World*, 5 vols (New York 1979), I:149, 151

44 Biggar, ed., *Voyages of Cartier*, 49–56

45 There is no exhaustive study of the European fur trade of the sixteenth century, although a beginning has been made for the French trade that was auxiliary to the fishery conducted out of Bordeaux in the last half of the century. Turgeon and Picot-Bermond, 'Pêcheurs basques,' 14–24

46 Quinn, *New American World*, I:281–9

47 Hoffman, 'Account of a Voyage,' 13

48 Quinn, 'Voyage of Etienne Bellenger,' 341

49 Marc Lescarbot, *The History of New France*, ed. W.L. Grant, 3 vols (Toronto 1907–14), II:362–3

50 Dean Snow, *The Archaeology of New England* (New York 1980), 34

51 Bruce J. Bourque and Ruth Holmes Whitehead, 'Tarrentines and the Introduction of European Trade Goods in the Gulf of Maine,' *Ethnohistory* 32:4 (Fall 1985), 337

52 Dean Snow and Kim Lanphear, 'European Contact and Indian Depopulation in the Northeast: The Timing of the First Epidemics,' *Ethnohistory* 35:1 (Winter 1988), 15–33

53 *Jesuit Relations*, III:105, 111

54 Philip Bock, 'Micmac,' in Trigger, ed., *Northeast*, 117; Virginia P. Miller, 'The Decline of Nova Scotia Micmac Population, A.D. 1600–1850,' *Culture* 2:3 (1982), 118; Snow, *Archaeology of New England*, 36

55 Bernard G. Hoffman, 'Historical Ethnography of the Micmac of the Sixteenth and Seventeenth Centuries' (PHD diss., University of California 1955), 589–90

56 Virginia P. Miller, 'Social and Political Complexity on the East Coast: The Micmac Case,' in Ronald J. Nash, ed., *The Evolution of Maritime Cultures on*

the Northeast and the Northwest Coasts of America (Burnaby 1983), 43; Bock, 'Micmac,' 109

57 *Jesuit Relations*, III:87

58 Miller, 'Social and Political Complexity,' 51

59 *Jesuit Relations*, III:89. Among the examples of Micmacs defying their saga-more are Biard's references to people apparently permanently leaving a sagamore's village.

60 Biard noted that when Micmac sagamores from different communities met, their assemblies were 'without order and subordination.' *Jesuit Relations*, III:91

61 Hoffman, 'Historical Ethnography of the Micmac,' 573; Miller, 'Social and Political Complexity,' 47–9

62 *Jesuit Relations*, III:89

63 Hoffman, 'Historical Ethnography of the Micmac,' 517; Miller, 'Social and Political Complexity,' 44–5

64 Chrestien Le Clercq, *New Relation of Gaspesia with the Customs and Religion of the Gaspesian Indians*, ed. W.F. Ganong (Toronto 1910), 237

65 Rogers and Leacock, 'Montagnais-Naskapi,' 181; Alfred G. Bailey, *The Con-flict of European and Eastern Algonkian Cultures, 1504–1700* (2nd ed.; Toronto 1969), 91–2

66 R.G. Matson, 'Intensification and the Development of Cultural Complexity: The Northwest versus the Northeast Coast,' in Nash, ed., *Evolution of Mari-time Cultures*, 125–48

67 Nicolas Denys, *The Description and Natural History of the Coasts of North America*, ed. William F. Ganong (Toronto 1908), 441

68 Lescarbot, *History of New France*, III:168; *Jesuit Relations*, III:69

69 *Jesuit Relations*, III:107; Denys, *Description and Natural History*, 444–51

70 *Jesuit Relations*, III:101–3

71 Denys, *Description and Natural History*, 444, 449

72 Bourque and Whitehead, 'Tarrentines,' 327–41

73 Trigger, *Natives and Newcomers*, 137

CHAPTER 3 1600–1650: Fish, Fur, and Folk

1 Graeme Wynn, Ralph Pastore, and Bernard G. Hoffman, 'The Atlantic Realm,' in R. Cole Harris, ed., and Geoffrey J. Matthews, Cartographer/Designer, *Historical Atlas of Canada I: From the Beginning to 1800* (Toronto 1987), 49

2 Adrien Huguet, *Jean de Poutrincourt, fondateur de Port-Royal en Acadie, Vice-Roi du Canada, 1557–1615: campagnes, voyages et aventures d'un colonisateur sous Henri IV* (Paris 1932), 159 ff; Gillian T. Cell, ed., *Newfoundland Discov-ered: English Attempts at Colonization, 1610-1630* (London 1982), 3

3 One of the most striking examples is to be found in the relationship of

Béarn with Paris; see M-P. Foursans-Bourdette, *Economie et finances en Béarn au XVIII siècle* (Bordeaux 1963), 12 ff.

4 Fernand Braudel, *The Identity of France; Vol. I, History and Environment*, trans. Sian Reynolds (London 1988), 37

5 E.L.J. Coornaert, 'European Economic Institutions and the New World: The Chartered Companies,' in E.E. Rich and C.H. Wilson, eds, *Economic History of Europe; Vol. IV, The Economy of Expanding Europe in the Sixteenth and Seventeenth Centuries* (Cambridge 1967), 246

6 T.H. Rabb, *Enterprise and Empire: Merchant and Gentry Investment in the Expansion of England 1575–1630* (Cambridge 1967), 2

7 Barthelmew Laffemas, 'The Aristocrat in Business,' *Explorations in Entrepreneurial History* 6:2, 3 (1953, 1954), passim

8 Rabb, *Enterprise and Empire*, 13

9 Coornaert, 'European Economic Institutions,' 254

10 An excellent discussion of this is to be found in L.C. Green and Olive P. Dickason, *The Law of Nations and the New World* (Edmonton 1989), ix ff.

11 Bruce G. Trigger, *Natives and Newcomers: Canada's `Heroic Age' Reconsidered* (Kingston and Montreal 1985), 298

12 See Fernand Braudel, *Civilization and Capitalism 15th–18th Century; Vol. I, The Structures of Everyday Life: The Limits of the Possible* (New York 1981), 21, 108 ff.

13 While his work has been criticized, expanded, and developed, H.A. Innis's *The Cod Fisheries: The History of an International Economy* (Toronto 1978), first published in 1940, remains the classic work in English about the subject. In French, a similar position is held by that of Charles de La Morandière, *Histoire de la pêche française de la morue dans l'Amérique septentrionale (des origines à 1789)*, 2 vols (Paris 1962). The relevant maps and articles in the *Historical Atlas of Canada I* provide a succinct and clear presentation of much of the evidence about the question.

14 Innis, *The Cod Fisheries*, 12, 45

15 H.P. Biggar, *The Early Trading Companies of New France: A Contribution to the History of Commerce and Discovery in North America* (Toronto 1901), 24

16 Gillian T. Cell, *English Enterprise in Newfoundland, 1577–1660* (Toronto 1969), 23; and W. Gordon Handcock, *'Soe longe as there comes noe women': Origins of English Settlement in Newfoundland* (St John's 1989), 24

17 Innis, *The Cod Fisheries*, 47–9

18 For dry fishing techniques I have followed Wynn et al., 'The Atlantic Realm,' and John J. Mannion and C. Grant Head, 'The Migratory Fisheries,' in the *Historical Atlas of Canada I*. Mannion and Head report sixty tons as the size of the smallest ship engaged in dry fishing.

19 Wynn et al., 'The Atlantic Realm,' *Historical Atlas of Canada I*, 48

20 Innis, *The Cod Fisheries*, 59

21 La Morandière, *Histoire de la pêche française*, I:257

22 K.G. Davies, *The North Atlantic World in the Seventeenth Century* (Minneapolis 1974), 14

23 Innis, *The Cod Fisheries*, 40–1; Cell, *English Enterprise in Newfoundland*, passim

24 H.A. Innis, *The Fur Trade in Canada: An Introduction to Canadian Economic History* (New Haven 1930; rev. ed. Toronto 1956) is still a classic introduction to the topic. But see also W.J. Eccles, 'A Belated Review of Harold Adams Innis, *The Fur Trade in Canada*,' *Canadian Historical Review* 60 (1979), 419–41, and Hugh M. Grant, 'One Step Forward, Two Steps Back: Innis, Eccles and the Canadian Fur Trade,' as well as W.J. Eccles, 'A Response to Hugh M. Grant on Innis,' *Canadian Historical Review* 62 (1981), 304–29.

25 Marcel Trudel, *Histoire de la Nouvelle France; Vol. I, Les vaines tentatives, 1524–1603* (Montreal 1963), 219

26 Richard Hakluyt, 'Discourse Concerning Westerne Planting,' in *Collections of the Maine Historical Society, Second Series, Documentary History of the State of Maine*, 24 vols (Portland 1869–1916), II:34

27 See Trudel, *Les vaines tentatives*, esp. ch. 5.

28 James Axtell, *The European and the Indian: Essays in the Ethnohistory of Colonial North America* (New York 1981), 246; see also Cornelius J. Jaenen, '"L'autre" en Nouvelle France / The "Other" in Early Canada,' *Historical Papers* (1989), 1–12.

29 See Paul Slack, *The Impact of Plague in Tudor and Stuart England* (Oxford 1985).

30 See Pierre Biard in Reuben Gold Thwaites, ed., *The Jesuit Relations and Allied Documents*, 73 vols (Cleveland 1896–1901), III:109. Also Virginia P. Miller, 'Aboriginal Population: A Review of the Evidence,' *Ethnohistory* 23 (1976), 117–27; Dean R. Snow and Kim M. Lanphear, 'European Contact and Indian Depopulation in the Northeast: The Timing of the First Epidemics,' *Ethnohistory* 35 (1988), 15–33; David Henige, 'Primary Source by Primary Source? On the Role of Epidemics in New World Depopulation,' *Ethnohistory* 33 (1986), 293–312; Ralph Pastore, 'Native History in the Atlantic Region during the Colonial Period,' *Acadiensis* 20:1 (Autumn 1990), 209–13; and Pastore, 'The Sixteenth Century,' in ch. 2 in this volume, 22–39.

31 Axtell, *The European and the Indian*, 250–1

32 David B. Quinn, 'Colonies in the Beginning: Examples from North America,' in Stanley H. Palmer and Dennis Reinhartz, eds, *Essays on the History of North American Discovery and Exploration* (Texas 1988), 10–34

33 This document is published in full in a number of works. One of the most easily accessible is in the introduction to Marc Lescarbot, *The History of New France*, ed. W.L. Grant, 3 vols (Toronto 1907–14), II:211–26.

34 Commission, 29 Jan. 1603, France, Archives des Colonies (AC), C11A, 8 ff; George MacBeath, 'Pierre Du Gua de Monts,' in George W. Brown et al.,

eds, *Dictionary of Canadian Biography*, 12 vols to date (Toronto 1966–; hereafter *DCB*), I:291–4

35 Huia Ryder, 'Jean de Biencourt de Poutrincourt et de Saint-Just,' *DCB*, I:96–9; Marcel Trudel, 'Samuel Champlain,' *DCB*, I:186–99; René Baudry, 'Marc Lescarbot,' *DCB*, I:469–72; George MacBeath,'Claude de Saint-Etienne de La Tour,' *DCB*, I:596–7

36 'The Commission Directed by the Counsaill to John Guy for His Government There in Newfoundland,' 15 May 1610, Nottingham University, Middleton, MS 1/1, ff 14–15; Gillian T. Cell, 'John Guy,' *DCB*, I:349–51

37 Cell, *English Enterprise in Newfoundland*, 65

38 Gillian T. Cell, 'Sir William Vaughan,' *DCB*, I:654–6; Cell, 'Sir William Whitbourne,' *DCB*, I:668–9; Allan M. Fraser, 'Sir George Calvert,' *DCB*, I:162–3

39 See two works that are of major help in understanding this: George A. Rawlyk, *Nova Scotia's Massachusetts: A Study of Massachusetts–Nova Scotia Relations, 1630-1784* (Montreal 1973) and John G. Reid, *Acadia, Maine, and New Scotland: Marginal Colonies in the Seventeenth Century* (Toronto 1981).

40 John G. Reid, *Six Crucial Decades: Times of Change in the History of the Maritimes* (Halifax 1987), 22

41 An excellent work on one particular enterprise is Luca Codignola, *The Coldest Harbour of the Land: Simon Stock and Lord Baltimore's Colony in Newfoundland 1621–1649* (Kingston and Montreal 1988). The incremental nature of the growth of English population in Newfoundland has been well explored in Handcock, *'Soe longe as there comes noe women.'*

42 M. Lescarbot, *Nova Francia*, trans. Erondelle (1609), ed. H.P. Biggar (London 1928), 13

43 Cell, *English Enterprise in Newfoundland*, 69

44 *Jesuit Relations*, II:229 ff; III:4–14, 275–83; Cell, *English Enterprise in Newfoundland*, 67

45 Reported by Guy in a letter to the company's council, 11 May 1611, cited in Cell, *English Enterprise in Newfoundland*, 64

46 Handcock, *'Soe longe as there comes noe women,'* 34–5

47 Ibid., 35; Allan M. Fraser, 'Sir George Calvert,' *DCB*, I:162; John S. Moir, 'Sir David Kirke,' *DCB*, I:404–07

48 Handcock, *'Soe longe as there comes noe women,'* 35; D.W. Meinig, *The Shaping of America: A Geographical Perspective on 500 Years of History, Volume I, Atlantic America, 1492–1800* (New Haven 1984), 87

49 See Jean Daigle, 'L'Acadie, 1604–1763: Synthèse historique,' in Daigle, ed., *Les Acadiens des Maritimes: études thématiques* (Moncton 1980), 17–48; Reid, *Six Crucial Decades*, 3–24; also, for an introduction to these years, John Bartlet Brebner, *New England's Outpost: Acadia before the Conquest of Canada* (New York 1927).

50 *Jesuit Relations*, I:127–37, 139–45; II:81–5; III:171–9

51 W. Austin Squires, 'Sir Samuel Argall,' *DCB*, I:67–9

52 See Reid, *Acadia, Maine, and New Scotland*, 23–4.
53 See Geneviève Massignon, *Les parlers français d'Acadie: enquête linguistique*, 2 vols (Paris 1962), passim.
54 See Leslie Phyllis Choquette, 'French Emigration to Canada in the 17th and 18th Centuries' (PHD diss., Harvard University 1988).
55 Massignon, *Les parlers français d'Acadie*, I:72
56 Ibid., I:37
57 George MacBeath, 'Jeanne Motin,' *DCB*, I:515
58 J.A. Maureault, *Histoire des Abénakis depuis 1605 jusqu'à nos jours* (Sorel 1888), 84
59 See M.A. MacDonald, *Fortune and La Tour: The Civil War in Acadia* (Toronto 1983).
60 'Registre des concessions en Acadie,' 17 Oct. 1672, in Pierre-Georges Roy, *Inventaires, concessions en fief et seigneurie ... conservés aux archives de la province de Québec* (Quebec 1927), 1; Azarie Couillard-Després, *Charles de Saint-Etienne de La Tour, gouverneur, lieutenant-général en Acadie, et son temps 1593–1666* (Arthabaska 1930), 130-1
61 Massignon, *Les parlers français d'Acadie*, I:69; Edme Rameau de Saint-Père, *Une colonie féodale en Amérique: l'Acadie, 1604–1881*, 2 vols (Paris 1889), II:348
62 René Baudry, 'Charles de Menou d'Aulnay,' *DCB*, I:502–6
63 While Brebner's *New England's Outpost*, 28–30, has an interesting account, it is also worthwhile reading John Winthrop, *The History of New England from 1630-1640*, ed. James Savage (Boston 1883), passim.
64 What follows is based upon Andrew Hill Clark, *Acadia: The Geography of Early Nova Scotia to 1760* (Madison, Wis. 1968), 94–107.
65 Nicolas Denys, *The Description and Natural History of the Coasts of North America (Acadia)*, ed. William F. Ganong (Toronto 1908), 123–4
66 See N.E.S. Griffiths, *The Acadians: Creation of a People* (Toronto 1973), and Daigle, 'L'Acadie, 1604–1763.'
67 Handcock, *'Soe longe as there comes noe women,'* 9

CHAPTER 4   1650–1686: 'Un pays qui n'est pas fait'

1 'Mémoire de Meneval,' 10 Sept. 1688, France, Archives des Colonies (AC), C11D, vol. 2, 98
2 Motto of the Bonasses of Béarn, ancestors of Jean-Vincent d'Abbadie de Saint-Castin. Robert LeBlant, *Une figure légendaire de l'histoire acadienne: le baron de Saint-Castin* (Dax 1934), 86
3 Naomi Griffiths, 'The Golden Age: Acadian Life, 1713–1748,' *Histoire sociale / Social History* 17:33 (May 1984), 21–34
4 Muriel K. Roy, 'Settlement and Population Growth in Acadia,' in Jean Daigle, ed., *The Acadians of the Maritimes: Thematic Studies* (Moncton 1982), 138; Andrew H. Clark, 'Acadia and the Acadians: The Creation of a Geo-

graphical Entity,' in John Andrews, ed., *Frontiers and Men: A Volume in Memory of Griffith Taylor, 1880-1963* (Melbourne 1966), 115

5 C. Grant Head, *Eighteenth Century Newfoundland: A Geographer's Perspective* (Toronto 1976), 2–29; John Mannion and Gordon Handcock, 'Fisheries of the 17th Century,' in R. Cole Harris, ed., and Geoffrey J. Matthews, cartographer/designer, *Historical Atlas of Canada I: From the Beginning to 1800* (Toronto 1987), pl. 23; Charles de La Morandière, *Histoire de la pêche française de la morue dans l'Amérique septentrionale (des origines à 1789)*, 2 vols (Paris 1962), I:425–6

6 Head, *Eighteenth Century Newfoundland*, 36–41

7 Gerald S. Graham, 'Britain's Defence of Newfoundland: A Survey from the Discovery to the Present Day,' *Canadian Historical Review* 23 (1942), 260–79

8 Gillian T. Cell, *English Enterprise in Newfoundland, 1577–1660* (Toronto 1969), 4

9 La Morandière, *Histoire de la pêche française*, 407; Sigmund Diamond, 'An Experiment in "Feudalism": French Canada in the Seventeenth Century,' *William and Mary Quarterly*, 3rd ser., 18 (1961), 4–6

10 Gustave Lanctôt, *L'administration de la Nouvelle-France* (Paris 1929), 24

11 John Humphreys, *Plaisance: Problems of Settlement at this Newfoundland Outpost of New France, 1660–1690* (Ottawa 1970), vi

12 René Baudry, 'Thalour Du Perron,' in George W. Brown et al., eds, *Dictionary of Canadian Biography*, 12 vols to date (Toronto 1966–; hereafter *DCB*), I:296; Baudry, 'La Poippe,' *DCB*, I:418–19; La Morandière, *Histoire de la pêche française*, 414–17

13 Jacques Rousseau and George W. Brown, 'The Indians of Northeastern North America,' *DCB*, I:5; Barrie Reynolds, 'Beothuk,' in Bruce G. Trigger, ed., *Northeast*, vol. 15 of the *Handbook of North American Indians* (Washington 1978), 106; Ingeborg Marshall, 'Beothuk and Micmac: Re-Examining Relationships,' *Acadiensis* 17:2 (Spring 1988), 56; Marshall, 'Disease as a Factor in the Demise of the Beothuk Indians,' *Culture* 1 (1981), 70–4

14 Alaric Faulkner and Gretchen Faulkner, *The French at Pentagoet, 1635–1674: An Archaeological Portrait of the Acadian Frontier* (Augusta and Saint John 1987), 29; Chrestien Le Clercq, *New Relation of Gaspesia, with the Customs and Religion of the Gaspesian Indians*, ed. William F. Ganong (Toronto 1910), 159–206

15 Alfred G. Bailey, 'Richard Denys de Fronsac,' *DCB*, I:259–61; Jean Daigle, 'La toponymie française de l'Acadie jusqu'en 1744,' *450 ans de noms de lieux français en Amérique du Nord* (Québec 1986), 276–80; Sebastien Rasles, 'A Dictionary of the Abenaki Language in North America,' in John Pickering, ed., *Memoirs of the American Academy of Arts and Sciences* 1 (1833) 383, 389, 405, 454–5

16 René Baudry, 'Charles de Menou d'Aulnay,' *DCB*, I:502–6; Mason Wade, 'Emmanuel Le Borgne,' *DCB*, I:433–5; on the commercial relationship

between Le Borgne and d'Aulnay, see M. Delafosse, 'La Rochelle et le Canada au XVIIe siècle,' *Revue d'histoire de l'Amérique française* 4 (1950–1), 471–2.

17 George MacBeath, 'Charles de Saint-Étienne de La Tour,' *DCB*, I:592–6; Fonds Placide Gaudet, Université de Moncton, Centre d'études acadiennes (CÉA), RG1, box 46, f.14

18 'Nicolas Denys et la Cie de Miskou,' AC, C11D, vol. 1, 93–4; Bernard Pothier, 'Nicolas Denys the Chronology and Historiography of an Acadian Hero,' *Acadiensis* 1:1 (Autumn 1971), 54–70; Rosemonde Cormier, 'Miscou au XVIIe siècle,' *Revue de la Société historique Nicolas Denys* 17:2 (1989), 3–45

19 William I. Roberts, 3rd, 'Robert Sedgwick,' *DCB*, I:604–5

20 'Mémoire des commissaires du roi, 4 octobre 1751,' *Mémoires des commissaires du Roi et ceux de Sa Majesté Britannique* (Paris 1755), I:48–50

21 A French memoir of 1667 described Temple's regime as not having made 'the slightest improvement.' Quoted in John G. Reid, *Acadia, Maine and New Scotland: Marginal Colonies in the Seventeenth Century* (Toronto 1981), 138; Huia Ryder, 'Sir Thomas Temple,' *DCB*, I:636–7

22 René Baudry, 'Madame de Brice,' *DCB*, I:129; Candide de Nant, *Pages glorieuses de l'épopée canadienne: une mission capucine en Acadie* (Montreal 1927)

23 Roy, 'Settlement and Population Growth in Acadia,' 133

24 Delafosse, 'La Rochelle et le Canada au XVIIe siècle,' 469–511

25 Rod Scarlett, 'Acadia and Massachusetts before 1670: Diplomatic and Economic Conditions' (MA thesis, Carleton University 1985), 87

26 Jean Daigle, 'Nos amis les ennemis: les relations commerciales entre l'Acadie et le Massachusetts, 1670–1711,' PHD diss., University of Maine 1975), 66–8; see also Nicolas Denys, *The Description and Natural History of the Coast of North America (Acadia)*, ed. William F. Ganong (Toronto 1908), 474.

27 Dièreville, *Relation of the Voyage to Port Royal in Acadia or New France*, ed. John Clarence Webster (Toronto 1933), 258

28 Nicole Bujold and Maurice Caillebeau, *Les origines françaises des premières familles acadiennes: le sud loudunais* (Poitiers 1979); Denys, *Description and Natural History,* 474; Yves Cormier, *Les aboiteaux en Acadie hier et aujourd'hui* (Moncton 1990), 30–1; Jean-Claude Dupont, 'Les défricheurs d'eau,' *Culture vivante* 27 (Dec. 1972), 6–9; Dupont, *Histoire populaire de l'Acadie* (Montreal 1979), 310

29 The French observer Dièreville commented that 'idleness pleases them, they like to take it easy.' Dièreville, *Relation*, 256; 'ces peuples [Acadians] sont fainéans,' 'Ministre à Costebelle' 2 Mar. 1714, AC, B, 36, 434 1/2

30 Jean Daigle 'Settlement of the Marshes by the Acadians,' *Historical Atlas of Canada* I, pl. 29

31 Ile Saint-Jean, already included in the grant to Nicolas Denys, was conceded to François Doublet in 1663; in 1686 the island was regranted to Gabriel Gauthier of the Sedentary Fishery Company. See Georges Arsenault, *The Island Acadians, 1720–1980* (Charlottetown 1989), 20.

32 'Ordre du roi d'Angleterre au colonel Temple de restituer l'Acadie à la France,' 8 Mar. 1669, AC, C11D, vol. 1, 133

33 Geneviève Massignon, *Les parlers français d'Acadie: enquête linquistique*, 2 vols (Paris 1962), I:68–75; Jean Daigle, 'Michel Le Neuf de La Vallière, seigneur de Beaubassin et gouverneur d'Acadie (1678–1684)' (MA thesis, Université de Montréal 1970), 75–80; Clarence-J. d'Entremont, 'Les Melansons d'Acadie sont français de père et anglais de mère,' *La société historique acadienne: les cahiers* 40 (July-Sept. 1973), 416–19; Bona Arsenault, *Histoire et généalogie des Acadiens*, II (Québec 1965), 550

34 'Mémoire concernant l'Acadie par le chevalier de Grandfontaine,' AC, C11D, vol. 1, 139

35 Ibid., 'Stores desired by Mr. Marson,' 16 July 1677, Massachusetts Archives (MA), vol. 61, 157; René Baudry, 'Jacques de Chambly,' *DCB*, I:185. See also John Bartlet Brebner, *New England's Outpost: Acadia before the Conquest of Canada* (New York 1927); George A. Rawlyk, *Nova Scotia's Massachusetts: A Study of Massachusetts–Nova Scotia Relations, 1630 to 1784* (Montreal 1973).

36 Azarie Couillard-Després, *Charles de Saint-Etienne de La Tour, gouverneur, lieutenant-général en Acadie et son temps, 1593–1666* (Arthabaska 1930), 12

37 'A Journal of a Voyage from Salem in the Ketch Supply to Cape Sable,' *Collections of the Maine Historical Society*, Second Series, *Documentary History of the State of Maine*, 24 vols (Portland 1869–1916), VI:179–84; 'Petition of William Tayler,' 16 July 1677, MA, vol. 61, 156; 'Ordonnance du roi concernant la traite des fourrures,' 12 May 1678, AC, F3, vol. 5, 43–5

38 Louis-André Vigneras, 'Letters of an Acadian Trader, 1674–1676,' *New England Quarterly* 13 (1940), 98–110; 'Autorisation de La Vallière à John Nelson,' 22 Oct. 1682, National Archives of Canada (NAC), MG11, 55, 188; Jean Daigle, 'La pêche en Acadie au 17e siècle,' *La société historique acadienne: les cahiers*, 5 (1974), 227–9

39 'Baron de Saint-Castin à Denonville,' *Collection des manuscrits contenant lettres, mémoires et autres documents historiques relatifs à la Nouvelle-France*, 4 vols (Québec 1883–5), I:400; see also W.J. Eccles, 'François-Marie Perrot,' *DCB*, I:540–2.

40 'Lettre de Frontenac au roi,' 6 Nov. 1679, *Rapport de l'archiviste de la province de Québec, 1926–1927* (Quebec 1927), 111; A. Augustin-Thierry, ed., *Un colonial au temps de Colbert: mémoires de Robert Challes, écrivain du roi* (Paris 1931), 275. See also Bernard Cartier and Marc Rébillon, 'Robert Challe, l'aventurier philosophe,' *Historia* 520 (Apr. 1990), 77–84.

41 Daigle, 'Michel Le Neuf de La Vallière,' 81–2; Andrew Hill Clark, *Acadia: The Geography of Early Nova Scotia to 1760* (Madison 1968), 120

42 'De Meulles au Ministre,' 12 Nov. 1683, AC, C11A, vol. 7, 81; see also Marcel Trudel, *Initiation à la Nouvelle-France* (Montreal 1968), 72–3.

43 'Vous "too"' for 'vous aussi,' and 'pas "yet"' for 'pas encore.' Thomas

Hutchinson, *The History of the Colony and Province of Massachusetts Bay*, 3 vols (Cambridge, Mass. 1936), II:93

44 'Recensement par Laurent Molins,' AC, G1, 466

45 'Perrot au Ministre,' 26 Aug. 1686, AC, C11D, vol. 2, 14; Faulkner and Faulkner, *The French at Pentagoet*, 3

46 Micheline Dumont-Johnson, *Apôtres ou agitateurs: la France missionaire en Acadie* (Trois-Rivières 1970), 150; G.-M. Dumas, 'Chrestien Le Clercq,' *DCB*, I:438–41; Le Clercq, *New Relation of Gaspesia*, ch. 11

47 De Goutin au Ministre, 3 Dec. 1704, AC, C11D, vol. 5, 34; Bernard Pothier, 'Mathieu de Goutin,' *DCB*, II:257–8

48 W. Gordon Handcock, 'English Migration to Newfoundland,' in John J. Mannion, ed., *The Peopling of Newfoundland: Essays in Historical Geography* (St John's 1977), 16–19; Peter Pope, 'Historical Archeology and the Demand for Alcohol in the 17th Century,' *Acadiensis* 19:1 (Autumn 1989), 72–90

49 Gillian T. Cell, 'John Downing,' *DCB*, I:277–8; C.M. Rowe, 'William Hinton,' *DCB*, I:369–70; Rowe, 'Sir John Berry,' *DCB*, I:92–3; Head, *Eighteenth Century Newfoundland*, 38–40, 63, 82–3; Keith Matthews, *Lectures on the History of Newfoundland, 1500–1830* (St John's 1988), 84–5

50 The census results are reproduced in *Mémoires de la société généalogique canadienne-française* 10:2 (Apr. 1959), 179–81. See also La Morandière, *Histoire de la pêche française*, 428; P.L. Le Jeune, *Tableaux synoptiques de l'histoire de l'Acadie: fascicule spécial (1500–1760)* (Québec 1918), 83; Mannion and Handcock, 'Fisheries of the 17th Century,' *Historical Atlas of Canada* I, pl. 23.

51 'Recensement général de l'Ile de Terre-Neuve, novembre 1687,' *Mémoires de la société généalogique canadienne-française* 13:10 (Oct. 1962), 204–6; La Morandière, *Histoire de la pêche française*, 284–335, 429; René Baudry, 'Antoine Parat,' *DCB*, I:530; Humphreys, *Plaisance*, 7–9, 10–11

52 Humphreys, *Plaisance*, 10–11

53 Jean-Baptiste de la Croix Chevrières de Saint-Vallier, *Estat présent de l'Eglise et de la colonie française dans la Nouvelle-France par M. l'Evêque de Québec* (Québec 1856), 34; the company enjoyed extensive fiscal privileges and the power to grant land. See 'Extraits du Conseil d'État,' 3 Mar. 1684, AC, C11D, vol. 1, 179. See also 'Bergier à Seignelay,' [1682], AC, C11D, vol. 1, 163; 'Voyage of Monsieur De Meulles to Acadie,' in W.I. Morse, ed., *Acadiensia Nova (1598–1779)*, 2 vols (London 1935), I:118.

54 'Denonville au Ministre,' 6 Nov. 1687, *Collection de manuscrits* I:406; Daigle, 'Nos amis les ennemis,' 107–110

55 De Meulles, 'Mémoire touchant le Canada et l'Acadie,' *Revue d'histoire de l'Amérique française* 2 (1948–9), 433–9; W.J. Eccles, 'Jacques de Meulles,' *DCB*, II:470–3

56 Jean Daigle, 'La famine de 1699 en Acadie,' *La société historique acadienne: les cahiers* 7 (1976), 147–9

57 Dièreville, *Relation*, 92; Gisa Hynes, 'Some Aspects of the Demography of
    Port Royal, 1650–1755,' *Acadiensis* 3:1 (Autumn 1973), 3–17
58 'Original and Unpublished Census of Acadie by Gargas,' in W.I. Morse,
    Acadiensia Nova, I:35–160; Raymond Roy, 'La croissance démographique en
    Acadie, 1671–1763' (MA thesis, Université de Montréal 1975), 32; Clark, *Aca-
    dia*, 123; Jacques Houdaille, 'Quelques aspects de la démographie ancienne
    de l'Acadie,' *Population* 3 (1980), 582, 585
59 Those estimates are drawn from Clark, *Acadia*, 123, 130; Edme Rameau de
    Saint-Père, *Une colonie féodale en Amérique: l'Acadie 1604–1881*, 2 vols (Mont-
    réal 1889), II:205–6; Denis Héroux, *La Nouvelle-France* (Montréal 1967), 222;
    W.J. Eccles, *France in America* (Toronto 1973), 88; Douglas R. McManis, *Colo-
    nial New England: A Historical Geography* (New York 1975), 68.
60 Saint-Vallier, *Estat présent de l'Eglise*, 28–42; Adrien Caron, *De Québec en
    Acadie sur les pas de Mgr de Saint-Vallier, avril-août 1686. Études et plans* (Que-
    bec 1975), 22; Alfred Rambaud, 'Jean-Baptiste de La Croix de Chevrières de
    Saint-Vallier,' *DCB*, II:328–34; C.-J. Russ, 'Louis Geoffroy,' *DCB*, II:243–4; G.-
    M. Dumas, 'Louis Petit,' *DCB*, II:521–2; Noel Baillargeon, 'Claude Trouvé,'
    DCB, II:637–9
61 Clark, *Acadia*, 216. Several generations could live in one household, but as a
    general rule, census data indicate that the presence of two generations
    under the same roof – parents and unmarried children – was the norm.
62 David J. Christianson, *Belleisle 1983: Excavations at a Pre-expulsion Acadian
    Site*, Nova Scotia Museum, Curatorial Report no. 48 (Halifax 1984), 97;
    André Crépeau and Brenda Dunn, *L'etablissement Melanson: un site agricole
    acadien (vers 1664–1755)*, Bulletin de recherche no. 250 (Ottawa 1986), 18.
    This architectural style can be found in France, in the Vendée region. See
    Pierre Drobecq, *La cheminée dans l'habitation* (Paris 1942), 58.
63 Kenneth M. Morrison, *The Embattled Northeast: The Elusive Ideal of Alliance in
    Abenaki-Euramerican Relations* (Berkeley 1984), 133–64; W.F. Ganong, 'Cen-
    sus by Richard Denys of the Residents of Perce, Restigouche, Nepisiguit
    and Miramichi in 1688,' *Collections of the New Brunswick Historical Society* 7
    (1907), 32–7
64 'Subercase au Ministre,' 3 June 1710, AC, C11D, vol. 7, 49

CHAPTER 5 1686–1720: Imperial Intrusions

1 [Jacques de Meulles], 'Mémoire 1686 sur ce que l'on peut faire dans l'acadie,'
   France, Archives des Colonies (AC), C11D, vol. 2, 33; Reuben Gold Thwaites,
   ed., *New Voyages to North America by the Baron de Lahontan*, 2 vols (orig. ed.
   1703; Chicago 1905), I:330; George Larkin to the Board of Trade, 20 Aug.
   1701, Great Britain, Public Record Office (PRO), CO194/2, no. 44. During the
   period covered by this chapter, the Julian (Old Style) calendar was in force in
   England and (from 1707) in Great Britain, while the Gregorian (New Style)

calendar was in force in France. In the chapter, dates will be rendered in whichever style is appropriate to each reference, except that the years will be modernized to begin on 1 January, and New Style will be used in references to international negotiations and agreements. The author wishes to thank the Senate Research Committee of Saint Mary's University for supporting research towards the writing of this chapter.

2 See Philip K. Bock, 'Micmac,' in Bruce G. Trigger, ed., *Northeast*, vol. 15 of the *Handbook of North American Indians* (Washington 1978), 117; Vincent O. Erickson, 'Maliseet-Passamaquoddy,' in Trigger, ed., *Northeast*, 125–6; Dean R. Snow, 'Eastern Abenaki,' in Trigger, ed., *Northeast*, 145; Ingeborg Marshall, 'Disease as a Factor in the Demise of the Beothuk Indians,' *Culture* 1 (1981), 71–3.

3 Antoine Parat to [the Minister], 9 July 1688, AC, C11C, vol. 1, 90–1; N.E.S. Griffiths, 'The Acadians,' in George W. Brown et al., eds, *Dictionary of Canadian Biography*, 12 vols to date (Toronto 1966–; hereafter *DCB*), IV:xviii

4 Commissioners of Customs to Sir Edmund Andros, 12 Jan. 1687, PRO, CO5/904, 410

5 René Baudry, 'Antoine Parat,' *DCB*, I:530; Baudry, 'Jacques-François de Mombeton de Brouillan,' *DCB*, II:478; Baudry, 'Louis-Alexandre Des Friches de Meneval,' *DCB*, II:182; Viola Florence Barnes, *The Dominion of New England* (New Haven 1923), 47–9, 69–72

6 Treaty of Peace between Great Britain and France for a Neutrality in America, 6 Nov. 1686, in Clive Parry, ed., *The Consolidated Treaty Series*, 18 (Dobbs Ferry 1969), 94. See also John G. Reid, *Acadia, Maine, and New Scotland; Marginal Colonies in the Seventeenth Century* (Toronto 1981), 179–80.

7 Andros to James II, 9 July 1688, PRO, CO1/65, no. 20; Meneval to the Minister, 10 Sept. 1688, AC, C11D, vol. 2, 96; Reid, *Acadia, Maine, and New Scotland*, 180

8 Meneval to the Minister, [1689], AC, C11D, vol. 2, 113; Kenneth M. Morrison, *The Embattled Northeast: The Elusive Ideal of Alliance in Abenaki-Euramerican Relations* (Berkeley 1984), 114–16. On the raid on Chedabucto, see A. Augustin-Thierry, ed., *Un colonial au temps de Colbert: mémoires de Robert Challes, écrivain du roi* (Paris 1931), 272.

9 Morrison, *The Embattled Northeast*, 123–5; Joseph Denys to [the Minister], 28 Aug. 1689, AC, C11C, vol. 1, 140–1; Letter of Petit, Trouvé, Dubreuil, Meneval, et al., 19–27 May 1690, in *Collection de manuscrits contenant lettres, mémoires, et autres documents historiques relatifs à la Nouvelle-France*, 4 vols (Québec 1883–5), II:8; Villebon to the Marquis de Chevry, 1690, in John Clarence Webster, ed., *Acadia at the End of the Seventeenth Century* (Saint John 1934), 27

10 Journal of Sir William Phips, 1690, PRO, CO5/855, no. 109:6–7; Villebon to Pontchartain, 1693, in Webster, *Acadia at the End of the Seventeenth Century*, 47

11 Resolutions of the House of Representatives, 18 Dec. 1696, Massachusetts

Archives (hereafter MA), vol. 2, 583; Letter of William Stoughton, 24 December 1696, MA, 3, 523. On the trading relationship between Acadia and New England at this time, see Jean Daigle, 'Nos amis les ennemis: relations commerciales de l'Acadie avec le Massachusetts, 1670–1711' (PHD diss., University of Maine 1975), 132–51.

12 Mathieu de Goutin to the Minister, 9 Sept. 1694, AC, C11D, vol. 2, 232–3; Charles Melanson to [Governor Stoughton], 5 Feb. 1696, MA, vol. 2, 587–8; Villebon to Pontchartain, 1693, in Webster, *Acadia at the End of the Seventeenth Century,* 46; Daigle, 'Nos amis les ennemis,' 150

13 Webster, *Acadia at the End of the Seventeenth Century,* 46; Memorial, 14 Feb. 1693, AC, B, 16 (1693), 42

14 Stephen Sewall to Edward Hull, 2 Nov. 1696, PRO, CO5/859, no. 40. See also Charles E. Clark, *The Eastern Frontier: The Settlement of Northern New England* (New York 1970), 72; Morrison, *The Embattled Northeast,* 140–1; George A. Rawlyk, *Nova Scotia's Massachusetts: A Study of Massachusetts–Nova Scotia Relations, 1630 to 1784* (Montreal and London 1973), 78–81. Insights on the conduct of the war by the Maliseet can be gained from the captivity narrative of John Gyles, 'Memoirs of Odd Adventures, Strange Deliverances, etc., in the Captivity of John Gyles, Esq ... Written by Himself,' in Samuel G. Drake, ed., *Indian Captivities* (Boston 1839), 73–109.

15 Alan F. Williams, *Father Baudoin's War: D'Iberville's Campaign in Acadia and Newfoundland, 1696, 1697* (St John's 1987), 24–96, passim; George F.G. Stanley, 'Nicolas Daneau de Muy,' *DCB,* II:168–9

16 Board of Trade to the King, 21 Jan. 1697, PRO, CO195/2, 71; on the founding and the activities of the Board of Trade, see I.K. Steele, *Politics of Colonial Policy: The Board of Trade in Colonial Administration, 1696–1720* (Oxford 1968).

17 John Gibsone to Board of Trade, 28 June 1697, PRO, CO194/1, no. 81; Colonel John Gibsone's Narrative, 29 Nov. 1697, PRO, CO194/1, no. 90

18 [John Norris], Abstract of the planters and boatkeepers in Newfoundland, 27 Sept. 1698, PRO, CO194/1, no. 125 (i); Keith Matthews, 'A History of the West of England–Newfoundland Fisheries' (DPHIL diss., Oxford University 1968), 246–80, passim; W. Gordon Handcock, *'Soe longe as there comes noe women': Origins of English Settlement in Newfoundland* (St John's 1989), 45–6; C. Grant Head, *Eighteenth Century Newfoundland: A Geographer's Perspective* (Toronto 1976), 56; Glanville James Davies, 'England and Newfoundland: Policy and Trade, 1660–1783' (PHD diss., University of Southampton 1980), 57–8; Williams, *Father Baudoin's War,* 109–15

19 William Popple to John Pulteney, 10 May 1698, PRO, CO194/25, 216

20 Keith Matthews, *Lectures on the History of Newfoundland, 1500–1830* (St John's 1988), 96–8; Davies, 'England and Newfoundland,' 44–5; Christopher English, 'The Development of the Newfoundland Legal System to 1815,' *Acadiensis* 20:1 (Autumn 1990), 99; Matthews, 'History of the West of England-Newfoundland Fisheries,' 259–76

21 Andrew Hill Clark, *Acadia: The Geography of Early Nova Scotia to 1760* (Madison 1968), 115–21

22 Villebon to the Minister, 3 Oct. 1698, AC, C11D, vol. 3, 105; Villebon and de Goutin to Massachusetts, 5 May 1699, MA, vol. 2, 590–1; Clark, *Acadia*, 128, 145–7

23 Report of Peter Schuyler and Godfrey Dellius, 2 July 1698, PRO, CO5/1040, no. 78 (ix)

24 Memorial of heads and propositions, 3 June 1701, MA, vol. 30, 467; on this entire sequence of events, see also Morrison, *The Embattled Northeast*, 146–57.

25 Letter of Antoine Gaulin, 24 Oct. 1701, Public Archives of Nova Scotia (PANS), RG1, vol. 4, 39

26 The Minister to Villebon, 26 Mar. 1698, AC, B, vol. 20, f24; Stoughton to Board of Trade, 24 Oct. 1698, PRO, CO5/860, no. 37

27 On the English empire at this time, see Richard R. Johnson, *Adjustment to Empire: The New England Colonies, 1675–1715* (New Brunswick, N.J. 1981). Though for a rival interpretation and a stimulating debate, see also Stephen Saunders Webb, *The Governors-General: The English Army and the Definition of the Empire, 1569–1681* (Chapel Hill 1979); Richard R. Johnson, 'The Imperial Webb: The Thesis of Garrison Government in Early America Considered,' *William and Mary Quarterly*, 3rd ser., 43 (1986), 408–30; Stephen Saunders Webb, 'The Data and Theory of Restoration Empire,' *William and Mary Quarterly*, 3rd ser., 43 (1986), 431–59. On French imperial institutions as they applied to Newfoundland, see Roland Plaze, 'La colonie royale de Plaisance, 1689–1713: impact du statut de colonie royale sur les structures administratives' (MA thesis, Université de Moncton 1991).

28 Brouillan to [the Minister], 6 Oct. 1701, AC, C11D, vol. 4, 46–7

29 Brouillan to [the Minister], 25 Nov. 1703, AC, C11D, vol. 4, 277; Samuel Sewall, *The Diary of Samuel Sewall, 1674–1729*, vol. II, *1699/1700–1714*, Massachusetts Historical Society *Collections*, 5th ser., 6 (Boston, 1879), 87; Morrison, *The Embattled Northeast*, 158–9

30 Brouillan to [the Minister], 25 Nov. 1703, AC, C11D, vol. 4, 280; Joseph Dudley to Board of Trade, 10 Oct. 1704, PRO, CO5/863, no. 118; Daniel d'Auger de Subercase to [the Minister], 22 Oct. 1705, AC, C11C, vol. 4, 196

31 Rawlyk, *Nova Scotia's Massachusetts*, 99–101

32 Joseph Dudley to John Leverett, 26 July 1707, MA, vol. 71, 370–2; Dudley to George Paddon and Charles Stuckley, 23 Aug. 1707, MA, vol. 71, 390; The Case of Samuel Vetch, [20 Feb. 1707], PRO, CO5/864, no. 89; Rawlyk, *Nova Scotia's Massachusetts*, 101–6

33 Costebelle to [the Minister], 26 Feb. 1709, AC, C11C, vol. 6, 179; William Keen's Journal of the Taking of St John's, 1709, PRO, CO194/4, no. 100 (ii); Proposals of the Inhabitants, 2 Feb. 1709, PRO, CO194/4, no. 100 (iii); Ratification of Articles, 6 May 1709, PRO, CO194/4, no. 100 (iv); John Moody to

Board of Trade, 23 Dec. 1709, PRO, CO194/4, no. 103; Bernard Pothier, 'Joseph de Mombeton de Brouillan, dit Saint-Ovide,' *DCB*, III:454–5; Georges Cerbelaud Salagnac, 'Philippe Pastour de Costebelle,' *DCB*, II:511

34 Francis Nicholson and Samuel Vetch to [Lord Dartmouth], 16 Sept. 1710, PRO, CO5/9, 65; Articles of Capitulation, 2 Oct. 1710, PRO, CO5/9, no. 66; Proclamation of Nicholson et al., 12 Oct. 1710, PRO, CO5/9, no. 73

35 Dale Miquelon, *New France, 1701–1744: `A Supplement to Europe'* (Toronto 1987), 44–5; Letter of Costebelle, 24 July 1711, English translation, MA, vol. 2, 625; Letter of Antoine Gaulin, 5 Sept. 1711, AC, C11D, vol. 7, 177–8; Samuel Vetch to Lord Dartmouth, 18 June 1711, PRO, CO5/9, no. 99

36 Vetch to Lord Dartmouth, 8 Aug. 1712, PRO, CO5/9, 109; Articles of Capitulation, 2 Oct. 1710, PRO, CO5/9, no. 66; Paul Mascarene to Francis Nicholson, 6 Nov. 1713, PANS, RG1, vol. 9, 1

37 See William G. Godfrey, *Pursuit of Profit and Preferment in Colonial North America: John Bradstreet's Quest* (Waterloo 1982), 2–3.

38 Principal inhabitants of Port Royal to Vaudreuil, 12 Nov. 1710, AC, C11D, vol. 7, 98–9; Paul Mascarene to Francis Nicholson, 6 Nov. 1713, PANS, RG1, vol. 9, 1

39 Jean-Pierre Proulx, 'The Military History of Placentia: A Study of the French Fortifications,' *History and Archaeology* 26 (1979), 49–51, 59–60; Matthews, 'History of the West of England–Newfoundland Fisheries,' 305, 318–20; Head, *Eighteenth Century Newfoundland*, 75; Carson I.A. Ritchie, 'George Skeffington,' *DCB*, II:609; Davies, 'England and Newfoundland,' 75–6

40 Report of Board of Trade, 18 Dec. 1710, PRO, CO194/22, no. 79; Letter of Mayor of Dartmouth et al., 17 Dec. 1710, PRO, CO194/22, no. 78; Joseph Crowe to Board of Trade, 31 Oct. 1711, PRO, CO194/5, no. 8

41 Board of Trade to Secretary St John, 5 Apr. 1712, PRO, CO195/5, 267–9; Treaty of Peace and Friendship between France and Great Britain, 11 Apr. 1713, in Parry, ed., *Consolidated Treaty Series*, 27:485

42 Augustin-Thierry, ed., *Un colonial au temps de Colbert*, 24; on Oxford's impeachment, see Davies, 'England and Newfoundland,' 68; and Matthews, 'History of the West of England–Newfoundland Fisheries,' 305.

43 Jean-Pierre Proulx, 'Placentia, 1713–1811,' *History and Archaeology* 26 (1979), 120–1; Handcock, *'Soe longe as there comes noe women,'* 81

44 Ralph Pastore, 'The Collapse of the Beothuk World,' *Acadiensis* 19:1 (Autumn 1989), 52–71; Report of Board of Trade, 29 Feb. 1716, PRO, CO194/26, 209–10; Report of Commodore Perry, 13 Oct. 1720, PRO, CO194/7, no. 2; Ralph Pastore, *The Newfoundland Micmacs* ([St John's] 1978), 12

45 Board of Trade, to George I, 19 Dec. 1718, PRO, CO195/6, 451–2, 463

46 Andrew Hill Clark, *Three Centuries and the Island: A Historical Geography of Settlement and Agriculture in Prince Edward Island, Canada* (Toronto and Buffalo 1959), 27–8; Kenneth Donovan, 'Ile Royale, 18th Century,' in R. Cole Harris, ed., and Geoffrey J. Matthews, cartographer/designer, *Historical*

Atlas of Canada I: From the Beginning to 1800 (Toronto 1987), pl. 24; D.C. Harvey, *The French Régime in Prince Edward Island* (New Haven 1926), 40–6; Mary McD. Maude, 'Robert-David Gotteville de Belile,' *DCB*, II:254–5; Miquelon, *New France, 1701–1744*, 117. The term 'Ile Royale' is a confusing one, in that it could be applied specifically to Cape Breton Island or to the entire French colony that encompassed other Gulf islands, including Ile Saint-Jean. In this chapter, Ile Royale normally refers to Cape Breton.

47 Clark, *Acadia*, 269–71; Terence A. Crowley, 'France, Canada, and the Beginning of Louisbourg: In Search of the Great Fortress Myth,' in *Papers and Abstracts for a Symposium on Ile Royale during the French Régime* (Ottawa 1972), 53–63; Miquelon, *New France, 1701–1744*, 108–12

48 See Kenneth Donovan, 'Emblems of Conspicuous Consumption: Slaves in Ile Royale, 1713–1760,' paper delivered at the Southeastern American Society for Eighteenth Century Studies, Birmingham, Alabama, Mar. 1993: 1, 8–11; Bridglal Pachai, *Beneath the Clouds ... of the Promised Land: The Survival of Nova Scotia's Blacks, Volume I, 1600–1800* (Halifax 1987), 41; Robin W. Winks, *The Blacks in Canada: A History* (New Haven 1971), 27. Mathieu Acosta (or deCoste), who is believed to have travelled to Acadia as a Micmac-French interpreter with the sieur de Monts in 1604, was the first of several Blacks recorded in French Acadia; see Marcel Trudel, *Histoire de la Nouvelle-France: le comptoir, 1604–1627* (Ottawa 1966), 465, 485.

49 Christopher Moore, 'The Other Louisbourg: Trade and Merchant Enterprise in Ile Royale, 1713-58,' *Histoire sociale / Social History* 12:23 (May 1979), 79. See also Moore, 'The Maritime Economy of Ile Royale,' *Canada: An Historical Magazine*, 1:4 (June 1974), 34–9; Bernard Pothier, 'Acadian Emigration to Ile Royale after the Conquest of Acadia,' *Histoire sociale / Social History* 3:6 (Nov. 1970), 116–31; B.A. Balcom, *The Cod Fishery of Isle Royale, 1713–58* (Ottawa 1984), 12–15, 20–1; J.S. McLennan, *Louisbourg from Its Foundation to Its Fall, 1713–1758* (London 1918), 11–21.

50 Moore, 'The Other Louisbourg,' 74–81; Pothier, 'Acadian Emigration to Ile Royale,' 129–30

51 Treaty of Peace and Friendship, 11 Apr. 1713, in Parry, *Consolidated Treaty Series*, 27:486; Letter of Queen Anne, 23 June 1713, PRO, CO217/1, no. 19; Vetch to Board of Trade, 24 Nov. 1714, PRO, CO217/1, no. 20

52 Felix Pain to Costebelle, 23 Sept. 1713, PANS, RG1, vol. 3, 64. For a revealing recent insight into Acadian material culture in a well-established settlement at this time, see David J. Christianson, *Belleisle 1983: Excavations at a Pre-Expulsion Acadian Site*, Nova Scotia Museum, Curatorial Report no. 48 (Halifax 1984).

53 Vetch to Board of Trade, 24 Nov. 1714, PRO, CO217/1, no. 20; Report of Board of Trade, 17 Mar. 1715, PRO, CO218/1, 170–83

54 Costebelle to the Minister, 5 Nov. 1715, AC, C11B, vol. 1, 143

55 Pothier, 'Acadian Emigration to Ile Royale,' 129–30; Gisa I. Hynes, 'Some Aspects of the Demography of Port Royal, 1650–1755,' *Acadiensis* 3:1 (Autumn 1973), 7–8; Clark, *Acadia*, 200–61; Naomi Griffiths, 'The Golden Age: Acadian Life, 1713–1748,' *Histoire sociale / Social History* 17:33 (May 1984), 21–34

56 Capt. Christopher Aldridge to Francis Nicholson, 15 Jan. 1714, PRO, CO217/2, no. 7

57 French Inhabitants of Minas to John Doucett, 10 Feb. 1718, PRO, CO217/2, no. 51 (iv); French Inhabitants of the River to Richard Philipps, [1720], PRO, CO217/3, no. 6 (v); Acadian Inhabitants to Saint-Ovide, 6 May 1720, PANS, RG1, vol. 3, 59; Philipps to the Lords Justices, 26 May 1720, PRO, CO217/3, no. 6 (i); Vaudreuil to [the Minister], 31 Oct. 1717, AC, C11A, vol. 38, 155

58 Olive Patricia Dickason, 'Louisbourg and the Indians: A Study in Imperial Race Relations,' *History and Archaeology* 6 (1976), 33–7, 66–70; Morrison, *The Embattled Northeast*, 161–4, 166–76

59 John Doucett to Board of Trade, 10 Feb. 1718, PRO, CO217/2, no. 51; Memorial of Richard Philipps, [1718], PRO, CO217/2, no. 37 (i); Report of Board of Trade, 30 May 1718, PRO, CO194/23, no. 30; Instructions to Philipps, 19 June 1719, PRO, CO218/1, 439–40; Conference of Governor Philipps with the Indians of St John's River: Speech of the Indians, [July 1720], PRO, CO217/3, no. 18 (x); Governor Philipps' Reply, [July 1720], PRO, CO217/3, no. 18 (xi); Indian Chiefs of Passamaquoddy to Philipps, 23 Nov. 1720, PRO, CO217/3, no. 19 (i); Philipps to Board of Trade, 27 Sept. 1720, PRO, CO217/3, no. 18

60 Indians of Les Mines to Richard Philipps, 2 Oct. 1720, PRO, CO217/3, no. 18 (xiv); L.F.S. Upton, *Micmacs and Colonists: Indian-White Relations in the Maritimes, 1713–1867* (Vancouver 1979), 40–1

61 David Jeffries and Charles Shepreve to Robert Mears, 6 July 1715, PRO, CO217/2, no. 2 (i)

62 Instructions to Peter Capon and Thomas Button, nd, in Archibald MacMechan, ed., *Nova Scotia Archives II: A Calendar of Two Letter-Books and One Commission-Book in the Possession of the Government of Nova Scotia, 1713–1741* (Halifax 1900), 12; Peter Capon, 'A Journall of a Voyage to Cape Britton on the Kings Account,' MA, vol. 38A, 11–15; Letter of Costebelle, 1 Oct. 1715 (summary), AC, C11B, 334–6; Dickason, 'Louisbourg and the Indians,' 74; Morrison, *The Embattled Northeast*, 172–3

63 John Doucett to Richard Philipps, 13 Dec. 1718, PRO, CO217/2, no. 64; Daniel Pulteney to Charles Delafaye, 10 Sept. 1720, PRO, CO217/3, no. 8 (i)

64 Instructions to Thomas Smart, [1718], PRO, CO217/2, no. 74; Saint-Ovide to [Samuel Shute], 23 Sept. 1717 [*sic*, for 1718], PRO, CO217/2, no. 75; Capon, 'Journall,' 13; Instructions to Philipps, 19 June 1719, PRO, CO218/1, 440

65 Board of Trade to the Lords Justices, 19 June 1719, PRO, CO218/1, 419

CHAPTER 6   1720–1744: Cod, Louisbourg, and the Acadians

1 Bernard Bailyn, *The Peopling of British North America* (New York 1985), 3
2 C. Grant Head, *Eighteenth Century Newfoundland: A Geographer's Perspective* (Toronto 1976), 54–61; W. Gordon Handcock, *'Soe longe as there comes noe women': Origins of English Settlement in Newfoundland* (St John's 1989), 91–120; Ingeborg Marshall, 'Disease as a Factor in the Demise of the Beothuk Indians,' *Culture* 1 (1981), 71–7
3 Nicolas de Jong, 'The French Regime, 1534–1758,' in F.W.P. Bolger, ed., *Canada's Smallest Province: A History of P.E.I.* (Charlottetown 1973), 18–24; L.F.S. Upton, *Micmacs and Colonists: Indian-White Relations in the Maritimes, 1713–1867* (Vancouver 1979), 32–3
4 Upton, *Micmacs and Colonists,* 32–3; Philip K. Bock, 'Micmac,' in Bruce G. Trigger, ed., *Northeast,* vol. 15 of the *Handbook of North American Indians* (Washington 1978), 117
5 W.B. Weeden, *Economic and Social History of New England, 1620–1789,* 2 vols (Boston 1890), II:594–5
6 Head, *Eighteenth Century Newfoundland,* 65; Handcock, `Soe longe as there comes noe women,' 73
7 Head, *Eighteenth Century Newfoundland,* 33
8 Handcock, *'Soe longe as there comes noe women,'* 88–9
9 Head, *Eighteenth Century Newfoundland,* 27; Handcock, *'Soe longe as there comes noe women,'* 97
10 B.A. Balcom, *The Cod Fishery of Isle Royale, 1713–58* (Ottawa 1984), 18
11 Christopher Moore, 'The Other Louisbourg: Trade and Merchant Enterprise in Ile Royale, 1713–58,' *Histoire sociale / Social History* 12:23 (May 1979), 4–5, 50, 79
12 Ibid., 4
13 J.S. McLennan, *Louisbourg from Its Foundation to Its Fall 1713–1758* (London 1918), 14, 34–6, 53–4. See also Bernard Pothier, 'Acadian Emigration to Ile Royale after the Conquest of Acadia,' *Histoire sociale / Social History* 3:6 (Nov. 1970), 116–31.
14 Balcom, *The Cod Fishery of Isle Royale,* 7
15 McLennan, *Louisbourg,* 222
16 G.A. Rawlyk, *Nova Scotia's Massachusetts: A Study of Massachusetts–Nova Scotia Relations, 1630 to 1784* (Montreal 1973), 135–6
17 E. Eis, *The Forts of Folly* (London 1959), 221
18 G.M. Wrong, ed., *Louisbourg in 1745: The Anonymous Lettre d'un Habitant de Louisbourg* (New York 1897), 39. See also McLennan, *Louisbourg,* 126.
19 This is an important theme in J.R. McNeill, *Atlantic Empires of France and Spain: Louisbourg and Havana, 1700–1763* (Chapel Hill 1985).
20 De Jong, 'The French Regime,' 14; 'New Style' dates will be used through-

out this chapter even though it was not until 1752 that the British finally adopted the Gregorian reform of the calendar.

21 Ibid., 16. See also J.H. Blanchard, *The Acadians of Prince Edward Island, 1720–1964* (Quebec 1964), 22; and Andrew Hill Clark, *Three Centuries and the Island: A Historical Geography of Settlement and Agriculture in Prince Edward Island, Canada* (Toronto 1959), 28.

22 Quoted in Blanchard, *The Acadians of Prince Edward Island*, 23

23 D.C. Harvey, *The French Regime in Prince Edward Island* (New Haven 1926), 67–8, 103–8; Clark, *Three Centuries and the Island*, 28–31; Bernard Pothier, 'Louis Du Pont Duchambon De Vergor,' in George W. Brown, et al., eds, *Dictionary of Canadian Biography*, 12 vols to date (Toronto 1966–; hereafter *DCB*), IV:249–51

24 J.B. Brebner, *New England's Outpost: Acadia before the Conquest of Canada* (New York 1927), 145

25 N.E.S. Griffiths, 'The Acadians,' *DCB*, IV:xiii

26 John Adams to the Lords of Trade, 8 Dec. 1739, National Archives of Canada (NAC), Nova Scotia A Series (NSA), 24

27 Quoted in Brebner, *New England's Outpost*, 77–8

28 Capt. Young to Council of Trade and Plantations, 21 Oct. 1720, *Calendar of State Papers Colonial, 1719–1720*, 32

29 'Armstrong's Journal, 1722,' quoted in McLennan, *Louisbourg*, 68

30 Armstrong to Council of Trade and Plantations, 22 Feb. 1722, *Calendar of State Papers Colonial, 1722–1723*, 3

31 Philipps to Council of Trade and Plantations, 19 Sept. 1722, ibid., 142

32 *Massachusetts House Journals, 1721–1722* (Boston 1922), 82

33 Philipps to Council of Trade and Plantations, 19 Sept. 1722, *Calendar of State Papers Colonial, 1722–1723*, 142

34 Ibid.

35 For different views of these events see B.M. Moody "A Just and Disinterested Man": The Nova Scotia Career of Paul Mascarene, 1710–1752' (PHD diss., Queen's University 1976), 84–9, and Kenneth M. Morrison, *The Embattled Northeast: The Elusive Ideal of Alliance in Abenaki-Euramerican Relations* (Berkeley 1984), 185–90.

36 Quoted in Beamish Murdoch, *History of Nova-Scotia, or Acadie*, 3 vols (Halifax 1865), I:428, 'Articles of Submission'

37 See H.A. Innis, ed., *Select Documents in Canadian Economic History, 1497–1783* (Toronto 1929), 158–9; see also 'State of codd fishery, 1735,' *Calendar of State Papers Colonial, 1735–1736*, 109–10, and 'State of codd fishery ... Whale Fishery, 1736', 324; 'Account of fish made at Canso ... Whale Fishery, 1737,' *Calendar of State Papers Colonial, 1737–1738*, 270

38 J. Corbett (Sec. to the Admiralty) to a John Scrope, 31 May 1744, NAC, Admiralty Papers, II:483

39 Paul Mascarene to King Gould, 14 June 1744, NAC, PRO, A26

40 Brebner, *New England's Outpost*, 86–7. See also Maxwell Sutherland, 'Lawrence Armstrong,' *DCB*, II:21–4.
41 Quoted in Brebner, *New England's Outpost*, 89
42 Quoted in ibid., 92
43 Philipps to the Duke of Newcastle, 2 Sept. 1730, in T.B. Akins, ed., *Selections from the Public Documents of the Province of Nova Scotia* (Halifax 1869), 86
44 This translation is from Griffiths, 'The Acadians,' xxii.
45 Brebner, *New England's Outpost*, 97
46 Quoted in ibid., 97–8
47 Griffiths, 'The Acadians,' xii. This argument is enthusiastically supported in T.G. Barnes, '"The Dayly Cry for Justice": The Juridical Failure of the Annapolis Royal Regime, 1713–1749,' in Philip Girard and Jim Phillips, eds., *Essays in the History of Canadian Law*, III: *Nova Scotia* (Toronto 1990), 10–41.
48 Andrew Hill Clark, *Acadia: The Geography of Early Nova Scotia to 1760* (Madison 1968), 200–37
49 For a sophisticated discussion of the evolution of the phrase 'neutral French,' see Brebner, *New England's Outpost*, 97–8.
50 Ibid., 40–1
51 'Removal of the French Inhabitants ...,' University of Edinburgh, Andrew Brown Papers (hereafter Brown Papers), 23, 52–5
52 Ibid., 61–3
53 Ibid., 68
54 Griffiths, 'The Acadians,' xxiii
55 Brown Papers, 53–4. For archaeological support for this eighteenth-century description, see B. Preston, *An Archaelogical Survey of reported Acadian Habitation Sites in the Annapolis Valley and the Minas Basin Area 1971*, Nova Scotia Museum, Curatorial Report no. 20 (Halifax 1971); David J. Christianson, *Belleisle 1983: Excavations at a Pre-Expulsion Acadian Site*, Nova Scotia Museum, Curatorial Report no. 48 (Halifax 1984); A. Crépeau and B. Dunn, *The Melanson Settlement: An Acadian Farming Community (ca 1664–1755)*, Research Bulletin Parks Canada, no. 250, Sept. 1986.
56 J. Demos, *A Little Commonwealth: Family Life in Plymouth Colony* (New York 1970). See also Nancy McMahon, 'Andrew Brown and the Writing of Acadian History' (MA thesis, Queen's University 1981), 112–14, and Barnes, '"The Dayly Cry for Justice,"' 25–8.
57 Brown Papers, 58; McMahon, 'Andrew Brown,' 119–20; Jacqueline Cyr, 'Le costume traditionnel en Acadie,' *Revue historique de l'Université de Moncton* 10 (1977), 99. For a general discussion of the rural economy see M. Mitterauer and R. Sieder, *The European Family: Patriarchy to Partnership from the Middle Ages to the Present* (Chicago 1983).
58 Brown Papers, 56
59 McMahon, 'Andrew Brown,' 131

60 Brown Papers, 57; see also Clark, *Acadia*, 233–5.

61 Brown Papers, 59

62 Brown Papers, 66–7. For a more detailed description of Acadian celebrations, see M.A. Downie and G.A. Rawlyk, *A Proper Acadian* (Toronto 1980).

63 Griffiths, 'The Acadians,' xxiii–xxiv. There is a particularly good discussion of Acadian life in Naomi Griffiths, 'The Golden Age: Acadian Life, 1713–1748,' *Histoire sociale / Social History* 17:33 (May 1984), 21–34. Griffiths has enlarged on this theme in *The Contexts of Acadian History 1686–1784* (Montreal and Kingston 1992), 33–61.

64 See G.A. Rawlyk, *Yankees at Louisbourg* (Orono 1967), 2; Blaine Adams, 'Jean-Baptiste-Louis Le Prévost Duquesnel,' *DCB*, III:392–3; T.A. Crowley and Bernard Pothier, 'François Du Pont Duvivier,' *DCB*, IV:251–5.

65 Paul Mascarene to King Gould, 14 June 1744, NAC, PRO A26. See also W.G. Godfrey, *Pursuit of Profit and Preferment in Colonial North America: John Bradstreet's Quest* (Waterloo 1982); Rawlyk, *Yankees at Louisbourg*, 5–15.

66 See 'Le Loutre's Autobiography,' in J.C. Webster, *The Career of the Abbé Le Loutre in Nova Scotia with a Translation of this Autobiography* (Shediac 1933), 35. See also N. McL. Rogers' sympathetic article 'The Abbé Le Loutre,' *Canadian Historical Review* 2 (1930), 112, and Gérard Finn's 'Jean-Louis Le Loutre,' *DCB*, IV:453–8.

67 Quoted in Brebner, *New England's Outpost*, 104, from 'Brown MS' in the British Museum Additional MSS, 19071, f61

68 Mascarene to the Indians, 3 July 1744, in Murdoch, *History of Nova-Scotia*, II:30

69 *Pennsylvania Journal*, 26 July 1744

70 Duvivier's 'Journal of the Annapolis Royal Expedition, 16 May 1745,' NAC, AC E169. I have used, throughout, my 1967 English translation of the manuscript 'Journal.' See also Bernard Pothier, *Course à l'Acadie: journal de campagne de François DuPont Duvivier en 1744* (Moncton 1982).

71 Duvivier's 'Order to the inhabitants of Mines, Piziquid, River Canard and Cobequid, 27 Aug. 1744,' in Akins, ed., *Selections from the Documents*, 134

72 See Duvivier's 'Journal,' NAC, AC E169.

73 Maurepas to the Bishop of Quebec, 12 May 1745, NAC, B, 81

74 Mascarene to Shirley, Dec. 1744, Akins, ed., *Selections from the Public Documents*, 143

75 Ibid., 144–5

76 Duvivier's 'Journal,' NAC, AC E169

77 *Boston Weekly News-Letter*, 15 Nov. 1744; Duchambon to Maurepas, 18 Nov. 1744, NAC, AC C 11 B, 26

CHAPTER 7 1744–1763: Colonial Wars and Aboriginal Peoples

1 Among the best treatments of the Natives in the region during the eigh-

teenth century are: L.F.S. Upton, *Micmacs and Colonists: Indian-White Relations in the Maritimes, 1713–1867* (Vancouver 1979); Andrew Hill Clark, *Acadia: The Geography of Early Nova Scotia to 1760* (Madison 1968), esp. 56–70; Olive Patricia Dickason, *Louisbourg and the Indians: A Study in Imperial Relations, 1713–1760* (Ottawa 1976); Olive Patricia Dickason, 'Amerindians between French and English in Nova Scotia, 1713–1763,' *American Indian Culture and Research Journal* 10:4 (1986), 31–56.

2 Yves F. Zoltvany, 'The Frontier Policy of Philippe de Rigaud de Vaudreuil, 1713–1725,' *Canadian Historical Review* 48 (1967), 227–50, esp. 230–2; Zoltvany, 'Philippe de Rigaud de Vaudreuil,' in George W. Brown, et al., eds, *Dictionary of Canadian Biography,* 12 vols to date (Toronto 1966–; hereafter *DCB*), II:565–74; Alfred Goldsworthy Bailey, *The Conflict of European and Eastern Algonkian Cultures, 1504–1700* (2nd ed.; Toronto 1969), 32–34, 50

3 Francis Jennings, 'The Constitutional Evolution of the Covenant Chain,' *Proceedings of the American Philosophical Society* 115 (1971), 88–96; Jennings, *The Ambiguous Iroquois Empire: The Covenant Chain Confederation of Indian Tribes with English Colonies from Its Beginning to the Lancaster Treaty of 1744* (New York 1984)

4 For a discussion of the limits of Native support of French interests, see W.J. Eccles, 'Sovereignty-Association, 1500–1783,' *Canadian Historical Review* 65 (1984), 475–510, esp. 503–4.

5 Jean Pariseau, 'Jean-Baptiste-Nicolas-Roch de Ramezay,' *DCB*, IV:650–3, 651; Barry M. Moody, 'Arthur Noble,' C.J. Russ, 'Louis La Corne,' *DCB*, III:483–4, 331–2; Messrs de Beauharnois and Hocquart to Count de Maurepas, Quebec, 12 Sept.1745, 'Military and Other Operations in Canada during the years 1745–1746,' and 'Journal of Occurrences in Canada; 1746, 1747,' in E.B. O'Callaghan, ed., *Documents Relative to the Colonial History of New-York*, X: *Paris Documents* (Albany 1858), 11, 14, 44, 57, 89, 90, 126

6 As quoted by J. Murray Beck, 'Edward Cornwallis,' *DCB*, IV:168–71, quotation at 168

7 Maxwell Sutherland, 'John Brewse'; A.A. MacKenzie, 'John Fillis'; L.R. Fischer, 'Michael Francklin'; Stephen E. Patterson, 'Benjamin Gerrish,' 'Joseph Gerrish'; Donald F. Chard, 'Joshua Mauger'; Phyllis R. Blakely, 'Charles Morris'; S. Buggey, 'Malachy Salter,' *DCB*, IV:92–3, 266–7, 272–6, 290–2, 525–9, 559–63, 695–7; C.E. Thomas, 'William Tutty,' *DCB*, III:634–5

8 Council Minutes, 13–14 Aug. 1749, Public Archives of Nova Scotia (PANS), RG1, vol. 186

9 Micmacs to Gov. Cornwallis, [22 Sept.] 1749, Great Britain, Public Record Office (PRO), CO217/9, 116. Translated here from the French. Maillard sent a copy of the letter written in Micmac and a French translation to his superior in Paris, later printed in *Collection de documents inédits sur le Canada et L'Amérique publié par le Canada-Français,* 3 vols (Quebec 1888), I:17–19. See also Micheline D. Johnson, 'Pierre Maillard,' *DCB*, III:415–19.

10 Council Minutes, 18 Sept. 1749, PANS, RG1, vol. 186

11 29 July 1749, as quoted by Gérard Finn, 'Jean-Louis Le Loutre,' *DCB*, IV:455

12 Council Minutes, 1–2 Oct. 1749, PRO, CO217/9, 117–18

13 John Clarence Webster, *The Career of the Abbé Le Loutre in Nova Scotia with a Translation of his Autobiography* (Shediac 1933)

14 See, for example, Micheline D. Johnson, 'Jean Baptiste Cope,' *DCB*, III:136–7.

15 John Clarence Webster, *The Forts of Chignecto* (Shediac 1930); Max Savelle, *The Origins of American Diplomacy* (New York 1967), 386–419

16 For a full discussion of population and the difficulties of precision, see Clark, *Acadia*, 200–12. See also J.-H. Blanchard, *Histoire des Acadiens de L'Ile du Prince-Edouard* (Moncton 1927), 21–8; Bona Arsenault, *History of the Acadians* (Quebec 1966), 113–14.

17 Finn, 'Le Loutre,' *DCB*, IV:456, 453; Webster, 'Le Loutre's Autobiography,' 33

18 Webster, 'Le Loutre's Autobiography,' 35

19 Ibid., 33–42

20 Gov. Cornwallis to [Lt] Gov. [Spencer] Phips [of Massachusetts], Halifax, 3 May 1750; Cornwallis to Board of Trade, Halifax, 10 July 1750, PRO, CO217/10, 48–9, 1–8; Major Charles Lawrence, 'A Journal of the Proceedings of the Detachment under My Command after Entering the Basin of Chignecto [Apr. 1750],' in John Clarence Webster, ed., *The Journal of Joshua Winslow* (Saint John 1936), 32–4. See also the estimates of Acadian population in Raoul Dionne, 'L'origine acadienne de Moncton Le Coude,' *Revue d'histoire de l'amérique française* 37 (1983), 410–11.

21 Capt. John Rous to Cornwallis, Chignecto, 6 Sept. 1750; Cornwallis to Duke of Bedford, Halifax, 20 Sept. 1750; Cornwallis to Board of Trade, Halifax, Sept. 22, 1750, in Webster, ed., *Journal of Joshua Winslow*, 36–9

22 Cornwallis to Board of Trade, Halifax, 27 Nov. 1750, in Webster, ed., *Journal of Joshua Winslow*, 39–40; Beamish Murdoch, *A History of Nova Scotia or Acadie*, 3 vols (Halifax 1865–7), II:192–3

23 Cornwallis to Board of Trade, Halifax, 19 Aug. 1750, PRO, CO217/10. The letter is immediately followed by 'Extract[s] of some letters found in the sloop London taken in Baie Verte by Captain LeCras.' See also Cornwallis to Duke of Bedford, Halifax, 19 Aug. 1750, in Webster, ed., *Journal of Joshua Winslow*, 35–6; Cornwallis to Board of Trade, Halifax, 27 Nov. 1750, PRO, CO217/11.

24 Murdoch, *History of Nova Scotia*, II:200–1; Cornwallis to Board of Trade, 24 June 1751, PRO, CO217/12

25 Paul Mascarene to Gov. Cornwallis, Falmouth, Maine, 27 Aug. 1751; Cornwallis to Board of Trade, Halifax, 16 Feb. 1752, PRO, CO217/13; Council Minutes, 17 July 1752, PANS, RG1, vol. 186

26 Micheline D. Johnson, 'Jean-Baptiste Cope,' *DCB*, III:136–7; Prevost to [?], Louisbourg, 10 Sept. 1752, NAC, MG1, C11B, vol. 33, 163–6 (microfilm copy read at Le centre d'études acadiennes, Université de Moncton)

27 Council Minutes, 14 Sept., 24 Nov. 1752, PANS, RG1, vol. 186; Treaty proposal,

16 Sept. PRO, 1752, CO217/13, 306–7; Treaty of 1752, 22 Nov. 1752, PRO, CO217/40, 229; Prevost to Minister [of Marine], Louisbourg, 12 May 1753, NAC, MG1, C11B, vol. 33, 159 ff

28 Council Minutes, 2, 12, and 16 Apr. and 16 May 1753, PANS, RG1, vol. 186; Hopson to Board of Trade, 14 and 16 Apr. 1753; 'An Examination ... of James Grace and John Conner taken April 16th 1753,' PRO, CO217/14, 151–5. 'Deposition of Anthony Casteel,' 30 July 1753, PRO, CO217/14, 199. Casteel's deposition presents an abbreviated version of his story, which appears in its complete form in 'The Diary of Anthony Casteel,' *Le Canada-Francais* (1889), II:111–26. A transcript of this document is located in the Brown MSS, PANS. See also Upton, *Micmacs and Colonists*, 55.

29 Prevost to Minister, 12 May 1753 and 17 June 1753, NAC, MG1, C11B, vol. 33, 159 ff, 181–3. Hopson to Board of Trade, two letters of 23 July 1753, PRO, CO217/14, 185–96; Letter Book, PAC/NS/A:54, in N.E.S. Griffiths, ed., *The Acadian Deportation: Deliberate Perfidy or Cruel Necessity?* (Toronto 1969), 84–5

30 Hopson to Board of Trade, Halifax, 29 May 1753, PRO, CO217/14, 177–8

31 Winthrop Pickard Bell, *The 'Foreign Protestants' and the Settlement of Nova Scotia* (Toronto 1961), 315, 397–475

32 Webster, 'Le Loutre's Autobiography,' 44–8; 'Anthony Casteel's Journal,' *Le Canada-Francais*, II:125–6

33 Gov. Duquesne to de la Martinière, Montreal and Quebec City, 27 July and 10 Sept. 1753, Webster Collection, New Brunswick Museum (NBM); 'Journal of Louis de Courville, 1755,' in John Clarence Webster, ed., *Journals of Beauséjour* (Halifax 1937), 45–50, esp. 45

34 Abbé Daudin to Abbé de l'Isle Dieu, 26 Sept. 1754, Webster Collection; Webster, 'Le Loutre's Autobiography,' 47

35 Lawrence to Board of Trade, 1 Mar., 1 June 1754, PRO, CO217/15, 25–9, 32

36 Council Minutes, 16 Nov. 1753, and 29 July 1754, PANS, RG1, vol. 187; William Cotterell to Captain Hamilton, 3 June 1754, in Thomas Beamish Akins, ed., *Selections from the Public Documents of the Province of Nova Scotia* (Halifax 1869), 210

37 Council Minutes, 9 Sept. 1754, PANS, RG1, 187. See also Savelle, *Origins of American Diplomacy*, 394, 413; Savelle, *Diplomatic History of the Canadian Boundary, 1749–1763* (New Haven 1940), 36–40.

38 Micheline D. Johnson, 'Paul Laurent,' *DCB*, III:358–9; Council Minutes, 12–13 Feb. 1755, PANS, RG1, vol. 187

39 Arsenault, *History of the Acadians*, 41, 93, 113–14, 116; Blanchard, *Histoire*, 21–2, 28, 30; Lawrence to Board of Trade, 5 Dec. 1753, 4 Mar. 1754, and 1 Aug. 1754, Akins, ed., *Selections from the Public Documents*, 205–8, 212–14. See also Clark, *Acadia*, 260–1, 333–4, and 347, for the difficulties in sorting out population movements in this period and references to trade patterns.

40 Arsenault, *History of the Acadians*, 120; Council minutes, 21 June 1754,

Akins, ed., *Selections from the Public Documents*, 212. See also 'Judge Morris' Account of the Acadians ... 1753,' 'Judge Morris' Remarks ... [1755],' and Secretary Bulkeley's account of the expulsion, 18 Aug. 1791, 'The Acadian French,' *Report and Collections of the Nova Scotia Historical Society* (Halifax 1881), II:149–60.

41 Lawrence to Board of Trade, 1 Aug. 1754; Murray to Council, 22 Sept. 1754; Council Minutes, 2 Oct. 1754; Lawrence's Proclamation, 17 Sept. 1754; 'Explanation of the Corn Act so far as relates to the French Inhabitants,' Akins, ed., *Selections from the Public Documents*, 212–14, 219–21, 222–26

42 Lawrence to Shirley, Halifax, 5 Nov. 1754, Akins, ed., *Selections from the Public Documents*, 376–9

43 Webster, ed., 'Journal of Louis de Courville,' *Journals of Beauséjour*, 45–50; 'Journal of Abijah Willard,' N.B. Historical Society *Collections* 13 (1930), 3–75, esp. 25; Thomas Pichon's Diary of Beauséjour, typescript in the John Clarence Webster Collection, NBM; Lawrence to Board of Trade, 18 July 1755, PRO, CO217/15

44 Griffiths, 'The Acadians,' *DCB*, IV:xxvi–xxvii

45 'Journal of Colonel John Winslow ... 1755,' *Report and Collections of the Nova Scotia Historical Society* (Halifax 1879), I:71–196; Jean Daigle and Robert LeBlanc, 'Acadian Deportation and Return,' in R. Cole Harris, ed., and Geoffrey J. Matthews, cartographer/designer, *Historical Atlas of Canada I: From the Beginning to 1800* (Toronto 1987), pl. 30; Phyllis E. LeBlanc, 'Charles Deschamps de Boishébert et de Raffetot,' *DCB*, IV:212–15; Dionne, 'L'origine acadienne de Moncton,' 412–15

46 The variety of interpretations of the expulsion is explored by N.E.S. Griffiths, ed., *Acadian Deportation*. See also Jean Daigle, 'Acadia, 1604–1763: An Historical Synthesis,' in Daigle, ed., *The Acadians of the Maritimes: Thematic Studies* (Moncton 1982), 17–46; Naomi Griffiths, *The Acadians: Creation of a People* (Toronto 1973), 48–85; and Griffiths, 'The Acadians,' *DCB*, IV:xvii–xxxi. Griffiths takes the view that the Deportation was unjustified because the Acadians were genuinely neutrals.

47 Governor Lawrence to Board of Trade, 11 Aug. 1755, PRO, CO217/15. See also Thomas Garden Barnes, '"The Dayly Cry for Justice": The Juridical Failure of the Annapolis Royal Regime, 1713–1749,' in Philip Girard and Jim Phillips, eds, *Essays in the History of Canadian Law, III: Nova Scotia* (Toronto 1990), 10–41, who argues that the lenity of the British judicial system prevented Acadians from recognizing the importance the British attached to loyalty oaths.

48 Governor Lawrence to Board of Trade, 1 Aug. 1754, PRO, CO217/15

49 'Journal of Occurrences,' 14

50 Governor Lawrence to Board of Trade, 1 Aug. 1754, PRO, CO217/15; l'abbé Daudin à l'abbé de l'Isle Dieu, [Minas], 26 Sept. 1754, Webster Collection

51 Micheline D. Johnson, 'Henri Daudin,' *DCB*, III:165–6

52 See, for example, Vaudreuil to the Minister [of Marine], Montreal, 19 Apr. 1757; Drucourt and Prévost to the Minister, Louisbourg, 6 Apr. 1756 and 12 May 1757, Webster Collection.

53 Governor Lawrence to Board of Trade, 18 Oct. 1755, PRO, CO217/15

54 14 and 25 May 1756, PRO, CO217/16; Council Minutes, 14 May 1756, PANS, RG1, vol. 187

55 Drucourt and Prévost to the Minister [of Marine], Louisbourg, 6 Apr. 1756; Prévost to Minister, Louisbourg, 27 Sept. and 2 Oct. 1756; Vaudreuil to Minister, Montréal, 19 Apr. 1757, Webster Collection; Prévost to unknown, Louisbourg, 12 May 1756, NAC, MG1, C11B, vol. 33, 105–6; accounts: 29 Nov. 1756; 20 Dec. 1756; 30 Sept. 1757, NAC, MG1, C11B, vol. 37, 209 ff; 36:221 ff; 37:128 ff

56 Franquer to [?], Louisbourg, 18 June 1757, NAC, MG1, C11B, vol. 37, 289–91; Prévost to Minister [of Marine], Louisbourg, 12 July and 16 Sept. 1757; Drucourt to Minister, Louisbourg, 12 July 1757; Vaudreuil to Minister, Montreal, 14 July 1757, Webster Collection

57 C.P. Stacey, 'Jeffery, 1st Baron Amherst,' DCB, IV:20–7. The Articles of Capitulation, dated 26 July 1758, are found in the Amherst Manuscripts, a microfilm copy of which is located in the Harriet Irving Library, University of New Brunswick. The most complete account of the military career of Louisbourg is J.S. McLennan, Louisbourg from Its Foundation to Its Fall, 1713–1758 (Sydney 1957). For numbers of men and details of the initial attack in 1758, see especially 247–60.

58 Lawrence to General Amherst, Halifax, 17 Sept. 1759, PRO, WO34/11. The prowess of the Micmac at sea is explored by Olive Patricia Dickason, 'La "guerre navale" contre les Britanniques, 1713–1763,' in Charles A. Martijn, ed., Les Micmacs et la mer (Quebec 1986), 233–48.

59 Council Minutes, 30 Nov. 1759, PANS, RG1, 188. Several bands of Micmacs were represented by Roger Morris and four others who came directly to Halifax on 9 Jan. 1760, and were given formal permission to come and go until a treaty could be negotiated: Council Minutes, PANS, RG1, vol. 188.

60 Council Minutes, 21, 22, 29 Feb., 10 Mar. 1760, PANS, RG1, vol. 210, 114, 115–16, 117–18. The Maliseet and Passamaquoddy Treaty was drafted and negotiated in French and the draft appears in PANS, MG1, vol. 258, 66–83. Final drafts appear under date of 23 Feb. 1760, in PRO, CO217/18. The first Micmac treaties were signed on 10 Mar.: see the La Have Treaty in the Andrew Brown MSS, PANS, 19071, 174. Gov. Lawrence reported to the Board of Trade that he had 'made a peace on the same terms with the Tribes of Richibuctou, Musquadoboit and La Have, who sent their Chiefs here for that purpose': 11 May 1760, PRO, CO217/17, 59.

61 See Council Minutes of 13, 14, and 16 Feb. 1760, PANS, RG1, vol. 188; Extracts of Minutes of the House of Assembly, 18 and 19 Feb. 1760, PRO, CO217/20; Patterson, 'Benjamin Gerrish,' DCB, IV:290–1; Extracts of Minutes of House

of Assembly, 18 and 19 Feb. 1760; 'Remarks on the Indian Commerce Carried on by the Government of Nova Scotia in the Year 1760, 1761 and Part of 1762,' 15 Apr. 1763, PRO, CO217/20.

62 The Miramichi Treaty of 25 June 1761 is found in PANS, RG1, 165, 162–5; the Treaty of Miramichi, Restigouche, Richibucto, and Shediac bands of 26 Sept. 1779 is in PRO, CO217/54, 252–7; 'Ceremonials at Concluding a Peace,' 25 June 1761, PRO, CO217/18, 276–84.

63 W.S. MacNutt, 'The Beginnings of Nova Scotia Politics,' *Canadian Historical Review* 16 (1935), 41–53; S. Buggey, 'Jonathan Belcher,' *DCB*, IV:50–3

64 Graeme Wynn, 'A Province Too Much Dependent on New England,' *Canadian Geographer* 31 (1987), 100–3; Graeme Wynn and Debra McNabb, 'Pre-Loyalist Nova Scotia,' *Historical Atlas of Canada I*, pl. 31

65 'A Report of the Present State of the Several Townships with the Numbers of Inhabitants in the Province of Nova Scotia, 1766,' PRO, CO217/21, 272–3

66 Georges Cerbelaud Salagnac, 'Charles-Henri Louis d'Arsac de Ternay,' William H. Whitely, 'Sir Hugh Palliser,' *DCB*, IV:30–2, 597–601

67 Council Minutes, 3 July 1762; Lt Gov. Belcher to Col. Denson, Halifax, 17 July 1762; S. Zauberbuhler et al. to Belcher, Lunenburg, 15 and 21 July 1762; Address of House of Representatives to Belcher, [July 1762], PRO, CO217/19, 106–29; Council Minutes, 26 and 30 July 1762; Thomas Hancock to Capt. James Brooks, Boston, 27 Sept. 1762, PRO, WO34/11, 128–9, 151

68 Gov. Wilmot to Board of Trade, Halifax, 10 Dec. 1763, PRO, CO217/20, 354–8; Benjamin Green to Board of Trade, Halifax, 24 Aug. 1766; Michael Franklin to Board of Trade, 3 Sept. 1766, PRO, CO217/21, 269–79; 342–47

69 For a discussion of the role of the Micmac in the extinction of the Beothuk, see Ingeborg Marshall, 'Beothuk and Micmac: Re-examining Relationships,' *Acadiensis* 17:2 (Spring 1988), 52–82. For a view that stresses the declining food sources, see Ralph Pastore, 'The Collapse of the Beothuk World,' *Acadiensis* 19:1 (Autumn 1989), 52–71.

CHAPTER 8 1763–1783: Resettlement and Rebellion

1 Adam Shortt and Arthur G. Doughty, eds, *Documents Relating to the Constitutional History of Canada 1759–1791* (Ottawa 1907), 73–92

2 J.M. Bumsted, 'The Canada-Guadeloupe Debate and the Origins of the American Revolution,' *Man and Nature / l'Homme et la Nature* 5 (1986), 51–62

3 Shortt and Doughty, eds, *Constitutional Documents*, 126–48

4 L.F.S. Upton, *Micmacs and Colonists: Indian-White Relations in the Maritimes, 1713–1867* (Vancouver 1979), 61–5

5 Bernard Bailyn, *Voyagers to the West: A Passage in the Peopling of America on the Eve of the Revolution* (New York 1986)

6 John Bartlet Brebner, *The Neutral Yankees of Nova Scotia: A Marginal Colony*

during the Revolutionary Years (New York 1937). See also W.B. Kerr, 'Nova Scotia in the Critical Years, 1775–6,' *Dalhousie Review* 12 (1932), 97–107; Kerr, 'The Merchants of Nova Scotia and the American Revolution,' *Canadian Historical Review* 12 (1932), 20–36; Kerr, *The Maritime Provinces of British North America and the American Revolution* (Sackville 1941); G.A. Rawlyk, *Nova Scotia's Massachusetts: A Study of Massachusetts-Nova Scotia Relations, 1630 to 1784* (Montreal 1973).

7 C. Grant Head, *Eighteenth Century Newfoundland: A Geographer's Perspective* (Toronto 1976), 82–100; John J. Mannion, ed., *The Peopling of Newfoundland: Essays on Historical Geography* (St John's 1977), 15–76; W. Gordon Handcock, *'Soe longe as there comes noe women': Origins of English Settlement in Newfoundland* (St John's 1989), 219–63

8 Quoted in Head, *Eighteenth Century Newfoundland*, 149

9 Margaret Conrad, ed., *They Planted Well: New England Planters in Maritime Canada* (Fredericton 1988); Graeme Wynn, 'A Province Too Much Dependent on New England,' *Canadian Geographer* 31 (1987), 98–113

10 Harold Innis, ed., *The Diary of Simeon Perkins 1766–1780* (Toronto 1948)

11 Wynn, 'A Province Too Much Dependent,' esp. 100–2

12 J.M. Bumsted, 'Henry Denny Denson,' in George W. Brown et al., eds, *Dictionary of Canadian Biography,* 12 vols to date (Toronto 1966–; hereafter *DCB*), IV:208–9

13 R.J. Morgan, 'Joseph Frederick Wallet DesBarres,' *DCB*, VI:192–7; D. Murray Young, 'Planter Settlements in the St. John Valley,' in Conrad, ed., *They Planted Well*, 29–35

14 Mason Wade, 'After the *Grand Dérangement*: The Acadians Return to the Gulf of St. Lawrence and to Nova Scotia,' *American Review of Canadian Studies* 5 (1975), 42–65

15 Georges Arsenault, *The Island Acadians, 1720–1980* (Charlottetown 1989), 51–8; Robert G. LeBlanc, 'The Acadian Migrations,' *Canadian Geographical Journal* 81:1 (1970–1), 10–19

16 J.M. Bumsted, *Land, Settlement and Politics on Eighteenth-Century Prince Edward Island* (Kingston and Montreal 1986)

17 J.M. Bumsted, 'Sir James Montgomery and P.E.I., 1767–1803,' *Acadiensis* 7:2 (Spring 1978), 76–102

18 J.M. Bumsted, 'Highland Emigration to the Island of St. John and the Scottish Catholic Church, 1769–1774,' *Dalhousie Review* 54 (1978), 511–27

19 F.L. Pigot, 'Thomas Desbrisay,' *DCB*, V:249–50

20 H.T. Holman, 'Robert Clark,' *DCB*, IV:152–3; D.C. Harvey, ed., 'Voyage of Thos. Curtis,' in *Journeys to the Island of St. John or Prince Edward Island, 1775–1832* (Toronto 1955), 9–69

21 Beverly Waugh Bond, *The Quit-Rent System in the American Colonies* (New Haven 1919)

22 L.K. Ingersoll, 'William Owen,' *DCB*, IV:596–7

23 Lois Kernaghan, 'A Man and his Mistress: J.F.W DesBarres and Mary Cannon,' *Acadiensis* 11:1 (Autumn 1981), 23–42

24 Donald MacKay, *Scotland Farewell: The People of the* Hector (Toronto 1980)

25 Brebner, *The Neutral Yankees of Nova Scotia*, 102

26 Quoted in ibid., 102n.

27 1767 Nova Scotia Census in 'Census of Canada: 1665 to 1871,' in *Census of Canada 1870–71*, IV (Ottawa 1876)

28 Gordon T. Stewart and George A. Rawlyk, *A People Highly Favoured of God: The Nova Scotia Yankees and the American Revolution* (Toronto 1972), 3–27

29 Quoted in Brebner, *The Neutral Yankees of Nova Scotia*, 309–10

30 Innis, *Diary of Simeon Perkins*, 98

31 Quoted in Brebner, *The Neutral Yankees of Nova Scotia*, 280

32 Innis, *Diary of Simeon Perkins*, 129

33 Ibid., 134

34 Stan Rogers, 'Barrett's Privateers,' on *Between the Breaks ... Live!* (1979)

35 Brebner, *The Neutral Yankees of Nova Scotia*, 284

36 J.M. Bumsted, *Understanding the Loyalists* (Sackville 1986), 47–8

37 Ibid., 38

38 J.M. Bumsted, 'Helen MacDonald of Glenaladale,' *DCB*, V:513–14

39 John MacDonald to J.F.W Desbarres, 8 Nov. 1795, DesBarres papers, National Archives of Canada (NAC)

40 Margaret Ells, 'Clearing the Decks for the Loyalists,' *CHA Report* (1933), 43–58

41 Bumsted, *Land, Settlement and Politics*, 83–97

42 Head, *Eighteenth Century Newfoundland*, 196–202

43 Bumsted, 'The Patterson Regime and the Impact of the American Revolution on the Island of St. John, 1775–1786,' *Acadiensis* 13:1 (Autumn 1983), 47–67

44 Quoted in Brebner, *The Neutral Yankees of Nova Scotia*, 295n

45 A useful bibliography may be found in G.A. Rawlyk, ed., *Henry Alline: Selected Writings* (New York 1987), 336–8.

46 J.M. Bumsted, ed., *The Hymns of Henry Alline* (Sackville 1987)

47 G.S. French, 'William Black,' *DCB*, VI:62–8; E.A. Betts, *Bishop Black and His Preachers* (Sackville 1976); Goldwin French, *Parsons and Politics: The Role of the Wesleyan Methodists in Upper Canada and the Maritimes from 1780 to 1855* (Toronto 1962)

48 J.M. Bumsted, 'Benjamin Chappell,' *DCB*, VI:130–2; Patrick O'Flaherty, 'Laurence Coughlan,' *DCB*, IV:175–7; Jacob Parsons, 'The Origin and Growth of Newfoundland Methodism, 1765–1855' (MA thesis, Memorial University of Newfoundland 1964)

49 Quoted in Upton, *Micmacs*, 69

50 Ibid., 78

51 Paul H. Smith, 'The American Loyalists: Notes on their Organization and

Numerical Strength,' *William and Mary Quarterly,* 3rd ser., 25 (1968), 259–77

52 Mary Beth Norton, 'Eighteenth-Century American Women in Peace and War: The Case of the Loyalists,' *William and Mary Quarterly,* 3rd ser., 33 (1976), 386–409

53 See Bumsted, *Understanding the Loyalists,* for bibliography and historiography.

54 Esther Clark Wright, *The Loyalists of New Brunswick* (Fredericton 1955)

55 D.G. Bell, *Early Loyalist Saint John: The Origin of New Brunswick Politics 1783–1786* (Fredericton 1983), 35–61; Marion Robertson, *King's Bounty: A History of Early Shelburne, Nova Scotia* (Halifax 1983), 51–82

56 Neil MacKinnon, *This Unfriendly Soil: The Loyalist Experience in Nova Scotia 1783–1791* (Kingston and Montreal 1986); Bumsted, *Land, Settlement and Politics,* 98–138; Robert J. Morgan, 'The Loyalists of Cape Breton,' *Dalhousie Review* 55 (1975), 5–17

57 Wallace Brown, *The King's Friends: The Composition and Motives of the American Loyalist Claimants* (Providence 1965)

58 Norton, 'Eighteenth-Century American Women,' 388, 393

59 James St G. Walker, *The Black Loyalists: The Search for a Promised Land in Nova Scotia and Sierra Leone, 1783–1879* (New York 1976); Ellen G. Wilson, *The Loyal Blacks* (New York 1976); see also Walker's 'Blacks as American Loyalists: The Slave War for Independence,' *Historical Reflections* 2 (1975), 51–67. On Nova Scotia Blacks before the arrival of the Loyalists, see Gary Hartlen, 'Bound for Nova Scotia: Slaves in the Planter Migration, 1759–1800,' in Margaret Conrad, ed., *Making Adjustments: Change and Continuity in Planter Nova Scotia, 1759–1800* (Fredericton 1991), 123–8; Bridglal Pachai, *Beneath the Clouds ... of the Promised Land: The Survival of Nova Scotia's Blacks, Volume I, 1600–1800* (Halifax 1987), 41.

60 Robin Winks, *The Blacks in Canada: A History* (Montreal 1971)

61 Graeme Wynn, 'A Region of Scattered Settlements and Bounded Possibilities: Northeastern America 1775–1800,' *Canadian Geographer* 31 (1987), 319–38; J.M. Bumsted, 'The Cultural Landscape of Early Canada,' in Bernard Bailyn and Philip D. Morgan, eds, *Strangers within the Realm: Cultural Margins of the First British Empire* (Chapel Hill 1991), 363–92

62 Howard Temperley, 'Frontierism, Capital, and the American Loyalists in Canada,' *Journal of American Studies* 13 (1979), 5–27

CHAPTER 9 1783–1800: Loyalist Arrival, Acadian Return, Imperial Reform

1 Ann Gorman Condon, *The Envy of the American States: The Loyalist Dream for New Brunswick* (Fredericton 1984), 43–71; R.M. Calhoon, *The Loyalists in Revolutionary America, 1760–1781* (New York 1973); Wallace Brown, *The Good Americans: The Loyalists in the American Revolution* (New York 1969)

2 Neil MacKinnon, 'The Enlightenment and Toryism: A Loyalist's Plan for

Education in British North America,' *Dalhousie Review* 55 (1975), 307–14, and MacKinnon, *This Unfriendly Soil: The Loyalist Experience in Nova Scotia 1783–1791* (Kingston and Montreal 1986)

3 William H. Nelson, *The American Tory* (Toronto 1961); MacKinnon, *This Unfriendly Soil*, 53–66; Esther Clark Wright, *The Loyalists of New Brunswick* (Fredericton 1955), 151–67; R. Cole Harris, ed., and Geoffrey J. Matthews, cartographer/designer, *Historical Atlas of Canada I: From the Beginning to 1800* (Toronto 1987), pl. 32

4 John Bartlet Brebner, *The Neutral Yankees of Nova Scotia: A Marginal Colony during the Revolutionary Years* (New York 1937); Gordon Stewart and George A. Rawlyk, *A People Highly Favoured of God: The Nova Scotia Yankees and the American Revolution* (Toronto 1972)

5 W.S. MacNutt, *The Atlantic Provinces: The Emergence of Colonial Society, 1712–1857* (Toronto 1965), 86–102, and MacNutt, *New Brunswick: A History, 1784–1867* (London 1963), 44–7; Vincent T. Harlow, *The Founding of the Second British Empire*, 2 vols, I (London 1954), 483, and II (London 1964), 727; Gerald S. Graham, *Sea Power and British North America, 1783–1820: A Study on British Colonial Policy* (Cambridge, Mass., and London 1941), 19–55

6 C. Grant Head, *Eighteenth Century Newfoundland: A Geographer's Perspective* (Toronto 1976), 198–212; Peter Neary and Patrick O'Flaherty, *Part of the Main: An Illustrated History of Newfoundland and Labrador* (St John's 1983), 38–51

7 MacNutt, *Atlantic Provinces*, 106, 110; Patrick O'Flaherty, 'The Seeds of Reform: Newfoundland, 1800–1818,' *Journal of Canadian Studies* 23 (1988), 42; Head, *Eighteenth Century Newfoundland*, 231, 244–5

8 Robert Morgan, 'The Loyalists of Cape Breton,' *Dalhousie Review* 55 (1975), 5–22, and 'Ranna Cossit,' in George W. Brown et al., eds, *Dictionary of Canadian Biography*, 12 vols to date (Toronto 1966–; hereafter *DCB*), V:204–5; Brian Tennyson, ed., *Impressions of Cape Breton* (Sydney 1980), 60

9 J.M. Bumsted, *Land, Settlement, and Politics on Eighteenth Century Prince Edward Island* (Kingston and Montreal 1986), 98–174

10 Condon, *Envy of the American States*, 89–151. The Petition of 55 is reprinted in Wright, *Loyalists of New Brunswick*, 251–2.

11 D.G. Bell, *Early Loyalist Saint John: The Origin of New Brunswick Politics, 1783–1786* (Fredericton 1983), 62–117

12 Condon, *Envy of the American States*, 141, 149–51

13 MacKinnon, *This Unfriendly Soil*, 16–53

14 Ibid., 118–36; J. Murray Beck, *The Politics of Nova Scotia*, 2 vols (Tantallon 1985), I:43–67; Margaret Ells, 'Governor Wentworth's Patronage,' Nova Scotia Historical Society, *Collections* 25 (1942), 49–73

15 MacKinnon, *This Unfriendly Soil*, 137–79; Charles Wetherell and Robert W. Roetger, 'Notes and Comments: Another Look at the Loyalists of Shelburne,' *Canadian Historical Review* 70 (1989), 76–91

16 Howard K. Temperley, 'Frontierism, Capital, and the American Loyalists in Canada,' *Journal of American Studies* 13 (1979), 5–27

17 MacNutt, *Atlantic Provinces*, 114–16

18 Judith Fingard, *The Anglican Design in Loyalist Nova Scotia, 1783–1816* (London 1972); Brian Cuthbertson, *The First Bishop: A Biography of Charles Inglis* (Halifax 1987)

19 Neil MacKinnon, 'The Enlightenment and Toryism,' 307–14, and *This Unfriendly Soil*, 77–9; Katherine MacNaughton, *The Development of the Theory and Practice of Education in New Brunswick, 1784–1900* (Fredericton 1947); Condon, *Envy of the American States*, 184–6, 193–6

20 Ann Gorman Condon, 'The Celestial World of Jonathan Odell: Symbolic Unities within a Disparate Artifact Collection,' in Gerald Pocius, ed., *Living in a Material World: Canadian and American Approaches to Material Culture* (St John's 1991), 92–126; George A. Rawlyk, *Ravished by the Spirit: Religious Revivals, Baptists, and Henry Alline* (Kingston and Montreal 1984); Barry Moody, *Repent and Believe: The Baptist Experience in Maritime Canada* (Hantsport 1980); MacNutt, *Atlantic Provinces*, 105–7, 118–23

21 MacNaughton, *Education in New Brunswick*, 25–46; Condon, *Envy of the American States*, 193–200; MacNutt, *Atlantic Provinces*, 105, 122; Lois K. Kernaghan, 'Deborah Cottnam How,' *DCB*, V:429–30

22 Gwendolyn Davies, 'A Literary Study of Selected Periodicals from Maritime Canada, 1789–1872' (PHD diss., York University 1979), 15–41

23 Patrick Campbell, *Travels in the Interior Inhabited Parts of North America*, ed. Hugh M. Langton and William F. Ganong (Toronto 1937), passim

24 Debra McNabb, 'The Role of Land in Settling Horton Township, Nova Scotia, 1766–1830,' in Margaret Conrad, ed., *They Planted Well: New England Planters in Maritime Canada* (Fredericton 1988); MacNutt, *New Brunswick*, 38–41

25 Condon, *Envy of the American States*, 82–3, 159–67; William G. Godfrey, 'James Glenie and the Politics of Sunbury County,' in Larry McCann, ed., *People and Place: Studies of Small Town Life in the Maritimes* (Fredericton 1987); W.O. Raymond, ed., *Winslow Papers, A.D. 1776–1826* (Saint John 1901), 399

26 Susan Buggey, 'Churchmen and Dissenters: Religious Toleration in Nova Scotia, 1758–1835' (MA thesis, Dalhousie University 1981), 1–7

27 Jean Daigle, ed., *The Acadians of the Maritimes: Thematic Studies* (Moncton 1982), 47–55; Béatrice Craig, 'Immigrants in a Frontier Community: Madawaska, 1785–1850,' *Histoire sociale / Social History* 58 (1986), 277–97

28 Ann-Marie Desdouits, 'La famille acadienne de sud-ouest de la Nouvelle-Ecosse,' *Revue de l'université Sainte-Anne* (1987), 90–106; N.E.S. Griffiths, 'The Acadians,' *DCB*, IV:xxx; Robert G. LeBlanc, 'The Acadian Migrations,' *Canadian Geographical Journal* 81:1 (1970), 10–19

29 James W. St G. Walker, *The Black Loyalists: The Search for a Promised Land in*

Nova Scotia and Sierra Leone, 1783–1870 (New York 1976), 40–93; William A. Spray, *The Blacks in New Brunswick* (Fredericton 1972)

30 Walker, *Black Loyalists*, 94 ff

31 Bridglal Pachai, *Beneath the Clouds ... of the Promised Land: The Survival of Nova Scotia's Blacks, Volume I, 1600–1800* (Halifax 1987), 55–60

32 L.F.S. Upton, *Micmacs and Colonists: Indian-White Relations in the Maritimes, 1713–1867* (Vancouver 1979), 61–141; Ellice B. Gonzalez, *Changing Economic Roles for Micmac Men and Women: An Ethnohistorical Analysis* (Ottawa 1981), 34–69

33 Upton, *Micmacs and Colonists*, 153–81; Judith Fingard, 'The New England Company and the New Brunswick Indians, 1786–1826: A Comment on the Colonial Perversion of British Benevolence,' *Acadiensis* 1:2 (Spring 1972), 28–43

34 Douglas Campbell and R.A. MacLean, *Beyond the Atlantic Roar: A Study of the Nova Scotia Scots* (Toronto 1974), 7–69, 193–228

35 J.M. Bumsted, *The People's Clearance: Highland Emigration to British North America, 1770–1815* (Edinburgh 1982); MacNutt, *Atlantic Provinces*, 117–18

36 Patrick Campbell, *Travels in the Interior*, 55

37 Beatrice Ross Buzek, '"By Fortune Wounded": Loyalist Women in Nova Scotia,' *Nova Scotia Historical Review* 7 (1978), 45–62; Raymond, ed., *Winslow Papers*, 225–7, 229–34, 300–1; Odell Family Papers and Robinson Family Papers, New Brunswick Museum; Botsford Family Papers, Beauséjour Collection, Mount Allison University Archives

38 Griffiths, 'The Acadians,' *DCB*, IV:xxix

39 Gonzalez, *Changing Economic Roles for Micmac Men and Women*, 34–69

40 Chipman Papers, Hazen Collection, New Brunswick Museum; Margaret Conrad, Toni Laidlaw, and Donna Smyth, eds, *No Place Like Home: Diaries and Letters of Nova Scotia Women, 1771–1938* (Halifax 1988), 45–59

41 Mary Bradley, *A Narrative of the Life and Christian Experience of Mrs. Mary Bradley ...* (Boston 1849); Jo-Ann Carr Fellows, 'Mary [Bradley] Coy,' *DCB*, VIII:176–7

42 Beamish Murdoch, *A History of Nova Scotia or Acadie*, 3 vols (Halifax 1865–7), III:99–210

43 David S. Macmillan, 'The "New Men" in Action: Scottish Mercantile and Shipping Operations in the North American Colonies, 1760–1825,' in David S. Macmillan, ed., *Canadian Business History: Selected Studies, 1497–1971* (Toronto 1972), 69–103

44 Charles Foss, *Cabinetmakers of the Eastern Seaboard* (Toronto 1977)

45 Head, *Eighteenth Century Newfoundland*, 225–48

46 Tennyson, ed., *Impressions of Cape Breton*; MacNutt, *Atlantic Provinces*, 113–14; Bumsted, *Land, Settlement, and Politics*, 175–200; W.S. MacNutt, 'Fanning's Regime on Prince Edward Island,' *Acadiensis* 1:1 (Autumn 1971), 37–53

47 Ann Gorman Condon, 'Les réactions des anglophones des maritimes face à

la révolution française,' *La société historique acadienne: les cahiers* 21 (1990), 131–46; Wallace Brown, 'William Cobbett in the Maritimes,' *Dalhousie Review* 56 (1976–7), 448–62

48 George F.G. Stanley, 'The Acadian Renaissance,' in David Jay Bercuson and Phillip A. Buckner, eds, *Eastern and Western Perspectives: Papers from the Joint Atlantic Canada / Western Canadian Studies Conference* (Toronto 1981); Gerald C. Boudreau, 'L'influence religieuse du Père Sigogne sur les Acadiens du sud-ouest de la Nouvelle-Ecosse,' *Revue de l'Université Sainte-Anne* (1987), 32–53

CHAPTER 10 1800–1810: Turning the Century

1 B.C. Cuthbertson, *The Loyalist Governor: A Biography of Sir John Wentworth* (Halifax 1983), 108–11; *Royal Gazette and Nova Scotia Advertiser*, 16 Sept. 1800

2 Howard Temperley, ed., *Gubbins' New Brunswick Journals, 1811 and 1813*, Entry for 20 July 1811 (Fredericton 1980), 28

3 J.D. Wood, 'Grand Design on the Fringes of Empire: New Towns for British North America,' *Canadian Geographer* 26 (1982), 243–55; Mrs Hunter to E. Bell, 7 Aug. 1804, Provincial Archives of New Brunswick (PANB), tps, MYO/ H/76; Stephen J. Hornsby, *Nineteenth Century Cape Breton: A Historical Geography* (Montreal and Kingston 1992), 25–8; J. Stewart, *An Account of Prince Edward Island* (London 1806), 9–10

4 See pls 25 to 28 of R. Cole Harris, ed., and Geoffrey J. Matthews, cartographer/designer, *Historical Atlas of Canada I: From the Beginning to 1800* (Toronto 1987); G. Handcock, 'The Poole Mercantile Community and the Growth of Trinity, 1700–1839,' *Newfoundland Quarterly* 15:3 (1984), 19–30; Graeme Wynn, 'A Region of Scattered Settlements and Bounded Possibilities: Northeastern America 1775–1800,' *Canadian Geographer* 31 (1987), 319–38

5 D.A. Muise, 'A Descriptive and Statistical Account of Nova Scotia and Its Dependencies,' *Acadiensis* 2:1 (Autumn 1972), 91

6 Graeme Wynn, 'Late-Eighteenth-Century Agriculture on the Bay of Fundy Marshlands,' *Acadiensis* 8:2 (Spring 1979), 80–9; Robert MacKinnon, 'Farming the Rock: The Evolution of Agriculture around St. John's, Newfoundland, to 1945,' *Acadiensis* 20:2 (Spring 1991), 32–61

7 Judith Fingard, *The Anglican Design in Loyalist Nova Scotia 1783–1816* (London 1972), 67, and Fingard, 'Robert Stanser,' in George W. Brown et al., eds, *Dictionary of Canadian Biography*, 12 vols to date (Toronto 1966–; hereafter *DCB*), VI:731–2

8 Cited by S.F. Wise, 'The 1790s,' in J.M.S. Careless, ed., *Colonists and Canadiens, 1760–1867* (Toronto 1971), 83

9 N.L. Nicholson, *The Boundaries of the Canadian Confederation* (Toronto 1979),

27–30; R.D. Tallman and J.I. Tallman, 'The Diplomatic Search for the St. Croix River, 1796–1798,' *Acadiensis* 1:2 (Spring 1972), 59–71

10 D.A. Sutherland, 'William Sabatier,' *DCB*, VI:676–7; Mary Sparling, *Great Expectations: The European Vision in Nova Scotia, 1749–1848* (Halifax 1980), 28–9; John Wentworth to Bishop Inglis, 25 Mar. 1801, Public Archives of Nova Scotia (PANS), RG1, 53

11 The late-eighteenth-century migrations are well treated in Bernard Bailyn, *Voyagers to the West: A Passage in the Peopling of America on the Eve of the Revolution* (New York 1986) and J.M. Bumsted, *The People's Clearance: Highland Emigration to British North America, 1770–1815* (Edinburgh 1982).

12 W. Gordon Handcock, *'Soe longe as there comes noe women': Origins of English Settlement in Newfoundland* (St John's 1990); John J. Mannion, *Irish Settlements in Eastern Canada: A Study of Cultural Transfer and Adaptation* (Toronto 1974), 15–21

13 M. Gray, *The Highland Economy, 1750–1850* (Edinburgh 1957) and Gray, 'Scottish Emigration. The Social Impact of Agrarian Change in the Rural Lowlands, 1775–1875,' *Perspectives in American History* 7 (1973), 96–174; J. Hunter, *The Making of the Crofting Community* (Edinburgh 1976); S.J. Hornsby, 'Scottish Emigration and Settlement in Early Nineteenth Century Cape Breton,' in Graeme Wynn, ed., *People, Places, Patterns, Processes* (Toronto 1990), 110–38

14 D.S. Macmillan, 'The "New Men" in Action: Scottish Mercantile and Shipping Operations in the North American Colonies, 1760–1825,' in David S. Macmillan, ed., *Canadian Business History: Selected Studies, 1497–1971* (Toronto 1972), 44–103; J.M. Bumsted, 'Scottish Emigration to the Maritimes: A New Look at an Old Theme,' *Acadiensis* 10:2 (1981), 65–85. The consequences were enduring; see A.H. Clark, 'Old World Origins and Religious Adherence in Nova Scotia,' *Geographical Review* 50 (1960), 317–44 .

15 Reprinted in J.M. Bumsted, ed., *The Collected Writings of Lord Selkirk, 1799–1809* (Winnipeg 1984). The quotations that follow are taken from 168–86. See also J.M. Bumsted, 'Settlement by Chance: Lord Selkirk and Prince Edward Island,' *Canadian Historical Review* 59 (1978), 170–88.

16 F.B. MacMillan, 'Trade of New Brunswick with Great Britain, the United States and the Caribbean, 1784–1828' (MA thesis, University of New Brunswick 1954); H.H. Robertson, 'The Commercial Relationship between Nova Scotia and the British West Indies, 1788–1828: The Twilight of Mercantilism in the British Empire' (MA thesis, Dalhousie University 1975); S. Basdeo and H. Robertson, 'The Nova Scotia–British West Indies Commercial Experiment in the Aftermath of the American Revolution, 1783–1802,' *Dalhousie Review* 61 (1981–2), 58–69

17 Ann Gorman Condon, 'George Leonard,' *DCB*, VI:394–6

18 G.S. Graham, *Sea Power and British North America, 1783–1820: A Study in British Colonial Policy* (Cambridge, Mass., and London 1941), 153–76; G.S.

Graham, 'The Gypsum Trade of the Maritime Provinces,' *Agricultural History* 12:3 (1938), 209–23

19 Ward Chipman to Edward Winslow, 14 Dec. 1805, W.O. Raymond, ed., *Winslow Papers, A.D. 1776–1826* (Saint John 1901), 541

20 Cited by Graham, *Sea Power*, 174

21 D.A. Sutherland, 'Halifax Merchants and the Pursuit of Development, 1783–1850,' *Canadian Historical Review* 59 (1978), 1–17, and 'Sabatier,' 676–7

22 John Baker Holroyd, Lord Sheffield, *Strictures on the Necessity of Inviolably Maintaining the Navigation and Colonial System of Great Britain* (London 1804); Graham, *Sea Power*, 187

23 Cited by Graham, *Sea Power*, 195

24 Cited in J. Conlin, *The American Past: A Survey of American History* (New York 1984), 189

25 Graeme Wynn, *Timber Colony: A Historical Geography of Early Nineteenth Century New Brunswick* (Toronto 1981); A.R.M. Lower, *Great Britain's Woodyard: British America and the Timber Trade, 1763–1867* (Montreal 1973)

26 Edward Winslow to Edward Winslow, Jr, 13 June 1811, in Raymond, ed., *Winslow Papers*, 670

27 *Historical Atlas of Canada I*, pls 25, 27, 28 and Graham, *Sea Power*, 247–74

28 C. Grant Head, *Eighteenth Century Newfoundland: A Geographer's Perspective* (Toronto 1976), 221; Graham, *Sea Power*, 249, 266

29 L.F.S. Upton, *Micmacs and Colonists: Indian-White Relations in the Maritimes, 1713–1867* (Vancouver 1979), 84; A.H. Clark, 'Titus Smith, Junior, and the Geography of Nova Scotia in 1801 and 1802,' *Annals of the Association of American Geographers* 44 (1954), 313; T. Smith, *Report of the Eastern and Northern Parts of the Province in Years 1801 and 1802*, PANS, RG1, vol. 380, 131–2

30 *Report of the Committee on the Condition of the Indians*, 15 Apr. 1800, and *Report of the Joint Committee* [1800] both in PANS, RG1, vol. 430, docs 33 1/2, and 72 1/2; *Journal of the Legislative Assembly of Nova Scotia*, 1800, 75–6, 102–3

31 Upton, *Micmacs and Colonists*, 98–100, 113–15; W.D. Hamilton, 'Indian Lands in New Brunswick. The Case of the Little Southwest Reserve,' *Acadiensis* 13:2 (1984), 3–28

32 Judith Fingard, 'The New England Company and the New Brunswick Indians,' *Acadiensis* 1:2 (Spring 1972), 29–42

33 Cited in Upton, *Micmacs and Colonists*, 165. See also B. Pothier, 'Jean-Mandé Sigogne,' *DCB*, VII:800–6; L.F.S. Upton, 'John Noel,' *DCB*, VII:443, and 'John Julien,' *DCB*, V:464–5; V.O. Erickson, 'Noel Bernard,' *DCB*, V:73–4, and 'Pierre Tomah,' *DCB*, VI:774–5.

34 'Notes on New Brunswick History by Edward Winslow – 1804,' and 'Notes by Edward Winslow Respecting the Indians and Acadians,' Raymond, ed., *Winslow Papers*, 508–13

35 Temperley, *Gubbins' New Brunswick Journals*, entries for 10 and 18 July 1813, 66, 78

36 Bishop Denaut's 1803 report on the Acadians is summarized in E-F. Rameau de Saint-Père, *Une colonie féodale en Amérique: l'Acadie 1604–1881*, 2 vols (Paris 1889), II:255–66. Fertility rates of Acadian women were high: compare Denaut's figures with those in A. Chiasson, *Cheticamp: History and Acadian Traditions* (St John's 1986), 30; W.F. Ganong, 'A Monograph of the Origins of Settlements in the Province of New Brunswick,' Royal Society of Canada, *Transactions* (1904), sect. 2, 3–186.

37 Temperley, *Gubbins' New Brunswick Journals*, 78; Joyer cited by Léon Thériault, 'The Acadianization of the Catholic Church in Acadia (1763–1953),' in Jean Daigle, ed., *The Acadians of the Maritimes: Thematic Studies* (Moncton 1982), 292; Clark, 'Titus Smith, Junior,' 306

38 J.-O. Plessis, 'Journal de deux voyages apostolique dans le Golfe Saint-Laurent et les provinces d'en bas, en 1811 et 1812,' *Le foyer canadien* III (1865), 164

39 Cited in Chiasson, *Cheticamp*, 37

40 John Garner, *The Franchise and Politics in British North America, 1755–1867* (Toronto 1969)

41 Léon Thériault, 'Acadia, 1763–1978, An Historical Synthesis', in Daigle ed., *Acadians of the Maritimes*, 54; N.-E. Dionne, *Les ecclésiastiques et les royalistes français refugiés au Canada à l'époque de la Révolution, 1791–1802* (Quebec 1905); Léon Thériault, 'Les missionnaires et leurs paroissiens dans le Nord-est du Nouveau-Brunswick, 1766–1830,' *Revue de l'Université de Moncton* 9 (1976), 31–51; Pothier, 'Sigogne'

42 Wentworth's friends were described as the 'court' party in 1799; see Judith Tulloch, 'James Fulton,' *DCB*, VI:268. The terms are used in discussions of British North America by G.T. Stewart, *The Origins of Canadian Politics: A Comparative Approach* (Vancouver 1986), and Phillip A. Buckner, *The Transition to Responsible Government: British Policy in British North America 1815–1850* (Westport 1985).

43 C.B. Fergusson, ed., *The Diary of Simeon Perkins* (Toronto 1961), entry for 19 Jan. 1790, 7

44 Cited in S. Whiteside, 'Colonial Adolescence: A Study of the Maritime Colonies of British North America, 1790–1814' (MA thesis, University of British Columbia 1965), 142; see also Carole Anne Janzen, 'Sir Alexander Croke,' *DCB*, VII:216–20, and 'Tentacles of Power: Alexander Croke in Nova Scotia, 1801–1815' (MA thesis, University of New Brunswick 1978).

45 Judith Tulloch, 'William Cottnam Tonge,' *DCB*, VI:778–83; see also Tulloch, 'James Fulton,' *DCB*, VI:268, and Susan Buggey, 'Edward Mortimer,' *DCB*, V:611–12.

46 See Thomas B. Vincent, '"Creon": A Satire on New Brunswick Politics in 1802,' *Acadiensis* 3:2 (Spring 1974), 80–98.

47 F.W.P. Bolger, 'Land and Politics, 1787–1824,' in Bolger, ed., *Canada's Smallest Province: A History of P.E.I.* ([Charlottetown] 1973), 66–84; J.M. Bumsted, 'The Loyal Electors of Prince Edward Island,' *Island Magazine* 8 (1980), 8–14; and

D.C. Harvey, 'The Loyal Electors,' Royal Society of Canada, *Transactions* (1930), sect. 2, 101–10

48 Ann Gorman Condon, 'Edward Winslow,' *DCB*, V:868; Bolger, *Canada's Smallest Province*, 83; Whiteside, 'Colonial Adolescence,' 138

49 Judith Fingard, 'Charles Inglis and his "Primitive Bishoprick" in Nova Scotia,' *Canadian Historical Review* 49 (1968), 247–66, quote on 251, and 'Charles Inglis,' *DCB*, V:444–7; see also Judith Tulloch, 'Conservative Opinion in Nova Scotia during an Age of Revolution, 1789–1815' (MA thesis, Dalhousie University 1971).

50 Fingard, *Anglican Design*, 114–33, and G.A. Rawlyk, *Ravished by the Spirit: Religious Revivals, Baptists, and Henry Alline* (Kingston and Montreal 1984), 73–104

51 D.G. Bell, ed., *The Newlight Baptist Journals of James Manning and James Innis* (Saint John 1984), 37

52 Rawlyk, *Ravished by the Spirit*, 89–90, 126; and Fingard, *Anglican Design*, 124

53 A point illustrated by Rawlyk, *Ravished by the Spirit*, 124–8, in which he traces the spiritual journey of Nancy (Lawrence) DeWolf

54 Rawlyk, *Ravished by the Spirit*, 118; Bell, *Newlight Baptist Journals*, 34

55 Rawlyk, *Ravished by the Spirit*, 123, 103–5, 128–32

56 D.C. Goodwin, 'From Disunity to Integration: Evangelical Religion and Society in Yarmouth, Nova Scotia, 1761–1830,' in Margaret Conrad, ed., *They Planted Well: New England Planters in Maritime Canada* (Fredericton 1988), 190-200

CHAPTER 11 1810–1820: War and Peace

1 A.B. Warburton, *A History of Prince Edward Island* (Saint John 1923), 233–4

2 The ambiguous career of William Cooper is analysed by Harry Baglole, 'William Cooper,' in George W. Brown et al., eds, *Dictionary of Canadian Biography,* 12 vols to date (Toronto 1966–; hereafter *DCB*), IX:155–8. For background on the emergence of the escheat movement, see Ian Ross Robertson, 'Highlanders, Irishmen and the Land Question in Nineteenth Century Prince Edward Island,' in L.M. Cullen and T.C. Smout, eds, *Comparative Aspects of Scottish and Irish Economic and Social History, 1600–1900* (Edinburgh 1977), 227–40; and Kent R. (Rusty) Bittermann, 'Escheat: Rural Protest on Prince Edward Island, 1832–1842' (PHD diss., University of New Brunswick 1991).

3 The complex Anglo-American manoeuvring that led to the outbreak of war is open to various interpretations. This account is based on the work of J.C.A. Stagg, *Mr. Madison's War: Politics, Diplomacy and Warfare in the Early American Republic, 1783–1830* (Princeton 1983), Reginald Horsman, *The Causes of the War of 1812* (Philadelphia 1962), and Reginald C. Stuart, *United States Expansionism and British North America* (Chapel Hill 1988).

4 As quoted by Judith Tulloch, 'Conservative Opinion in Nova Scotia during the Age of Revolution' (MA thesis, Dalhousie University 1971) 129

5 Cited in Brian D. Tennyson, 'An Apostolic Visit to Cape Breton in 1812,' *Nova Scotia Historical Review* 5 (1985), 63

6 American war aims are surveyed by Stagg, *Mr. Madison's War*, 14–47. For initial colonial response to the threat of American invasion, see W.S. MacNutt, *New Brunswick: A History* (Toronto 1963), 154–8; Walter R. Copp, 'Military Activities in Nova Scotia during the War of 1812,' *Nova Scotia Historical Society Collections* 24 (1938), 57–74.

7 The extent to which the United States exercised economic domination over the adjacent colonies is noted by W.R. Copp, 'Nova Scotian Trade during the War of 1812,' *Canadian Historical Review* 18 (1937), 141–55; and Gerald S. Graham, *Sea Power and British North America, 1783–1820: A Study in British Colonial Policy* (Cambridge, Mass., and London 1941).

8 Stagg, *Mr. Madison's War*, 230–59. See also James M. Banner, Jr, *To the Hartford Convention: The Federalists and the Origins of Party Politics in Massachusetts, 1789–1815* (New York 1970); Paul A. Varg, *New England and Foreign Relations, 1789–1850* (Hanover and London 1983).

9 Peter Burroughs, 'Sir John Coape Sherbrooke,' *DCB*, VI:712–16; and D.M. Young, 'George Stracey Smyth,' *DCB*, IV:723–7

10 John Leefe, 'A Bluenose Privateer of 1812,' *Nova Scotia Historical Quarterly* 3 (1973), 1–20; Diane M. Barker and D.A. Sutherland, 'Enos Collins,' *DCB*, X:188–90

11 The traditional interpretation of Maritime privateering dominates the work of C.H.J. Snider, *Under the Red Jack* (Toronto 1928). The revisionist point of view is best expressed by Faye Kert, 'The Fortunes of War: Privateering in Atlantic Canada in the War of 1812' (MA thesis, Carleton University 1986).

12 An old but still informative analysis is A.T. Mahan, *Sea Power in its Relations to the War of 1812*, 2 vols (London 1905). For the celebrated events of June 1813, see H.F. Pullen, *The Shannon and the Chesapeake* (Toronto and Montreal 1970).

13 Keith Matthews, *Lectures on the History of Newfoundland* (St John's 1973), 213–27; Shannon Ryan, 'Fishery to Colony: A Newfoundland Watershed, 1793–1815,' *Acadiensis* 12:2 (Spring 1983), 34–52; D.W. Prowse, *A History of Newfoundland* (London 1895), 387–8

14 Graeme Wynn, *Timber Colony: A Historical Geography of Early Nineteenth Century New Brunswick* (Toronto 1981), 45

15 Marilyn G. Smith, *King's Yard: An Illustrated History of the Halifax Dockyard* (Halifax 1985), 9; John Mannion, 'Patrick Morris and Newfoundland Irish Immigration,' in C.J. Byrne and Margaret Harry, eds, *Talamh an Eisc: Canadian and Irish essays* (Halifax 1986), 193

16 An overview of life in the wartime Nova Scotia capital can be found in D.A. Sutherland, 'The Merchants of Halifax, 1815–1850: A Commercial Class in

Pursuit of Metropolitan Status' (PHD diss., University of Toronto 1975), 45–93. See also James S. Martell, 'Halifax during and after the War of 1812,' *Dalhousie Review* 23 (1943–44), 239–304, and Thomas H. Raddall, *Halifax, Warden of the North* (rev. ed.; Toronto 1971), 149–65.

17 Brian Cuthbertson, *The Old Attorney General: A Biography of Richard John Uniacke, 1753–1830* (Halifax 1980), 64

18 J.S. Martell, *A Documentary Study of Provincial Finance and Currency* (Halifax 1941); James Hannay, *History of New Brunswick* (Saint John 1909), 333–5

19 Thomas McCulloch, *The Mephibosheth Stepsure Letters*, ed. and intro. Gwendolyn Davies (Ottawa 1990); Marjory Whitelaw, ed., *The Dalhousie Journals*, 3 vols (Toronto 1978–82), I:176

20 Beamish Murdoch, *A History of Nova Scotia, or Acadie*, 3 vols (Halifax 1865–7), III:364

21 Kert, 'The Fortunes of War,' 23–6. For a description of a riot provoked in Halifax by press-gang activity, see Richard Tremain to Sir John Sherbrooke, 30 July 1813, Public Archives of Nova Scotia (PANS), RG1, vol. 226, no. 90. Local opposition to press gangs is also expressed in *Acadian Recorder*, 3 Dec. 1814.

22 Daniel C. Harvey, 'The Halifax-Castine expedition,' *Dalhousie Review* 18 (1938–39), 207–13; H.A. Davis, *An International Community on the St. Croix* (Orono 1950), 107–12

23 *Acadian Recorder*, 14 May 1814, as cited in D.A. Sutherland, 'Halifax Merchants and the Pursuit of Development, 1783–1850,' *Canadian Historical Review* 59 (1978), 4

24 John Young to William Young, 19 Feb. 1815, as cited in Daniel C. Harvey, 'Pre-Agricola John Young, or a compact Family in Search of Fortune,' *Nova Scotia Historical Society Collections* 32 (1959), 137

25 Sutherland, 'The Merchants of Halifax,' 53–5. See also Daniel C. Harvey, 'A Blueprint for Nova Scotia in 1818,' *Canadian Historical Review* 26 (1943), 397–409, and MacNutt, *New Brunswick*, 160–2.

26 Sutherland, 'The Merchants of Halifax,' 56–68. Contemporary attitudes can be found in John Homer, *A Brief Sketch of the Present State of the Province of Nova Scotia* (Halifax 1834), 6, and Walter C. Hartridge, 'Halifax to Savannah, Letters of Michael Wallace,' *Georgia Historical Quarterly* 45 (1961), 71–91, 171–86.

27 D.C. Harvey, ed., *Journeys to the Island of St. John or Prince Edward Island, 1775–1832* (Toronto 1955), 101. Newfoundland's interior posed an even greater challenge to would-be developers; see William E. Cormac, 'Account of a Journey across Newfoundland ...,' *Edinburgh Philosophical Journal* 10 (1823–24), as referred to by G.M. Story, 'William E. Cormac,' *DCB*, IX:158–62.

28 Whitelaw, ed., *Dalhousie Journals*, I:76

29 Shirley B. Elliott, *A history of Province House* (Halifax 1968), [5]

30 Whitelaw, ed., *Dalhousie Journals*, I:75. For analysis of theatre life in the

region, see: Yashdip S. Bains, 'The New Grand Theatre, Halifax, 1789–1814,' *Nova Scotia Historical Quarterly* 10:1 (Mar. 1980), 1–21; Bains, 'The Spectator's Eye: Impressions of Halifax Theatre in [the] Early Nineteenth Century'; Mary E. Smith, 'Theatre in Saint John: The First Thirty Years'; and Rebecca L. Smith, 'Charlottetown Amateur Theatre to 1824,' all in *Dalhousie Review* 59:1 (Spring 1979), 40–50; 5–27; 28–39.

31 Nova Scotia House of Assembly, Reports and Resolutions, 25 Mar. 1819, PANS, RG5, series R, vol. 3. Hangings remained a public spectacle into the 1840s; see Archibald MacMechan, *Old Provincial Tales* (Toronto 1924), 209–38. The last-minute reprieve of a woman sentenced to hang is reported in *Royal Gazette* [Halifax], 6 Feb. 1810.

32 For a detailed contemporary description of the Uniacke mansion, see Cyril Byrne, 'The Maritime Visits of Joseph-Octave Plessis, Bishop of Quebec,' *Nova Scotia Historical Society Collections* 39 (1977), 41. The fact that the site had been purchased from local Micmacs for £60 is reported by Elizabeth Hutton, 'The Micmac of Nova Scotia to 1834' (MA thesis, Dalhousie University 1961), 213. An account of the celebrated duel between R.J. Uniacke, Jr, and William Bowie can be found in Brian C. Cuthbertson, 'Richard John Uniacke,' *DCB*, VI:792.

33 Tennyson, 'An Apostolic Visit,' 67–8

34 Allan MacDonald, 'Angus Bernard MacEachern, 1759–1835: His Ministry in the Maritime Provinces,' in Terrence Murphy and Cyril J. Byrne, eds, *Religion and identity: The Experience of Irish and Scottish Catholics in Atlantic Canada* (St John's 1987), 53–67

35 Whitelaw, *Dalhousie Journals*, I:62–73. To put Dalhousie's views into perspective, see Peter Burroughs, 'George Ramsay,' *DCB*, VII:722–33.

36 Whitelaw, ed., *Dalhousie Journals*, I:47–9 and 86

37 This account comes from the memoirs of a French prisoner of war who escaped from Halifax to take refuge among the Acadians of western Nova Scotia; see J. Alphonse Deveau, ed., *Diary of a Frenchman* (Halifax 1990), and Gerald G. Ouellet, 'François-Lambert Bourneuf,' *DCB*, X:83.

38 Whitelaw, ed., *Dalhousie Journals*, I:7, 21–2; *Acadian Recorder*, 25 Jan. 1817, 27 Feb. 1818

39 *Acadian Recorder*, 1 Feb., 22 Apr., 7, 28 June, 9 Aug., 8, 29 Nov., 6 Dec. 1817, 25 Apr., 31 Oct. 1818, 27 Mar. 1819; Whitelaw, ed., *Dalhousie Journals*, I:89, 97

40 See Whitelaw, ed., *Dalhousie Journals*, I:156; *Free Press* [Halifax], 20 July 1819; Thomas C. Haliburton, *A General Description of Nova Scotia* (Halifax 1823); John G. Marshall, *A Patriotic Call to Prepare in a Season of Peace, for One of Political Danger ...* (Halifax 1819).

41 An overview of long-term trends in transatlantic trade is provided by Judith B. Williams, *British Commercial Policy and Trade Expansion, 1750–1850* (Oxford 1972).

42 Albert H. Imlah, *Economic Elements in the Pax Britannica: Studies in British*

Foreign Trade in the Nineteenth Century (New York 1969), and Douglass C. North and Robert P. Thomas, eds, *The Growth of the American Economy to 1860* (Columbia 1968)

43 *Acadian Recorder*, 14 Mar. 1818; Homer, *A Brief Sketch*, 5–6

44 McCulloch, *Stepsure Letters*, xxii; Prowse, *A History of Newfoundland* (London 1895), 403–6; Charles Pedley, *The History of Newfoundland* (London 1863), 299–318; Matthews, *Lectures*, 227–8

45 Gerald S. Graham, 'The Gypsum Trade of the Maritime Provinces,' *Agricultural History* 12:3 (1938), 209–23; Frederic F. Thompson, *The French Shore Problem in Newfoundland* (Toronto 1961), 21–5; Shannon Ryan, *Newfoundland-Spanish Saltfish Trade: 1814–1914* (St John's 1983), 5–23

46 Frank L. Benns, *The American Struggle for the British West Indies Carrying Trade, 1815–1830* (Bloomington 1923); Harold Robertson, 'The Commercial Relationship between Nova Scotia and the British West Indies, 1788–1822: The Twilight of Mercantilism in the British Empire' (MA thesis, Dalhousie University 1975)

47 Gerald S. Graham, 'The Origin of Free Ports in British North America,' *Canadian Historical Review* 22 (1941), 25–34

48 See Wynn, *Timber Colony*, and William A. Spray, 'The Irish in Miramichi,' in Peter M. Toner, ed., *New Ireland Remembered: Historical Essays on the Irish in New Brunswick* (Fredericton 1988), 55–62.

49 Brian W. Preston, 'The settlement of Scottish Immigrants in Nova Scotia, 1770–1830' (PHD diss., University of Glasgow 1986); Stephen J. Hornsby, *Nineteenth-Century Cape Breton: A Historical Geography* (Kingston and Montreal 1992); D. Campbell and R.A. MacLean, *Beyond the Atlantic Roar: A Study of the Nova Scotia Scots* (Toronto 1974); John J. Mannion, *Irish Settlements in Eastern Canada: A Study of Cultural Transfer and Adaptation* (Toronto 1974)

50 J.S. Martell, *Immigration to and Emigration from Nova Scotia, 1815–1838* (Halifax 1942); *Acadian Recorder*, 23 Dec. 1815, 14 Dec. 1816, 26 July 1817

51 D.A. Sutherland, 'Andrew Belcher,' *DCB*, VII:62–4; Keith Matthews, 'James MacBraire,' *DCB*, VI:417–20; D.A. Sutherland, 'William Sabatier,' *DCB*, VI:676–8

52 Gideon White to Cornelius White, 27 Nov. 1818, PANS, MG1, vol. 953, no. 1079. White's role as a community leader is outlined by Mary M. Harvey, 'Gideon White,' *DCB*, VI:813–14.

53 Phillip A. Buckner, *The Transition to Responsible Government: British Policy in British North America, 1815–1850* (Westport 1985)

54 Frederic F. Thompson, 'Francis Pickmore,' *DCB*, V:671–2

55 Patrick O'Flaherty, 'The Seeds of Reform: Newfoundland, 1800–1818,' *Journal of Canadian Studies* 23 (1988), 39–59; Patrick O'Flaherty, 'William Carson,' *DCB*, V:151–6

56 See G.M. Story, 'Demasduwit,' *DCB*, V:243–4; W. Gordon Handcock, 'John Peyton,' *DCB*, VI:580–1.

57 Various perspectives on this incident can be obtained from William Kirwan, 'David Buchan,' *DCB*, VII:114–15; John Hewson 'John Leigh,' *DCB*, VI:392–3; Patrick O'Flaherty, 'John Lundrigan,' *DCB*, VI:409–11.

58 Keith Matthews, 'The Class of '32: St. John's Reformers on the Eve of Representative Government,' *Acadiensis* 6:2 (Spring 1977), 80–94

59 Robert J. Morgan: 'Orphan Outpost: Cape Breton Colony, 1784–1820' (PHD diss., University of Ottawa 1972); Morgan, 'George R. Ainslie,' *DCB*, VII:9–11, 'Hugh Swayne,' *DCB*, VII:839–40, 'Archibald C. Dodd,' *DCB*, VI:212–14; and Morgan, 'Separatism in Cape Breton, 1820–1845,' in Kenneth Donovan, ed., *Cape Breton at 200: Historical Essays in Honour of the Island's Bicentennial 1785–1985* (Sydney 1985), 41–51

60 Phillip Buckner, 'Charles D. Smith,' *DCB*, VIII:823–8

61 F.W.P. Bolger, ed., *Canada's Smallest Province: A History of P.E.I.* (Charlottetown 1973), 75–90

62 As well as the work of Buckner and Bolger, cited above, see D.C. Harvey, 'The Loyal Electors,' Royal Society of Canada, Transactions, 3rd ser., 24 (1930), sect. 2, 101–10; Frank MacKinnon, *The Government of Prince Edward Island* (Toronto 1951).

63 Wynn, *Timber Colony*, 139–40; D.M. Young, 'George S. Smyth,' *DCB*, VI:724–7

64 MacNutt, *New Brunswick*, 181. See also MacNutt, 'The Politics of the Timber Trade in Colonial New Brunswick,' *Canadian Historical Review* 30 (1949), 47–65.

65 J. Murray Beck, 'Simon Bradstreet Robie,' *DCB*, VIII:754–7

66 R.A. MacLean, 'Edmund Burke,' *DCB*, V:123–5; Susan Buggey and Gwendolyn Davies, 'Thomas McCulloch,' *DCB*, VII:529–41; Patrick O'Flaherty, 'Sir Richard G. Keats,' *DCB*, VI:371–3

67 R.J. Morgan, 'Laurence Kavanagh,' *DCB*, VI:370–1

68 Judith Fingard, *The Anglican Design in Loyalist Nova Scotia, 1783–1816* (London 1972)

69 Susan Buggey, 'Churchmen and Dissenters: Religious toleration in Nova Scotia, 1758–1835' (MA thesis, Dalhousie University 1981), 120–203

70 Judith Fingard, 'Charles Inglis,' *DCB*, V:444–8; Fingard, 'Robert Stanser,' *DCB*, VI:731–2; Whitelaw, ed., *Dalhousie Journals*, I:162–3

71 Judith Fingard, 'Walter Bromley,' *DCB*, VII:107–9; Buggey and Davies, 'Thomas McCulloch,' *DCB*, VII:529–41

72 Daniel C. Harvey, 'Dalhousie University Established,' *Dalhousie Review* 18 (1938), 50–66; Harvey, 'The Early Struggles of Dalhousie,' *Dalhousie Review*, 17 (1937), 311–26

73 William Spray, *The Blacks in New Brunswick* (Fredericton 1972); C. Bruce Fergusson, *A Documentary Study of the Establishment of the Negroes in Nova Scotia* (Halifax 1948)

74 Fergusson, *Documentary Study*, 30

75 James Walker, 'The Establishment of a Free Black Community in Nova

Scotia,' in M.L. Kitson and R.I. Rotberg, eds, *The African Diaspora* (Cambridge, Mass. 1976), 205–36

76 Whitelaw, ed., *Dalhousie Journals*, I:99; Hutton, 'The Micmac Indians,' 213–17; L.F.S. Upton, *Micmacs and Colonists : Indian-White Relations in the Maritimes, 1713–1867* (Vancouver 1979), 87–101

77 Story, 'Demasduwit,' *DCB*, V:243–4

78 J.S. Martell, 'Military Settlements in Nova Scotia after the War of 1812,' *Nova Scotia Historical Society Collection*, 24 (1938), 75–106; Whitelaw, ed., *Dalhousie Journals*, I:91–2

79 Peter Thomas, *Strangers from a Secret Land : The Voyages of the Brig* Albion *and the Founding of the First Welsh Settlements in Canada* (Toronto 1986), 161–71

80 J. Murray Beck, *Politics of Nova Scotia*, 2 vols, I:1710–1896 (Tantallon 1985), 80–8; Sutherland, 'The Merchants of Halifax,' 57–83

81 Davies, ed., *Stepsure Letters*, 13–14, 42–5, 61, 81, 117–18, 123, 138, 142

82 *Acadian Recorder*, 4 July 1818

83 D.A. Sutherland, 'William Wilkie,' *DCB*, V:853–4

84 R.A. MacLean, 'John Young,' *DCB*, VII:930–5; Graeme Wynn, 'Exciting a Spirit of Emulation among the "Plodholes": Agricultural Reform in Pre-Confederation Nova Scotia,' *Acadiensis* 20:1 (Autumn 1990), 5–51

CHAPTER 12 The 1820s: Peace, Privilege, and the Promise of Progress

1 Accounts of travels by both residents and visitors highlight these features. Among the unpublished, see the travel journals of Bishop John Inglis of the Church of England, which refer to all four colonies between the 1820s and 1840s. They are available on microfilm in the Public Archives of Nova Scotia (PANS) and the National Archives of Canada (NAC). Among the published, see Joseph Howe, *Western and Eastern Rambles: Travel Sketches of Nova Scotia*, ed. M.G. Parks (Toronto 1973); John MacGregor, *Historical and Descriptive Sketches of the Maritime Colonies of British America* (London 1828); William Moorsom, *Letters from Nova Scotia: Comprising Sketches of a Young Country* (London 1830 [rpt 1986]).

2 Phillip A. Buckner, *The Transition to Responsible Government: British Policy in British North America, 1815–1850* (Westport 1985), 57–8

3 Peter Burroughs, 'James Kempt,' in George W. Brown et al., ed, *Dictionary of Canadian Biography*, 12 vols to date (Toronto 1966–; hereafter *DCB*), VIII:458–65; J. Murray Beck, *Politics of Nova Scotia*, 2 vols, I: 1710–1896 (Tantallon 1985), ch. 4

4 Robert Morgan, 'Separatism in Cape Breton 1820–1845,' in Kenneth Donovan, ed., *Cape Breton at 200: Historical Essays in Honour of the Island's Bicentennial 1785–1985* (Sydney 1985), 41–51

5 Susan Buggey, 'Churchmen and Dissenters: Religious Toleration in Nova Scotia, 1758–1835' (MA thesis, Dalhousie University 1981), ch. 4

6 D.C. Harvey, *An Introduction to the History of Dalhousie University* (Halifax 1938); Peter Burroughs, 'George Ramsay, 9th Earl of Dalhousie,' *DCB*, VII:722–33; Susan Buggey and Gwendolyn Davies, 'Thomas McCulloch,' *DCB*, VII:529–41; B. Anne Wood, 'Thomas McCulloch's Use of Science in Promoting a Liberal Education,' *Acadiensis* 17:1 (Autumn 1987), 56–73

7 D.M. Young, 'George Stracey Smyth,' *DCB*, VI:723–8

8 D. Murray Young, 'Sir Howard Douglas,' *DCB*, IX:218–22

9 W.S. MacNutt, 'Thomas Baillie,' *DCB*, IX:21–4, and *New Brunswick: A History, 1784–1867* (Toronto 1963), ch. 9

10 Elinor Vass, 'John Ready,' *DCB*, VII:740–3

11 Phillip Buckner, 'Charles Douglass Smith,' *DCB*, VIII:823–8, and 'John Edward Carmichael,' *DCB*, VI:122–3; F.L. Pigot, 'John Stewart,' *DCB*, VI:735–8; Francis W.P. Bolger, 'Land and Politics, 1787–1824,' and 'The Demise of Quit Rents and Escheat, 1824–1842,' in Francis W.P. Bolger, ed., *Canada's Smallest Province: A History of P.E.I.* (Charlottetown 1973), 66–114; Andrew Hill Clark, *Three Centuries and the Island* (Toronto 1959), ch. 4

12 A.H. McLintock, *The Establishment of Constitutional Government in Newfoundland, 1783–1832* (London 1941), 158

13 Phillip Buckner, 'Sir Charles Hamilton,' *DCB*, VII:376–7; Frederic F. Thompson, 'Sir Thomas John Cochrane,' *DCB*, X:178–80

14 J.S. Martell, ed., *Immigration to and Emigration from Nova Scotia 1815–1838* (Halifax 1942); H.J.M. Johnston, *British Emigration Policy, 1815–1830: 'Shovelling Out Paupers'* (Oxford 1972); W.S. MacNutt, *The Atlantic Provinces: The Emergence of Colonial Society, 1712–1857* (Toronto 1965), 159

15 Stephen J. Hornsby, 'Migration and Settlement: The Scots of Cape Breton,' in Douglas Day, ed., *Geographical Perspectives on the Maritime Provinces* (Halifax 1988), 15–24; Rusty Bittermann, 'Economic Stratification and Agrarian Settlement: Middle River in the Early Nineteenth Century,' in Kenneth Donovan, ed., *The Island: New Perspectives on Cape Breton History 1713–1990* (Fredericton and Sydney 1990), 71–87

16 William A. Spray, 'Reception of the Irish in New Brunswick,' T.W. Acheson, 'The Irish Community in Saint John, 1815–1850,' and P.M. Toner, 'The Irish of New Brunswick at Mid Century: The 1851 Census,' in P.M. Toner, ed., *New Ireland Remembered: Historical Essays on the Irish in New Brunswick* (Fredericton 1988), 9–26, 27–54, and 106–32

17 Kenneth G. Pryke, 'Poor Relief and Health Care in Halifax, 1827–1849,' in Wendy Mitchinson and Janice Dickin McGinnis, eds, *Essays in the History of Canadian Medicine* (Toronto 1988), 39–61

18 Quoted by William A. Spray, 'The Irish in Miramichi,' in Toner, ed., *New Ireland Remembered*, 57; Alan R. MacNeil, 'Cultural Stereotypes and Highland Farming in Eastern Nova Scotia, 1827–1861,' *Histoire sociale / Social History* 19:37 (May 1986), 39–56

19 Laurie Stanley, *The Well-Watered Garden: The Presbyterian Church in Cape Breton, 1798–1860* (Sydney 1983), ch. 8

20 Peter Burroughs, 'The Administration of Crown Lands in Nova Scotia, 1827–1848,' *Collections of the Nova Scotia Historical Society* 35 (1966), 79–108; Johnston, *British Emigration Policy*, chs. 4 and 7; Graeme Wynn, *Timber Colony: A Historical Geography of Early Nineteenth-Century New Brunswick* (Toronto 1981), ch. 6

21 Graeme Wynn, 'Exciting a Spirit of Emulation among the "Plodholes": Agricultural Reform in Pre-Confederation Nova Scotia,' *Acadiensis* 20:1 (Autumn 1990), 5–51

22 J.S. Martell, ed., 'The Achievements of Agricola and the Agricultural Societies 1818–25,' *Bulletin of the Public Archives of Nova Scotia*, 2:2 (1940); R.A. MacLean, 'John Young,' *DCB*, VII:930–5; M. Brook Taylor, *Promoters, Patriots, and Partisans: Historiography in Nineteenth-Century English Canada* (Toronto 1989), ch. 2; Cedric Lorne Haines, 'The Acadian Settlement of Northeastern New Brunswick, 1755–1826' (MA thesis, University of New Brunswick 1979)

23 John Garner, *The Franchise and Politics in British North America, 1755–1867* (Toronto 1969), ch. 10; Terrence Murphy, 'The Emergence of Maritime Catholicism, 1781–1830,' *Acadiensis*, 13:2 (Spring 1984), 29–49; Patrick O'Flaherty, 'Government in Newfoundland before 1832: The Context of Reform,' *Newfoundland Quarterly* 84:2 (Autumn 1988), 26–30

24 Judith Fingard, 'John Inglis,' *DCB*, VII:432–6, and 'John Thomas Twining,' *DCB*, VIII:901–2

25 T.W. Acheson, *Saint John: The Making of a Colonial Urban Community* (Toronto 1985), ch. 6

26 Judith Fingard, '"Grapes in the Wilderness": The Bible Society in British North America in the Early Nineteenth Century,' *Histoire sociale / Social History* 5:9 (April 1972), 5–31

27 W. Gordon Handcock, 'Samuel Codner,' *DCB*, VIII:164–7; Phillip McCann, 'The Newfoundland School Society 1823–1836: Missionary Enterprise or Culture [*sic?*] Imperialism?', unpublished Newfoundland Historical Society Lecture 1976

28 Judith Fingard, 'Attitudes towards the Education of the Poor in Colonial Halifax,' *Acadiensis* 2:2 (Spring 1973), 15–42, and Fingard, 'English Humanitarianism and the Colonial Mind: Walter Bromley in Nova Scotia, 1813–25,' *Canadian Historical Review* 54 (1973), 123–51; Acheson, *Saint John*, ch. 8

29 Stanley, *The Well-Watered Garden*, ch. 4

30 Ibid., ch. 8; W.A. Spray, *The Blacks in New Brunswick* (Fredericton 1972)

31 G.E. Hart, 'The Halifax Poor Man's Friend Society, 1820–27: An Early Social Experiment,' *Canadian Historical Review* 34 (1953), 109–23; Fingard, 'English Humanitarianism and the Colonial Mind'

32 *New Brunswick Courier* (Saint John), 1 Sept. 1827; Judith Fingard, 'The Win-

ter's Tale: The Seasonal Contours of Pre-Industrial Poverty in British North America, 1815–1860,' Canadian Historical Association, *Historical Papers* (1974), 80; Gertrude Himmelfarb, *The Idea of Poverty: England in the Early Industrial Age* (London 1984), ch. 6

33 Spray, *The Blacks in New Brunswick*, 53–7; L.F.S. Upton, *Micmacs and Colonists: Indian-White Relations in the Maritimes, 1713–1867* (Vancouver 1979), ch. 11; Judith Fingard, 'The New England Company and the New Brunswick Indians, 1786–1826: A Comment on the Colonial Perversion of British Benevolence,' *Acadiensis* 1:2 (Spring 1972), 29–42; Bernard Pothier, 'D'Or et de vieux plomb: la carrière acadienne de Jean-Mandé Sigogne,' *Revue de l'Université Sainte-Anne* (1987), 19–20

34 L.F.S. Upton, 'The Extermination of the Beothucks of Newfoundland,' *Canadian Historical Review* 58 (1977), 133–53; G.M. Story, 'William Eppes (Epps) Cormack,' *DCB*, IX:158–62

35 'The Indians,' *Novascotian* (Halifax), 6 Mar. 1828

36 D.C. Harvey, 'The Intellectual Awakening of Nova Scotia,' *Dalhousie Review* 13 (1933–4), 1–22; Taylor, *Promoters, Patriots, and Partisans*, ch. 2

37 M. Brook Taylor, 'T.C. Haliburton as a Historian,' *Acadiensis* 13:2 (Spring 1984), 68; Frank M. Tierney, ed., *The Thomas Chandler Haliburton Symposium* (Ottawa 1985); Wayne A. Hunt, ed., *The Proceedings of the Joseph Howe Symposium* (Sackville 1983); Ann Gorman Condon, 'Peter Fisher,' *DCB*, VII:288–91; J.M. Bumsted, 'John MacGregor,' *DCB*, VIII:547–9

38 David Alexander Sutherland, 'The Merchants of Halifax, 1815–1850: A Commercial Class in Pursuit of Metropolitan Status,' (PHD diss., University of Toronto 1975), ch. 3; Julian Gwyn, '"A Little Province Like This": The Economy of Nova Scotia under Stress, 1812–1853,' in Donald H. Akenson, ed., *Canadian Papers in Rural History*, VI (Gananoque 1988) 192–225

39 Sutherland, 'The Merchants of Halifax, 1815–1850,' ch. 4

40 D.A. Muise, 'The General Mining Association and Nova Scotia's Coal,' *Bulletin of Canadian Studies* 6:2; 7:1 (Autumn 1983), 76

41 W.S. MacNutt, 'The Politics of the Timber Trade in Colonial New Brunswick, 1825–1840,' *Canadian Historical Review* 30 (1949), 47–65, and 'Thomas Baillie,' *DCB*, IX:21–4; Wynn, *Timber Colony*, ch. 2

42 T.W. Acheson, 'The Great Merchant and Economic Development in St. John 1820–1850,' *Acadiensis* 8:2 (Spring 1979), 3–27

43 Shannon Ryan, *Fish out of Water: The Newfoundland Saltfish Trade 1814–1914* (St John's 1986), 118; S.D. Antler, 'A Plantation Fishery at Newfoundland, 1800–1840,' Canadian Economic Association *Papers*, 3 (1974), 143–67

44 Charles Hamilton to James Kempt, 8 Dec. 1821, PANS, RG1, 230 (1821–2), doc. 132

45 Clark, *Three Centuries and the Island*, ch. 5; Lewis R. Fischer, '"An Engine, Yet Moderate": James Peake, Entrepreneurial Behaviour and the Shipping Industry of Nineteenth-Century Prince Edward Island,' in Lewis R. Fischer

and Eric W. Sager, eds, *The Enterprising Canadians: Entrepreneurs and Economic Development in Eastern Canada, 1820–1914* (St John's 1979), 99–118

46 Carol Campbell, 'A Prosperous Location: Truro, Nova Scotia, 1770–1838,' (MA thesis, Dalhousie University 1988), chs 6, 7

47 Daniel C. Goodwin, 'Revivalism and Denominational Polity: Yarmouth Baptists in the 1820s,' in Robert S. Wilson, ed., *An Abiding Conviction: Maritime Baptists and Their World* (Hantsport 1988), 8–52; David Weale, 'The Ministry of Rev. Donald McDonald on P.E.I. 1826–1867: A Case Study of the Influence and Role of Religion within Colonial Society' (PHD diss., Queen's University 1976), ch. 5

48 Entries, 17 June 1826, 21 June 1827, John Inglis Journal 22, 24

49 See the chapters on Louisa Collins and Eliza Ann Chipman in Margaret Conrad, Toni Laidlaw, and Donna Smyth, eds, *No Place Like Home: Diaries and Letters of Nova Scotia Women, 1771–1938* (Halifax, 1988); Campbell, 'A Prosperous Location,' ch. 8

50 Letters of Mrs M. McDonald, secretary of the Miramichi Ladies Bible Society, 7 Aug. and 21 Nov. 1822, Foreign Correspondence, 1822 (162) and 1823 (10), Archives of the British and Foreign Bible Society, London; *Novascotian*, 18 Feb. 1826

51 Lois D. Kernaghan, 'A Man and His Mistress: J.F.W. DesBarres and Mary Cannon,' *Acadiensis*, 11:1 (Autumn 1981), 23–42; Julie Morris and Wendy L. Thorpe, 'Sarah Deblois,' *DCB*, VI:181–2; Occasional's Letter, *Acadian Recorder*, 25 May 1912; Campbell, 'A Prosperous Location,' 167

52 Entry, 15 Sept. 1826, John Inglis Journal, 23

53 Stephen J. Hornsby, 'Staple Trades, Subsistence Agriculture, and Nineteenth-Century Cape Breton Island,' *Annals of the Association of American Geographers*, 79:3 (Sept. 1989), 411–34; Keith Matthews, 'The Class of '32: St. John's Reformers on the Eve of Representative Government,' *Acadiensis* 6:2 (Spring 1977), 80–94

CHAPTER 13 The 1830s: Adapting Their Institutions to Their Desires

1 W.S. MacNutt, *The Atlantic Provinces: The Emergence of a Colonial Society, 1712–1857* (Toronto 1965). The author wishes to thank the Social Sciences and Humanities Research Council of Canada for a grant that allowed her to do the necessary research for this chapter, Barry Moody for consultation and detailed advice on religious history, and Phillip Buckner for the same on matters political. The title is adapted from John Plamenatz, *The English Utilitarians* (Oxford 1949), 151.

2 Phillip Buckner, 'The Colonial Office and British North America, 1801–50,' in George W. Brown et al., eds, *Dictionary of Canadian Biography*, 12 vols to date (Toronto 1966–; hereafter *DCB*), VIII:xxxv

3 J.M. Ward, *Colonial Self-Government: The British Experience 1759–1856* (Lon-

don 1976); Peter Burroughs, *British Attitudes towards Canada, 1822–49* (Scarborough 1971); Phillip Buckner, *The Transition to Responsible Government: British Policy in British North America, 1815–1850* (Westport 1985)

4 Catherine Estelle Saunders, 'Social Conditions and Legislation in Nova Scotia (1815–1851)' (MA thesis, Dalhousie University 1949), app. A

5 John Douglas White, 'Speed the Plough: Agricultural Societies in Pre-Confederation New Brunswick' (MA thesis, University of New Brunswick 1976), 151

6 Basil Greenhill and Ann Giffard, *Westcountrymen in Prince Edward's Isle* (Toronto 1976), 133

7 W. Gordon Handcock, *'Soe longe as there comes noe women': Origins of English Settlement in Newfoundland* (St John's 1989), 96–8. See also his 'English Migration to Newfoundland,' in John J. Mannion, ed., *The Peopling of Newfoundland: Essays in Historical Geography* (St John's 1977), 15–48.

8 See Mannion, *Peopling*, 28–9; Handcock, *'Soe longe as there comes noe women,'* 145–83; and Sean T. Cadigan, 'Economic and Social Relations of Production on the North-east Coast of Newfoundland, with Special Reference to Conception Bay, 1785–1855' (PHD diss., Memorial University of Newfoundland 1991), 74–7.

9. J.M. Bumsted, *The People's Clearance: Highland Emigration to North America, 1770–1815* (Edinburgh 1982); D.C. Harvey, 'Scottish Immigration to Cape Breton,' *Dalhousie Review* 21 (1941), 313–24; S.J. Hornsby, 'Staple Trades, Subsistence Agriculture, and Nineteenth-Century Cape Breton Island,' *Annals of the Association of American Geographers* 79:3 (Sept. 1989), 411–34; J.S. Martell, *Immigration to and Emigration from Nova Scotia, 1815–1838* (Halifax 1942); Rosemary E. Ommer, 'Highland Scots Migration to Southwestern Newfoundland: A Study of Kinship' (MA thesis, Memorial University of Newfoundland 1973); Ommer, 'Primitive Accumulation and the Scottish *Clann* in the Old World and the New,' *Journal of Historical Geography* 12:2 (1986), 121–41. There is some debate in the literature about the compulsory nature of the evictions: see my review of Bumsted in *Labour / Le Travail* 14 (Fall 1984), 291–4.

10 Kent R. (Rusty) Bittermann, 'Agrarian Alternatives: The Ideas of the Escheat Movement on Prince Edward Island, 1832–42,' paper presented to the Canadian Historical Association (Victoria 1990), 506

11 W.A. Spray, 'Moses Henry Perley,' *DCB*, IX:628–32

12 W.A. Spray, 'The Irish in Miramichi,' in P.M. Toner, ed., *New Ireland Remembered: Historical Essays on the Irish in New Brunswick* (Fredericton 1988), 12

13 Ivan J. Saunders, 'The New Brunswick and Nova Scotia Land Company and the Settlement of Stanley, New Brunswick' (MA thesis, University of New Brunswick 1969), 63, 78, 233–7

14 See Oliver MacDonagh, *A Pattern of Government Growth, 1800–1860: The Passenger Acts and Their Enforcement* (London 1961), 87, 88, 138, and chs 4–6 passim.

15 Spray, 'The Irish in Miramichi,' 12, 15–16; George A. Campbell, 'Social Life and Institutions of Nova Scotia in the 1830s' (MA thesis, Dalhousie University 1949), 54–66

16 Kent R. (Rusty) Bittermann, 'Middle River: The Social Structure of Agriculture in a Nineteenth Century Cape Breton Community' (MA thesis, University of New Brunswick 1987), ii, 115–17; see also R.G. Riddell, 'A Study of the Land Policy of the Colonial Office, 1763–1855,' *Canadian Historical Review* 18 (1937), 385–405.

17 Graeme Wynn, 'Exciting a Spirit of Emulation among the "Plodholes": Agricultural Reform in Pre-Confederation Nova Scotia,' *Acadiensis* 20:1 (Autumn 1990), 18

18 A.H. Clark, *Three Centuries and the Island*, (Toronto 1959), 69–71, 73; Greenhill and Giffard, *Westcountrymen*, 93, 123

19 Julian Gwyn, '"A Little Province Like This": The Economy of Nova Scotia under Stress, 1812–1853,' in Donald H. Akenson, ed., *Canadian Papers in Rural History* VI (1988), 192–225

20 See the diaries of Edward J. Ross of New Ross, Lunenburg County, Nova Scotia, which cover the 1830s, for a detailed account of the seasonal round of his farm: Ross Family Collection, Public Archives of Nova Scotia (PANS), MG1, Box 1, No. 794. See also Clark, *Three Centuries and the Island*, 78; and, for New Brunswick, Graeme Wynn, 'A Share of the Necessities of Life: Remarks on Migration, Development and Dependency in Atlantic Canada,' in Berkeley Fleming, ed., *Beyond Anger and Longing: Community and Development in Atlantic Canada* (Fredericton 1988), 35–40.

21 Wynn, 'Exciting a Spirit of Emulation'

22 Shannon Ryan, *Fish out of Water: The Newfoundland Saltfish Trade, 1814–1914* (St John's 1986), 55–6

23 Harold Innis, *The Cod Fisheries: The History of an International Economy* (rev. ed.; Toronto 1954), 241, 333; Alton A. Lomas, 'The Industrial Development of Nova Scotia, 1830–1854' (MA thesis, Dalhousie University 1950), has a good overview of the Banks fishery; see also B.A. Balcom, *History of the Lunenburg Fishing Industry* (Lunenburg 1977); Raymond McFarland, *A History of the New England Fisheries* (Philadelphia 1911), and Joseph W. Goode, ed., *The History and Methods of the Fisheries*, 2 vols (Washington 1884–7); Ryan, *Fish out of Water*, 55–6.

24 Keith Matthews, 'History of the West of England–Newfoundland Fishery' (DPHIL diss., University of Oxford 1968); Shannon Ryan, 'The Newfoundland Cod Fishery in the Nineteenth Century' (MA thesis, Memorial University of Newfoundland 1971); Ryan, *Fish out of Water*. See also Patricia A. Thornton, 'The Transition from the Migratory to the Resident Fishery in the Strait of Belle Isle,' in Rosemary E. Ommer, ed., *Merchant Credit and Labour Strategies in Historical Perspective* (Fredericton 1990), 138–66, and Rosemary E. Ommer, *From Outpost to Outport: A Structural Analysis of the*

Jersey-Gaspé Cod Fishery, 1767–1886 (Montreal and Kingston 1991).

25 MacNutt, *The Atlantic Provinces*, ch. 7; Floyd B. MacMillan, 'Trade of New Brunswick with Great Britain, The United States and the Caribbean, 1819–1849,' 2 vols (MA thesis, University of New Brunswick 1955), I:83; MacFarland, *New England Fisheries*, 167–8; Ryan, *Fish out of Water*, 81–3, 111, 116–17

26 Shannon Ryan, 'The Newfoundland Salt Cod Trade in the Nineteenth Century,' in James Hiller and Peter Neary, eds, *Newfoundland in the Nineteenth and Twentieth Centuries* (Toronto 1980), 44, 62–3

27 David Alexander, 'Newfoundland's Traditional Economy and Development to 1934,' in Hiller and Neary, *Newfoundland*, 20, table 1. For a detailed discussion of this issue, and a revisionist treatment, see Cadigan, 'Economic and Social Relations,' chs 2, 4, 8, and 9.

28 Martell, *Immigration*, 18, quoting the Minutes of June 1831

29 MacMillan, 'Trade of New Brunswick,' 84; Graeme Wynn, *Timber Colony: A Historical Geography of Early Nineteenth Century New Brunswick* (Toronto 1981), 48–9

30 Eric W. Sager with Gerald E. Panting, *Maritime Capital: The Shipping Industry in Atlantic Canada, 1820–1914* (Montreal and Kingston 1990); Frederick William Wallace, *Wooden Ships and Iron Men* (London 1924); Peter D. McClelland, 'The New Brunswick Economy in the Nineteenth Century' (PHD diss., Harvard University 1966); Richard Rice, 'The Wrights of Saint John: A Study in Shipbuilding and Shipping in the Maritimes, 1839–1855,' in D.S. Macmillan, ed., *Canadian Business History: Selected Studies, 1497–1971* (Toronto 1972)

31 Reginald D. Evans, 'Transportation and Communication in Nova Scotia, 1815–1830' (MA thesis, Dalhousie University 1936), 119; Campbell, 'Social Life,' 115

32 Marilyn Gerriets, 'The Impact of the General Mining Association on the Nova Scotia Coal Industry from 1826–1850,' *Acadiensis* 21:1 (Autumn 1991), 83–4; Hornsby, 'Staple Trades,' 423–4; J.S. Martell, 'Early Coal Mining in Nova Scotia,' *Dalhousie Review* 25 (1945), 156–72

33 Ommer, *Outpost*, 114–15

34 Balcom, *History*, 12–15

35 Dan L. Bunbury, 'From Philanthropy to Finance: The Halifax Government Savings Bank, 1832–67' (MA thesis, Saint Mary's University 1990), passim; J.S. Martell, 'A Documentary Study of Provincial Finance and Currency, 1812–1836,' *Bulletin of the Public Archives of Nova Scotia* 2:4, PANS, 1941; David Alexander Sutherland, 'The Merchants of Halifax, 1815–1850: A Commercial Class in Pursuit of Metropolitan Status' (PHD diss., University of Toronto 1975), 229–32

36 Bittermann, 'Middle River,' passim; Robert MacKinnon and Graeme Wynn, 'Nova Scotian Agriculture in the "Golden Age": A New Look,' in Douglas

Day, ed., *Geographical Perspectives on the Maritime Provinces* (Halifax 1988), 47–59; see also Ommer, 'Introduction,' *Merchant Credit*, 14–15.

37 Donald C. Mackay, 'Peter Nordbeck,' *DCB*, IX:599–600; Lois K. Kernaghan, 'Andrew Mackinley,' *DCB*, IX:510

38 Evans, 'Transportation and Communication,' 22: my calculations from his figures

39 See, for example, Gerald Tulchinsky, *The River Barons: Montreal Businessmen and the Growth of Industry and Transportation 1837–1853* (Toronto 1977); M.B. Katz, *The People of Hamilton, Canada West: Family and Class in a Mid-Nineteenth-Century City* (Cambridge, Mass. 1975); L.R. MacDonald, 'Merchants against Industry: An Idea and Its Origins,' *Canadian Historical Review* 56 (1975), 263–81; Douglas McCalla, 'An Introduction to the Nineteenth Century Business World,' in Tom Traves, ed., *Essays in Canadian Business History* (Toronto 1984), 13–23.

40 Sutherland, 'Merchants of Halifax,' 245–54, 295–7

41 T.W. Acheson, *Saint John: The Making of a Colonial Urban Community* (Toronto 1985), 5, 57–60

42 Martin Hewitt, 'The Mechanics' Institute Movement in the Maritimes, 1831–1889' (MA thesis, University of New Brunswick 1986), 25

43 Richard Rice, 'A History of Organised Labour in Saint John, New Brunswick, 1813–1890' (MA thesis, University of New Brunswick 1968)

44 Hewitt, 'Mechanics' Institute Movement,' 1–2, 20–3; Evelyn P. Costello, 'A Report on the Saint John Mechanics' Institute, 1838–1890' (MA thesis, University of New Brunswick 1974), 1–11

45 Campbell, 'Social Life,' 184–93; Saunders, 'Social Conditions,' 74–188; Kenneth Pryke, 'Poor Relief and Health Care in Halifax, 1827–1849,' in W. Mitchinson and J.D. McGinnis, eds, *Essays in the History of Canadian Medicine* (Toronto 1988), 39–61

46 Sandra Barry, '"Shades of Vice ... and Moral Glory": The Temperance Movement in Nova Scotia, 1828 to 1848' (MA thesis, University of New Brunswick 1986), 8, 326–8

47 Barry M. Moody, ed., *Repent and Believe: The Baptist Experience in Maritime Canada* (Hantsport 1980), ix, x, and Moody, 'The Maritime Baptists and Higher Education in the Early Nineteenth Century,' in *Repent and Believe*, 92. See also D.G. Bell, 'The Allinite Tradition and the New Brunswick Free Christian Baptists 1830–1875,' and Allison A. Trites, 'The New Brunswick Baptist Seminary, 1833–1895,' both in Moody, ed., *Repent and Believe*, 57–62, 105–6; Robert S. Wilson, ed., *An Abiding Conviction: Maritime Baptists and Their World* (Hantsport 1988); H. Miriam Ross, 'Shaping a Vision of Mission: Early Influences on the United Baptist Women's Missionary Union,' in Wilson, ed., *Abiding Conviction*, 89.

48 Philip G.A. Griffin-Allwood, 'The Attraction of Souls: Acadia College and the Local Church,' in Wilson, ed., *Abiding Conviction*, 41–2

49 Philip G.A. Griffin-Allwood, '"Joseph Howe Is Their Devil": Controversies among Regular Baptists in Halifax, 1827–1868,' and Moody, 'The Maritime Baptists,' both in Moody, ed., *Repent and Believe*, 77, 101

50 Campbell, 'Social Life,' 124–33

51 See Terrence Murphy and Cyril J. Byrne, eds, *Religion and Identity: The Experience of Irish and Scottish Catholics in Atlantic Canada* (St John's 1987), especially the paper by Allan MacDonald, 'Angus Bernard MacEachern, 1759–1835. His Ministry in the Maritime Provinces,' 53–65; Phillip McCann, 'Bishop Fleming and the Politicization of the Irish Roman Catholics in Newfoundland, 1830–1850,' in Murphy and Byrne, eds, *Religion and Identity*, 81–93; Mason Wade, 'Relations between the French, Irish and Scottish Clergy in the Maritime Provinces, 1774–1836,' *Canadian Catholic Historical Association Reports* 39 (1972), 9–33; for the complexities of Catholic hierarchy, see A.A. Johnston, *A History of the Catholic Church in Eastern Nova Scotia*, 2 vols (Antigonish 1971).

52 A.J.B. Johnston, 'The "Protestant Spirit" of Colonial Nova Scotia: An Inquiry into Mid-Nineteenth Century Anti-Catholicism' (MA thesis, Dalhousie University 1977), 10; T. Punch, 'The Irish in Halifax, 1836–71: A Study in Ethnic Assimilation' (MA thesis, Dalhousie University 1976), 13; T.W. Acheson, *Saint John*, ch. 5; Laurie Stanley, *The Well-Watered Garden: The Presbyterian Church in Cape Breton, 1798–1860* (Sydney 1983)

53 See Linda Little, 'Collective Action in Outport Newfoundland: A Case Study from the 1830s,' *Labour / Le Travail* 26 (Fall 1990), 7–36.

54 Ian Ross Robertson, 'Introduction,' *The Prince Edward Island Land Commission of 1860* (Fredericton 1986), ix–xxx, and Robertson, 'Highlanders, Irishmen and the Land Question in Nineteenth-Century Prince Edward Island,' in L.M. Cullen and T.C. Smout, eds, *Comparative Aspects of Scottish and Irish Economic and Social History 1600–1900* (Edinburgh 1977), 232; Francis W.P. Bolger, ed., *Canada's Smallest Province: A History of P.E.I.* (Charlottetown 1973), ch. 4; Bittermann, 'Agrarian Alternatives'

55 Thomas McCulloch, *The Stepsure Letters* (Toronto 1960)

56 Bittermann, 'Agrarian Alternatives,' 13; Cadigan, 'Economic and Social Relations,' ch. 8

57 See Phillip Buckner, 'Sir Archibald Campbell,' *DCB*, VI:139–42, and 'Sir John Harvey,' *DCB*, VIII:374–84; W.S. MacNutt, 'Thomas Baillie,' *DCB*, IX:21–4.

58 Phillip Buckner, 'Sir Colin Campbell,' *DCB*, VII:142–5; J. Murray Beck, 'Joseph Howe,' *DCB*, X:362–70; MacNutt, *Atlantic Provinces*, 200–1

59 Bolger, *Canada's Smallest Province*, ch. 4; J.M. Bumsted, 'The Origins of the Land Question on Prince Edward Island, 1767–1805,' *Acadiensis* 11:1 (Autumn 1981), 43–56; Greenhill and Giffard, *Westcountrymen*, 123–43; Harry Baglole, 'William Cooper,' *DCB*, IX:155–8, and Baglole, 'William Cooper of Sailor's Hope,' *The Island Magazine* 7 (Fall–Winter 1979), 3–11; Ian Ross Robertson, 'Introduction,' ix–xxx

60 Kent R. (Rusty) Bittermann, 'Escheat: Rural Protest on Prince Edward
   Island, 1832–1842' (PHD diss., University of New Brunswick 1991), chs 8 and
   9; Phillip Buckner, 'Sir Aretas William Young,' *DCB*, VI:820–2, 'Sir John Harvey,' *DCB*, VIII:374–84, 'Sir Charles Augustus FitzRoy,' *DCB*, VIII:295–7

61 Cadigan, 'Economic and Social Relations,' ch. 8; Patrick O'Flaherty, 'Wil-
   liam Carson,' *DCB*, VII:151–6; J.J. Mannion, 'Patrick Morris,' *DCB*, VII:626–9;
   Frederic F. Thompson, 'Sir Thomas John Cochrane,' *DCB*, X:178–80; S.J.R.
   Noel, *Politics in Newfoundland* (Toronto 1971) 1–10; Gertrude E. Gunn, *The
   Political History of Newfoundland 1832–1864* (Toronto 1966), 3–128; Keith Mat-
   thews, 'The Class of '32: St. John's Reformers on the Eve of Representative
   Government,' *Acadiensis* 6:2 (Spring 1977), 80–94

62. Cadigan, 'Economic and Social Relations,' ch. 9

63 John P. Greene, 'The Influence of Religion in the Politics of Newfound-
   land' (MA thesis, Memorial University of Newfoundland 1970), 5; Leslie
   Harris, 'The First Nine Years of Representative Government' (MA thesis,
   Memorial University of Newfoundland 1959), 46–50; Phillip McCann,
   'Culture, State Formation and the Invention of Tradition: Newfoundland,
   1832–1855,' *Journal of Canadian Studies* 23 (Spring–Summer 1988), 86–103;
   Hereward Senior and Elinor Senior, 'Henry John Boulton,' *DCB*, IX:70;
   Cyril Byrne, ed., *Gentlemen-Bishops and Faction Fighters* (St John's 1984), 4–
   27; Raymond Lahey, 'Michael Anthony Fleming,' *DCB*, VII:292–9; Phillip
   McCann, 'Bishop Fleming,' 82–98; Matthews, 'The Class of '32'; David Wil-
   son, 'The Irish in North America: New Perspectives,' *Acadiensis* 18:1
   (Autumn 1988), 127–32

CHAPTER 14   The 1840s: Decade of Tribulation

1 A.R.M. Lower, *Great Britain's Woodyard: British America and the Timber Trade,
   1763–1867* (Montreal 1973), 73

2 Lower, *Great Britain's Woodyard*, 93, 116, and Graeme Wynn, *Timber Colony:
   A Historical Geography of Early Nineteenth-Century New Brunswick* (Toronto
   1981), 50–2

3 Eric W. Sager with Gerald E. Panting, *Maritime Capital: The Shipping Industry
   in Atlantic Canada 1820–1914* (Montreal 1990), chs 2–5

4 Shannon Ryan, *Fish out of Water: The Newfoundland Saltfish Trade 1814–1914*
   (St John's 1986), 258–62

5 Wynn, *Timber Colony,* ch. 5; see also the articles in R.E. Ommer, ed., *Merchant
   Credit and Labour Strategies in Historical Perspective* (Fredericton 1990).

6 Judith Fingard, 'The Winter's Tale: The Seasonal Contours of Pre-Industrial
   Poverty in British North America, 1815–1860,' *Historical Papers / Communications Historiques* (1974), 65–94

7 T.W. Acheson, *Saint John: The Making of a Colonial Urban Community* (Toronto
   1985), ch. 9

8 William MacKinnon, *Over the Portage: Early History of the Upper Miramichi* (Fredericton 1984), ch. 4

9 Lower, *Great Britain's Woodyard*, 167–78; Wynn, *Timber Colony*, 146–7

10 Julian Gwyn, '"A Little Province Like This"': The Economy of Nova Scotia under Stress, 1812–1853,' in Donald H. Akenson, ed., *Canadian Papers in Rural History*, VI (1988), 216–18; David Alexander and Gerry Panting, 'The Mercantile Fleet and Its Owners: Yarmouth, Nova Scotia, 1840–1889,' *Acadiensis* 7:2 (Spring 1978), 3–28; Merseyside Museum, Liverpool, Register of Shipping for the Port of Liverpool

11 Judith Fingard, 'The Relief of the Unemployed Poor in Saint John, Halifax, and St. John's, 1815–1860,' *Acadiensis* 5:1 (Autumn 1975), 32–53

12 I.R. Robertson, 'Highlanders, Irishmen and the Land Question in Nineteenth-Century Prince Edward Island,' in L.M. Cullen and T.C. Smout, eds, *Comparative Aspects of Scottish and Irish Economic and Social History 1600–1900* (Edinburgh 1977), 227–48

13 T.W. Acheson, 'The Irish Community in Saint John, 1815–1850,' and Scott W. See, 'The Orange Order and Social Violence in Mid-Nineteenth Century Saint John,' in P.M. Toner, ed., *New Ireland Remembered: Historical Essays on the Irish in New Brunswick* (Fredericton 1988), 29–54, 71–89

14 See Ian Ross Robertson, 'Highlanders, Irishmen and the Land Question in Nineteenth-Century Prince Edward Island,' in J.M. Bumsted, ed., *Interpreting Canada's Past*, 2 vols (Toronto 1986), I:367–9

15 Gertrude E. Gunn, *The Political History of Newfoundland 1832–1864* (Toronto 1966), 70–1

16 Malcolm Ross, 'John Medley,' in George W. Brown et al., eds, *Dictionary of Canadian Biography*, 12 vols to date (Toronto 1966–; hereafter *DCB*), XII:713–17

17 W.S. MacNutt, *The Atlantic Provinces: The Emergence of Colonial Society, 1712–1857* (Toronto 1965), 220

18 G.A. Rawlyk, 'From New Light to Baptist: Harris Harding and the Second Great Awakening in Nova Scotia,' in B.M. Moody, ed., *Repent and Believe: The Baptist Experience in Maritime Canada* (Hantsport 1980), 1–14; G.A. Rawlyk, *Ravished by the Spirit: Religious Revivals, Baptists, and Henry Alline* (Kingston and Montreal 1984); David Bell, ed., *The Newlight Baptist Journals of James Manning and James Innis* (Saint John 1984), ch. 1, 56–99, 172–216

19 Raymond J. Lahey, 'Michael Anthony Fleming,' *DCB*, VII:292–9

20 Terrence Murphy, 'Trusteeism in Atlantic Canada: The Struggle for Leadership among the Irish Catholics of Halifax, St John's and Saint John, 1780–1850,' in Terrence Murphy and Gerald Stortz, eds, *Creed and Culture: The Place of English-Speaking Catholics in Canadian Society, 1750–1930* (Kingston and Montreal 1993); Acheson, *Saint John*, ch. 5

21 Wynn, *Timber Colony*, 81–2; Eric Sager, *Seafaring Labour: The Merchant Marine of Atlantic Canada 1820–1914* (Montreal 1989), 50–57, 82–96, 137–8

22 Colebrooke to Stanley, 26 Feb. 1842, Return of Average Wages in Saint John. Prepared by A. Wedderburn. Great Britain, Public Record Office (PRO), CO188/75
23 Alison Prentice, Paula Bourne, Gail Cuthbert Brandt, Beth Light, Wendy Mitchinson, and Naomi Black, *Canadian Women: A History* (Toronto 1988), 96–7
24 Gail G. Campbell, 'Disfranchised but Not Quiescent: Women Petitioners in New Brunswick in the Mid-19th Century,' *Acadiensis*, 18:2 (Spring 1989), 36–52
25 Constance Backhouse, 'Infanticide,' *University of Toronto Law Journal* 34 (1984), 447–78; Backhouse, *Petticoats and Prejudice: Women and Law in Nineteenth-Century Canada* (Toronto 1991), 187–8
26 Jean Daigle, ed., *The Acadians of the Maritimes: Thematic Studies* (Moncton 1982), 231, 295, 396–400; Naomi Griffiths, 'Longfellow's *Evangeline*: The Birth and Acceptance of a Legend,' *Acadiensis* 11:2 (Spring 1982), 28–41
27 Douglas F. Campbell, ed., *Banked Fires: The Ethnics of Nova Scotia* (Port Credit 1978), 28–9
28 L.F.S. Upton, *Micmacs and Colonists: Indian-White Relations in the Maritimes, 1713–1867* (Vancouver 1979), 89–116; W.D. Hamilton, 'Indian Lands in New Brunswick: The Case of the Little South West Reserve,' *Acadiensis*, 13:2 (Spring 1984), 3–28
29 MacNutt, *Atlantic Provinces*, 219–30
30 David Sutherland, 'J.W. Johnston,' *DCB*, x:383–8; J.M. Beck, 'Joseph Howe,' *DCB*, x:362–70
31 P.A. Buckner, *The Transition to Responsible Government: British Policy in British North America 1815–1850* (Westport 1985), 296–306
32 MacNutt, *Atlantic Provinces*, 229
33 W.S. MacNutt, *New Brunswick: A History, 1784–1867* (Toronto 1963), ch. 12
34 T.W. Acheson, 'The Great Merchant and Economic Development in St. John 1820–1850,' *Acadiensis* 8:2 (Spring 1979), 3–27, and Acheson, 'Charles Simonds,' *DCB*, VIII:805–11
35 Francis W.P. Bolger, ed., *Canada's Smallest Province: A History of P.E.I.* (Charlottetown 1973), 111–24
36 Buckner, *Transition to Responsible Government*, 317–21; I.R. Robertson, 'Sir John Vere Huntley,' *DCB*, IX:400–2
37 M. Brook Taylor, 'John Longworth,' *DCB*, XI:528–9
38 Gertrude E. Gunn, *The Political History of Newfoundland 1832–1864* (Toronto 1966), chs 5–7
39 P.A. Buckner, 'Sir John Harvey,' *DCB*, VIII:380–1
40 Phillip McCann, 'Culture, State Formation and the Invention of Tradition: Newfoundland 1832–1855,' *Journal of Canadian Studies* 23 (Spring–Summer 1988), 86–103; MacNutt, *Atlantic Provinces*, 222–30
41 MacNutt, *Atlantic Provinces*, 238–47

CHAPTER 15 The 1850s: Maturity and Reform

1 See table 5 in S.A. Saunders, *The Economic History of the Maritime Provinces* (2nd ed.; Fredericton 1984), 105. Saunders appears to have made an error in calculation: on the basis of the figures he gives, the percentage increase for New Brunswick is 30.0, not 30.4. The Prince Edward Island calculations presented here are based on the censuses of 1848 and 1861 as published in P.E.I., House of Assembly, *Journal*, 1849, app. Y, and 1862, app. A. See also R. Cole Harris and John Warkentin, *Canada before Confederation: A Study in Historical Geography* (Toronto 1974), 180, fig. 5.2.

2 Eric W. Sager and Lewis R. Fischer, *Shipping and Shipbuilding in Atlantic Canada 1820–1914* (Ottawa 1986), 7; Eric W. Sager with Gerald E. Panting, *Maritime Capital: The Shipping Industry in Atlantic Canada, 1820–1914* (Montreal and Kingston 1990), 91, graph 5.2; 92, table 5.1

3 See Sager with Panting, *Maritime Capital*, 93, graph 5.3; 55, table 3.1; 66, table 3.5. Concerning changes in the 'tonnage' measurement, see 55–6; 235 nn10, 11. The 'average life' calculation excludes transferred vessels.

4 Sager with Panting, *Maritime Capital*, 148, graph 7.1, and 48, 50, 59, 85–7, 96, 147

5 Calculations are based on Sager with Panting, *Maritime Capital*, 31, table 2.2; Saint John accounted for 48 per cent and Charlottetown 22.5 per cent.

6 See Sager with Panting, *Maritime Capital*, 66, table 3.5; Lewis R. Fischer, 'The Port of Prince Edward Island, 1840–1889: A Preliminary Analysis,' in Keith Matthews and Gerald Panting, eds, *Ships and Shipbuilding in the North Atlantic Region* (St John's 1978), 66, table 16, and 65, table 14; comments on the Fischer paper by Robin Craig on 71 and by Basil Greenhill on 72; Eric W. Sager and Lewis R. Fischer, 'Patterns of Investment in the Shipping Industries of Atlantic Canada, 1820–1900,' *Acadiensis* 9:1 (Autumn 1979), 25, table 2; Richard Rice, 'Measuring British Dominance of Shipbuilding in the "Maritimes," 1787–1890,' in Matthews and Panting, eds, *Ships and Shipbuilding*, 127, fig. 2.

7 See Keith Matthews, 'The Shipping Industry of Atlantic Canada: Themes and Problems,' in Matthews and Panting, eds, *Ships and Shipbuilding*, 9, app. 1.

8 Julian Gwyn and Fazley Siddiq, 'Wealth Distribution in Nova Scotia during the Confederation Era, 1851 and 1871,' *Canadian Historical Review* 73 (1992), 441–52, esp. 447, 449; Julian Gwyn, 'Golden Age or Bronze Moment? Wealth and Poverty in Nova Scotia: The 1850s and 1860s,' *Canadian Papers in Rural History* 8 (1992), 195–230; Rusty Bittermann, Robert A. MacKinnon, and Graeme Wynn, 'Of Inequality and Interdependence in the Nova Scotian Countryside, 1850–70,' *Canadian Historical Review* 74 (1993), 1–43; Rusty Bittermann, 'Farm Households and Wage Labour in the Northeastern Maritimes in the Early 19th Century,' *Labour / Le Travail* 31 (Spring 1993), 13–45

9 Sager with Panting, *Maritime Capital*, 107, graph 5.11; 104, graph 5.9; 105, graph 5.10

10 Sager and Fischer, 'Patterns of Investment,' 28, table 3; Sager with Panting, *Maritime Capital*, 176–8

11 Estimates are based on Sager with Panting, *Maritime Capital*, 178, graph 9.2.

12 Andrew Hill Clark, 'Contributions of Its Southern Neighbours to the Underdevelopment of the Maritime Provinces Area, 1710–1867,' in Richard A. Preston, ed., *The Influence of the United States on Canadian Development: Eleven Case Studies* (Durham, N.C. 1972), 183, n42

13 S.A. Saunders, 'The Maritime Provinces and the Reciprocity Treaty,' *Dalhousie Review* 14:3 (Oct. 1934), 360

14 Sager and Fischer, 'Patterns of Investment,' 28, table 3

15 C.M. Wallace, 'Saint John Boosters and the Railroads in Mid-Nineteenth Century,' *Acadiensis* 6:1 (Autumn 1976), 71

16 T.W. Acheson, *Saint John: The Making of a Colonial Urban Community* (Toronto 1985), 21, 23–4

17 Sager and Fischer, 'Patterns of Investment,' 20–2; Sager with Panting, *Maritime Capital*, 53, 83–5; David Sutherland, 'Halifax Merchants and the Pursuit of Development, 1783–1850,' *Canadian Historical Review* 59 (1978), 1–17

18 Loris Russell, 'Abraham Gesner,' in George W. Brown et al., eds, *Dictionary of Canadian Biography*, 12 vols to date (Toronto 1966–; hereafter *DCB*), IX:310–1

19 Eugene A. Forsey, *The Canadian Labour Movement 1812–1902* (Ottawa 1974), 3, 14; Forsey, *Trade Unions in Canada 1812–1902* (Toronto 1982), 9–14; K.G. Pryke, 'Labour and Politics: Nova Scotia at Confederation,' *Histoire sociale / Social History* 3:6 (Nov. 1970), 34–6, 38; C. Bruce Fergusson, *The Labour Movement in Nova Scotia before Confederation* (Halifax 1964), 14, 26; J. Richard Rice, 'A History of Organized Labour in Saint John, N.B. 1813–1890' (MA thesis, University of New Brunswick 1968), ch. 2; Ian McKay, 'Class Struggle and Mercantile Capitalism: Craftsmen and Labourers on the Halifax Waterfront, 1850–1902,' in Rosemary Ommer and Gerald Panting, eds, *Working Men Who Got Wet* (St John's 1980), 291–2

20 See W.S. MacNutt, *New Brunswick: A History, 1784–1867* (Toronto 1963), 245–6, 266, 298–9, 335, 381. Concerning public ownership, see Gene Lawrence Allen, 'The Origins of the Intercolonial Railway, 1835–1869' (PHD diss. University of Toronto 1991), 117, 193, 199, 234, 344, 462–3.

21 Allen, 'Origins of the Intercolonial Railway,' 62; also see 36–7, 48–9, 80–1, 87–8, 107, 265, 278–9.

22 J.M. Beck, 'Sir William Young,' *DCB*, XI:947; Peter Burroughs, 'George Augustus Constantine Phipps, 3rd Earl of Mulgrave and 2nd Marquess of Normanby,' *DCB*, XI:686

23 J.M. Beck, *Joseph Howe, Volume II: The Briton Becomes Canadian 1848–1873* (Kingston and Montreal 1983), 299 n70; Thomas R. Millman and A.R.

Kelley, *Atlantic Canada to 1900: A History of the Anglican Church* (Toronto 1983), 129, 132; V. Glen Kent, 'Hibbert Binney,' *DCB*, XI:75

24 See Peter R. Eakins and Jean Sinnamon Eakins, 'Sir John William Dawson,' *DCB*, XII:230–7. For a summary of his achievements as superintendent in Nova Scotia, see Stanley B. Frost, *McGill University: For the Advancement of Learning, Volume I 1801–1895* (Montreal 1980), 181–2.

25 D.C. Harvey, 'The Spacious Days of Nova Scotia,' *Dalhousie Review* 19:2 (July 1939), 139; B.C. Cuthbertson, 'Thomas Beamish Akins: British North America's Pioneer Archivist,' *Acadiensis* 7:1 (Autumn 1977), 88

26 Beck, *Joseph Howe*, II:135; also see 115.

27 W.S. MacNutt, 'The Politics of the Timber Trade in Colonial New Brunswick, 1824–1840,' in G.A. Rawlyk, ed., *Historical Essays on the Atlantic Provinces* (Toronto 1967), 122–40; on 1848, C.M. Wallace, 'Charles Fisher,' *DCB*, X:285; on 1854, W.A. Spray, 'John Ambrose Street,' *DCB*, IX:767

28 W.A. Spray, 'Peter Mitchell,' *DCB*, XII:741

29 J.K. Chapman, 'The Mid-19th Century Temperance Movements in New Brunswick and Maine,' in J.M. Bumsted, ed., *Canadian History before Confederation: Essays and Interpretations* (1st ed.; Georgetown, Ont. 1972), 461; C.M. Wallace, 'Sir Samuel Leonard Tilley,' *DCB*, XII:1051; MacNutt, *New Brunswick*, 362; Peter B. Waite, 'The Fall and Rise of the Smashers, 1856–1857: Some Private Letters of Manners-Sutton,' *Acadiensis* 2:1 (Autumn 1972), 65–70

30 Wallace, 'Charles Fisher,' *DCB*, X:286. Also see Millman and Kelley, *Atlantic Canada to 1900*, 153; Richard Wilbur, 'Edwin Jacob,' *DCB*, IX:408–9; J.E. Kennedy, 'William Brydone Jack,' *DCB*, XI:446–8; W.A. Spray, ed., 'The 1842 Election in Northumberland County,' *Acadiensis* 8:1 (Autumn 1978), 97–100; Acheson, *Saint John*, 110–12.

31 I am adopting the usage noted in Alan Rayburn, *Geographical Names of New Brunswick* (Ottawa 1975), 203: 'the entire E and N coasts from Baie Verte to Restigouche River.'

32 Ian Ross Robertson, 'Donald McDonald,' *DCB*, VIII:532

33 Summary report of House of Assembly debates for 10 Feb. 1852 in *Royal Gazette* (Charlottetown), 23 Feb. 1852

34 This argument is developed in Ian Ross Robertson, 'Reform, Literacy, and the Lease: The Prince Edward Island Free Education Act of 1852,' *Acadiensis* 20:1 (Fall 1990), 52–71.

35 Phillip A. Buckner, 'Sir Donald Campbell,' *DCB*, VII:146

36 Summary report of Assembly debates for 25 Feb. 1853 in *Royal Gazette*, 7 Mar. 1853. Palmer, also a landlord and agent, embodied the Charlottetown élite's fear of the rural grassroots. See Ian Ross Robertson, 'Edward Palmer,' *DCB*, XI:664–70.

37 M. Brook Taylor, 'Charles Worrell,' *DCB*, VIII:954; Ian Ross Robertson, 'William Henry Pope,' *DCB*, X:593–4

38 Ian Ross Robertson, 'The Bible Question in Prince Edward Island from 1856 to 1860,' *Acadiensis* 5:2 (Spring 1976), 3–25; 'Party Politics and Religious Controversialism in Prince Edward Island from 1860 to 1863,' *Acadiensis*, 7:2 (Spring 1978), 29–35

39 L.F.S. Upton, *Micmacs and Colonists: Indian-White Relations in the Maritimes, 1713–1867* (Vancouver 1979), 140–1, 95–7

40 Ruth Holmes Whitehead, *Elitekey: Micmac Material Culture from 1600 A.D. to the Present* (Halifax 1980), 9, 37–43; Joan M. Vastokas, 'Indian Art,' *The Canadian Encyclopedia*, 4 vols (2nd ed.; Edmonton 1988), II:1053; Harold F. McGee, Jr, 'The Micmac People: The Earliest Migrants,' in Douglas F. Campbell, ed., *Banked Fires: The Ethnics of Nova Scotia* (Port Credit 1978), 26–7

41 Ruth Holmes Whitehead, *Micmac Quillwork: Micmac Indian Techniques of Porcupine Quill Decoration: 1600–1950* (Halifax 1982), 45; see also 27–39, 41–60, 136–7.

42 See Whitehead, *Elitekey*, 44–5, *Micmac Quillwork*, 203, 210, and 'Mary Christianne Paul,' *DCB*, XI:679; Ruth Holmes Whitehead, ed., *The Old Man Told Us: Excerpts from Micmac History 1500–1950* (Halifax 1991), 252; Judith Fingard, 'Silas Tertius Rand,' *DCB*, XI:722–4; Upton, *Micmacs and Colonists*, 135–6, 167–9.

43 James W. St G. Walker, *A History of Blacks in Canada: A Study Guide for Teachers and Students* (Hull 1980), 43. Also see Frank S. Boyd, Jr, 'Richard Preston,' *DCB*, VIII:969.

44 William Arthur Spray, 'Robert J. Patterson,' *DCB*, XI:677–8, and Spray, *The Blacks in New Brunswick* (Fredericton 1972), 60–1

45 Jim Hornby, *Black Islanders: Prince Edward Island's Historical Black Community* (Charlottetown 1991), xv, 44, 54–8, 63–5, 68. No Island census bothered to count Black Prince Edward Islanders until 1881, and by that time 'the population [living in the Bog] may already have begun to decline' (53).

46 George A. Rawlyk and Ruth Hafter, *Acadian Education in Nova Scotia: An Historical Survey to 1965* (Ottawa 1970), 10–11; R.A. MacLean, 'Hubert Girroir,' *DCB*, XI:351–2; Daniel MacInnes, 'The Acadians: Race Memories Isolated in Small Spaces,' in Campbell, ed., *Banked Fires*, 58 n27; Léon Thériault, 'Acadia, 1763–1978: An Historical Synthesis,' in Jean Daigle, ed., *The Acadians of the Maritimes: Thematic Studies* (Moncton 1982), 55–8; Naomi Griffiths, *The Acadians: Creation of a People* (Toronto 1973), 75–6

47 Naomi Griffiths, 'François-Xavier-Stanislas Lafrance,' *DCB*, IX:451–2; Philippe Doucet, 'Politics and the Acadians,' in Daigle, ed., *Acadians of the Maritimes*, 229, 231

48 Maillet, *Rabelais et les traditions populaires en Acadie* (Québec 1980), 8; Thériault, 'Acadia, 1763–1978,' 58

49 Georges Arsenault, *The Island Acadians, 1720–1980* (Charlottetown 1989), 97. Also see Ian Ross Robertson, 'Religion, Politics, and Education in Prince Edward Island, from 1856 to 1877' (MA thesis, McGill University 1968), 161.

50 Katherine F.C. MacNaughton, *The Development of the Theory and Practice of Education in New Brunswick,1784–1900* (Fredericton 1947), 89, 149

51 John Garner, *The Franchise and Politics in British North America 1755–1867* (Toronto 1969), 155–6; of the three colonies, only in Nova Scotia were there recorded incidents of women voting prior to disfranchisement.

52 T.W. Acheson, 'Charles Simonds,' *DCB*, VIII:809–10. On appeal, three of the counts were erased, and two were reduced to assault with carnal intent.

53 Gail G. Campbell, 'Disfranchised but Not Quiescent: Women Petitioners in New Brunswick in the Mid-19th Century,' *Acadiensis* 18:2 (Spring 1989), 23–55

54 Constance Backhouse, *Petticoats and Prejudice: Women and Law in Nineteenth-Century Canada* (Toronto 1991), 44–5; 349–50 n8; 351–2 n15

55 James Snell, 'Marital Cruelty: Women and the Nova Scotia Divorce Court, 1900–1939,' *Acadiensis* 18:1 (Autumn 1988), 5; Margaret Conrad, Toni Laidlaw, and Donna Smyth, eds,'Introduction,' to *No Place Like Home: Diaries and Letters of Nova Scotia Women, 1771–1938* (Halifax 1988), 12; Backhouse, *Petticoats and Prejudice*, 187–91; 391 n59

56 Janet Guildford, '"Separate Spheres": The Feminization of Public School Teaching in Nova Scotia, 1838–1880,' *Acadiensis* 22:1 (Autumn 1992), 44–64

57 Ramsay Cook and Wendy Mitchinson, eds, *The Proper Sphere: Woman's Place in Canadian Society* (Toronto 1976), 8, 19, 21

58 Conrad, Laidlaw, and Smyth, eds, 'Afterword,' to *No Place Like Home*, 299–300

59 John G. Reid, 'The Education of Women at Mount Allison, 1854–1914,' *Acadiensis* 12:2 (Spring 1983), 3–33, esp. 9 n20; Margaret Conrad, 'Recording Angels: The Private Chronicles of Women from the Maritime Provinces of Canada, 1750–1950,' in Alison Prentice and Susan Mann Trofimenkoff, eds, *The Neglected Majority: Essays in Canadian Women's History* (Toronto 1985), II:48; James Doyle Davison, 'Alice Shaw and her Grand Pre Seminary: A Story of Female Education,' in Moody, ed., *Repent and Believe*, 124–37

60 Alison Prentice, Paula Bourne, Gail Cuthbert Brandt, Beth Light, Wendy Mitchinson, and Naomi Black, *Canadian Women: A History* (Toronto 1988), 74–5, 77–8

61 Alison Prentice, 'The Feminization of Teaching in British North America and Canada 1845–1875,' in J.M. Bumsted, ed., *Interpreting Canada's Past*, 2 vols, *Volume I: Before Confederation* (Toronto 1986), 379, table 1

62 Guildford,'"Separate Spheres,"' 57

63 Judith Fingard, *The Dark Side of Life in Victorian Halifax* (Porters Lake 1989), 99

64 Marilyn Porter, '"She Was Skipper of the Shore-Crew": Notes on the History of the Sexual Division of Labour in Newfoundland,' *Labour / Le Travail* 15 (Spring 1985), 107. The author emphasizes the provisional nature of her analysis (108); also see 114, 120; C. Grant Head, *Eighteenth Century New-*

foundland: A Geographer's Perspective (Toronto 1976), 218; Prentice et al., *Canadian Women*, 77–8.

65 Shannon Ryan, *Fish out of Water: The Newfoundland Saltfish Trade 1814–1914* (St John's 1986), 54–5; see also 49, 51, 237, 248, 250; Ryan, 'The Newfoundland Salt Cod Trade in the Nineteenth Century,' in J.K. Hiller and Peter Neary, eds, *Newfoundland in the Nineteenth and Twentieth Centuries* (Toronto 1980), 44–7; and Ryan, 'Seals Spelled Survival,' *Horizon Canada* 3:27 (Aug. 1985), 638–43.

66 E.W. Sager, 'The Port of St. John's, Newfoundland, 1840–1889: A Preliminary Analysis,' in Matthews and Panting, eds, *Ships and Shipbuilding*, 36; 22, table 2; 28, table 6; 23, table 3; also see 22, 29, 33–4, 37–8, and his comment on 73; Sager with Panting, *Maritime Capital*, 31.

67 J.K. Hiller, 'Philip Francis Little,' *DCB*, XII:564; Gertrude Gunn, *The Political History of Newfoundland 1832–1864* (Toronto 1966), 121–3

68 W.S. MacNutt, *The Atlantic Provinces: The Emergence of Colonial Society, 1712–1857* (Toronto 1965), 224, 254–5; Frederick Jones, 'Ker Baillie Hamilton,' *DCB*, XI:43–4; Gunn, *Political History of Newfoundland*, 142, 149–50, 206–8; J.K. Hiller, introduction to 'The 1855 Election in Bonavista Bay: An Anglican Perspective,' *Newfoundland Studies* 5:1 (Spring 1989), 69

69 MacNutt, *Atlantic Provinces*, 257; Frederic F. Thompson, *The French Shore Problem in Newfoundland: An Imperial Study* (Toronto 1961), 34–5

70 Gunn, *Political History of Newfoundland*, 145; Hiller, 'Philip Francis Little,' *DCB*, XII:565; Hiller, 'Sir Frederic Bowker Terrington Carter,' *DCB*, XII:161; 'GEB' [Geoff E. Budden], 'French Shore,' *Encyclopedia of Newfoundland and Labrador*, 5 vols (St John's 1984), II:411–12, 415; H.B. Mayo, 'Newfoundland and Confederation in the Eighteen-Sixties,' *Canadian Historical Review* 29 (1949), 126 n5; P.B. Waite, 'John Kent,' *DCB*, X:399

71 See Edward C. Moulton and Ian Ross Robertson, 'Sir Alexander Bannerman,' *DCB*, IX:27–31. Bishop Mullock also became critical at the Liberals' abuse of the public spending power soon after they gained office. See Frederick Jones, 'John Thomas Mullock,' *DCB*, IX:583.

72 Frederick Jones, 'Bishops in Politics: Roman Catholic v Protestant in Newfoundland 1860–2,' *Canadian Historical Review* 55 (1974), 408. Also see Raymond J. Lahey, 'Michael Anthony Fleming,' *DCB*, VII:292–4, 296, 299; Phyllis Creighton, 'Edward Troy,' *DCB*, X:687–8; Patrick O'Flaherty, 'Edward Kielley,' *DCB*, VIII:467–70; Jones, 'John Thomas Mullock,' *DCB*, IX:582–6; Shannon Ryan, 'John Dalton,' *DCB*, IX:189; David J. Davis, 'James William Tobin,' *DCB*, XI:881; Gunn, *Political History of Newfoundland*, 150–1.

73 Head, *Eighteenth Century Newfoundland*, 238–9; Shannon Ryan, 'Fishery to Colony: A Newfoundland Watershed, 1793–1815,' *Acadiensis* 12:2 (Spring 1983), 34–52

74 Ryan, 'Newfoundland Salt Cod Trade,' 40–66; Ryan, *Fish out of Water*, 64–5

75 Shannon Ryan, 'Fisheries: 1800–1900,' *Encyclopedia of Newfoundland and Labrador*, II:154–5, table

76 Cited in Charles W. Dunn, *Highland Settler: A Portrait of the Scottish Gael in Nova Scotia* (Toronto 1953), 79

77 K.G. Pryke, 'John Boyd,' *DCB*, X:85

78 Ursula Bohlmann, 'The Germans: The Protestant Buffer,' in Campbell, ed., *Banked Fires*, 185

CHAPTER 16   The 1860s: An End and a Beginning

1 *An Enquiry into the Merits of Confederation and the Duty of the Hour*, By One of the People (Halifax 1867), 5–7

2 Alexander Paterson, *The True Story of Confederation* (2nd ed.; Fredericton 1926), 7, 17–18, 31, 32

3 David Alexander, 'Economic Growth in the Atlantic Region, 1880–1940,' *Acadiensis* 8:1 (Autumn 1978), 47

4 For a different view see Julian Gwyn, 'Golden Age or Bronze Moment? The Economy of Nova Scotia in the 1850s and 1860s,' *Canadian Papers in Rural History*, 8 (1991), 195–230. He concludes that between 1851 and 1871 there was an annual overall net increase of wealth of 2 per cent per annum, a gain that he dismisses as negligible. Yet it seems to me to prove that these were years of real and substantial growth.

5 See S.A. Saunders, 'The Maritime Provinces and the Reciprocity Treaty,' *Dalhousie Review* 14 (1934), 355–71 and Saunders, 'The Reciprocity Treaty of 1854: A Regional Study,' *Canadian Journal of Economics and Political Science* 2 (1936), 41–53.

6 Peter Dean McClelland, 'The New Brunswick Economy in the Nineteenth Century' (PHD diss., Harvard University 1966)

7 Eric W. Sager with Gerald E. Panting, *Maritime Capital: The Shipping Industry in Atlantic Canada, 1820–1914* (Montreal 1990)

8 Rosemary Patricia Langhout, 'Public Enterprise: An Analysis of Public Finance in the Maritime Colonies during the period of Responsible Government' (PHD diss., University of New Brunswick 1989), 18. The quote within the quote comes from the concluding chapter of W.S. MacNutt's *The Atlantic Provinces*.

9 Graeme Wynn, 'Exciting a Spirit of Emulation among the "Plodholes": Agricultural Reform in Pre-Confederation Nova Scotia,' *Acadiensis* 20:1 (Autumn 1990), 5–51

10 T.W. Acheson, 'New Brunswick Agriculture at the End of the Colonial Era: A Reassessment,' in Kris Inwood, ed., *Farm, Factory and Fortune: New Studies in the Economic History of the Maritime Provinces* (Fredericton 1993), 41, 45

11 E.C. Bolton and H.H. Webber, *The Confederation of British North America* (London 1866), 4

12 Brian D. Tennyson, 'Economic Nationalism and Confederation: A Case Study in Cape Breton,' *Acadiensis* 2:2 (Autumn 1972), 40–3

13 Gwyn, 'Golden Age or Bronze Moment?' 18

14 Hugh M. Grant, 'Public Policy and Private Capital Formation in Petroleum Exploration,' in Paul A. Bogaard, ed., *Profiles of Science and Society in the Maritimes prior to 1914* (Fredericton 1990), 142–5

15 T.W. Acheson, *Saint John: The Making of a Colonial Urban Community* (Toronto 1985), 23, 24

16 L.D. McCann, 'The Mercantile-Industrial Transition in the Metal Towns of Pictou County, 1857–1931,' *Acadiensis* 10:2 (Spring 1981), 30–2 and McCann, 'Staples and the New Industrialism in the Growth of Post-Confederation Halifax,' *Acadiensis* 8:2 (Spring 1979), 57–8

17 Langhout, 'Public Enterprise,' 68–9

18 Burton Glendenning, 'The Burchill Lumbering Firm, 1850–1906: An Example of Nineteenth Century New Brunswick Entrepreneurship' (MA thesis, Concordia University 1978), 187–90

19 E.C. Moulton, 'The Political History of Newfoundland, 1861–1869' (MA thesis, Memorial University of Newfoundland 1961), 122–3

20 C.M. Wallace, 'Saint John Boosters and the Railroads in Mid-Nineteenth Century,' *Acadiensis* 6:1 (Autumn 1976), 83–4

21 Quoted in Langhout, 'Public Enterprise,' 69

22 Peter B. Waite, *The Life and Times of Confederation 1864–1867* (Toronto 1962), 232

23 Margaret Howard Blom and Thomas E. Blom, eds, *Canada Home: Juliana Horatio Ewing's Fredericton Letters, 1867–1869* (Vancouver 1983), 200

24 L.F.S. Upton, 'Indian Affairs in Colonial New Brunswick,' *Acadiensis* 3:2 (Spring 1974), 21–2, and Upton, 'Indian Policy in Colonial Nova Scotia,' *Acadiensis* 5:1 (Autumn 1975), 28–9

25 William Spragge in his annual report for 1869, quoted in W.D. Hamilton, *The Federal Indian Day Schools of the Maritimes* (Fredericton 1986), 11

26 Ralph T. Pastore, *The Newfoundland Micmacs: A History of their Traditional Life* (St John's 1978), 20–4; Carol Brice-Bennett, 'Missionaries as Traders: Moravians and the Inuit, 1771–1860,' in Rosemary Ommer, ed., *Merchant Credit and Labour Strategies in Historical Perspective* (Fredericton 1990)

27 Judith Fingard, *The Dark Side of Life in Victorian Halifax* (Porters Lake 1989), 12, 38, 104–5

28 Donald H. Clairmont and Dennis William Magill, *Africville: The Life and Death of a Canadian Black Community* (rev. ed.; Toronto 1987), 42

29 Savanah E. Williams, 'The Role of the African United Baptist Association in the Development of Indigenous Afro-Canadians in Nova Scotia' in Barry Moody, ed., *Repent and Believe: The Baptist Experience in Maritime Canada*

(Hantsport 1980), 51–3; Judith Fingard, 'Race and Respectability in Victorian Halifax,' *Journal of Imperial and Commonwealth History* 20 (1992), 170–2, 175, 179

30 See Sheila M. Andrew, 'French Participation in New Brunswick Local Government: St. Basile and Shippagan, 1850–1860' (MA thesis, University of New Brunswick 1983).

31 Della M.M. Stanley, *Pierre-Amand Landry: A Man for Two Peoples* (Fredericton 1988), 17–20

32 Rusty Bittermann, Robert H. MacKinnon, and Graeme Wynn, 'Of Inequality and Interdependence in the Nova Scotian Countryside, 1850–1870,' *Canadian Historical Review* 74 (1993), esp. 36. See also Rusty Bittermann, 'The Hierarchy of the Soil: Land and Labour in a 19th Century Cape Breton Community,' *Acadiensis* 18:1 (Autumn 1988), 33–55.

33 B.A. Balcom, *History of the Lunenburg Fishing Industry* (Lunenburg 1977), 10, 11–14, 17

34 Stuart W. Godfrey, *Human Rights and Social Policy in Newfoundland, 1832–1982* (St John's 1985), 21–2

35 Susan Buggey, 'Building Halifax 1841–1871,' *Acadiensis* 10:1 (Autumn 1980), 90–2, 110

36 Halifax City Mission Report for 1866, quoted in Fingard, *Dark Side of Life in Victorian Halifax*, 20

37 See Judith Fingard, 'The Relief of the Unemployed Poor in Saint John, Halifax and St. John's, 1815–1860,' *Acadiensis* 5:1 (Autumn 1975), 22–53.

38 See Gail A. Campbell, 'The Most Restrictive Franchise in British North America? A Case Study,' *Canadian Historical Review* 71 (1990), 161–88.

39 T. Wetmore Bliss to Tilley, 25 Mar. 1861, New Brunswick Museum (NBM), Saint John, Tilley Papers, 5-F1-36

40 Carl M. Wallace, 'Sir Samuel Leonard Tilley,' in George W. Brown et al., eds, *Dictionary of Canadian Biography*, 12 vols to date (Toronto 1966–), XII:105–9

41 John Livingstone to Tilley, 21 July 1860, NBM, Tilley Papers, 4-F5-43

42 William M. Baker, *Timothy Warren Anglin, 1822–96: Irish Catholic Canadian* (Toronto 1977), 39–41

43 Jonathan McCully to Tilley, 10 Jan. 1861, NBM, Tilley Papers, 5-F1-1

44 Margaret Conrad, '"An Abiding Conviction of the Paramount Importance of Christian Education": Theodore Harding Rand as Educator, 1860–1900,' in Robert S. Wilson, ed., *An Abiding Conviction: Maritime Baptists and Their World* (Hantsport 1988), 161; Kenneth G. Pryke, *Nova Scotia and Confederation, 1864–74* (Toronto 1979), 37

45 See Ian Ross Robertson, 'Party Politics and Religious Controversialism in Prince Edward Island from 1860–1863,' *Acadiensis* 7:2 (Spring 1978), 29–59.

46 Ian Ross Robertson, 'Introduction,' *The Prince Edward Island Land Commission of 1860* (Fredericton 1988), xviii–xxvii

47 Ian Ross Robertson, 'Political Realignment in Pre-Confederation Prince

Edward Island, 1863–1870,' *Acadiensis* 15:1 (Autumn 1985), 35–58

48 Phillip McCann, 'The Politics of Denominational Education in the Nineteenth Century in Newfoundland,' in William A. McKim, ed., *The Vexed Question: Denominational Education in a Secular Age* (St John's 1988), 45

49 J.K. Hiller, 'A History of Newfoundland 1874–1901' (PHD diss., Cambridge University 1972), 18; E.C. Moulton, 'Constitutional Crisis and Civil Strife in Newfoundland, Feb. to Nov. 1861,' *Canadian Historical Review* 48 (1967), 251–72

50 Charles Lindsey to S.L. Tilley, private and confidential, 28 Aug. 1860, NBM, Tilley Papers, 4-F5-50

51 Tilley to Lindsey, private and confidential, 4 Sept. 1860, ibid., 4-F5-52

52 See G.P. Browne, ed., Documents on the Confederation of British North America (Toronto 1969), 171–3.

53 Jonathan McCully to Tilley, 8 June 1866, quoted in Pryke, *Nova Scotia and Confederation*, 28; see also A.G. Bailey, 'The Basis and Persistence of Opposition to Confederation in New Brunswick,' in his *Culture and Nationality: Essays by A.G. Bailey* (Toronto 1972), 116; W.S. MacNutt, *New Brunswick: A History, 1784–1867* (Toronto 1963), 456–7. F.W.P. Bolger, *Prince Edward Island and Confederation, 1863–1873* (Charlottetown 1964), 89, declares that 'the moulding of public opinion [on P.E.I.] against Confederation was largely the result of the efforts of' Coles, Palmer, and Macdonald. It seems more plausible to assume that recognizing the unpopularity of the measures to which they had reluctantly agreed at Quebec, they allowed themselves to be moulded by public opinion on the Island.

54 Waite, *Life and Times*, 122

55 See Phillip A. Buckner, 'The Maritimes and Confederation: A Reassessment,' *Canadian Historical Review* 71 (1990), 10–13

56 Bailey, 'Basis and Persistence of Opposition,' 99

57 *Morning Telegraph* (Saint John), 23 Jan. and 1 Feb. 1865, quoted in C.M. Wallace, 'The Life and Times of Albert James Smith' (MA thesis, University of New Brunswick 1960), 44, 45

58 5 Apr. 1865, in Waite, *Life and Times*, 247–8

59 *Saint Croix Courier*, 3 Feb. 1866, quoted in David Graham Bell, 'The Confederation Issue in Charlotte County, New Brunswick' (MA thesis, Queen's University 1976), 150

60 Philippe Doucet, 'Politics and the Acadians,' in Jean Daigle, ed., *The Acadians of the Maritimes: Thematic Studies* (Moncton 1982), 232–42

61 Pryke, *Nova Scotia and Confederation*, 23, 27

62 Pope to Tilley, private and confidential, 29 Sept. 1866, NBM, Tilley Papers, 6-F1-6B

63 See A.M. Fraser, 'The Issue of Confederation, 1864–1870,' in R.A. MacKay, ed., *Newfoundland: Economic, Diplomatic, and Strategic Studies* (Toronto 1946),

411–43; H.B. Mayo, 'Newfoundland and Confederation in the Eighteen-Sixties,' *Canadian Historical Review* 29 (1948), 125–42.

64 James Hiller, 'Confederation Defeated: The Newfoundland Election of 1869,' in James Hiller and Peter Neary, eds, *Newfoundland in the Nineteenth and Twentieth Centuries: Essays in Interpretation* (Toronto 1980), 79

65 Frederick Jones, '"The Antis Gain the Day": Newfoundland and Confederation in 1869,' in Ged Martin, ed., *The Causes of Canadian Confederation* (Fredericton 1990), 147

66 D.A. Muise, 'Parties and Constituencies: Federal Elections in Nova Scotia, 1867–1896,' *Historical Papers* (1971), 188

67 D.F. Warner, 'The Post–Confederation Annexation Movement in Nova Scotia,' *Canadian Historical Review* 28 (1947), 156–65

68 *Morning Freeman*, 5 June 1870, quoted in Wallace, 'Smith,' 98

69 Canada, House of Commons, *Debates*, 1 Mar. 1870, quoted in John F. Baker, 'The Underdevelopment of Atlantic Canada 1867–1920: A Study of the Development of Capitalism' (MA thesis, McMaster University 1977), 207

70 G.A. Rawlyk, 'Nova Scotia Regional Protest, 1867–1967,' *Queen's Quarterly* 75 (1968), 103–23

71 W.S. Fielding, quoted in Colin Howell, 'W.S. Fielding and the Repeal Elections of 1886 and 1887 in Nova Scotia,' *Acadiensis* 8:2 (Spring 1978), 89

72 Alexander, 'Economic Growth in the Atlantic Region,' 76

Illustration Credits

Contributors

T.W. ACHESON teaches history at the University of New Brunswick and is the author of *Saint John: The Making of a Colonial Urban Community*.

PHILLIP A. BUCKNER is a member of the Department of History at the University of New Brunswick. He was the founding editor of *Acadiensis: Journal of the History of the Atlantic Region* and founder of Acadiensis Press.

J.M. BUMSTED is on the staff of St John's College, University of Manitoba. He has published extensively in many areas of Canadian history and recently produced the two-volume history *The Peoples of Canada*.

ANN GORMAN CONDON wrote an award-winning thesis for Harvard University that was subsequently published as *The Loyalist Dream for New Brunswick*. She teaches at the University of New Brunswick at Saint John.

JEAN DAIGLE specializes in Acadian history and was the editor of *The Acadians of the Maritimes: Thematic Studies*. He is a member of the history department at the Université de Moncton.

STEPHEN A. DAVIS is a member of the Department of Anthropology at Saint Mary's University. His publications focus on the early history of Atlantic Canada and its Native peoples.

JUDITH FINGARD is dean of graduate studies at Dalhousie University. Her publications have focused on social history and include *Jack in Port: Sailortowns of Eastern Canada*.

N.E.S. GRIFFITHS teaches at Carleton University and is the author of a number of studies in Acadian history, including most recently *The Contexts of Acadian History, 1686–1784*.

ROSEMARY E. OMMER recently published *From Outpost to Outport: A Structural Analysis of the Jersey-Gaspé Codfishery, 1767–1886* and is research director at the Institute of Social and Economic Research at the Memorial University of Newfoundland.

RALPH PASTORE has published extensively on the history of the Native peoples of Newfoundland and teaches in the Department of History at the Memorial University of Newfoundland.

STEPHEN E. PATTERSON is the author of *Provincial Politics in Revolutionary Massachusetts* and a specialist in early American and colonial history. He teaches at the University of New Brunswick.

GEORGE RAWLYK is a professor of history at Queen's University and the author of numerous publications on the Maritimes, among which is the recently published *Ravished by the Spirit: Religious Revivals, Baptists and Henry Alline*.

JOHN G. REID teaches at Saint Mary's University and has written many books and articles on the history of the Maritimes, including a two-volume history of Mount Allison University.

IAN ROSS ROBERTSON is a member of the faculty of Scarborough College, University of Toronto, and a specialist in the history of Prince Edward Island, about which he has published extensively.

D.A. SUTHERLAND is the author of a number of studies of nineteenth-century Nova Scotia and teaches in the history department at Dalhousie University.

GRAEME WYNN is a member of the geography department and associate dean of arts at the University of British Columbia. He has written extensively on the history of the Atlantic region and is the author of *Timber Colony*.

Index